CHRISTOLOGY FROM WITHIN AND AHEAD

BIBLICAL INTERPRETATION SERIES

VOLUME 49

TUTA SUB AEGIDE PALLAS · 1683 ·

CHRISTOLOGY FROM WITHIN AND AHEAD

Hermeneutics, Contingency and the Quest for Transcontextual Criteria in Christology

BY

MARK L.Y. CHAN

BRILL
LEIDEN · BOSTON · KÖLN
2001

This book is printed on acid-free paper.

Library of Congress Cataloging-in-Publication Data

Chan, Mark L.Y.
    Christology from within and ahead : hermeneutics, contingency,
and the quest for transcontextual criteria in christology / by Mark L.Y.
Chan.
       p.   cm. — (Biblical interpretation series, ISSN 0928-0731 ; v.49)
    Includes bibliographical references and index.
    ISBN 9004118446 (alk. paper)
    1. Jesus Christ—Person and offices.   2. Hermeneutics—Religious
    aspects—Christianity.   I. Title.   II. Series.
    BT205.C42   2000
    232—dc21   00-037924
                                                                     CIP

Die Deutsche Bibliothek – CIP-Einheitsaufnahme

Chan, Mark L.Y.:
Christology from within and ahead : hermeneutics, contingency and the
quest for transcontextual criteria in christology / by Mark L.Y. Chan.
- Leiden ; Boston ; Köln : Brill, 2000
      (Biblical interpretation series ; Vol. 49)
      ISBN 90-04-11844-6

                            ISSN   0928-0731
                            ISBN   90 04 11844 6

CONTENTS

PREFACE

Without the encouragement, guidance and support of friends and colleagues, this present work would not have seen the light of day. I am mindful of my indebtedness to the many who stood by me through the long process of getting this study to print.

I wish to express gratitude to two former teachers whose commitment to academic scholarship has been an inspiration to me. Professor Colin Brown of Fuller Theological Seminary exemplifies for me the art of judicious theological judgment. He is ever ready to break new grounds in his work without becoming a slave to the many fads and fashions in theological studies. It was he who first introduced me to the fascinating world of Christology.

Professor Canon Anthony C. Thiselton, Head of the Department of Theology at the University of Nottingham, gave of himself unreservedly in supervising my doctoral studies at Nottingham. He embodies in his gentle yet robust scholarship the virtues of accuracy, thoroughness and fairness. I am deeply grateful to him for his expert and patient guidance through the often undulating terrain of Hermeneutics. I have benefited hugely from his insights and gracious hospitality during my years in England.

Gratitude goes also to the *Overseas Research Award* (UK), to Dr Walter Hansen of the *Rivendell Stewards' Trust* and to Dr Leighton Ford from the *Sandy Ford Memorial Fund*, for their financial grants and interest in this project. Special thanks goes to the community at *Eagles Communications*, Singapore, Clarence and Mona Tan, and the many who sustained me by their unflinching support and belief. Finally, my gratitude to Dr David E. Orton for his helpful editorial comments and assistance throughout the preparation of this work for publication. Thank you all.

ABBREVIATIONS

Referenced Works

APHS	*A Pathway into the Holy Scripture*
ATP	*Anthropology in Theological Perspective*
BQT	*Basic Questions in Theology*
CF	*The Christian Faith*
FR	*Faith and Reality*
GS	*Gesammelt Schriften*
GW	*Gesammelte Werke*
HMP	*Hermeneutics and Modern Philosophy*
HT	*Hermeneutics and Truth*
JGM	*Jesus—God and Man*
MIG	*Metaphysics and the Idea of God*
NHH	*New Horizons in Hermeneutics*
NoC	*The Nature of Confession*
PH	*Philosophical Hermeneutics*
PHG	*The Philosophy of Hans-Georg Gadamer*
PI	*Philosophical Investigations*
RaH	*Revelation as History*
RAS	*Reason in the Age of Science*
ST	*Systematic Theology*
TaD	*Theology and Dialogue: Essays in Conversation with George Lindbeck*
TaH	*Theology as History*
TWP	*The Theology of Wolfhart Pannenberg: Twelve American Critiques*
TPS	*Theology and the Philosophy of Science*
TH	*The Two Horizon*
TKG	*Theology and the Kingdom of God*
TM	*Truth and Method*

Periodicals, Reference Works and Serials

AJT	*American Journal of Theology*
ATJ	*Asbury Theological Journal*
BBR	*Bulletin of Biblical Research*
Bib	*Biblica*
BJRL	*Bulletin of the John Rylands University Library of Manchester*
BMMLA	*Bulletin of the Midwest Modern Language Association*
CH	*Cultural Hermeneutics*
Chm	*Churchman*
Cont	*Continuum*
CSR	*Christian Scholars' Review*
CTJ	*Calvin Theological Journal*
CTSAP	*The Catholic Theological Society of America Proceedings*
DLGTT	*Dictionary of Latin and Greek Theological Terms*
DPL	*Dictionary of Paul and His Letters*
EA	*Ex Auditu*
EJT	*European Journal of Theology*

EKKzNT	*Evangelisch-katholischer Kommentar zum Neuen Testament*
FH	*Fides et Historica*
FT	*First Things*
Greg	*Gregorianum*
HeyJ	*Heythrop Journal*
HTR	*Harvard Theological Review*
Int	*Interpretation*
IJP	*Independent Journal of Philosophy*
JAAR	*Journal of the American Academy of Religion*
JBL	*Journal of Biblical Literature*
JBR	*Journal of Bible and Religion*
JETS	*Journal of the Evangelical Theological Society*
JHI	*Journal of the History of Ideas*
JP	*Journal of Philosophy*
JRel	*Journal of Religion*
JSSR	*Journal for the Scientific Study of Religion*
JSNT	*Journal for the Study of the New Testament*
JTC	*Journal for Theology and the Church*
JTS	*Journal of Theological Studies*
JTSA	*Journal of Theology for South Africa*
KuD	*Kerygma und Dogma*
LS	*Louvain Studies*
MidS	*Mid-Stream*
Monist	*The Monist*
MSP	*Midwest Studies in Philosophy*
MTh	*Modern Theology*
MW	*Man and World*
NGC	*New German Critique*
NIDNTT	*New International Dictionary of New Testament Theology*
NLH	*New Literary History*
NovT	*Novum Testamentum*
NTS	*New Testament Studies*
NZSTR	*Neue Zeitschrift für Systematische Theologie und Religionsphilosophie*
PAAPA	*Proceedings and Addresses of the American Philosophical Association*
PCTS	*Proceedings of the Catholic Theological Society*
PhT	*Philosophy Today*
Ph&T	*Philosophy and Theology*
PJ	*Preussische Jahrbücher*
PPR	*Philosophy and Phenomenological Research*
PRS	*Perspectives in Religious Studies*
RelS	*Religious Studies*
RGG	*Die Religion in Geschichte und Gegenwart*
RP	*Research in Phenomenology*
RR	*Reformed Review*
RSR	*Religious Studies Review*
SC	*Second Century*
SJT	*Scottish Journal of Theology*
SNTSMS	*Society for New Testament Studies Monograph Series*
SR	*Studies in Religion/Sciences Religieuses*
TB	*Theologische Beiträge*
TDNT	*Theological Dictionary of the New Testament*
Them	*Themelios*
Thomist	*The Thomist*
TJ	*Trinity Journal*

TS   *Theological Studies*
TT   *Theology Today*
TuP   *Theologie und Philosophie*
UnaS   *Una Sancta*
USQR   *Union Seminary Quarterly Review*
UUC   *Unitarian Universalist Christian*
VC   *Vigiliae Christianae*
VE   *Vox Evangelica*
WBC   *Word Biblical Commentary*
WesTJ   *Wesley Theological Journal*
WTJ   *Westminster Theological Journal*
WW   *Word & World*
ZTK   *Zeitschrift für Theologie und Kirche*

INTRODUCTION

The growing recognition of the necessary historical contingency of all human ideas and beliefs poses a challenge to Theology in general and Christology in particular. The postmodern revolt against the hegemony of Cartesianism, with its rejection of universal truth, comes out of a historicist mindset which valorizes contextuality and vilifies transcontextuality. This has repercussions for Christology, for the question of Christ is inseparable from the question of truth. To speak of Jesus as Lord and as the one in whom God has revealed himself definitively, and through whom God has effected salvation for the world, is to make a truth-claim about God, humanity, the world and the nature of reality.

Ostensively, the Christian faith has always understood its message about the crucified and resurrected Christ to be universally valid. Yet such a claim to universality is considered scandalous in a postmodern age accustomed to the rhetoric that there is no such thing as transcontextual truth. It is in such an intellectual climate, where perspectival plurality rather than metanarratival unity holds sway, that theology today must articulate its beliefs about Christ as the way to the truth about life.

This study aims to develop an approach to Christology which is hermeneutically sensitive and takes into account the temporal and historical nature of knowledge and understanding. It seeks a Christology beyond the objectivism of ahistorical truth and the relativism of absolutized contextuality. It takes as its departure a historico-eschatological framework grounded in a concept of divine transcendental immanence in history. God's revelatory and redemptive activity in universal history, centering in Jesus Christ, forms the backdrop for our argument that the truth of Christology is both historically mediated and transcendentally referential.

In what follows, we shall develop two interrelated models of Christology which reflect awareness of this eschatologically determined historicity. The by now stereotypical contrastive models of Christology "from above" and "from below" often seem perhaps unwittingly to presuppose an essentialist and atemporal metaphysics, even if the model "from below" within its own context was oriented towards a more temporal, contingent view of history. Yet together in the context of Christological debate, they tend to reflect an atemporal and hierarchical metaphorical framework. In contrast to these, we propose an alternate approach which entails an exploration of what is primarily a temporal rather than a spatial model. A Christology which is responsive to historical contingency and yet retains its universality, should, we suggest, be done "*from within*" and "*from ahead.*"

First, Christology is *from within* in two senses: (1) Christological reflections are invariably made from within a specific *tradition*; and (2) such formulations naturally arise on account of, or from within, the *experience* of the theologian or theological community. These two elements are interrelated: tradition is always experienced tradition, while experience is never mere interiority but always tradition-mediated and never wholly independent of theory. Second, we propose that Christology is *from ahead* in the Pannenbergian sense of proleptic eschatological fulfilment. The notion of prolepsis, vis-à-vis the prearrival in the resurrection of Christ of that totality of truth reserved for the end of time, infuses time now with an eschatological quality. That which *transcends* time has come *in* time, thus allowing for the coinherence of transcendence and historicity. We seek to situate Christological formulation within such a proleptic framework.

To explore and to attempt to substantiate these proposals, we have opted, in Gadamerian fashion, to interrogate and converse with a series of key thinkers, each of whom offers distinctive contributions towards our project. In chapter one, we shall set out the challenge of historical contingency for the question of truth, first by surveying the salient features of postmodernity before looking at Ernst Troeltsch's struggle with historicism. Troeltsch's work crystalizes for us the challenge of historicism and serves as the foil against which we clarify what we mean by a Christology which is beyond objectivism and relativism.

The formative impact of tradition for theology will be explored in the next two chapters, where we develop a Christology from within *tradition*. Chapter two will enlist Hans-Georg Gadamer's hermeneutical rehabilitation of tradition as a resource to formulate a hermeneutically sensitive Christology. The question of truth and relativism, and the possibility of critique in tradition, will then be discussed. This sets the stage for chapter three, where we shall trace the dynamic contours of Christological development, and argue the case for a "traditionary" Christology. Issues dealt with here include: the dialectic of continuity and discontinuity in Christological development; the ecclesiality of theological reflection; the criteriological role of Scripture in theology; and theological contextualization. A critical response to George Lindbeck's Postliberalism, with its emphasis on intra-systemic coherence, will conclude this chapter.

As a counterbalance to the stress on tradition and communality, chapter four will focus on the personal and experiential, as we grapple with Friedrich Schleiermacher's experiential approach to theological reflection. Schleiermacher is an appropriate dialogue partner in developing a hermeneutical Christology as he is widely regarded as the father of hermeneutics and modern theology. Not only did he make significant contributions to hermeneutics, he attempted as well an affective reinterpretation of Christology with roots which can be traced back to both romanticism and Reformed piety. We shall explicate a Christology *from within* experience, examining along the way his theology of subjectivity, particularly the reciprocity between experience, belief and tradition in his Christology. If Gadamer provides impetus for a traditionary Christology, then Schleiermacher invites the development of a Christology of the Heart.

The notion of eschatological proleptic fulfilment which undergirds the prodigious work of Wolfhart Pannenberg will be central to our argument for a Christology *from ahead* in chapter five. Pannenberg's views on revelation as history, as well as his eschatologically-oriented Christology with its focus on the retroactive power of Christ's resurrection, together constitute an eschatologically oriented temporality which allows us to hold together elements of both contingency and universality. This will be followed by a critical appropriation of Pannenberg's insights to help us sketch a profile of a Christology *from ahead*.

Chapter six will look at the hermeneutical Christology of the apostle Paul, which, we shall argue, nicely combines both the *from within* and *from ahead* approaches. The impact of his conversion/call experience at the Damascus Christophany on the shape of his Christology will be explored, as we investigate the ways in which his theological frame of reference was reconfigured as a result of his experiential encounter with the living Christ. The conceptual categories and symbolic universe bequeathed to him from the tradition of his pharisaic Judaism provided Paul with the terms by which he reinterpreted Christ and his tradition. Further, as we shall argue, this was carried out within a framework of eschatological fulfilment. We hope to show that there is present in Paul's Christology, a confluence of tradition, experience and eschatology.

What we are attempting here has the character of a *theologia viatorum*, a theology on-the-way. In one sense, our explorations, proposals and arguments constitute a progress report on a journey of theological reflection on how best to confess Christ today. In another sense, the proposed models of Christology *from within* and *from ahead* are truly "on-the-way" because they arise from the fundamental premise that the transcontextual truth about God, Christ and reality are grasped through the contingency of history. As such, they constitute an approach to Christology which takes seriously the temporality of truth. Theology done along the axis of temporality will inevitably have an "on-the-way" quality about it.

CHAPTER ONE

HISTORICAL CONTINGENCY AND THE QUESTION OF TRUTH IN CHRISTOLOGY

I. *Christological Particularity & the Scandal of Universality*

The idea that truth is universally valid has been increasingly pilloried in a postmodern age and jettisoned as a relic from a spent Cartesianism whose hegemonic grip on philosophical thought is deemed to be over. Whereas the challenge to incarnational Christology came in the past from those steeped in Enlightenment rationalism and empiricism, the challenge today is more likely to come from those who see themselves as post-Enlightenment denizens of a new and postmodern age. If modernity finds the particularity of Christology scandalous, postmodernity by contrast finds the universality implicit in Christological claims positively unacceptable; for postmodernism is, among other things, allergic to the notion of universality and transcontextual truth.

How then does one understand the confession that Jesus of Nazareth is at once the incarnate Son of God and Lord of the universe when the very idea of transcendental and universal truth is in question? To clarify the challenge which Christological scholarship faces today, it is necessary to briefly describe the "postmodern condition"[1] which attends much of contemporary intellectual discussion. Our intention is not to provide a comprehensive assessment of postmodernity, only to set the stage for our quest for transcontextual criteria in Christological formulation.

This chapter will (1) trace the contours of postmodernity and argue that its aversion to metanarratival truth-claim (arising from a strong view of historical contingency) is in many ways a heightening of the problem of faith and history which has dogged Christological formulations since the nineteenth-century. We will (2) examine the challenge of historical contingency by way of a case study of Ernst Troeltsch

---

[1] Jean-François Lyotard, *The Postmodern Condition: A Report on Knowledge*, tr. Geoff Bennington & Brian Massumi (Minneapolis: University of Minnesota Press, 1984).

whose critical historicism not only precipitated a de-absolutization of
Christology, but anticipated some of the trends in postmodern thought.
In view of the apparent impasse created by the objectivism of modernity on the one hand, and the relativism which postmodernity (at
least the deconstructive wing of the movement) seems to foster on
the other, we will (3) argue for a hermeneutical approach as the way
forward, vis-à-vis a Christology beyond objectivism and relativism.
The conventional division of Christological approaches to either "from
above" or "from below" will be reviewed as a prelude to our proposal for a Christology *from within* and *from ahead* which we shall flesh
out in subsequent chapters. Having mapped the way forward, we
turn now to an overview of postmodern thought.

Postmodernism is famously difficult to define. It is a complex and
hydra-headed phenomenon not amenable to easy characterization.[2]
Such is the diversity of postmodernism that one is hard-pressed to
give a complete and systematic account of it. In any case, a *systematic* and *definitive* treatment of postmodernism would be anathema to
postmodern sensibilities, and ironic to say the least. Rather than
being a unified and monolithic movement with a clear centre and
sharp boundaries, it is a plurality of viewpoints and positions.
Nevertheless, there are leitmotifs which seem to coagulate into a
fairly discernible shape such that one is justified in painting a por-
trait of it, albeit with broad impressionist strokes.

It is generally acknowledged that postmodernity or postmodernism[3]
represents a new chapter in the cultural history of the world, even
though the extent to which it is related to modernity is a matter of

---

[2] The literature on various aspects of postmodern thought is immense. Besides
Lyotard's *Postmodern Condition*, see for instance: Zygmunt Bauman, *Intimations of
Postmodernity* (London & New York: Routledge, 1992); Richard J. Bernstein, *The New
Constellation: The Ethical-Political Horizons of Modernity/Postmodernity* (Cambridge: Polity
Press, 1991); Steven Best and Douglas Kellner, *Postmodern Theory: Critical Interrogations*
(Basingstoke & London: Macmillan, 1991); Albert Borgmann, *Crossing the Postmodern
Divide* (Chicago: University of Chicago Press, 1992); David Harvey, *The Condition of
Postmodernity: An Enquiry into the Origins of Cultural Change*, 2d ed. (Oxford: Blackwell,
1989); Ihab H. Hassan, *The Postmodern Turn: Essays in Postmodern Theory and Culture*
(Columbus: Ohio State University Press, 1987); Frank Lentricchia, *After the New
Criticism* (Chicago: University of Chicago Press, 1980); David Lyon, *Postmodernity*
(Buckingham: Open University Press, 1994); Christopher Norris, *The Truth about
Postmodernism* (Oxford: Blackwell, 1993).
[3] While some, like Best and Kellner, *Postmodern Theory*, 5, distinguish between
"postmodernity" and "postmodernism", for our purpose, we shall use these terms
interchangeably.

debate.[4] Postmodernism results from a confluence of various developments in architecture, epistemology, philosophy of science, literary criticism, philosophy of language, ethics, and critical theory in the last quarter of the twentieth century, all of which converge on a common revolt against modernity and its key ideas.[5] Nietzsche's rejection of system-building in philosophy, the pragmatism of Dewey and James, Heidegger's critique of western metaphysics, and the later Wittgenstein's reflections on language use, combined to prepare the ground for the postmodern turn away from a naïve realism to an epistemological perspectivalism. Developments in French literary criticism after the Second World War provided added impetus in the shift to postmodernity. The decentering of the Cartesian autonomous subject in Saussurean Structuralism—which entails an understanding of the self as a linguistic construct, constituted by its relation within language, rather than as a centre of efficacy—led to the severing of

---

[4] Periodization of history is always a risky affair, and often strays into the minefield of ethnocentrism. Nevertheless, the Enlightenment of 1700 is usually regarded as the beginning of the modern world, even though elements of it were already present as far back as 1470 with the dawn of the Italian Renaissance. Modernity is marked by confidence in the scientific and technological prowess of human beings, and a spirit of progress characterized modern western history through the nineteenth and the beginning of the twentieth-century. Two world wars and a string of atrocities later (the Holocaust, Cambodia, ethnic-cleansing in the Balkans, Rwanda, etc.), that confidence quickly evaporated, and modernity is judged to have failed to deliver on its promises. Postmodernity as a movement follows in the wake of the dismantling of the underlying assumptions and convictions of modernity. There are distinguishing characteristics which mark postmodernity off from modernity even though some regard the former as a developed or an extreme form of the latter rather than something new altogether. See Frederic Jameson, *Postmodernism: Or, The Cultural Logic of Late Capitalism* (Durham: Duke University Press, 1991). On modernity and its relation to postmodernity, see Bauman, *Intimations of Modernity*, 187f; J. Habermas, "Modernity versus Post-Modernity," *NGC* 22(1981): 3–22; Richard J. Bernstein's "Introduction," in R. J. Bernstein, ed., *Habermas and Modernity* (Cambridge: Polity Press, 1985), 1–32; J. Richard Middleton & Brian J. Walsh, *Truth is Stranger Than It Used to Be: Biblical Faith in a Postmodern Age* (Downers Grove: InterVarsity, 1995), 9–27; James B. Miller, "The Emerging Postmodern World," in Frederic B. Burnham, ed., *Postmodern Theology: Christian Faith in a Pluralist World* (San Francisco: Harper & Row, 1989), 1–19; and Stephen Toulmin, *Cosmopolis: The Hidden Agenda of Modernity* (New York: Free Press, 1990).

[5] The impact of this shift from modern to postmodern philosophical assumptions is felt not only in the halls of academia but in popular culture as well. See Walter Truett Anderson, *Reality Isn't What It Used to Be: Theatrical Politics, Ready-to-Wear Religion, Global Myths, Primitive Chic, and Other Wonders of the Postmodern World* (San Francisco: Harper & Row, 1990); Gene Edward Veith, *Guide to Contemporary Culture* (Leicester: Crossway Books, 1994); and Stanley J. Grenz, *A Primer on Postmodernism* (Grand Rapids: Eerdmans, 1996).

the necessary relation between the signifier and that which is signified in Poststructuralism. Instead of meaning being guaranteed by a referential relation between subject (signifier) and object (signified), Derridean poststructuralism argues that meaning is necessarily indeterminate, since it is rooted in a never-ending process of indefinite signification. Once the hegemony of authorial intention in textual interpretation is broken, fixity of meaning gives way to the frolic of word play and the celebration of differences. It is but a small step from this reappraisal of the subject-object relation in textual understanding to a reinterpretation of human knowledge.

The distinguishing features of the postmodern mutiny against a modernity defined by the Enlightenment include the following, which are by no means incontestable: (1) rejection of an essentialist metaphysics; (2) a nonfoundationalist epistemology;[6] (3) the historical contingency of all ideas and a constructivist view of knowledge; (4) an aversion to metanarratives; and (5) the decentering of the self in a movement away from atomistic individualism to a stress on tradition and community. These characteristics interpenetrate so that the discussion of one invariably points to the others. We shall look at these briefly, with an eye toward unpacking the rationale behind postmodernism's rejection of the notion of metanarratival truth.

Firstly, postmodernity rejects an essentialist metaphysics and a representationalist understanding of knowledge.[7] The distinction between knowledge or reality and its varied expressions in history is integral to the intellectual tradition of the West since Plato distinguished between knowledge and opinion, between appearance and reality. Nature exists independently of the human mind. Knowledge is what conforms or corresponds to the nature of things, independent of their

---

[6] The language of foundationalism and nonfoundationalism is widely used in philosophical discourse, especially in the North American context. By foundationalism is meant a Cartesian rationalistic approach to knowledge, while nonfoundationalism points to a post-Cartesian, post-Enlightenment form of rationality. This picturesque expression however is not without its ambiguities, especially when it migrates from philosophical to theological discourse. Nonfoundationalism has the unfortunate connotation—no doubt unintended—of assertions which are ungrounded in the sense of being unsubstantiated. Theology as discourse about God *founded* on God's revelation, definitively given in Jesus Christ (1 Cor 3:11) and mediated through apostolic and scriptural witness (Eph 2:20), can hardly be said to be nonfoundational. Nevertheless, despite the infelicity of the language of foundationalism and nonfoundationalism, we employ it because it is already widely used in the literature.

[7] See essays in Hilary Lawson & Lisa Appignanesi, eds., *Dismantling Truth: Reality in the Post-Modern World* (New York: St. Martin's Press, 1989).

being known. This realism underlies Newtonian and Baconian science which is paradigmatic for all human knowledge in modernity. Just as science seeks to discover the inner workings of Nature, so all other fields of human enquiry are judged by their approximation to Nature or what is objectively distinct from the enquiring mind.

Such an optimistic view of knowledge is problematic in postmodernity. Richard Rorty's is an eloquent voice crying in the wilderness of positivistic science, seeking to retire the Enlightenment model of the mind as the mirror of nature.[8] Though not personally enthused by the term *postmodern*, Rorty has, alongside his American pragmatist forebears,[9] Nietzsche, Heidegger, Foucault, Derrida, and others, provided postmodernity with its intellectual underpinnings. In a Rortyan universe, nature is utterly mute; it "speaks" only insofar as human conventions have first put words in its mouth. This being the case, words have no corresponding referents in reality. Although not the first to repudiate the theory of language which sees words as representational of things,[10] it is in pragmatic postmodernism that the correspondence theory of language and truth is most severely criticized. Pragmatists, Rorty reminds us, regard the latter notion of truth as "an uncashable and outworn metaphor."[11] The edifice of words, instead of being grounded in a solid subterranean platform

---

[8] Richard Rorty, *Philosophy and the Mirror of Nature* (Oxford & Cambridge: Blackwell, 1980). See also his *Consequences of Pragmatism* (Minneapolis: University of Minnesota Press, 1982); *Contingency, Irony, and Solidarity* (Cambridge: Cambridge University Press, 1989); *Objectivity, Relativism, and Truth. Philosophical Papers, Vol. 1* (Cambridge University Press, 1991); *Essays on Heidegger and Others. Philosophical Papers, Vol. 2* (Cambridge University Press, 1991).

[9] John Patrick Diggins writes: "In America the revolt against theory long antedated the arrival of European existential philosophy by way of the neopragmatists of our time. The revolt began after the decline of Puritanism and manifested itself in the founding of the Republic in 1787.... Doctrines, treatises, and systems were alien to a national character more interested in improving life than in perfecting thought." *The Promise of Pragmatism: Modernism and the Crisis of Knowledge and Authority* (Chicago & London: University of Chicago Press, 1994), 408–9. See also: Roger Lundin, *The Culture of Interpretation: Christian Faith and the Postmodern World* (Grand Rapids: Eerdmans, 1993).

[10] Already at the end of the eighteenth century and the beginning of the nineteenth-century, we find, with the rise of German Romanticism in Europe, a shift away from the understanding of language as correspondence. As Michel Foucault describes it, "words cease to intersect with representations". *The Order of Things: An Archaeology of the Human Sciences* (London: Tavistock, 1970), 304. On this, see Andrew Bowie, *From Romanticism to Critical Theory: The Philosophy of German Literary Theory* (London & New York: Routledge, 1997).

[11] *Objectivism*, 79.

called reality, is in actuality a linguistic construct, the product of an
"unforced agreement"[12] by members of a particular community,
rooted in pragmatic usefulness or social practice. Knowledge is not
so much a matter of getting reality right as acquiring habits of action
for dealing or coping with reality.

Related to the nonessentialism of postmodernity is, secondly, its
rejection of a foundationalist epistemology. The search for firm philosophical foundations has exercised philosophers since the Middle
Ages, and Descartes' nomination of the thinking *cogito* as a philosophical first principle[13] should be seen as a continuation of this
desire for certitude in philosophy. Classical foundationalism divides
beliefs into two types: beliefs "which need support from others and
those which can support others and need no support themselves.
The latter constitute our epistemological foundations, the former the
superstructure built on those foundations."[14] Knowledge is depicted
metaphorically as a building sitting on firm foundations, and the
justifiability of beliefs depends on their being anchored in indubitable
foundational beliefs. Only then does one have a rule by which to
judge if a knowledge claim is warranted or not. Descartes' expectation that philosophy be thus grounded became paradigmatic of foundationalist epistemology; and this characterizes modern philosophy
whether in the form of idealism, rationalism, or empiricism.

This modern epistemological tradition has been severely criticized
by philosophers from very different persuasions, not all of whom are
necessarily postmodern in the sense employed in this essay. These
range from old school pragmatists like Peirce, James, and Dewey to
the new pragmatism of Rorty; from the analytic tradition of Wittgenstein to Reformed philosophers like A. Plantinga and N. Wolterstorff.[15]

---

[12] Ibid., 38.

[13] René Descartes, *Discourse on the Method of Rightly Conducting the Reason and Seeking
for Truth in the Sciences*, in *The Philosophical Works of Descartes, Vol. 1* (New York: Dover
Publications, 1955).

[14] Jonathan Dancy, *An Introduction to Contemporary Epistemology* (Oxford: Blackwell,
1985), 53. For philosophical discussion on foundationalism, see: William P. Alston,
"Two Types of Foundationalism," *JP* 73(1976): 165–85; Ernest Sosa, "The Foundations
of Foundationalism," *Nous* 14(1980): 547–64; idem, "The Raft and the Pyramid,"
MSP 5(1980): 3–25; Nicholas Wolterstorff, *Reason Within the Bounds of Religion* (Grand
Rapids: Eerdmans, 1976; 2d ed., 1984), 28f; and the "Introduction" in Alvin Plantinga
& Nicholas Wolterstorff, eds., *Faith and Rationality: Reason and Belief in God* (Notre
Dame: University of Notre Dame, 1983), 1–15.

[15] For an overview of changes in epistemological thinking and the rise of nonfoundationalist epistemology and its impact on theology, see Jeffrey Stout, *Flight from*

Apart from a lack of unanimity in deciding what constitutes foundational beliefs, some of these supposedly universal principles of understanding are, upon closer inspection, found to be conceptually dependent themselves. Nietzsche's devastating dismantling of the Cartesian noninferential ego and the policy of methodical doubt is a case in point. He argues that it is fallacious to regard, "I think" (in Descartes' pithy conclusion, "I think, therefore I am") as something which offers immediate and unambiguous certainty. A host of unproved assumptions are implied by the expression, "I think," so that its meaning can only be explicated in terms of what we already know about ourselves.[16] Furthermore, Sellars' exposé on "the Myth of the Given,"[17] Quine's critique of the dogmas of empiricism,[18] and Wittgenstein's "philosophical investigations" have rendered problematic the notion of a firmly established and independent starting point for theory. Instead of foundational beliefs holding up the house of theory, Wittgenstein suggests that it may well be that the whole house is held up by the foundation's walls.[19] The rules of logic, Wittgenstein argues in his notion of "language games," are not principles inherent in the nature of thought in the sense of a single calculus of logic;

Authority: Religion, Morality, and the Quest for Autonomy (Notre Dame: University of Notre Dame Press, 1981) and John E. Thiel, "Nonfoundationalism as Philosophical Criticism," in *Nonfoundationalism* (Minneapolis: Fortress, 1994), 1–37; Ronald F. Thiemann, *Revelation and Theology: The Gospel as Narrated Promise* (Notre Dame: University of Notre Dame Press, 1985). On the difficulties inherent in foundationalism, see Wolterstorff, *Reason*, 35–55; and Dancy, *Contemporary Epistemology*, 58f.

[16] Nietzsche writes: "When I analyze the process that is expressed in the sentence, 'I think,' I find a whole series of daring assertions that would be difficult, perhaps impossible, to prove; for example, that it is *I* who think, that there must necessarily be something that thinks, that thinking is an activity and operation on the part of a being who is thought of as a cause, and that there is an 'ego,' and finally that it is already determined what is to be designated as thinking—that I *know* what thinking is. For if I had not already decided within myself what it is, by what standard could I determine whether that which is just happening is not perhaps 'willing' or 'feeling'? In short, the assertion 'I think' assumes that I *compare* my state at the present moment with other states of myself which I know, in order to determine what it is; on account of this retrospective connection with further 'knowledge,' it has, at any rate no immediate certainty for me." F. Nietzsche, "Beyond Good and Evil," in Walter Kaufmann, ed., *The Basic Writings of Nietzsche* (New York: Modern Library, 1969), 213.

[17] Wilfred Sellars, *Science, Perception and Reality* (New York: Humanities Press, 1963).

[18] Willard V. O. Quine, "Two Dogmas of Empiricism," in *From a Logical Point of View*, 2d rev. ed. (New York: Harper & Row, 1963).

[19] Ludwig Wittgenstein, *On Certainty*, §248 (New York: Harper Torchbooks, Harper & Row, 1969), 33.

they are more like grammatical rules in language. Their efficacy depends on the context in which they function and their relations to other beliefs within a network of ideas which are mutually constitutive.[20] The mutual dependence of ideas and beliefs militates against the hierarchism implicit in foundationalism.

Postmodern epistemology is characteristically nonfoundational, or more accurately, post-foundational. A pragmatic understanding of knowledge occupies a prominent spot in the postmodern firmament, and truth is accordingly determined not on the basis of conformity to first principles but by its regulative function within a social context and its ability to yield practical results. An antifoundationalist approach accentuates the contextuality, and thus revisability, of all human knowledge. It probes epistemological claims in the light of human limits, and sees the goal of philosophy as maintaining the discussion between differing interpretations, all of which are exactly that: interpretations.

Thirdly, postmodernity is thoroughly committed to the notion of contingency. All ideas are constructed from raw materials supplied by historical and social conditionedness. Modernity's confidence in the availability of an absolute and constant viewpoint is illusory, as Nietzsche is quick to point out. Reality is marked by a "Heraclitean concept of absolute becoming";[21] and insofar as it is embedded in the necessarily metaphoric nature of language,[22] it is essentially a

---

[20] Ludwig Wittgenstein, *Philosophical Investigations*, 2d ed., tr. G. E. M. Anscombe (Oxford: Basil Blackwell, 1953, 1958, rpt. 1963; hereafter *PI*). On the idea of "language-games" in Wittgenstein, see Hans-Johann Glock, *A Wittgenstein Dictionary. The Blackwell Philosopher Dictionaries* (Oxford: Blackwell, 1996), 193–98. Note that the concept of "language games" is used in Wittgenstein as a heuristic device to remind us of the various ways in which language works. References to it are deliberately unsystematic, and Wittgenstein refuses to define the essence of a language-game. See Anthony C. Thiselton, *The Two Horizons: New Testament Hermeneutics and Philosophical Description* (Grand Rapids: Eerdmans, 1980; hereafter *TH*), 374.

[21] Robin Small, "Nietzsche" in C. L. Ten, ed., *The Nineteenth Century. Routledge History of Philosophy, Vol VII* (London & New York: Routledge, 1994), 181.

[22] Nietzsche relocates truth from the realm of logic to that of rhetoric when he describes truth as "a mobile army of metaphors, metonyms, and anthropomorphisms—in short, a sum of human relations, which have been enhanced, transposed, and embellished poetically and rhetorically, and which after long use seem firm, canonical, and obligatory to a people: truths are illusions about which one has forgotten that this is what they are; metaphors which are worn out and without sensuous power; coins which have lost their pictures and now matter only as metal, no longer as coins." "On Truth and Lie in an Extra-Moral Sense," in Walter Kaufmann, ed., *The Portable Nietzsche* (New York: Penguin, 1976), 46–47.

human construct. This philosophical critique is abetted by developments both in philosophy of science and sociology of knowledge, where Geertz, Berger and Luckmann make the case for the social construction of knowledge.[23] The positivistic ideal of scientific knowledge in modernity, with its quest for empirical objectivity and its phobia of subjectivity is shown to be a mirage by historians and philosophers of science like Hanson, Hesse, Kuhn, and Feyerabend.[24] Objectivity is dependent on the regnant scientific paradigm of the day, and this, as Kuhn argues, is far from inviolable. When paradigms change, so does the notion of objectivity. Any interpretation of data is theory-laden and no clear cut distinction between facts and theories, or observations and theories, can be maintained.[25] The impact of these developments in the philosophy of science on the shape of postmodernity is widely recognized.[26]

The upshot of this is a deabsolutizing of knowledge claim and a heightening of perspectivalism. To enquire into the nature of knowledge or truth can only be, according to Rorty, "a sociohistorical account of how various people have tried to reach agreement on what to believe."[27] Pragmatism replaces modernity's "desire for objectivity" with a "desire for solidarity" in community. While modernity signaled a turn to the autonomous subject, in postmodernity, it is a turn to communal subjectivity shaped by language, history, and social context.

---

[23] Clifford Geertz, *Local Knowledge: Further Essays in Interpretive Anthropology* (New York: Basic Books, 1983); Peter Berger & Thomas Luckmann, *The Social Construction of Reality: A Treatise in the Sociology of Knowledge* (London: Penguin, 1966).

[24] Norwood Hanson, *Patterns of Discovery* (Cambridge: Cambridge University Press, 1958); Mary Hesse, *Revolutions and Reconstructions in the Philosophy of Science* (Bloomington: Indiana University Press, 1980); Thomas S. Kuhn, *The Structure of Scientific Revolutions*, 2d ed. (Chicago: University of Chicago Press, 1962, 1970); Paul Feyerabend, *Against Method* (London: New Left Books, 1975). See also: Mary Gerhart and Allan Russell, *The Metaphoric Process: The Creation of Scientific and Religious Understanding* (Fort Worth: Texas Christian University Press, 1984); Richard J. Bernstein, *Beyond Objectivism and Relativism: Science, Hermeneutics, and Praxis* (Philadelphia: University of Pennsylvania Press, 1983).

[25] See: Gerald Doppelt, "Kuhn's Epistemological Relativism: An Interpretation and Defense," *Inquiry* 21(1978): 33–86. See also Thomas Guarino, "Contemporary Theology and Scientific Rationality," *SR* 22(1993): 314–5; & Nancey Murphy, *Theology in the Age of Scientific Reasoning* (Ithaca & London: Cornell University Press, 1990), 51f.

[26] See for example: Christopher Norris, "Truth, Science and the Growth of Knowledge: On the Limits of Cultural Relativism," in *Reclaiming Truth: Contribution to a Critique of Cultural Relativism* (London: Lawrence & Wishart, 1996), 154–79.

[27] R. Rorty, "Solidarity or Objectivity," in *Objectivism*, 24.

Following the emphasis on historical contingency, there is fourthly in postmodernity what Lyotard calls an "incredulity toward meta-narratives",[28] an incredulity prompted by the suspicion that any form of totalizing discourse is a mask for manipulation and power interests. Since there is no panoptical perspective from which reality is grasped but only historically conditioned and linguistically mediated perspectives, there can be no Archimedean point from which we may adjudicate between differing epistemic frameworks. Heterogeneity is thus celebrated and diversity valorized. Teleology is eschewed while the aleatoric is esteemed. As Eagleton observes, if postmodernism is enthusiastic about history, it is only history in the sense of an arbitrary conjunction of narratives, and not History as a purposeful and meaningful entity.[29] The aversion to unity and universality results in a pluralization and a parochialization of truth. The notion of an overarching Truth gives way to multiple truths, each a legitimate perspective and none having priority over the others. Truth is tribalized in postmodernity. Such an egalitarianism means that criteria for truth are strictly immanent to the form of life or sociality in which truth-claimants live and have their being.

The historical apriorism of beliefs is further evidenced by the presence of embedded interest in all forms of discourse. Ever since Nietzsche, Freud and Marx, there is a heightened suspicion that totalizing metanarratives are masks for vested interests, some of which operate just beneath the surface of discourse while others exert their influence from chambers burrowed deep in the subconscious.[30] This loss of discursive innocence is sharpest in Foucault, whose output helped shape the postmodern landscape.[31] He pursues the Nietzschean

[28] Lyotard, *Postmodern Condition*, xxiv.

[29] Terry Eagleton, *Illusions of Postmodernism* (Oxford: Blackwell, 1996), 30. As David Hoy, "Jacques Derrida," in Quentin Skinner, ed., *The Return of Grand Theory in the Human Sciences* (Cambridge: Cambridge University Press, 1985), 48–49, notes, poststructuralists like Foucault and Derrida assume that there is no such thing as "history".

[30] For a discussion on Nietzsche, Freud and Marx as masters of suspicion, see Merold Westphal, *Suspicion and Faith: The Religious Uses of Modern Atheism* (Grand Rapids: Eerdmans, 1993). Also: Anthony C. Thiselton, *Interpreting God and the Postmodern Self: On Meaning, Manipulation and Promise* (Grand Rapids: Eerdmans, 1995).

[31] Though Foucault does not explicitly take on the postmodern tag himself. As Best and Kellner, *Postmodern Theory*, 74 n. 2, note, "Foucault rarely mentions and nowhere adopts the discourse of the postmodern." While he is consistently included as a formative thinker in postmodernism, there are nevertheless significant differences between him and other postmodern luminaries such as Derrida and Baudrillard. See ibid, 43–45. Nevertheless, his critique of modernity and the postmetaphysical character of his proposals put him in the postmodern camp.

connection between power and knowledge, decenters the self as an epistemologically constituting subject, and detotalizes history and society as unified wholes through locating all supposedly timeless categories of discourse firmly within the flux of history.[32] He champions an insurrection against the "tyranny of globalizing discourses",[33] rejecting a positivistic or emancipatory (Marxist) view of knowledge. The modern confidence in the liberating benefits of the pursuit of knowledge is rejected by Foucault, for whom the carceral nature of totalizing discourse makes it an instrument of manipulation rather than freedom. Knowledge is inseparably tied to regimes of power, hence the suspicion of universal truth-claim.

Postmodernity's historicist understanding of knowledge sets the stage for our fifth characteristic: the displacement of individualism by an emphasis on tradition and communitarianism. The imperious and unified ego of modernity is replaced by a fragmented and "saturated self"[34] in postmodernity. As Thiselton observes, the postmodern self has become decentred, and unlike the Cartesian or Kantian self, it is no longer an active agent but "an opaque product of variable roles and performances which have been imposed upon it by the constraints of society and by its own inner drives or conflicts."[35] The postmodern self is a multiphrenic self,[36] and like notions of truth and falsehood, it is contingent on the social and linguistic tradition within which a person stands. Hence fidelity to one's tradition and the irreducibility of community are highly prized.[37] Chauvinism of any kind is vilified in the culture of the postmodern, and political correctness stands ready to censure any claim to speak the Truth for fear that it might open the pandora box of imperialism and undermine the equal standing of all cultures.

To reiterate, the distinguishing and interlacing features of postmodernity are: antiessentialism; a nonfoundational epistemic stance; the contingency of ideas and a constructivist view of knowledge; antipathy to metadiscourses; and the eclipse of the autonomous self with

---

[32] See M. Foucault, *Order of Things*; idem, *The Archaeology of Knowledge* (New York: Random House, 1972).

[33] M. Foucault, *Power/Knowledge* (New York: Pantheon Books, 1980), 83.

[34] Kenneth J. Gergen, *The Saturated Self: Dilemmas of Identity in Contemporary Life* (New York: Basic Books, 1991).

[35] *Postmodern Self*, 121.

[36] Gergen, *Saturated Self*, 174.

[37] See Alasdair MacIntyre, *After Virtue: A Study in Moral Theory*, 2d ed. (Notre Dame: University of Notre Dame Press, 1981, 1984); Robert Bellah *et al.*, *Habits of the Heart* (Berkeley: University of California Press, 1985).

a corresponding emphasis on community and tradition. As noted earlier, postmodernity is a highly protean and polymorphous phenomenon; any description of it risks being labeled tendentious at best and distortive at worst. Nevertheless, we consider such an overview of postmodern thinking, however cursory, a necessary preamble to our discussion on Christology and transcontexual criteriology. Our intention is not so much to offer a critique of postmodernism as to examine the nature of theological method or christological formulation within an intellectual climate marked by its concerns. Specifically, we are interested to see how Christology can be affirmed as a claim about God and reality, while at the same time take cognizance of what to us are some legitimate postmodern criticisms of modernity. Enlightenment rationalism has not always been kind to Christian truth-claims. The unmasking of its pretensions by postmodern thinkers such as Rorty can only be applauded. Yet the sword of postmodernity cuts both ways; the same slicing thrusts that render modernity mortally wounded can have equally telling effects on traditional theology.

The question of the relationship between postmodernity and theology[38] hinges on what we mean by the former, and which aspects

---

[38] See David Ray Griffin, ed., *Varieties of Postmodern Theology* (Albany: SUNY Press, 1989) for a categorization of different types of postmodern theologies. The jury is still out on what shape theology should take given the postmodern tenor in current intellectual discussion. The response to postmodernism in theology is mixed: (1) Those who endorse its deconstructive possibilities: e.g., Carl Raschke, *The Alchemy of the Word: Language and the End of Theology* (Missoula: Scholars Press, 1979); Thomas J. J. Altizer, Max A. Myers, Carl A. Raschke, Robert P. Scharlemann, Mark C. Taylor, & Charles Winquist, *Deconstruction and Theology* (New York: Crossroad, 1982); Mark C. Taylor, *Deconstruction in Context* (Chicago: University of Chicago Press, 1986); idem, *Erring: A Postmodern A/theology* (Chicago: University of Chicago Press, 1984); Charles Winquist, *Epiphanies of Darkness: Deconstruction in Theology* (Philadelphia: Fortress, 1986).

(2) Those who question the compatibility of deconstructive postmodernity with the theistic claims of Christian theology while recognising that there are strengths in it: e.g., D. A. Carson, *The Gagging of God: Christianity Confronts Pluralism* (Grand Rapids: Zondervan, 1996), 96f; Thomas C. Oden, *After Modernity . . . What? Agenda for Theology* (Grand Rapids: Zondervan, 1990), 77, regards the postmodern as a form of the ultramodern; Roger Lundin, "The Pragmatics of Postmodernity," in Timothy R. Phillips & Dennis L. Okholm, eds., *Christian Apologetics in the Postmodern World* (Downers Grove: InterVarsity Press, 1995), 24–38.

(3) Those who are selective in following the postmodern lead, embracing for instance its nonfoundationalist epistemic stance and seeing in this a rallying point for a new paradigm in theology: e.g., Thiemann, *Revelation and Theology*; Thiel, *Nonfoundationalism*; George A. Lindbeck, *The Nature of Doctrine: Religion and Theology in a Postliberal Age* (Philadelphia: Westminster Press, 1984); William Placher, *Unapologetic Theology: A Christian Voice in a Pluralistic Conversation* (Louisville: Westminster/John

of postmodernity we are referring to. For our purpose, the aversion
to ontological claims and universal truth in deconstructive postmodernity, as we have outlined it, is antithetical to Christology as
a universal truth-claim. Nevertheless, theology cannot ignore the challenge of postmodernity or brush aside the difficulties it poses to the
very possibility and shape of theology. Unless one opts for a thoroughgoing intra-systemic view of Christology (the tribalization of
truth?)—and this, we shall argue, is fundamentally unfaithful to the
Christian tradition—it is imperative that we face up to the issue of
the intelligibility and plausibility of its extra-systemic claims. And one
of the chief questions posed by postmodernity is that of the historicality of knowledge.

Postmodernity rejects a metanarratival notion of universal truth
and finds it scandalous because of its strong view of the historicality of all understanding. If the provenance of all ideas can be traced
to the social context in which we are historically situated, then, it is
argued, we can no longer retain belief in divinely revealed truths.
Christological convictions would thus be construed as parochial expressions of what Christians consider to be true *for them*. We suggest that
this is akin to the historicist critique of incarnational Christology
which has dogged the course of Christological debate from Reimarus
to Hick by way of Lessing, Strauss, and Schweitzer.

That the Incarnation is a mythical or metaphorical construct with
affinities to Greco-Roman religious ideas is often cited as an argument
against the uniqueness of Christ. Traditional incarnational doctrine,
according to its critics, makes the categoric mistake of transforming
metaphor into ontology.[39] This line of argument is not unlike the
historicist rejection of transcendental truth. The thread which ties

---

Knox Press, 1989); D. Allen, *Christian Belief in a Postmodern World: The Full Wealth of
Conviction* (Louisville: Westminster/John Knox, 1989); Nancey Murphy & James Wm.
McClendon, Jr., "Distinguishing Modern and Postmodern Theologies," *MTh* 5(1989):
191–214; Nancey Murphy, *Theology in the Age of Scientific*; idem, *Beyond Liberalism &
Fundamentalism: How Modern and Postmodern Philosophy set the Theological Agenda* (Valley
Forge: Trinity Press International, 1996); Daniel Liechty, *Theology in a Postliberal
Perspective* (London: SCM; Philadelphia: Trinity Press International, 1990); Stanley
Hauerwas, Nancey Murphy & Mark Nation, eds., *Theology Without Foundations: Religious
Practice & The Future of Theological Truth* (Nashville: Abingdon, 1994); Terrence W.
Tilley *et al.*, *Postmodern Theologies: The Challenge of Religious Diversity* (Maryknoll: Orbis,
1995).
[39] See John Hick, *The Metaphor of God Incarnate* (London: SCM, 1993); Sallie
McFague, *Metaphorical Theology: Models of God in Religious Language* (Philadelphia:
Fortress, 1982).

a modern rationalistic rejection of ontological Christology and the postmodern aversion to universal truth is their common historicism. Postmodernity radicalizes the historicism which has questioned the transcendental nature of Christology since the Enlightenment. In a sense, the challenge confronting Christology today is really an intensification of the longstanding question of how theology can affirm the presence of the divine and absolute in the midst of the human and finite.

This does not mean that the postmodern challenge is merely a repristination of the old rationalistic rejection of incarnational Christology. We are simply highlighting the isomorphism between both challenges to Christology. Modernity rejects incarnational Christology on account of its particularity because such exclusivism contravenes the plurality of access to Ultimate Reality. Implicit in this is the assumption of a universal reality which transcends all religious instantiations. With postmodernity however, such a universal reality is dispensed with. Significantly, the platform from which it criticises Christology as a universal truth-claim is the same historicist platform from which the rationalism and empiricism of modernity launched their attack. The scandal of universality which characterizes postmodernity is thus the follow-through of the scandal of particularity which distinguishes modern criticism of Christology.

To flesh out this observation, we will examine once again the issue of faith and history in relation to Christology, and compare the difficulties posed by previous critics of Christology and the challenge of historical contingency in postmodernity. There is no better case study on the interface between faith, history and Christology than Ernst Troeltsch, who is generally regarded as the father of historicism in modern theology. We shall examine his theological method and assess its impact on the shape of his Christology.

II. *The Challenge of Historical Contingency*

Christology, Macquarrie reminds us, is not only about who Jesus *was*, but also who he *is*, not only about what he *did* but what he *does*.[40] While one may argue the extent to which historical questions

---

[40] John Macquarrie, *Jesus Christ in Modern Thought* (London: SCM; Philadelphia: Trinity Press International, 1990), 1–6. In the same vein, Colin Brown suggests that

are determinative of Christology, Macquarrie asserts that "the historical problem is part of the christological complex". And it is in Christology that the problem of faith and history comes to its sharpest focus. This question is encountered on two fronts: (1) The historical front, where questions are raised about the historical basis for the Christian faith in general and Christology in particular. This coincides with the rise of biblical criticism with its questioning of the historical reliability of the Gospels, and lies behind the still on-going quest of the historical Jesus. (2) The philosophical front, where the metaphysical incompatibility between historical particularity and religious universality is raised.

Lessing's famous dictum that "accidental truths of history can never become the proof of necessary truths of reason"[41] poses this conundrum succinctly. Since then, the question as to how a historical "event" can at the same time be "truth"[42] has occupied a firm spot on the agenda of Christology. This same problem hovers behind the postmodern embrace of historical contingency and its rebellion against absolute truth. Whereas in modernity absoluteness is defined in terms of universal rationality, in postmodernity, it is cloaked in contingency. To examine again the relationship between faith and history, we turn to Troeltsch's historicist approach as an example of an attempt to deal with the challenge of historical contingency.

A. *The Historicism of Ernst Troeltsch*

The question of historicity and theology exercised Ernst Troeltsch (1865–1923) deeply.[43] Like no other theologian of his time, he perceived

---

"Christology has two poles: the historical Jesus and our ongoing human experience." "Christology and the Quest for the Historical Jesus," in Donald Lewis & Alister McGrath, eds., *Doing Theology for the People of God: Studies in Honour of J. I. Packer* (Leicester: Apollos, 1996), 78.

[41] *Lessing's Theological Writings: Selections in Translation with an Introductory Essay*, tr. Henry Chadwick (London: A & C Black; Stanford: Stanford University Press, 1956), 53. On Lessing, see Colin Brown, *Jesus in European Protestant Thought: 1778–1860* (Durham: Labyrinth, 1985), 16–29; and Gordon E. Michalson, Jr., *Lessing's "Ugly Ditch": A Study of Theology and History* (University Park & London: Pennsylvania State University Press, 1985).

[42] Gordon E. Michalson, Jr., "Faith and History," in Alister E. McGrath, ed., *The Blackwell Encyclopedia of Modern Christian Thought* (Oxford: Blackwell, 1993), 211.

[43] See for instance: Ernst Troeltsch, "Glaube: Glaube und Geschichte" in F. M. Schiele and L. Zscharnack, eds., *Die Religion in Geschichte und Gegenwart*, 5 vols. (Tübingen: J. C. B. Mohr (Paul Siebeck], 1909–1914; hereafter *RGG*), 2:1437–56; *The Absoluteness of Christianity and the History of Religions*, 2d ed. (London: SCM, 1972);

"the upsetting and urgent features of the relation between faith and history"[44] and consistently called Protestantism to face up to the challenge of historicism. The rise of historical consciousness in the nineteenth-century, spurred on by Vico, Herder, Croce, Ranke, Hegel, and Dilthey,[45] posed such a challenge to theology that Barth's revelational positivism may justifiably be regarded as a trenchant reply to the historicization of theological claims which emerged at the turn of the century. This development in theological method was due in no small part to Troeltsch. "His chief claim upon our attention", writes R. Morgan, "resides not in the substance of his doctrinal position, but in his method for doing theology in a historically conscious age".[46] Despite the sharp criticisms leveled at him, notably by K. Barth and F. Gogarten, the question of faith and history which Troeltsch posed so sharply, cannot be easily sidestepped.[47] Like Kant in phi-

---

"On the Historical and Dogmatic Methods in Theology," in *Gesammelte Schriften*, 4 vols. (Tübingen: J. C. B. Mohr [Paul Siebeck), 1913; hereafter *GS*), 2:728–53; *Die Historismus und seine Probleme, Erstes Buch: Das logische Problem der Geschichtsphilosophie*, *GS* 3; & *The Social Teaching of the Christian Churches*, tr. Olive Wyon, 2 vols. (London: George Allen & Unwin; New York: Macmillan, 1931). For a complete bibliography of works by Troeltsch, see Hans-Georg Drescher's biography, *Ernst Troeltsch: His Life and Work*, tr. John Bowden (London: SCM, 1992), 318–40.

The literature on Troeltsch is substantial; see for example: K. A. Apfelbacher, *Frömmigkeit und Wissenschaft: Ernst Troeltsch und sein theologisches Program* (Munich: Paderborn, 1978); L. Allen, "From Dogmatik to Glaubenslehre: Ernst Troeltsch and the Task of Theology," *FH* 12(1980): 37–60; John Powell Clayton, ed., *Ernst Troeltsch and the Future of Theology* (Cambridge: Cambridge University Press, 1976); Sarah Coakley, *Christ Without Absolutes: A Study of the Christology of Ernst Troeltsch* (Oxford: Clarendon Press, 1988); Hans Frei, "The Relation of Faith and History in the Thought of Ernst Troeltsch," in Paul Ramsey, ed., *Faith and Ethics: The Theology of H. Richard Niebuhr* (New York: Harper & Brothers, 1957), 53–64; Benjamin A. Reist, *Toward a Theology of Involvement: The Thought of Ernst Troeltsch* (London: SCM, 1966); Robert Morgan & Michael Pye, eds. & trs., *Ernst Troeltsch: Writings on Theology and Religion* (London: Duckworth, 1977); cf. Thiselton, *TH*, 69–74.

[44] Hans-Georg Drescher, "Das Problem der Geschichte bei Ernst Troeltsch," *ZTK* 57(1960): 186.

[45] On the rise of historicism, see Thiselton, "The Emergence of Historical Consciousness," in *TH*, 63–69; and Paul Hamilton, *Historicism* (London & New York: Routledge, 1996), 30–50.

[46] Robert Morgan, "Introduction: Ernst Troeltsch on Theology and Religion," *Writings*, 39. "Troeltsch's formal delineation of method in theology has proved more permanent than his more frequently discussed attempts to provide a modern substitute for the old natural theology." 43.

[47] According to Darrell Davis Perkins, Jr., the questions which Troeltsch raised have not so much been answered as sidestepped by Barth and his fellow critics. *Explicating Christian Faith in a Historically Conscious Age: The Method of Ernst Troeltsch's Glaubenslehre* (Ph.D. diss., Vanderbilt University, 1981), 3.

losophy, Troeltsch represents a critical turning point in theology.[48]

It is our contention that key features in Troeltsch's thought antic-ipate in a significant way some of the issues confronting theology today as it seeks to understand itself in a postmodern age. Troeltsch's rejection of revelational apriorism in favour of a historicized reli-gious apriorism is not unlike the postmodern assault on authority and its emphasis on historical contingency. Without sidestepping the differences between the two, one nevertheless detects thematic reso-nance, if not continuity, between his emphases and those in post-modernity. Before delineating how this resonance is evident and exploring how it is germane to our project, we must first unpack the salient features of Troeltsch's critical historicism.

The breadth and variety of Troeltsch's interests and writings make it difficult to identify the unifying thread which joins these together.[49] Nevertheless, there are recurrent themes, the most prominent of which is that all human thoughts and cultural phenomena must be evaluated from the standpoint of their historical situatedness. He calls this *Historismus*: a "fundamental historicizing of all our thinking about human beings, its culture, and its values."[50] The Enlightenment is to Troeltsch a watershed, signalling the start of the modern world. It renders untenable the dogmatic approach of traditional theology with its naïve interventionist view of the way the divine relates to the human. To Troeltsch's mind, the attempt to justify knowledge on the basis of compliance with external authorities, such as an eccle-siastical body, miraculous events, e.g., the resurrection, scriptures, etc., is outdated, unscientific, and fundamentally ahistorical.[51] The dawning of historical consciousness signals the passing of an age

---

[48] As Claude Welch observes, "one cannot go around him in the attempt to recover a prior state of theological reflection; one must rather go through the crit-ical perspective that he embodied." *Protestant Thought in the Nineteenth Century, Vol. 2: 1799–1870* (New Haven & London: Yale University Press, 1985), 267.

[49] Different suggestions have been made on what constitutes the heart of Troeltsch's thought. On these, see Toshimasa Yasukata's introduction in *Ernst Troeltsch: Systematic Theologian of Radical Historicality* (Atlanta: Scholars Press, 1986), xiii–xxvi. The devel-opmental nature of Troeltsch's works and his early death compound the difficulty involved in identifying a centre in his thinking.

[50] Troeltsch, *GS* 3:102. Or what Yasukata, *Troeltsch*, 151 n. 27, calls, "radical his-toricality".

[51] Troeltsch laments that dogmatic theology in academia has "everywhere aban-doned the demonstration of scientifically valid general truths in favour of personal, subjective convictions of a confessional sort". "Half a Century of Theology: A Review," in *Writings*, 58.

where the authority of the church held sway.[52] The Bible is critically dissected like any other literary work, while miracles, once accepted as an indubitable foundation for belief, must be reappraised according to the principles of the historical method.

In his polemical essay, "On the Historical and Dogmatic Methods in Theology," he contrasts the historical method with the dogmatic method:

> It [dogmatic method] begins from a point fully removed from history and its relativity, and from that point it derives unconditionally valid statements which at best can be brought only later into touch with the knowledge and understanding of other aspects of human life. . . . Its essential characteristic is the possession of an authority that avoids the overall interconnectedness of history, analogy with other historical events, and everything historical criticism has to say along with the uncertainty of its results. It wants to bind men to individual historical facts that claim to dissolve all historical analogies. It can contrive this binding power because its facts are different from all normal history and can neither be established nor shaken by criticism. Rather they are confirmed by a miraculous tradition and an inner seal or verification in the heart.[53]

By contrast, the historical method subjects all phenomena to criticism, including those "authorities" which the dogmatic approach looks to as foundations for knowledge. There can be no privileging of any idea or notion; only an indiscriminating application of the critical apparatus of historical investigation will offer a proper basis of knowledge.

The historical method, which Troeltsch regards as his own "theological method," comprises three related principles: *criticism, analogy* and *correlation*. The principle of criticism means that all traditions are to be uniformly evaluated from a critical-historical standpoint, and historical judgment yields only degrees of probability, not absolute certainty. In the dogmatic approach, one either believes or disobeys. The historical method, by contrast, is more nuanced; it is often a matter of "both-and" rather than "either-or."[54] The principle of analogy makes possible historical criticism in that past events are

---

[52] Troeltsch explores this in a series of essays in the closing years of the nineteenth-century: "Historical and Dogmatic Methods"; "Die christliche Weltanschauung und die wissenschaftlichen Gegenströmungen," *ZTK* 3(1893): 493–528; 4(1894): 167–231; "Die Selbständigkeit der Religion," *ZTK* 5(1895): 361–436; 6(1896): 71–110, 167–218; "Geschichte und Metaphysik," *ZTK* 8(1898): 1–69.

[53] "Historical and Dogmatic Methods in Theology," *GS* 2:7.

[54] Troeltsch, *Absoluteness*, 35.

intelligible on account of their perceived correspondence to events or situations in the present.[55] This presupposes a certain homogeneity between people everywhere and at all times.[56] Troeltsch's third principle is related to the second: historical events are interconnected so that they are simultaneously the causes and results of other historical events.[57] But more than just a methodology, a historical way of thinking must be a world-view.

If history is a network of interconnected phenomena, it is no longer viable to absolutize any single moment of history and make it a definitive and exclusive act of divine intervention.[58] Doctrines are invariably tied to their cultural milieu and are expressive of the religious sentiments of the period; they are not repositories of timeless truths. Christianity and Christian origins must be explained in terms of the wider cultural context in which they are situated. In this, he is one with the *religionsgeschichtliche Schule*, a movement which Troeltsch served as dogmatician. History is thus the only acceptable avenue

---

[55] See E. Troeltsch, "Historiography," in John Macquarrie, *Contemporary Religious Thinkers: From Idealist Metaphysicians to Existential Theologians* (London: SCM, 1968), 81. It should be noted that Troeltsch is prepared to accept the probability of a past event even when it has no analogy to our present experience, so long as we can see an "analogy between similar events of the past." "Historical and Dogmatic Methods," 3.

[56] The understanding of human nature as essentially uniform is true of the early Troeltsch, in whose argumentation one detects the lingering effects of German Idealism. See Michael A. Quigley, "Ernst Troeltsch and the Problem of the Historical Absolute," *HeyJ* 24(1983): 25–26. Such an idealistic view has the feel of a metaphysical ground, and seems to go against a thoroughgoing historical stance. Troeltsch appears to move away from this unwitting metaphysicality in his later works. See Coakley, *Christ Without Absolutes*, 41.

[57] The interconnection between historical events and ideas is seen for example in Troeltsch's explication of the relation between Reformation thought and the Middle Ages, particularly in his understanding of Protestant ethics. To him, none of the fundamental ideas arising from the Reformation are in the last resort original creations. They are grounded in prior questions and dependent on concepts from Medieval theology. The concept of grace for instance has its roots in Medieval theology and Augustine. See Drescher, *Troeltsch*, 135–6. The historian's task is to locate and explain any movement in history in terms of the web of causal relations of which it is a part. See Troeltsch, "Historiography," 83.

[58] Ernst Troeltsch, *Glaubenslehre nach Heidelberger Vorlesungen aus den Jahren 1911 und 1912*, (Munich & Leipzig: Duncker & Humblot, 1925), 90. In Troeltsch's words, the historical method entails "the renunciation of a history possessing dogmatic, ready-made criteria and the assumption of a history which produces its basic concepts out of its own work. A firmly delimited normative truth, presented as available in the Bible or in the church, and both accredited and recognisable on the basis of divine authority is dispensed with." Troeltsch, "What Does 'Essence of Christianity' Mean?," *Writings*, 131.

to meaning, and a rigorous historical method renders it impossible to posit the presence of the eternal within the changing matrix of history. If there is any divine meaning in the world, it can only be sought from within history.[59] Criteriology for truth is firmly planted within history, not apart from it.

Troeltsch's commitment to history accounts for his varied interests. He was involved in interdisciplinary academic work[60] before it became fashionable, adding to his works on theology significant contributions in areas such as philosophy, religion, sociology, ethics and politics. His decision to move from the theological faculty at the university of Heidelberg to assume the chair of philosophy at Berlin in 1914 was not, as Barth would have us believe,[61] a case of giving up theology for philosophy. Rather, it should be seen as a natural transition given his markedly historical orientation and his understanding of theology as a discipline founded in the philosophy of history and religion.[62] We find in Troeltsch a metaphysics of history with a porous divider between theology and philosophy. To his mind, it is the business of theology to demonstrate the compatibility (*Zusammenbestehbarkeit*) between secular culture and religious truth.[63] Such an inclusiveness is integral to the scientific thrust of the historical method when applied to theology, vis-à-vis the programme of *religionsgeschichtliche Theologie*.

His *modus operandi* in theology is to first examine the history of the Christian faith to see how it has developed historically, and then

---

[59] Quigley, "Historical Absolute," 23.

[60] Trutz Rendtorff & Friedrich Wilhelm Graf, "Ernst Troeltsch," in Ninian Smart, John Clayton, Patrick Sherry, & Steven T. Katz, eds., *Nineteenth Century Religious Thought in the West*, 3 Vols. (Cambridge: Cambridge University Press, 1985), 3:307.

[61] K. Barth, "Evangelical Theology in the 19th Century," in *The Humanity of God* (Atlanta: John Knox Press, 1960). On reasons for Troeltsch's decision to leave Heidelberg, see Yasukata, *Troeltsch*, 123–5.

[62] Of the move, biographer Drescher notes: "We are to think less in terms of a violent break or renunciation on his part than of a transition to something new, in both his specific work and its external setting." *Troeltsch*, 127. Troeltsch himself confessed that in the intervening years between the publication of *The Absoluteness of Christianity* in 1902 and the move to Berlin in 1914, his outlook or horizon had broadened even further in the direction of a universal history. See Yasukata, *Troeltsch*, 126; and Helmut Thielicke, *Modern Faith and Thought* (Grand Rapids: Eerdmans, 1990), 538.

[63] Troeltsch, "Weltanschauung," 495. As Morgan avers, "Troeltsch forced Christian theology to take seriously the reality of the world—a world which includes nature as well as history, society as well as ideas, other religions as well as Christianity." "Troeltsch and Christian Theology," *Writings*, 214.

seek out what is enduring in the Christian tradition and match that with needs in the present.[64] To understand what is abiding or absolute in theology, one must first situate Christianity within the larger context of world religions, and then through a process of comparison discern the validity and superiority of Christianity.[65] Troeltsch has no intention of reducing theology to a general science of religion; probing the universal history of religions is but preliminary and auxiliary to theology. Nor does he dispense with the role of faith in theological formulation. Faith and history must coexist harmoniously.

Theology is a scientific enterprise in that it takes serious account of the total historical phenomenon of Christianity, while at the same time it provides "support for a living religious preaching."[66] His interest in history is not confined to a past distinct from the present. Rather he regards the past and present as conjoined and linked in the continuum of history. The present is invariably a product of the past; and the past is in turn understood and perceived from the standpoint of the present. Furthermore, the past is interrogated to search out its significance for the present. He sought throughout his intellectual life to bring about a mediation between the pastness of Christian tradition and the concerns and needs of the present.

Given the interlacing of Christianity with the universal history of religions, how then does one affirm its absoluteness? Neither the way of supernatural presuppositionalism nor Hegel's nomination of Christianity as the evolutionary realization of the universal "idea" of religion is acceptable to Troeltsch; the first because it is an ahistorical imposition and the second because it undermines the integrity of historical data by fitting them within Hegel's procrustean framework.[67] In that Hegelian speculation assumes a vantage point from

---

[64] This is discernible in Troeltsch's essays, "Historical and Dogmatic Methods in Theology"; "Prinzip, religiöses," in *RGG*, as well as the methodological prolegomenon in his *Glaubenslehre*.

[65] This is true of his early works, particularly in *The Absoluteness of Christianity*, where Troeltsch assumes and tries to demonstrate the superiority of Christianity. As we shall see below, he moves away from this position in his mature years.

[66] Troeltsch, "Half a Century of Theology," *Writings*, 77.

[67] See James Luther Adams' introduction, and chapter 2 of Troeltsch's *Absoluteness*. Troeltsch argues against Hegel when he contends that there exists "no *a priori* ready-made criterion" for the history of religions. "Selbständigkeit," 6:167. It should be noted that in his earlier essays, Troeltsch was not unsympathetic to Hegel. In his "Geschichte und Metaphysik" and "Historical and Dogmatic Methods," we find signs of a Hegelian slant. But by the time he wrote *Absoluteness*, especially in the second edition, he became critical of Hegel. See Coakley, *Without Absolutes*, 58, 74–75.

which the movement of the divine life as a causal, teleological and
unitary life-process is perceived, it is but "a philosophical substitute
for the dogmatic supernaturalism of the church."[68] History, according to Troeltsch, knows no values which are part of a universal principle which serves as a norm for all individual historical realities.

What Troeltsch offers instead is a two-pronged approach: first,
redefine the "absolute" in historical terms; and second, locate it
within the historicity of human experience. With regards to the first,
he argues that historical thinking need not preclude Christianity as
the highest religious truth. In fact, one might say on the basis of
historical investigation that Christianity is the focal point and cul-
mination of all religious developments.[69] Yet this evaluation can only
be normative *for the time being*, and *for the adherents* of Christianity; it
is by no means a universal and timeless absoluteness.[70] This need
not open the door to "unlimited relativism;" Troeltsch is not saying
that history is without norms, only that we understand these as products of history. In a manner which anticipates Pannenberg's eschatological view of universal history, Troeltsch asserts that the realization
of absoluteness is a goal which is ever "out in front".[71] Absolute
truth is futural and will appear only at the close of earthly history.

Troeltsch has no wish to relativize the claim of Christianity on
account of it being a purely historical phenomenon. To avoid the

---

[68] Troeltsch, *Absoluteness*, 55.

[69] Chapter 4 of *Absoluteness*, cf. 114. Troeltsch himself illustrates the corrigibility of ideas, for one detects shifts in his views on the absoluteness of Christianity.
In his early (1894) essay on the Christian world-view and its counter-currents,
"Weltanschauung," 4:224, he presents a largely Ritschlian view on the problem of
absoluteness, i.e., Christianity's superiority is attested by its pure spiritual and moral
character, in opposition to other religions of nature. By 1898, we find a movement
away from this dogmatic bias, a movement clearly evident in *Absoluteness*. See his
essay, "Zur theologischen Lage," *Die Christliche Welt* 12(1898): 627–31; 650–57.

[70] Troeltsch writes: "Faith may regard Christianity . . . as a heightening of the
religious standard in terms of which the inner life of man will continue to exist.
But we cannot and must not regard it as an absolute, perfect, immutable truth."
Absoluteness, 115. He goes on: "To wish to possess the absolute in an absolute way
at a particular point in history is a delusion. It shatters not only because of its
impracticability but also because it runs counter to the nature of every historical
expression of religion." 122.

[71] Troeltsch, *Absoluteness*, 99. As Drescher, *Troeltsch*, 162, describes it: "For Troeltsch,
the comparability of historical formations presupposes a universal; not, however,
one which is arrived at through abstraction but one which appears in the phenomena of life itself as the goal or ideal which is envisaged at any point. This goal
is not realized anywhere, but remains an idea which is envisaged as a final purpose of the whole. For Troeltsch, this notion from the philosophy of history is without doubt an analogy to the eschatology of Christianity."

extremes of ahistorical supernaturalism and a relativism arising from
an absolutization of historicality, he seeks a "fresh, durable, and creative synthesis"[72] centered on the dynamics between the individual
and his or her historical context. This idea of a creative synthesis
will go on to play an important role in his later theological development. Troeltsch rejects history as fate, and wants to allow for the
formative possibility of individuals acting within history. Here the
second part in his two-pronged approach comes into the discussion
on the subject of absoluteness in history: religious experience.

Troeltsch's strong historicism led him increasingly to locate the
divine in the historicity of the human heart, particularly in the religious intuition to seek out meaning. Instead of searching for the
divine objectively in the past, the focus is now on the present and
the search directed at the inner dimension.[73] In this, he considers
himself an heir of Schleiermacher.[74] Revelation is not about supernatural events like the incarnation or resurrection within time and
space. It is understood as intuition and resides in religious experience, which in turn is grounded in the historicity of the experiencing (religious) subject. Troeltsch's method combines historicist and
existential elements in a coherent way, so much so that Gogarten,
his former student and one of his sharpest critics, even describes him
as a "romanticist" and charges him, alongside Schleiermacher, with
compromising the otherness of divine revelation by locating it within
the romantic subjectivism of an innate human faculty for experiencing God.[75] But this existential and romantic side to Troeltsch is
not incompatible with his historicism. According to Perkins, the existential features represent not so much a weakening of historicism as
the realistic means by which its demands may be fulfilled.[76] The

---

[72] Troeltsch, *Absoluteness*, 90.

[73] Miracles, in Troeltsch's estimation, are not so much events in history as "events"
within the hearts of people in the form of an inner perception of God's power and
influence. See his *Glaubenslehre*, 34; and *Absoluteness*, 48.

[74] Troeltsch, "Metaphysik," 27–28, 40. Also his "Half a Century of Theology: A
Review," in *Writings*, 80. On the relationship between Troeltsch and Schleiermacher,
see B. A. Gerrish, "Ernst Troeltsch and the Possibility of a Historical Theology,"
Clayton, ed., *Troeltsch and the Future of Theology*, 100–35; and Yasukata, *Troeltsch*, 79.

[75] Friedrich Gogarten, "Wider die romantische Theologie," in Jürgen Moltmann,
ed., *Anfänge der dialektischen Theologie*, 2 vols. (Munich: Chr. Kaiser Verlag, 1967),
2:148. Frei alludes too to the combination of the historical and the existential in
Troeltsch. "Faith and History," 63.

[76] Perkins, *Explicating*, 13. Troeltsch's existentialism is also noted by James Luther
Adams in his introduction to Troeltsch's *Absoluteness*, 12. Elsewhere, Adams suggests

challenges thrown up by the historical method can only be resolved
or addressed through an existential response. Historical study must
lead to existential decision, and the criterion for such a decision must
in the end be a personal one.[77]

Absoluteness is impossible since its historicity necessarily relativizes
it. Yet the pious are wont to speak of their religious experiences in
absolute existential terms. How then does one reconcile the necessary relativity of historical events and the assertion of finality by the
religious? Troeltsch responds by interpreting the relationship between
human beings and God as something direct and immediate. Although
revelation is associated with Jesus and developed in history, it is ultimately found in "individual religiosity and illumination"; the core
definition of revelation lies in "inner sensing and certainty of God".[78]
History is but the arena in which this immediate encounter with
God takes place.

In addition to Kant's theoretical a priori, moral a priori, and aesthetic a priori in his *Critique of Pure Reason*, *Critique of Practical Reason*,
and *Critique of Judgment* respectively, Troeltsch adds a fourth: humans
are imbued with a "religious a priori."[79] Human consciousness is
marked by an innate and immediate predisposition toward self-transcendence. While he concurs with the empiricists that all thought
must be grounded in an analysis of human experience, he parts company with them by insisting that such an analysis is inadequate if it
is restricted to sense data and does not take into account the relation
between human consciousness and the absolute. A strictly positivistic

---

that Troeltsch's integration of existential elements in his historical method is a "har-
binger of contemporary existentialism". "Ernst Troeltsch as Analyst of Religion,"
JSSR 1(1961): 98. Thielicke too observes an existential affinity between him and
Kierkegaard, whom Troeltsch knew and wrestled with in his thinking. *Modern Faith*,
521. However, Perkins notes, Troeltsch is not a thoroughgoing existentialist in the
mold of a Kierkegaard, Heidegger or Sartre. The style of his theologizing reflects
sufficiently the formal emphases of existentialism that one is justified in designating
him as one among the existentialists. Perkins, *Explicating*, 16–19.

[77] Troeltsch, *Absoluteness*, 96–97, writes: "Such a criterion is, then, a matter of
personal conviction and is in the last analysis admittedly subjective. However, there
is no other way to obtain a criterion that will enable us to choose among competing historical values. It is, in short, a personal, ethically oriented, religious conviction acquired by comparison and evaluation."

[78] Troeltsch, "Offenbarung," in *RGG*, quoted in Coakley, *Without Absolutes*, 93.

[79] Troeltsch, "Zur Frage des religiösen Apriori," *GS* 2:754–68. Cf. Paul Tillich,
Perspectives on Nineteenth and Twentieth Century Protestant Theology, ed. Carl E. Braaten
(London: SCM, 1967), 231.

treatment of religion will invariably be reductionistic.[80] It is this relation of consciousness to the absolute that constitutes the religious a
priori.

Troeltsch adopted the genre of *Glaubenslehre* which Schleiermacher
introduced to theological writing.[81] Up till Schleiermacher, the dogmatics of Protestantism were essentially construals based on the Bible.
The shift from dogmatics to *Glaubenslehre*, reflects the movement away
from a reliance on an essentially timeless authority to a descriptive
analysis of religiosity in the present. The existential dimension in
theology comes to the fore in the approach of *Glaubenslehre*, with the
spotlight falling on the subjectivity entailed in an experience of God,
a subjectivity conditioned by history. This is evident in Troeltsch's
view of the relationship between faith and history. Faith cannot establish historical facts—only a critical historical method can; it can only
interpret them.[82] And that interpretation entails a grappling with
those images, ideas, and symbols which are given in the Christian
tradition.

B. *Historical Relativism and Christology*

How then does Troeltsch's commitment to historicism militate against
an incarnational Christology? As Coakley notes, this is the crux of
the criticisms leveled against Troeltsch's Christology. Coakley's treatise on his Christology is particularly helpful in two ways: firstly, in
pointing out the equivocality of the concept of relativism and noting
that its occurrence in Troeltsch is not always clear and consistent;
and secondly, in outlining the development in Troeltsch's Christological position over the years,[83] so that any characterization of his

---

[80] "Religion and the Science of Religion," *Writings*, 82–84; 106f. Cf. Troeltsch,
"Empiricism and Platonism in the Philosophy of Religion," *HTR* 5(1912): 401–22.

[81] Troeltsch's *Glaubenslehre* was published posthumously. On his *Glaubenslehre*, see
Gerrish, "Possibility of Theology"; Perkins, *Troeltsch's* Glaubenslehre; Walter E.
Wyman, Jr., *The Concept of Glaubenslehre: Ernst Troeltsch and the Theological Heritage of
Schleiermacher* (Chico: Scholars Press, 1983).

[82] "The Significance of the Existence of the Historical Jesus for Faith," *Writings*, 198.

[83] Troeltschean scholarship usually traces the development of Troeltsch's thought
through three phases: the early period up to 1903, the period of disengagement
from Ritschlianism; the middle period to about 1914, the most productive period;
and the final period leading up to his untimely death in 1923. Examples of the
way Troeltsch changed his mind include: amendments which he made in the second edition (1912) of *Absoluteness* (1902); and the over seventy alterations he made
to his 1903 essay, "What Does 'Essence of Christianity' Mean?" for inclusion in
his collected works. See Sykes' note in *Writings*, 180.

views on Christology should take into account the contexts of his
developing thought. The following comments may be made about
Troeltsch's de-absolutized or relativized Christology:

First, there is a lack of definitional precision in the use of the
word "relativism" in Troeltsch. While words like "relativising," "relativity," and "relativism" are employed in his early works,[84] it does not
necessarily follow that he is advocating a strong epistemological relativism. Coakley distinguishes between various types of relativism,
and warns against applying it univocally.[85] In so doing, she provides
a schema by which Troeltsch's claims for relativism, made at different
times in his career, may be appraised. While there is ambiguity as
to whether, and in what sense, Troeltsch espouses relativism in his
early works, the overall impression one gets, as a close reading of
his *The Absoluteness of Christianity* indicates, is that he does not come
out on the side of a strong or conscious epistemological relativism
at this point in his life.[86] He seems at this stage explicitly to reject
any ethical or value scepticism. His concern is to accentuate the
importance of religion within history, and for this to happen, it is
necessary to discern from within the ebb and flow of history, instantiations of critical religious insights which mark them out from all
other elements in history. An absolute relativism on matters of religion and ethics would nullify this.

However, from Troeltsch's "middle period" (to about 1914) on,
we find evidence of an increasing tilt in a more radical direction.
Essays from this period[87] reveal a basic vacillation or "indecision"
on his part which inclined him gradually towards an epistemologi-

---

[84] E.g., "Metaphysik;" "Historical and Dogmatic Methods;" and *Absoluteness*.
[85] See Coakley, *Without Absolutes*, 8–23.
[86] While the principles of criticism, analogy and correlation, which together form
the pillars of Troeltsch's historical method, have been cited as evidence of Troeltsch's
relativism, it is not certain that his position is that of epistemological relativism.
Granted that the principle of criticism with its implication of the corrigibility of historical judgments may be read as a form of epistemological relativism, especially in
view of Troeltsch's later espousal of Hegelian metaphysics, it is neither a very strong
nor a conscious form; and it seems to be restricted to specifically religious truths
only.
[87] See: Troeltsch, "What Does 'The Essence of Christianity' Mean?", written in
response to Harnack's *Das Wesen des Christentums* in 1903. ET in *Writings*, 124–81.
Troeltsch made about seventy alterations in his revision in 1913. See S. W. Sykes,
"Ernst Troeltsch and Christianity's Essence," in Clayton, ed., *Future*, 139–71 and
his note in *Writings*, 180–81. Also: "The Dogmatics of the 'Religionsgeschichte
Schule'," *AJT* 17(1913): 1–21.

cal relativism. On the issue of Christianity's essence, Coakley captures the dilemma facing Troeltsch nicely:

> Should he move to a consistent espousal of epistemological relativism in the case of doctrinal truth, admitting that this might, in principle, lead to a range of disjunctive "truths"; or should he still attempt to ward off that particular possibility by a continued appeal to a unified teleological metaphysic?[88]

His grip on the belief that there is ultimately one essence in Christianity proves tenuous, as we find in his essay on Christianity's essence intimations of an epistemological relativism. If the very act of doctrinal definition has a constituting effect on the essence, does that not make it context-dependent? Troeltsch mitigates this relativism by espousing a metaphysical perspectivism whereby contingently formulated "essences" somehow correspond to the real "essence" of Christianity. By the time of the essay on the dogmatics of the "history of religions" school, metaphysical perspectivism is quietly dropped and we are left with an essentially epistemological relativism.[89] If one's approach is to be consistently historical, then it is futile to speak of a univocal essence. Contrary to Harnack, Christianity has as many "essences" as there are epochs and contexts in history.

Ambiguity on the nature of his relativism again attends Troeltsch's mature works from the final period of his career, even though he appears to countenance a thesis of incommensurability at the end of his life. In *Der Historismus und seine Probleme*, Troeltsch espouses a kind of value relativism in the sense that there are no permanent criteria by which one may make value judgment, only criteria arising from a given context. Identifying what these contextual criteria are is important if one is to avoid "unlimited relativism" and discern what is of value from among the plethora of values which historical investigation throws up. Troeltsch argues in *Historismus* that criteria for value judgment are given in the particularity of historical situation, but these come to light only by means of a cultural synthesis which takes place within the historical horizon or subjectivity of the historian. We shall return to this idea later; suffice it to say that this is Troeltsch's way of affirming historical relativity without falling foul of an indiscriminate endorsement of values.

---

[88] *Without Absolutes*, 31.
[89] Ibid., 33.

Nevertheless, in the essay of 1923, "The Place of Christianity among the World Religions" (which Troeltsch planned to deliver in England, but he died before he could do so), he departs from his earlier position in *Absoluteness*, and argues for an epistemological relativism: Christianity can be said to be true only in the sense of being "true for" adherents of a particular social and cultural context.[90] He adheres to a perspectival view of reality whereby different religions offer perspectives on the whole of reality. What is significant to note is that for Troeltsch now, Christianity is neither unique nor supreme; it is but one among other possible apprehensions of reality. In this he is a value- and an epistemological relativist.[91]

Second, Troeltsch's Christology seems to oscillate between on the one hand, ascribing a sense of uniqueness to Christ with a corresponding appeal to his inner experience which is not hostage to historical scholarship, and on the other hand, repudiating the subjectivism of any claim to a direct relationship with Christ which is not mediated through historical investigation.[92] This variegation seems to be calibrated to his ambivalence towards Hegel and his attempt to come out from under the shadow of Ritschl.[93] His 1898 essay, "Geschichte und Metaphysik," shows signs of this tension. He questions the possibility of reconstructing the personality of the historical Jesus with certainty, yet asserts a strong linkage between Jesus and the Christian principle (*Prinzip*),[94] in such a way that the "security" (*Bürgschaft*) of the believers' relationship with God is attainable only by means of a return to the historical Jesus. He wants to hold on to the Ritschlian notion that Jesus' inner life testifies to his unique rela-

---

[90] The essay is included in *Christian Thought: Its History and Application*, ed. Baron F. von Hügel (London: University of London Press, 1923), 3–35. See Coakley, *Without Absolutes*, 37f.

[91] Coakley cautions against equating Troeltsch's relativism with the sort of strong incommensurability canvassed by contemporary writers like D. Z. Phillips, Feyerabend or Winch. Neither is it unrestricted in application—Troeltsch's epistemological relativism for instance does not concern perception—nor does it contravene a correspondence doctrine of truth. *Without Absolutes*, 43.

[92] See his essay, "Geschichte und Metaphysik," written in response to criticisms by the Ristchlian Julius Kaftan in 1898.

[93] To the extent that Yasukata avers: "it would hardly be an overstatement to say that the entire course of Troeltsch's theological development was strongly determined by his Oedipean struggle to overcome the flaws which he exposed in his great teacher's doctrines." *Troeltsch*, 2.

[94] This linkage is one which Troeltsch continues to maintain in his essay of 1911, "The Significance of the Historical Existence of Jesus for Faith," *Writings*, 197.

tionship with God, while simultaneously affirming the lack of certainty about Jesus' personality which the application of the historical critical method brings. This is due, in Coakley's opinion, to his basic indecision at this point as to whether to follow through, as far as Christology is concerned, the full implications of a "theology of historicism"; and this ambivalence continues in *The Absoluteness of Christianity*, where in the first edition of 1902, we find him "back tracking towards Ritschlianism".[95] Only in the period from 1902–1912 that he finally disengaged from the Christology of Ritschl and Herrmann. Any variances or lack of clarity in his statements may be put down to the torturous tension he laboured under in seeking to reconcile the absolute and the historically contingent[96] while at the same time affirm the significance of Jesus Christ.

Third, we encounter in Troeltsch's understanding of God, revelation, and redemption a tendency which might best be described as a depivotalization of Christology. Instead of the particularity of Christ being pivotal to one's definition of God, revelation, and redemption, in Troeltsch's mature thought, the latter are grounded not so much in Christology as in a metaphysics of history. In his desire to combat the dualistic understanding of God's relation to the world whereby his activity is bifurcated into the ordinary and humdrum on the one hand, and the salvifically significant on the other (i.e., distinction between normal history and *Heilsgeschichte*), he puts the accent on God's immanence, and in so doing dissolves the distinction between the sacred and the ordinary.

Theology is incarnational in the sense that it is in the nature of God to reveal himself in and through humanity.[97] And the idea that God is mediated through history means that one can only speak of a full revelation of God at the end of time, thus relativizing the traditional claim that in Jesus we have the full revelation of God. His

---

[95] Coakley, *Without Absolutes*, 67, explains: "in some passages Troeltsch explicitly adopts a position uncannily close to Herrmann, and that this actively flouts the tenets of the 'historical method' as laid down in his most recent essay on 'historical and dogmatic method'." Cf. 62–63.

[96] Paul Tillich is right when he suggests that the core (*Kern*) of Troeltsch's *Lebensproblematik* is "the tension between the absolute and the relative" (*Spannung von Absoluten und Relativen*). Cited in Yasukata, *Troeltsch*, xv.

[97] There is a seemingly panentheistic dimension to Troeltsch's doctrine of God which correlates his being to positive human response. See Coakley, *Without Absolutes*, 116.

progressive understanding of revelation[98] puts in question the finality
and exclusivity of revelation in Christ. Moreover, there is in Troeltsch
a "democratization of revelation"[99] which extends revelatory significance
to mediatorial figures besides Jesus. His immanentized view of divine
activity is joined by an existential understanding of redemption.
Rather than being restricted to a past event, redemption is perpet-
ual and recurrent, and takes place at the existential level of religious
experience, which is at once self-authenticating and immediate, requiring no postulation of incarnational Christology. There is thus in his
redefinition of theology proper, of redemption and revelation, a loosening of ties with an incarnational Christology.

Fourth and finally, Troeltsch's own Christological reflections provide additional material for his case against an incarnational Christology.[100] His Enlightenment-inspired metaphysics of history rules out
of court the patristic idea of a God-Man,[101] and regards the thought-
form and language of Chalcedon irrelevant to modern "preaching,
devotion and catechism".[102] His anti-metaphysical predilection betrays
the lingering presence of Ritschlianism, and contributes to his rejection of Chalcedonian Christology. The application of critical methods to the Gospels and to patristic formulations of Christology yields
a historical and "humanized" Jesus as the starting point for dogmatic reflection, making it problematic to retain belief in the incarnation of a pre-existent Logos. In place of a metaphysical Christology,
he proposes a sociological and psychological approach which takes
history seriously yet retains (at least tries to) a place of significance
for the historical Jesus. The divinization of Christ in the creeds owes
more to the need of the early Christians for a central galvanising
and unifying figure than a metaphysical incarnation. One detects in
this reading of the rise of Christology more than a hint of Ebionism.

Troeltsch argues for the importance of Christology on sociological grounds in his essay, "The Significance of the Historical Existence
of Jesus for Faith," written in response to Arthur Drews' tendentious
book, *Die Christusmythe.*[103] Unlike Drews who regards the historical

---

[98] See Troeltsch, "Historiography," and *Glaubenslehre*, 39f, 118f.
[99] Coakley, *Without Absolutes*, 117; also 164–87. In this, Troeltsch anticipates contemporary non-incarnational pluralists like John Hick and Paul Knitter.
[100] See ibid., 123–35.
[101] Troeltsch, *Historismus*, GS 3:14.
[102] Troeltsch, "Significance," 206.
[103] Troeltsch, "Significance," in *Writings*, 182–207; Arthur Drews, *Die Christusmythe*

Jesus of the Gospels as a personified ideal or a historicized myth, he affirms the indispensability of the historical Jesus to Christianity, though it is not entirely clear how he regards the former as necessary for the latter.[104] In any case, his concern is to offer a historical argument for the rise of Christology. Christ, he contends, is the "rallying-point" of the early "Christ cult," and the rise of the Christological dogma is a natural sociological consequence. "It was the requirement of community and cult which gave to the personality of Christ its central position."[105] Troeltsch's is a functional rather than an ontological Christology, in which Christ's divinity is a sociological and psychological necessity, not an ontological postulate. While it would be incorrect to say that Christology is for him nothing more than a socio-psychological necessity—he still wants to make a strong claim for the "revelatory" significance of Jesus—the functional element is nevertheless conspicuous, given its compatibility with a committed historicism.

C. *The Long Shadow of Troeltsch*

Troeltsch is extraordinarily perceptive to the implications of the rise of historical consciousness for theology. One may not agree with his reinterpretation of Christ and Christianity, but one cannot ignore the fact that the historicization of thought poses a challenge to the revelatory finality of Jesus Christ. We find in Troeltsch's work emphases which comport with some of the features of postmodernity identified above. It appears to us that contemporary postmodern rejection of

---

(Jena: E. Diedrichs, 1909), ET from the 3rd German edition by C. Delisle Burns, *The Christ Myth* (London: Fisher Unwin, 1910). Troeltsch discusses Drews most directly in "Aus der religiösen Bewegung der Gegenwart," in *GS* 2:22–24, 36–43. Cf. B. A. Gerrish, "Jesus, Myth and History: Troeltsch's Stand in the 'Christ-Myth' Debate," *JRel* 55(1975): 13–35.

[104] Gerrish, "Jesus, Myth and History," 26, suggests that the efficacy of the image of Christ for Christianity in Troeltsch's social-psychological argument does not require it to be demonstrably grounded in an actual historical life. Troeltsch himself seems to say as much with his emphasis on the decisive role of religious experience for the individual. While conceding many of Gerrish's points, Coakley nevertheless defends Troeltsch against this charge. In Troeltsch's metaphysics of history, religious truth arises in and through history, which would make it necessary to tie the truth of Christology to the historical Jesus. See *Without Absolutes*, 155–63.

[105] Troeltsch, "Significance," 203; also *Absoluteness*, 161; *Social Teaching*, 994: "The only peculiarly primitive Christian dogma, the dogma of the Divinity of Christ, first arose out of the worship of Christ, and this again developed out of the fact that the new spiritual community felt the necessity for meeting together."

unifying truth comes out of a form of argumentation not unlike the critical historicism of Troeltsch. Perhaps today's postmodern consciousness is a radicalized version, an evolved form, of nineteenth-century historical consciousness of which Troeltsch is a proponent.

There are of course differences between Troeltsch's project and postmodernity. To begin with, there is absent in Troeltsch that dismissiveness of absolute truth which is virtually *de rigueur* in deconstructive postmodernity. He would not have subjected himself to such torment in trying to reconcile the absolute with the historical if truth were not important to him. There is a rather different spirit in him. The largely Enlightenment *Weltanschauung* under which Troeltsch laboured is another point of dissimilarity. His historiography is essentially positivistic insofar as it assumes that what really happened in history can be abstracted from the superstitious or supernatural forms in which events are couched. His confidence in historiography as a science, as well as the premium he pays to values like objectivity and impartiality, are all indicative of his Enlightenment mindset. Unlike the postmetaphysical slant of postmodernity, he does not hesitate to embrace metaphysics. It may well be that in assigning *a priori* status to subjectivity and consciousness, he is still operating within the Cartesian framework of searching out a firm platform to overcome Renaissance scepticism, which would clearly differentiate him from postmodernity.

Yet in one sense, he goes beyond the Enlightenment in endorsing a brand of epistemic and criterial relativism towards the end of his career; and this highlights the "family resemblance" between Troeltsch's thoughts and contemporary philosophical concerns. For a start, this comparison is not inappropriate considering the influence which Nietzsche evidently had on his philosophy of history. Though not uncritical of Nietzsche, he nevertheless took on board elements of his philosophy in his understanding of historical existence. Quigley observes:

> Troeltsch appears to be directly indebted to the work of Nietzsche, who, in his essay of 1874 *On the Use and Abuse of History*, had outlined a radical understanding of historical existence, the principle elements of which are to be found in Troeltsch's formulation of the absolute and incorporated in his text of 1903. It is well to remember that in his essay "On Historical and Dogmatic Method in Theology", Troeltsch not only gave evidence of being aware of Nietzsche's essay, but con-

sidered it "brilliant" in that it articulated the most precise understanding of historical existence.[106]

We might even say that Troeltsch belongs to that stream in German philosophy emanating from Herder which feeds into the relativism which is so much a feature of contemporary thought.[107] Moreover, that strong humanistic assertion of the will, evident in Descartes and the Enlightenment, and alchemized in Nietzsche into "the will to power," is a theme in Troeltsch's system. His repudiation of determinism and strong emphasis on consciousness, freedom, and human subjectivity, his elevation of the volitional above other human faculties, and his view of faith as a responsible decisional act, are variations of an existential assertion of the will which has both a Nietzschean and a contemporary feel to it. If history may be said to have any teleological significance, it would be a "volitional teleology, which forms and shapes the future out of the past in the present moment."[108]

Secondly, and perhaps the area where Troeltsch intersects most with postmodern thought, is in their common allegiance to historicism, albeit defined differently and employed for different purposes (with differing effects). The replacement of the dogmatic method by a historical one is, in Kuhnian parlance, nothing short of a "paradigm shift." In this regard, it is interesting to compare Troeltsch and Rorty's startling pronouncements before their respective colleagues. Sensing the monumental changes which historicism would make to theology, Troeltsch stood before the Friends of the *Christliche Welt* gathering in 1896 and declared: "Meine Herren, es wackelt alles! (Gentlemen, everything is tottering!)"[109] With comparable panache,

---

[106] Quigley, "Historical Absolute," 30. Troeltsch considers Nietzsche (alongside Dilthey) "as 'the great master' who has expounded for all the psychological elements of historical existence." A survey of his *Gesammelte Schriften* will provide ample evidence of Troeltsch's understanding of Nietzsche's work. 20.

[107] Patrick Gardiner, "German Philosophy and the Rise of Relativism," *Monist* 64(1981): 138–53. There are elements in Herder's works which Troeltsch regards as containing the germs of a *religionsgeschichtliche* theology. "Religionswissenschaft und Theologie des 18. Jahrhunderts," *PJ* 114(1903): 55–56.

[108] "... sondern die Teleologie des seine Vergangenheit zur Zukunft aus dem Moment herausformenden und gestaltenden Willens." Troeltsch, *Historismus*, 112. Translation by Peter C. Hodgson in *God in History: Shapes of Freedom* (Nashville: Abingdon, 1989), 137, cf. 268 n. 73.

[109] As Walter Köhler recounts it, after an erudite lecture on the meaning of the

Rorty shocked the 1979 gathering of the *American Philosophical Association*
by announcing "the end of philosophy."[110] Just as Troeltsch presided
over what he perceived to be the demise of the dogmatic method,
Rorty eulogized the death of philosophy. Troeltsch's rejection of the
dogmatic method is a consequence of the older nineteenth century
historicism, while Rorty's deconstruction of philosophy shares the
same historicist impulse. After all, his strategy in the assault on philosophy as the mirror of nature lies in exposing its contingency.

Historicism, so conspicuous in the human sciences of the last century, is enjoying a resurgence since the late 1980s in the form of a
"new historicism," which has become somewhat of a catchphrase in
literary criticism and in American philosophy. William Dean characterizes the claim for the ultimacy of historical categories in contemporary writers like Rorty, Bernstein, Goodman, Putnam, Lentricchia,
West and Stout, as a "new historicism" which is different though
not unlike the older historicism represented by Kant, Schleiermacher,
Hegel, Dilthey, and Troeltsch.[111] In that the latter retains ontological and theological dimensions, it describes the kind of historicism
present in Heidegger, Gadamer, Habermas, and Pannenberg.
Interestingly, the historical method which Troeltsch seized upon is
one which is still operative today, albeit in a different form. Fixed
external criteria for knowledge are set aside in favour of criteria
which are grounded in history. It is in this sense that postmodern
consciousness is a radicalized version of the kind of historical consciousness represented by Troeltsch.

A third area of comparison is the anticipation of postmodernity's
perspectivalism and democratization of truth in Troeltsch's rejection

---

logos-doctrine by Julius Kaftan, a young Troeltsch went to the rostrum and began
his statement on the changing scene of theology with his "*es wackelt alles*" exclamation. This appalled the older scholars present, and Troeltsch was rebuked by the
spokesman Ferdinand Kattenbusch; whereupon Troeltsch left the room, slamming
the doors behind him. *Ernst Troeltsch* (Tübingen: J. C. B. Mohr [Paul Siebeck],
1941), 1. Cf. Drescher, *Troeltsch*, 86.

[110] Diggins, *Promise of Pragmatism*, 11.

[111] "The Challenge of the New Historicism," *JRel* 66(1986): 261–81. On the "new
historicism," see also: Hodgson, *God in History*, 31–36; Brook Thomas, *The New
Historicism and Other Old-Fashioned Topics* (Princeton: Princeton University Press, 1991);
H. Aram Veeser, ed., *The New Historicism* (New York & London: Routledge, 1989);
Georg G. Iggers, "Historicism: The History and Meaning of the Term," *JHI*
56(1995): 129–52; David D. Roberts, *Nothing But History: Reconstruction and Extremity
after Metaphysics* (Berkeley: University of California Press, 1995); also Hamilton,
Historicism, 150f.

of an absolutized Christianity on account of the immensity of human history. Troeltsch argues:

> Man's age upon earth amounts to several hundred thousand years or more. His future may come to still more. It is hard to imagine a single point of history along this line, and that the centre-point of our own religious history, as the sole centre of all humanity. That looks far too much like the absolutising our [sic] own contingent area of life. That is in religion what geocentricism and anthropocentricism are in cosmology and metaphysics.[112]

A deabsolutization of truth results in a pluralization of truth-claims. Adams characterizes Troeltsch's approach to reality as multi-perspectival or "meroscopic" rather than "holoscopic"; the latter seeks to unify everything under a unitary perspective while the former "presupposes that different spheres of reality should be described by means of quite different types of concept."[113] The concept of unitary truth, under the hammer blow of historicism, disintegrates into fragments of truths. Consequently, one can speak of truth only from within one's own historical, cultural and social context. Truth is *for us* rather than *for all*. Troeltsch says as much in an essay in 1910, where he alludes to "an infinite plurality of spiritual worlds" and cautions against speaking of the "cosmic significance of Jesus".[114] Truth assertions reflect only what different religious adherents regard as true. Through further study of non-Christian religions, and an appraisal of the individuality of Christianity, he came to see Christianity as inextricably tied to the civilization of Greece, Rome and Northern Europe, and not universal. It is true only for those who have grown up with it. In the face of religious pluralism, he avers:

> one has only to resolve to let each complex go untroubled on its way, and to live in each according to its own special demands, without elevating any one of them monistically into a universal basis or a single all-determining accent. One can only demand for the most universal community, which is that of *Humanity*, a mutual understanding and tolerance, and a feeling of fundamental human obligation, without any very definite content.[115]

---

[112] "Significance," 189.
[113] J. L. Adams, "Troeltsch as Analyst," 100.
[114] "On the Possibility of a Liberal Christianity," *UUC* 29(1974): 31.
[115] "Place of Christianity," 26.

Troeltsch is prophetic here, for such a tolerance, borne of pluralism, has become virtually a touchstone of political correctness in the halls of academia today. The egalitarian thrust of his view of revelation surely resonates with the pluralization of truth in postmodernity.

Fourthly, the view of doctrine enshrined in Troeltsch's *Glaubenslehre*, with its grounding of belief in the subjectivity of the Christian and its understanding of doctrine as expressive of the Christian's personal experience, and fulfilling a regulative function within the community, bears comparison with the social constructivist notion of belief-formation in postmetaphysical thought. Despite criticism that his construal of subjectivity is too individualistic,[116] there is certainly present in Troeltsch a strong emphasis on faith as a communal experience,[117] especially in his *Social Teaching of the Christian Churches*. He eschews the individualism which marks modern life, and calls for a greater respect for tradition even though the latter is neither beyond reproach nor correction. The faith of the individual is sustained by resources which come through the heritage of churches. Community and cult are thus indispensable to religious faith, and the consciousness of the community necessary for the construction of doctrine.[118] Doctrines not only reflect and grow out of the faith-experience of the Christian community, they perform a regulatory function within the religious cultus as well. In that doctrines express experiences which are prior to conceptualization, they have the ability to unite and preserve the Christian fellowship.[119] Theology's task is to articulate how beliefs of the specific religious community have normative validity for its members. This, we suggest, is akin to the "retreat

---

[116] Gerrish for instance chides Troeltsch for "the apparent neglect of intersubjectivity". "Possibility," in Clayton, ed., *Future of Theology*, 127. See also F. von Hügel's introduction to Troeltsch's *Christian Thought*, xvii.

[117] Troeltsch asserts that "the whole idea of a piety that simply springs from every man's heart and nevertheless forms a harmony, that does not need reciprocity and yet remains a living power" is "utopian". "Significance," *Writings*, 196. See also: "Glaube: Glaube und Geschichte," *RGG* 2:1448–9; cf. Perkins, *Explicating*, 77f.

[118] Troeltsch, *Glaubenslehre*, 14; also "Kirche," *RGG* 3:1153–54. Troeltsch writes: "The religious doctrine was the expression of the religious vitality and development of thought which was focused first of all in the cultus, and then radiated forth from it again, so far as for this purpose ideas were necessary at all." *Social Teaching*, 2:995.

[119] If our reading of Troeltsch (and Schleiermacher) is correct, it would seem that the dividing line between what Lindbeck, *Nature of Doctrine*, designates as the "Experiential-expressive" and the "Cultural-linguistic" models is not a sharp one. They often interpenetrate. See discussion in chapter 3 below on Lindbeck's postliberalism.

to community"[120] in socio-pragmatic postmodernity. One can see how such an understanding of doctrine lends itself easily to a functional rather than an ontological Christology.

Troeltsch's historicism, perspectivalism, and his communal take on doctrine make him an interesting dialogue partner given the current postmodern condition. How then is he germane to our project? We begin with a warning from Coakley which she makes at the end of her book on Troeltsch's Christology: "any contemporary exposition of 'incarnational' Christology for today . . . will I believe attempt to side-step the problems raised by Troeltsch only at the peril of its own credibility."[121] What critical issues has Troeltsch put his finger on that must be taken into account today? How are these pertinent to Christological formulation? We suggest that it is his answers to methodological questions, rather than his relatively sparse dogmatic outputs, that are of interest. And here we find themes which cohere at different points with Gadamer, Schleiermacher and Pannenberg, all of whom we shall consider in subsequent chapters. While some may judge Troeltsch's theological project a failure,[122] we think there are insights in his work which are relevant to theological formulation today.

For a start, it is no longer viable to immunize the Christian faith against historical criticism by planting it within an ahistorical zone, and posting a guard to ward off prying questions aimed at its foundational beliefs. The "flight from authority" (Stout) which took off in the Enlightenment is still airborne, and there is no turning back. The challenge now is to steer the plane of theological inquiry toward a new airport of normativity without crashing into the mountains of nihilism. In an age of historical consciousness, it seems feeble to simply declare that Christ is the basis of theological formulation without grappling with the question of how Christology can function as theological criterion when it is itself mediated through history.[123] In

---

[120] The title of William W. Bartley, III's critique of absolutized intra-traditionality: *The Retreat to Commitment*, 2d rev. ed. (LaSalle & London: Open Court, 1984).

[121] *Without Absolutes*, 191.

[122] Reist speaks of "The Collapse of Troeltsch's Theology," *Theology of Involvement*, 154f; while Walter Bodenstein, *Neige des Historismus: Ernst Troeltschs Entwicklungsgang* (Gütersloh: Gütersloher Verlagshaus Gerd Mohn, 1959), 207, regards him as a "wrecked theologian" (*ein gescheiterter Theologe*).

[123] This unwitting failure to take into account the historicity of one's theological first principle(s) unfortunately characterizes Alister E. McGrath's attempt to differentiate

other words, one needs to contend with the issue of how a yard-stick, bearing all the marks of history, can serve a transcendental and criteriological function. To say this is not to deny the central-ity of Christ as theological norm, only to alert us to the challenges involved in affirming it and the inadequacy of a wholly assertional approach. Christology must come to terms with the historicality of knowledge, the validating potential of religious experience, and the impact of sociality in belief-formation. Not to do so would, in Troeltsch's view, repeat the mistake of a "theology of claims."

Troeltsch's struggle to explicate the "essence" of Christianity from a historical standpoint, evident in his essay on the essence of Christianity,[124] has a hermeneutical feel to it. The method he pro-poses for determining the essence of Christianity is, as Sykes rightly points out, Schleiermacherian in nature.[125] Essence, according to Troeltsch, is an abstraction:

> The "essence" can only be found in *a broad view over the totality of all the manifestations which are related to this idea,* and its discovery demands the exercise of historical abstraction, *the art of seeing the whole, both the details and the fullness of the various methodically studied materials, with a synoptic vision.*[126]

the Christology of Evangelicalism from modernist Christologies. The latter are instances of the "mastery" of Christ by cultural trends and interpretations, where Nietzschean redefinition makes "Jesus of Nazareth conform to the personal norms of individual interpreters, or the ideological tribes to which they belong." Unlike these, "Evangelicalism does not believe it has the right or the resources to recon-struct Christ", and its "emphasis on the authority of Jesus Christ *as he is revealed in Scripture* [emphasis his] (rather than as he is constructed by human interest groups or power blocks) is profoundly liberating." *A Passion for Truth: The Intellectual Coherence of Evangelicalism* (Leicester: Apollos, 1996), 33–35. While we hold no brief for the-ological liberalism and agree entirely with McGrath's Christocentrism, we think the argument would be strengthened if it is acknowledged that insofar as all Christological statements, evangelical or otherwise, are human formulations, they are necessarily constructions arising from specific contexts. It will not do to say that "modernist Christologies" are contingent on "human interest groups or power blocks" as though the Evangelical position is immune from contingency or power interests. Even if one accepts divine revelation as a presuppositional backdrop, one still has to con-tend with the fact that all knowledge, including that of revealed truth, is histori-cally mediated. To acknowledge the authority of Jesus as revealed in Scripture surely entails an act of interpretation. In short, a mere assertional approach is not sufficient. Only an approach which reconciles the revelatory (universality) and the historical (contingent), will serve as a viable theological prolegomenon in a historicized age.
[124] "What Does 'Essence of Christianity' Mean?" in *Writings*, 124–79.
[125] Stephen Sykes, *The Identity of Christianity: Theologians and the Essence of Christianity from Schleiermacher to Barth* (Philadelphia: Fortress, 1984), 157.
[126] Troeltsch, "'Essence'," 130 (emphasis his).

Evident in this is Schleiermacher's notion of the hermeneutical circle. To understand the *parts*, one must posit the *whole*, "a synoptic vision" or "essence," and this in turn is dependent on investigation of the parts. Essence as an abstraction serves a critical function (differentiating between legitimate and illegitimate development), and is "a developing spiritual principle" or a "germinative principle" flexible enough to bring forth new and creative formulations.[127] What is of interest to us is the way in which the personal attitude and judgment of the historian—in short her subjectivity—affects the definition of Christianity's essence. As Sykes again rightly notes, to permit the personal and the subjective dimension to intrude is to affirm the situatedness of the historian-cum-theologian within a particular interpretive horizon.[128] It is from within this horizon, a situatedness encompassing the past and oriented to the future, that the identity of Christianity is determined anew in the present.[129]

This personalistic stance is maintained in subsequent works,[130] and is discernible in his later reflections on historicism. To seek out what is normative in a historically conditioned Christianity, one must investigate it as an "individual totality" (*individuelle Totalität*, a concept he develops in his *Historismus*). But as a historical phenomenon, it passes through time and this invariably results in it taking on a diversity of forms. And unless the historian is prepared to settle for a multiplicity of unrelated forms—in which case Christianity loses any claim to a coherent identity—one is confronted with the challenge of discerning continuity in the midst of discontinuity; and this essentially ushers the historian into the realm of philosophy and theology. If Christianity as a-totality-in-process is to have an identity or essence, its many temporal expressions must be synthesized within a unified or unifying framework. In this, Troeltsch finds himself needing to assume the existence of a suprahistorical realm much like Vico, Hegel

---

[127] Ibid., 140–41, 151. Troeltsch admits that a definition of Christianity's essence is "an extremely complicated undertaking". It can be said to be "an intuitive abstraction, a religious and ethical critique, a flexible developmental concept and the ideal to be applied in the work of shaping and recombining for the future." Ibid., 164.

[128] Sykes, *Identity*, 161.

[129] Troeltsch, "'Essence'," 162, writes: "To define the essence is to shape it afresh. It is the elucidation of the essential idea of Christianity in history in the way in which it ought to be a light for the future, and at the same time it is a living view of the present and the future world together in this light."

[130] E.g., in the 1913 essay, "The Dogmatics of the 'Religionsgeschichtliche Schule'," 11 & 16, where the definition of essence is regarded as a matter of personal intuition.

and Dilthey did.[131] He then posits the notion of "development" (*Ent-wicklung*); for all historical entities, Christianity included, "are a part of an uninterrupted flow of becoming and must be set into this flow."[132] Such a move is needed to avoid the intellectual and moral anarchy which a radical pluralism inevitably spawns. Our thinking must be both historical and "universal-historical".[133] Christianity must be appraised within the totality of human history, and the drive towards universal history is in Troeltsch's opinion an instinctual human capacity.[134]

What then does this universal history consist of? Since Troeltsch has already rejected argumentation by way of dogma and authority and any notion of Hegelian *a priori* teleology as ahistorical, this *Universalgeschichte* cannot be a transcendental given. It is instead a construct of the historian, serving a function not unlike his earlier definition of the essence of Christianity. Just as "essence construction" is bound up with the judgment of the historian,[135] so the postulate of universal history is a determination made by the historian qua philosopher, and this must arise from within history. At which point, Troeltsch confronts again the issue of how history may be criticized when the very instrument of critique is itself born of history.

His approach to the challenge of historicism is paradoxical: history is the source of problems as well as the source of their solu-

---

[131] Though Vico, Hegel and Dilthey strongly embraced history, they each relied on something suprahistorical and metaphysical; see Roberts, *Nothing But History*, 22–39.
[132] *Historismus*, 54.
[133] Troeltsch, "The Ideas of Natural and Humanity in World Politics," in Otto Gierke, *Natural Law and the Theory of Society, 1500–1800* (Cambridge: Cambridge University Press, 1934), 218. In this sense, Troeltsch may be said to be Hegelian in his instincts. His position in the essay, "Metaphysik," exhibits "considerable similarities" with Hegel and has been described as a developmental-historical idealism (*entwicklungsgeschichtlicher Idealismus*). See George Rupp, *Christologies and Cultures: Toward a Typology of Religious Worldviews* (The Hague: Mouton, 1974), 227.
[134] Troeltsch brings to his attempt to search for norms in history two presuppositions: that there is an ultimate value, a final end or a goal which is universally valid; and that human beings, endowed with a religious *a priori*, are able to synthesize actual historical values into a value system. "According to Troeltsch," Yasukata observes, "the concept of development has its ultimate root in the *essence* and *capability* of the human spirit. Human being is essentially disposed to integration and is capable of giving a unified interpretation to a multiple complex of historical events. The historian or the thinker conceives historical development by creating from the multiple diversity of historical phenomena a logically comprehensible succession of events which gives the impression of a movement with an inner consistency." *Troeltsch*, 132, cf. 88.
[135] Sykes, *Identity*, 155.

tions; and his strategy is encapsulated in the motto: *Geschichte durch Geschichte überwinden*, "to overcome history with history",[136] a strategy which Hodgson regards as "strikingly relevant to the postmodern temper."[137] While escape from the gravitational bonds of historicity is impossible, there are always at work in the historical process personalistic acts of "damming and shaping the historical stream of life" (*Dämmung und Gestaltung des historischen Lebensstromes*)[138] so as to prevent history from dissipating into chaos. Troeltsch writes:

> The task of damming and shaping is . . . essentially incapable of completion and essentially unending; and yet it is always soluble and practicable in each new case. A radical and absolute solution does not exist; there are only working, partial, synthetically uniting solutions. Yet the stream of life is always surging upward and onward. History within itself cannot be transcended. . . . The kingdom of God and nirvana lie outside all history. In history itself there are only relative victories; and these relative victories themselves vary greatly in power and depth, according to time and circumstance.[139]

The overcoming of history is accomplished through "a cultural synthesis," a *Gestaltung*, a shaping, or an activity of configuration, whereby new syntheses are brought about through "a creative fusion of the ethically and rationally universal with the historically individual." These syntheses or fusions, though new and spontaneous, "entail a reforming and further development of what has already been shaped in the great nexus of historical tradition; they create out of what has been, not out of nothing."[140] In a synthesis of culture:

> Every formation of a standard in relation to historical matters thus arises out of the particular living context (*Lebenszusammenhang*), and is at the same time the critique and the improvement of this. As every calculation of motion in the natural sciences is dependent on the position of the reckoner, so also in history is every standard indelibly determined by the position out of which it arises. In fact it arises continually in living connection with the shaping of the future (*Zukunftsgestaltung*).[141]

This notion of *Gestaltung* expresses an insight which comes into its own later in the philosophical hermeneutics of Gadamer; for like

---

[136] *Historismus*, 772.
[137] *God in History*, 41.
[138] Troeltsch, "Ethics and the Philosophy of History," in *Christian Thought*, 37.
[139] Ibid., 128–29.
[140] *God in History*, 139.
[141] *GS* 3:169, quoted in Reist, *Involvement*, 66.

Troeltsch, Gadamer is decidedly historical in his view of human understanding. At the risk of anachronism, one might say that this configurative act of synthesis in which the ideal (the ethically-rationally universal) and the real (the historically individual) are commingled is not incompatible with Gadamer's notions of "effective historical consciousness" (*wirkungsgeschichtliches Bewusstsein*) and the fusion of horizons. Like the Gadamerian interpreter, the Troeltschean synthesizer works within the stream of history, and both operate under the conditionality of their situatedness. Just as understanding is born in a fusion of the interpreter's horizon with that of the object of interpretation, the definition of Christianity's essence is accomplished through a synthesis of what is recognized to be the universal ideal, and the specific historical situation. In both cases, the fusion or synthesis occurs within the realm of human subjectivity.

Troeltsch though differs from Gadamer in two ways: (1) in the strong ethical and practical emphasis which he brings to the concept of *Gestaltung*, and (2) its future orientation.[142] Reconfiguration or synthesis in the present is needed because the Christian faith is a living religion, the essence of which must be constituted afresh. (Thus we find in the later Troeltsch, a contemporary cultural synthesis involving a new shaping of a European culture for which Christianity is normative.) And this reconfiguration of history is oriented to the future, not in the sense that history is moving toward a *telos*, but because the future lies open and uncertain before us. If we do not shape history responsibly, then the future will descend into the abyss of destruction and dehumanizing anarchy. In all these, Troeltsch's ethical and practical concern remains in the forefront.

D. *Theology in the Wake of Historical Consciousness*

It is time to gather the pieces and see how Troeltsch is instructive, and what qualifications are needed before his insights can be enlisted in the service of theological construction today. There are four broad areas where we think he points the way ahead for theology, and these revolve around the motif of historicity: (1) historicity and revelation; (2) the communal and experiential dimension in revelatory

---

[142] As Yasukata, *Troeltsch*, 138, observes, his philosophy of history "bore an eminently *practical* and, in this sense, ethical tone." It was also "trained exclusively on the task of 'the shaping of the future' (*Zukunftsgestaltung*). . . . Troeltsch's point was, however, not to speculate about the future but to shape or form it."

history; (3) continuity and the shaping of the new in theology; and (4) the ethical and praxis-orientation of theological configuration.

First, any claim to truth as universal is necessarily made from somewhere in time and space, and Troeltsch is surely right to draw our attention to the undeniable contingency of theological assertions. Where Troeltsch paints himself into a corner—unnecessarily we think—is to regard contingency as antithetical to supernaturalism. The historicization of theology could just as well be understood as a robust affirmation of the immanence of God in his self-revelation and redemptive action within history. While God is not contingent on his creation, it is not inconceivable that he could, by an act of divine will, subject himself to the terms of contingency in order to make himself known or accomplish his redemptive purposes.

The epistemological dualism which absolutizes the partition between the eternal, unchanging and divine on the one hand, and the temporal, mutable and human on the other, has a long history, stretching back to Parmenides and Plato and reaching to Kant and beyond.[143] Troeltsch's difficulty stems from an implicit obedience to the terms of this dualism, which is procrustean as it pertains to the supranatural. In this regard, Pannenberg's view of "revelation as history"[144] has, in our opinion, an edge over Troeltsch in that it allows him to be thoroughly committed to the historical process without dismissing from the outset the possibility of divine involvement. While Pannenberg overtly endorses the breaking in of divine revelation in history, Troeltsch resists such explicit acknowledgement even though closer inspection reveals the presence of an underlying metaphysics with features which betray an origin in theological soil, notwithstanding its Hegelian slant. In his notion of "creative synthesis," he speaks of a deep movement operating in and through the contingency and accidents of history. The claim that there is an "inner movement of the divine spirit in the finite spirit"[145] entails, as Hodgson observes, a metaphysical or "a religious faith" which "helps to distinguish authentic configurations of value from mere subjectivism because it is expressive of the sense of being grasped and pulled by

---

[143] On this philosophical dualism and its impact on the shape of both patristic and modern critical Christology, see Colin E. Gunton, *Yesterday & Today: A Study of Continuities in Christology* (Grand Rapids: Eerdmans, 1983).

[144] Wolfhart Pannenberg *et al.*, *Revelation as History*, tr. David Granskou (New York: Macmillan; London: Collier-Macmillan, 1968; hereafter *RaH*).

[145] See Troeltsch, *Historismus*, 166–68, 173–79.

something that transcends the subject."[146] We need not assess the merits of this (qualified) Hegelian turn in Troeltsch, except to say that his attempt to overcome history with history is not free from presuppositions. Despite his attempt to disavow reliance on dogma and ecclesiastical authority, one detects the presence of a basic faith-commitment which makes his approach not all that different method-ologically from one which confesses divine revelation as a presupposition for theology.

The same might be said of those deconstructive savants who decry the possibility and presupposition of objective truth. Even in the per-suasive rhetoric of some of these postmodern thinkers, there is an implicit commitment to some form of universality. Those who inveigh against truth as metanarratival and universally binding, operate with a tacit assumption of ultimacy in their appeals. Paradoxically, Nietz-sche's critique of truth is, in P. Berkowitz's opinion,[147] a protest aris-ing from a commitment to truth! In demonstrating the contingency of what is seemingly suprahistorical and normative, Nietzsche was led to posit the notion of an "eternal recurrence" or eternal return, so that what is encountered in history—the particular and the con-tingent—is not a stepping stone en route to future realization (as in Hegelian teleology) but a true apprehension of what is. As a con-ception of the totality of history, the notion of eternal recurrence is needed to put a cap on indefinite novelty and creativity which is endlessly being generated from one historical moment to another. In other words, Nietzsche too cannot escape the demand for some universalizing totality.[148]

Furthermore, does not his recommendation of "the will to power" suggest that he thinks it is in principle universally true and applic-able in all situations? And is not Rorty's pragmatism in the final analysis a transcendentalization of contingency or the elevation of contingency to a universal principle? Foucault's unmasking of power interests in the human sciences is an outworking of a commitment

---

[146] *God in History*, 141. Hodgson sees "striking similarities between Troeltsch's the-ory of historical configuration and Hegel's image of the fabric of history." 140.

[147] Peter Berkowitz, *Nietzsche: The Ethics of an Immoralist* (Cambridge & London: Harvard University Press, 1995).

[148] See F. Nietzsche, *The Will to Power*, tr. Walter Kaufmann and R. J. Hollingdale, ed. by Walter Kaufmann (New York: Vintage, 1967), 536 (#1041); and *The Gay Science*, tr. Walter Kaufmann (New York: Random House, Vintage, 1974), 273-4 (#341); also D. Roberts, *Nothing But History*, 70-78, on the theme of eternal recur-rence in Nietzsche.

to an ideology of protest and subversion, an antipolitical political ideology. Evidently, there is no escaping an overarching presuppositional framework. Reasoning is in a sense circular in nature since no one can proceed from a position of absolute neutrality. Given this, it is not improper from a methodological standpoint to embrace revelation as a framework by which we conduct our quest for transcontextual truth within contingent history.

Now the claim of revelation necessarily entails a claim for the possibility of transhistorical criteria or metanarratival truth; and this, as we have noted, goes against the grain of deconstructive postmodernity. Yet contingency need not exclude transcontextuality. Two comments may be relevant here:

(1) *There is a need to make the case or persuade others to accept the cogency of that case, whether one is claiming that there is universal truth, or arguing against it.* If it is not enough to simply assert that there is such a thing as revelation in history, it is equally inadequate to simply pronounce (like Rorty does peremptorily in his *Philosophy as the Mirror of Nature*) that there is no universal truth or mind-independent Reality outside of human description. One cannot simply proclaim or dismiss the possibility of the Incarnation and that God has revealed himself in Christ *in history*, without first investigating the validity of the claim and furnishing reasons for it. We contend that even if one were to do away with the subject-object dualism of Cartesianism, it does not follow that reality collapses into subjectivism. The strong claim for the historicity and subjectivity of knowledge need not entail an anti-realist epistemology. One can be an anti-Cartesian non-foundationalist and still be a theological realist.[149]

---

[149] While knowledge has become problematic in anti-foundationalist postmodernity, it does not mean that knowledge is impossible. The absence of the kind of certitude offered by Cartesian epistemology need not lead one to posit the impossibility of knowing outside of description. The same applies to the question of language and its referent. The fact that language involves more than just words as representations of things does not warrant a wholesale indeterminacy of language. As Borgmann notes: postmodern criticism gets arrested prematurely when, "having considered critically the modern arrogation of reality, it accepts naively the legacy of that arrogance, namely, the disappearance of reality." *Postmodern Divide*, 117. One must differentiate between a critique directed at the way in which reality is claimed to be represented in knowledge claims, and the idea that reality itself is absent. The problem is one of a lack of epistemic clarity, of modesty in the project of epistemology, rather than the absence of objective truth distinct from the knowing subject. Of course, one is entitled to the rejoinder: but how can we be sure that there is objective truth "out there"? But by the same token, the question can equally be

To say that argument is needed is to assume some tacit agreement on an operative rationality or a grammar of discourse which would umpire debate and allow investigators to weigh evidence and render judgment. On this, we think the later Wittgenstein's idea that the common life within a particular cultural-social community serves as the interpretive or reference point for language use, as well as Karl-Otto Apel's "transcendental pragmatics" (a Wittgensteinian notion), the establishing of an intersubjectively valid knowledge within an ideal and unlimited community of interpretation, and Habermas' metacritical stance grounded in social communicative interaction, together provide theoretical underpinning for our suggestion.[150] Given the presupposed norms of social interaction implicit in all rational behaviour, or what Apel calls "the indubitability of certain paradigmatic evidence in the language game of philosophical argumentation",[151] it is possible for reasoned persuasion between participants in dialogue. A minimal logic is operational here; and the ability to mount a critique or make a point, in short, a critical rationality, is an inescapable part of human judgment. One cannot deny it or persuade that it does not exist without invoking it.

In this regard, the principle of the criticizability of all beliefs enshrined in the "pancritical rationalism" (a modification of Popper's

---

turned on the questioner: how can one be sure that there is no truth which is independent of our construct?

On the possibility of epistemic realism, see William P. Alston, *A Realist Conception of Truth* (Ithaca & London: Cornell University Press, 1996); Alan Musgrave, *Common Sense, Science and Scepticism: A Historical Introduction to the Theory of Knowledge* (Cambridge: Cambridge University Press, 1993); Roger Trigg, *Reality at Risk: A Defence of Realism in Philosophy and the Sciences*, 2d ed. (New York: Harvester Wheatsheaf, 1980, 1989).

[150] Wittgenstein's notion of "language games" seeks the meaning of language in its use in ordinary life, and is closely connected to what he calls "forms of life." See: L. Wittgenstein, *PI* §§7, 19, 23, 241, pp. 174, 226; cf. Glock, *Wittgenstein Dictionary*, 124–9; Karl-Otto Apel, "Wittgenstein and the Problem of Hermeneutic Understanding," and "Scientism or Transcendental Hermeneutics? On the Question of the Subject of the Interpretation of Signs in the Semiotics of Pragmatism," in *Towards a Transformation of Philosophy* (London, Boston & Henley: Routledge & Kegan Paul, 1980), 1–45, 93–135; idem, "The Problem of Philosophical Foundations in Light of a Transcendental Pragmatics of Language," in Kenneth Baynes, James Bohman & Thomas McCarthy, eds., *After Philosophy: End or Transformation?* (Cambridge & London: MIT Press, 1987), 250–90; Jürgen Habermas, *Knowledge and Human Interests*, 2d ed. (London: Heinemann, 1978); idem, *The Theory of Communicative Action*, 2 vols. (Cambridge: Polity Press, 1984, 1987). See also Thiselton, *TH*, 370–85; idem, *New Horizons in Hermeneutics: The Theory and Practice of Transforming Biblical Reading* (Grand Rapids: Zondervan, 1992, hereafter *NHH*), 380–93; 401–5.

[151] Apel, "Philosophical Foundations," 272.

critical rationalism) which Bartley develops in his critique of *The Retreat to Commitment*,[152] has much to commend it. It is therefore the better part of wisdom to be upfront about this, as it is to admit that presuppositions about divine revelation form an integral part of our interpretive horizon. The question then becomes one of inquiring whether our framework is cogent, coherent, persuasive and plausible; and this line of inquiry invites discussion and opens up debate. We hasten to add that subscribing to such an operative rationality does not make one a card-carrying rationalist. The former makes argument possible, while the type of Humean rationalistic empiricism represented by the latter makes it unnecessary, since its anti-supernaturalism has already precluded the possibility of an Incarnation. Reason is here understood as a test of truth, and not, as in rationalism, a source of truth.

(2) *The claim that there is universal truth is not the same as saying that one has absolute or full possession of it, or that there is complete transparency of perception.* To posit the reality of transcontingent truth is to invite attention to, and initiate a probe of, the contours of this truth; it need not presuppose a total absence of ambiguity. As Vanhoozer reminds us, a passion for truth is not the same as a possession of the (whole) truth, and our inability to grasp the truth comprehensively is no argument against the reality of such truth.[153] To pick up Rorty's image of philosophy as a mirror of nature, and apply it in a way quite different from him, we submit that the mirror of human perception which we hold up to Reality, despite its inadequacy on account of its finitude, is capable of revealing what is before it. A mirror's image need not contain *all* of nature to reflect what is really and truly there in front of it. Neither does it need to be totally free of ambiguity. A mirror does not need to reflect perfectly for it to reflect truly. By the same token, it is possible to maintain that Reality or Truth is mediated through what is historically contingent without

---

[152] Bartley, *Retreat to Commitment*, 109f. Note that Apel is critical of this "pancritical rationalism" because its principle of criticism is, according to him, dependent on logical rules which are themselves fundamental postulates beyond rational revision. One is able to subject all beliefs to criticism only because a "transcendental language-game" already exists, i.e., the conditions for intersubjectively validated knowledge are presupposed. See Apel, "Philosophical Foundations," 274f. We think it is possible to concede Apel's point and still see value in Bartley's pancritical rational principle as a methodological approach.

[153] Kevin J. Vanhoozer, "Exploring the World; Following the Word: The Credibility of Evangelical Theology in an Incredulous Age." *TJ* 16 NS (1995), 25.

the immodest claim that everything entailed by universal truth is apprehended, boxed and neatly packaged in our mind. The truth, though perceived, remains larger than our perception.[154]

Second, the immanental view of God's revelation is highly compatible with human experience and agency, especially the emphasis on the Christian community as the channel and context in which Christ is mediated and experienced. Troeltsch's view that the knowledge of God "comes to the individual only through history by the medium of Christian community",[155] as well as the Schleiermacherian move he makes to conjoin God's revelatory and salvific act with human response, are significant and needed emphases for Christology today. We will look briefly at these elements of communality and experience.

(1) *That Christ is experienced in the context of Christian community should exorcize any remaining traces of individualism associated with the process of doing theology.* Community, tradition and context constitute a living and interpenetrating matrix out of which beliefs are formed and faith nurtured. And because we are social beings, "the institutional embodiment and posture of the Church has a profound impact upon our consciousness."[156] We submit that it is out of such a consciousness,

---

[154] Insofar as theology concerns the Creator-God in distinction from his creation, it invariably assumes a correspondence theory of truth. Theologians seek to make statements which correspond to the truth of God. Yet this need not exclude a coherence theory of truth. It is mandated by our argument for revelatory presuppositionalism, i.e., something is true in that it coheres with the overall structure of thought. The critical question is whether our presuppositions are true or not, i.e., do they correspond with what is in reality. While the correspondence theory is usually assumed in everyday life (e.g., the statement, "It is raining," can be shown to be true by matching it with the actual state of rain falling on the streets) it is not so straightforward as far as God and his revelatory and redemptive activity in history are concerned. Yet as a methodological procedure, one might decide on these beliefs as presuppositions and commend them to be debated in the public sphere. The question as to whether these presuppositions are true or not can only be established, as we have already suggested, through rational inquiry. Now once this qualified correspondence theory of truth is accepted, it is entirely proper to work with a coherence theory of truth. In this sense, we might say that coherence is contingent on correspondence.
On theories of truth, see: Anthony C. Thiselton, "Truth" in Colin Brown, ed., *New International Dictionary of New Testament Theology, 3 vols.* (Exeter: Paternoster, 1978; hereafter *NIDNTT*), 3:874–902; and John Macquarrie, "Truth in Theology" in his *Thinking about God* (London: SCM, 1975), 15–27; and Richard L. Kirkham, *Theories of Truth: A Critical Introduction* (Cambridge & London: MIT Press, 1995).
[155] *Glaubenslehre*, 339. The same communal focus is evident in Troeltsch's *Social Teaching*, 995, where he reminds theologians to keep Christological assertions closely tied to "worship" and "cultus".
[156] Sykes, *Identity*, 32.

whereby one is simultaneously steeped in tradition and critical of it, that we forge a contemporary witness to Christ. Such an approach is essentially hermeneutical in nature, and as our examination of Gadamer's view on the role of tradition in the next chapter will demonstrate, theological understanding develops within and in dialogue with tradition. The attention to the Church as context for truth in theology is characteristic of postliberal and narrative theologians like Lindbeck, Frei, Hauerwas, Thiemann, Placher, Stroup, and Wood.[157] In accentuating the importance of intra-traditional fidelity in doctrinal formulation, they hope to forge a coherent platform upon which the voice of theology may win a hearing in a pluralized world. We shall engage Lindbeck's postliberalism in the third chapter where we take up the issue of the relation between intra and extra traditionality in Christological formulation.

(2) *The emphasis on the self-involving character of faith continues a theme which goes back to the Reformers.* On this, both Troeltsch and Schleiermacher are following through on the Protestant principle that faith is an act which must be consciously undertaken. As Gerrish points out, unlike the medieval doctrine of implicit faith, the reformers insisted that all must do their own believing.[158] There is thus a personalistic, volitional and psychological dimension to faith. Word and faith are correlative in Luther, and the movement toward psychological transparency is present in Calvin as well.[159] Schleiermacher and

---

[157] Lindbeck's *Nature of Doctrine* articulates the agenda of a Postliberal theology in response to the liberal and revisionist trends in theology. This has also been described as "the Yale School," even though some of the names cited are not comfortable with the tag. See: Hans W. Frei, *The Eclipse of Biblical Narrative: A Study in Eighteenth and Nineteenth Century Hermeneutics* (New Haven & London: Yale University Press, 1974); Stanley Hauerwas, *A Community of Character* (Notre Dame: University of Notre Dame Press, 1981); idem, "The Church as God's New Language," in Garrett Green, ed., *Scriptural Authority and Narrative Interpretation* (Philadelphia: Fortress, 1987), 179–98; idem, "The Church's One Foundation is Jesus Christ Her Lord; Or, In a World Without Foundations: All We Have is the Church," in Hauerwas, Murphy & Nation, eds., *Theology Without Foundations*, 143–62; Placher, *Unapologetic Theology*; George W. Stroup, *The Promise of Narrative Theology* (London: SCM, 1981, 1984); Thiemann, *Revelation and Theology*; Charles Wood, *The Formation of Christian Understanding* (Philadelphia: Westminster, 1981).

[158] B. A. Gerrish, "Theology and the Historical Consciousness," in Mary Potter Engel & Walter E. Wyman, Jr., eds., *Revisioning the Past: Prospects in Historical Theology* (Minneapolis: Fortress, 1992), 289. See also his "From 'Dogmatik' to 'Glaubenslehre': A Paradigm Change in Modern Theology?" in Hans Küng & David Tracy, eds., *Paradigm Change in Theology* (New York: Crossroad, 1991), 161–73.

[159] B. A. Gerrish alerts us to connections between Schleiermacher and Calvin; see his "Theology Within the Limits of Piety Alone: Schleiermacher and Calvin's

Troeltsch, in explicating doctrine as *Glaubenslehre*, are examples of
that "tradition of inwardness"[160] which is an integral part of the history of Christian faith and thought. This is strikingly compatible with
the self-involving hermeneutics articulated by Donald Evans.[161] Truth
in Christology we suggest must engage with this experiential dimension, which is in turn anchored in a context of tradition. As we shall
argue in chapter four below, experience is invariably mediated, and
the communal tradition in which one stands provides the terms and
framework in which experience is possible. The existential and the
traditional are dialectically related in that one is understood in terms
of the other.

Third, Troeltsch's view of theology as something anchored to the
times and opened to the future offers scope for creativity and innovation in theological articulation. His emphasis on the need for the
ongoing definition and redefinition of the essence of Christianity
guards against the fossilization of doctrines and ensures that they
retain their dynamic contemporaneity. If one may speak of a "system" in him, it is an open and flexible one, attuned at once to the
givens of the theologian's context, culture and community, as well
as the needs of the present. Systematic theology for Troeltsch is not
the mere handing down of tradition; it is "the task of orienting the
tradition in view of the intellectual and religious life of the present
day."[162]

Where we differ from Troeltsch is in the assessment of the importance of the history of Jesus to theology. As Dyson notes, "Troeltsch
would prefer to see the revelation associated with Jesus and his tra-

---

Notion of God," in *The Old Protestantism and the New: Essays on the Reformation Heritage*
(Edinburgh: T&T Clark, 1982).

[160] Sykes, *Identity*, 35f.

[161] *The Logic of Self-Involvement* (London: SCM, 1963).

[162] Troeltsch, *GS* 2:227. This present and future orientation is noted by A. O.
Dyson, *The Immortality of the Past* (London: SCM, 1974), 47: "the programme which
Troeltsch has in mind gives greater emphasis to theology, not as a past-centred,
but as a present-centred discipline and therefore as a discipline which can respond
to the pull of the future. Theology does not so much bring a theological world-
view from the past to see how far, by adjustment and restatement, it can be given
force for the present. Rather it reflects directly upon issues of the present in the
light of the values which the cultural historian brings from the religious past. Thus
theology is not primarily an expository discipline. It is a critical and inventive discipline whose subject-matter concerns the quality and content of the personal, intellectual, social and religious life of the present and the directions which it must take
for the future."

dition as the presupposition of theology rather than its working content."[163] The historical Jesus represents the starting point of tradition. What theology needs to concern itself with, is the continuous shaping of this tradition; this undertaking is not dependent on what we know about Jesus. That is why Troeltsch does not seem too perturbed by questions about the historical reliability of the New Testament documents.[164]

Contrary to Troeltsch, we do not see any necessity to dichotomize between revelation associated with Jesus and his tradition as "presupposition" and as "working content." Any theological *Gestaltung*, we suggest, requires both. Theological reflection takes place on a temporal bridge suspended between the historical Jesus and the eschaton. What happened *then*, and what has happened *since*, are brought to bear on what is being shaped *now*, and this is carried out in the light of the *future*. Again, we think Pannenberg is strong where Troeltsch is weak. Expressing a sentiment with which Troeltsch would concur, Pannenberg asserts that the truth of God "must prove itself anew in the future".[165] But unlike Troeltsch, the future is not a *tabula rasa* for Pannenberg; it is Christologically defined. The incisive way in which he brings together past, present and future in his proleptic-eschatological Christology is, in our opinion, an approach which keeps the revelatory and salvific work of God firmly centred in Christ as well as allows that truth to be simultaneously transcendental and historical.

Fourth, the practical and ethical concern which fires Troeltsch's philosophy of history must also characterize Christology today. Theology is not just about creating creeds and polishing propositions; it is about shaping the world. To be conscious of history, theology must consciously engage history. The transformation of the present for the sake of the future is a theme writ large in Troeltsch. In Yasukata's opinion,

> The historical and existential concern with the fate of Christianity in the modern world . . . penetrated his entire scientific endeavor. Accordingly, Troeltsch's thought, despite his constant emphasis on scientific objectivity, broadness of scope, and impartiality of judgment, is in the last analysis burdened considerably with predetermined values.[166]

---

[163] Ibid., 47–48.
[164] Troeltsch. "Metaphysik," 9.
[165] *BQT*, 2:8.
[166] Yasukata, *Troeltsch*, 178.

These values are essentially ethical, religious and metaphysical concerns. His idea of cultural synthesis thus has a distinctly active and ethical character. The way he frames the challenge of "damming and shaping the historical stream of life" suggests a commitment to *shape* historical life so that the future will turn out for the good. Yet despite his full-throttled commitment to responsible and ethical action in history (usually couched in humanistic terms), he is not always clear as to how one decides what constitutes the ethical or the ultimate good. If we are to shape present history for the future, one might legitimately ask, what pattern are we to follow? How do we tell a proper configuration from an improper one? All of which brings us back to the problem of finding norms in the relativity of history, one which Troeltsch identified but found extremely difficult to resolve given the naturalism of his historiography.

Divine revelation, once granted as a possibility and accepted as normative, can, we suggest, function as the theoretical basis and criterion for our praxis. In the perspective of Scripture and Christian tradition, the truth is not only to be *known*, it is to be *done* as well. And the doing of truth in history is determined by the "what-ness" of truth, which in turn comes into sharper focus as one acts in accordance with it. This reciprocity stems from the fact that the question of truth is about the knowledge of God in Christ (revelation) and the experience of God's salvation through him (reconciliation). The Johannine interchange between knowing God and receiving eternal life in Christ suggests that truth is both epistemic and salvific. Christ is both revealer and redeemer; he is not only the truth about the way to life (Jn. 14:6), but the way to life as well (Jn. 1:12). And the work of reconciliation inaugurated by the life, death and resurrection of Christ encompasses the renewal of a world flawed by sin. This is a historical process which will culminate at the Parousia. The question of truth is thus inextricably tied to Christology understood not just in terms of revelation but also God's redemptive activity in history.

The truth about Christ is therefore more than mere contemplation of Christ or propositions about who he is in himself; it has a this-worldly praxis-orientation aimed at the soteriological re-alignment of human life in all its manifold dimensions. In essence, it is the project of Shalom and the Kingdom of God on earth in the perspective of the Old and New Testaments respectively. The linkage between knowing God in Christ (epistemology) and serving God with

Christ (salvific praxis) lies at the heart of the relationship between Christology, truth, and history.[167]

To recapitulate, in our examination of Troeltsch's response to historicism, we have argued that in some significant ways he prefigured trends in contemporary deconstructive postmodernity, particularly on the matter of the possibility of the absolute and universal within the contingent. Our reconnaissance of the postmodern landscape indicates that the question of contingency which captivated Troeltsch is still being posed today, albeit in different conceptual contexts. Troeltsch's reflections on doing theology in a historicized age continue to have relevance as starting points for theological method today, even though one might decline to follow him into the arid desert of criterial relativism and a deabsolutized Christology. His attempt to "overcome history with history" has a hermeneutical feel to it, and holds out potential for our proposal of a hermeneutical Christology. And with Troeltsch as dialogue partner, we have identified four main areas which theology must take into account in the wake of historical consciousness: (1) the conceivability of divine revelation in and through history; (2) the compatibility between an immanental view of revelation and human experience, agency and self-involvement; (3) the possibility and necessity of ongoing doctrinal redefinition in conscious dialogue with the history of Jesus and Christian tradition; and finally, (4) the salvific and this-worldly responsibility which must characterize the outworking of theological truth in history. With these in mind, we turn next to explicate a hermeneutical approach to Christological formulation which embraces contingency as a necessary part of our quest for that which is universal and transcontextual. The four areas just mentioned will feature prominently in what follows.

III. *Toward a Christology beyond Objectivism and Relativism*

The resurgence of historicism in postmodernity means that the question of truth will have to be tackled anew, particularly as it relates to Christology. In this section, we wish to establish the basis for

---

[167] The inviolable connection between revelation and reconciliation is highlighted recently by Stephen N. Williams, *Revelation and Reconciliation: A Window on Modernity* (Cambridge: Cambridge University Press, 1995), who suggests that the problem

progress towards an approach to Christology which takes into account the historicality of understanding. As a point of departure for our discussion, we turn to Christoph Schwöbel's diagnosis of the crisis situation in Christology today. Schwöbel categorizes the ills which haunt modern Christology into three main classes or antinomies:[168]

(1) The antinomy between the historical and the necessary highlighted by Lessing's thesis that contingent truths can never be proof of necessary or ultimate truths of reason. This epistemological dualism troubled Troeltsch greatly as we have seen, and it lies behind difficulties with Chalcedonian two-natures Christology, typically expressed in the query: how could the eternal God be at one and the same time the Jesus of Nazareth since the eternal and the temporal are ontologically opposed? This antinomy often leads to a tenuous relationship between historical investigation into the person of Jesus and the theological appraisal of Christ and his (dogmatic) relationship with God and reality. Furthermore, it tends to serve as the impetus behind the polarization of Christological method into either a "from above" or a "from below" approach, depending on which side of the divine-human divide one chooses to start from.

(2) A second antinomy is that between the past and the present. In what sense can an event which transpired in the past have ultimate significance for our present understanding of reality? The rise of historical consciousness, with its sharpened sensitivity to the pastness of the past, makes the gap between the historical Jesus and us today virtually unbridgeable. The result of this historical relativism is seen in the fact that the quest for the historical Jesus and the question about the significance of Christ today are increasingly dichotomized.[169] Again, on method in Christology, one is presented with the option either of beginning with the historical Jesus, or with the *Christus praesens* or the contemporary experience of faith.

(3) The third antinomy is the disjunction between being and meaning, between soteriology and Christology. The key issue here is whether Christ's work provides the only legitimate access to Christology;

---

which critics such as Nietzsche and Don Cupitt have with Christianity hinges not so much on the untenability of revelational truth (i.e., epistemology) as it does on a rejection of, or an unwillingness to submit to, the moral and ethical demands entailed in the Gospel message of reconciliation.

[168] "Christology and Trinitarian Thought," in Christoph Schwöbel, ed., *Trinitarian Theology Today: Essays on Divine Being and Act* (Edinburgh: T&T Clark, 1995), 113–9.

[169] Schwöbel laments: "What seems no longer possible in modern Christology is to present an integrated picture of Jesus Christ's past and his presence for the church and the cosmos." Ibid., 117.

in which case the spotlight falls on soteriology rather than ontology. The dilemma is whether to choose "between a non-soteriological ontology (being without meaning) and a non-ontological soteriology (meaning without being)."[170] In short, it is the dichotomy between a functional and an ontological Christology.

Taking these three antinomies as symptomatic of the malaise confronting Christology today, Schwöbel concludes that modern Christological reflection seems to be directed, seemingly without much success, at finding ways of integrating the historical Jesus with the Christ of faith in a new synthesis, or reuniting what cannot be divided in the first place. The reason for this, he suggests, lies in a failure to situate Christological reflection within a trinitarian framework. Only by a return to the "trinitarian logic of Christian faith" and the application of a "trinitarian hermeneutic of Christology" can we hope to overcome these antinomies in modern Christology.

While we think Schwöbel's trinitarian focus is timely, correct, and much needed—with some of his recommendations for Christological reflection highly pertinent to our thesis—we suspect that it would not satisfy Troeltsch and those like him who wish to do theology outside "the house of authority."[171] To transpose the music of Christology to a trinitarian key would only postpone the question of why one should accept trinitarianism, a contingent faith-postulate like Christology, as foundational. A strong and absolute historicism challenges all claims to universal truth, whether Christology or Trinitarian Theology. The methodological reconciliation of contingency with metanarrativity must still be reckoned with. And as suggested earlier, it seems inescapable that any attempt at the justification of beliefs will have to run on a set of presuppositions.

Rather than being covert about it, Christian theologians should frankly acknowledge and locate the basis of their argument in divine revelation. Of course, a self-involving act of nailing one's colours to the mast is but the first step. As we argued earlier, one needs to go on to make the case for the plausibility of one's presuppositions. By so doing, one opens up one's beliefs and operating assumptions to public scrutiny. The intention is not to claim triumphalistically that one has cornered the market on truth, or that one's beliefs are incorrigible and beyond criticism, but merely to establish a starting point

---

[170] Ibid., 119.
[171] This characterization is by Edward Farley, *Ecclesial Reflection: An Anatomy of Theological Method* (Philadelphia: Fortress, 1982).

from which one may embark on a journey of hermeneutical inquiry
oriented to the quest for transcontextual truth. Once this procedural
matter is settled, it is entirely proper, and arguably even necessary,
to adopt a trinitarian framework and all that it implies as the way
forward to a hermeneutic of Christology.

The Christological antinomies identified by Schwöbel—between
the historical-accidental and the ultimate-universal, between the past
and the present, between being and meaning—are the sorts of
difficulties which lend themselves to hermenuetical reflection. Insofar
as these prompt questions like the nature of truth and understanding
in history, theological investigation will do well to pay attention to
the hermeneutic tradition, represented by Schleiermacher, Dilthey,
Heidegger, and Gadamer, which occupies a firm spot in discussions
about the challenge of historicism.[172] A hermeneutical orientation is
increasingly incorporated into theological construction today even as
much of contemporary philosophy is marked by an "interpretive
turn."[173] It remains for us to demonstrate why we think the above
Christological antinomies invite a hermeneutical approach; and using
this as a launching pad, we will trace the contours of a hermeneu-
tically-informed Christological method. We begin with the last two
of the three above-mentioned antinomies.

The second antinomy concerns the chronological distance which
separates the historical Jesus from the present, and asks in what sense
this past event may be said to have ultimacy for the present. From
a hermeneutical standpoint, we suggest that the historical gap between
past and present is not a chasm without a bridge. As far as Christology
is concerned, this time-gap is *not vacuous but is tradition-filled*. Suspended

[172] See P. Hamilton, *Historicism*, 51–98; and Roberts, *Nothing But History*, 111–79.
[173] Theology since Schleiermacher has become increasingly hermeneutical. For a
review of this development, see James M. Robinson, "Hermeneutic since Barth" in
James M. Robinson & John B. Cobb, Jr., eds., *New Frontiers in Theology. Vol. 2: The
New Hermeneutic* (New York: Harper & Row, 1964), 1–77; and Thiselton, *TH*, 85–114.
On the place of hermeneutics in theology today, see Werner G. Jeanrond, *Theological
Hermeneutics: Development and Significance* (London: SCM, 1991, 1994); David Tracy,
"Theological Method," in Peter C. Hodgson & Robert H. King, eds., *Christian
Theology: An Introduction to Its Traditions and Tasks*, 2d rev. & enlarged ed. (Philadelphia:
Fortress, 1982, 1985), 35–59; idem, "Hermeneutical Reflections in the New Paradigm,"
in Küng & Tracy, eds., *Paradigm Change*, 34–62.
On the interpretive turn in the social sciences and philosophy, see: Zygmunt
Bauman, *Hermeneutics and Social Science: Approaches to Understanding* (London: Hutchinson,
1978); David R. Hiley, James F. Bohman & Richard Shusterman, eds. *The Interpretive
Turn: Philosophy, Science, Culture* (Ithaca & London: Cornell University Press, 1991);
and essays in Baynes, Bohman & McCarthy, eds., *After Philosophy*.

between theologians in the present and the Jesus-event in the past is the living bridge of Christian tradition, that complicated ecclesial mix of personalities, events, ideas, doctrines, creeds, aesthetic expressions, liturgy, commentaries, etc., all of which interpenetrate, knitting and knotting to form the rich tapestry that is church history.

And because Christian tradition is in the public domain, involving followers of Christ endowed with volitional powers and entrusted with the responsibility to engage and shape the world according to God's creational design, it is a living, lively and constantly evolving tradition. In confessing Christ and serving his cause, Christian believers participate in the process of "traditioning." And this is done not in a historical vacuum, but invariably from within a specific tradition: interrogating what is given in that tradition in the light of what we are confronted with in the present, for the purpose of articulating who Jesus Christ is today. This process, we suggest, is essentially a hermeneutical undertaking. The stress on the situatedness of understanding in postfoundationalist thinking, owed in no small part to Gadamer's influence, is not only appropriate as a description of Christian traditioning but provides an intellectual resource to overcome the second antinomy identified by Schwöbel.

The third antinomy—the impasse between Christology as essentially a soteriological expression (meaning) or a statement about Christ's ontological identity (being)—is problematic because it is rooted in a Cartesian subject-object dualism which, on the one hand, objectifies knowledge as something distinct from and independent of the knowing subject, and, on the other, reduces knowledge to its subjective effects on the knower. The former veers towards transparent objectivism while the latter approaches anti-realist relativism. Once again, an approach which goes beyond such a dualism, and espouses knowledge as a dialectic between the "subjectivity" of the interpreter and the "objectivity" of the interpretandum, provides a way out of this antinomy.

It is fundamentally misguided to force a choice between an *ontological* and a *functional* Christology. Apart from the fact that we cannot avoid ontological reference in any functionalized view of Christology,[174]

---

[174] See: MacQuarrie, *Christ in Modern Thought*, 7; D. M. MacKinnon notes that any confession about Christ already involves an ontological dimension. "'Substance' in Christology—a cross-bench view," in S. W. Sykes & J. P. Clayton, eds., *Christ, Faith and History: Cambridge Studies in Christology* (Cambridge: Cambridge University Press, 1972), 288.

the self-involvement of the theologian in the process of hermeneutical understanding entails a dispositional stance shaped by the continuing effects of Christ's ministry. The hermeneutic-theological community
is soteriologically determined in that its confession of Christ's ontological identity as the Incarnate Son of God comes out of an existential engagement with the tradition of Jesus mediated through
Scripture and the history of the Christian religion.[175] Wittgenstein's
notions of "language games" and "forms of life" are relevant here,
for without the appropriation of the symbolic universe or grand narratival background of tradition, one would not have the requisite linguistic apparatus to testify to the ontic character of Jesus Christ. The
being and the *meaning* of Christ are thus inextricably tied, from a
hermeneutical perspective.

The historical process thus figures prominently in a hermeneutical response to Schwöbel's second and third Christological antinomies. The same is true in the case of his first antinomy, that between
the historical and the ultimate. In our examination of Troeltsch, we
responded to the challenge of historical consciousness with a cock-
tail of ideas which includes the following: the inescapability of a postulate of totality or universality in dealing with phenomenological
particularity; Pannenberg's idea of revelation as history; the unavoid-
ability of argumentation for one's position with regard to the possibility of universal truth; Apel's notion of a transcendental pragmatics;
and the acknowledgment of the limitation and finitude of human
apprehension of truth. The upshot of our argument is that the universal and the contingent need not be mutually exclusive, and that
a theological framework involving the revelatory immanence of God
in history and the Pannenbergian idea of proleptic eschatological
fulfilment centering on Christ can provide a means of correlating
the two. Such a move locates knowledge and understanding within
the temporal axis of history, and it is here that the relevance of a
hermeneutical approach becomes clear.

The distinctiveness of a hermenuetical theology becomes clearer
when we change the underlying metaphor for knowledge and perception from a spatial to a temporal one. Enlightenment epistemological

---

[175] On the relationship between the historical Jesus and the origin and development of the church, see Francis Schüssler Fiorenza, *Foundational Theology: Jesus and
the Church* (New York: Crossroad, 1984), 108–73, where he applies insights from
Speech-Act theory and Hans Robert Jauss' reception hermeneutics to the question
of the ongoing interpretation of Jesus in the history of the church.

foundationalism, that ubiquitous dartboard at which modern philosophers squint and aim their learned projectiles, is metaphorically hierarchical and vertical in orientation. In place of this spatial-vertical framework, we propose a temporal-horizontal one, one which has been characterized as a "hermeneutical foundationalism" or "dialectical foundationalism." In this understanding, Bruce Coriell argues,

> the foundation is simply the beginning (to change from a spatial to a temporal metaphor) of any system of knowledge. This dialectical foundationalism maintains that the limited adequacy of any foundation must be continually adjusted in light of conclusions. The process of knowledge is at worst a vicious circle which leads to complete skepticism and at best a helical movement which leads to a provisional approximation of truth. A prominent contemporary form of this tradition can be characterized as hermeneutical foundationalism, in which any starting point for understanding is recognized as conditioned by human experience and yet discloses truth.[176]

Unlike Cartesian foundationalism, justification of knowledge in a hermeneutical approach is not based on arguments resting on universal first principles, but on prior conditioned perceptions which in turn precipitate new understanding. It is hermeneutically *foundational* in the sense that present understanding is always founded on and takes off from previous understanding, and this in turn becomes the basis or foundation for yet newer interpretations.

Applying this shift in metaphor to Christological formulation, we suggest that the common bifurcation of Christological method to either a "from above" or a "from below" approach[177] needs to be reassessed. We shall review these approaches briefly and then move on to propose an alternative approach which is hopefully more in tune with a historical, hermeneutical and eschatological perspective. The basic difference between these two approaches lies in the starting point and direction of Christological investigation. Represented

---

[176] Unpublished essay, "A Hermeneutics of Solidarity: A Conversation between Richard Bernstein and Alfred North Whitehead," quoted by Sallie McFague, "The Theologian as Advocate," in Sarah Coakley & David A. Pailin, eds., *The Making and Remaking of Christian Doctrine: Essays in Honour of Maurice Wiles* (Oxford: Clarendon, 1993), 157–58.

[177] On these approaches, see: Gerald O'Collins, *What Are They Saying About Jesus?* (New York: Paulist, 1977); Edward L. Krasevac, "'Christology from Above' and 'Christology from Below'," *Thomist* 51(1987): 299–306; and Karl Rahner, "The Two Basic Types of Christology," *Theological Investigations. Vol. XIII: Theology, Anthropology, Christology*, tr. David Bourke (London: Darton, Longman & Todd, 1975), 213–23.

quintessentially by Karl Barth,[178] a "Christology from above" begins
with the decision of the triune God to send the prexistent Son into
the world. This approach assumes the divinity of Jesus and follows
his move from eternity to time in the Incarnation. Its appraisal of
the humanity of Christ is done from the standpoint of his divinity.
By contrast, a "Christology from below," advocated by Küng, Pannenberg, Robinson, Schillebeeckx, Sobrino,[179] etc., begins with the man
Jesus (through critical-historical reconstructions) and traces the steps
leading to the apostolic acclamation of this man as the Incarnate
and divine Son of God. It moves from time to eternity, and attention is paid especially to the humanity of Jesus and the process by
which his divinity is recognized and confessed.

The "from above" and "from below" approaches should not be
construed as advocating a "high" and "low" Christology respectively.[180] Apart from the fact that one is hard-pressed to be thoroughly "from below" without smuggling in "from above" elements
and vice-versa, the use of the metaphor of "above" and "below"
tends, as Nicholas Lash points out, to obscure rather than clarify. It
is not our intention to provide a comprehensive critique of their use;
we concur with Lash's trenchant observations about the conceptual
difficulties inherent in them, not the least of which is the supposi-

---

[178] See his *Church Dogmatics, 12 vols.*, ed. G. W. Bromiley & T. F. Torrance
(Edinburgh: T&T Clark, 1936–1962; hereafter *CD*). On Barth's Christology, see
Karl-Josef Kuschel, *Born Before All Time? The Dispute over Christ's Origin* (New York:
Crossroad, 1992), 61–123.

[179] On the prominence of a "from below" approach in modern Christology, see
Monika Hellwig, "Re-Emergence of the Human, Critical, Public Jesus," *TS* 50(1989):
466–80. Wolfhart Pannenberg is often identified as a prime representative of a
Christology from below approach; see his *Jesus—God and Man*, tr. Lewis L. Wilkins
& Duane A. Priebe, 2d ed. (Philadelphia: Westminster, 1968, 1977; hereafter *JGM*),
33f. Pannenberg has however gone on to restate his position in a more nuanced
way in his *Systematic Theology*, 3 vols., tr. Geoffrey W. Bromiley (Grand Rapids:
Eerdmans, 1991, 1994, 1997; hereafter *ST*), 2:277f, 289, where he asserts that a
"from below" approach cannot be absolutized, and argues that both "from below"
and "from above" approaches are complementary. Other advocates of a "from
below" approach include: John A. T. Robinson, *The Human Face of God* (London:
SCM, 1973); Hans Küng, *On Being a Christian* (London: Collins, 1977); Edward
Schillebeeckx, *Jesus: An Experiment in Christology*, tr. Hubert Hoskins (London: Collins,
1979); Jon Sobrino, *Christology at the Crossroads: A Latin American Approach* (London:
SCM, 1978). It should be noted that the tag, "from below," is used rather equiv-
ocally and with a diversity of meaning by different proponents. See Nicholas Lash,
"Up and Down in Christology," in Stephen Sykes & Derek Holmes, eds., *New Studies
in Theology* (London: Duckworth, 1980), 33.

[180] See Krasevac, "'Christology from Above' and 'Christology from Below'," 299f.

tion that the terms "above" and "below" (read divinity and human-ity respectively) are unambiguous.[181] Suffice to say that they are com-plementary rather than mutually exclusive.[182]

What interests us however is the way in which they are depend-ent on an up/down spatial metaphorical framework or the super-natural/natural dichotomy which has by and large typified theology since the Patristic period. In such a bifurcated metaphysics, God sits "above" the world in his transcendent timelessness while history exists "below" in time and space. God and the supernatural realm are spa-tially separated from humanity and the realm of the natural. Such an ontology renders the "from above" and "from below" methods susceptible to the kind of logical conundrums involved in trying to "squeeze" two seemingly incompatible natures or elements—divinity and humanity; universality and contingency—into one person with-out compromising the integrity of either. How can the divine and the human subsist in the same "space" of a single person or phe-nomenon? Questions of this ilk, we suggest, are sparked off by an up/down spatial mindset.

Instead of a Christology "from above" or "from below," we sug-gest, in line with our proposed shift to a temporal metaphor, that Christology be done simultaneously *from within* and *from ahead*. This is intended to reflect greater sensitivity to "the interpretive turn," or the historical and processual character of understanding, and takes as its departure a historico-eschatological framework grounded in a concept of divine transcendental immanence in history. Pannenberg's critique of theology's bondage to the Greek philosophical notion of timelessness and his neo-Hegelian eschatological interpretation of God, metaphysics and history, provides the building blocks for our temporalized hermeneutical framework.[183] Before concluding, we shall

---

[181] Lash, "Up and Down".

[182] Significantly, both Pannenberg and Barth, supposedly occupying polar posi-tions on Christological method, affirm the complementarity of the two approaches. We have already alluded to Pannenberg's restatement of his position in his later *Systematic Theology*. Lash helpfully points out that Barth regards the two as different not in their subject matter but in the "order" and "sequence" of their concern for knowledge. "Up and Down," 36.

[183] See W. Pannenberg, *BQT* 2:1–27; 201–49; idem, *Metaphysics and the Idea of God*, tr. Philip Clayton (Edinburgh: T&T Clark, 1990; hereafter *MIG*). For a dis-cussion on classical theology's appropriation of the Greek notion of true being as that which is unaffected by the flux of history, and its divergence from the bibli-cal understanding of God as personal and truth as historic, see Laurence W. Wood, "Above, Within or Ahead Of? Pannenberg's Eschatologicalism as a Replacement

set out briefly what we mean by "from within" and "from ahead",
and explicate how these go into our project of articulating a Christology
beyond objectivism and relativism. It will be evident from our explanation that the points raised in response to Troeltsch set out in the
above section, "Theology in the Wake of Historical Consciousness,"
will be incorporated into what we mean by Christology from *within*
and *ahead*.[184]

Christology is "from within" in two senses: (1) in the sense that
all Christological reflections are invariably made *from within* a specific
context and a particular tradition; and (2) the experience of the theologian plays a formative role in the shaping of theological understanding, i.e., the inward tradition of Christian experience. The
operative words for a Christology "from within" are thus *tradition*
and *experience*. Let us look at these in turn.

First, in the wake of the rejection of Cartesian Scientism in Kuhnian
post-empiricist philosophy of science, and developments in the sociology of knowledge and hermeneutics, it is virtually a truism in our
postmodern age to say that understanding is contextual and rooted
in tradition. The task of interpreting the significance of Christ for
today is therefore one necessarily undertaken from within the framework of a living and ongoing tradition. Gadamer's notion of "effective
historical consciousness" is especially helpful in throwing light on the
dynamics of such a traditionary Christology. Furthermore, a hermeneutical approach to Christological construction will pay attention to the

---

for Supernaturalism," *ATJ* 46(1991): 43–72. By "Above", Wood refers to the "Supernaturalism," developed from the thirteenth century on, from Aquinas and the
Scholastics through to Kant's deistic supernaturalism, where the absolute God coex-
ists "above" us. His "supernaturalism" parallels what we have called, "an up/down
spatial metaphor" or a hierarchical ontology. By "Within", Wood has in mind the
kind of pantheistic mysticism which blurs the distinction between God and the
world, i.e., God is somehow collapsed into the system. This usage of "within" is
very different, as we shall see, from what I mean by a Christology *from within*. Wood
essentially embraces Pannenberg's ontology of anticipation (hence "Ahead of" in
his title) as a *via media* between an absolute transcendence ("Above") and an absolute
monistic immanence ("Within").

[184] In proposing new models for Christology, we do not mean that the "from
above" and "from below" approaches are invalid or have no distinctive contributions to make. We are merely highlighting their limitations and wish to provide
additional (hermeneutically sensitive) tools by which to understand and testify to the
significance of Christ. The truth of Incarnation and the realization of God's redemptive design in the world and in history are surely too profound a mystery to be
exhausted by any single model; and the multiplying of Christological models and
metaphors can only accentuate the many-sided splendour of the Incarnation.

relation between a Christocentric form of life in community and confessional statements concerning Christ: what one does and what one
believes and confesses are interconnected. Such a form of life is not
a closed system. Tradition, or the paradigm under which one for-
mulates Christology, is not deterministic but open,[185] albeit in a
qualified way. Exploring the dialectic between the conventionality of
tradition and the intentionality of those operating within that tradition is what is entailed in a Christology "from within." The call to
situate Christology within the "form of life" of the Christian community is echoed in Schwöbel's argument for a return to a trinitarian logic in Christology. The task of Christology, he asserts, should
be interpreted as "the conceptual reconstruction of the truth claims
concerning the person and work of Jesus Christ asserted, presupposed and implied in Christian faith as it is practised in worship,
proclamation, confession and the Christian life."[186]

This brings us, secondly, to the personalistic and the experiential
dimension in Christological belief. Ever since Schleiermacher sought
to get around the deistic implications of Kant's epistemology by situating theology in the realm of piety and the feeling of God-consciousness, questions have been raised about the place of experience in
theology.[187] Whatever one may think of the viability of romanticism
for theological construction, the role of the interpreter's subjectivity
in the determination of meaning and understanding certainly invites
attention to the experiential and existential dimension of Christological
formulation. The self-involvement entailed in hermeneutics makes
such a move both prudent and necessary. In this respect, Michael
Polanyi's metaphor of "indwelling" as the way by which one comes

---

[185] Thomas Guarino, "Contemporary Theology and Scientific Rationality," *SR*
22(1993): 311–22, examines the implications for theology of a postpositivistic scientific
rationality, and suggests that it, like contemporary philosophy of science, must seek
a *via media* between correspondence and constructivism. He helpfully points out that
we need to distinguish between a strong determinism of contingency from a softer
version, one which accepts the inescapable fact of contingency without succumbing
to determinism. In other words, historical situatedness and the ability to transcend
our conditionedness are not incompatible.

[186] Schwöbel, "Christology," 138. Accordingly, Christological reflection arises "*from
within* [emphasis mine] the community which sees itself as part of the divine economy in that it celebrates the trinitarian being of God as the condition for its own
being and acknowledges its participation in the life of the triune God by grace in
its witness and eucharistic practice."

[187] See Donald L. Gelpi, *The Turn to Experience in Contemporary Theology* (New York
& Mahwah: Paulist, 1994).

to knowledge, is pertinent to our project. Gunton appropriates Polanyi's
metaphor of indwelling to argue that we can only begin to understand the Christology of the NT when we personally participate in
the reality which it depicts. In other words, we can only converse
with, critique, and build upon the Christological formula bequeathed
to us by tradition if we indwell it.[188] The notion of "indwelling"
coheres with our proposal for a Christology "from within."

In positing a Christology *from ahead*, we take on board Pannenberg's
sagacious view of truth as essentially eschatological in nature, and
apply this to Christological reflection insofar as the latter concerns
the apprehension of truth in Jesus Christ. The proleptic realization
of the Eschaton in Christ's resurrection, i.e., the forward grasp within
history of that which lies only at the end of history, provides the
critical element needed in hermeneutical inquiry. (In our opinion, a
Christology "from ahead" seems more propitious and representative
of the thrust of Pannenberg's theological position than his earlier
Christology "from below.") If understanding takes place in a hermeneutical spiral between the part (contingency) and the whole (universality),
then the notion of a proleptic-eschatological Christ fulfils the role of
the "whole" within that dialectical polarity of whole and part. In
this sense, a Christology "from ahead" serves a criteriological function.

In that this eschatological realization is centred in the person of
Jesus, Christology "from ahead" is ineluctably chained to the unique
and inviolable historicity of Jesus of Nazareth. The eschatological
future is thus not an absolute indeterminacy but a Jesus-qualified
openness. In this proleptic perspective, we have the presence of the
future ahead of time. This eschatological criteriology is paradoxically
linked with the pastness of the historical Jesus. In addition, the future
orientation suggested by "from ahead" reminds one of the provisionality of all theological constructs, and should disinfect us of the
virus of theological complacency. Just as the truth is always *ahead*,
Christology is a pilgrim enterprise, ever en route toward the eschatological denouement where history will end at the feet of Christ.

The advantage of Christology *from within* and *from ahead* (as set out
above) is that it allows Christology to be simultaneously retrospective and prospective, enabling the old and the traditional to feast at

---

[188] Gunton, *Yesterday and Today*, 149; cf. Michael Polanyi, *Personal Knowledge* (London:
Routledge and Kegan Paul, 1958); idem, *The Tacit Dimension* (London: Routledge
and Kegan Paul, 1966).

the same table as the new and the innovative; and makes possible the coinherence of the contingent and the universal. The elements of tradition, experience, and the eschatological, interpenetrate and are dialectically related in the sense that they set the parameters for each to function within the paradigm. The generative potential of experience means that the introduction of new, even unprecedented, theological constructs is to be expected. Yet it does not mean there are no limits or guidelines for innovation; not all new offerings are by definition proper and right. The dialectical relationship between experience and tradition means that the latter provides guidance to the former even as the former transforms the latter.

It is hoped that the combination of the fiduciary and the critical in a *from within* and *from ahead* paradigm would lead to a Christology "beyond objectivism and relativism." Like a boat sailing down river, Christology in an age of critical historicism must avoid crashing against the jagged rocks of objectivism on the one side and relativism on the other side. Our proposal seeks to affirm simultaneously the meta-narratival truthfulness of Christ and the necessary contingency of all Christological affirmations. How Christology can ride the waves and navigate the waters between objectivism and relativism will be the task of the chapters that follow. The rubric of Christology *from within* and *from ahead* will form the overarching structure of our discussion. We begin in the next chapter with the issue of tradition in Christological formulation, and seek, in dialogue with Gadamer, to probe the implications of *wirkungsgeschichtliches Bewusstsein* for Christological development.

CHAPTER TWO

A CHRISTOLOGY FROM WITHIN—TRADITION (I): THE HERMENEUTICAL REHABILITATION OF TRADITION

Postmodernity's rejection of the ahistorical epistemic stance of the Enlightenment has ramifications for all claims to knowledge. Theological claims are no exception. In the wake of historical consciousness, theology must come to terms with the contingency and temporality of knowledge and understanding. And as we suggested in the previous chapter, attending to the historicity of knowledge makes the task of articulating what one believes concerning Christ a hermeneutical one. We wish to argue for a Christological approach which takes into account, first, the hermeneutical situatedness and experience of the theological community, and second, the eschatological character of theological truth. To incorporate both these aims, we proposed earlier that Christology be done *from within* and *from ahead* respectively. We shall take up the *from within* aspect in this and the next two chapters.

To recapitulate, Christology *from within* is understood in two related senses: (i) Christology is rooted in, and arises from within, a particular tradition; and (ii) Christology is the formulation of a belief or stance which germinates and blossoms within Christian experience. We are *not* using the term to denote some individual or subjective interiority. Reflecting on Christology *from within* entails paying attention first to the dialogical relation between the theological interpreter and Christian tradition; and second to the formative and transformative role of Christian experience. We shall examine Christology's situatedness within tradition in chapters two and three, and leave the existential self-involvement implicit in theological understanding to chapter four. The treatment of the *traditionary* and the *experiential* dimensions in separate chapters is but a heuristic expedient which should not obscure the fact that they are inextricably related.

We shall explore in this chapter the hermeneutics of Hans-Georg Gadamer en route to explicating the place of tradition in theological understanding and construction. Gadamer has laboured hard to rehabilitate tradition and authority in human understanding, and is thus ideally suited as a dialogue partner in our attempt to articulate a hermeneutically sensitive Christology *from within tradition*. His reflections on the process of understanding will serve as a conceptual backdrop for our discussion on the relationship between the historicality of understanding and Christology as truth-claim. Two key areas will be examined: (1) whether an emphasis on tradition necessarily leads to the relativizing of truth or the reinforcement of entrenched beliefs; and (2) whether it is possible to mount a critique of tradition.

I. *Hans-Georg Gadamer's Philosophical Hermeneutics*

As a discipline, hermeneutics has evolved from its early focus on philology and textual interpretation to one today which engages virtually all of the humanities (*Geisteswissenschaften*). Schleiermacher paved the way for the integration of hermeneutics and philosophical concerns when he made room for the psychology and individuality of the author/speaker in interpretation. This broadening of hermeneutics' embrace was carried on by Dilthey, who defended the autonomy of the human and historical sciences against the encroachment of the methodologically-minded natural sciences. However, it is not until Heidegger that we witness the shift from a methodical focus to a thorough philosophization of hermeneutics.[1] Seizing upon Dilthey's view of texts as expressions of life which can be grasped through the "lived experience" and self-understanding of the interpreter, Heidegger argues that investigation into what Life entails necessarily raises the question of ontology, i.e., what is the nature of Being itself? He proposes an existential ontology in which Being is understood as Being-in-the-world, *Dasein*. The ontological structure of human life lies in the inescapable temporality of existence; being-in-the-world is being-in-time. Given this fundamental ontology, time is regarded as the basic horizon in which interpretation takes place. Hermeneutics in Heidegger's view is contingent on the given structure of life, and cannot be construed as an atemporal exercise. In bringing to light the many hidden but enveloping dimensions of

---

[1] As Grondin observes, in Heidegger's thought, "hermeneutics is elevated to the center of philosophical concern." Jean Grondin, *Introduction to Philosophical Hermeneutics*, tr. Joel Weinsheimer (New Haven/London: Yale University Press, 1994), 91.

being which define human thought, Heidegger puts to rest any notion of the human subject as a passive receptor of experience. Inasmuch as the interpreter partakes of *Dasein*, he or she does not approach interpretation with a blank slate but comes equipped with a pre-understanding which conditions understanding.

Heidegger's hermeneutics of *Dasein* exerted a deep influence on his student Hans-Georg Gadamer (1900–), who openly confesses his indebtedness to his teacher, even though his was not the only inspiration for his philosophical hermeneutics.[2] Since the publication of his magnum opus *Wahrheit und Methode*[3] in 1960, he has, through his substantial output, demonstrated the applicability of hermeneutical insights to the fundamental questions of human knowledge.[4] Gadamer's hermeneutics has already been analysed in the literature.[5] What follows is but an overview of the salient features of his hermeneutical reflections, drawing principally from his *Truth and Method*. In its published form,[6] the work begins with a consideration of art and the

---

[2] Gadamer acknowledges: "What was most important for me, however, I learned from Heidegger." "Reflections on My Philosophical Journey," in Lewis Edwin Hahn, ed., *The Philosophy of Hans-Georg Gadamer* (Chicago/La Salle: Open Court, 1997; hereafter *PHG*), 9. Other contributing factors include his reading of the Greek classics, Plato and Aristotle in particular, Kierkegaard, and Hegel. See Gadamer, *Philosophical Apprenticeships*, tr. R. R. Sullivan (Cambridge & London: MIT Press, 1977); Jean Grondin, *Sources of Hermeneutics* (Albany: SUNY Press, 1995); Robert R. Sullivan, *Political Hermeneutics: The Early Thinking of Hans-Georg Gadamer* (University Park & London: Pennsylvania State University Press, 1989); and James Risser, *Hermeneutics and the Voice of the Other: Re-reading Gadamer's Philosophical Hermeneutics* (Albany: SUNY Press, 1997), 25–53.

[3] *Wahrheit und Methode: Grundzüge einer philosophischen Hermeneutik*, 4th edition (Tübingen: J. C. B. Mohr, 1960, 1975), ET: *Truth and Method*, 2d rev. ed. & translation revision by Joel Weinsheimer & Donald G. Marshall (London: Sheed & Ward, 1975. 1989; hereafter *TM*).

[4] See Richard E. Palmer's comprehensive compilation of Gadamer's published works in *PHG*, 555–602.

[5] See: Thiselton, *TH*; Bernstein, *Beyond Objectivism*; Grondin, *Philosophical Hermeneutics*, 106–123; essays in Hahn, ed., *PHG*; Sullivan, *Political Hermeneutics*; Josef Bleicher, *Contemporary Hermeneutics: Hermeneutics as Method, Philosophy and Critique* (London, Boston & Henley: Routledge & Kegan Paul, 1980), 108f; Richard E. Palmer, *Hermeneutics: Interpretation Theory in Schleiermacher, Dilthey, Heidegger, and Gadamer* (Evanston: Northwestern University Press, 1967), 162–217; Hugh J. Silverman, ed., *Gadamer and Hermeneutics* (New York & London: Routledge, 1991); Georgia Warnke, *Gadamer: Hermeneutics, Tradition and Reason* (Stanford: Stanford University Press, 1987); Joel C. Weinsheimer, *Gadamer's Hermeneutics: A Reading of "Truth and Method"* (New Haven: Yale University Press, 1985); Kathleen Wright, ed., *Festival of Interpretations: Essays on Hans-Georg Gadamer's Work* (Albany: SUNY Press, 1990). See also: Hans Herbert Kögler, *The Power of Dialogue: Critical Hermeneutics after Gadamer and Foucault* (Cambridge & London: MIT Press, 1996); and Risser, *Hermeneutics*.

[6] For an account of the genesis of *TM* from its handwritten manuscript stage to its final published form, see Grondin, *Sources*, 83–98.

aesthetic consciousness, and moves to the historicality of understanding in the human sciences, before culminating with linguisticality as the ontological condition of the hermeneutic experience. Consciously using the word "Method" in an ironic, disparaging or pejorative sense in his title, Gadamer makes it clear that he is not commending any particular method of interpretation. His aim is to explore philosophically the question, "how is understanding possible?", a question "which precedes any action of understanding on the part of subjectivity, including the methodical activity of the 'interpretive sciences' and their norms and rules."[7]

The development of Gadamer's philosophy must be appraised against the backdrop of the flowering of Phenomenology and its critique of Neo-Kantianism in the 1920s. Husserl's phenomenology, critically explicated by Heidegger,[8] provided Gadamer with a way to correct the false priority of self-consciousness in Neo-Kantianism. To Gadamer, Husserl's concept of the life-world (*Lebenswelt*), with its stress on the pre-reflective givenness of things and inclusion of the wider field of everyday experience in perception, demonstrates the inadequacy of the justification of knowledge based on the objectivism of the natural sciences.[9] He considers the attempts by Dilthey, Droysen and Neo-Kantianism at the end of the nineteenth and the beginning of the twentieth-century to secure a methodology for the human sciences (*Geisteswissenschaften*) akin to that in the natural sciences (*Naturwissenschaften*), as fundamentally misguided. The scientific status of the human sciences does not rest on their having a methodology. *Truth and Method* may be regarded as a trenchant remonstration against the hegemonic grip of scientific positivism on what constitutes legitimate knowledge. Not that he is against method per se;[10] his concern

---

[7] *TM*, xxx.

[8] Gadamer attended Heidegger's 1925 lecture course, "The History of the Concept of Time" at Marburg University where he defended Husserl's concept of intentionality against the bifurcation of subject and object in Neo-Kantianism. See: Heidegger, *History of the Concept of Time: Prolegomena*, tr. Theodore Kisiel (Bloomington: Indiana University Press, 1985). Nevertheless, Heidegger differs from Husserl at fundamental points; see Thiselton's comments on approaching Heidegger from the standpoint of Husserl's phenomenology, *TH*, 144–5; cf. John McGinley, "Heidegger's Concern for the Lived-World in his Dasein-Analysis," *PhT* 16(1972): 92–116.

[9] See Gadamer, "The Phenomenological Movement" and "The Science of the Life-World" in *Philosophical Hermeneutics* (Berkeley, Los Angeles & London: University of California Press, 1976; hereafter *PH*), 130–81; 182–97.

[10] Gadamer acknowledges that in his desire to pry open the stranglehold of *techne* or method on the sciences, he may have unwittingly contributed to a rather polemical

is rather to show that hermeneutics is more a matter of ontology than methodology. If temporality is to be taken seriously, no "method" can be selected in interpretation *in advance of* its application. This would distort what is to be understood by subjecting it to the "control" of the subject.

Drawing on Heidegger's analysis of *Dasein* and his "hermeneutics of facticity,"[11] Gadamer calls into question the latent-Cartesian dichotomy between what is subjective and objective in Romantic hermeneutics. Heidegger's notion of the fore-structure (*Vorstruktur*) of understanding[12]— interpretation depends on a fore-having (*Vorhabe*), a fore-sight (*Vorsicht*), and a fore-conception (*Vorgriff*)—provided Gadamer with the philosophical underpinning for his hermeneutics. He seeks to reverse the repression of temporality in scientific methodologism, charting a course away from an atomistic view of meaning-determination, and affirming the constitutive role of preunderstanding in understanding.[13] Instead of a neutral objectivity, a point zero from which one begins the process of interpretation, understanding in the human sciences takes off from a situation of "facticity" or "thrownness," by which is meant the inescapable particularity of life.

On the basis of Dasein as a mode of being rather than an "act" of subjectivity, Gadamer explores the ontological conditions of knowledge. Instead of the Cartesian dualism of subject and object, in Gadamer's Heideggerian perspective, the questioner finds himself interrogated by the "subject-matter" (*Sache*).[14] Gadamer explicates the ontic nature of understanding by appealing to the experience of art and the playing of games (*Spiel*). In a game, the players acknowl-

---

heightening of the tension between truth and method. *TM*, xxi; and his "Afterword" in 2d. ed. of *TM*, 555.

[11] Heidegger develops his "hermeneutics of facticity" in his lecture courses of 1919–1923, in particular those of 1921–22 and 1923 published as volumes 61 and 63 of his *Gesamtausgabe: Phänomenologische Interpretationen zu Aristoteles: Einführung in die phänomenologische Forschung* (Frankfurt: Klostermann, 1985); and *Ontologie: Hermeneutik der Faktizität* (Frankfurt: Klostermann, 1988), respectively. On the influence of Heidegger (and Kierkegaard) on Gadamer, see Risser, *Hermeneutics*, 25–53.

[12] Martin Heidegger, *Being and Time*, tr. John Macquarrie & Edward Robinson (Oxford & Cambridge: Blackwell, 1962, rpt. 1992), §32, 188–95. Heidegger's rejection of "calculative" (method-based) thinking and preference for "meditative" (*Gelassenheit* or "releasement") thinking is carried through in Gadamer's repudiation of hermeneutics understood solely in terms of method. See Heidegger, *Discourse in Thinking* (New York: Harper & Row, 1966), 54; and Thiselton, *NHH*, 319–20.

[13] Gadamer, *TM*, 262–71.

[14] Palmer, *Hermeneutics*, 165.

edge the priority of the game over their subjectivity and submit to its norms and requirements. "[P]lay has its own essence, independent of the consciousness of those who play."[15] Yet a game is not simply the sum of its codified rules and strategies; it is a transubjective event actualized by the players' playing of the game. The play however is not constituted by the players; it constitutes an event which is brought about through the performative participation of the players. "The players are not the subjects of play; instead play merely reaches presentation (*Darstellung*) through the players."[16] The play exists through the playing of the players; the game "absorbs the player into itself."[17]

Something similar occurs in the experience of art. A work of art stands over its viewers and draws them out of their existence. Its meaning has no independent subsistence apart from its relation to the viewer. Just as a game happens only when players play it, so the meaning of an object of art emerges only when viewers engage it.[18] In unpacking the hermeneutical structure entailed in the experience of a work of art, one realizes that its meaning is not exhausted in a concept. When a viewer engages a work of art, she not only apprehends the ideational content expressed therewith, she also learns something about herself, as well as seeing the world afresh. Art expands the viewer's horizon.[19] We shall take up Gadamer's ontological analysis of the picture (*Bild*) below in our discussion on hermeneutics and truth. Suffice for now that the experience of art illuminates what is entailed in the process of understanding. There is an inexhaustibility of meaning in interpretation which makes the search for the meaning of a text an unending process.[20]

Understanding rooted in a pre-given conceptual scheme or a set of assumptions is never a presuppositionless apprehending of what

---

[15] *TM*, 102; see Warnke, *Gadamer*, 48–56.

[16] *TM*, 103.

[17] *TM*, 105.

[18] It is not adventitious that *Truth and Method* begins with the experience of art. The task of construing the relevance of art to philosophy is one which Gadamer took on board very early in his career. See his "Reflections," *PHG*, 6.

[19] See H-G. Gadamer, *The Relevance of the Beautiful*, tr. N. Walker & ed. by Robert Bernasconi (Cambridge: Cambridge University Press, 1986).

[20] Gadamer speaks of "the inexhaustibility of the experience of meaning" in "Text and Interpretation," Brice R. Wachterhauser, ed., *Hermeneutics and Modern Philosophy* (Albany: SUNY Press, 1986, hereafter *HMP*), 381. The "discovery of the true meaning of a text . . . is never finished; it is in fact an infinite process." *TM*, 298.

is presented to us. Accordingly, attention must be paid to the historicality (*Geschichtlichkeit*) of understanding. Contrary to Schleiermacher and Dilthey who see the task of hermeneutics as the avoidance of misunderstanding and the methodical reconstruction of historical reality respectively, Gadamer argues that such reconstruction is never free from the influence of historical tradition insofar as all who undertake reconstructive work are themselves rooted in history.[21]

The Enlightenment's "prejudice against prejudice"[22] and historicism's displacement of prejudices with methods, do not do justice to the historical situatedness of the interpreter. Understanding is never prejudice-free. Instead of polarizing situated subjectivity and objectivity in understanding, Gadamer argues that prejudices or "pre-judgments" (*die Vorurteile*) are the conditions of understanding.

> It is not so much our judgments as it is our prejudices that constitute our being. . . . Prejudices are not necessarily unjustified and erroneous, so that they inevitably distort the truth. In fact, the historicity of our existence entails that prejudices, in the literal sense of the word, constitute the initial directedness of our whole ability to experience.[23]

Rather than cordoning off her dispositional stances or prejudices, the interpreter acknowledges these and makes them transparent in the process of interpretation. Gadamer calls for a non-pejorative view of prejudice and authority, and argues for the epistemic value of tradition (*Überlieferung*). Situatedness in tradition is the condition for "hermeneutic productivity,"[24] and not, as the Enlightenment insists, the enemy of understanding. In rejecting prejudice, the Enlightenment is blind to its own historically mediated prejudice; and in opposing tradition to reason, it fails to recognize that reason itself is historically contingent.

Prejudice has a threefold character in Gadamer:[25] (1) our prejudices are inherited from tradition and they shape what we are now,

---

[21] On Gadamer's critique of Schleiermacher and Dilthey, see *TM*, 184–97; 218–42. Dilthey too affirms the historical conditionality of the knower, but he does not wish to sacrifice the ideal of objectivity in historical understanding. To Gadamer, Dilthey is ultimately still operating under the shadow of Enlightenment Cartesianism. His demand for objectivity is so strong that "the historicity of historical experience is never truly integrated in his thought." *TM*, 241.

[22] *TM*, 270.

[23] Gadamer, "The Universality of the Hermeneutical Problem," *PH*, 9. On Gadamer's discussion of prejudice or prejudgment, see *TM*, 277–85.

[24] *TM*, 283.

[25] See Richard Bernstein, "From Hermeneutics to Praxis," *HMP*, 90.

whether we are aware of it or not; (2) they are the reason why we have a sense of affinity (*Zugehörigkeit*) with, or a sense of belonging to, tradition;[26] and (3) there is a projective or anticipatory dimension to our prejudices and prejudgments. In interpretation, initially one invariably projects the meaning of the text in advance, and this initial anticipation of meaning is then revised in the process of engaging the text. In short, we have here the idea of the hermeneutical circle: the constant interplay between the movement of tradition and the movement of the interpreter.[27] By being aware of the initial bias of her own preunderstanding, the interpreter is able to let the otherness of the text modify her own fore-meanings.

Understanding emerges in the intersection between a tradition-conditioned preunderstanding and the text's otherness. Interpretation is never simply a reproduction of a meaning which is objectively there in the text; it is always productive in the sense that something new is born as the interpreter engages the text in dialogue. In this way, Gadamer hopes to rehabilitate the authority of tradition while at the same time allowing for the expansion of the interpreter's horizon. As tradition is questioned from the vantage point of a specific moment in history, a new layer of meaning is generated. Whether Gadamer's hermeneutics simply confers privilege upon the status quo, or genuinely allows for the possibility of a critique of tradition, is a debated question which we shall take up below. It is perhaps enough that understanding in Gadamer is more a participation in an event of transmission than an act of subjectivity. Tradition is "not simply a permanent precondition". In understanding, we participate in the evolution of tradition or the happening of tradition (*Überlieferungsgeschehen*).[28] Tradition is meaning within the historicity of understanding, and as such is dynamic, not static; it always contains within it an element of freedom befitting its historical nature.

In contrast to nineteenth-century hermeneutics which sees "temporal distance" (*Zeitenabstand*) in historical understanding as an obstacle,

---

[26] See H-G. Gadamer, "The Problem of Historical Consciousness," Paul Rabinow & William M. Sullivan, eds., *Interpretive Social Science: A Reader* (Berkeley, Los Angeles & London: University of California Press, 1979), 155.

[27] *TM*, 269. Gadamer's notion of the hermeneutical circle differs from the nineteenth-century model which focuses on the interplay between whole and part in the process of interpretation. His is more in line with the later Heidegger's ontological conception, and has to do primarily with the movement between interpreter and text. See Risser, *Hermeneutics*, 75.

[28] *TM*, 293.

Gadamer sees it as something to be embraced. For in making explicit the prejudices and prejudgments which go into the tradition-filled temporal space between the pastness of the text and the present, the interpreter is able to reexamine such prejudices critically, and through this to allow the meaning of the text to be grasped. Temporal distance is productive in that it enables understanding.[29] In interpretation, we are not so much interested in the individuality of the author as we are in the "truth" which comes to being as we engage the text.

The interpreter's situatedness in history and tradition is captured in Gadamer's use of the Husserlian notion of "horizon" and his idea of "historically effected consciousness" (*wirkungsgeschichtliches Bewusstsein*). The term has been variously translated.[30] A "horizon is the range of vision that includes everything that can be seen from a particular vantage point."[31] And this vantage point is shaped by the interpreter's historical and cultural situatedness, including all the prejudices of her tradition. In this sense, the consciousness of the interpreter is historically effected. By the expression, *wirkungsgeschichtliches Bewusstsein*, Gadamer underscores the fact that the interpreter is always "already in the middle of history". He describes effective historical consciousness thus:

> I call it consciousness of being affected by history because on the one hand I want to say that our consciousness is historically [*wirkungs-geschichtlich*] determined, that is, it is determined by real events [*wirkliches Geschehen*] rather than left on its own to float free over against the past. On the other hand I want to say it is important to produce within ourselves always again a consciousness of this being effected [*ein Bewusstsein dieses Bewirktseins*]—just as the past which comes to us to experience forces us to deal with it, and in a certain respect to take its truth upon ourselves.[32]

---

[29] *TM*, 298–300; cf. Grondin, *Philosophical Hermeneutics*, 112.

[30] See *TM*, 299–300. "Historically effected consciousness" is the translation of *wirkungsgeschichtliches Bewusstsein* adopted by Weinsheimer and Marshall in the 2d rev. ed. of *TM*, see xv & 300. The German phrase has been variously translated: "consciousness exposed to the effects of history" or "consciousness of historical efficacy" (Ricoeur); "historically operative consciousness" (Kisiel); "authentically historical consciousness" (Palmer); and "the consciousness of standing within a still operant history" (Hoy). See Risser, *Hermeneutics*, 228, n. 37; Palmer, *Hermeneutics*, 191.

[31] *TM*, 302; cf. 245. On the genesis of the concept of "horizon" in Nietzsche, and the difference between Gadamer's use of "horizon" and Husserl's, see Walter Lammi, "Hans-Georg Gadamer's 'Correction' of Heidegger," *JHI* 52(1991): 493–95.

[32] Risser's modification of Thomas Wren's translation of H-G. Gadamer, "Die Kontinuität der Geschichte und der Augenblick der Existenz," which appears as "The Continuity of History and the Existential Moment," *PhT* 16(1972): 230–40. See Risser, *Hermeneutics*, 79.

In line with Heidegger's call to make transparent one's fore-under-standings, *wirkungsgeschichtliches Bewusstsein* concerns the exposing of one's own consciousness in dealing with texts or traditions. This is an ongoing fore-grounding of historically engendered consciousness which can never be completed. Gadamer means by this expression *the effect*, as well as *the awareness of the effect of history*.[33] The interpreter's historicality is summed up in Gadamer's pithy remark: "history does not belong to us; we belong to it."[34] To him, historically-effected consciousness is "more being than consciousness" (*mehr Sein als Bewusstsein*); it is both a condition and a task.[35]

Consciousness as historically effected has a protensive character which renders the interpreter's horizon open rather than fixed or closed. A horizon moves and changes with the interpreter;[36] it is constantly being shaped and reformed. Understanding takes place in the interface between past tradition and the interpreter's present, or a fusion of the interpreter's horizon and that of the past or text. This "fusion of horizons" (*Horizontverschmelzung*) does not mean a dis-solving of the tension between the horizons; rather it highlights the fact that understanding always involves the emergence of a shared truth.[37] In Warnke's assessment, this consensus over meaning in a fusion of horizons has two senses:

> on the one hand we understand the object from the point of view of our assumptions and situation; on the other, our final perspective reflects the education we have received through our encounter with the object. Such fusion, then, does not entail any concrete agreement. It means merely that we have learned to integrate a certain point of view and have thereby advanced to a new understanding of the issues in question.[38]

In a fusion of horizons, the subject-matter represented by the hori-zon of the text is taken on board by the interpreter, resulting in a transformation of the latter's consciousness. Through this "fusion," the "truth" of the object of interpretation and the "truth" which the interpreter brings are constituted as a new layer of tradition. Hence Gadamer prefers to speak of experience as *Erfahrung*, which has the

---

[33] *TM*, xxxiv. As Risser describes it, "Hermeneutical consciousness is a conscious-ness of history's effects and a consciousness effected by history." *Hermeneutics*, 9.
[34] *TM*, 276.
[35] Gadamer, *PH*, 38; also *TM*, xxiv; cf. Grondin, *Philosophical Hermeneutics*, 114.
[36] *TM*, 304; cf. 245.
[37] See Weinsheimer, *Gadamer's Hermeneutics*, 183.
[38] Warnke, *Gadamer*, 107.

sense of being led along to something new, rather than *Erlebnis*, a
term which Dilthey used, which simply refers to having lived through
an experience. Historically effected consciousness thus consciously
effects history by contributing to the protend march of tradition.

The self-involving character of interpretation is accentuated in
Gadamer's contention that application (*Anwendung*) is an integral part
of understanding since the latter is invariably tied to a specific historical situation. Gadamer alludes to legal hermeneutics and the interpretation of Scripture to illustrate how application is inseparably
meshed with understanding.[39] Just as legal counselors interpret the
law with an eye to its application to current cases, and biblical scholars interpret Scripture with a view to bringing home its message to
today's audience, application is an inalienable part of interpretation.

Gadamer makes a case for the linguisticality (*Sprachlichkeit*) of hermeneutical experience in the third part of *Truth and Method*. The Heideggerian view of language as the "house of being" is taken up in his
notion of language as the ontological horizon of hermeneutical understanding.[40] Drawing on the linguist Wilhelm von Humboldt, Gadamer
asserts that language is not merely a possession; it is the means by
which we have a world (*Welt haben*) at all. "*Language is the universal
medium in which understanding occurs*. . . . All understanding is interpretation, and all interpretation takes place in the medium of a language."[41]
In that language makes possible intersubjective communication, it
constitutes the "universal aspect of hermeneutics". There is a pri-
mordial unity between language and world in Gadamer's ontology
such that the finite and the infinite interpenetrate in linguisticality.
"Being that can be understood", he suggests, "is language."[42] And
tradition comes into being through the finitude and possibility inher-

---

[39] *TM*, 308–309.

[40] Heidegger writes: "Language is the house of Being in which man ek-sists by
dwelling, in that he belongs to the truth of Being, guarding it." "Letter to Humanism,"
in M. Heidegger, *Basic Writings: From Being and Time (1927) to The Task of Thinking
(1964)*, F. Krell, ed. (London: Routledge & Kegan Paul, 1978), 213. It should be
noted that Gadamer's exposition of historically-effected consciousness, though indebted
to Heidegger, is not merely a hermeneutical extension of Heidegger's *Being and Time*.
Gadamer's primary concern is not that of the question of being. He looks to the
reflections of the later Heidegger on the artwork and language as a resource to
help him explicate the practice of hermeneutics. See Gadamer, "Reflections," *PHG*,
34f; and Risser, *Hermeneutics*, 12–13.

[41] *TM*, 389; emphasis his.

[42] *TM*, 474, cf. *PH*, 103.

ent in language. It is a language which "expresses itself like a Thou",[43] yet paradoxically not a Thou in the sense that tradition is apart from us, but tradition as that in which we stand and with which we converse. Language is "not only an object in our hands, it is the reservoir of tradition and the medium in and through which we exist and perceive our world."[44]

The universality of hermeneutics lies in the indissoluble connection between language and rationality. Concurring with Wittgenstein, Gadamer avers that language is such a naturalized part of who we are that it is "the element in which we live, as fishes live in water."[45] By the fundamental linguisticality of the human lifeworld, Gadamer is not denying the reality of nonlinguistic, prelinguistic or metalinguistic awareness in human contact with the world,[46] only that understanding itself cannot but be grounded in language. It is in language, the living language of conversation, of intersubjective speech, that we have the experience of the world.

Language as a social phenomenon is formally oriented toward intersubjectivity. "To speak means to speak *to* someone." And speaking, Gadamer adds, "does not belong in the sphere of the 'I' but in the sphere of the 'We.'"[47] Dialogue as inter-subjective speech or conversation (*Gespräch*) is the paradigmatic form of linguisticality; it belongs to the ontological make-up of humanity. A conversation between individuals depends on both parties sharing a symbolic commonality which in turn prestructures the way understanding takes place in that conversation. And in a dialogue or a dialectic of question and answer,[48] the subject matter is the controlling factor, not the interlocutors involved, even though they are indispensable to the coming-into-being of the subject matter. Their views are significant insofar

---

[43] *TM*, 358.

[44] Gadamer, *PH*, 29.

[45] "Reflections," *PHG*, 22, cf. 25.

[46] Gadamer writes in "Reflections," *PHG*, 28: "Naturally, the fundamental linguisticality of understanding cannot mean that all experiencing of the world can only take place as and in language, for we know all too well those prelinguistic and metalinguistic inner awarenesses, those moments of dumbfoundedness and speaking silences in which our immediate contact with the world is taking place. And who would deny that there are real factors conditioning human life, such as hunger, love, labor, and domination, which are not themselves language or speaking, but which for their part furnish the space within which our speaking to each other and listening to each other can take place."

[47] Gadamer, *PH*, 65.

[48] While indebted to Collingwood's work on the logic of question and answer,

as they are related to the coming into agreement (*Verständigung*) about the subject matter (*Sache*).[49] Genuine hermeneutical experience occurs only when dialogue partners give themselves over to productive conversation in which something new is born. And the subject-matter brought forth in dialogue in turn raises questions which move the dialogue further along. Dialogue is thus fundamental to hermeneutical understanding.

Gadamer moves hermeneutics from the domain of the specialists to the wider human community by construing it as a practical philosophy. The point of philosophical hermeneutics, like philosophy in general, is

> to defend practical and political reason against the domination of technology based on science. . . . It corrects the peculiar falsehood of modern consciousness: the idolatry of scientific method and of the anonymous authority of the sciences and it vindicates again the noblest task of the citizen—decision-making according to one's own responsibility—instead of conceding the task to the expert.[50]

In this, the influence of Aristotle's practical philosophy is unmistakable.[51] Philosophical hermeneutics is itself a practical philosophy, since its concern extends beyond the text to the experiences of the interpreter, providing her with knowledge and insight appropriate to the practical matters of moral decision-making in life. Aristotle's category of *phronesis* ("practical wisdom" or "practical knowledge") is considered the most viable alternative to the monological rationality of objectivistic science.[52] *Phronesis* is a virtue or a form of reasoning which mediates between the universal and the particular, and this

---

Gadamer goes beyond Collingwood in his view on the question-raising capacity of the subject-matter of dialogue. See Gadamer, *Reason in the Age of Science*, tr. Frederick G. Lawrence (Cambridge & London: MIT Press, 1981; hereafter *RAS*), 45–47; "Reflections," *PHG*, 43; *TM*, 370–72; "Man and Language" in *PH*, 66; and John P. Hogan, "Hermeneutics and the Logic of Question and Answer: Collingwood and Gadamer," *HeyJ* 28(1987): 263–84.

[49] *TM*, 295.

[50] H-G. Gadamer, "Hermeneutics and Social Science," *CH* 2(1975): 316.

[51] Bernstein suggests that "Gadamer's own understanding of philosophic hermeneutics can itself be interpreted as a series of footnotes on his decisive intellectual encounter with Aristotle." *Beyond Objectivism*, 146. See: *TM*, 312–24; Gadamer, *RAS*, 88–138; idem, "Practical Philosophy as a Model of the Human Sciences," *Research in Phenomenology* 9(1980): 74–85. See also Sullivan, *Political Hermeneutics*, 119–35; Günter Figal, "*Phronesis* as Understanding: Situating Philosophical Hermeneutics," Lawrence K. Schmidt, ed., *The Specter of Relativism: Truth, Dialogue, and Phronesis in Philosophical Hermeneutics* (Evanston: Northwestern University Press, 1995), 236–47.

[52] Gadamer, "Reflections," 31.

is acquired not apart from, but in the course of history and in the midst of life.

Our review of Gadamer's hermeneutics underscores the constitutive role of tradition in understanding. Before applying its insights to Christological development, we need to grapple with two issues which relate to our project: (1) the question of *truth and relativism*: How do we affirm the radical historicality of understanding without sacrificing truth as transcontextually valid?; (2) the question of *tradition and critique*: Does traditionality imply a conservatism which merely perpetuates what is given in the past without the possibility of a critique of tradition? The first issue concerns the relationship between tradition and truth, and asks if Christology as truth-claim is even possible given Gadamer's claims. The second enquires into the questionability of tradition and what that means for doctrinal development. We shall examine these in sequence.

II. *Historicality and Transcontextuality: Truth as Understanding or Understanding Truth?*

Given Gadamer's view on the insuperable historicity of understanding and the impossibility of attaining to absolute knowledge, are we not left with a situation of intrinsic uncertainty? In view of this, how helpful can Gadamer be as a dialogue partner for Christology when the latter is unapologetically about the revelatory and redemptive activity of a God who transcends the bonds of history? In this section, we will (1) look at the concept of truth operative in Gadamer's hermeneutics, and (2) ask if traditionality necessarily leads to relativism.

A. *Truth in Philosophical Hermeneutics*

Truth is in fact one of the most elusive concepts in Gadamer.[53] Part of the reason, one suspects, for his reluctance, even refusal, to give a clear definition is the fear that it might lead back to the reductionism of positivistic science. Contrary to what the title *Truth and Method* might suggest, the question of truth is not explicitly dealt with in the work.[54] Only in connection with his analysis of the experience

---

[53] Bernstein, "Praxis," 96.

[54] A point noted by Francis J. Ambrosio, "Dawn and Dusk: Gadamer and Heidegger on Truth," *Man and World* 19(1986): 39; cf. Brice R. Wachterhauser,

of art is the issue thematized, and even there the point is often lost since the analysis of hermeneutic experience has not yet been given.[55] In essays which predate *Truth and Method*,[56] Gadamer argues that truth in the human sciences cannot be defined solely in terms of the verifiability of propositions. It is not something which corresponds to an independent objective reality,[57] but that which coinheres with the emergence of meaning in the historical "performance" or "play" of understanding.

Gadamer's view on truth is closely connected to his analysis of the nature of the image or picture (*Bild*). Explaining the ontology of the *Bild*, he argues that the relation between a presented picture and the original is not that of a copy and an original. (We will look at the idea of *Bildung* below.) He uses the concept of *mimesis*, not in the sense that art mimics reality *as it is*, but a *mimesis* in which an image, by virtue of it being a Re-Presentation (*Darstellung*) of the original (*Urbild*), is already the real, the original.[58] It *is* the original as it presents itself through the picture, just as in the performing arts, the presentation of the play is not a mere copy of the original but has integrity in itself *as* the play. In fact, it is only through the picture that the original actually becomes original.[59] The *Urbild* is (re)pre-

---

"Must We Be What We Say? Gadamer on Truth in the Human Sciences," *HMP*, 219, 238 n. 7.

[55] Risser, *Hermeneutics*, 139.

[56] H-G. Gadamer, "Truth in the Human Sciences" (1954) and "What is Truth?" (1957); ET in Wachterhauser, ed., *HT*, 25–32; 33–46; cf. idem, "The Eminent Text and Its Truth," *BMMLA* 13(1980): 3–10.

[57] Gadamer, "What is Truth?", 36–37. He rejects a correspondence theory of truth, and essentially affirms the finitude of all truth-assertions. In the foreword to the second edition of *TM*, xxxvi, Gadamer writes: "I regard statements that proceed by wholly dialectical means from the finite to the infinite, from human experience to what exists in itself, from the temporal to the eternal, as doing no more than setting limits, and am convinced that philosophy can derive no actual knowledge from them." On the historical conditionedness of truth, see his "Truth in the Human Sciences."

[58] An image "has an essential relation to its original"; the image in the mirror is the image of what is represented, it is not a copy in that it does not exist apart from the presence of the original. "A copy effaces itself in the sense that it functions as a means and, like all means, loses its function when it reaches its end." *TM*, 137–38. The impact of Heidegger's "The Origin of the Work of Art," *Poetry, Language, Thought*, tr. Albert Hofstadter (New York: Harper & Row, 1971), 15–87, on Gadamer is evident here. See: Gadamer, "Heidegger's Later Philosophy," *PH*, 213–28; Lammi, "'Correction' of Heidegger," 479–501.

[59] *TM*, 137, 142. See Warnke, *Gadamer*, 58; and James Risser, "The Remembrance of Truth: The Truth of Remembrance," *HT*, 123–36.

sented in the *Bild*. The coming into presentation of the original in the image is an ontological event. Risser summarizes it thus:

> There is a question of truth in hermeneutic experience, but it is certainly not that of *adequatio* whereby there is an agreement between the re-presentation and the thing, for the character of the image play is no longer tied to the image/original distinction. Philosophical hermeneutics, in other words, is not engaged in a metaphysical quest of seeing truth itself instead of an image but in its own paradoxical way, precisely the inverse: of getting entangled in the image that entangles us in truth.[60]

Heidegger's interpretation of truth as uncovering (*Unverborgenheit*) and disclosure (*Erschlossenheit*) is clearly discernible in Gadamer's view of truth. Alongside this, we have resonances of the Neoplatonic concept of emanation, and Hegel's notion of truth as that which emerges dialectically in history, even though he would not subscribe, as Hegel does, to a self-objectifying transcendental subject or a dialectical telos of absolute knowledge.[61]

Truth has no substantiality apart from its actualization as performance.[62] It is a speculative finite assertion which is presented to us, and emerges, through the continuing "play" of dialogical inquiry. While Gadamer affirms the Heideggerian notion of *Unverborgenheit*, he departs from Heidegger's quasi-religious view of truth as immediate (i.e., that which suddenly arrests a person), and argues instead for a mediated view of truth. The experience of truth emerges from

---

[60] *Hermeneutics*, 151.

[61] On Gadamer's indebtedness to Heidegger's view of truth, see Gadamer, *PH*, 50; J. Grondin, *Hermeneutische Wahrheit? Zum Wahrheitsbegriff Hans-Georg Gadamers* (Königstein: Forum Academicum, 1982); Theodore Kisiel, "The Happening of Tradition: The Hermeneutics of Gadamer and Heidegger," Robert Hollinger, ed., *Hermeneutics and Praxis* (Notre Dame: University of Notre Dame Press, 1985; hereafter *HP*), 3–31; Brice R. Wachterhauser, "Introduction," and Robert J. Dostal, "The Experience of Truth for Gadamer and Heidegger: Taking Time and Sudden Lightning," *HT*, 4f & 47–67; Bernstein, "Praxis," 97. On the Neoplatonic notion of emanation, see *TM*, 140, 502–4, and David Carpenter, "Emanation, Incarnation, and the Truth-Event in Gadamer's *Truth and Method*," *HT*, 98–122. That so little attention is paid to the rootage of Gadamer's concept of truth-event in Neoplatonic emanationism and in the Christian doctrine of the Incarnation is, in Carpenter's opinion, surprising. He further contends that Gadamer's notion of truth is not as elusive as Bernstein suggests, when one takes these "roots" into account. Gadamer differentiates his position from Hegel clearly in *PH*, 128; see H-G. Gadamer, *Hegel's Dialectic: Five Hermeneutical Studies* (New Haven & London: Yale University Press, 1976), 75–116; cf. Merold Westphal, "Hegel and Gadamer," *HMP*, 65–86.

[62] For a helpful exposition of truth as performance in Gadamer, see Weinsheimer, *Gadamer's Hermeneutics*, 100–17.

the discursive temporality of conversation. It is only in the to-and-fro of question and answer that propositions may be said to be true. He asserts:

> There can be no proposition that is purely and simply true. . . . Every proposition is motivated. Every proposition has presuppositions that it does not express. Only they who comprehend these presuppositions can really judge the truth of a proposition. Now I maintain that the the ultimate logical form for such motivation of every proposition is the question. . . . The primacy of the question over against the proposition implies, however, that the proposition is essentially an answer. There is no proposition which does not represent a type of answer.[63]

Truth is not so much what we seek to understand as what comes about in understanding. It is construed *as* understanding, or more precisely, the truth-event of understanding. Just as there is no world-in-itself apart from the world which comes through language, and just as the world is not exhausted by any single language or linguistic play, but comes to being again and again through the multiplicity of such plays, truth can never be exclusively connected to a single linguistic perspective. The only element which comes closest to acting as a criterion in Gadamer's view of truth is the concept of an "anticipation of perfection" (*Vorgriff der Vollkommenheit*), a kind of transcendental expectation where meaning is deferred to the future rather than definite and definitive.[64] This indefinite openness of meaning has prompted critics like Betti and Hirsch to charge Gadamer with surrendering the objectivity of author-intended meaning, and confusing understanding with application, or meaning with significance.[65]

Gadamer does not believe philosophical hermeneutics can lay claim to foundational knowledge about ultimate or final truth since we can never step outside of language and our historicity. Truth cannot be had prior to its situated emergence from the dialogue of history. Even though he advocates a practical philosophy to guide human conduct and behaviour, Gadamer nevertheless explicitly states that it is not his intention "to make prescriptions for the sciences or the

---

[63] "What is Truth?", 41–42.

[64] See David Couzens Hoy, *The Critical Circle: Literature, History, and Philosophical Hermeneutics* (Berkeley: University of California Press, 1978), 107.

[65] See Emilio Betti, "Hermeneutics as the General Methodology of the Geisteswissenschaften," in Bleicher, *Contemporary Hermeneutics*, 51–94; E. D. Hirsch, *Validity in Interpretation* (New Haven: Yale University Press, 1967).

conduct of life," and suggests that there "can be no anterior certainty concerning what the good life is directed towards as a whole."[66] This accounts for his reticence in recommending any specific action to tackle the concrete issues of global order and disorder,[67] a reticence which stems perhaps from his tendency to regard critical questions about what constitutes good and evil as signs of "technique" at work. He warns against assuming the presence of objective norms prior to their being "birthed" in dialogue. In the same vein, he cautions against looking to the philosopher as one who has all the answers and who is capable of prescribing what should be done in the concrete.[68]

While Gadamer elucidates the process in which truth is disclosed, he is however not altogether neutral vis-à-vis the advocacy of a particular notion of truth. There appears to be a prescriptive element, a specific moral (humanistic) vision of "the good,"[69] undergirding his arguments. As Ingram observes, there is an implicit "teleological dimension" in Gadamer,[70] such that his descriptive analysis of hermeneutics has prescriptive overtones.[71] The conjoining of temporality and truth in Gadamer may be inimical to epistemic absolutism, and may at first sight seem to support relativism, yet his is not an unqualified endorsement of relativism. The expansion of one's interpretive horizon through a hermeneutical dialogue with the "thou" of the interpretendum is part and parcel of *Bildung*, "a process of cultivation, or education, whereby egoistic individuality is elevated to the moral plane of free, universal self-consciousness."[72] Thus the very dialogical process of human understanding is teleologically oriented

---

[66] *TM*, xxiii, and 321.

[67] See H-G. Gadamer, "Notes on Planning for the Future," *Daedalus* 95(1966): 572–89.

[68] See Frederick Lawrence's critique in "Responses to 'Hermeneutics and Social Science'," *Cultural Hermeneutics* 2(1975): 321–25; and Gadamer's reply to responses to his lecture, "Hermeneutics and Social Science," "Summation," 329–30. Matthew Foster suggests that one reason why Gadamer is reluctant to specify concrete involvement is the negative example of Heidegger's association with German National Socialism. *Gadamer and Practical Philosophy: The Hermeneutics of Moral Confidence* (Atlanta: Scholars Press, 1991), 271–2.

[69] See Gadamer, *RAS*, 118; Foster, *Practical Philosophy*, 230.

[70] David Ingram, "Hermeneutics and Truth," *HP*, 32–53.

[71] This is pointed out by Lawrence Hinman, "Quid Facti or Quid Juris? The Fundamental Ambiguity in Gadamer's Understanding of Hermeneutics," *PPR* 40(1980): 512–35.

[72] Ingram, "Hermeneutics and Truth," 42.

toward the movement from an isolated self-referentiality to a respect-
ful and productive engagement with the other in dialogue. In short,
there is in the hermeneutical process a movement towards an implicit
telos, a movement spurred on by reciprocity. There is thus a sense
in which reciprocity is regarded in Gadamer as a necessary transcendental condition which makes possible human communication, even
though he remains equivocal as to whether this should be regarded
as normative and universal.

Significantly, even though Gadamer repudiates the notion that
truth is prior to interpretation and corresponds to what is antecedently
given, in practice he seems to operate with an already assumed concept of truth. To regard understanding as movement along a teleologically circumscribed path presupposes an antecedently determined
truth. Despite his insistence that the projection of a universal history is always provisional and that one can never postulate a fixed
end-point to history, he appears to subscribe to a teleology which
invests dialogical reciprocity with prescriptive significance. Ingram
suggests that this is "tantamount to a transcendental justification of
a norm having considerable prescriptive, critical impact."[73] In addition, one might say that his privileging of the Heideggerian view of
truth as disclosure further suggests that truth in Gadamer, though a
matter of process and oriented to a state of openness (*Offenheit*), is
not without determinate features. It seems that truth in Gadamer is
as much a prior commitment (exercising a criteriological role) as it
is a futural "something" which comes to being only in the process
of understanding.

If having an underlying truth-commitment is logically compatible
with the belief that truth is disclosed only through the hermeneutical
process, it follows that one can affirm simultaneously the presence
of revelatory truth as criterion for interpretation *and* the open-ended
character involved in the "play" of meaning; especially, as we shall
argue in chapter five below, if this is construed in terms of the dialectic between finality and provisionality within a proleptic eschatological framework. Suffice it for now to affirm that it is not illegitimate
to begin with an antecedent set of theological assumptions in explicating the process of understanding Christ. This is doing no more
than making explicit what is inherent within the Christian's preunderstanding. Given the inescapable situatedness of the interpreter in

---

[73] Ibid., 49.

Gadamer's hermeneutics, beginning with one's inherited tradition is not unwarranted. In the case of Christology, one cannot be faulted for invoking the fundamental convictions of Christian theology. This brings us to the question of how the essential historicality of understanding can be reconciled with truth as history-transcending.

B. *Traditionality and Relativism*

Is Gadamer's philosophical hermeneutics inherently relativistic, as Leo Strauss suggests?[74] If new dimensions of meaning are encountered through every new act of interpretation as in the experience of art or play, will this not lead to an endless parade of "meanings" with none definitive and absolute? In short, in taking the hermeneutical turn, are we sliding down the greasy pole of relativism?

As noted earlier, relativism is a slippery word with a wide range of possible meanings.[75] While Gadamer would agree that understanding is inescapably perspectival on account of the interpreter's historicality, he would not deny that there is reality outside of the interpreter. Philosophical hermeneutics may not offer an objective warrant for truth, but it nevertheless wants to affirm the presence of genuine truth. If by relativism one means there are no criteria to validate knowledge claims or there is no such thing as truth, then Gadamer cannot be labelled a relativist since he has consistently argued that one can arrive at "truth" through dialogue, and that it is possible to differentiate between true and false prejudices, despite the ambiguity which surrounds this aspect of his exposition. But if one means by relativism that what counts as knowledge is dependent on the particular tradition and social context in which it is articulated, then in this sense, truth is, for Gadamer, "relative."

There are parallels between Gadamer's view on the tradition-boundedness of understanding and Kuhn's notion of "paradigm" in his influential work, *The Structure of Scientific Revolutions*. It may therefore be instructive to examine briefly Kuhn's thesis, and the criticisms and clarifications which surround it, as a way of wrestling with

---

[74] Leo Strauss & Hans-Georg Gadamer, "Correspondence Concerning *Wahrheit und Methode*," *Independent Journal of Philosophy* 2(1978): 5–12. On Strauss's critique and Gadamer's response, see Foster, *Practical Philosophy*, 81f.

[75] Not only are there different types of relativism, there are different types of absolutism as well. See Rom Harré & Michael Krausz, *Varieties of Relativism* (Oxford & Cambridge, Mass.: Blackwell, 1996).

traditionality and relativism. It is hoped that a critique of Kuhn will redound to our analysis of the viability of Gadamer's argument for tradition.

Despite the ambiguity and the lack of precision in Kuhn's definition of a "paradigm"—a point noted by his critics[76]—the general thrust of his argument is clear. Contrary to the stereotypical image of scientific research as wholly rational and value-free, Kuhn points to the roles played by community and corporate prejudices. He dissolves the distinction between science as a purely cognitive and theoretical undertaking, and science as a social system comprising scientists in enclaves governed by accepted norms and values.[77] Science depends on a body of achievements accepted by a community of practitioners, and together these constitute a paradigm, a "disciplinary matrix,"[78] or framework under which "normal science" is done, i.e., science done within an erstwhile operative paradigm. Questions of selection, evaluation, criticism and legitimacy of argumentation in science take off from the accepted paradigm, which gains its status because it is more successful in solving problems than its competitors.

Paradigms though are not immutable. As scientists come upon anomalies which cannot be adequately accounted for by the regnant paradigm, science is plunged into crisis, and "normal science" gives

[76] See for instance, Margaret Masterman, "The Nature of a Paradigm," I. Lakatos & A. Musgrave, eds., *Criticism and the Growth of Knowledge* (Cambridge: Cambridge University Press, 1970), 59–89; and Dudley Shapere's review of the first edition of Kuhn's *Structure*, "The Structure of Scientific Revolutions," in Gary Gutting, ed., *Paradigms and Revolutions: Appraisals and Applications of Thomas Kuhn's Philosophy of Science* (Notre Dame & London: University of Notre Dame Press, 1980), 27–38. Kuhn responds to criticisms about ambiguities in his work in a postscript to the second edition of *Structure*. He acknowledges the equivocity of his earlier analysis of paradigm and proposes that a paradigm be understood in two distinctive senses: (1) a constellation of beliefs, values, techniques shared by practitioners in a community; and (2) a model or an experimental exemplar based on the constellation of beliefs which then serve to unravel puzzles in normal science. For our purpose, we shall understand paradigm in the general sense of an overarching set of commitments and presuppositions which characterize a particular approach to inquiry.
[77] Herein lies, according to Gary Gutting, Kuhn's distinction as a philosopher of science. See his "Introduction," in Gutting, ed., *Paradigms and Revolutions*, 9. For an analysis of Kuhn's proposals, see: Paul Hoyningen-Huene, *Reconstructing Scientific Revolutions: Thomas S. Kuhn's Philosophy of Science* (Chicago: University of Chicago Press, 1993).
[78] This nomenclature is proposed by Kuhn as a way of clarifying what he means by "paradigm" in the "Postscript" to the second edition of *Scientific Revolutions*, 182; also his "Second Thoughts on Paradigm," in *The Essential Tension: Selected Studies in Scientific Tradition and Change* (Chicago & London: University of Chicago Press, 1977), 297.

way to "revolutionary science." Discoveries and insights, usually initiated by an individual or a small group, spark a "scientific revolution" in which the paradigm is either modified, expanded, or replaced.
Paradigms change to absorb anomalies. This "paradigm shift" is
likened to a "gestalt switch" in perception or a "conversion experience"; it is not the result of a rational process.[79] The new paradigm
is non-cumulative and discontinuous, and, according to Kuhn, "incommensurable" with the old, since the criteria used to evaluate paradigms are internal to them. When paradigms clash, there is no appeal
to a universally valid logic to arbitrate. It is this component of his
thesis which has generated most controversy.

Kuhn's interest lies in developing a new approach to the nature
of scientific rationality which takes into account historical and sociological factors. His arguments are decidedly Wittgensteinian, even
though he does not explicitly allude to Wittgenstein in his work.[80]
He appears to be advocating, at least in *The Structure of Scientific
Revolutions*, a strong case for incommensurability whereby meaning is
so thoroughly paradigm-dependent that "after a revolution scientists
are responding to a different world".[81] In suggesting that criteria of
rationality operate only *within*, rather than *across*, paradigms, Kuhn
opens himself to the charge of a strong epistemic relativism.[82] Such
an interpretation is perhaps fueled by his provocative rhetoric, particularly the use of the word "incommensurability." In this regard,
the ambivalence in Gadamer on differentiating true interpretations
from false ones, makes him susceptible to the same criticisms leveled at Kuhn.[83]

---

[79] Kuhn, *Structure*, 120f; 151. Larry Laudan thinks Kuhn is claiming that choos-
ing between competing scientific theories is a wholly "irrational" move. *Progress and
Its Problems* (Berkeley: University of California Press, 1977), 3; cf. James F. Harris,
Against Relativism: A Philosophical Defense of Method (LaSalle: Open Court, 1992), 80.

[80] That Kuhn's arguments are similar to Wittgenstein's reflections in *On Certainty*
is noted by A. C. Thiselton, "Knowledge, Myth and Corporate Memory," in *Believing
in the Church: The Corporate Nature of Faith*, A Report by the Doctrine Commission of
the Church of England (London: SPCK, 1981), 57–58.

[81] Kuhn, *Structure*, 111.

[82] See the criticism of Israel Scheffler, *Science and Subjectivity*, 2d ed. (Indianapolis:
Hackett, 1967, 1982); Carl R. Kordig, *The Justification of Scientific Change* (Dordrecht:
D. Reidel, 1971); and Harvey Siegel, *Relativism Refuted: A Critique of Contemporary
Epistemological Relativism* (Dordrecht: D. Reidel, 1987).

[83] This tension and ambivalence in Gadamer has been identified by Weinsheimer,
Gadamer's Hermeneutics, 110f; Warnke, *Gadamer*, 156–76; and Bernstein, *Beyond Objectivism*,
158. See Thiselton, *NHH*, 327–28.

Responding to his critics, Kuhn categorically rejects "charges of irrationality, relativism, and the defence of mob rule";[84] and in the postscript to the second edition of the work, as well as in *The Essential Tension*,[85] he seems to moderate his position on incommensurability. It is, he suggests, a serious misconstrual of his view to say that paradigm-choice is irrational and void of argumentation. In place of an algorithm of theory-choice, Kuhn points to "values" shared by scientists which influence their assessment of paradigms, providing them "good reasons" for paradigm choice.[86] Nevertheless, one is not sure if Kuhn succeeds in softening his incommensurability stance, or overcoming the apparent inconsistency between his later remarks and his earlier postulate.[87] It is unclear how his "values" actually serve as criteria for paradigm choice.[88] What is clear though is that a denial of cross-paradigm intelligibility leads to a determinism of paradigm. In our view, situatedness in paradigm need not entail the epistemic relativism of incommensurability.

---

[84] Kuhn, "Reflections on My Critics," in Lakatos & Musgrave, eds., *Criticism*, 234.

[85] See "Postscript," *Structure*, 198f; and the essays, "Second Thoughts," and "Objectivity, Value-Judgment, and Theory Choice," *Essential Tension*, 293–319 & 320–39 respectively. For an analysis of Kuhn's response, see Ian G. Barbour, *Myths, Models and Paradigms: The Nature of Scientific and Religious Language* (London: SCM, 1974), 108–12. For a clarification and defense of Kuhn's concept of incommensurability, see Gerald Doppelt, "Kuhn's Epistemological Relativism: An Interpretation and Defense," *Inquiry* 21(1978): 33–86.

[86] Kuhn asserts that nothing in the rejection of an algorithm theory of choice "implies either that there are no *good reasons* for being persuaded or that these reasons are not ultimately decisive for the group." "Postscript," *Structure*, 199. In *Essential Tension*, 330–331, he writes: "Values and norms provide . . . clear examples of effective guidance in the presence of conflict and equivocation. . . . Two men deeply committed to *the same values* may nevertheless, in particular situations, make different choices as, in fact, they do. But that difference in outcome ought not to suggest that the values scientists share are less than *critically important either to their decisions or to the development of the enterprise in which they participate*." (Emphasis mine.) The type of rationality which Kuhn sees at work is similar to the Aristotelian notion of practical discourse or *phronesis*. See Bernstein, *Beyond Objectivism*, 54.

[87] See Harris, *Against Relativism*, 89–92. After a close analysis of Kuhn's various responses to his critics, Siegel suggests that he "continually tries both to retract the more radical claims of his earlier writing, and at the same time to maintain them under different guises." *Relativism Refuted*, 57.

[88] Bernstein, *Beyond Objectivism*, 58, alludes to the equivocity surrounding the epistemological status of Kuhn's criteria or values: "Are the criteria or values accepted by the scientific communities rational because these are the values *accepted* by scientific communities, *or* are they accepted by scientific communities because they are *the criteria of rationality*?"

Ian Barbour is correct to say that paradigm-dependency does not mean there is no rational appraisal of the validity of knowledge claims. He builds on Kuhn's observations without adopting their relativistic implications, and makes the following observations:

1. All data are paradigm-dependent, but there are data on which adherents of rival paradigms can agree.
2. Paradigms are resistant to falsification by data, but data does [sic] cumulatively affect the acceptability of a paradigm.
3. There are no rules for paradigm choice, but there are shared criteria for judgment in evaluating paradigms.[89]

The fact that in practice one can differentiate between paradigms, say, between Newtonian physics and Einsteinian relativity, renders a strong incommensurability thesis untenable. In Barbour's view, it is possible to reconcile a paradigm-circumscribed traditionality and the possibility of transcontextual argumentation. Though communities differ, they are not so radically different as to make cross-contextual comparison and communication impossible.[90] Just as Wittgenstein's "language games" interpenetrate, overlap, and demonstrate family resemblances, paradigms are not shut out from interaction with other paradigms or traditions. The commonality of a shared life enables the transcending of one's situatedness in paradigms and tradition.

A similar line of argument is found in Karl-Otto Apel's notion of transcendental-pragmatics.[91] Apel's reflections on the transcendental conditions of subjectivity allow us to break out of the solipsistic prison of Kuhnian paradigm incommensurability. According to Apel, implicit in any cognitive claim or argument is an ideal or unlimited communication community.[92] Unlike Kant's solitary subject, Apel contends that subjectivity always entails intersubjectivity, and that the assertions of the individual are always assertions made within a necessary relational web. Like Gadamer, Apel regards understanding as linguistically constituted; language is critical as a transcendental condition of human knowledge. The transcendental subject is intersubjective in that it is constituted by relations to others. For instance,

---

[89] *Religion in an Age of Science* (New York: Harper, 1990), 53–54.
[90] See Terence W. Tilley, "Incommensurability, Intratextuality, and Fideism," *MTh* 5(1989): 90.
[91] See above, p. 63, n. 150, for references to Apel's works; also: Hoy, *Critical Circle*, 107–17; Thiselton, *NHH*, 401–405.
[92] See K.-O. Apel, "The Communication Community as the Transcendental Presupposition for the Social Sciences," *Transformation of Philosophy*, 136–79.

the statement, "I believe x," not only describes a person's *self-reflection*, namely, what in her judgment she considers to be a valid claim about x,—which in itself presupposes a fundamental operative rationality—but also a *self-expression* in which she seeks to communicate her thoughts on x to others. As Gamwell sees it, cognition to Apel is "a performance or a public act."[93] In that cognition is an offer to communicate, subjectivity is inherently intersubjective. And this intersubjectivity entails the presence of transcontextual standards, or transcendental conditions of rationality, which make possible evaluation and validation of claims as well as discursive argumentation between people.

Apel concurs with Gadamer's critique of methodological objectivism, and applauds his emphasis on historicality and tradition in understanding. His stress on intersubjectivity is certainly congruent with Gadamer's dialogical hermeneutics. But Apel thinks Gadamer "goes too far" in collapsing "criteria" into interpretation, thus failing to incorporate a critical dimension in his hermeneutics.[94] He opines that Gadamer (like Heidegger) replaces "the *counterfactual* and, therefore, *per se intersubjective* validity of truth . . . with the *facticity* of *meaning* as it becomes *manifest* to us in the particular historical situation." A temporal-ontology of understanding as truth-happening alone, according to Apel, has no answer to the question of the validity of understanding. One needs "*regulative ideas* for a *normative* orientation of understanding."[95] A concept of truth as a regulative principle is needed, understood in the Peircean sense as something which has achieved consensus over time within a community of interpreters.

To Apel, Gadamer's idea that one understands differently if one understands at all,[96] is at one level indisputable since finite creatures immured in history necessarily understand differently in differing contexts. But at a more crucial level, Apel thinks it is important that we not only understand *differently* but also understand *correctly* and

---

[93] Franklin I. Gamwell, *The Divine Good: Modern Moral Theory and the Necessity of God* (San Francisco: Harper, 1990), 131.

[94] Apel, "Scientists, Hermeneutics and the Critique of Ideology: Outline of a Theory of Science from a Cognitive-Anthropological Standpoint," *Transformation of Philosophy*, 63.

[95] K.-O. Apel, "Regulative Ideas or Truth-Happening?: An Attempt to Answer the Question of the Conditions of the Possibility of Valid Understanding," *PHG*, 68; 70–71.

[96] *TM*, 297.

understand *better*. For this to happen, "regulative ideas" are needed. We shall examine in a moment the possibility and place of critique in philosophical hermeneutics. For now, it is hoped that our critique of Kuhnian incommensurability and our appeal to Apel's transcendental intersubjectivity would indicate that an emphasis on tradition in understanding need not lead to epistemic relativism. It is one thing to say that knowledge claims are invariably situated, i.e., relative to their contexts, and quite another to assert a strong relativism.

To argue for the possibility of inter-paradigmatic communication is to argue against the absolute contextualism of meaning. We question the paradigmatic determinism or "strong holism" in which all understanding is interpretively tied to other beliefs and dependent on the background and context of the interpreter.[97] The main problem with this, Bohman avers, lies in its confusing "limiting conditions" with "enabling conditions;" the former are determinate and fixed, while the latter variable and alterable. Bohman illustrates the difference by distinguishing between being linguistically capable in general ("it is a formal property of my linguistic ability that I can speak some language"), and being fluent in a specific language in particular ("it is a material property of my linguistic competence that I specifically speak English"). The first is a formal condition which enables communication, while the second is a material condition which limits it.[98]

The way one's background conditions interpretation is likened to an enabling conditioning. "Thus, like speaking a particular language, interpreting within a certain background is best understood as presenting a set of loose constraints, rather than strict limits, upon activities of interpretation and understanding."[99] Conditionality and the possibility of a critical assessment of interpretations are not incompatible. Instead of a strong holism, Bohman puts forward a transcendental argument for a "weak holism" which allows for the element of circularity in the process of interpretation without doing away

---

[97] James F. Bohman, "Holism Without Skepticism: Contextualism and the Limits of Interpretation," David R. Hiley, James F. Bohman, & Richard Shusterman, eds., *The Interpretive Turn: Philosophy, Science, Culture* (Ithaca & London: Cornell University Press, 1991), 129–54. Bohman includes Gadamer among the strong holists.

[98] Bohman, "Holism," 141.

[99] Ibid., 144. See John Searle's hypothesis of the "Background" in his *Intentionality: An Essay in the Philosophy of Mind* (Cambridge: Cambridge University Press, 1983), 19–20, 144–59; cf. Thiselton, *NHH*, 45–46, 266, 362–63, 540, 559 & 562.

with epistemic norms like coherence and correctness.[100] It is therefore possible to reconcile the conditioning which comes through background, context or tradition with the open-ended nature of that
situatedness.

By the same token, the opposite of relativism need not be the
kind of non-temporal non-contextual "objectivism" that nowadays is
often rightly or wrongly known as foundationalism. The prospect of
being saddled with an ahistorical foundationalism has driven many
a postpositivist to the strong arms of epistemic incommensurability.
But this overlooks a third alternative: *an in-principle-corrigible and nonfoundational transcendentalism.* The strident certitude of a Cartesian epistemological objectivism is not the only alternative to relativism. Just
as viable, if not more so, is what we might call a *contingent transcendentalism,* which not only acknowledges the finite contextuality of
human understanding but also the reality of transcontextual transcendental postulates. In this latter, understanding is simultaneously
contextual and open-ended, situated but not stagnant. Along the
same line, Thiselton warns against making the mistake of confusing
"the role of historical contingency and contextualism in challenging
the status of some absolutized foundationalism outside time, place
and history, with *a positive dialectical relation between contextual contingency
and ongoing metacritical exploration and testing in the form of an open system.*"[101]

It is important to differentiate between *a*historicality and *trans*historicality. The former is inherent in what might be called an absolutized
objectivistic transcendentalism which is non-temporal in orientation,
while the latter describes a "contingent transcendentalism" which is
thoroughly historical yet capable of providing a *trans*historical perspective. To be transhistorical is to transcend the historical, not to
be outside history or impervious to historical permutations. Belief in
revelatory truth is certainly a claim to truth as transhistorical in the
sense that its truthfulness is not confined to the historical particularity in which it is situated. What we call a contingent transcendentalism could be better described as a *transcendental contextualism.* The
transhistoricality of revelatory truth means that truth is historically
situated yet not exhausted by that historical situatedness. It is universality *in* particularity, not universality consumed by particularity.
This is the thrust of the message of the Incarnation. The histori-

---

[100] Bohman, "Holism," 147.
[101] *NHH*, 401 (emphasis added).

cality of God's revelation is a necessary "enabling condition" if there is to be any genuine encounter between God and people.

III. *The Possibility and Place of Critique*

Gadamer's questioning of the Enlightenment's "prejudice against prejudice" has not gone unchallenged. He has been criticized for overplaying the prejudice hand,[102] and advocating an authoritarianism of authority, or a virtual determinism of tradition and linguistic conditionality. The situation is not helped by the ambiguity of his explanation. On the one hand he expressly argues that it is impossible to uphold a radical alterity in that given our linguistically structured preunderstanding, we understand only in terms of our experiential and conceptual schemes.[103] On the other hand, he rejects the suggestion that his concept of truth leads to conservatism and an uncritical acceptance of tradition.[104] Furthermore, his view on history and tradition has been censured for being equivocal, optimistic and too inclusive, failing to recognize their complex and multifarious nature. T. Eagleton, for instance, wonders whose and what "tradition" Gadamer has in mind since his theory operates with "the enormous assumption" that tradition and history form a single, unbroken, and monolithic continuum. This, he suggests, is "a grossly complacent theory of history" and does not face up to the reality that tradition can be oppressive as well as liberating, and that history is often the arena of intense struggle and conflict.[105]

Eagleton's reading of Gadamer however is questionable, for Gadamer does not subscribe to or endorse the notion of tradition as a unitary

---

[102] James DiCenso, *Hermeneutics and the Disclosure of Truth: A Study in the Work of Heidegger, Gadamer, and Ricoeur* (Charlottesville: University Press of Virginia, 1990), 98, feels that the word "prejudice" has an unavoidable negative meaning which renders its use unwise. In pressing for an archaic and specialized use of the word "prejudice" rather than its regular everyday-language meaning, Gadamer "contradicts the cultural and historical orientation of his own hermeneutical approach and engages in a form of the 'originary' thinking for which he rebukes Heidegger." In ordinary use, prejudice has the connotation of a rigidified prejudgment which is irrationally closed to dialogue and transformation, the very opposite of what Gadamer is arguing for.

[103] See *TM*, 269. A same line of argument is presented by Donald Davidson, "On the Very Idea of a Conceptual Scheme," *PAAPA* 47(1974): 5–20.

[104] Gadamer, "Problem of Historical Consciousness," 108.

[105] *Literary Theory: An Introduction* (Minneapolis: University of Minnesota Press; Oxford: Blackwell, 1983), 72–73.

and monolithic "super-subject". Nor does he commend a servile
acquiescence to the "mainstream" tradition.[106] In defense of Gadamer,
Bruns maintains that "tradition" in his philosophical hermeneutics
can neither be equated with institutional structures or construed as
a single master narrative, a sort of code by which to judge interpretations. Rather, tradition refers to "the historicality of open-ended,
intersecting, competing narratives that cannot be mastered by any
Great Code."[107] Tradition is not so much a repository of official interpretations as it is a historically mediated readiness or openness to
embrace conflicting interpretations.

Moreover, one might conceivably argue on Gadamer's own terms,
that tradition is not the implacable foe of freedom and creativity.
Delwin Brown cites three elements in Gadamer's analysis which support a liberational view of tradition:[108] (1) Prejudices need not be
contrary to creativity; they are the conditions out of which creativity in understanding emerges. (2) Tradition exists only within the
multifariousness of voices, and there is always present within tradition a plurality of possibilities which are then worked out or realized
as tradition develops. The dynamism created by the interaction of
multiple voices within tradition propels it forward, causing it to evolve,
to move from its conditioned situation into something new and
different. (3) Traditions are not hermetically sealed and insulated from
encounters with other traditions, and are therefore open to change.

Nevertheless, despite his remonstrations about the possibility of
freedom in tradition, there remains the lingering impression of conservatism in Gadamer's hermeneutics.[109] Does not a strong emphasis

---

[106] Risser considers Eagleton's treatment of Gadamer as "the most extreme misreading of Gadamer's position imaginable". *Hermeneutics*, 225, n. 22; cf. 71. To characterize Gadamer's view of tradition as a kind of unifying essence cannot be further
from his intentions. Gadamer rebuts the charge that tradition is treated as a kind
of "super-subject": "It seems very misleading to me for someone to say that just
because I emphasize the role of tradition in all our posing of questions and also in
the indication of answers, I am asserting a super-subject and this . . . reducing
hermeneutical experience to an empty word [*parole vide*]. There is no support in
Truth and Method for this kind of construction. When I speak there of tradition and
of conversation with tradition, I am in no way putting forward a collective subject." Gadamer, "*Destruktion* and Deconstruction," Diane P. Michelfelder & Richard
E. Palmer, eds., *Dialogue and Deconstruction: The Gadamer-Derrida Encounter* (Albany:
SUNY Press, 1989), 111.
[107] Gerald L. Bruns, "What is Tradition?" *NLH* 22(1991): 11.
[108] *Boundaries of Our Habitation: Tradition and Theological Construction* (Albany: SUNY
Press, 1994), 40–41; cf. *TM*, 277, 284, 304.
[109] A point noted for instance by critic, John D. Caputo, *Radical Hermeneutics*

on belongingness to history invariably stifle differences and resist innovation? How one deals with this question has repercussions for Christology. Is it possible to root Christology in tradition and still allow for interpretive diversity and theological creativity?

The issue of critique in tradition is central to the debate between Gadamer and Jürgen Habermas,[110] a debate between philosophical hermeneutics and critical theory. While Habermas agrees with Gadamer that dialogue is critical for understanding, he nevertheless thinks that there are societal impediments which block and distort communication. These must be unmasked and dealt with before dialogical interchange can be successful. He sees the lack of a platform for critique as a weakness in Gadamer's philosophy, making it susceptible to the subtle manipulation of ideology.[111] What is needed is a depth-herme-

---

(Bloomington: Indiana University Press, 1987), 108–15; cf., idem, "Gadamer's Closet Essentialism: A Derridean Critique," in Michelfelder & Palmer, eds., *Dialogue and Deconstruction*, 258–64.

[110] The debate was carried out in the late sixties and early seventies in a series of essays by the two of them, and these are chronologically: Jürgen Habermas, "A Review of Gadamer's *Truth and Method*," (originally in 1967) in Fred Dallmayr & Thomas A. McCarthy, eds., *Understanding and Social Inquiry* (Notre Dame: University of Notre Dame Press, 1977), 335–63; H-G. Gadamer, "On the Scope and Function of Hermeneutical Reflection" (1967), tr. G. B. Hess & R. E. Palmer with minor additions by Gadamer in *Cont* 8(1970): 77–95, reprinted in Gadamer, *PH*, 18–43; J. Habermas, "The Hermeneutic Claim to Universality" (1970), tr. by Joseph Bleicher in his *Contemporary Hermeneutics*, 181–211; Gadamer, "Hermeneutics and Social Science," *CH* 2(1975): 307–16.

Subsequent essays by both parties continue to refer to the theoretical problems entailed in the debate. See e.g., Gadamer, "The Hermeneutics of Suspicion," Gary Shapiro & Alan Sica, eds., *Hermeneutics: Questions and Prospects* (Amherst: University of Massachusetts Press, 1984), 54–65; and J. Habermas, *The Theory of Communicative Action, Vol. 1: Reason and the Rationalization of Society*, tr. Thomas McCarthy (Boston: Beacon Press, 1984), 134–36; idem, *On the Logic of the Social Sciences*, tr. Shierry Weber Nicholsen & Jerry A. Stark (Cambridge: Polity Press, 1988), 162–70.

On this debate, see also: Warnke, *Gadamer*, 107–38; Foster, *Practical Philosophy*, 121–79; Kögler, *Dialogue*, 73–77; 148–55; Hoy, *The Critical Circle*, 117f; Karl-Otto Apel, *et al.*, eds., *Hermeneutik und Ideologiekritik: Theorie-Diskussion* (Frankfurt: Suhrkamp, 1971), 45f, 57f; Martin Jay, "Should Intellectual History Take a Linguistic Turn? Reflections on the Habermas-Gadamer Debate," in Dominick LaCapra & Steven L. Kaplan, eds., *Modern European Intellectual History: Reappraisals and New Perspectives* (Ithaca: Cornell University Press, 1982), 86–110; Jack Mendelson, "The Habermas-Gadamer Debate," *NGC* 18(1979): 44–73; Paul Ricoeur, "Ethics and Culture: Habermas and Gadamer in Dialogue," *PhT* 17(1973): 153–65; idem, "Hermeneutics and the Critique of Ideology," in *HMP*, 300–39; Demetrius Teigas, *Knowledge and Hermeneutic Understanding: A Study of the Habermas-Gadamer Debate* (Lewisburg: Bucknell University Press; London & Toronto: Associated University Presses, 1995); also Donn Welton and Hugh Silverman, eds., *Critical and Dialectical Phenomenology* (Albany: SUNY Press, 1987).

[111] Habermas, "Hermeneutic Claim to Universality," 207.

neutical analysis (akin to the critique of delusion in psychoanalysis) which posits a transcendental vantage point from which to judge language use, specifically, to distinguish speech in the interest of power from speech in the service of freedom.

Gadamer acknowledges that ideology does pose a problem (though he rarely uses the word "ideology," preferring instead to speak of the claims of tradition or authority) and that some form of critique of false social prejudices or "false claims" is necessary. Where he parts company with Habermas is in the need to posit a non-hermeneutical source of knowledge as basis of critique. Contra Habermas, Gadamer does not think that authority is inevitably domineering. "Authority," he maintains, "is not *always* wrong."[112] Moreover, one can be situated in tradition and still retain a critical stance since one is free to accept or reject authority. "The obedience that belongs to true authority is neither blind nor slavish."[113] In addition, Gadamer rejects as illegitimate Habermas' application of psychoanalysis to ideological critique, for it presupposes the presence of a "knowing" analyst able to guide the delusional patient to reality. In reality, Gadamer contends, there is no such uninvolved vantage point.[114] Any critique mounted is necessarily implicated in a person's conditionality. It is pretentious to think that one can have insights superior to historically situated knowledge. In a sense, Gadamer continues to argue for a privileging of tradition in response to Habermas's criticism.[115]

---

[112] Gadamer, *PH*, 33.

[113] Gadamer, *PH*, 34. Teigas, *Knowledge*, 125, observes: "The transparency and the recognition of a prejudice has been worked upon by reason and its *acceptance* or *rejection* is also based upon rational choice. The individual retains the choice of *rejecting* an unjustified (unproductive) prejudice and this is clear in Gadamer's view of prejudices, thus disproving Habermas's accusation that hermeneutic reflection legitimates all prejudices."

[114] Gadamer, "Rhetorik, Hermeneutik und Ideologiekritik," *Gesammelte Werke*, 10 vols. (Tübingen: J. C. B. Mohr [Paul Siebeck], 1985–95; hereafter *GW*), 2:232–50. In a sense, Habermas' critique, arising as it does from the critical "tradition" of the Frankfurt school and utilizing traditional theoretical tools, serves only to underscore Gadamer's point that understanding is always situated in tradition.

[115] It appears that Gadamer, for all his commitment to understanding through a fusing of horizons, seems in the case of Habermas to have subsumed the latter's horizon to his own. The fact of dialogue alone is no guarantee that one hears what the other is saying. More often than not, a person hears only what he wants to hear. One wonders if Gadamer is guilty of this in relation to Habermas. The same sublation of the other's horizon into one's own may be said of Habermas as well. Habermas seems to think that Gadamer's view on the linguisticality of all experience means the rejection of ways of conceiving the world in terms of "domination," "power" and "work." Teigas, *Knowing*, 63–64, observes that Habermas "confronts

In defense of Gadamer against Habermas, Grondin and Foster suggest that while Gadamer seeks to rehabilitate tradition and authority which have been marginalized by the high premium placed on reason in the Enlightenment, he is not subsuming reason under authority, even though some of his statements may appear to point in this direction. Habermas's criticism that Gadamer has raised authority or tradition over reason may be faulted for not taking into account the fact that Gadamer "never gave authority and tradition precedence over reason, but only recalled that they depend on a situated reason that plays itself out in communication."[116]

Gadamer would argue furthermore that there is in philosophical hermeneutics a potential for a critique of prejudice. Rather than situating critique outside our colloquial use of language, he contends that critique is already a part of language use. He asserts:

> The fact that we move in a linguistic world and grow into our world through linguistically performed experiences, does not deprive us of the potential for critique. Quite the contrary. . . . Indeed we owe our aptitude for critique to the linguistic capacity of our reason; and we are not in any way obstructed from our reason by language.[117]

Although he argues strongly that the world or being is verbally-constituted, he nevertheless wants to say that this is not necessarily a barrier to the genuine enlargement and alteration of one's perception. On the contrary, it is the very condition for such a change. He writes: "the verbal world in which we live is not a barrier that prevents knowledge of being-in-itself but fundamentally embraces everything in which our insight can be enlarged and deepened."[118]

Despite his positive spin on prejudice, Gadamer is equally concerned that one should not become uncritically biased. We must, he cautions, let the otherness of the text confront us. While interpretation necessarily entails working out appropriate projections which are

---

Gadamer as if the latter had proposed that language alone creates political domination or that the causes of such domination could be solely attributed to linguistic properties. His understanding of Gadamer on this point is limited. He does not wish to grasp the philosophical discourse of Gadamer on language, fearing that the latter's statement leads to a subjectivist withdrawal into the linguisticality of experience, which in the end neglects the 'materiality' of the forces of domination."

[116] Grondin, *Philosophical Hermeneutics*, 131. In fact, Grondin notes, Gadamer himself chides Karl Jasper and Gerhard Krüger for elevating authority over reason in their accounts of tradition. See *TM*, 280, n. 206.

[117] H-G. Gadamer, *GW* 2:203–4, quoted in Kögler, *Dialogue*, 75.

[118] *TM*, 447.

always anticipatory in nature, it is also the constant task of understanding to await confirmation of meaning "by the things" themselves.

> A person trying to understand something will not resign himself from the start to relying on his own accidental fore-meanings, . . . Rather, a person trying to understand a text is rather prepared for it to tell him something. That is why a hermeneutically trained consciousness must be sensitive to the other of the text from the beginning.[119]

One's fore-understanding is constantly amended through encounter with the object of interpretation. Such a readiness to let the other break through into one's ego-centeredness is a "Kierkegaardian motif" which has guided Gadamer "from the beginning."[120] This openness to the other is reinforced by his encounter with the poet Paul Celan and certainly comes to the fore in his response to Deconstruction, where he contends, contra Derrida, that in hermeneutical dialogue, the voice of the other is not appropriated in the sense of being completely subsumed.[121]

Having said that, one does get the impression that at points, Habermas and Gadamer appear to be talking past each other, owed no doubt to the fact that they are looking at different aspects of the one phenomenon of understanding. We might say that they are both highlighting what each considers as blind-spots in the other's argument. Both "truth" and "untruth" are present in tradition, and if Gadamer is contending for the possibility of truth in tradition, Habermas is warning against the possibility of deception in tradition.[122] Both are in a sense right in their concerns, and the antinomies between them should not be absolutized. They both have something to contribute to the development of a critical stance towards civilization.[123]

While it is clear that for Gadamer, the voice of the other must be allowed to confront us in all of its foreignness, there is nevertheless sufficient ambiguity in his formulation that questions have been

---

[119] *TM*, 269, also 267.

[120] In his autobiographical reflections, "Reflections," *PHG*, 46, Gadamer writes: "According to Kierkegaard, it is the other who breaks into my ego-centeredness and gives me something to understand. This Kierkegaardian motif guided me from the beginning, and entered completely into my 1943 lecture, 'The Problem of History in Modern German Philosophy.'"

[121] Gadamer, "*Destruktion* and Deconstruction."

[122] Teigas, *Knowledge*, xix, 118f.

[123] Ricoeur, "Ethics and Culture," 164, suggests that "only the conjunction between the critique of ideologies, animated by our interests in emancipation, and the reinterpretation of the heritages of the past, animated by our interest in communication, may yet give a concrete content to this effort."

raised as to the genuineness of his dialogical openness to the other. Roberts wonders if Gadamer is "simply ambiguous" or is "caught up in a metaphysically grounded authoritarianism"?[124] Take this quote for instance, where Gadamer warns that meaning cannot be arbitrarily understood:

> Just as we cannot continually misunderstand the use of a word without its affecting the meaning of the whole, so we cannot stick blindly to our own fore-meaning about the thing if we want to understand the meaning of another. Of course this does not mean that when we listen to someone or read a book we must forget all our fore-meanings concerning the content and all our own ideas. All that is asked is that we remain open to the meaning of the other person or text. *But this openness always includes our situating the other meaning in relation to the whole of our own meanings or ourselves in relation to it.*[125]

Is Gadamer taking back with one hand what he has given with the other? Is openness to the other a genuine openness, or is it only relatively so? Is understanding which is supposedly dialogical, in the end only self-referential, and an echo of traditionalism or collective consciousness?[126]

Hans Herbert Kögler suggests that with adjustments, Gadamer's philosophical hermeneutics, particularly his concept of dialogue, can take on a critical dimension. He argues that the commonality of a single-world entailed in Gadamer's linguistic ontology need not entail that disparate views be in total agreement with regard to the subject matter. Relatedness to a common subject matter, Kögler suggests, simply highlights that dialogue takes off from a shared linguistic commonality. We need not infer from this "a *shared view* of the subject matter. On the contrary, it is quite possible that we can agree in *identifying* a common theme or subject matter while acknowledging that certain concepts, valuations, and views necessarily exclude one another."[127] Commonality need be no more than a "mere consensus necessary for disagreement."[128]

---

[124] Roberts, *Nothing But History*, 176.
[125] *TM*, 268; emphasis mine.
[126] These queries have been raised against Gadamer by: John D. Caputo, "Beyond Aestheticism: Derrida's Responsible Anarchy," *RP* 18(1988): 67; idem, *Radical Hermeneutics* (Bloomington: Indiana University Press, 1987), 108–19; and Gianni Vattimo, *The End of Modernity*, tr. Jon R. Snyder (Baltimore: Johns Hopkins University Press, 1991), 130–44.
[127] Kögler, *Dialogue*, 70; cf. 154–55.
[128] Ibid., 71. Kögler understands Gadamer's concept of fusion of horizons in the

According to Kögler, a weakness in Gadamer's strong focus on language as the ontological horizon of understanding is the sublation of the contributions of individuals. Individuality is submerged in the linguistic universality which comes into expression in dialogue. He thinks it is important to establish the individuality and alterity of the subject within language, rather than submerge the individual subject in cultural meaning systems of language or predetermined discursive limits. In view of this, Gadamer's hermeneutic theory needs to be expanded and modified to circumvent the deficiences of his strong linguistic-ontological grounding of understanding. While the concept of dialogic understanding is retained, it must nevertheless be conceived afresh.

> Dialogic understanding can no longer proceed from the idea of a universal consensus or from the idea of a prior being-in-the-truth; rather, it must pursue the more modest objective of seeking to make present one's own constraints through an understanding of the other, and of gaining knowledge of certain limits of the other through one's own perspective. Understanding becomes a reciprocal, critically challenging process with the other, but without the metaphysical guarantee of a comprehensive truth and without the further, albeit assured goal of a final consensus.[129]

One needs to develop the hermeneutical competence of self-distanciation, i.e., a kind of functionally sufficient self-transcendence, which makes possible a self-critique mounted from the standpoint and perspective of the other. Instead of sublating the alterity of the other into one's own horizon, this calls for a conscious effort at letting the voice of the other be heard. Such a respect for otherness, though present in Gadamer, must nevertheless be accentuated lest it be subsumed under a linguistic ontology. In short, the dialectical tension which exists between one's horizon and the horizon of the other, must be retained. Only a dialogical interaction between the two, not the erasure of their distinctiveness, makes possible a critical hermeneu-

---

light of his language ontology, and characterizes his view on the "integrative overcoming of differences and divergences in dialogue" as quasi-Hegelian. "Although Gadamer correctly perceives that it is not impossible to *understand* other symbolic orders, he is wrong to infer that, inasmuch as we are able to overcome our own horizonal limitations through language, we are *ontologically guaranteed consensual unity*. By contrast, it is essential—even and precisely for dialogic understanding—that the indissoluble difference of symbolic orders be retained and properly recognized." 72.

[129] Kögler, *Dialogue*, 84.

tics. The horizon-expansion engendered by dialogue cannot be obtained at the expense of dissolving distinction of voices in that dialogue.[130]

Kögler calls for the replacement of "historically effected consciousness" with a "dialogically critical consciousness" because "a strong linguistic-ontological account" leads to a situation where the subjective experience of the interlocutor in the dialogue is so thoroughly dependent on a universal event of meaning (which conditions and constrains meaning possibility), that it is virtually effaced. This seems to dispense with the subjective "hermeneutic attitude" of the interpreter since it has no impact whatsoever on the outcome of the actual hermeneutic event. Unless reflective subjectivity is allowed to contribute and play a genuinely codeterminate role in the production of (dialogical) meaning, it remains vacuous to speak of a hermeneutic or historically effected *consciousness*.[131] Without this participation of the interpreter, dialogue cannot be said to be truly productive. Kögler argues:

> Productive dialogue presupposes that both interlocutors mutually learn from one another, and both are thereby potentially able to revise their views. Yet because tradition is present in the text as well as in the preunderstanding of the interpreter, the Gadamerian theory demotes the interpreter from the position of a dialogic equal vis-à-vis tradition to that of a mere medium for tradition. Tradition, as a comprehensive meaning context, appears so powerful that a critique of traditional paradigms can never be made on a firm basis, because every such basis is itself situated in tradition.[132]

Whereas Apel underscores intersubjectivity in interpretation, Kögler seeks to preserve the integrity of alterity in hermeneutical dialogue. The interpreter's voice must be allowed to reflect on, thematize, and criticize tradition; and the interpreter's experiences must be allowed

---

[130] The same insistence on retaining the differentiation between horizons is found in Hans Robert Jauss' development of Gadamer. The alterity of the other in dialogue, according to Jauss, has priority over oneself. It is only through the strange, new and unfamiliar otherness of the other that understanding is possible. See Hans Robert Jauss, *Question and Answer: Forms of Dialogic Understanding* (Minneapolis: University of Minnesota Press, 1989), 215.

[131] Kögler, *Dialogue*, 116–18.

[132] Kögler, *Dialogue*, 133. Gadamer writes: "we are always situated within traditions, and this is no objectifying process—i.e., we do not conceive of what tradition says as something other, something alien. It is always part of us, a model or exemplar, a kind of cognizance that our later historical judgment would hardly regard as a kind of knowledge but as the most ingenuous affinity with tradition." *TM*, 282.

to contradict the conventionality of tradition. While Gadamer espouses this in his exposition of dialogue, there is a sense in which the traditionalism of his linguistic ontology tends to overshadow, if not overwrite, the formative contribution of the experiences of the interlocutors in the hermeneutical conversation.

While tradition to some degree determines the questions the interpreter brings to the text, one recognizes as well that tradition is dynamic and the interpreter's participation in that tradition changes it or adds to its evolution. The questions we put to tradition shape that tradition which in turn shapes us. This dialectic between interpreter and a tradition-mediated text, a dialectical interaction which takes place within a shared and anterior linguistic structure allows for tradition to influence as well as change. Again, this is not alien to Gadamer. What we wish to underscore is that the tension between a differentiation of horizons and a fusion of horizons should be maintained, and that concern for the latter should not be at the expense of the former.

To recapitulate, after reviewing the salient features of Gadamer's hermeneutics, we examined two key issues precipitated by his hermeneutics which are germane to our agenda, namely the question of truth and the possibility of critique in tradition. In the first, we looked at the notion of truth in philosophical hermeneutics and explored the issue of traditionality and relativism; in the second, we took up the question as to whether and how a critical stance may be incorporated into a tradition-based hermeneutical approach. It remains for us in the next chapter to see how Gadamer's hermeneutical reflections can assist in formulating an approach to Christology from within tradition.

CHAPTER THREE

A CHRISTOLOGY FROM WITHIN—TRADITION (II):
DYNAMICS OF A TRADITIONARY CHRISTOLOGY

The place of a basic belief in the aseity of God within theology, together with his transcendence over history, might seem incompatible at first sight with Gadamer's ambivalence on the possibility of transcendental truth apart from the event of human interpretation. Yet there remains much in his reflections on the dynamics of understanding which is helpful to the project of Christological formulation. In this chapter, we shall explore, in dialogue with Gadamer, the relation between tradition and Christology. This chapter is in two sections. In the first, we will examine the process of "traditioning," focussing on (1) the dialectic of continuity and discontinuity in tradition, (2) the impact of ecclesial life and praxis on Christology, (3) Scriptures as canon or criterion for theological reflection, and (4) the dialogical context of Christological formulation. In the second section, we will make a case for the regulatory and referential nature of Christology.

Our hope is to engage in an exploratory crystalizing of what is entailed in the process of Christological formulation. Such a dialogical appropriation is congruent with Gadamer's insistence that application is an ineluctable part of understanding. It is, in his words, "a good test of the idea of hermeneutics itself" if it can be carried over into other fields.[1] In view of this invitation, we shall attempt here a dialogical application of Gadamer's reflections to Christology.

Gadamer's observation that to understand is always to understand from within tradition is one which readily applies to theological

---

[1] "Reflections," *PHG*, 17. Hermeneutics is increasingly being appropriated by disciplines other than textual interpretation and philosophy, as Gadamer himself does in *The Enigma of Health: The Art of Healing in a Scientific Age*, tr. Jason Gaiger & Nicholas Walker (Cambridge: Polity Press, 1996). See also: Shaun Gallagher, *Hermeneutics and Education* (Albany: SUNY Press, 1992); Charles V. Gerkin, *The Living Human Document: Re-visioning Pastoral Counseling in a Hermeneutical Mode* (Nashville: Abingdon, 1984); Stanley B. Messer, Louis A. Sass & Robert L. Woolfolk, eds., *Hermeneutics and Psychological Theory: Interpretive Perspectives on Personality, Psychotherapy, and Psychopathology* (New Brunswick & London: Rutgers University Press, 1988).

understanding. Our attempt to articulate a Christology *from within* tradition follows from this hermeneutical insight, and is in line with the renewed emphasis currently on the sociality of theology.[2] In the aftermath of the displacement of Enlightenment foundationalism, theology is emboldened to embrace a dispositional stance in favour of faith. Christology in a postmodern ethos, or what Dulles calls "a postcritical theology",[3] is the disciplined reflection on the significance of Christ *from within* a faith tradition and community. What follows is an attempt to underscore and unpack the ecclesiality entailed in a postcritical Christology.

Situating Christology in tradition means that it is implicated in the historicality of tradition and necessarily partakes of its dynamism and fluidity. The liveliness of tradition should not be confused with the funereal aridity of traditionalism. As Pelikan perceptively notes: "Tradition is the living faith of the dead, traditionalism is the dead faith of the living."[4] As a historical phenomenon, tradition is ever changing; and Christology, situated in tradition, develops and evolves along with it. For Christology is not only faith's confession of what happened *in* history, the confession itself is historical and exhibits all the marks of historicity. Understanding the process of "traditioning" would therefore shed light on the nature and development of Christology in (our) history.

I. *Christology and the Process of "Traditioning"*

Tradition is like culture, and a parallel may be drawn between tradition and recent analyses of cultures and their development. Unlike the dominant nineteenth century depiction of culture as an organ-

---

[2] This emphasis is especially evident in works affiliated with narrative theology, e.g., Hans W. Frei, *The Identity of Jesus Christ: The Hermeneutical Bases of Dogmatic Theology* (Philadelphia: Fortress, 1975); Paul Holmer, *The Grammar of Faith* (New York: Harper & Row, 1978); Lindbeck, *Doctrine*. Also: Thiselton, "Corporate Memory". Stanley J. Grenz, in *Revisioning Evangelical Theology: A Fresh Agenda for the 21st Century* (Downers Grove: InterVarsity Press, 1993), 72 & 75, argues that theology must be done "from within" the vantage point of the community of faith. He follows through on that programmatic essay with a systematic theology rooted in Christian community: *Theology for the Community of God* (Nashville: Broadman & Holman, 1994).
[3] Avery Dulles, *The Craft of Theology: From Symbol to System* (New York: Crossroad, 1992), 3–15.
[4] Jaroslav Pelikan, *The Vindication of Tradition* (New Haven & London: Yale University Press, 1984), 65.

ism which grows and matures, recent anthropological and sociological analyses suggest that cultural identity is not a settled entity but something which is constantly being negotiated.[5] Culture, in the Geertzian sense of a social symbol system, is tensive, malleable and vulnerable to innovative interests. Current analogies for understanding cultures are thus more hermeneutical than organic.[6] In summing up the processual and interpretive character of culture, Brown describes it as analogous to "play," which recalls Gadamer's analysis:

> Culture is the play of conflicting symbols, conflicting interests, and conflicting symbols and interests. . . . With these as its players, the game of culture is as much process as structure, stability as change, dissolution as construction, past as present, action as giveness [sic], the collective as the individual. Culture is a struggle—the negotiation of identity amid chaos and order.[7]

Brown defines tradition as "the cultural negotiation of identity that takes place within, and with, a canon", the latter understood religiously as "a privileged locus of thought or action, to which relevant thinking and acting must conform because it is somehow derived from deity."[8] This "negotiation of identity" takes place in the "space" of tradition, and is carried out in accordance with the terms and conditions mediated by tradition. But negotiation is also *with* canon in the sense that the parameters of tradition and canon themselves are subject to negotiation. There is thus a dialectical relation between tradition as *supplier* of the terms of negotiation, and tradition as the *subject* of negotiation. Tradition is both a *given* and a *task*.

The Christological creeds of the past form the "given" of tradition; they are part and parcel of the preunderstanding which theologians bring to the task of interpreting Christ today. Christology is thus paradoxically the presuppositional launching pad as well as the destination of theological reflection. Owing to the historicality of

---

[5] See for instance: Clifford Geertz, *The Interpretation of Cultures* (New York: Basic Books, 1973); James Clifford, *The Predicament of Culture: Twentieth Century Ethnography, Literature, and Art* (Cambridge: Harvard University Press, 1988); Roy Wagner, *The Invention of Culture*, rev. & exp. ed. (Chicago: University of Chicago Press, 1981); Marshall Shalins, *Islands of History* (Chicago: University of Chicago Press, 1985). Cf. Delwin Brown, *Boundaries of Our Habitation: Tradition and Theological Construction* (Albany: SUNY Press, 1994), 59–67.

[6] Brown, *Boundaries*, 62; & Clifford, *Predicament*, 274.

[7] Brown, *Boundaries*, 66–67. "[L]ike a game, the traditioned life is playing *and* being played." 89.

[8] Ibid., 67, cf. 83f.

all theological interpreters, the task of Christology is a hermeneutical one, since human existence is necessarily contextual and the way past formulae are received varies from situation to situation.

And because the church's Christology is a foundational symbol[9] which is meant to be universally relevant, it is by definition open to reinterpretation since people from different parts of the world and at different times of history necessarily respond to Christ differently. One cannot even repeat past formulae without at the same time reinterpreting them, since "historical experience changes, and the differences generate meanings different from what was originally intended."[10] If Gadamer is right that all understanding is interpretative, then any attempt at understanding Christ will of necessity be an interpretive undertaking. The past is always being updated, and the morphological transformation of traditional symbols through reinterpretation is what we mean by "traditioning." The forward movement of tradition through time is thus hermeneutically propelled.

Not only is the process of "traditioning" hermeneutical, in terms of Christology, the very object of theological investigation, namely Christ, is a result of earlier hermeneutical appraisals. The Christ-symbol is already meaning-laden and symbolically structured. The very sources for our understanding of the historical Jesus are already theologically pregnant.[11] Warnke's explication of Gadamer's view on the transformation of tradition aptly describes this phenomenon:

> The text that is handed down to us is a fusion of previous opinions about it, a harmony of voices, as Gadamer often puts it, to which we add our own. But this means that object of hermeneutic understanding is already a fusion of the interpretations of a tradition and our encounter with it is an encounter with tradition.[12]

That the object of interpretation is hermeneutically layered suggests that a radical bifurcation of the Christ of faith and Jesus of history

---

[9] By "symbols" we refer to all historical or finite elements, e.g., creeds, Scripture, propositions, etc., which are recognized as the conduits through which the transcendental reality of God and truth is made present and known. See Karl Rahner, "The Theology of the Symbol," *Theological Investigations, Vol IV: More Recent Writings* (Baltimore: Helicon; London: Darton, Longman & Todd, 1966), 221–52.

[10] Roger Haight, *Dynamics of Theology* (New York: Paulist, 1990), 172.

[11] F. S. Fiorenza, *Foundational*, 291. The fact that the Gospels are theologically tendentious (as redaction criticism reveals) does not impugn their historical reliability. In fact, Gadamer's positive take on prejudice makes the theological orientation of the Gospels something to be embraced rather than a barrier to historical knowledge.

[12] Warnke, *Gadamer*, 90.

is facile since our knowledge of the historical Jesus is already "prejudiced" in the Gadamerian sense.

The unity of the Jesus-event and Christological interpretation—a viewpoint Gadamer would undoubtedly endorse—means that dogmatic Christology cannot be construed simply as a conceptual dress draped over the historical Jesus as Harnack does in his kernel-husk model of Christology. Neither is the attempt to reconstruct the picture of the historical Jesus free from the presuppositional stance of tradition, for our encounter with the historical Jesus is already an encounter with tradition. Gadamer has demonstrated that there are no pure data free from the web of historicity. A historical "given" about Jesus is already an interpretation since only "in the light of interpretation does something become a fact".[13] All objects within history present themselves to the investigative historian as inextricably fastened to a nexus of factors in history known as "tradition." The effective-historicality of meaning means that what happened in history continues to happen as the past is fused with the present horizon of the interpreter. Investigation into the Jesus of history is thus as much a hermeneutical undertaking as theological reflection on the significance of Christ.[14]

---

[13] Gadamer, "Text and Interpretation," 388; cf. *TM*, 281–3.

[14] The disciplines of systematic theology and historical theology converge at the point of hermeneutics. Thomas B. Ommen notes that the tension between dogmatic theology and historical investigation can be eased "if the *systematic dimension of historical method* and the *historical dimension of systematic method* are kept in view." *The Hermeneutic of Dogma* (Missoula: Scholars Press, 1975, emphasis added), 231. Space does not permit further explorations into the hermeneutical relationship between the dogmatic Christ and the historical Jesus. Suffice to say that the belief that Jesus was raised from the dead and the (still ongoing) practice of the worship of Jesus as God-incarnate, are elements present in the earliest layer of Christian tradition, suggesting that already from the very beginning, Christology and the historical Jesus cannot be sharply differentiated in such a way that we can isolate a brute historical datum which served as nucleus for later Christology. The intertwining of the language of faith and history is noted by James M. Robinson and Helmut Koester: "it is by no means easy, and perhaps it is impossible, to extrapolate from any particular creed an objective historical event, a seemingly stable historical datum, as it were, that could be used as a criterion to evaluate critically the diverse creeds and symbols of faith." *Trajectories through Early Christianity* (Philadelphia: Fortress, 1971), 208. This means that it will not do to characterize the distinction between dogmatic formulation and a historically given revelation as that between form and substance or content. While such a distinction offers a neat way to deal with the contextualization of doctrine,—decide what the core of a doctrine is, detach it from its historically conditioned form and then transplant it into a new context—it is problematic since there is no "essence" of Christology which can be abstracted from its external historical form, e.g., the Chalcedonian model, since the very notion of "essence"

Christian tradition locates the genesis of Christology in Jesus of Nazareth and the salvific events devolving from his life. What makes the historical Jesus indispensable is the belief that in him we have the definitive revelation of God and the locus of salvation. Christology's validity depends on its being anchored in the history of Jesus. If Gadamer is right, then the temporal distance separating present believers from the historical Jesus is not empty but filled with the continuity of custom and tradition. To posit a disjunction, as Kähler does, between the Christ of faith and the Jesus of history is, from a Gadamerian standpoint, unwarranted.[15] The historical Jesus is integral to Christology in that a contemporary witness to Christ must be done on the basis of as accurate a picture of the historical Jesus as critical historiography can possibly provide. While hermeneutical meaning is never a mere methodical manoeuvre, it does not mean that it is free from constraints or that all interpretations are equally valid. Critical historiography keeps vigil and rightfully challenges all unwarranted (even fanciful) reconstructions of the historical Jesus, and as such serves as a criterion for Christological development.

In one sense, this is a propaedeutic to the hermeneutical development of the tradition of Christology; in another, it is already a part of the "traditioning" process as the historical genesis of Christology is brought to bear again and again on subsequent interpretations. This brings us back to our earlier characterization of tradition as *given* and *task*. If tradition is viewed as both the *habitus* and *goal* of theological reflection, how then are they related? In what way is theological development an extension of the "given" of tradition, and how does tradition remain identifiably constant despite its varied historical forms?

---

is itself apprehended historically. As Edward Schillebeeckx asserts, the distinction between "dogmatic essence" and its historical form is "virtually meaningless and unmanageable precisely because this 'essence' is never given to us as a pure essence, but is always concealed *in* a historical mode of expression." "Towards a Catholic Use of Hermeneutics," in *God the Future of Man* (New York: Sheed and Ward, 1968), 12. The inextricability of Christology and the historical Jesus is reflected in the title of Stephen Evans' book, *The Historical Christ and the Jesus of Faith* (Oxford: Clarendon Press, 1996). A similar critique of the dichotomy between the Christ of faith and the Jesus of history, this time from a dogmatic standpoint, is mounted by Eberhard Jüngel, "The Dogmatic Significance of the Question of the Historical Jesus," in *Theological Essays II*, ed. with introduction by J. B. Webster, tr. Arnold Neufeldt-Fast and J. B. Webster (Edinburgh: T&T Clark, 1995), 82–119.

[15] Martin Kähler, *The So-Called Historical Jesus and the Historic Biblical Christ*, ed. Ernst Wolf, tr. Carl Braaten (Philadelphia: Fortress, 1964).

A. *The Dialectic of Continuity and Discontinuity in Tradition*

The rejection of the notion of tradition modeled after that of an organism which grows and matures may be compared to Gadamer's rejection of truth as predeterminately given. John Henry Newman's idea of doctrinal development set out in his *An Essay on the Development of Christian Doctrine*,[16] is a prime example of an organic model of tradition, in which doctrinal formulation means making explicit what is already implicit in the primal revelation. This allows him to affirm simultaneously the "unity" of the "idea" of Christianity and the fact that doctrines do in fact change and develop in history. Later doctrines are regarded as explicit appropriations of aspects of the one idea of revelation. Newman perceives a grand superintending Providence in the development of doctrine, and compares the historical eventuation of doctrines to the fulfilment of prophecies. The focus of his theory is undeniably on continuity and internal order in doctrine.

We cannot engage Newman on doctrinal development given the limitations of this paper,[17] though his view on the "illative" sense and the nature of religious knowledge is not only compatible with Gadamer[18] but also pertinent to our project, as we shall show in chapter four. Suffice it to note that his idea of doctrinal development has been justly criticized for the ambiguity of his notion of the seminal "idea," and its uncritical and procrustean historiography.[19]

---

[16] First published in 1845, the work was revised twice, 1846 and 1878. References will be from the 1878 (3rd.) edition reproduced in J. H. Newman, *Conscience, Consensus, and the Development of Doctrine* (New York: Image Books, Doubleday, 1992), 38–385. Newman's essay was published in 1845 at the time of his conversion from Anglicanism to Catholicism. While not a full statement on the rationale for his change of ecclesiastical allegiance, it does reveal the frame of mind which pointed him in the direction of Rome.

[17] On Newman, see Sykes, *Identity*, 102–22; Owen Chadwick, *From Bossuet to Newman: The Idea of Doctrinal Development* (Cambridge: Cambridge University Press, 1957); Ian T. Ker, *The Achievement of John Henry Newman* (London: Collins, 1990); Nicholas Lash, *Change in Focus: A Study of Doctrinal Change and Continuity* (London: Sheed & Ward, 1973), 83–103; idem, *Newman on Development: The Search for an Explanation in History* (Shepherdstown: Patmos Press, 1975); Aidan Nichols, *From Newman to Congar: The Idea of Doctrinal Development from the Victorians to the Second Vatican Council* (Edinburgh: T&T Clark, 1990); Jaroslav Pelikan, *Historical Theology: Continuity and Change in Christian Doctrine* (Philadelphia: Westminster, 1971).

[18] As Thomas K. Carr demonstrates in his *Newman & Gadamer: Toward a Hermeneutics of Religious Knowledge* (Atlanta: Scholars Press, 1996).

[19] In Lash's opinion, *Change*, 91, Newman is "notoriously erratic and often uncritical" as a historian. Cf. R. P. C. Hanson, *The Continuity of Christian Doctrine* (New York: Seabury, 1981), 73. Sykes, *Identity*, 119, notes that Newman does not seem

Despite his preference for an organic model of development, one wonders if he does not treat doctrines mechanistically as products of logical deduction. Such an approach tends to drain history of its blood and reduces the genuine unpredictability of historical decision-making to an anaemic inevitability.

What is needed instead is an approach which allows for a discriminatory appropriation and critical extension of tradition, simultaneously reenforcing tradition, criticising and moving it forward. The way ahead lies in a dialectical understanding of the relationship between continuity and discontinuity in Christological development. We will flesh out this dialectic in two ways: (1) by taking up Gadamer's view of truth in art and arguing that Christology is an evocative symbol which stands in a hermeneutical relation to the revelatory and redemptive reality which it mediates; and (2) by enquiring into the phenomenon of continuity in discontinuity in the history of Christological development. It is hoped that together they will accentuate the fact that Christology is first, "*from* within" tradition in the innovative sense of departure and discontinuity, and second, "from *within*" in the conservative sense of continuity.

We note firstly that the hermeneutical nature of the relationship between Christology as a historical construct and the transcendental Reality which it represents and re-presents, means that Christology is simultaneously rooted in a history of tradition and open to change as the Gospel of Christ, the truth of God's redemptive self-communication centred on Jesus Christ which is grasped anew in different historical situations. Christology as conceptual construct is a consequence of a hermeneutics of the Gospel of Christ, which constitutes the revelation of God sedimented in tradition and the New Testament, particularly the Gospels. Insofar as the Gospel of Christ is realized historically in the temporal space between the "already" of the Incarnation and the "not yet" of eschatological consummation, Christology, as the evocative and mediating symbol of the truth of the Gospel, is an ongoing venture in history. And owing to its historicality, Christology, like all historical entities, is *situated in* and *changes with* tradition.

---

to appreciate the force of objections to his project arising from biblical and historical criticism. See also: F. S. Fiorenza's critique of the developmental model in his *Foundational*, 155–70; and Bradford E. Hinze, "Narrative Contexts, Doctrinal Reform," *TS* 51(1990): 417–33.

As Macquarrie observes, Gadamer's musings on the emergence of truth in art are applicable to Christology.[20] An "objectified" work of art is in Gadamer's aesthetic reflection, the means by which truth, in the Heideggerian sense of *aletheia*, is disclosed in the act of interpretation. Analogous to this, we differentiate between the dogmatic symbol of Christology (work of art) and the divine reality (truth) which precedes it, precipitates it, and is "presented" through it. While the truth of God's self-revelation is expressed in Christological formulae, it remains distinct from the latter.

Just as the meaning of art has a plenitude and depth which is not exhausted by any one viewing or interpretation, no single historical Christological formula can totally encapsulate the truth or reality of God vis-à-vis Christ and the world. The mysterious plenitude and alterity of the truth of God is always larger than any human formulation can express, however clear its truth-mediating capability. All ecumenical creeds, dogmas and doctrines, while disclosive of truth, are "solutions" to specific problems in church history, and are as such relative to these situations.[21] That is why every generation of Christian believers, confronted with challenges very different from those which exercised their spiritual ancestors, must confess Christ anew. It is therefore in the very nature of Christology as historically mediated and situated to be polysemous. The dynamism and contextuality intrinsic to its hermeneutical nature makes it conducive to the fostering of new insights on Christ. Diversity of Christological interpretations is thus to be expected.

Plurality of interpretations however need not end in an absolute incommensurability of viewpoints. For just as the possible meanings of art are constrained by the materiality of the artwork being interpreted,—it is *this* particular configuration of shapes and colours on *this* particular canvass—there must be a recognisable continuity between a freshly minted Christological interpretation and what is given in tradition. Moreover, insofar as meaning is based on specific rules of human interaction situated within specific historical contexts, it does not have an unlimited range of interpretive possibilities. Openness does not entail an infinity of meanings.

---

[20] Macquarrie, *Christ*, 15.

[21] Avery Dulles, *The Survival of Dogma* (New York: Crossroad, 1971), 179, asserts: "No doctrinal decision of the past directly solves a question that was not asked at the time."

Secondly, we may explore the continuity-discontinuity dialectic of tradition from the standpoint of the history of Christological interpretations. While the conceptual and linguistic character of early Christology reflects the philosophical and religious environment of the Greco-Roman world, one must not ignore the equally clear fact that at key points it contravenes its context. The consistently *discriminatory* way in which elements from historical contexts were appropriated *and* rejected suggests the presence of operative norms or criteria.

For instance, Wisdom in Hellenistic Judaism and Philo's Logos-concept may have furnished the conceptual building blocks for an incarnational Christology, yet the latter differs from them in significant ways. The coming of the Son into history may parallel the coming of Wisdom into the world—an observation not lost on the early Christians,[22]—yet the former is not completely explained by the latter. Colossians 1:15–20 may be couched in the language of wisdom, but there is "no parallel in Jewish wisdom literature (or in the rest of the extant Jewish materials for that matter) to the statement about Christ as the goal of creation: 'all things have been created through him and *for him* . . .', verse 16."[23] Similarly, the Johannine Logos goes beyond the abstraction of Philo's logos-concept. The philosophical and religious milieu may be an influencing factor, but it alone cannot account for the rise of incarnational Christology. In fact, the Incarnation, as Hanson argues, is essentially unlike Greek thought.[24] There appears to be a dialectic between the internal convictions of

---

[22] On the connection between Wisdom and Christology, see John Balchin, "Paul, Wisdom and Christ" in H. H. Rowdon, ed., *Christ the Lord: Studies in Christology presented to Donald Guthrie* (Leicester: Inter-Varsity Press, 1982), 204–19; James D. G. Dunn, *Christology in the Making: A New Testament Inquiry into the Origins of the Doctrine of the Incarnation* (Philadelphia: Westminster, 1980), 163–212; R. G. Hamerton-Kelly, *Pre-existence, Wisdom, and the Son of Man* (SNTSMS 21; Cambridge: Cambridge University Press, 1973); Seyoon Kim, *The Origin of Paul's Gospel* (Grand Rapids: Eerdmans, 1981), 258f; Ben Meyer, *The Aims of Jesus* (London: SCM, 1979), 65, 270 n. 28 & 31; Ben Witherington III, *Jesus the Sage: The Pilgrimage of Wisdom* (Minneapolis: Fortress, 1994).

[23] Peter T. O'Brien, *Colossians, Philemon*, WBC (Waco: Word, 1982), 40.

[24] Hanson, *Continuity*, 46–47. He argues that the Greek association of truth with timeless immaterial permanence makes it inhospitable to the notion of God coming into history and being subjected to the mutability of time and space. While Greek culture may be open to notions of epiphanic and/or apotheotic "incarnation", the suggestion that the divine actually enters history as an actual and true human being is philosophically anathema. Oskar Skarsaune calls the Incarnation an "impossible dogma" when seen against the background of Jewish theology and Hellenistic philosophy, *Incarnation: Myth or Fact?* (St Louis: Concordia, 1991), 13–23.

the faith-community and external influences. The early Christians were mindful of the need to remain faithful to the tradition shaped by and emanating from Jesus.

We contend that despite the plurality of Christologies in history, there is arguably *a retrospectively discernible trajectory* in Christological development which is animated by an internal resolve to remain faithful to the early tradition concerning Christ. We shall examine this a little closer; not so much to "prove" that an identical Christology is shared by all in church history—it is not—but to suggest that a certain directionality of development is discernible, and that it is possible to speak of continuity in discontinuity or cohesiveness in plurality. Obviously one cannot be dogmatic, yet it is important that there be doctrinal continuity, for on it hangs not only the identity of Christianity but also Christology. As Lash notes, if Christ is God's definitive word, then there must be a sense in which the word proclaimed in every successive age is the *same* word, otherwise God's promise is not fulfilled.[25]

Opinions are deeply divided on the rise of orthodoxy or normative Christianity judging from the various historical scenarios on offer.[26] Clearly if by orthodoxy one means a structured body of

---

[25] Lash, *Change*, 59.

[26] We may discern for example five main models which have been proposed. Our categorization is adapted from the taxonomy used in Arland Hultgren's *The Rise of Normative Christianity* (Minneapolis: Fortress, 1994):

(1) *Heresy preceded Orthodoxy*: the view of Walter Bauer, *Orthodoxy and Heresy in Earliest Christianity*, ed. Robert A. Kraft & Gerhard Krodel (Philadelphia: Fortress, 1971), and the Tübingen school of F. C. Baur. Primitive Christianity was an amorphous and variegated tapestry of highly distinctive, even contradictory beliefs with no clear cut distinction between orthodoxy and heresy. Second centuries heresies were in fact theological descendents of first century variations of Christianity. Bauer's tendentious oversimplification of the problems faced by the early Christian communities, the lack of precision and clarity on what "orthodoxy" and "heresy" mean, as well as his arguments from silence, are flaws which have been highlighted by his critics. Moreover, he fails to take seriously enough the distinction which New Testament Christians seemed to make between truth and error, e.g. Gal. 1:8–9; 1 Jn. 2:22; Heb. 2:1–2. See the critical analyses by: H. E. W. Turner, *The Pattern of Christian Truth: A Study in the Relations between Orthodoxy and Heresy in the Early Church* (London: Mowbray, 1954); Thomas A. Robinson, *The Bauer Thesis Examined: The Geography of Heresy in the Early Christian Community* (Lewiston: Edwin Mellen, 1988); Michael Desjardins, "Bauer and Beyond: On Recent Scholarly Discussions of *Hairesis* in the Early Christian Era," *SC* 8(1991): 65–82; Daniel J. Harrington, "The Reception of Walter Bauer's *Orthodoxy and Heresy in Earliest Christianity* during the Last Decade," *HTR* 73(1980): 289–98; I. Howard Marshall, "Orthodoxy and Heresy in Earlier Christianity," *Them* 2(1976): 5–14; and Frederick W. Norris, "Ignatius, Polycarp, and I Clement: Walter Bauer Reconsidered," *VC* 30(1976): 23–44.

propositions linguistically akin to the formulae of either Nicea or
Chalcedon, then orthodoxy is undoubtedly absent from the New

---

(2) The classical model of *Truth before Error*: the view which sees the truth of the
gospel or some form of orthodoxy, however rudimentary, as already established and
operating as norm for beliefs from the very beginning. Appeal is made to early
confessions and traditional teachings which are reflected in the New Testament.
See: V. H. Neufeld, *The Earliest Christian Confessions* (Grand Rapids: Eerdmans, 1963),
and O. Cullmann, *The Earliest Christian Confessions* (London: Lutterworth, 1949). Also
invoked as support is the patristic notion of the "rule of faith" (e.g. Tertullian: "our
rule of faith came first and that all heresy is of more recent emergence", *Adv. Marc.*
5.19). Critiques of this model include: its historical anachronism; its overly uniform
and static construal of orthodoxy, giving it a fixity of form which it probably did
not have in its early history; and its failure to account for the inherent diversity
within the Christian tradition itself. On this last point, see James D. G. Dunn, *Unity
and Diversity in the New Testament* (Philadelphia: Westminster, 1977).

(3) *Deviation via Accretions*: early Christian dogmas owed their origin and form to
the impact of Hellenistic ideas (e.g., Gnosticism) on the simple ethico-religious mes-
sage of Jesus, and are as such deviations from the message of Jesus. See Adolf von
Harnack, *History of Dogma*, 7 vols., tr. from 3rd German ed. by Neil Buchanan
(London: Williams & Norgate, 1905); idem, *What is Christianity?*, tr. Thomas Bailey
Saunders, (New York: Harper & Brothers, 1957). A more radical variation of
Harnack's thesis is found in Martin Werner, *The Formation of Christian Dogma: An
Historical Study of its Problems*, tr. & intro. by G. F. Brandon (London: Adam &
Charles Black, 1957), who argues that the doctrines of later orthodoxy arose in the
aftermath of the failure of the Parousia. Bultmann may also be included here, even
though he differs at points from Harnack and Werner.

(4) *Interplay of Fixed and Flexible Elements*: the view of Turner who sees doctrinal
development as an interaction between "fixed and flexible elements", *Pattern*, 26–31.
The fixed or constant elements which were in place very early include: (a) the religious factity of God and Christ; (b) the acceptance of authoritative biblical revelation; and (c) the "Creed and the rule of faith" which eventually developed into "an
Agreed Syllabus". *Pattern*, 475. These constants are balanced by flexible elements
such as: (a) "differences in Christian idiom", e.g., Christianity can be expressed
either eschatologically or ontologically; (b) selection and use of technical terms; and
(c) idiosyncrasies of leading theologians.

(5) *Diversity of Trajectories from Beginning*: this approach essentially revitalizes Bauer's
thesis on diversity in early Christianity. Dogmas are not regarded as immutable and
monolithic truths; they are historical constructs. According to Robinson and Koester
in *Trajectories through Early Christianity*, 9, the background or environment to the New
Testament must be understood historically, and not in terms of a static and essence-
oriented metaphysics. An historicist approach points to "trajectories" in the Hellenistic
world, and regards distinctions between orthodoxy and heresy as obsolete. "Orthodoxy"
is not a fixed thing but is a fluid historical construct which takes its form and direction from the dynamic interaction between interpreters and their contexts. Early
Christologies were the products of a combination of the religious and cultural contexts of the early Christians and their faith-motivation. See Koester, "The Structure
and Criteria of Early Christian Beliefs," in *Trajectories*, 211–29. It is undeniable that
early Christian beliefs reflect their historical situatedness, and Koester and Robinson
are correct to warn against the naïveté of positing a simplistic single-line developmental model for the rise of orthodoxy. However, one cannot but note the reduc-
tionistic and speculative tenor of their conclusions. A supposedly "pure" historical
reading can often be as tendentiously anti-supernatural as the historiography of a
fundamentalist is tendentiously supernaturalistic!

Testament. This does not, however, mean that there was no concern for a differentiation between true and false teachings there or in the Christian communities of the first century. Early Christianity may be a diverse phenomenon caught in a tangled mass of religious ideas, but it was not so amorphous as to be bereft of distinctive identifying beliefs.

It seems best to speak of an embryonic orthodoxy with blurred edges gradually gaining acceptance in the numerous nascent Christian groups around the Mediterranean. Their search for normative beliefs was prompted no doubt by their need for greater self-definition, and the experience of salvation through the risen Christ in the formative period of the church precipitated Christological reflection in the patristic period.[27] And despite the variety of expressions and understanding, there were nevertheless commonly held beliefs and patterns of behaviour which served as "limiting factors"[28] to diversity within the broad stream of trajectories in early Christianity. The specifics of these unifying beliefs may be debated, but the fact seems incontrovertible that some normative beliefs and prescriptive behaviour patterns, however rudimentary, were present in the earliest Christian communities.[29]

---

[27] The experience of forgiveness of sin, the indwelling power of the Spirit, and the new life of faith within Christian community, led the early Christians to ask themselves: "What sort of being must Jesus be for us to experience what we experienced in him?" Soteriology thus provided the initial impetus for Christological formulation. The early Christians were drawn to two basic conditions which Jesus Christ must meet if he is to be effective as Saviour: he must be truly human and truly divine. Christology as the outworking of the logic of salvation runs like a line through the first five Christian centuries; see e.g., Irenaeus' doctrine of recapitulation (*Haer.* 3.16.6); Tertullian's emphasis on the redemptive function of the incarnation: Christ had to be born a real man if he was to die (*De carne Christi* 6.6f) and if he is to be the forerunner of the resurrection (*Res.* 48.8; 56.6). See: J. Pelikan, *The Christian Tradition: A History of the Development of Doctrine, Vol. 1: The Emergence of the Catholic Tradition (100–600)* (Chicago/London: University of Chicago Press, 1971), 232.

[28] Hultgren, *Normative*, 86–104; cf. Robert L. Wilken, "Diversity and Unity in Early Christianity," *SC* 1(1981): 106–10.

[29] Without delving into the complex issue of the rise of Christology, we submit that the Christologies of the early Christians had their genesis in the earthly ministry of Jesus, and that the traditions concerning Jesus served to orientate development in the early church. See: Craig A. Evans, "The Historical Jesus and the Deified Christ: How Did the One Lead to the Other?" Stanley E. Porter, ed., *The Nature of Religious Language: A Colloquium* (Sheffield: Sheffield Academic Press, 1996), 47–67; Graham N. Stanton, "The Gospel Traditions and Early Christological Reflection" in Sykes & Clayton, eds., *Christ, Faith and History*, 201; Ben Witherington, III, *The Christology of Jesus* (Minneapolis: Fortress, 1990). Such a primitive understanding of the rise of Christology would challenge Bauer's thesis that orthodoxy

It is patently clear from the works of Grillmeier, Pelikan, Kelly, Studer, Young, and others,[30] that patristic Christological reflection is both immensely complex and pluralistic. It would be simplistic to posit a single line of development. What we have, as Robinson and Koester argue, is a host of trajectories, a plurality of traditions and lines of development. We want to ask if it is not in fact possible to discern a confluencing of the divergent trajectories such that one might conceivably speak of a *complex and composite directionality* which somehow unite different Christological interpretations.

We have no wish to defend a simple single-line linear developmental model with its chronological contiguity of ideas. Neither do we want to overlook the presence of genuine conflicts in the history of Christology. Yet it is conceivable that one might discern a certain lineality of development retrospectively as one looks at the diverse and apparently discontinuous lines of historical development.[31] A complex lineality is broad enough to include differences of perspec-

---

came much later. This critique of Bauer gains further weight when we consider the interchangeable way in which God and Christ are referred to in Paul's epistles, which strongly suggests that the link between the two was already made in the first-century. On this interchange, see Neil Richardson, *Paul's Language about God* (Sheffield: Sheffield Academic Press, 1994); Don N. Howell, Jr., "God-Christ Interchange in Paul: Impressive Testimony to the Deity of Jesus," *JETS* 36(1993): 467–79. That Christ was worshipped very early on in the history of the church clearly indicates the primitive attribution of deity-status to Jesus. See R. T. France, "The Worship of Jesus," Rowden, ed., *Christ the Lord*, 19–23; Donald A. Hagner, "Paul's Christology and Jewish Monotheism" in Marguerite Shuster & Richard Muller, eds., *Perspectives on Christology: Essays in Honor of Paul K. Jewett* (Grand Rapids: Zondervan, 1991), 19–38; L. W. Hurtado, *One God, One Lord: Early Christian Devotion and Ancient Jewish Monotheism* (Philadelphia: Fortress, 1988). On whether the New Testament addresses Jesus as God, see Murray J. Harris, *Jesus as God: The New Testament Use of Theos in Reference to Jesus* (Grand Rapids: Baker, 1992).

[30] Aloys Grillmeier, *Christ in Christian Tradition. Vol. I: From the Apostolic Age to Chalcedon (451)*, tr. John Bowden, 2d rev. ed. (Atlanta: John Knox, 1975); Pelikan, *Christian Tradition*; J. N. D. Kelly, *Early Christian Doctrines* (New York: Harper & Row, 1960); Basil Studer, *Trinity and Incarnation: The Faith of the Early Church* (Edinburgh: T&T Clark, 1993); Frances Young, *From Nicea to Chalcedon* (Philadelphia: Fortress, 1983); Gerald O'Collins, *Christology: A Biblical, Historical, and Systematic Study of Jesus* (Oxford: Oxford University Press, 1995), 153–93.

[31] The way in which the dogmatic achievement of one generation becomes the basis for the dogmatic reflection of the next bespeaks the idea of a trajectorial directionality. The development of Christological doctrine cannot be accounted for historically if not for the determination of faith achieved at Nicea (325) and efforts at resolution at Ephesus (431). There is a sense in which succeeding debates are conducted as it were on the shoulders of theological predecessors, as resources from the past are invoked to deal with the pressing situations of the moment. The debate on the coinherence of the human and divine in Christ was one in which all parties involved saw themselves as arguing from within the accepted tradition of the church.

tives, false starts, failures, setbacks, overstatements, and other permutations characteristic of historicity and finitude. It must be emphasized that it is only from a retrospective and diachronic perspective that one discerns that pattern of Christian truth which we are characterizing as a complex-composite lineality. Admittedly, this makes our postulate conjectural and corrigible. Nevertheless, it is arguable that there is sufficient coherence to this retrospective reading (or sufficient family resemblances present) that one may speak of a *functionally unified Christian identity* which aids in determining if a development is faithful to tradition. Such a cumulative directionality comes out of the past like a trajectory, a trajectory which plots the path for a traditionary (i.e., congruent with tradition) development of Christology.

The plausibility of our proposal will of course depend on a careful historical reconstruction of the rise and development of Christology, a task which is clearly beyond our scope. We can only allude to the way in which key components of patristic Christological reflection seem often to have been intimated in earlier developments.[32] The

---

[32] Gerald O'Collins identifies four such "early intimations", *Christology*, 166–69: (1) The double eternal/temporal generation of the Son (Rm. 1:3–4), an idea found in Irenaeus (*Haer.* 2.28.6; 3.10.2) which flowered later in Lactantius (Lact.*Inst.* 4.8.1–2), in Cyril of Alexandria's pre-Chalcedon description of the Word's double generation (*Chr.un.; Ep.Nest.*), and in Leo's *Tome*. (2) The notion of double consubstantiality in Tertullian (*Prax.* 27.10–11) figures later in Nicea's view of the Son as "of one substance (*ousia*) with the Father", and in Chalcedon's statement that Christ is "of one substance (*homoousios*) with the Father in his divinity and of one substance (*homoousios*) with us in his humanity." O'Collins opines: "Chalcedon's teaching on Christ's double consubstantiality did little more than unpack the language of 'double substance' fashioned by Tertullian more than 200 years earlier." Ibid., 167. (3) The unity of Christ as subject, a theme which both Irenaeus (*Haer.* 3.16; 2.8) and Tertullian (*Prax.* 27.2, 10–11) stressed over against the Gnostics' attempt to "divide" the Son of God. This was reiterated in the Cappadocians' repudiation of any talk of Christ as two sons, one derived from the Father and the other from his mother. This thematic trajectory can be traced through Cyril's letters to Nestorius and the Chalcedonian confession of Christ as "one and the same Son". (4) The *communicatio idiomatum* or interchange of properties which follows naturally from the unity of divinity and humanity in the one incarnate Son. Although generally associated with the Council of Ephesus (431) and Cyril of Alexandria, this idea had already been anticipated in Ignatius of Antioch, Melito of Sardis, Tertullian, Gregory of Nazianzus, Leo, and, arguably, even in the New Testament itself, where the one who was crucified could be simultaneously described as both "Jesus of Nazareth" (Mk. 16:6) and "Lord of glory" (1 Cor. 2:8; Gal. 6:14). This notion of *communicatio idiomatum* flows like a stream from its conceptual intimations in the New Testament through subsequent patristic refinements into the theological pond from which emerged the Christology of Chalcedon. On the influence of the *communicatio idiomatum*, see Richard A. Muller, *Dictionary of Latin and Greek Theological Terms: Drawn Principally from Protestant Scholastic Theology* (Grand Rapids: Baker, 1985; hereafter *DLGTT*), 72.

relation between early intimations and later development in Christology
lends support to our idea of a trajectory of continuity in discontinuity. The idea of an overarching trajectory, though by no means
probative, is not implausible either.

It may be objected that lineality presupposes that one has a view
of history as a totality, which opens us to the same criticisms leveled at Newman. In response, we maintain that a postulate of totality is a natural and necessary concomitant of the Christian belief in
the finality of revelation in Christ. It is as such a coherent assertion
given the framework of Christian belief. Furthermore, even if we
bracket off this item of Christian belief, it is not at all clear why it
is illegitimate to posit a totality of meaning, provided that one includes
the disclaimer that such a totality is provisional in nature, and is in
principle revisable.

This is none other than the hermeneutical circle at work: the dialectic between a provisional "whole" (universal) and the concrete
parts (particulars). The point is not to prove the finality of revelation in Christ in an epistemologically irresistable way, but merely to
say that the form of the theological argument for a totality to history is not unlike that which goes on in everyday hermeneutical
deliberations. This harks back to our earlier proposal that there is
sufficient coherence to Christian identity that it is capable of exercising a criteriological function.

The metaphor of a trajectory is illuminating because it highlights
the "inherent dynamic"[33] of Christology and carries the dual idea of
coming from and *going to*. A trajectory has the effect of nudging us in a
particular interpretive direction, and orientates future doctrinal development without predetermining its outcome, much like preunderstanding
does in interpretation. In short, there is directionality without pre-
destined specificity. The trajectory of development is sufficiently broad
to accommodate different lines of enquiries. Only such a reading
can hold together the need for fidelity and the demands of creativity.

Evidently, this notion of trajectorial directionality is conceptually
compatible with Gadamer's *wirkungsgeschichtliches Bewusstsein*, and it is
not unlike the way "anticipation of perfection" functions in his herme-

---

[33] John Macquarrie alludes to trajectory as "a useful metaphor" and the "inher-
ent dynamic" of ideas in his essay, "Doctrinal Development: Searching for Criteria,"
Sarah Coakley & David A. Pailin, eds., *The Making and Remaking of Christian Doctrine:
Essays in Honour of Maurice Wiles* (Oxford: Clarendon Press, 1993), 163–64.

neutics. If the dogmatic achievements of the past are understood as interpretations of Christ sedimented in tradition, then the present interpreter of Christ, standing within tradition, invariably brings to the task a Christ-shaped orientation. This brings us to a consideration of the relational links between revelation, Christ, Church and tradition.

To begin with, we suggest that our notion of trajectory is congruent with the view of divine revelation as something which is not merely given and received *immediately*, but also *mediately*. There is a "mediated immediacy" to God's revelation which follows from revelation as historicized truth.[34] The witness of Scriptures and church tradition are the mediate means by which the decisive revelation and efficacious redemptive work of God through Jesus Christ is historically extended. We will defer for now the question of Scriptures and theology, and look briefly at the relation between Jesus and the Church, and how that impinges on our understanding of theology as that which occurs along the axis of a trajectory of tradition.

While it is generally accepted that the genesis of the Church has its historical foundation in the person of Jesus, there is dissension on the nature of the connection between the two, as Francis S. Fiorenza's judicious analysis of the various construals of the relationship between the two indicates. In his opinion, it is no longer possible after Gadamer and Ricoeur to simply equate the meaning of a text or an institution with the intentionality of its author or founder. Neither is the implicit-explicit organic developmental model tenable, seeing that it does not really allow for genuine discontinuity and diversity.[35] What is needed instead is a "reconstructive hermeneutics" of the relation between Jesus and Christology or Church.

Fiorenza draws on developments in the philosophy of action, linguistic theory and hermeneutics to make his case for a "reconstructive hermeneutics." Meaning, he argues, ought to be understood as retrospective.[36] History is more than just an itemization of events; it

---

[34] While God's self-revelation comes through certain salvific events in history, e.g., the Exodus, the life and ministry of Jesus Christ, etc., it is not merely episodic but is historically mediated. Gerard Loughlin, *Telling God's Story: Bible, Church and Narrative Theology* (Cambridge: Cambridge University Press, 1996), 188, asserts, "The immediacy of God's event is always mediated." On the mediated nature of revelation, see also: Francis Watson, "Is Revelation an 'Event'?" *MTh* 10(1994): 383–99 and Colin Gunton, *A Brief Theology of Revelation* (Edinburgh: T&T Clark, 1995).
[35] Fiorenza, *Foundational*, 109; 166–8.
[36] Ibid., 111–2.

attempts a coherent chronicling of what happened, and this entails the demonstration of continuity. The meaning of the Jesus-event is thus retrospectively perceived in that it includes the historical consequences which follow (contiguity) and flow (continuity) from it.

Fiorenza explicates this further by means of an appeal to the Speech-Act theory of Austin and Searle.[37] Speech is correlated with rule-governed behaviour in that meaning involves not just the saying of something (locutionary actions) but the doing of something (illocutionary force) and the bringing about of something by means of what is said (perlocutionary acts). Language is a performative act and entails conventions and constitutive rules, i.e., rules (like those in chess) which create the possibility of action. The meaning of an utterance or action,[38] is therefore not to be equated simply with the intention of a speaker or agent. To grasp the meaning of sentences requires knowledge of the context and background in which they are spoken as well as the implicit rules of language and behaviour which govern their use.

From the perspective of Speech-Act theory, we might say that Jesus as the Logos of God cannot be adequately understood without reference to what God has effected and continues to effect in history following the "utterance" of the Logos at the Incarnation. The existence of the Church,[39] its ongoing testimony to what God has done in Christ, and its engagement in Christ's "ministry of reconciliation" (2 Cor. 5:18) in the world, are dimensions of the meaning of the Incarnation as God's Speech-Act. Not only does this perspective cohere with our understanding of revelation as historically

---

[37] Fiorenza, *Foundational*, 113f; John L. Austin, *How To Do Things With Words*, 2d ed. (Cambridge: Harvard University Press, 1962, 1975); John R. Searle, *Speech-Acts: An Essay in the Philosophy of Language* (Cambridge: Cambridge University Press, 1969); idem, *Expression and Meaning: Studies in the Theory of Speech-Acts* (Cambridge: Cambridge University Press, 1979).

[38] Paul Ricoeur extends the correlation between language and act in Speech-Act theory to human action so that the meaning of the latter is appreciated not just in terms of its place within a specific temporal context, but also its illocutionary force, vis-à-vis what it effects in history. See Ricoeur, "The Model of the Text: Meaningful Action Considered as a Text," *Human Sciences*, 197–221.

[39] In interpreting the meaning of Jesus' proclamation and actions, Fiorenza asserts, "the significant question is not what did Jesus intend, or whether he intended a Church. . . . Instead, the question should be whether his proclamation and actions have a meaning that legitimates the emergence of a Church. Do they have a meaning so that the Church does not simply stand after Jesus in time, but that its existence and meaning are entailed in the meaning that Jesus' proclamation and actions can have?" *Foundational*, 114.

mediated, it situates Christology squarely within the continuing life and practice of the Christian community.

The meaning of the Christ-event as diachronically discerned in the ongoing history of the Church gains conceptual clarity in the light of the "reception hermeneutics" of Hans Robert Jauss and the "Konstanz School."[40] Although primarily a literary theory, reception hermeneutics has been increasingly appropriated, particularly by Roman Catholic theologians, as a helpful way of dealing with the question of doctrinal continuity in history.[41] Following in the footsteps of his teacher Gadamer, Jauss affirms the participative role of the reader in the interpretation of a text. The reader is "the intermediary between the past and the present, the work and its effects".[42] To determine the effects of a work, one has to reconstruct the "expectation horizon" which every reader brings to the text.

The novelty of a work often goes against the expectation-horizon and spurs changes to it. To the degree that a work consistently explodes conventions, challenges and changes the horizon of its readers, it is considered a "classic." Whereas understanding in Gadamer comes through a fusion of horizons, in Jauss it is by means of a differentiation of the text's horizon and that of the interpreter. It is the alterity or strange unfamiliarity of the text which provokes changes to the reader's expectation-horizon. Jauss describes receptions of a text as different "concretizations" of the work in history.[43] As the

---

[40] See works by Hans Robert Jauss which have been translated into English: *Question and Answer: Forms of Dialogic Understanding* (Minneapolis: University of Minnesota Press, 1989); *Toward an Aesthetic of Reception* (Minneapolis: University of Minnesota Press, 1982); *Aesthetic Experience and Literary Hermeneutics* (Minneapolis: University of Minnesota Press, 1982); also, "The Theory of Reception: A Retrospective of its Unrecognized Prehistory," in Peter Collier & Helga Geyer-Ryan, eds., *Literary Theory Today* (Oxford: Polity Press, 1990), 53–73. See also: Robert C. Holub, *Reception Theory: A Critical Introduction* (London: Methuen, 1984); idem, "Constance School of Reception Aesthetics," in Irena R. Makaryk, ed., *Encyclopedia of Contemporary Literary Theory: Approaches, Scholars, Terms* (Toronto: University of Toronto Press, 1993), 14–18.

[41] See Fiorenza, *Foundational*, 118f; Ormond Rush, "Reception Hermeneutics and the 'Development' of Doctrine: An Alternative Model," *Pacifica* 6(1993): 125–40; idem, "Living Reception of the Living Tradition: Hermeneutical Principles for Theology," Neil J. Byrne, ed., *Banyo Studies* (Banyo, Queensland: Pius XII Seminary, 1991), 242–90; David Tracy, *Plurality and Ambiguity: Hermeneutics, Religion, Hope* (San Francisco: Harper & Row, 1987). One should note though that it is the concept of reception in general, rather than reception hermeneutics specifically, which tends to characterize Catholic views of tradition and doctrinal development.

[42] Jauss, *Question and Answer*, 224.

[43] Jauss is indebted to Prague structuralists Jan Mukarovksy and Felix Vodicka for the concept of "concretization." *Aesthetic of Reception*, 72–73; also 147–8.

reader engages a text, her expectation horizon is either confirmed or challenged, and a new Gestalt emerges. The formation of a new Gestalt constitutes a new concretization of the text. Only through a diachronic history of the different "concretizations" of a work's reception does one discover what is creative and paradigmatic about it. As O. Rush summarizes it,

> Jauss' theory not only highlights the effects which a work produces on a reader, but also the element of active reception on the part of the reader. Effect and reception are correlative principles. The schemata of the text constitute the former (the effect) and set limits to possible interpretations. Yet within those limits the work is open; through its necessary concretization there is open creativity for manifold meanings to be revealed. A work has potential for unlimited concretization down through history.[44]

Interpretation is therefore concerned not just with the original reception of a text and the present horizon of the interpreter, but also the work's receptions through history. Revelation as history means that the disclosure of the truth of the Christ-event continues through history, and a hermeneutics of Christology must take into account its provocations and receptions in history. Reception hermeneutics accentuates the degree to which Jesus' teachings and actions went against the expectation-horizons of his contemporaries.[45] The full paradigmatic meaning and significance of Christ is seen only through the history of successive receptions of Jesus. "The concretization of the creative tension between successive expectations and receptions", Fiorenza asserts, "makes manifest how the relation between Jesus and the Church is not one of simple contiguity, but rather one of a foundation based upon the breaking through of the horizons of expectation."[46]

Similarly, the historical development of doctrines and dogmas may be characterized as a diachrony of receptions or concretizations. This emphasis on tradition as a living, evolving phenomenon is evident

---

[44] Rush, "Reception Hermeneutics," 130; cf. Jauss, "Theory of Reception," 59–60.

[45] See Thiselton, *NHH*, 34. Fiorenza points out that the attempt by the "history-of-religions" school to interpret Jesus primarily in terms of the horizon of his background "minimizes, indeed overlooks, the extent to which the meaning of Jesus consists precisely in his changing of the horizons of expectation and his creation of new horizons." *Foundational*, 120.

[46] Ibid., 121; cf. Francis S. Fiorenza, "The Crisis of Scriptural Authority: Interpretation and Reception," *Int* 44(1990): 365f.

in contemporary Catholicism where the primary meaning of tradition has shifted from *tradita* (body of truths within a *depositum fidei*) to *traditio* (corporate life of the church in passing on its grasp on revelation).[47] The formation of new Gestalts means that certain themes, images, narratives, etc., from tradition will be appropriated (and thus gain prominence) while others fade to the background. This discriminatory and hermeneutical appropriation of tradition, spurred on by contextual considerations, as well as a fundamental commitment to remain faithful to tradition, accent the dialectic of continuity and discontinuity in tradition.

This perspective, we submit, is consonant with Gadamer's emphasis on the history of effects in interpretation, as well as Pannenberg's notion of *Überlieferungsgeschichte*, "the history of the transmission of traditions" (which we shall take up in chapter five). Tradition lives through the continuous constitution of new Gestalts which re-express the transcendental (revelatory) truth of God in Christ. In so doing, they often need to go beyond the linguistic forms of previous formulations. "The sameness of meaning can only be a sameness in difference."[48] Tradition lives on in history precisely through it being continually appropriated and concretized.

Another way of unraveling the dialectic of evocative newness (discontinuity) on the one hand and trajectorial directionality (continuity) on the other, is in terms of Ricoeur's threefold narrative movement of prefiguration, configuration and refiguration.[49] For to inhabit tradition is to be taken up by its story, the extension of which equals

---

[47] See Michael J. Himes, "The Ecclesiological Significance of the Reception of Doctrine," *HeyJ* 33(1992): 151–2; and Yves Congar, *Tradition and Traditions: An Historical and a Theological Essay* (New York: Burns and Oates, 1966).

[48] Haight, *Dynamics*, 178. In line with this, Ormond Rush cites the trinitarian controversies in the fourth century as an illustration of "the way the continuous living tradition provokes discontinuity in linguistic expression, precisely in order to maintain continuity of truth." Athanasius' defence of Nicea against the Arians amounts to the claim that "a living reception of the truth of Christian belief expressed in scripture *requires* discontinuity, a going-beyond scriptural language, precisely in order to maintain the proclamation of that scriptural truth with fidelity." The Nicean formulation of 325 did not gain normativity until the Council of Constantinope in 381, and the historical bridge linking the two may be understood as "a process of living reception of the living tradition" rather than an organic development from the less formed to the more fully formed. "Reception Hermeneutics," 132–3.

[49] The prolific and complex nature of Ricoeur's works poses difficulties for anyone wishing to enlist his insights. For his view on narrative, see P. Ricoeur, ET: *Time and Narrative*, 3 vols. (Chicago & London: University of Chicago Press, 1984, 1988, 1990); "The Narrative Function," *Human Sciences*, 274–96; "Life in Quest of

the expansion or development of tradition. The notion of trajectory
as a movement of *coming from* and *going to* has the character of a narrative plot. The themes of participatory apprehension of knowledge,
human finitude, openness to new possibilities and the enlargement
of horizons, leitmotifs in Ricoeur's narrative hermeneutics,[50] are certainly congruent with our understanding of tradition as a dialectical
trajectory of continuity and discontinuity.[51]

If tradition may be described as the ongoing redemptive narrative of Jesus Christ through his Church in history, the task of moving that narrative along comes via a process of configuration, where
the multiplicity of events are gathered up into a coherent and unified
story. This configurative move does not take place in a narratival
vacuum; it is preceded by the prefiguration of events and actions.
There is already a narratival character to life prior to the continuation of that narrative through our configurative involvement. We
might say, in a fashion after Ricoeur, that Christological formulation or configuration within a narratival framework takes place "in
front of" the "text" of past formulae. Yet this configuration is not
apart from what is "behind," in the dual sense of one, behind in
time, and two, the reality which lies behind previous formulations.[52]
The consequence of configuration is a "refiguration" of our horizon
as the latter is first distantiated and then fuses with the horizon of
the narrative. This refiguration leads to an expansion of our horizon,
and it is this ability of narrative to open up new worlds and possibilities in life which drew Ricoeur early in his career to narrative.[53]

Narrative," in David Wood, ed., *On Paul Ricoeur: Narrative and Interpretation* (London
& New York: Routledge, 1991), 20–33. Also: Thiselton, *NHH*, 351f; Kevin
J. Vanhoozer, *Biblical Narrative in the Philosophy of Paul Ricoeur* (Cambridge: Cambridge
University Press, 1990), especially 86f.

[50] See Thiselton, *NHH*, 344f; cf. P. Ricoeur, *Human Sciences*, 61–62.

[51] Ricoeur's reflections on narratival configuration are applicable to our project
despite its ambiguity on the relation between historical and fictive narratives. On
this ambiguity, see Vanhoozer's critique, *Ricoeur*, 11–12, 90–99, 175–8, 281–3;
Thiselton, *NHH*, 356–8.

[52] See Thiselton's use of the Speech-Act theory of Austin, Searle and Recanati
to surmount the intra-linguistical bent and ambivalence on extralinguisticality in
Ricoeur. Certain states of affairs "behind" the text is presumed in what goes on
"in front of" it. *NHH*, 361f. Also: David E. Klemm, *The Hermeneutical Theory of Paul
Ricoeur: A Constructive Analysis* (Lewisburg: Bucknell University Press; London &
Toronto: Associated University Presses, 1983), 93.

[53] See P. Ricoeur, *Freedom and Nature: The Voluntary and the Involuntary* (Evanston:
Northwestern University Press, 1966); cf. Kevin J. Vanhoozer, "Philosophical Antecedents to Ricoeur's *Time and Narrative*," in Wood, ed., *On Paul Ricoeur*, 48. Ricoeur

Prefigurative givenness, narratival configuration, and horizonal refiguration aptly describes the process of traditioning, a process which is simultaneously continuous and discontinuous. As the story of Jesus Christ given in tradition is retold, something is added to the story in the retelling. Telling, as Loughlin reminds us, "is always retelling, and retelling changes the story."[54] Yet it is recognizably the same story which is being narrated. Paradoxically, Christology moves forward only by looking backward and following after that which has been given in tradition, just as new meaning comes through the already interpreted text, not apart from it.

To recapitulate, in explicating the dialectic between continuity and discontinuity in tradition, we looked firstly at the nature of truth as that which comes to the fore in a hermeneutics of the Christ-symbol. The revelatory truth of God's redemptive work in Christ is distinct from, and larger than, any dogmatic formula; and while the former is truly expressed in doctrinal achievements of the past, it is not exhausted by any. Alongside this, we have the contextuality which characterises all theological formulations, and together they render Christology both polysemic and reformulable in principle. Secondly, we proposed that a retrospectively discernible trajectory in the historical development of Christology provides a certain predisposing directionality which serves as a counterpoise to the openness of theological development. Christology is both *"traditioned"* and *"traditioning"*; and the process of "traditioning" coinheres with, and takes place in, the life and praxis of the ecclesial community.

B. *Ecclesial Embodiment and Christological Reflection*

The dialectical and interactive connection between theoretical reflection and action has been noted by social scientists and theologians.[55] While

---

alludes to the intervention of the world of the text in the world of action which results in a new configuration or transfiguration of the latter. P. Ricoeur, "On Interpretation," in Alan Montefiore, ed., *Philosophy in France Today* (Cambridge: Cambridge University Press, 1983), 185.

[54] Loughlin, *Telling*, 191.

[55] See for instance: Nicholas Lobkowicz, *Theory and Practice: History of a Concept from Aristotle to Marx* (Notre Dame: University of Notre Dame Press, 1967); Richard Bernstein, *Praxis and Action: Contemporary Philosophies of Human Activity* (Philadelphia: University of Pennsylvania Press, 1971); Clodovis Boff, *Theology and Praxis: Epistemological Foundations* (Maryknoll: Orbis, 1987); & Edmund Arens, *Christopraxis: A Theology of Action*, tr. John F. Hoffmeyer (Minneapolis: Fortress, 1995).

attention is often given to the analytical dimension of negotiations in tradition, the affective, behavioural and communal elements tend to be neglected. Such a bias in favour of the conceptual fails to recognise that the dynamism of "traditioning" owes as much to practical, non-cognitive elements as it does to revolutions in thought or beliefs. Theological construction cannot ignore or bypass the actualities of life in Christian community. Theology, like religion, "is as much a way of life as it is a view of life."[56]

An examination of the first three centuries of church history reveals that the entire life of the church served as "the bearer of the tradition".[57] The life, worship, and praxis of the early communities of faith provided the impetus for doctrinal development just as much as polemics and controversies moved them to clarify their beliefs. The connection between liturgical worship and credal development is evident in the intermingling of early confessional materials with hymns and doxologies in the New Testament, e.g., 1 Cor. 15:3–5; Phil. 2:6–11. A seminal Christology is already suggested by the wor-

---

[56] R. J. Schreiter, *Constructing Local Theologies* (Maryknoll: Orbis, 1985), 43.

[57] Lash, *Change*, 39. There is evidently an interdependence between belief and community ethos in the evolving orthodoxy of the patristic church. Hultgren, *Normative*, 21, points to the tendency to emphasize the *confession* side of the relationship at the expense of the *community ethos* dimension. The expansive *koinonia*-web of ecclesiastical bodies, connected by leadership and epistolary interchanges, formed the setting for the formulation of doctrines and creeds. See Rowan Williams, "Does it Make Sense to Speak of Pre-Nicene Orthodoxy?" in Rowan Williams, ed., *The Making of Orthodoxy: Essays in Honour of Henry Chadwick* (Cambridge: Cambridge University Press, 1989), 11–12. The continuity of community life is a much overlooked factor in doctrinal development. J. Pelikan, *Development of Christian Doctrine: Some Historical Prolegomena* (New Haven & London: Yale University Press, 1969), 49, notes that historians of doctrine tend to be drawn more to change in doctrinal development than to continuity. Their preoccupation with doctrinal controversy and theological speculation creates the impression that the development of doctrine is far more erratic and fitful than it has in fact been.

The preservation and transmission of theological traditions are achieved not only through conciliar dialogues, ecumenical statements, and the normal ecclesiastical activities of the gathered community, but through artistic objects as well. Up till the eighth century, Sister Charles Murray argues, art was apparently "the only unifying theological force in the early church." "Artistic Idiom and Doctrinal Development," *Making of Orthodoxy*, 290. Where the content of belief was disputed, the aesthetic creations of the patristic church, by virtue of their allusive character, performed their silent duty of carrying the torch of orthodoxy forward. Art as theological idiom facilitated "the transfer of orthodoxy from one area and milieu and from one age to another in the continuity of community." Ibid., 302. While one may question the ability of artistic creations as adequate vehicles *by themselves* for the preservation and transmission of orthodox beliefs, one cannot deny their role in "the transfer of orthodoxy" when seen alongside the other facets of community life.

ship of Jesus and the prayer invocation of Jesus as *kurios*, a title allusive of the divine name in the OT.[58] A Trinitarian understanding of God developed out of a desire to "glorify God appropriately",[59] given the divine status accorded to Jesus. The law of prayer is the law of believing: *lex orandi, lex credendi*.

Praise within the Christian community is simultaneously retrospective and prospective. Worship recalls what God has done in Christ and anticipates what God will do for all of creation in the consummation. Praise and worship are thus eschatological in character. To participate in the corporate worship of the Church is to be involved in a proleptic prefiguring of the final restoration of the world. The liturgical activities of the church are thus more than just exercises in social cohesion. They are profoundly theological, and it is our contention that they are the theatre in which Christology *from within* tradition is played out.

The intertwining of beliefs and life is again seen in the early practice of catechetical instruction and baptism. Interestingly, catechetical lessons on the basic tenets of Christian beliefs included moral instruction as well (*Didache* 1–6; Justin Martyr, *1 Apol.* 61), indicating that continuity with the tradition of Jesus is a matter of both belief and behaviour. Like beliefs and creeds, rites and rituals are important carriers and transformers of tradition as Gadamer notes,[60] and this is certainly the case with baptism and the eucharist. Baptism

---

[58] Maurice Wiles observes: "The continuing practice of invoking the name of Jesus in worship helped to ensure that when the time came for more precise doctrinal definition of his person it would be in terms which did not fall short of the manner of his address in worship." *The Making of Christian Doctrine: A Study in the Principles of Early Doctrinal Development* (Cambridge: Cambridge University Press, 1967), 65. On the connection between liturgy and doctrinal development in the early church, see: John Barton & John Halliburton, "Story and Liturgy," *Believing in the Church*, 85–94; and Geoffrey Wainwright, *Doxology: The Praise of God in Worship, Doctrine and Life* (New York: Oxford University Press, 1980).

[59] Daniel W. Hardy & David F. Ford, *Praising and Knowing God* (Philadelphia: Westminster, 1985), 59. This doxological characteristic is true also of the confessions of the early ecumenical councils, though this is more apparent of the pre-Chalcedonian councils than in the statement of Chalcedon itself. See Edmund Schlink, "Die Struktur der dogmatischen Aussage als Oekumenisches Problem," *KuD* 3(1957): 251–306, esp. 266. Confessions of faith which exercised a doxological function in liturgical contexts gradually shifted in the fifth century to a regulative role. As Lash notes interestingly, unlike the earlier Nicene and Constantinople creeds, the Chalcedonian creed never made it into liturgy. Lash, *Change*, 50.

[60] "Zur Phänomenologie von Ritual und Sprache," *GW* 8:400–440. Sykes avers: "Communal worship includes the use of rituals which plainly imply doctrines." *Identity*, 267.

provided an occasion for the overt confession of faith in Christ, both through the recitation of the Baptismal Symbol (anticipating perhaps in its substance the later Apostles' Creed) as well as through the symbolic enactment of identification with the death and resurrection of Christ. Baptism is thus Christologically oriented.[61] It grounds the experience of the individual in the once-for-all saving and founding events of community (Rom. 6:3, 10).[62]

The same is true of the eucharistic meal. Participation in the eucharist proclaims Christ's death, resurrection and return, and constitutes a remembrance (*anamnesis*). In the eucharist, believers are taken up into the story of what God has done, is doing, and will do through Christ. This Christological framework undergirded the observance of the Lord's supper which in turn became the means through which the significance of Christ continued to be impressed upon the corporate consciousness of the Church.

Christian community plays a pivotal role in the transmission of tradition or the "corporate memory"of the church. The consciousness effected by the history of Jesus continues to be shaped by participation in the communal life of the church. It is important to maintain, as Thiselton asserts, "that degree of continuity which is necessary for Christian *identity* and more especially for participation in the *patterns of behaviour which have been instituted and prescribed* by those events on which the community itself has been founded."[63] Theological constructions are to be carried out within the tradition-mediating community of faith, and should never be divorced from the practice of Christian piety.[64]

---

[61] See Nils Alstrup Dahl, "Trinitarian Baptismal Creeds and New Testament Christology," *Jesus the Christ: The Historical Origins of Christological Doctrine*, ed. Donald H. Juel (Minneapolis: Fortress, 1991), 165–86; Lars Hartman, "Early Baptism— Early Christology," Abraham J. Malherbe & Wayne Meeks, eds., *The Future of Christology: Essays in Honor of Leander E. Keck* (Minneapolis: Fortress, 1993), 191–201; idem, "'Into the Name of Jesus': A Suggestion concerning the Earliest Meaning of the Phrase," *NTS* 20(1973/4): 432–40; cf. Oscar Cullmann, *Early Christian Worship*, tr. A. Stewart Todd & James B. Torrance (London: SCM, 1953), 25–6.

[62] Thiselton, "Corporate Memory," 63.

[63] Ibid., 64 (emphasis his).

[64] We shall return to this in chapter four when we take up the issue of theological reflection and experience. Cf. Ronald F. Thiemann, "Piety, Narrative, and Christian Identity," *WW* 3(1983): 148–59. Whatever the merits of Newman's reflections on doctrinal development, he is right to emphasize the inseparability of belief and devotion. The unfolding of doctrines is not a purely intellectual theological exercise untouched by matters of piety and morality. On the contrary, doctrines develop in step with the holiness and devotion of the church. There is in Newman a pro-

The notions of "custom", "training", "rules" and "forms of life" in the later Wittgenstein are highly relevant here. Not only are they consonant with Gadamer's positive stance towards tradition,[65] they underscore two points: first, our confession of Christ is always enmeshed within the ongoing stream of life, for only with reference to the latter do words have meaning; and second, we are sensitized to discern the reality of Christ through involvement in ecclesial life. A Christologically rooted "form of life" is both the environ for faith and the basis for new articulations of that faith. Wittgenstein likens inhabiting a linguistic tradition to being perched on a branch.[66] We suggest, it is only from the vantage point of this "branch" (which we "must not saw off") that we are able to do what Wittgenstein invites us to do: to "look and see",[67] to trace the contours of Christology.

As indicated earlier, truth is not only something to be known but also something to be done, and tradition is not only a *habitus* but also a *task*. The process of "traditioning" entails an interpretive "performance of Christian identity",[68] an active re-presenting of what has been given in tradition. Like a symphonic score, the scriptural testimony to Christ is "performed" through participatory engagement in the redemptive work of Christ in the world. Christology as a "performative" utterance commits Christian believers "to ways of understanding towards God and others which transcend the limits of a strictly 'private' or individual world."[69] It is in the context of the ecclesial community's involvement in the multifaceted work of the

---

foundly democratic view of tradition. Tradition is not the preserve of clergy and academics; it resides in the faith of the ordinary faithful in the church. Tradition filters up from the faithful till it becomes a subject for discussion at councils by bishops and theologians. See Pelikan, *Vindication*, 30.

[65] See Wittgenstein, *PI* §5, 23, 143–242; *The Blue and Brown Books* (New York: Harper, 1958), 80. Gadamer's disquisition on game-playing parallels the concept of "language games" in the later Wittgenstein. See Gadamer, "The Phenomenological Movement," *PH*, 130–81. He confesses: "very shortly after I had completed *Truth and Method* in 1960, I had myself begun to read the later Wittgenstein and found there much that had long been familiar to me." "Reflections," *PHG*, 19, cf. 39. See also: P. Christopher Smith, "Gadamer's Hermeneutics and Ordinary Language Philosophy," *Thomist* 43(1979); 299f.

[66] Wittgenstein, *PI* §55.

[67] Wittgenstein, *PI* §66; cf. §122.

[68] Sykes, *Identity*, 265. On this idea of performance of beliefs, see Thiselton, "Corporate Memory," 74; Nicholas Lash, "Performing the Scriptures," in *Theology on the Way to Emmaus* (London: SCM, 1986), 37–46; Frances Young, *The Art of Performance: Towards a Theology of Holy Scripture* (London: Darton, Longman & Todd, 1990).

[69] Thiselton, "Corporate Memory," 75.

Kingdom of God in the world that Christology is forged. In a way
analogous to Gadamer's ethico-phronetic concept of play, Christian
believers, through their participation in the "play" of Christ's redemptive work in the world, are the means by which the latter is actualized and concretized in the world.

The identification of the story of the Church as a continuation of
the story of Jesus in Narrative Theology reinforces our point. As
Loughlin characterizes it: "The story of Christ is not finished. It
includes the stories of all those people who were touched by him,
and of the people touched by them, and so on through the Church's
touching history". The aliveness of Jesus from the dead and his continuing activity in and through his earthly Church ensures that his
story continues. "The Church is shaped by a story that is even now
being told. It is shaped *within* a story that it has also shaped and is
shaping: the story of the body of Christ."[70] The ecclesial locus of
theological reflection and speech, with its strong emphasis on intrasystemic congruence, is, as we shall see, characteristic of "postliberal" theology.

C. *Scriptures as Canon for Christological Interpretation*[71]

That critical investigation of the Bible demonstrates its contingency
can hardly be denied today. Equally incontrovertible is the traditional acknowledgement of Scriptures as the *norma normans non nor-
mata*, the norm or rule that rules but is not itself ruled. However,
affirming both contingency and normativity raises the question as to
whether, and in what sense, we can continue to appeal to the Bible
as canon for Christology, especially when the former is as historically contingent as the latter. We are told that the "scripture principle", along with the "house of authority" to which it belongs, has

---

[70] Loughlin, *Telling*, 86. On the Church as an integral part of our understand-
ing of Christ, see: Macquarrie, *Christ*, 19–22; Frei, "The Church as Christ's Presence,"
Identity, 157–64; G. Lindbeck, "The Story-shaped Church: Exegesis and Theological
Interpretation," in Garrett Green, ed., *Scriptural Authority and Narrative Interpretation*
(Philadelphia: Fortress, 1987), 161–78; John Knox, *The Church and the Reality of Christ*
(New York: Harper & Row, 1962); Peter C. Hodgson, *Jesus—Word and Presence: An
Essay in Christology* (Philadelphia: Fortress, 1971).

[71] I differentiate between "canon of Scriptures" and "Scriptures as canon." The
former refers to the historic ecclesial determination of books which ought to be recognized as belonging to the canon of Scriptures. By the latter, I mean Scriptures
as the Old and New Testaments employed as a norm to determine the legitimacy
of theological construct.

been smashed by the wrecking ball of deconstructive post-Cartesianism.[72] How can Scriptures be simultaneously normative *and* a
subject of negotiation within the ever evolving "play" of tradition?[73]

Just as tradition entails a dialectic of continuity and discontinuity,
we suggest that *Scriptures as transcendental norm and Scriptures as a contingent implicate of tradition are dialectically related.* The relationship between
Scriptures and tradition has been variously described in the history
of Christian thought.[74] We propose a construal which affirms simultaneously (1) the *sola Scriptura* formula of the Reformation, and (2)
the role of tradition in any appeal to Scriptures as norm. In short,
we wish to combine the traditional view of Scriptures as the transcendental and authoritative Word of God and the Gadamerian
emphasis on the role of tradition in grasping the meaning of Scriptures.
The Bible is understood only within tradition, yet paradoxically it
stands over churchly tradition as its judge.[75]

---

[72] See Farley, *Ecclesial Reflection*; cf. Stout, *Flight from Authority*. On the crisis arising from the waning of biblical authority, see W. Pannenberg, "The Crisis of the
Scripture Principle," *BQT* 1:1–14; Fiorenza, "Scriptural Authority," 353–68.

[73] Delwin Brown would not adhere to Scripture as normative even though he
accepts it as a canon for theology. He criticizes conservative theologies for failing
to grasp that canons are themselves negotiable items, and in effect chides them for
their "pious possessiveness". While he understands their fear that allowing for such
fluidity would remove constraints and thereby jeopardize the maintenance of Christian
identity, he nevertheless feels that they are underestimating the power of tradition
to redefine itself through the participation of people in the "play" of tradition. To
him, there is everything to be played for, including the canon of Scripture in the
play of tradition. See *Boundaries*, 127.

[74] A. N. S. Lane, "Scripture, Tradition and Church: An Historical Survey," *VE*
9(1975): 37–55, summarises the various ways of conceiving the relationship between
tradition and scripture since the ancient church into four main categories: (1) the
coincidence view as articulated in Irenaeus and Tertullian, where the apostolic tradition coincides with the content of Scripture; (2) the *supplementary view*, or the "two-
source theory of revelation," prominent in the Middle Ages and represented in
post-Tridentine Catholicism, sees Scripture as insufficient by itself and in need of
supplement by tradition, whether written or unwritten; (3) the *ancillary view* of six-
teenth-century Protestantism in which tradition aids, rather than serves as norm for,
scriptural interpretation; and finally, (4) the *unfolding view*, the modern Roman Catholic
view arising from Newman, regards tradition not as something static but as the
gradual unfolding of the full meaning of the apostolic message. See also Congar,
Tradition; Richard Bauckham, "Tradition in Relation to Scripture and Reason," in
R. Bauckham & B. Drewery, eds., *Scripture, Tradition and Reason: A Study in the Criteria
of Christian Doctrine* (Edinburgh: T&T Clark, 1988), 117–45; R. P. C. Hanson, *Tradition
in the Early Church* (London: SCM, 1962); Maurice Wiles, "The Patristic Appeal to
Tradition," in *Explorations in Theology 4* (London: SCM, 1979), 41–52; Donald F.
Winslow, "Tradition," in Everett Ferguson, ed., *Encyclopedia of Early Christianity*
(Chicago & London: St James Press, 1990), 906–10.

[75] David Tracy's "Scripture in tradition" model seems closest to what we have

This means that the ability of Scriptures to serve as canon for theology is closely tied to Christian tradition and community. While *sola Scriptura* underscores the normative authority and sufficiency of Scriptures, it does not mean that Scriptures are *the* only source or resource for theological reflection, or that they exist and function independent of the ecclesial hermeneutics of tradition.[76] The ecclesial preunderstanding which comes through tradition enables the theological interpreter to understand Scriptures, without which it makes no sense to speak of them as canon. Doctrines are not simply read off from the surface of the biblical text, and the mere citation of scriptural references does not establish or validate a theological position. Hermeneutical judgment is needed when invoking Scriptures as a basis for our Christological confession. The Gospels are not mere collations of brute facts about Christ; they are interpretations of Christ which invite further theological interpretations.

Interpretation is thus presupposed in the appeal to Scriptures as criterion. Before Scriptures can serve as canon, their meaning has to be first ascertained. In this sense, the criteriological identity of Scriptures is hermeneutically established. Doctrines are products of the sustained interaction between a number of elements: the Bible, ecclesiastical tradition, experience, questions raised from within the context of the community of faith, and the form of rationality and discursive argumentation operative at a given time. A scripturally informed Christology is hermeneutically grounded, and is as such rooted in the historicality of tradition.[77]

---

in mind. See his "On Reading the Scriptures Theologically," in Bruce D. Marshall, ed., *Theology and Dialogue: Essays in Conversation with George Lindbeck* (Notre Dame: University of Notre Dame Press, 1990; hereafter *TaD*), 37–38; idem, *The Analogical Imagination: Christian Theology and the Culture of Pluralism* (New York: Crossroad, 1981), 233–339; and Robert M. Grant & David Tracy, *A Short History of the Interpretation of the Bible* (London: SCM, 1984), 174–87. A "Scripture in tradition" approach places a high premium on the intertwining of Scripture and tradition, and is akin, as Tracy notes, to George Lindbeck's intrasystemic emphasis. This will become clear when we examine Postliberalism below.

[76] Anthony N. S. Lane, "*Sola Scriptura?* Making Sense of a Post-Reformation Slogan," in Philip E. Satterthwaite & David F. Wright, eds., *A Pathway into the Holy Scripture* (Grand Rapids: Eerdmans, 1994; hereafter *APHS*), 297–327, argues convincingly that tradition can serve as both resource and source for theology even when one adheres to the sufficiency and authority of Scripture as theological norm. The commitment of the Reformers and the Protestant orthodox to *sola Scriptura* did not preclude their use of tradition as a subordinate norm in theology, even though it is understandable, given the battles they were fighting, that tradition was depicted as ancillary to tradition. See Richard Muller, "sola Scriptura" in *DLGTT*, 284.

[77] See Darrell Jodock's argument that both scriptural study and theological

In one sense, one may speak of scriptural authority and normativity from a wholly functional standpoint, vis-à-vis describing how
the Bible, as a "classic" text, shapes the church's identity and "autho-
rizes" theology.[78] Despite the plurality of genres, emphases, and
expressions in Scriptures, there is sufficient internal coherence there
for them to act as a criterion for theological proposals.[79] The Bible's
message is not so nebulous that any construal is permitted. By being
accorded a place of prominence in the community of faith, Scriptures shape the subjectivity of those labouring within the hermeneutical community. In reading Scriptures and retelling the foundational
story of Jesus Christ, members of the Christian community participate in that ongoing story by becoming characters in that narrative.
As Scriptures are performed or enacted, they effect a salvific form
of life which authenticates their transformative potential as the char-
acter-forming Word of God.[80]

However, explicating the normativity of Scriptures in terms of
their function alone yields only a *de facto* authority. One needs to
move on to consider its status as the inscripturated Word of God
as well. Only then will we secure the *de jure* authority of Scriptures.
The *functional-descriptive* must be joined by the *ontic-prescriptive*. To
merely describe how Scriptures and tradition interrelate only highlights the contingent pole of the dialectic; one needs to grab hold
of the transcendental pole as well. In speaking of Scriptures as both

---

reflection are activities of the community of faith. "The Reciprocity Between Scripture
and Theology: The Role of Scripture in Contemporary Theological Reflection," *Int*
44(1990): 369–82.

[78] On the idea of Scripture as "classic," see Tracy, *Short History*, 153–87; also
idem, *Plurality*; James Barr, *The Bible in the Modern World* (London: SCM, 1973),
118f. On the identity-shaping and transformative function of Scripture, see David
H. Kelsey, *The Uses of Scripture in Recent Theology* (Philadelphia: Fortress, 1975).

[79] From a strictly descriptive standpoint, one may argue for a procedural privileging of Scriptures as regulatory canon for theological reflection and development,
even though one accepts that all constructs (including those which have achieved
canonical status) are in principle subject to negotiation and revision. Since there is
no escaping the necessity of some privileged starting point—even the suggestion that
nothing can be normative is itself a normative suggestion—it is not unreasonable
to accept and begin with Scriptures as the inherited norm for theology. The fact
that Scripture has long been recognized as canon cannot be easily dismissed. Of
course, in itself the longevity of a belief is no guarantee of its legitimacy or reason
for its perpetuity; but neither should it be cavalierly dismissed either. That a canon
is not intrinsically normative does not mean that in practice, it cannot be defended
as a more adequate normative rule than any other norms proffered or available.
On this last point, see Brown, *Boundaries*, 69.

[80] This is forcefully stated by Kelsey, *Uses of Scripture*, who argues that the authority of Scripture consists in its ability to shape identities and transform them.

transcendental and contingent, we are led back to the key issue we grappled with in chapter one, namely the coinherence of the infinite with the finite in an age of historical consciousness. We suggested there that a hermeneutical approach offers a way forward for theology after foundationalism, and recommended a switch of metaphor, from a hierarchical-vertical model to a temporal-horizontal one, where universality or truth is hermeneutically apprehended through the particularity of history. Such an approach, we think, is equally applicable to the issue of scriptural authority. Both Fiorenza and Thiselton have demonstrated the viability of a hermeneutical response to the question of scriptural authority, the former enlists Jauss's reception hermeneutics while the latter appeals to speech-act theory as resource.[81] We shall look at these in turn.

Fiorenza discusses the relative merits of two approaches to the nature and authority of the Scriptures: the *functional* approach of Kelsey and the *canonical* approach of Paul Achtemeier and James Sanders.[82] The first sees the normative value of Scriptures in terms of their function within the Christian communities, while the second looks to the origin of the scriptural texts and their canonical formation to gain insight into their normativeness. Fiorenza combines the two and argues that Scriptures function less as a "classic" (à la Tracy) than as the "constitution of an ongoing community."[83] Scriptures as our primary sources for the confession of Jesus as Messiah constitute the foundational documents for the church, and as such have hermeneutical primacy both for our knowledge of the historical Jesus and his relation to Christology.

Nevertheless, the authority of Scriptures does not rest on a single meaning that is received and then interpreted. Rather, Fiorenza maintains on the basis of Jauss's reception hermeneutics, the meaning of Scriptures "is construed in relation to the integrity of the events and traditions expressed in the Scriptures along with the ongoing process of reception of these interpretations."[84] In other words, the criterio-

---

[81] Fiorenza, "Scriptural Authority"; Anthony C. Thiselton, "Authority and Hermeneutics: Some Proposals for a More Creative Agenda," *APHS*, 107–41. We have already alluded earlier to both reception hermeneutics and Speech-Act theory.

[82] Fiorenza, "Scriptural Authority," 359–63; cf. Paul Achtemeier, *The Inspiration of Scripture: Problems and Proposals* (Philadelphia: Westminster, 1980); James A. Sanders, *From Sacred Story to Sacred Text* (Philadelphia: Fortress, 1987).

[83] Fiorenza, "Scriptural Authority," 363.

[84] Ibid., 367.

logical or "canonical" status of Scriptures is dependent on a dialectic
between Scriptures and tradition/community, and this is diachronically discerned.

Like Fiorenza, Thiselton emphasizes the interpretive interaction
between Scriptures and the ongoing life of Christian communities in
seeking a way out of the "over worn grooves" into which the debate
about scriptural authority has been mired. The polarization between
those who locate authority in the propositions of the Bible and those
who understand it in terms of its function, can be overcome by
attending to insights from hermeneutical theory and the philosophy
of language. The upshot of Thiselton's thesis is that the question of
authority is inextricably tied to the question of interpretation. Appealing
to Berkouwer's assertion that authority is inseparably linked with hermeneutics, i.e., obedient listening to Scriptures, he contends that
scriptural authority consists in the Bible's ability to perform acts of
salvation, liberation, forgiveness, renewal, etc., which affect its readers, and presuppose certain extra-linguistic states of affairs.[85]

He notes the parallels between the debate over Christological
method and that over biblical authority and interpretation. Many of
the conundrums surrounding the "from above" and "from below"
approaches in Christology, he observes, stem from either a Platonic
or Kantian view of reality which conceptualizes perfection and transcendence primarily in spatial imagery (above or below? this or that?
human or divine?). A more profitable approach would be to adopt
a temporal perspective (one which we have taken on board in this
essay). Drawing on Cullmann, Moltmann and Pannenberg,[86] Thiselton situates the debate about biblical authority along a temporal-
eschatological axis, and applies insights from Speech-Act theory to
overcome the putative dichotomy between acknowledging the Bible's
authority as truth-claim and construing its authority in terms of its
function. For an utterance to be authoritative and effective, the identity of the speaker and certain institutional states of affairs are presumed.[87] The authority of Scriptures as the Word of God is thus

---

[85] Thiselton, "Authority and Hermeneutics," 113–6; cf. G. C. Berkouwer, *Studies in Dogmatics: Holy Scripture* (Grand Rapids: Eerdmans, 1975), 105–38.
[86] Oscar Cullmann, *Christ and Time* (London: SCM, 1951); Jürgen Moltmann, *Theology of Hope* (London: SCM, 1967); idem, *The Crucified God: The Cross of Christ as the Foundation and Criticism of Christian Theology* (London: SCM, 1974); Pannenberg, *JGM*.
[87] See Thiselton's application of insights from the Speech-Act theory of J. L.

never abstracted from their performative effectiveness in the Christian community.

Any attempt to set apart the canonical status and function of Scriptures will lead to the diriment of its authority as the normative and transformative Word of God. While the Bible, and for that matter the creeds, serves as canon for the negotiated development of Christology, it is not immune from critical reappraisal insofar as Scripture is hermeneutically appropriated. And since this task is dependent on the givenness of the tradition in which one stands, it is essentially a dialectical undertaking carried out *within* and *with* tradition.

Christ, Church and Scriptures are so inseparably and indispensably webbed, that one may speak of a triune reciprocity between them. The church as the historical community of faith is the locus in which the scripturally constituted Christ is encountered. As Loughlin asserts, "Christ and the Church are understood properly only in the light of Scripture, and Scripture is understood properly only in the light of Christ and the Church."[88] He goes on to explicate the interrelations between them:

> Christ is the rule for the Church's reading of Scripture. He is the norm by which the text is judged. . . . But Christ himself is given in the text; given in the Church's reading or performance of the text. Christ, as the norm of Christian reading, is realised only in the practice of faithful reading. He is not given apart from that for which he is normative. The Church is better able to read Scripture the more the Scripture lives in the Church; the more the Scripture is faithfully read and performed.[89]

Our Christology affects our reading and understanding of Scriptures as much as the ongoing investigation of Scriptures shapes and reshapes our Christology. Such a construal of the hermeneutical relationship between Christ, Scriptures, Church and tradition is integral to a traditionary Christology *from within*.

Austin, J. Searle, D. Evans & Recanati in his "Christology in Luke, Speech-Act Theory, and the Problem of Dualism in Christology after Kant," in Joel B. Green & Max Turner, eds., *Jesus of Nazareth: Lord and Christ: Essays on the Historical Jesus and New Testament Christology* (Grand Rapids: Eerdmans; Carlisle: Paternoster, 1994), 453–72; *NHH*, 283–307.

[88] *Telling*, 113.
[89] Ibid., 119.

D. *Context, Dialogue and Dialogical Transcontextualization*

Our inquiry into the dynamics of a traditionary Christology so far reveals that tradition is both cohesive and open-ended, a given as well as a task. The dialectic between continuity and discontinuity at the heart of the process of traditioning is coterminous with the embodiment and ongoing enactment of the narratival truth of Jesus Christ in the corporate life, worship and praxis of the Christian community. And inasmuch as any Christological formulation must arise from within tradition and be scripturally mediated, it is necessarily hermeneutical in nature. We turn now to explore the ramifications for Christology of Gadamer's notion of dialogue and the inescapable contextuality entailed in hermeneutical understanding.

The Gadamerian view that application is entailed in understanding highlights two related points pertinent to Christological construction: first, the influence of the interpreters' interests and concerns; and two, the impact of the context in which interpretation is undertaken. Personal and contextual considerations mix to form the horizon of the interpreters. We leave till the next chapter the personal, self-involving and experiential dimension, and focus our attention here on the dialogical and contextual nature of Christological reflection.

If Gadamer is right that language "is most in itself not in propositions but in dialogue",[90] then the language of Christology or propositions concerning Christ cannot be understood except within the context of dialogue. Knowledge claims in Gadamer are ineluctably embedded in the dialogue of tradition. As the Christologies of previous generations arose out of past conversations carried out with tradition in answer to questions raised by their contexts, our attempts at articulating a contemporary witness to Christ must therefore take into account not only the dogmatic achievements of the past, but also questions generated from within our historical, political and cultural contexts. Context colours our hermeneutics of tradition, which in turn shapes our Christology.

---

[90] H-G. Gadamer, "Grenzen der Sprache," *Evolution und Sprache: Über Entstehung und Wesen der Sprache, Herrenalber Texte* 66(1985): 98. While we agree in general with Gadamer at this point, it is not necessary, as Gadamer seems to do, to devalue the import of propositions. One may regard propositions as progress reports, which have referential significance even though they are in principle corrigible. It is the interconnectedness of propositions, not individual proposition, that remains fundamental for theology. New things can repair or extend this web of beliefs or propositions without dismantling it.

One thinks for example of the birth of liberation theology within the violent womb of poverty, oppression, and injustice; or the efforts by Christian feminist theologians to punch holes in the asphyxial canopy of patriarchalism; or the attempts by the emergent churches in the so-called Two-Third (non-Western) World to fashion theological responses to questions which are peculiar to their vastly different contexts as well as formulate new ways of confessing Christ.[91] Gadamer's attention to the impact of the interpreter's horizon on understanding means that *all* theological constructs, whether developed in the North-Atlantic West or forged in the churches of Africa, Asia, and Latin America, are contextual. When expressions such as "contextual theology" or "local theologies" are often used to describe non-Western theological output,[92] one needs to be reminded that the Christologies of Aquinas or Barth are just as contextual and local as the Christologies of Pannikar or Sobrino. The contextuality of all theologies means there is no one generic and acultural Theology which is then instantiated in an African theology, a Latin American theology, a black theology, a feminist theology, and so forth.

Having said that, it is equally important that one does not lose sight of the fact that all who are in Christ have dual citizenship: they are humans in the "city of man" and Christians in the "city of God." Not only is their identity defined by the inalienable features of humanity, i.e., gender, ethnicity, nationality, temperament, etc., they are concurrently members of the transhistorical Body of Christ. There is thus a sense in which the doctrinal heritage of the Christian faith, mediated largely (for better or worse) through Western Christianity, is as much a part of who a Christian is as his or her social and cultural identity. Augustine, Anselm, Aquinas, Luther, Calvin are theological ancestors to all Christian theologians insofar as they stand within the trajectory of Christian tradition, whether they hail

---

[91] For a survey of non-Western Christologies, see Priscilla Pope-Levison & John R. Levison, *Jesus in Global Contexts* (Louisville: Westminster/John Knox, 1992); cf. Anton Wessels, *Images of Jesus: How Jesus is Perceived and Portrayed in Non-European Cultures* (Grand Rapids: Eerdmans, 1990).

[92] On theological contextualization, see Schreiter, *Constructing Local Theologies*; Stephen B. Bevans, *Models of Contextual Theology* (Maryknoll: Orbis, 1992). Both Schreiter and Bevans make the point that contextuality is implicit in all theological constructions. See also: Douglas John Hall, "The Meaning of Contextuality in Christian Thought," in *Thinking the Faith: Christian Theology in a North American Context* (Minneapolis: Augsburg, 1989), 69–144.

from Bombay or Birmingham, Osaka or Oxford. While non-Western theologians are justly sensitive to the hegemony of Western (academic) theology in a post-colonial age and wary of simply blessing the status quo, it is a mistake to jettison the entire doctrinal heirloom bequeathed to us by the history of the Christian church. Just as the phenomenology of Gadamer's hermeneutics reminds us that there is no point-zero from which interpretation begins, all attempts to interpret Christ today must be undertaken in dialogue with the Christologies of Christian tradition.

The hermeneutical community of faith, standing within the tradition emanating from the received Christology of church history, enters into dialogue with its situation and context, for it is in this process of dialogue that the truth about Christ is born anew and recontextualized. Dialogue or the conversational to-and-fro of question and answer lies at the heart of the hermeneutical process according to Gadamer. In terms of Christological development, this dialogue takes place at multiple levels: between interpreters and the Scriptures, between current interpreters and interpretations from the past, and between coeval interpreters in ecumenical dialogue. Contextual considerations such as determination of identity and implementation of social change precipitate queries which then become occasions for the expansion of the interpreter's horizon. An ecumenical intersubjectivity involving dialogical exchanges between different communions offers greater balance and, when judiciously implemented, can lead to a sharpening of corporate theological acumen. If safeguarding the truth is our concern, then the check and balance offered by the intersubjectivity of communions in dialogue promises to provide greater protection. If our concern is to see how the truth can be better grasped and embodied in the world today, then surely the sharing of wisdom and theological insights made possible through ecumenical fellowship can only have positive effects.

Yet before re-contextualization through a fusion of horizons can take place, a prior move must first be made. Distantiation and critical reciprocity in dialogue must be allowed to operate before the horizons in question are amalgamated. Such a step is necessary to prevent a premature sublation of distinctions. In other words, before there is recontextualization, there must first be what we call a process of *dialogical transcontextualization*. By dialogical transcontextualization, we refer to the resultant transcending of one's own historical conditionality through a dialogical encounter with that which is in turn

situated and mediated through history.[93] This assumes that historical conditionality is not deterministic and that one is able to experience a self-distantiation whereby one's beliefs and belief-structures
are brought into sharp relief through being confronted by the other
in dialogue.

Such dialogical confrontation allows one to see the radical contingency of one's own ideas, as well as unmasking hitherto hidden
assumptions and practices, without denying the situatedness of the
interpreter. And it is precisely in looking at ourselves through the
eyes of the other—or to change the metaphor, speaking to ourselves
through the voice of the other—that we exemplify a form of reflexivity
which makes possible the transcending of our contingency. In such
a distantiation, we attempt to make transparent our preunderstanding as we reconstruct the implicit structures behind our interpretations. This moment of transcendence, or the attainment of a perspective
external to one's pregiven disposition and perception, is what we
mean by *transcontextualization*; and this takes place in and through
dialogical engagement. To be sure, this transcontextualizing move
does not take place in a non-linguistic realm; Gadamer is correct to
insist on the essential linguisticality of all understanding. Nevertheless,
a distinction must be maintained between linguisticality as the condition which makes thought possible, and linguisticality as the pre-
determinant of the content of what is thought.

Christology can thus be said to be simultaneously traditional (situated) and traditionary—in the sense of moving along the historical
(space-time) trajectory of tradition—when theologians, in dialogue
with the biblical texts, credal formulae and the Christological heritage of church history, and with other differently situated theolo-

---

[93] While the expression, "dialogical transcontextualization" is our way of describing the process of critical "traditioning," the concept itself is theoretically indebted
to, and consonant with, Kögler's "dialogically critical hermeneutics" as laid out in
his *The Power of Dialogue*. Kögler critically appropriates elements from both Gadamer
and Foucault to construct a hermeneutical approach which combines the ineluctabil-
ity of preunderstanding and the possibility of critique. In a dialogical/critical
hermeneutics, Kögler asserts, "we do not attempt interpretively to remove alterity
but rather seek to employ alterity productively toward a *different experience of ourselves*.
This productive use arises from the fact that only in the experience of a foreign or
unfamiliar order do we recognize this *as* a symbolic order. Rather than recasting
this experience in our own terms . . . this *external point of view* can be used to gain
insight into the specific structuration of world pictures. . . . If this succeeds, then
one's own basic assumptions and patterns of meaning can in turn be made distinct
and *reflexively accessible*." 212–3.

gians, are gathered up in a process of transcontextualization so that they are able to see how and in what ways their tradition-mediated belief concerning Christ can undergo transformative development. Such a transformative development of tradition, or what might be called, *critical "traditioning" in Christology*, is accomplished through a process of transcontextualization principally carried out through dialogue. The ongoing task of re-contextualizing Christology is thus contingent on the prior task of dialogical transcontextualization. *Before one contextualizes Christology, one needs to transcontextualize*, to fore-ground the distantiation between the horizon into which one is "thrown," and the horizon of the other, vis-à-vis our dialogue partner(s). Respecting the alterity of that which is foreign is the starting point of new understanding. Such an approach, we maintain, is broadly congruent with the terms of Gadamer's view on understanding as the consequence of a fusion of horizons. The otherness of a divergent voice in dialogue should be recognized and allowed to do its work of critique rather than neutralized through dissolution within an idealist linguistic ontology.

II. *The Regulatory and Referential Nature of Christology*

The emphasis on corporate knowledge and tradition in our case for Christology *from within* echoes in general what may be described as "the ecclesial turn" or "the turn to the Bible" in Postliberalism or the so-called New Yale Theology.[94] George Lindbeck minted the

---

[94] The nomenclature, "New Yale School" is by Brevard S. Childs, "The Canonical Approach and the 'New Yale Theology'," *The New Testament as Canon: An Introduction* (Philadelphia: Fortress, 1984), 541–46. See also: Mark Wallace, "The New Yale Theology," *CSR* 17(1987): 154–70. Members of this loose fraternity are generally affiliated with Yale University and Divinity School. Though distinctive in their own ways, the works of Hans Frei, Garrett Green, Stanley Hauerwas, Paul Holmer, George Hunsinger, David Kelsey, George Lindbeck, Bruce Marshall, William Placher, Ronald Theimann, Kathryn Tanner, etc., demonstrate sufficient family resemblances that their voices may be harmonized in a postliberal chorus, despite reservations raised by a few of these thinkers about being so labeled. For an overview of postliberalism, see: William C. Placher, "Postliberal Theology," in David F. Ford, ed., *The Modern Theologians: An Introduction to Christian Theology in the Twentieth Century*, 2d ed. (Oxford: Blackwell, 1997), 343–56; Delwin Brown and Sheila Greeve Davaney, "Postliberalism," in McGrath, ed., *Modern Christian Thought*, 325–30. See also Kevin J. Vanhoozer, "The Spirit of Understanding: Special Revelation and General Hermeneutics," Roger Lundin, ed., *Disciplining Hermeneutics: Interpretation in Christian Perspective* (Grand Rapids: Eerdmans, 1997), 131–65, for a comparison of the Yale and Chicago schools.

word "postliberal," and his *The Nature of Doctrine* is widely regarded as a manifesto for this approach to theology.[95] The book grew out of his reflection on the way doctrines function in ecclesial traditions through his long years of involvement in ecumenical discussions.[96] A conceptual archaeology of Lindbeck's seminal work unearths the influence of Frei, Barth, Aquinas, Wittgenstein, Kuhn, sociologist Peter Berger, and anthropologist Clifford Geertz. A nonfoundationalist, Lindbeck regards fundamentalists and liberals as both doing theology a disservice by grounding it in something external to itself; in the case of the former, an objectivistic rationality, and in the latter, an alleged universal human experience. He criticizes in particular the theological revisionism of Protestant Liberalism, and recommends a dose of *post*liberal medicine to revitalize theology from the vapid state into which it had fallen.

Lindbeck characterizes postliberalism as a "research program" which seeks to "recover premodern scriptural interpretation in contemporary form."[97] We shall first summarise the principal tenets of this "research program" before moving on to a critical appropriation of its main proposals for our own project. The following are key features of postliberalism: (1) Christianity is best understood as a cultural-linguistic system which provides its adherents the idiom, language, or overarching framework by which to construe reality, express experiences and order life.[98] Following Geertz, Lindbeck argues for a *cultural-linguistic* interpretation of religion in contrast to, firstly, a *cognitive-propositionalist* approach which sees doctrines as informative propositions corresponding to objective realities; and secondly, an *experiential-expressivist* approach which "interprets doctrines as noninformative and nondiscursive symbols of inner feeings, attitudes, or

---

[95] Lindbeck's work has precipitated much discussion; see for instance: essays in *Modern Theology* 4(1988); *Thomist* 49(1985): 393–472; Burnham, ed., *Postmodern Theology*; Marshall, ed., *TaD*; Alister E. McGrath, *The Genesis of Doctrine: A Study in the Foundations of Doctrinal Criticism* (Oxford: Basil Blackwell, 1990), 14–34; Timothy R. Phillips & Dennis L. Okholm, eds., *The Nature of Confession: Evangelicals & Postliberals in Conversation* (Downers Grove: InterVarsity, 1996; hereafter *NoC*); Placher, *Unapologetic*; Tilley, "Incommensurability".

[96] Lindbeck, *Doctrine*, 7–9; Hans Frei notes the importance of the "ecumenical matrix" in Lindbeck's *Nature of Doctrine*. "Epilogue: George Lindbeck and *The Nature of Doctrine*," *TaD*, 277.

[97] Lindbeck in "A Panel Discussion" with Hunsinger, McGrath and Fackre, in *NoC*, 246.

[98] Lindbeck, *Doctrine*, 47–8, 117.

existential orientations." By contrast, a cultural-linguistic model regards doctrines as "communally authoritative rules of discourse, attitude, and action."[99] It assumes that humans are social beings, whose perceptivity is socially and historically formed as they interiorize a particular narratival form of life.

(2) Religions as cultural-linguistic systems are like languages; they are governed by grammatical rules or doctrines. Drawing on the traditional view of doctrines as *regulae fidei*, and in a manner akin to the later Wittgenstein's notion of theology as grammar,[100] Lindbeck advances a *regulative* or *rule theory* of doctrine. A distinction is made between first-order ontological statements, which have specific cognitive content, and second-order statements which serve as a grammar to regulate first-order religious language and praxis.

> Just as grammar by itself affirms nothing either true or false regarding the world in which language is used, but only about language, so theology and doctrine, to the extent that they are second-order activities, assert nothing either true or false about God and his relation to creatures, but only speak about such assertions.[101]

Doctrines are not propositions about ontological realities or symbols expressive of experiences. They are "second-order guidelines for Christian discourse rather than first-order affirmations about the inner being of God or of Jesus Christ."[102] As rules they are second-order statements *concerning* proper belief and behaviour, not first-order statements *of* belief. They are normative for religious communities in that they discipline both belief and action, much like a grammar disciplines the way language functions. If Christianity is a language, then theology is its grammar.

There are many different *doctrines* as first-order propositions, but these are understood as specific instantiations of the idea of *Doctrine* understood as a unified set of grammatical rules.[103] First-order doctrines differ and change, but second-order propositions, insofar as

---

[99] Ibid., 16–18.
[100] Wittgenstein, *PI* §373.
[101] Lindbeck, *Doctrine*, 69.
[102] Ibid., 94.
[103] Brad J. Kallenberg, "Unstuck From Yale: Theological Method After Lindbeck," *SJT* 50(1997): 195, distinguishes between first-order doctrines (lower case "d", plural) and second-order Doctrine (capital "D", singular). See also: Lee C. Barrett, "Theology as Grammar: Regulative Principles or Paradigms and Practices," *MTh* 4(1988): 155–72.

they regulate first-order propositions, remain constant. Lindbeck distinguishes three senses of truth, corresponding to his taxonomy of theories of religion: *propositional* truth, *symbolic* truth, and *categorial* truth (or adequacy).[104] He favours the last of these, and appears to argue for an intrasystemic, rather than an ontological, view of truth.

(3) The canonical Scriptures and the narrative world which they conjure lay at the heart of Christianity as a cultural-linguistic system, forming the basis for an intratextually determined theology. The scriptural texts constitute a distinct semiotic world which is absolutely real to those steeped in it.[105] Lindbeck's insistence on the primacy of the story of the Bible in relation to our stories and the world's stories echoes that of Hans Frei. Just as Frei rejects the subjugation of theology to some definition of reality external to the biblical narratives, Lindbeck maintains that believers do not

> find their stories in the Bible, but rather that they make the story of the Bible their story. . . . Intratextual theology redescribes reality within the scriptural framework rather than translating Scripture into extrascriptural categories. It is the text, so to speak, which absorbs the world, rather than the world the text.[106]

In Wolterstorff's opinion, this reversal of "the direction of conformation" is a deep "guiding metaphor" in Lindbeck's postliberalism.[107] Instead of the world absorbing the text—as in liberalism's redefinition of scriptural truth in categories acceptable to the "cultured despisers" of Christianity,—it is the scriptural text or framework which absorbs the world.

Truth in theology is measured by its consistency with the narratival framework of Scripture, and it functions by constituting a particular form of life.[108] Lindbeck argues strenuously for an inviolable

---

[104] Lindbeck, *Doctrine*, 47f.

[105] Ibid., 117: "For those who are steeped in them [i.e., canonical writings], no world is more real than the ones they create. A scriptural world is thus able to absorb the universe".

[106] *Doctrine*, 118; cf. G. Lindbeck, "Atonement & The Hermeneutics of Intratextual Social Embodiment," *NoC*, 239; Frei, *Eclipse*; idem, *Types of Christian Theology*, ed. George Hunsinger & William C. Placher (New Haven: Yale University Press, 1992). See David E. Demson, *Hans Frei & Karl Barth: Different Ways of Reading Scripture* (Grand Rapids: Eerdmans, 1997).

[107] Nicholas Wolterstorff, *What New Haven and Grand Rapids Have to Say to Each Other*, Stob Lectures of Calvin College and Calvin Theological Seminary (Grand Rapids: Calvin College, 1993), 2.

[108] The truth of a theological statement is "a function of [its] role in constituting

link between religious propositions and patterns of behaviour. The truth or meaningfulness of the assertion, "Christ is Lord," is evident only when accompanied by an appropriate form of life.[109] The truth of Christology is thus contingent on its situatedness in the narratival framework of the Christian story. Theology is intrasystemically determined. The vitality of faith depends on believers mastering and re-learning "the language of Zion".[110] Thus for example the truth about the resurrection of Jesus is determined by its function within the overall narrated identity of Jesus Christ in the biblical texts, not so much by its reference to actual historical events.[111] The rationality of theology is a matter of acquiring a language, or imbibing the particular narrative of God's activity in Christ.

How then should we respond to this postliberal proposal? We will first look at some aspects of Lindbeck's work which we think cohere with our emphasis on the traditionary and ecclesial-performative character of Christology, before moving on to some areas of critique. Three areas where Lindbeck might lend support to our thesis are: (1) his unequivocal rooting of scriptural and theological interpretation in the life and practice of the Christian community,[112] which is a laudable advance over the individualism which tended to mark hermeneutics after Descartes and Kant, a move which would undoubtedly warm the cockles of Gadamer's heart; (2) his refusal to subject theology to alien definitional categories or rules,[113] recognizing that the voice of theology has as much right to be heard and serve a paradigmatic role as any other in the cacophonous pluralism of postmodernity; and (3) his unapologetic commitment to the primacy and

---

a form of life." Lindbeck, *Doctrine*, 65. On this, his view is akin to that of D. Z. Phillips who characterizes religious beliefs ostensibly as (Wittgensteinian) language-games. See Phillips, "Religious Beliefs and Language Games," *Faith and Philosophical Enquiry* (London: Routledge and Kegan Paul, 1970), 77–110.

[109] See Bruce D. Marshall's explication of Lindbeck's view of truth in "Aquinas as Postliberal Theologian," *Thomist* 53(1989): 353–402; and Lindbeck's "Response to Bruce Marshall," in the same issue, 403–6.

[110] G. Lindbeck, "The Church's Mission in a Postmodern Culture," Burnham, ed., *Postmodern Theology*, 55.

[111] See Frei, *Eclipse*, 315.

[112] Lindbeck, "Atonement," 225, advocates a return to the way premodern Christians read the Bible, and argues for the "priority of practice". He writes: "theory that is relevant to practice is not first learned and then applied, but rather is chiefly useful as part of an ongoing process of guarding against and correcting errors while we are engaged in practice."

[113] See John Milbank, *Theology and Social Theory: Beyond Secular Reason* (Oxford: Blackwell, 1990); Placher, *Unapologetic*.

metanarrativity of the Scriptural framework, which provides the historical backdrop of a narrational continuity for Christological interpretation. Thus for instance, John the Baptist's exclamation, "Behold the Lamb of God!" (Jn. 1:29), is meaningful only when appraised against the levitical sacrificial system of Israel instituted at Sinai. This confession assumes the continuity of that grand-narrative of God's relation to his world which joins the First (Old) and Second (New) Testaments.

Nevertheless, there are ambiguous and questionable elements in Lindbeck which invite critique. The main issue that concerns us is whether Christology should be construed merely as a cultural-linguistic construct which gives identity to Christian communities and regulates their discourse and behaviour. In other words, does an emphasis on the traditionality of Christology mean that its truthfulness is understood primarily (and only?) at the level of intrasystemic coherence? In what sense then can we speak of Christology as a truth-claim? We wish to argue that it is a false dilemma to force a choice between doctrines as regulatory and doctrines as referential of reality. *Intrasystemic coherence and extrasystemic correspondence coalesce in Christology*. We shall unpack this by way of a critical response to Lindbeck's proposals.

Postliberal intratextualism has been criticized for being antirealist and fideistic, and a cultural-linguistic approach to Christian doctrine for promoting (unwittingly?) a totalitarianism of tradition, foreclosing the possibility of a prophetic critique, and consigning theology to an intellectual ghetto.[114] The great reservation about a rule-theory of doctrine is that its self-referentiality is inherently relativistic. At this point, we are greeted by a sense of déjà vu, for the worries engendered by Lindbeck's proposals seem to be of the same genus as those raised in our earlier discussions on incommensurability and the possibility of critique in tradition. Accordingly, the (meta)critique

---

[114] Lindbeck seems to have anticipated this criticism and deals with it in *Doctrine*, 128f, though obviously not to the satisfaction of his detractors. See e.g., Tilley, "Incommensurability"; Mark Corner's review of Lindbeck's *Nature of Doctrine* in *MTh* 3(1986): 110–13; Michael Root, "Truth, Relativism and Postliberal Theology," *Dialog* 25(1986): 175–80; Charles M. Wood's and Timothy P. Jackson's ("Against Grammar") reviews of Lindbeck's *The Nature of Doctrine* in "The Nature of Doctrine: Religion and Theology in a Postliberal Age," *RSR* 11(1985): 235–45; James F. Gustafson, "The Sectarian Temptation: Reflections on Theology, the Church, and the University," *PCTS* 40(1985): 83–94.

of Apel, Habermas and Kögler which we brought to bear on the socio-pragmatic side of Gadamer and Kuhn's thesis of incommensurability, are equally applicable to the perceived absolutization of intratextuality in Lindbeck. In addition to these, the following overlapping comments may be made in the hope of surmounting the false dichotomy between doctrine as intrasystemic rule and doctrine as extrasystemic reference:

(1) *The relationship between truth statements as intrasystemically coherent and pragmatic on the one hand, and truth statements as ontological on the other, is ambiguous in Lindbeck.* The general impression is that the latter, though affirmed, tend nevertheless to be eclipsed by the former. Mark Wallace observes that Lindbeck, in speaking of the truth of a statement in terms of its function within a semiotic system rather than its referentiality to extra-systemic reality, has confused "notions of truth and reference in theological language with notions of meaning and use."[115] To say that the Bible absorbs the world and not the other way round already assumes that something can be known about that world. Wallace writes:

> If we say that the world outside the biblical texts *should* conform to the biblical world, then we imply that the outside world *can* in fact do this. But if we mean that the external world *can* conform to the Bible's world, then we must assume that our language does, in some sense, *tell us something about the external world as such*, namely, that it is that reality which can be molded and shaped by the biblical view of things. If this is the case ... then we do operate with some sort of realist assumption about the world outside the Bible because we are claiming that it should and can conform to our biblical world.[116]

Ironically, Hensley makes the same point in defending Lindbeck against the charge of antirealism. In differentiating between "text"

---

[115] Mark Wallace, *The Second Naiveté: Barth, Ricoeur, and the New Yale Theology* (Macon: Mercer University Press, 1990), 106. Wallace appeals to both Wittgenstein and Putnam who argue that language use depends on certain extralinguistic states of affairs. See Wittgenstein, *PI* §7, 19; H. Putnam, *Meaning and the Moral Sciences* (London: Routledge & Kegan Paul, 1978). A similar critique is found in Colman E. O'Neill, "The Rule Theory of Doctrine and Propositional Truth," *The Thomist* 49(1985): 417–42.

[116] Wallace, *Second Naiveté*, 107 (emphasis his). Note that this line of argument is similar to the one we made in chapter two in response to Kuhnian incommensurability, with regard to one's capability of transcending one's paradigm and apprehending another before one can render the verdict that the paradigms concerned are incommensurable.

and "world," Hensley argues, Lindbeck shows that he is not denying the existence of an ontologically real world distinct from the
text.[117] In the same vein, Loughlin, *pace* Wallace, points to statements
by Lindbeck which apparently indicate that a cultural-linguistic approach to religious truth and meaning need not entail a denial of
ontological referentiality. Lindbeck states quite unequivocally that
doctrines as second-order propositions can function symbolically as
first-order propositions:

> There is nothing in the cultural-linguistic approach that requires the
> rejection (or acceptance) of the epistemological realism and corre-
> spondence theory of truth which, according to most of the theologi-
> cal tradition, is implicit in the conviction of believers that when they
> rightly use a sentence such as "Christ is Lord" they are uttering a
> first-order proposition.[118]

Again, he seems to allow for a certain ontological correspondence
when he says that doctrines function grammatically only because
they *as a whole* do conform to ultimate reality:

> There is ... a sense in which truth as correspondence can retain its
> significance even for a religion whose truth is primarily categorial rather
> than propositional. A religion thought of as comparable to a cultural
> system, as a set of language games correlated with a form of life, may
> *as a whole* correspond or not correspond to what a theist calls God's
> being and will. As actually lived, a religion may be pictured as *a sin-
> gle gigantic proposition*. It is a true proposition to the extent that its objec-
> tivities are interiorized and exercised by groups and individuals in such
> a way as to *conform them in some measure in the various dimensions of their
> existence to the ultimate reality* and goodness that lies at the heart of things.[119]

Be that as it may, the ambivalence in his designation of doctrines
as (primarily?) second-order, and (sometimes?) first-order propositions funds the impression that his sympathies rest with antirealism.[120]

---

[117] Jeffrey Hensley, "Are Postliberals Necessarily Antirealists? Reexamining the
Metaphysics of Lindbeck's Postliberal Theology," *NoC*, 76. Like Hensley, Placher,
"Postliberalism," 351, considers it a "misinterpretation" to pin the relativist label
on Lindbeck, even though he concedes that it is easy to do so. Cf. Demson, *Hans
Frei and Karl Barth*, 62–67.
[118] *Doctrine*, 68–9, cf. 80; also Loughlin, *Telling*, 158–9; Hensley, "Antirealists," 79.
[119] *Doctrine*, 51 (emphasis added).
[120] Apart from Hensley's essay on Lindbeck's view of truth, see also: Marshall,
"Aquinas as Postliberal Theologian," and Lindbeck's response that Marshall has
captured accurately his position, 403–6; also Bruce D. Marshall, "Absorbing the
World: Christianity and the Universe of Truths," *TaD*, 69–102; cf. idem, "'We

One is not sure how to reconcile his attempt to construe religion as "a single gigantic proposition" which corresponds to reality, with his assertion that religion is like a language.[121] Does adding up all the grammatical rules of a language somehow allow one to do what he himself says cannot be done, namely cross the dividing wall between *how* something should be said (grammar) and *what* is being said (content)?

Despite his effort to clear a space for ontological truth and correspondence, it is not clear if he succeeds in doing so. His contention that a cultural-linguistic approach "is open to the possibility that different religions and/or philosophies may have incommensurable notions of truth" and that there is "no common framework"[122] by which to compare religions, makes it difficult to see how his model can be hospitable to a realist alethiology. Moreover, while Lindbeck wants to say that there is ontological truth in doctrinal statements, he "makes *contextual* and *performative* aspects essential requirements to the *ontological* truth of statements."[123] By so qualifying it, he effectively redefines what ontological referentiality means. His overtures to a correspondence theory of truth notwithstanding, it seems that the weight of his arguments rests primarily on a pragmatic-coherence theory of truth.

(2) Related to the above, we suggest that *the distinction between doctrines as first-order and second-order propositions cannot be drawn too sharply. Religious language is both assertional and performative.* While Lindbeck allows doctrines to function symbolically as a first-order proposition,[124] as

---

Shall Bear the Image of the Man of Heaven': Theology and the Concept of Truth," *MTh* 11(1995): 93–117.

[121] See Jay Wesley Richards, "Truth and Meaning in George Lindbeck's *The Nature of Doctrine*," *RelS* 33(1997): 37–8.

[122] Lindbeck, *Doctrine*, 49.

[123] Richards, "Truth and Meaning," 38, cf. 43. Lindbeck, *Doctrine*, 64–65, avers: "An intrasystemically true statement ... is ontologically true if it is a part of a system that is itself categorically true (adequate)." Kenneth Surin, "'Many Religions and the One True Faith': An Examination of Lindbeck's Chapter Three," *MTh* 2(1988): 187–209, notes that Lindbeck appears to want to combine elements of correspondence, coherence and pragmatic theories of truth. Lindbeck's work may be described as an attempt to tread a middle path between the objectivism of a cognitive-propositionalist model and the relativism of an experiential-expressivist model. In this, it may be regarded as an instantiation of the larger conflict between realism and pragmatism. In Jackson's view, he pleases neither the realist nor the pragmatist. "Against Grammar," 242.

[124] Lindbeck, *Doctrine*, 80.

in the language of worship, doctrines *qua* doctrines must be seen as second-order statements. How this differentiation actually works is far from clear, and one wonders what its cash-value really is. Presumably when God is worshipped as Triune and praised for sending his Son in the Incarnation in worship, we are making first-order truth statements. But does changing the location, say to a theology classroom, suddenly make these same statements second-order propositions, effective as rules but ontologically vacuous? Does this not turn one into a Bultmannian schizophrenic who is kerygmatically assertorial in the pulpit but a demythologizer in the lecture hall?

In Lindbeck's rule-theory of doctrine, the Nicene and Chalcedonian creeds do not make truth-claims or positive propositional *assertions* about extralinguistic realities. They are *rules* or *procedures* which discipline speech about God and Christ. The rejection of a referential theory of meaning is not new—Lindbeck takes his cue here from the semiotic theorizing of post-positivism. Neither is the observation that doctrines function as rules; what is novel is that their function is not dependent on first-order reference.[125] Alluding to Austin's speech-act theory, Lindbeck regards the confessing of the creeds a performative utterance, a case of "performatory" language use[126] which brings about certain effects in the lives of their adherents.

Now it is undoubtedly correct to say, after the later Wittgenstein and Austin, that language use cannot be confined to just ostensive referencing. There are clear instances, as Austin has shown, when language is used performatively, as in, "I hereby baptise you . . .", or "I do" in a wedding ceremony. Yet in saying that religious language does *more than* make assertions, and often functions performatively, it does not follow that it cannot have an ostensive referent. While Lindbeck rightly points to the incongruity of the crusader's battle cry, "*Christus est Dominus*" when used to authorize the cleaving of the infidel's skull,[127] he commits a categoric mistake by making the truth (or falsity) of the confession hostage to its *use*. He seems to understand truth only in terms of an intrasystemic congruence between belief and practice, making it inimical, if not antithetical, to ontological truthfulness. So while damaging the skull of an infidel is incompatible with the confession, "Jesus is Lord," the truth of the latter is not established by or dependent on it.

---

[125] Stephen Williams, "Lindbeck's Regulative Christology," *MTh* 4(1988): 174.
[126] Lindbeck, *Doctrine*, 65.
[127] Ibid., 64.

Commenting on Lindbeck's use of this illustration, Charles Wood offers two alternate ways of reading and responding to the problem which are preferable to Lindbeck's strategy: (i) the crusader's utterance is false because he is asserting an ontologically false proposition. Judging by what he means by *Dominus*, Christ is not this sort of Lord; (ii) the crusader's utterance is true, but he is making an improper use of it or drawing wrong implications from it. Christ is in fact Lord, despite the crusader's reprehensible action. A distinction is thus made between *meaning* and *use*, one which Lindbeck is reluctant to make. In Wood's opinion, to say as Lindbeck does, that "intrasystemic truth" is "a *necessary* condition of ontological truth gives a religion an odd sort of veto power over assertions".[128]

Contrary to Lindbeck, Richards argues that creeds are not performative utterances but are more accurately "propositional attitude statements."[129] He questions Lindbeck's suggestion that the theologians who crafted the Nicaenum and the Chalcedonian formulae were setting out second-order rules for belief rather than making assertions about God and Christ.[130] Not only is this counter-intuitive to how one would normally understand the creeds, i.e., as making extralinguistic truth-claims, it is difficult to abstract rules from cognitive content. Rules are invariably parasitic on particular propositions. Richards asserts:

> It would be confounding for someone to insist on the rule that *We should ascribe to Christ all the human and divine attributes we can*, but blush at the assertion that *Jesus is fully human and fully divine*. Of course, if we believe this latter claim is true, it would probably inspire such rules as the one we mentioned. But belief in the truth of some proposition *precedes* normative rules like this one; such rules make little sense apart from a willingness to assent to the truth of certain propositions which inspire them. Doctrines may function as rules, but they are clearly not primarily rules, and still less can they be reduced to rules.[131]

It would seem that Lindbeck is too quick to dismiss the cognitive and referential capability of propositions. It is not necessary to polarize

[128] "Nature of Doctrine," 237.
[129] Richards, "Truth and Meaning," 46, 48–53.
[130] Ibid., 47, 50; cf. Lindbeck, *Doctrine*, 94. Williams, "Regulative Christology," criticizes Lindbeck's interpretation of the Nicaenum.
[131] Richards, "Truth and Meaning," 49; cf. Barrett, "Theology as Grammar," points to the difficulties involved in trying to isolate rules from proposition or cognitive content, and argues against too sharp a distinction between doctrines as second-order regulative principles and first-order truth-claims.

between language-reference and language-use. Richards rightly asks: "what if one of the *uses* of language is to make reference to things that are extra-linguistic?"[132]

Lindbeck's distinction between first-order religion and second-order theological reflection is too sharp, and does not "do justice to first-order involvement of the mind in relating to God."[133] Perhaps we may ask: which comes first? Is a doctrine true because it regulates, or does it regulate because it is true? What gives a doctrine its power to shape lives and define behaviour? We contend that when a belief is recognized as reflecting what is there in reality, it has greater regulatory force than the argument that the doctrine is right because it works. Christology regulates because it makes ontological claims, however flawed and imperfect its extralinguistic referentiality may be.

(3) *Postliberalism assumes the givenness and validity of Christianity as a semiotic system, but fails to explain (a) how this particular cultural-linguistic phenomenon came to be binding, and (b) why it is preferable to other semiotic systems.* It is not enough to analyse how the confession "Jesus is Lord" governs the belief and action of believers; one has to ask why this claim came to be in the first place. The question of history refuses to be nudged aside by the question of use or intrasystemic function. According to Lindbeck, three "regulative principles" were at work historically in the formation of Trinitarian and Christological affirmations:

> First, there is the monotheistic principle: there is only one God, the God of Abraham, Isaac, Jacob, and Jesus. Second, there is the principle of historical specificity: the stories of Jesus refer to a genuine human being ... Third, there is the principle of ... Christological maximalism: every possible importance is to be ascribed to Jesus that is not inconsistent with the first rules.[134]

---

[132] Richards, "Truth and Meaning," 52. In his *Genesis of Doctrine*, 16–20, and "An Evangelical Evaluation of Postliberalism," *NoC*, 29–30, McGrath thinks that Lindbeck's portrayal of the cognitive-propositional approach does not do justice to the historical and linguistic sophistication of cognitive approaches to doctrines. Doctrines do not need to be *purely* cognitive for them to *truly* convey cognitive content. Cf. J. Kellenberger, *The Cognitivity of Religion: Three Perspectives* (Berkeley & Los Angeles: University of California Press, 1985). Along the same line, Janet Martin Soskice, *Metaphor and Religious Language* (Oxford: Clarendon, 1985), 150, argues in her defence of theological realism against an empiricist and an idealistic view of religious language, that it is not conceptually incredulous to make metaphysical claims even though the language used is metaphoric and rooted in a particular linguistic tradition of investigation. The contextuality of reference in no way deprives it of its referential status.

[133] David F. Ford's review of *The Nature of Doctrine*, in *JTS* 37(1986): 281.

[134] *Doctrine*, 94.

Apart from asking how one decides what constitutes a regulative principle, one still needs to enquire into the historical grounding for these proposed principles. What made Israel believe in one God when the prevailing culture was thoroughly polytheistic? Why was Jesus "maximalized" and not someone else?

What prompted the lavishing of high esteem upon Jesus? It is surely not enough to say that these are simply historical accidents. McGrath and Jackson are right to ask: Why Jesus? Why this particular confession? Why the Bible?[135] Not only is there insufficient attention to the genesis of Christology, the ongoing discriminatory mediation and critical reception of doctrinal traditions in history are conspicuous by their absence as well.

Moreover, the three mentioned rules are far from "self-evident." Their equivocality makes it difficult to see how they play a regulative function. What it means to ascribe "every possible importance" to Jesus depends on how the interpreter defines "importance." As David S. Cunningham in his friendly critique points out, more often than not, this is, in effect, "to make Jesus more like whatever it is that we already believe."[136] The language in which supposedly theological rules are expressed is equivocal and open to different interpretations. The ability of terms such as *monotheism, historical existence,* and *importance* to function as rules is therefore questionable since their meaning are themselves in dispute.[137] Insofar as they are expressed in language, they are necessarily equivocal and in need of interpretation. This is ironic given Lindbeck's espousal of a cultural-*linguistic* theory of religion.

(4) *The ambiguous relationship between the intratextual biblical "text" and the extratextual "world" in Lindbeck's reversal of "the direction of conformation" does not do justice (a) to the interpenetrating relation between them, and*

---

[135] Alister E. McGrath, "An Evangelical Evaluation of Postliberalism," *NoC*, 39–41; idem, *Genesis of Doctrine*, 30–33, writes: "The Christian idiom cannot simply be taken as 'given': it must be interrogated concerning its historical and theological credentials. . . . [T]he question of the *genesis* of the Christian language becomes significant. What brought it into being? The Christian idiom is not a perennial feature of the intellectual landscape: it came into being, and developed within history." Jackson, "Against Grammar," 241: "even if religions are thought to be akin to idioms or cultures . . . one must still be able to explain *why* this particular confession is embraced rather than that."

[136] *Faithful Persuasion: In Aid of a Rhetoric of Christian Theology* (Notre Dame & London: University of Notre Dame, 1990–91), 210.

[137] Ibid., 211.

*(b) the dialectic between intra-traditional fidelity and extra-traditional responsi-
bility.* Lindbeck's strong intra-traditional emphasis makes him susceptible to the same Habermasian criticism of Gadamer, namely a
failure to take into account the impact of power and interest on the
shape of our interpretation. In Cunningham's opinion, he fails to
grapple with *"the politics of doctrine"*, for the "force of a doctrinal
rule ... depends largely on the political and ethical authority under
which it is invoked."[138] Attention ought therefore to be given to the
connections between, on the one hand, *what* is formulated and *how*
it is being formulated, and, on the other hand, the extra-systemic
context in which this is done.

Miroslav Volf offers a sustained argument against the apparent
segregation of text and world into discrete compartments in Lindbeck,
and argues that "we need more complex ways of relating the 'world'
and the 'text' than the dichotomy between conforming the text to
the world (liberal translation) and conforming the world to the text
(postliberal absorption)".[139] The "scriptural world" of the community
of faith is not an ahistorical environ into which one may step and
from which one may absorb the world.[140] Interpretation is needed
to access this world. And this in turn demands attention to the specific historical-cultural context of interpretation. Lindbeck underscores
the impact of the text on the world, but does not seem to reckon
with the effect of the world on our construal of the text. The fact
is, intratextuality and extratextuality overlap and intersect. Traditionality
and contextuality intertwine; hermeneutical historicality means "inhabiting" simultaneously a scripture-shaped tradition *and* a specific
cultural context. Theologians are denizens of two worlds: the world
of Scripture and the everyday world.

Lindbeck seems to presume "a normality, a stability, of a religious
framework, independent of its actual instantiations in multiple cultural contexts."[141] He gives the impression that Christianity as a cultural-linguistic system is uniformly the same, despite the manifest
diachronic pluralism of its instantiations in history and the synchronic

---

[138] Ibid.
[139] "Theology, Meaning & Power: A Conversation with George Lindbeck on
Theology & the Nature of Christian Difference," *NoC*, 47.
[140] Volf asks: "If I am supposed to be located in a Christian 'cultural-linguistic
system,' where is that 'system' itself located?" Ibid., 54.
[141] Tilley, "Incommensurability," 96.

differentiation of social locations in which it is expressed. Here we think our historical-trajectorial developmental model which takes into account the varied receptions of a doctrine in history has an advantage over a monolithic understanding of a seemingly single and stable Christian semiotic system.

Postliberalism rightly challenges attempts to translate the uniqueness of the Christ-event into some ethical principle or reduce it to an instantiation of a generic religious experience. But in its zeal to preserve the integrity of the text and the irreducible narratival identity of Jesus, it risks dissolving the reality of Christ into "an irreplaceable chain of religious intersignifications."[142] While Jesus Christ is encountered in the narrative of Scriptures as these are embodied and proclaimed in the ecclesial community, the semiotic system is not alone in mediating Christ. It is part of a network of factors which includes nonsemiotic elements like personal experiences, contextual issues, and the work of the Holy Spirit. Textual and non-textual components interact within this skein of influences on theological construction.

What the Church does in discharging its extra-textual and "worldly" responsibility as God's "unworldly" people, has as much an effect on how it understands the truth of Scripture as its intratextual encounter with the scriptural narratives of Jesus has on determining what it should do in the world and how it should behave. This is what we mean by intratraditional fidelity and extratraditional responsibility. Volf depicts the "reversal of the direction of conformation" in terms of a dialectic between intratextuality and extratextuality, and asserts:

> The reversal takes place not in that we inhabit the texts in order to absorb the world, but in that we let the story, lived out in the communities of believers, shape our culturally situated selves . . . so that we in turn, as inhabitants of our cultures, can embody "Christian difference" and insert it wherever needed and whenever possible. The goal here is not to situate symbolically the extratextual realities within the Christian semiotic system, but to insert the Christian difference into the extra-textual realities by practicing the fine and methodologically nonspecifiable art of accepting, transforming, subverting or replacing from within various aspects of the cultures we inhabit.[143]

---

[142] Volf, "Theology," 56.
[143] Ibid., 62–63.

(5) Finally, *one wonders if Lindbeck's dichotomous polarity between intratextual and extratextual, and his tacit reliance on a social-scientific interpretive structure, do not in effect domesticate and constrict the present activity of the Holy Spirit and lead to an enervation of the transformative power of spiritual experiences.* In his desire to steer clear of the experiential-expressivist model of liberalism, Lindbeck sublimates tradition over experience, even though theoretically, tradition (cultural-linguistic system) and experience are supposed to be dialectically related.[144] Which prompts one to ask: what room is there for the *experience* of the present activity of God in the Holy Spirit? Are the Spirit's "activities" merely mythic equivalents for social-scientific permutations within a cultural-linguistic system? Does one need to dismiss the possibility of the experience of the transcendent God just because experience is invariably embedded in a cultural-linguistical system?

Stephen L. Stell pointedly observes that the Holy Spirit has "a logically odd existence within Lindbeck's program." Lindbeck, Stell continues, boldly identifies the reality and work of the Spirit with a particular cultural-linguistic reality, and does not clarify how the Spirit is distinct from the Christian semiotic system.[145] By ignoring the interrelations between "inside" and "outside", and by subsuming experience under tradition, Lindbeck does not consider the way in which a vital experience of the Spirit "must concomitantly reshape one's cultural-linguistic tradition, thereby challenging hermeneutical and theological presuppositions embedded within one's theoretical framework."[146]

What is absent in Lindbeck is precisely what is needed, namely a way to integrate traditionality and the alterous newness and critique which present spiritual experiences bring. In other words, how can experience be, on the one hand, intrasystemically conditioned, and, on the other, a conditioning factor in shaping the Christian semiotic system? The robust intra-traditional bias of Lindbeck is not unlike Gadamer's prejudice in favour of prejudice in interpretation.

---

[144] Lindbeck is not unaware that religion and (extra-religious, extra-textual, culturally mediated) experience condition each other. *Doctrine*, 33. Yet he seems to regard the intratextual scriptural world of the Christian community as capable of interpreting extratextual realities, but not itself an interpreted phenomenon. Cf. Volf, "Theology," 51.

[145] Stephen L. Stell, "Hermeneutics in Theology and the Theology of Hermeneutics: Beyond Lindbeck and Tracy," *JAAR* 61(1993): 691f; cf. Lindbeck, *Doctrine*, 100.

[146] Stell, "Hermeneutics," 693.

Our earlier review of Kögler's critique of Gadamer is equally relevant here. Gadamer's tendency to sublate individuality within a strong linguistic ontology parallels the apparent submersion of individual experience within the overpowering primacy and priority of the cultural-linguistic system in Lindbeck. Kögler calls for the integrity of individuality to be respected in the interpretive process, and seeks to factor in the contribution of the individual in the emergence of hermeneutical meaning. That call, we maintain, applies *mutatis mutandis* to Lindbeck as well. Only then will we fully appreciate the dynamism of a traditionary Christology. We shall examine this reciprocity between experience and tradition in the next chapter. The theological constructs of tradition, we contend in summation, are not only a regulatory ascesis for communal reflection and behaviour, but also ostensibly referential of extrasystemic and extralinguistic (transcendental) realities.

We have sought in this chapter to explore the dynamics of a traditionary Christology in view of Gadamer's hermeneutical reflections. We argued for a non-positivistic view of tradition, and maintained that the dialectic of continuity and discontinuity inherent in tradition makes it both a given and a task. Gadamer's Heideggerian view of truth as disclosure and the portrayal of tradition as a retrospectively discerned trajectory formed our analysis of the dialectic of constancy and openness in tradition. Ecclesial life and praxis, we suggested, are the dynamo for an animated tradition, while the Scriptures provide criteriological guidance to the dialogical and contextual development of Christology. Lindbeck's postliberalism was revisited as a foil for our contention that Christology as a doctrine must be understood both descriptively as a regulative principle and prescriptively as an assertion about reality. Our case for a Christology "from within" has so far been focussed on the corporate and ecclesial level. In the next chapter, we shall look at the personal and experiential dimension involved in hermeneutical theologization.

CHAPTER FOUR

A CHRISTOLOGY FROM WITHIN—EXPERIENCE: TOWARD A CHRISTOLOGY OF THE HEART

The formulation of Christology takes place along that bridge of tradition which connects the living community of faith today to the genesis of Christianity in the history of Jesus Christ. Gadamer and his rehabilitation of the authority of tradition framed our attempt in the previous chapter to explore the dynamics of Christology along the axis or trajectory of tradition. It is our contention that only by attending to the historical, contextual and ecclesial situatedness of theological reflection are we able to fulfill the purpose outlined above, and to transcend the "timeless" subject-object dualism of Cartesianism which has hugely influenced the shape of theology since the Enlightenment.

While the Gadamerian emphasis on tradition and the positive function of prejudice in understanding is a needed corrective to an atomistic individualism in theological hermeneutics, one must not swing with the proverbial pendulum to the other extreme, where the element of creative imagination and individual contribution is eclipsed. For this reason, we wish to argue that Christology *from within* should be understood in two senses: first in the sense of *from within tradition*, and second, *from within* in the sense of the inner *experience* of the theological interpreter as this emerges in terms of his or her public stance. It is hoped that this will strike a balance between the traditionary and the experiential in theological reflection. A reciprocity of hermeneutical disciplining exists between the *sensus communis* of tradition and the idiosyncratic interpretive perspective of individuals. It should be emphasized at the outset that by experience, we do not mean a mere interiority or psychological state. As we shall demonstrate below, the experiential is invariably intersubjectively determined and dependent on a conceptual framework.

We shall explore in this chapter the experiential dimension entailed in theological construction and examine the dialectic between tradition and experience in Christology. We will argue that Christian tradition as the horizon of theological understanding lives and expands through the imaginative contribution or authorship of the individual theologian, for whom Christ is experientially encountered. Christology is truly *from within* when the effectivity of history in tradition and the affectivity of faith in experience are conjoined.

Speech of subjectivity and experience in Christology invariably brings to mind Friedrich E. D. Schleiermacher (1768–1834), who has been described as the father of modern theology and modern hermeneutics. Inasmuch as Schleiermacher has made distinctive contributions in hermeneutics, Christology and theological method, particularly in the way he correlates experience and theological formulation, he is immensely suited as a dialogue partner for our project. This chapter will: (1) examine his hermeneutics before tracing the contours of his theology, specifically his reinterpretation of Chalcedonian Christology; (2) assess critically the viability of his theological method en route to arguing that a dialectical relationship exists between the personal and experiential on the one hand and the communal and traditional on the other. We hope to show that Christological confession is a self-involving undertaking which entails the interpenetration of the inward dimension of faith and the outward dimension of cultural-linguistic ecclesiality. We maintain that experience is necessarily traditioned, and that tradition must be experienced, if it is to do its work of shaping individual and communal consciousness.

I. *Friedrich Schleiermacher's Hermeneutical Christology*

Schleiermacher is "a phenomenon of church history" (Gerrish) who founded not so much a school as a whole epoch in theology (Barth).[1] Besides being a theological author of note (having written on virtually every branch of theological studies with the exception of the OT) he was also a conscientious preacher, churchman, apologist, prolific letter-writer, translator and theology professor. To understand his thoughts, one must first situate him within his historical

---

[1] B. A. Gerrish, "Schleiermacher and the Reformation: A Question of Doctrinal Development" in *Old Protestantism*, 179–95; Karl Barth, *Protestant Theology in the Nineteenth Century* (Valley Forge: Judson Press, 1973), 425. C. W. Christian observes: "theology since his day sometimes seems to be little more than a series of footnotes on Schleiermacher." *Friedrich Schleiermacher* (Waco: Word, 1979), 13. "[T]he whole tree of the 19th and 20th centuries", H. Thielicke, *Faith and Thought*, 160, suggests, "is present in seed-form in him so far as the link between theological and intellectual history is concerned."

and intellectual context, and take into account biographical elements
of his life and experiences.[2]

The shape of Schleiermacher's theology was hammered out at a
time when great changes were demanded of theology as a result of
the pervasive spread of Enlightenment rationalism. He picked up the
gauntlet that Kant had thrown down, and sought an answer to the
question of the possibility of theology in the face of Kant's attempt
to locate "religion within the limits of reason." Schleiermacher
attempted to do theology at a time of great intellectual ferment, and
what he did will be of interest to the contemporary discussion on
theological methodology, since the very possibility of theology is again
called into question in these our postmodern times.

The eighteenth-century of Schleiermacher's youth saw the gradual
loosening of the church's hold over Europe as the Cartesian *cogito*
began more and more to displace *credo* as the source of assurance.
Developments in the sciences, as well as in politics, religion, literature, and philosophy, combined to create an ethos where the assertion
of autonomy from authority became increasingly dominant.[3] G. E.
Lessing's (1729–1781) play, *Nathan the Wise* (1779), celebrated the
ideal of independent enquiry, an ideal guided by enlightenment ration-

---

[2] Standard works on Schleiermacher's life and thought include: Karl Barth,
Protestant Thought, 425–73; idem, *The Theology of Schleiermacher: Lectures at Göttingen,
1923–24*, ed. Dietrich Ritschl (Grand Rapids: Eerdmans, 1982); Keith W. Clements,
ed., *Friedrich Schleiermacher: Pioneer of Modern Theology* (Minneapolis: Fortress, 1991),
7–65; B. A. Gerrish, *A Prince of the Church: Schleiermacher and the Beginnings of Modern
Theology* (Philadelphia: Fortress, 1984); idem, "Friedich Schleiermacher," in Ninian
Smart *et al.*, eds., *Nineteenth Century Religious Thought in the* West, 3 vols. (Cambridge:
Cambridge University Press, 1985), 1:123–56; Richard R. Niebuhr, *Schleiermacher on
Christ and Religion* (New York: Scribners, 1964); Martin Redeker, *Schleiermacher: Life
and Thought*, tr. John Wallhausser (Philadelphia: Fortress, 1973); Gerhard Spiegler,
The Eternal Covenant: Schleiermacher's Experiment in Cultural Theology (New York: Harper
& Row, 1967).

For a complete listing of Schleiermacher's works, see Terrence N. Tice, *Schleiermacher Bibliography 1784–1984*, Princeton Pamphlets no. 101 (Princeton: Princeton
Theological Seminary, 1985). For review of recent publications on Schleiermacher,
see Richard Crouter, "Friedrich Schleiermacher: A Critical Edition, New Work,
and Perspectives," *RSR* 18(1992): 20–27.

[3] For a historical overview of the period in which Schleiermacher's ideas took
shape, see: Colin Brown, *European Protestant Thought*, 105–32; Martin H. Prozesky,
"The Young Schleiermacher: Advocating Religion to An Age of Critical Reason
(1768–1807)," *JTSA* 37(1981): 51–55; Paul Tillich, *Perspectives on Nineteenth and Twentieth-
Century Protestant Theology*, ed. Carl E. Braaten (London: SCM, 1967), 92f; Claude
Welch, *Protestant Thought in the Nineteenth Century, Vol 1: 1799–1870* (New Haven &
London: Yale University Press, 1972), 52–55; 59–85.

alism. The impact of the latter is certainly felt in theology as the rise of the English Deists and biblical criticism attests. Not everyone, however, was enamored by rationalism; there arose towards the end of the eighteenth-century those who sought fulfilment instead in the romantic realm of the imagination, aesthetics and the emotions. Romanticism offered a counterbalance to the increasing influence of scientific rationalism. By the time Schleiermacher was a young man, the revolt led by the romantics was already well underway.

Perhaps the one person whose ideas exercised Schleiermacher most was the Königsberg philosopher, Immanuel Kant (1724–1804). His analysis of the dynamics of human knowledge continued the line of inquiry begun in his predecessors Descartes and Hume. Kant's view that human rationality is incapable of dealing with transcendental matters led to a situation where the very possibility of the knowledge of God is called into question. The string that tied truth and dogma firmly together began to dissolve under the Kantian distinction between fact and value. Schleiermacher was profoundly disturbed by this challenge to the possibility of faith, and applied himself to the advocacy of religion and the commendation of theology in and to an age of critical reason. It is a matter of debate as to whether he succeeded in doing so. What is clear is his belief that religion will not only withstand but will indeed thrive, despite the scrutiny of enlightenment rationalism. Prozesky rightly regards Schleiermacher as "the first great Christian theologian to come to terms with a Europe no longer dominated intellectually by the church."[4]

Schleiermacher's early years with the Herrnhuters (Moravians) instilled in him a deep pietism which never left him even when fierce winds of scepticism pounded him at different times of his life. He was born into a devout home, where his grandfather and father were both Reformed ministers. "Religion," he confessed, "was the maternal womb in whose holy darkness my young life was nourished and prepared for the world still closed to it."[5] There are many references to the love of the Saviour (*Heilandsliebe*), his own unworthiness, and his longing for deeper spiritual experiences in letters dating back to his days at the Moravian school at Niesky.

---

[4] Martin H. Prozesky, "The Young Schleiermacher", 51; cf. Paul Ricoeur, "Schleiermacher's Hermeneutics", *Monist* 60(1977): 181–97.
[5] Friedrich Schleiermacher, *On Religion: Speeches to its Cultured Despisers*, introduced and tr. Richard Crouter, (Cambridge: Cambridge University Press, 1988), 84.

Yet alongside his piety was an inquisitive scepticism which would neither allow his honest questions to be ignored nor silenced by the closed-minded conservatism of his superiors at the pietistic seminary at Barby. While other Moravians might want piety without critical thinking, Schleiermacher would have none of that. He left the seminary and enrolled at the nearby University of Halle in the spring of 1787 where he immersed himself in the study of philosophy, particularly Kant's. He had to grasp doubt by its horns, and resolve the tension between his heart and his head. Besides Kant, Schleiermacher grappled with the thoughts of the ancient Greeks, as well as the philosophical ideas of Pierre Bayle and Friedrich H. Jacobi.[6] It was only after emerging from his engagement with critical thought at Halle, able to reconcile pietism and critical reason, that he returned to the Moravians in 1802 and described himself with those famous words: "I have become a Herrnhuter again, only of a higher order."[7] This reconciling of intellectual rigour with the piety of the redeemed life is arguably one of his most significant achievements.[8]

His lifelong work as a preacher and churchman underscored for him the ecclesial and praxis-orientation of theology, while his involvement with the literary elites which gathered around Henrietta Herz, while he was chaplain to the Charity hospital in Berlin, helped shape his thoughts. His friendship with Friedrich Schlegel in the period 1797 to 1798 left indelible marks on him, many of which found their way into his works.[9] His first book, *On Religion: Speeches to its Cultured Despisers*, was composed with these cultured Berlin Romantics in mind, those who were "despisers" of the Christian religion.

A. *Schleiermacher's Hermeneutics*

Schleiermacher's work as a NT exegete and philologist (a translator of Plato's works) prompted him to think seriously about the notion of interpretation. His musings on the process of interpretation are

---

[6] Prozesky, "The Young Schleiermacher", 59.
[7] Quoted in Gerrish, *Prince*, 13.
[8] Prozesky, "Young Schleiermacher", 58.
[9] On Schleiermacher's relationship with Schlegel, see Jack Forstman, *A Romantic Triangle: Schleiermacher and Early German Romanticism* (Missoula: Scholars Press, 1977); and Sabine Wilke, "Authorial Intent versus Universal Symbolic Language: Schleiermacher and Schlegel on Mythology, Interpretation, and Communal Values," *Soundings* 74(1991): 411–425.

collected in a series of handwritten manuscripts dating from 1805.[10] Largely through the mediation of Dilthey, Schleiermacher's philosophy of understanding has found a firm and permanent place in the philosophical tradition of Europe. Schleiermacher's hermeneutical theory has already been comprehensively analysed in the literature,[11] and what follows will simply be a rehearsing of its salient features. Following the Enlightenment assumption, he believes that the Bible is to be understood like any other literary work, and interpretation of Scripture must be congruent with a general hermeneutics.[12] His concern is to conceive hermeneutics in universal terms, and commend it as universally applicable.[13]

As Schleiermacher himself acknowledged in his Academy Address of 1829, he developed his hermeneutical ideas in conscious dialogue with philologists Friedrich Ast (1778–1841) and Friedrich August Wolf (1759–1824), both of whom may be regarded as "forerunners" of Schleiermacher.[14] With Wolf he affirms the need for linguistic and reconstructive understanding, but faults him for restricting hermeneutics to just the classical writings. He regards Wolf's philological

---

[10] Schleiermacher's reflection on hermeneutics evolved over a period of nearly three decades, 1805–1833. References in this essay are from Friedrich Schleiermacher, *Hermeneutics: The Handwritten Manuscripts*, ed. Heinz Kimmerle, tr. James Duke & Jack Forstman, (Atlanta: Scholars Press, 1977, rpt 1986); German edition: *Hermeneutik: Abhandlung der Heidelberger Akademie der Wissenschaften* (Heidelberg: Carl Winter, 1959). Cf. Peter Szondi, *Introduction to Literary Hermeneutics* (Cambridge: Cambridge University Press, 1995), 109–10; Thiselton, *NHH*, 209.

[11] Richard L. Corliss, "Schleiermacher's Hermeneutic and Its Critics," *RelS* 29(1993): 363–79; Gadamer, *TM*, 184–97; H-G. Gadamer, "The Problem of Language in Schleiermacher's Hermeneutic," in Robert Funk, ed., *Schleiermacher As Contemporary, Journal for Theology and the Church*, 7 (New York: Herder & Herder, 1970), 68–84; Grondin, *Philosophical Hermeneutics*, 63–75; W. Jeanrond, "The Impact of Schleiermacher's Hermeneutics on Contemporary Interpretation Theory," in David Jasper, ed., *The Interpretation of Belief: Coleridge, Schleiermacher and Romanticism*, (New York: St Martin's Press, 1986), 81–96; idem, *Theological Hermeneutics*, 44–50; Heinz Kimmerle, "Hermeneutical Theory or Ontological Hermeneutics," in *Journal for Theology and the Church*, 4: *History and Hermeneutic* (Tübingen: Mohr; New York: Harper & Row, 1967), 107–21; Palmer, *Hermeneutics*, 84–97; Ricoeur, "Schleiermacher's Hermeneutics"; Szondi, *Literary Hermeneutics*, 109–34; Thiselton, *NHH*, 204–36; T. F. Torrance, "Hermeneutics According to F. D. E. Schleiermacher," *SJT* 21(1968): 257–67; J. B. Torrance, "Interpretation and Understanding in Schleiermacher's Theology: Some Critical Questions," *SJT* 21(1968): 268–82.

[12] Schleiermacher, *Hermeneutics*, 67, 216.

[13] Kimmerle, "Hermeneutical Theory", 107.

[14] Palmer, *Hermeneutics*, 75–83. It should be noted that Schleiermacher's earliest notes on hermeneutics were written in 1805, *before* the publication of Wolf's and Ast's works. See Szondi, *Literary Hermeneutics*, 112.

observations as limited in their usefulness since they are aimed only at interpreting particular written texts. Schleiermacher shares with Ast in pressing into service the concept of the hermeneutical circle (a concept anticipated in Ast, though in a simpler form than Schleiermacher's), and agrees with his view that events, institutions, and texts are in essence objectifications of the creative spirit which animates life in the world.[15] Where Schleiermacher differs from both Wolf and Ast is in the way in which he seeks to integrate the various dimensions of interpretation into a comprehensive theory of understanding.

Schleiermacher secured a permanent place in the history of hermeneutical scholarship by locating hermeneutics within the larger problem of human understanding. Knowing what the process of understanding involves will, in Schleiermacher's assessment, provide the key to a comprehensive theory on how we may understand human discourses, both verbal and literary. He begins his Compendium of 1819 with the observation that there does not yet exist a "general hermeneutics as the art of understanding but only a variety of specialized hermeneutics",[16] and then proceeds to offer a general theory of understanding. His concern is with the basis, possibility, and conditions of human understanding and communication. Can one get a message across to another in such a way that the receiver of that message understands what is being communicated? How does one circumvent misunderstanding in communication? Hermeneutics is, as such, applicable to all areas of life, apart from and including, textual interpretation. Anticipating the hermeneutics of self and action in late twentieth-century thought, he extends the applicability of hermeneutics beyond the interpretation of texts, or texts written in a foreign language. As Schleiermacher himself says, "I often make use of hermeneutics in personal conversation".[17]

The task of hermeneutics is, in Schleiermacher's view, to reconstruct and re-experience the mental processes leading up to an author's production of the text under consideration. Since this entails thinking the thoughts of the author, hermeneutics is necessarily tied to the art of thinking.[18] And the very possibility of thinking is in turn dependent on the existence of concepts and language conventions

---

[15] Schleiermacher, *Hermeneutics*, 195–6.
[16] Ibid., 95.
[17] Ibid., 181–82.
[18] Ibid., 107.

CHRISTOLOGY OF THE HEART

which are necessarily prior to the very production of thought itself.
Thinking can never be totally self-referential; it is parasitic on patterns of thought which exist independent of both writer and reader.
This is bound up with his hermeneutics of the self. To understand
the thought of an author as it is communicated requires knowledge
not just of the language conventions used, but also of the specific
ways in which words are chosen, framed and placed in relation to
each other by the author so as to convey a particular idea. Understanding invariably takes place along the two inseparable axes of
generality (universal and common) and individuality (unique and singular),[19] the first seen in terms of the range of language possibilities
open to the writer, the second in terms of a specific instantiation of
language possibility. In this, Schleiermacher anticipates Saussure's
discussion on the relationship between *la langue* (generality) and *la
parole* (particularity).[20]

Richard Corliss defends Schleiermacher from critics who tend to
interpret him on their own terms rather than appreciate his hermeneutical agenda. Gadamer, for instance, does not seem interested in
Schleiermacher's project of understanding, and is apparently concerned only with a phenomenological and descriptive analysis of the
conditions in which understanding takes place.[21] Schleiermacher's
hermeneutics, according to Corliss, is essentially founded on the sup-
position that words are linguistic acts which must be understood
according to the role they play in the context of communication.
Instead of treating words like objects, Schleiermacher invites us to
see them as action rather than things. Thought is action, not an
object; and insofar as hermeneutics seeks the meaning of thoughts,
it may be compared to the speech-act theory of Austin and Searle.[22]

1. *Grammatical and Technical or Psychological Interpretation*
Perhaps the clearest element in Schleiermacher's hermeneutics is his
view of the "double-character" of understanding: "understanding by
reference to the language and understanding by reference to the one

---

[19] Thiselton, *NHH*, 217.
[20] See James Duke & Jack Forstman, "Translators' Introduction" in Schleiermacher,
Hermeneutics, 12.
[21] Corliss, "Schleiermacher's Hermeneutic," 363–79; cf. Gadamer, *TM*, 184f.
[22] Corliss, "Schleiermacher's Hermeneutic," 368. According to Jeanrond, "The
Impact of Schleiermacher", 95 n. 8, Schleiermacher was probably the first to use
the term *Sprechakt*.

who speaks."[23] The first is called *grammatical* interpretation, and the second, *technical* interpretation, which he later describes alternatively as "psychological interpretation."[24] Every text has an "external form" and an "inner form;" the first is discerned through grammatical interpretation, while the second through psychological interpretation. From a phenomenological standpoint, grammatical interpretation has to do with the objective dimension, while the technical has to do with the subjective. "The more objective the statement," Schleiermacher writes, "the more grammatical; the more subjective, the more technical."[25] Understanding entails an integration of these two aspects in such a way that a text cannot be understood grammatically unless it is also understood psychologically, and vice-versa.[26]

Grammatical interpretation seeks the sense (*Sinn*) of a statement by locating its meaning within the language convention shared by the author and his readers. It requires knowledge of language. Technical or psychological interpretation is a reconstructive act in that the interpreter seeks to reverse the process of composition and arrive at the originating thought or situation in the lifeworld of the author, which expresses itself in terms of the text. Such a reconstructive process is premised on the view that thinking and speaking are the inner and outer sides of the same process. Speech is the outer side of thought.[27] If grammatical interpretation requires knowledge of language in order to understand the text, technical/psychological interpretaton requires knowledge of person in order to understand the person in the text.

In that interpretation must gather together and combine these two aspects in a dynamic interplay or "oscillation," hermeneutics is an "art doctrine" (*Kunstlehre*) requiring both knowledge of language and of person. The two feed upon each other. "One must already know a man in order to understand what he says, and yet one first becomes acquainted with him by what he says."[28] As Heinz Kimmerle has

---

[23] Schleiermacher, *Hermeneutics*, 68.

[24] According to Jeanrond, the terminology between psychological and technical remains unclear. Only from a note by Schleiermacher in 1833 that we learn that *psychological* refers to the development of thoughts from the whole of the *Lebensmoment*; whereas *technical* refers to the reduction to a certain thinking, or *Darstellenwollen* from which a series of thoughts arises. "The Impact of Schleiermacher," 84.

[25] Schleiermacher, *Hermeneutics*, 69.

[26] Barth, *Theology of Schleiermacher*, 180.

[27] Schleiermacher, *Hermeneutics*, 97.

[28] Ibid., 56.

argued over against those who see the psychological as displacing the grammatical in Schleiermacher's later writings, the two aspects are always held in tandem in Schleiermacher.[29] Schleiermacher is explicit on the inseparability of the two:

> Understanding always involves two moments: to understand what is said in the context of the *language* with its possibilities and to understand it as a fact in the thinking of the *speaker* . . . these two hermeneutical tasks are completely equal, and it would be incorrect to label the grammatical interpretation the "lower" and psychological interpretation as the "higher" task.[30]

Schleiermacher holds out the possibility of understanding an author as well as, if not better than, he understands himself.[31] This stems from his assumption that there may be factors at work in shaping the way an author wrote, factors which the author had no knowledge of. The modern reader has an advantage over the author in this respect. Nevertheless, as Thiselton notes, for Schleiermacher, understanding acquired through the interaction between grammatical and psychological interpretations must remain provisional and corrigible since it is impossible to have complete knowledge of either language or person.[32]

To understand both text and person involves a process where the parts are understood in terms of the whole, and the whole in terms of the parts; or what is known as the hermeneutical circle. "The understanding of a particular is always conditioned by an understanding of the whole."[33] Understanding, for Schleiermacher, is a matter of degree; it is a process of having a provisional and imperfect understanding of the whole which is then revised as the parts are examined.

2. *Comparative and Divinatory Modes of Understanding*

The interrelating polarity between unity and individuality, generality and specificity, an approach not untypical of Romantic discourse,

---

[29] Schleiermacher is presented in Dilthey's biography as gradually emphasing the psychological dimension at the expense of the grammatical. On Kimmerle's rebuttal, see *Hermeneutics*, 21–40, 229–34; "Hermeneutical Theory," 107–21. Also Thiselton, *NHH*, 206.

[30] Schleiermacher, *Hermeneutics*, 98–99.

[31] Ibid., 64, 69. Ricoeur notes that this is not original with Schleiermacher; Kant anticipated this in his Critiques. "Schleiermacher's Hermeneutics", 184, 193 n. 10.

[32] Schleiermacher, *Hermeneutics*, 100; Thiselton, *NHH*, 219.

[33] Schleiermacher, *Hermeneutics*, 59.

plays a major role as an operational principle in Schleiermacher's hermeneutics. A speech or a writing, considered from both the grammatical as well as the psychological perspective, may be regarded from two different standpoints which lead to two different interpretive functions or strategies, what Schleiermacher calls, the comparative and the divinatory. In his "Compendium of 1819" he differentiates between a masculine and a feminine approach to interpretation and relates these to comparative as well as divinatory knowledge:

> By leading the interpreter to transform himself, so to speak, into the author, the divinatory method seeks to gain an immediate comprehension of the author as an individual. The comparative method proceeds by subsuming the author under a general type. It then tries to find his distinctive traits by comparing him with the others of the same general type. Divinatory knowledge is the feminine strength in knowing people; comparative knowledge, the masculine.[34]

The divinatory process is thus an imaginative and intuitive grasp of the individuality of an author as it is expressed in what is communicated (text). As Frei characterises it, "the interpreter in his divination as it were transcends his own individuality or subjectivity without losing it, and becomes the other in the form of understanding him intuitively."[35] The interpreter "transforms" himself as it were into the author, and "seeks to gain an immediate comprehension of the author as an individual." It should be noted that the divinatory process is not thorough subjectivism since it is always done in conjunction with the comparative or the philological. The comparative strategy analyzes the use of language and sees how it is similar or different from what is conventional or current at the time of composition. A comparative analysis of the author's linguistic use will amply demonstrate his or her dependence upon a shared "form of life", and this would most assuredly guard against any pure idiosyncratic subjectivism.[36] Furthermore, it should also be noted that the two functions, comparative and divinatory, relate individually to both grammatical and psychological interpretations, even though in practice, the comparative tends to gravitate in the direction of a grammatical interpretation while the divinatory in that of psychological interpretation.

We observe in Schleiermacher's hermeneutics the combined influ-

---

[34] Ibid., 150.
[35] Frei, *Eclipse*, 297.
[36] Thiselton, *NHH*, 223.

ence of romantic ideas as well as implicit Reformed theological
assumptions. While it is debatable to what degree Schleiermacher
has imbibed the spirit of Romanticism, it is quite clear that its
influence is evident in his theology[37] and hermeneutics. Granted that
he is not uncritical in his appropriation of romantic ideas,—his *Speeches*
were after all a critique of his fellow romantics for excluding the
religious dimension in their preoccupation with the aesthetic and
the creative matters of the spirit—the notion that one can tap into
the creative moments of an author's life in order to intuit the lived
experience out of which a text is born bears the unmistakable marks
of Romanticism. The notion that psychological interpretation is possible through a divinatory approach may be regarded as the point
at which his assumptions about consciousness, experience, or "feeling" overlap with his hermeneutics. The philosophical commitments
which undergird his inaugural work, *On Religion* in 1799, run like a
subterranean stream through his hermeneutics.[38]

Schleiermacher's theological roots lie decidedly within the Reformed
tradition,[39] and one can discern its underlying influence in his
hermeneutics. We see this in at least two ways: (1) the interconnection between his notion of the "feeling of absolute dependence" and
his doctrine of God; and (2) a common humanity which unites people across the barriers of time and space. To him, the "feeling of
absolute dependence" is commensurable with the conviction that
anthropology and theology are inviolably tied. All forms of theological propositions are derived from the *Grundform*,[40] the fundamental

---

[37] The language of Schleiermacher's dogmatics certainly bears the stamp of
Romanticism, and he was undoubtedly influenced by the Romanticism of the Berlin
of his time. Nevertheless he was not given over to a thoroughgoing poetic and aesthetic subjectivism in his theology. Martin Redeker, *Schleiermacher*, 63f, notes that
though Schleiermacher participated in the cultural world of his romantic friends,
he "ultimately did not succumb to the temptations of romantic fantasy and senti-
mentality ... because his decisive religious and theological conceptions were not
rooted in romanticism."

[38] Frei, *Eclipse*, 297 & 299, doubts if a link can be established between "intuition" and "feeling" in Schleiermacher's hermeneutics. According to him, the notion
of "feeling" hardly figures in his hermeneutical musings, even though at the point
of his most mature writing on hermeneutics (1819), he was working on the first
edition of his *Glaubenslehre*, a work in which feeling has a pivotal role.

[39] See Gerrish, "Schleiermacher and the Reformation," 179–95. On the connection between hermeneutics and theology in Schleiermacher, see Bruce D. Marshall,
"Hermeneutics and Dogmatics in Schleiermacher's Theology", *JRel* 67(1987): 14–32.

[40] F. Schleiermacher, *Der christliche Glaube nach den Grundsätzen der evangelischen Kirche*

form, and are attempts at describing the correlation of God and the
world as this is apprehended immediately in religious consciousness.
God is a constituent part of the immediate, original and originating
religious experience.

The second way in which Schleiermacher's hermeneutics is theological in orientation lies in his assumption about a pre-given shared
language and a common humanity which bind author and reader
together. We might say that the appeal is one made to the ontological structure of human life. The overlap of worlds between interpreter and writer goes beyond the commonality of a shared language;
it assumes that there are sufficient similarities between the reader's
and the author's very different and historically conditioned contexts
to enable the former to know what moved the latter to put pen to
paper in the first place. For Schleiermacher, the chasm between
reader and author is bridgeable only because they both share a common humanity. While this assumption of a common given reality is
not without its detractors,[41] we think the basic orientation animat-
ing Schleiermacher's approach is essentially a theological one. As we
shall argue, Schleiermacher's position is not unlike the creational
anthropology of Reformed theology. The oneness of creation life
which draws people everywhere and at all times together is a fundamentally theological conviction.

B. *Contours of Schleiermacher's Theology of Subjectivity*

Schleiermacher contended throughout his life that theology must be
grounded in the life-matrix of piety and be in dialogue with philosophy. He wanted "in all circumstances to be a modern man as well

---

im Zusammenhange dargestellt. 2 vols. 2d. ed. of 1830–31, ed. Martin Redeker (Berlin:
Walter de Gruyter, 1960); ET: *The Christian Faith,* H. R. Mackintosh & J. S. Stewart,
eds., tr. from 2d German ed. (Philadelphia: Fortress, 1976; hereafter, *CF*), §§30–31,
125–8.

[41] Cornel West, "Schleiermacher's Hermeneutics and The Myth of the Given,"
USQR 34(1979): 71–84, for instance, dismisses Schleiermacher's hermeneutics as fundamentally flawed because its operating assumption that there is a universal element implicit in every human expression is a "myth." According to West, the Myth
of the Given consists of the following epistemological assumption: "the justification
of our employment of concepts, utterance of sentences, or intelligent use of words
rests on non-linguistic awareness, that is, on special, felt, incommunicable qualities."
71. See also Charles E. Scott, "Schleiermacher and the Problem of Divine Immediacy",
RelS 3(1967): 499–512; and Wayne Proudfoot, *Religious Experience* (Berkeley, Los
Angeles & London: University of California Press, 1985).

as a Christian theologian",[42] by which is meant a pietistic religion of the heart. Streetman too notes that there is throughout his life and work a tension between a deep experiential faith rooted in a *sensus numinis* and a critical rationalistic intelligence engendered by the Enlightenment. As a mature theologian, he "refused to relax either pole of this tension. Rather he formulated and maintained positions which continually played one pole against the other as a check to extremes."[43]

We have already noted the philosophical context in which Schleiermacher worked. His approach to theology may be characterized as a phenomenology of experience, which is grounded in an ontology which posits a necessary relationality between God and the world. This correlation between God and world is given immediately in religious consciousness. In *The Christian Faith*, the relation between God and all created reality is described in terms of the former as the transcendental conditioning-principle of the latter. According to Robert Williams, such an appraisal of the God-world relationship echoes the kind of Platonic theological thought associated with Nicolas Cusa,[44] whose philosophical principle of *coincidentia oppositorum*, the coincidence of opposites, specifically the coincidence of the infinite and the finite, played a not uncritical part in shaping Romanticism.[45] Whether there is direct historical or literary influence on Schleiermacher cannot be established.[46] Nevertheless, his conceptualisation of God in terms of a bipolar coincidence of opposites bears comparison with Nicholas's philosophy. Such a principle seems promising to Schleiermacher in his attempt to overcome Kant's subject-object dualism, by providing an ontological bridging of the gap between the self as subject (world) and God as object.

We will look at three key elements in his theology which exemplify how his particular methodology works. After an examination

---

[42] Barth, *Protestant Thought*, 314. Hans Küng likewise regards Schleiermacher the theologian as "a modern man through and through." *Great Christian Thinkers* (London: SCM, 1994), 161.

[43] Robert F. Streetman, "Romanticism and the *Sensus Numinis* in Schleiermacher," in Jasper, ed., *Interpretation of Belief*, 107.

[44] Robert R. Williams, *Schleiermacher the Theologian: The Construction of the Doctrine of God* (Philadelphia: Fortress, 1978), 14.

[45] Tillich, *Perspectives*, 77.

[46] Wolfgang Sommer, "Cusanus und Schleiermacher", *NZSTR* 12(1970): 85–102; cf. Williams, *Schleiermacher*, 18 n. 23.

of Schleiermacher's theory of consciousness and its impact on his understanding of the genesis and nature of theological assertions, we will move on to consider his Christology with an eye on how it serves as an instantiation of his theological method. This will culminate with an analysis of the relation between his hermeneutics and his theology, specifically asking in what way his theological approach can be said to be hermeneutical.

1. *Consciousness and the Genesis of Theology in Redemptive Experience*
Experience or human receptive subjectivity plays a pivotal role in Schleiermacher's theological system. He is the first modern European theologian to attempt to base theology on self-consciousness (*Selbstbewusstsein*).[47] All doctrines are understood from within what Thielicke calls, the "believing subjectivity" of the theologian or believer. Christian doctrines are, in Schleiermacher's view, "accounts of the Christian religious affections set forth in speech".[48] This believing subjectivity from which all Christian beliefs and doctrines must arise, is characterized as *das Gefühl der schlechthinnigen Abhängigkeit*, which is the *Leitbegriff* of his theory of religion and serves as foundation for his interpretation of the tradition of Christian doctrine.[49] Theology for Schleiermacher is human reflection spurred on by the Christian's experience of redemption in Christ.

Schleiermacher does not provide a thorough and systematic analysis of the term *Gefühl*. Nevertheless, from his *Speeches* and *Christian Faith*, as well as his other works, particularly *Psychologie* and *Dialektik*,[50] one finds a consistent description of "feeling" as immediate self-

---

[47] Louis Roy, "Consciousness according to Schleiermacher," *JRel* 77(1997): 217.

[48] Schleiermacher, *CF*, 76.

[49] This is the view of Hans-Joachim Birkner, "Gefühl schlechthinniger Abhängigkeit," in *Historisches Wörterbuch der Philosophie*, Vol. 3, ed. J. Ritter & K. Gründer (Darmstadt: Wissenschaftliche Buchgesellschaft, 1974), 98. According to Thomas H. Curran, *Doctrine and Speculation in Schleiermacher's Glaubenslehre* (Berlin & New York: Walter De Gruyter, 1994), 272f, the terminology of *Abhängigkeitsgefühl* was already found in Fichte's *Wissenschaftslehre*, e.g., J. G. Fichte, *Grundlage der gesamten Wissenschaftslehre: Als Handschrift für seine Zuhörer (1794)* (Hamburg: Felix Meiner, 1988), 42, particularly in his later *Darstellung der Wissenschaftslehre (1801/1802)*, ed. Reinhard Lauth & P. K. Schneider (Hamburg: Felix Meiner, 1977), 60, 75, 76, 79, where we find repeated references to "das unmittelbare Gefühl der *Gewissheit* (d.i. Absolutheit, Unerschütterlichkeit, Unveränderlichkeit des wissens)."

[50] See F. Schleiermacher, *Psychologie*, aus Schleiermachers Handschriften Nachlasse und nachgeschriebenen Vorlesungen, h.g. von Ludwig George, *sämmtliche Werke*, III/6 (Berlin: G. Reimer, 1862); idem, *Dialektik 1814/15*, ed. Andreas Arndt (Hamburg: Felix Meiner Verlag, 1988).

consciousness (*unmittelbares Selbstbewusstsein*), a prereflective consciousness which constitutes the very structure of human existence.[51] Feeling is the comprehensive term which encompasses the cognitive, volitional and affective. As immediate self-consciousness, it is the hinge or "pivot" (*Angelpunkt*), the midpoint (*Mittelpunkt*) or passage-crossing (*Übergang*),[52] which enables traffic between thinking and willing. Schleiermacher differentiates immediate (prereflective) self-consciousness from the kind of (reflective) self-consciousness which is "more like an objective consciousness, being a representation of oneself, and thus mediated by self-contemplation."[53]

While "feeling" entails a person's capacity to apprehend reality, i.e., consciousness as subjectivity, it is never simply a psychological or emotive state.[54] Since the self participates in, and is always conditioned by, the larger social whole of which it is a part, immediate self-consciousness is always a consciousness of the self in reciprocal co-existence with another.[55] The 'feeling' subject is conscious of himself in relation to the co-determining other or object.[56] To say that feeling is subjective for Schleiermacher is to say that it is subjectivity or consciousness as such. "Feeling is not primarily a self-directed

---

[51] On the translation of *Gefühl* as "feeling," see C. Brown, *Jesus*, 116, 310 n. 69. Schleiermacher's understanding of "feeling" was developed over a long period of time. See Roy, "Consciousness," 217–221, for the different significance assigned to "feeling" between the first and second editions of *Der christliche Glaube*. Despite the variety of usage in his different works, there are certain continuities. See "Translators' Introduction" in F. D. E. Schleiermacher, *On the Glaubenslehre: Two Letters to Dr. Lücke*, tr. James Duke & Francis Fiorenza (Chico: Scholars Press, 1981), 12–13. For his early use of *Gefühl*, see Julia A. Lamm, "The Early Philosophical Roots of Schleiermacher's Notion of *Gefühl*, 1788–1794," *HTR* 87(1994): 67–105.

[52] See Friedrich Beisser, *Schleiermachers Lehre von Gott dargestellt nach seinen Reden und seiner Glaubenslehre* (Göttingen: Vanderhoeck & Ruprecht, 1970), 60. Schleiermacher speaks of *ein Übergang*; see Roy, "Consciousness," 221. Cf. Marianne Simon, *La philosophie de la religion dans l'oeuvre de Schleiermacher* (Paris: Vrin, 1974), 130–31; and John E. Thiel, *God and World in Schleiermacher's "Dialektik" and "Glaubenslehre"* (Berne: Peter Lang, 1981).

[53] Schleiermacher, *CF*, §3.2. The same twofold distinction is found in his *Dialektik* and *Speeches*.

[54] As Roy, "Consciousness," 219, asserts, what is often overlooked is that "having emotions or feelings (usually plural: *Erregungen, Gefühle*) belongs to the realm of the antithesis (Schleiermacher gives us examples: pleasure/pain, objective/introvertive), whereas feeling (singular: *Gefühl*) is found in the realm where the antithesis between subject and its objects is abolished". See *CF*, §§5 & 34.

[55] Schleiermacher, *CF*, §§30.1 & 32.2; cf. Robert Roy Williams, *Consciousness and Redemption in the Theology of Friedrich Schleiermacher* (Th.D. diss., Union Theological Seminary, 1971), 47.

[56] Schleiermacher, *Psychologie*, 71; *CF*, §4.4.

consciousness; rather it is the precondition and presupposition of such a determinate mode of consciousness."[57]

In setting the stage for his contribution to dogmatics, Schleiermacher is careful not to say that the feeling of absolute dependence is conditioned by some prior knowledge of God.[58] This would defeat his apologetic intentions. He seeks instead a secure starting point which would command assent from the secular world; to begin with God when God is in question does not seem a sensible way to start his expedition into the highlands of dogmatics. He sees in the phenomenon of human consciousness an acceptable entrée into the exposition of Christian claims. Nevertheless, Schleiermacher introduces the word *God* as a corresponding term, an existential reference, for the feeling of absolute dependence. "[T]o feel oneself absolutely dependent and to be conscious of being in relation with God are one and the same thing."[59] God is presented as a correlate of the human feeling of absolute dependence, the "*Whence* of our receptive and active existence"[60] implied in our self-consciousness. Human *Gefühl* invariably involves God as the co-present (*mitgesetzt*), "the pre-given intentional correlate of religious consciousness".[61]

The view of "feeling" as both immediate self-consciousness and determinate subjectivity means that there is in the self a dialectic of freedom and dependence, of assertion and reception. The self is at once a stable constant and a dynamic entity, simultaneously self-positing (*ein Sichselbstsetzen*) and non self-positing (*ein Sichselbstnichtsogesetzthaben*).[62] There is a coinherence of "activity" (*Selbsttätigkeit*) and receptivity (*Empfänglichkeit*). Schleiermacher maintains, against the criticism of Hegel and others, that far from denying human freedom, the feeling of absolute dependence, transcends the either-or dichotomy between human freedom and absolute dependence.[63]

---

[57] Williams, *Consciousness*, 57.
[58] Schleiermacher, *CF* §4.4.
[59] Ibid., 17; see Thielicke, *Faith & Thought*, 218–19.
[60] *CF*, 16.
[61] Williams, *Schleiermacher*, x; cf. 11. To say that Schleiermacher's *Glaubenslehre* is fundamentally an anthropology with God tacked on so as to fulfill the need for continuity with previous Christian theology (as Barth does) is in Williams' opinion, a "caricature".
[62] *CF*, §4.1–2.
[63] Hegel fears that piety defined as a feeling of absolute dependence would compromise human freedom and reduce humans to the level of animals. He writes cuttingly in his "Foreword to Hinrich's *Religionsphilosophie*,": "Should feeling constitute

Schleiermacher prefaced his *The Christian Faith* with a quote from Anselm of Canterbury which serves to orientate his dogmatics: "Nor do I seek to understand in order that I may believe, but I believe in order that I may understand."—"For he who does not believe does not experience, and he who does not experience, does not understand."[64] Faith-experience is prior to faith-expression. As we shall see below, Christology for Schleiermacher develops out of the believing community's experience of the redemption brought on by the Redeemer. All ecclesiastical Christological constructions are rooted in the "original consciousness" of the activity of the Redeemer.[65] There is here more than a strong echo of Melanchthon's dictum, "to know Christ is to know his benefits" (*hoc est Christum cognoscere, eius beneficia cognoscere*). We might say that for Schleiermacher, the Christian Faith is the verbal outworking of the Christian's faith. Faith, for him, is first a verb before it is a noun.

This privileging of the experiential stands behind Schleiermacher's bias for the feminine principle of intuition and affective attention to spiritual values as opposed to the allegedly masculine principle of rationalistic objectivity. This is clearly evident in his *Christmas Eve* (1806) dialogue.[66] While the males (Leonhardt, Ernst & Eduard) in the parable indulged in intellectual matters concerning the historicity of Jesus and the philosophical possibility of the incarnation, the women were revelling in the joy of Christmas through the expression of feelings. Josef, Schleiermacher's alter-ego in the dialogue and the final speaker in the story, invites the company to sing Christmas carols, for only in the affective language of music can the subject of Christmas create in us "a speechless joy". This exaltation of the feminine is consistent with Romanticism.[67]

---

the basic determination of human nature, then humans are equated with animals, for feeling is what is specific to animals. . . . Consequently, a dog would be the best Christian, since a dog is most strongly characterized by this feeling and lives primarily in this feeling." Quoted in Duke & Fiorenza, "Translators' Introduction," *On the Glaubenslehre*, 15. See Richard Crouter, "Hegel and Schleiermacher at Berlin: A Many-Sided Debate," *JAAR* 48(1980): 19–43.

[64] "*Neque enim quaero intelligere ut credam, sed credo ut intelligam.—Nam qui non crediderit, non experietur, et qui expertus non fuerit, non intelliget.*" These quotes from Anselm's *Proslogion* and *De Incarnatione* respectively are found in the title page of the original *Der Christliche Glaube*. They are omitted in the (Mackintosh and Stewart) English translation.

[65] Schleiermacher, *CF*, 389.

[66] F. Schleiermacher, *Christmas Eve: Dialogue on the Incarnation*, tr. Terrence N. Tice (Richmond: John Knox, 1967). See C. Brown's analysis of this work in *Jesus*, 110–14.

[67] As Sabine Wilke, "Authorial Intent", 413, notes, recent scholarship has shown

Not that Schleiermacher dissolves altogether any objective referent in his notion of feeling. It would be a misreading of Schleiermacher
to label him an out and out subjectivist, who elevates consciousness
to criteriological status. The consciousness is, for Schleiermacher, the
place where the historical person of Christ is appropriated by the
believer; it is not the *norm* of that appropriation.[68] Furthermore, one
may argue that even in his parabolic *Christmas Eve*, the feminine
dimension of aesthetic appropriation is highlighted over against the
rationalistic theologizing of the males, not because the latter is unnecessary or irrelevant, but because by itself it can never fully capture
the essence of the Christian message. Rationalistic engagement with
theological propositions has its place, but it is not enough, and it is
certainly no substitute for a religion of the heart.

Theology is the articulation of the common life of faith shared by
all within the community of faith, and is therefore practical and
ecclesial. To Schleiermacher, theological reflection must take place
within the historical religion of the Christian community.[69] Faith,
understood as the bringing into consciousness of the human awareness of the divine, is something engendered by the Christian tradition, particularly as this is mediated through the preaching of the
church. He asserts: "For since Christian piety never arises independently and of itself in an individual, but only out of the communion
and in the communion, there is no such thing as adherence to Christ
except in combination with adherence to the communion."[70] We
might say that Schleiermacher operated with an empiricism which
is oriented to the phenomenology of religious experience which takes
place within the communion of Christian believers.

---

the extent to which Schleiermacher identified with the feminine role in hermeneutics. Cf. Kurth Lüthi, *Feminismus und Romantik: Sprache, Gesellschaft, Symbole, Religion*
(Wien u.a.: Böhlau, 1985), 92; cf. Ruth Drucilla Richardson, *The Role of Women in
the Life and Thought of the Early Schleiermacher, 1768–1806: An Historical Overview* (Lewiston:
Edwin Mellen Press, 1992). In a letter dated 1799, Schleiermacher expressed himself: "This tendency to attach myself more closely to women than to men, is deeply
rooted in my nature; for there is so much in my soul that men seldom understand." F. Schleiermacher, *The Life of Schleiermacher, as Unfolded in His Autobiography
and Letters*, tr. Frederica Rowan, 2 vols. (London: Smith, Elder & Co., 1860), 1:198.
He muses in a letter to a close friend, Charlotte von Kathen: "from whatever side
I look at it, the nature of woman seems to me nobler than that of man, and their
life more happy. Therefore, if I ever find myself sportively indulging in an impossible wish, it is that I were a woman." 1:382.

[68] Thielicke, *Faith & Thought*, 215.
[69] Niebuhr, *Schleiermacher*, 141.
[70] *CF*, 106.

2. *An Anthropologically Paradigmatic Christology*

Christology lies at the centre of Schleiermacher's theological enterprise. It figures in virtually all his writings, beginning with the *Speeches*, through his lectures on the *Life of Jesus*,[71] right through to his magnum opus, *The Christian Faith*. Even in his hermeneutics, the "Being and Spirit of Christ" is said to stand behind the individuality of the New Testament writers as the underlying unity of their faith.[72] But his was neither the eighteenth-century view of Jesus as a great, but all too human, ethical teacher, nor a regurgitation of the traditional Christological formulae of Chalcedon.

Given Kant's critique of rationalistic metaphysics, a reductionistic Christology may be an understandable outcome, but it would be profoundly unsatisfactory to Schleiermacher. To render the Christian faith merely in terms of propositional knowledge is just as wrong as reducing it to ethical activism. Such a Christology does not cohere with the biblical testimony to the reality of God "in Christ" and the redemptive accomplishments of Jesus of Nazareth. At the same time, Schleiermacher rejects the traditional two-natures Christological language of Chalcedon, and reinterprets the traditional understanding of the divine nature in Christ in terms of the potency of the God-consciousness regnant in him. This is in line with his programmatic assertion that the "ecclesiastical formulae about the person of Christ need an ongoing critical treatment."[73]

Richard A. Muller rightly observes that it is one thing to disagree with Schleiermacher's reformulation of Christology and judge it inadequate, but quite another to charge him with deliberately setting out to deny the divinity of Christ or to set aside the fundamental dogmatic intention of the classical formulate.[74] While some of his views may be questionable, particularly in his critical lectures on the historical

---

[71] F. Schleiermacher, *Das Leben Jesu. Vorlesungen an der Universität Berlin im Jahr 1832*, ed. K. A. Rutenik (Berlin: G. Reimer, 1864); ET: *The Life of Jesus*, ed. J. C. Verheyden, tr. S. M. Gilmour (Philadelphia: Fortress, 1975).

[72] Schleiermacher, *Hermeneutics*, 125–6, 139.

[73] *CF*, §95, p. 389; cf. *CF*, §94. On Schleiermacher's Christology, see: Alister McGrath, *The Making of Modern German Christology: 1750–1990*, 2d ed. (Leicester: Apollos; Grand Rapids: Zondervan, 1987, 1994), 36–49; MacQuarrie, *Christ*, 192–211; Jürgen Moltmann, *The Way of Jesus Christ: Christology in Messianic Dimensions*, tr. Margaret Kohl (San Francisco: Harper, 1990), 59f.

[74] Richard A. Muller, "The Christological Problem as Addressed by Friedrich Schleiermacher: A Dogmatic Query", in Shuster & Muller, eds., *Perspectives on Christology*, 142; also Gerrish, "Schleiermacher," 149.

Jesus,[75] it was certainly not his intention to cast aspersion on the divine status of Christ. What he wanted to do instead was to provide an alternative to the traditional dogmatic language, which to his mind was no longer usable.

In criticising the "two-natures, one person" formula of Chalcedon, Schleiermacher is simply highlighting the immense conceptual difficulties involved in affirming the unity of the person of Christ while positing simultaneously the presence of two wills in Jesus. The difficulty appears insoluble to him: does Christ, the one person with two natures have "two wills according to the number of natures, or only one according to the number of the person?"[76] His desire is to emphasize the unity of the person of Jesus. Schleiermacher's reinterpretation, according to Muller, cannot be dismissed as heterodox simply because it highlights the problematic aspects of the Chalcedonian formulation. In all fairness, Muller goes on to argue, Schleiermacher's doctrinal intention stands well within the bounds of the doctrinal intention of the patristic fathers.

> Schleiermacher's Christological construction, resting as it does on an alternative to the person/nature language of the early church, cannot be judged heterodox or otherwise unsuccessful on the basis of that language: he cannot, in other words, be classed as teaching Adoptionism or a Nestorianism or some other doctrine defined as problematic on patristic grounds because the language of natures is as inherent to the patristic heresies as it is to patristic orthodoxy.[77]

Since human nature is the same everywhere, the redeemer is the same as all other human beings. Christ as the last Adam is a more appropriate formulation than the two-nature Christology of Chalcedon. Jesus is the prototypical, paradigmatic, or archetypal man, the human *Urbild*; he is what all human beings should be in terms of their being

---

[75] Schleiermacher's Christological assumptions are reflected in some of his historical assessments of the *Life of Jesus*. Thus for instance, Jesus' sinlessness is not dependent on his supernatural birth since the latter rests on the notion of original sin, which Schleiermacher does not see as essential to Christian belief. On the miraculous in the Gospels, he maintains that "Christ's performance of healing miracles was incidental and occasional." *Life of Jesus*, 197. Jesus' God-consciousness is so emphasized that it overshadows the importance of Christ's death and resurrection. His ambivalence about the supernatural is evident also in his view on the resurrection and ascension of Christ. See Brown, *Jesus*, 127–30.

[76] *CF*, 394. For a summary of Schleiermacher's criticism of the two-natures doctrine, see Macquarrie, *Christ*, 209.

[77] Muller, "Christological Problem," 155.

filled with a thorough God-consciousness. Schleiermacher's Christology is shaped largely by his prior notion of "the feeling of absolute dependence." It is the impression of his person which constitutes the redemptive efficacy of his life.[78]

His redemptive work is defined in terms of his communication of the potency of his God-consciousness. In his *Letters to Lücke*, Schleiermacher maintains that Christology has its roots not in the idea of a redeemer (as critics have charged), but in the effect which Jesus has on religious consciousness. Since sin is defined entirely in terms of a lack of God-consciousness, redemption consists in translating people from a state of "God-forgetfulness" to one of absolute dependence on God. The distinguishing feature of Christianity lies in the subordination of its content to the redemption accomplished by Jesus Christ, understood as the engendering of the "feeling of absolute dependence" in the corporate consciousness of the Christian community through the effects of Christ's achievement.[79]

Owing to his assumption concerning the nature of a theological assertion, some have characterized Schleiermacher's Christology as "humanistic" (Macquarrie) or "anthropological" (Moltmann).[80] Questions remain as to whether the Christ of Schleiermacher is different from all other humans only in terms of degree rather than in kind. In summary, we concur with Michael Root's assessment that the way Schleiermacher handles theological subjects indicates that he is both traditional and innovative. His view on the relationship between God and the world shows signs of being the product of his innovative reflection on religious feeling as well as being a reassertion of the Augustinian understanding of God. Root says:

> Tradition and innovation go hand in hand. An assessment of Schleiermacher's theology cannot then be simply an assessment of Schleiermacher as the father of liberalism. Any evaluation of Schleiermacher's treatment of the central doctrinal loci must also assess Schleiermacher as the child of Calvin and Augustine.[81]

---

[78] See *CF*, §89.1, p. 367.

[79] On the soteriological connection between dogmatics and God-consciousness in Schleiermacher, see Alister E. McGrath, *Iustitia Dei: A History of the Christian Doctrine of Justification. Vol. 2: From 1500 to the Present Day* (Cambridge: Cambridge University Press, 1986), 154–8; idem, *Modern German Christology*, 41–45.

[80] Macquarrie, *Christ*, 192f; Moltmann, *Way of Jesus Christ*, 55f.

[81] Michael Root, "Schleiermacher as Innovator and Inheritor: God, Dependence, and Election," *SJT* 43(1990): 87–110.

3. A Hermeneutical and Phenomenological Theology

Instead of the conventional doctrine of the verbal inspiration of the Bible, Schleiermacher speaks of Scripture as a "mausoleum of religion"[82] in his *Speeches*. Scripture is a memorial to the religious experience of the apostles which provided the original impetus for its production. Following Herder (and Ast), he looks to the creative spirit which stands behind documents, institutions, events, etc. Like the smoky trail which remains suspended in the sky after a jetplane has flown by, we have in the scriptural texts the afterglow or residual effects of a reality which is no more. In other words, Schleiermacher wants to affirm the inspiration of the biblical *writers* rather than the biblical *writings*. "[T]he biblical authors were not simply moved by the Holy Spirit to write (see 2 Peter 1:21). They had already been "moved," and in this condition spoke and wrote."[83]

The "condition" under which the apostles wrote is something which is universal, and therefore not, in principle, unique to the apostles. Others too can establish contact with the divine or infinite, and be similarly inspired.[84] Consequently, one finds in Schleiermacher neither a high view of the uniqueness of the Bible nor much attention given to exegesis in his theological exposition. Not that he lacks interest or expertise in biblical exegesis, having taught courses in exegesis at the University of Berlin, and published critical studies on the biblical texts.[85] This conspicuous absence owes more to his view that the basis of dogmatics lies in experience and in the articulation of the faith of the church rather than in exegesis. The latter has its place alongside dogmatics, but is not subservient to it.[86]

---

[82] *Speeches*, 134; cf. Thiselton, *NHH*, 210, 215.

[83] Roy A. Harrisville & Walter Sundberg, *The Bible in Modern Culture: Theology and Historical-Critical Method from Spinoza to Käsemann* (Grand Rapids: Eerdmans, 1995), 77.

[84] Barth considers Schleiermacher's understanding of inspiration as simplistic: "He seems not to have known, considered, or at any rate understood it except in the very crude form that the biblical authors were recording instruments of the Holy Spirit." *Theology of Schleiermacher*, 183.

[85] For instance, his essay, "Ueber den sogenannten ersten Brief des Paulos an den Timotheos. Ein kritisches Sendschreiben an J. C. Gass," *Sämmtliche Werke*, 2:221–320; and *A Critical Essay on the Gospel of Luke*, tr. Connop Thirlwall, (London: John Taylor, 1825). On Schleiermacher and New Testament studies, see William Baird, *History of New Testament Research, Vol. 1: From Deism to Tübingen* (Minneapolis: Fortress, 1992), 212–20. In Baird's opinion, "one is tempted to say that he would have been a great biblical scholar if he had not been preoccupied with theology!" 220.

[86] *CF*, §19, postscript; cf. §15. See also B. A. Gerrish, "Theology Within the Limits of Piety Alone: Schleiermacher and Calvin's Notion of God" in *Old Protestantism and the New*, 202.

Schleiermacher's view on the nature of Scripture has direct bearings on his hermeneutical methodology. If the Bible is not unlike other products of human inspiration, then the rules which govern its interpretation are not, and need not, be different from those used in the interpretation of all other writings. The legacy of Spinoza and Reimarus lives on in Schleiermacher in his view that the Bible is to be understood like any other book.[87] Given his position on Scripture, in what sense then can we characterize his theology as hermeneutical? Is there a way in which we may provide some sort of linkage between his pioneering work in hermeneutics, his theological method, and the substance of his theology? The way to do this, we propose, is to recognise that *Schleiermacher's hermeneutics and his theological method share a common quest for understanding.* Just as hermeneutics seeks to penetrate the fog of possible misunderstandings in a given text so as to better understand the person communicating (author) and the message communicated (text), so in theological reflection, we need to penetrate the confessional, liturgical and homiletical legacy of the historical church in order to understand and grasp the faith-consciousness which stands behind it. The process in which one approaches the latter is not unlike, we suggest, the search for understanding in Schleiermacher's hermeneutics.

Just as it is possible for the interpreter to penetrate, through the process of divination, into the text-generating experience of the author on account of the shared humanity which spans the spatial-temporal divide between interpreter and writer, so the theologian seeks to tap into the faith-generating consciousness of the church, represented both in Scripture and in the tradition of Christianity, before he goes about the task of "setting it forth in speech." And just as a self-involving element is necessarily present in the hermeneutical dialogue that goes on between interpreter and text, so in theology's on-going dialogue with the church, the present situatedness of the theologian will necessarily intersect with the past. In a real sense, the theologian only understands the faith-horizon or consciousness of the church if he or she is standing *within* the circle of faith, not as an uninvolved observer but as an insider. In this sense, Schleiermacher's position is not unlike Barth's.

In recasting Christological language in terms of the (mediatorial)

---

[87] Harrisville & Sundberg, *Bible in Modern Culture*, 78.

work of Jesus (as given through the believing community) rather than in terms of his person, Schleiermacher's Christology may be said to be "from below".[88] Here again we encounter the Kantian constraints under which Schleiermacher laboured. True to his apologetic intentions, Schleiermacher wants no radical separation between transcendence and immanence, and opts instead for a fusing of the two in his attempts at rooting all theological assertions in the faith consciousness of the believer. His view on the nature of Christian doctrines necessarily implies, as Manfred Frank notes, the contingency of all human meaning systems, including theological statements.[89] Furthermore, dogmatic theology, understood as "the science which systematizes the doctrine prevalent in a Christian Church", must be articulated "*at a given time*."[90] All these add up to a world-grounded and conditioned faith.

The ontological relatedness between God and world is an idea which has been seized upon by more than one modern thinker. The other-worldly can only be perceived and processed within the concreteness and tangibility of this-worldly reality. As human constructs, theological assertions are necessarily anthropological in character.[91] It is not enough to have inner coherence; theology must be engaged in conversation with differing perspectives in the face of the complexity of knowledge. As a "worldly" theologian, Schleiermacher seeks to bring God back into the ebb and flow of ordinary life. It may well be that he is guilty of over-compensating for the transcendence of God in the direction of a panentheistic immanentism. Yet this is not so much a comprehensive world-view as it is his attempt at spell-

---

[88] C. W. Christian, *Schleiermacher*, 118–21.

[89] Manfred Frank, *Das Individuelle Allgemeine: Textstrukturierung und Interpretation nach Schleiermacher* (Frankfurt am Main: Suhrkamp, 1977); Manfred Frank, ed., *Hermeneutik und Kritik* (Frankfurt am Main: Suhrkamp, 1977, 1990); cf. Crouter, "Schleiermacher", 24.

[90] *CF*, §19, emphasis added; cf. Niebuhr, *Schleiermacher*, 152.

[91] See David A. Pailin, *The Anthropological Character of Theology: Conditioning Theological Understanding* (Cambridge: Cambridge University Press, 1990). In a work which probes the question of God in the common quest of both Christian believers and non-believers alike, Paul R. Sponheim, *God—The Question and the Quest: Toward a Conversation Concerning Christian Faith* (Philadelphia: Fortress, 1985), argues that all speech about God necessarily carries with it speech about the self, world, and history. Pointing to both Schleiermacher and Schillebeeckx, Sponheim contends that Christian faith speaks of that which is known through human experience. The self can know only *in* the world. The "self must have recourse beyond itself in order to know and to know that it knows." 26.

ing out the nature of God's relation to the world.[92] The "worldliness" of Schleiermacher is also manifested in his commitment to offer an *apologia* for the Christian message. For what is his *Speeches* if not a piece of apologetic writing? Schleiermacher criticises and challenges his culture by using terms prevalent in his time and context.[93]

II. *The Reciprocity of Experience, Belief and Tradition in Christology*

We shall attempt next a critical assessment of Schleiermacher's project with an eye on how we might appropriate his insights for our own reflection on a Christology *from within*, namely a Christology of the heart which takes into account the experiential dimension of theological construction. As indicated above, Schleiermacher's (Anselmian) decision to root Christology in experience should not be construed as an ahistorical move unhinged from ecclesial tradition. On the contrary, we contend that Schleiermacher understands experience not so much as an undifferentiated existential apprehension but as something firmly rooted in history and in the corporate memory and witness of the community of faith. It is hoped that this will lead to a re-enchantment of subjectivity in Christological reflection which is not abstracted from tradition.

A. *Subjectivity as Transcendental, Mediated and Intersubjective*

Two principal elements in Schleiermacher's life had a profound effect on the shape of his theology: his pietistic roots, and the priority he placed on friendship and interpersonal communion. We already noted how Schleiermacher's pietism stayed with him throughout his life despite his intellectual doubts. It is therefore not surprising to find theology described as an *inward* fact and dogmatics understood as something pursued *from within* the inner experience of the theologian. *Glaubenslehre* presupposes the vibrancy of personal faith.[94] Friendship is the other priority for Schleiermacher. Acknowledging that he is a

---

[92] Warren Lee Holleman, "Schleiermacher's 'Liberalism'," *JTSA* 62(1988): 30.

[93] Holleman, ibid., 29–42, notes that Schleiermacher's *Speeches* is a tract cleverly structured as a response to the moralism, rationalism (Deism and Scholasticism), and romanticism of his time.

[94] *CF* §33.3, p. 136: "Dogmatics must therefore presuppose intuitive certainty or faith; and thus, as far as the God-consciousness in general is concerned, what it has to do is not to effect its recognition but to explicate its content."

"virtuoso in friendship",[95] he writes in one of his letters, "it is in my
nature not to have any independent existence ... all my activity is
but the product of communion."[96] So it is again not surprising that
the theme of Christian community should figure prominently in his
works. These two emphases, inwardness of experience and out-
wardness of friendship, must be held in tandem if we are to appreciate his theology.

The idea that Schleiermacher's theology is experientially oriented
has been worn smooth through repetition by theologians. However, one needs to take into account both his determination to
situate theological reflection within ecclesial tradition and the historical dimension in his reinterpretation of the pattern of the theological
encyclopaedia. Theology, for Schleiermacher, is always undertaken
within a particular church tradition, and is aimed at helping the
church define its identity. The latter entails adopting a critical stance
so that tradition may be assessed. It is with the aim of evaluating
and reconceiving Christian tradition in terms of the challenge posed
by Kant and the Enlightenment that he promulgates the notion of
Gottesbewusstsein. Experience in Schleiermacher is not mystical in the
sense of an intuitive groping after that which is ineffable and eludes
human description. His emphasis on ecclesial mediation renders his
position closer to Bernard Lonergan's notion of "mediated immediacy"[97] than a pure interiority and immediacy of experience.

We wish to argue that *Schleiermacher's claim that God-consciousness is
present in all people is a natural implicate of his theological anthropology; and
that the concept of experience in his theological system is inalienably rooted in
history and ecclesiality.* Arguably, Schleiermacher's understanding of subjectivity is a restatement of the theological anthropology of his pietistic and Reformed faith. The quality of being simultaneously active
and receptive inherent in his idea of the feeling of absolute depend-

---

[95] In his letter to Elenore Grunow, Schleiermacher writes: "You have declared
me to be a virtuoso in friendship, and you may be right, for I do believe that I
am this by the grace of God." *Letters*, 1:322; cf. Redeker, *Schleiermacher*, 18.

[96] *Letters*, 1:309. At another point, he writes: "every human being must, as a matter of course, live in a state of sociableness; he must have one or more persons to
whom he can communicate his innermost thoughts and feelings, and the ways in
which he is led. In a word, everything that is in him ought, if possible, to be communicated to another. Thus it is ordained in accordance with the divine dictum:
'It is not good for man that he should be alone.'" 1:200f. See also F. Schleiermacher,
Soliloquies: An English Translation of the Monologen, tr. Horace Leleand Freiss (Westport:
Hyperion Press, 1926), 74.

[97] *Method in Theology* (New York: Herder & Herder, 1972), 77, 273.

ence may be compared with Calvin's correlation of the knowledge of God and the knowledge of man at the beginning of his *Institutes*.[98] Just as God and man are ontologically distinct yet correlated in Calvin, in Schleiermacher's estimation, human consciousness is inviolably and fundamentally oriented towards God. We find here an echo of Calvin's idea of the *divinitatis sensus* inscribed on all human hearts, even though Schleiermacher's exposition is rather different from Calvin's.[99] While he may not describe it as such, Schleiermacher's view of consciousness as God-infused, intersubjectively determined, and universally true of all humans, is conceptually consonant with the *imago Dei*. Redemption as the restoration of the sin-marred image of God in humankind is in Schleiermacherian rhetoric, the reversal of the elision of God-consciousness in people through the salvific influence of Christ.

Besides this transcendental/theological orientation, experience has both an historical and an ecclesial character in Schleiermacher. As we noted earlier, his understanding of "feeling" or consciousness is not an abstract sensation or psychological state. His construal of subjectivity as meaning-filled, pre-reflective human existence in lived interaction with the world, anticipates the phenomenology of Husserl. Schleiermacher's correlation of self and world in his analysis of consciousness may be compared with the primacy of the life-world (*Lebenswelt*) as the foundation of theoretical cognition and judgment in Husserl.[100] All this is to underscore the fact that far from being an ineffable interiority, subjectivity in Schleiermacher is about human experience irretrievably entangled in the web of intersubjectivity. In him we find intimations of Husserl's transcendental subjectivity.

Support for this interpretation of Schleiermacher comes from his view on the positivity of the Christian faith and a "sacramental" notion of history. Christianity is for Schleiermacher a positive and revealed religion historically rooted in the "miraculous fact" (*wunderbare Erscheinung*) of the divine causality of Christ.[101] Theology is a

---

[98] J. Calvin, *Institutes of the Christian Religion*, 2 vols., ed. John T. McNeill, tr. Ford Lewis Battles (London: SCM, 1961), I.1.1–2: "Without knowledge of self there is no knowledge of God." "Without knowledge of God there is no knowledge of self."

[99] *Institutes*, I.3.3.

[100] Edmund Husserl, *Crisis of European Science and Transcendental Phenomenology*, tr. David Carr (Evanston: Northwestern University Press, 1970), 124. See Williams, *Schleiermacher*, 26–34.

[101] The historical facticity of revelation is for Schleiermacher the origin of Christianity. *CF*, §10.

"positive science".[102] The redemptive significance of the mission and nature of Christ is explicated in terms of the Church, the Body of Christ, as the community through which the Kingdom of God is realized in history and the divine election consummated.[103] The idea of the Kingdom of God provides him with a theological interpretation of history, and is prominent in the *Glaubenslehre*.[104] Hinze characterizes this as a "sacramental" view of history in that the Church is seen as the concrete medium in history of God's gracious salvation effected through Christ. History, in this understanding, is an "organic unity",[105] not in Newman's sense that everything which happens in history is already implicitly given and anticipated, or that history since Christ is uniform and homogeneous, but in the sense that there is continuity of identity in the midst of changes and development. This "organic dialectic" view of history, according to Hinze, combines two insights:

> On the one hand, organic unity conveys the great romantic equation of life: the whole is everything and each part must be viewed in relation to that whole. On the other hand, this affirmation of the whole must be balanced with the romantic appreciation of the individual part; each individual historical part—person, event, community, nation— has its own integrity as a part and each part must also be viewed as a reflection of a larger whole. The attempt to discern the organic unity in history requires correctly constructing the relation of part to whole.[106]

---

[102] CF, §93; and Schleiermacher, *Kurze Darstellung des theologischen Studiums zum Behuf einleitender Vorlesungen*, ed. H. Scholz (1910; rpt., Darmstadt: Wissenschaftliche Buchgesellschaft, 1973); ET: *Brief Outline on the Study of Theology*, tr. Terrence N. Tice (Atlanta: John Knox, 1966), §1. By "positive theology," Schleiermacher means a definite or particular religion which is concretely historical; from Latin *positus* or (less commonly) *positivus*, meaning something given, or something "put there." See Sykes' discussion in *Identity*, 87f.

[103] *CF*, §87.3, cf. pp. 119–20, 123–5. Schleiermacher affirms that the Church as the Body of Christ "is related to Christ as the outward to the inward, so that in its essential activities it must also be a reflection of the activities of Christ. And since the effects produced by it are simply the gradual realization of redemption in the world, its activities must likewise be a continuation of the activities of Christ Himself." *CF*, §127, pp. 589–90. See also: Gerrish, "Schleiermacher," 144; idem, "The Nature and Theater of Redemption: Schleiermacher on Christian Dogmatics and the Christian Story," in *Continuing the Reformation: Essays on Modern Religious Thought* (Chicago & London: University of Chicago Press, 1993), 196–216.

[104] See for instance: *CF*, §9, p. 43; §§102–5, pp. 439–75; §113, p. 528. The importance of the language of the Kingdom of God in Schleiermacher's dogmatics is often overlooked. For a summation of his view on the Kingdom of God, see Bradford E. Hinze, *Narrating History, Developing Doctrine: Friedrich Schleiermacher and Johann Sebastian Drey* (Atlanta: Scholars Press, 1993), 37–50; cf. 170.

[105] Hinze, *Narrating History*, 6–11, 62f.

[106] Ibid., 70; & *Brief Outline*, §150.

The historical actualization of salvation through the sacramental mediation of the Church gives history the character of an organic unity, yet not in such a deterministic manner that individual contribution is elided. History is narrated in terms of the organic growth of the Kingdom of God in history. This framework, involving a reciprocity of influence between the whole and the individual, as well as between the organic life of the Church and external factors in the world,[107] allows Schleiermacher to forge a new understanding of doctrinal identity and change. We have in Schleiermacher, Thiel suggests, a "far more interesting and original theory of [doctrinal] development" than that in Newman's *Essay*.[108] Theology is positive in that it concerns the specific tradition in which theology is rooted. In view of this, Thiel suggests that the theologian must

> address the historical continuity of the tradition he claims as his own and which he serves. In Schleiermacher's understanding, it is the theologian's task first, to identify the definitive elements of that tradition; second, to elucidate the tradition's past and delineate its shape in the present; and third . . . to establish principles for the proper guidance of the tradition in the present and into the future.[109]

Seen in this light, Schleiermacher's anchoring of theological reflection in a tradition which flows from the past, engages the present and orientates the future, is not that different from Gadamer's rehabilitation of tradition in hermeneutics. Gadamer's reading of Schleiermacher, like Dilthey's, tends to accentuate the psychologizing tendency and the element of interiority in him at the expense of his concern for tradition and historicity,[110] a neglect similarly found in critics like

---

[107] The Christian community as a living organism is not hermetically sealed off from the world, and as such is not immune to "diseases" and corruption. Schleiermacher alerts us to this possibility in *Brief Outline*, §35 ("Diseased conditions do occur in historical entities, no less than in organic."), §54; *CF*, §21; *Die christliche Sitte*, ed. L. Jonas, *sämmtliche Werke*, I/12, 2d ed. (Berlin: G. Reimer, 1884), 118–21, 200–205.

[108] John E. Thiel, "Orthodoxy and Heterodoxy in Schleiermacher's Theological Encyclopedia: Doctrinal Development and Theological Creativity," *HeyJ* 25(1984): 142; also his, *Imagination & Authority: Theological Authorship in the Modern Tradition* (Philadelphia: Fortress, 1991).

[109] Thiel, "Orthodoxy," 146. "Schleiermacher argued throughout his career that the theologian's work is only legitimate to the degree that it represents, and in so doing speaks *from within*, a particular Church." 147 (emphasis added). See also Gerrish, *Tradition and the Modern World: Reformed Theology in the Nineteenth Century* (Chicago: University of Chicago Press, 1978), 13–48.

[110] Gadamer says as much in his "Afterword" to *TM*, 565: "Perhaps I overemphasized Schleiermacher's tendency toward psychological (technical) interpretation rather than grammatical-linguistic interpretation." See: Thiel, *Imagination*, 55–56.

Barth, Brunner, Bender and Flückiger.[111] The element of historicality is more implicit than it is explicit in Schleiermacher. And it is
entirely understandable that Gadamer, in his critique of consciousness as interiority, may have overstated his criticism of Schleiermacher.
What we seek to do is to make explicit what is implicit in Schleiermacher, vis-à-vis that his understanding of experience presupposes a
framework of historicity. That Schleiermacher is implicitly committed to historicality, can be seen in his *Kurze Darstellung*, where the
historical dimension of theology is elevated to a level of importance
unprecedented in the history of theological encyclopedia.[112]

The relationship between inwardness and historicality is consonant
with Schleiermacher's hermeneutical reflections. The differentiation
between grammatical and technical (psychological) interpretations
bears testimony to the tension between the empirical givenness of
linguistic tradition and discursive categories on the one hand, and
the intuitive or divinatory dimension on the other.[113] This tensive
polarity between the "objective" and "subjective" is a key feature of
Schleiermacher's thought,[114] and is true of his theological method as

---

[111] Barth, *Schleiermacher*; Emil Brunner, *Die Mystik und das Wort: Der Gegensatz zwischen moderner Religionsauffassung und christlichen Glauben dargestellt an der Theologie Schleiermachers*
(Tübingen: J. C. B. Mohr [Paul Siebeck], 1924); Wilhelm Bender, "Schleiermachers
Lehre vom schlechthinnigen Abhängigkeitsgefühl im Zusammenhang seiner Wissenschaft," in *Jahrbücher für deutsche Theologie*, 16 (Gotha: Rudolf Besser, 1871), 79–146;
Felix Flückiger, *Philosophie und Theologie bei Schleiermacher* (Zollikon-Zurich: Evangelischer Verlag, 1947).

[112] Thiel, *Imagination*, 41. In this regard, one should note that Schleiermacher
regards dogmatic propositions as descriptions of the consciousness of the *Church*, and
that these be judged on the basis of their coherence with the "Evangelical confessional documents" and the "New Testament Scriptures". *CF*, §§27, 30–31; cf. Sykes,
Identity, 99. In Hinze's descriptive label, *Narrating*, 177f., the theologian in Schleiermacher's view, is an "organic leader" who is firmly situated in the life of the
Christian community and working toward a consensual agreement between Christian
doctrines and the faith of the Church. See *Brief Outline*, §202; *CF*, §§153–5. Besides
ecclesial criteria, the formulation of doctrines must take into account extra-ecclesial
cultural factors, i.e., dogmatics evaluated in terms of their responsiveness and adequacy to modern scientific and philosophical discourses. See *Brief Outline*, §§160,
167, 177; *On the Glaubenslehre*, 64.

[113] It is clear from Schleiermacher's *Hermeneutics*, that consciousness is linguistically mediated and that subjectivity is understood from the standpoint of language.
Hinze observes: "for Schleiermacher there is a dialectical relationship between the
inner consciousness of the Church and the linguistic heritage of the Scriptures,
ecclesial creeds, and doctrinal formulations." *Narrating*, 102. See also: Eduardo
Mendieta, "Metaphysics of Subjectivity and the Theology of Subjectivity: Schleiermacher's Anthropological Theology," *Ph&T* 6(1992): 276–90.

[114] Schleiermacher refuses to bifurcate the intellectual (reason) and the affective
(faith/feeling) into separate compartments. His *Glaubenslehre* was written as a response

a whole. Failure to appreciate this balance between linguistic tradition (corporate) and intuitive apprehension (individual) in him will
lead, as in the case of Lindbeck, to a misunderstanding, if not mis-
representation, of his project.[115] The importance of the linguistic heritage of Christianity in Schleiermacher, specifically his view on the
realization of the Kingdom of God through the Church in history,
should caution us against portraying him as an advocate of a pure
mystical interiority.

It is in the relationship between the experience of the individual
and the inherited linguistic tradition of the Church that Schleiermacher's understanding of doctrinal development is instructive. Theological development in his view involves a dialectic between orthodoxy
and what he calls an "inspired heterodoxy"[116] or a "divinatory heterodoxy." Orthodoxy refers to the inherited dogmas and doctrines
of the Church, while "heterodoxy" refers not so much to deviations
from the faith—for which Schleiermacher reserves the word "heresy"—
as that which is new, contemporaneous, innovative, and different
from what had been expressed in the past.[117] It is important to note
that he is *not* downplaying the difference between orthodoxy and
heresy. On the contrary, one of the tasks of theology, he asserts, is
to sift and interrogate the Christian past to discern the orthodox
from the heretical.[118] What he wants to say is that the acknowledged
"orthodox" beliefs are always open to critical reassessment.

---

to F. H. Jacobi, who had described himself as a pagan in intellect but a Christian
in feeling. In Jacobi's metaphor, the speculative intellect and the pious heart are
like two bodies of water that cannot come together. Schleiermacher rejects this
dichotomy and argues that they necessarily belong together in a "galvanic pile". In
his letter to Jacobi, he speaks of "the two foci of my own ellipse". This letter is
reproduced in Martin Cordes, "Der Brief Schleiermachers an Jacobi: Ein Beitrag
zu seiner Entstehung und Überlieferung," *ZTK* 68(1971): 195–212, esp. 208–11; cf.
Curran, *Schleiermacher's Glaubenslehre*, 26f; Gerrish, "Schleiermacher," 125–26.

[115] See Lindbeck, *Doctrine*, 21, 32f; Georg Behrens, "Schleiermacher *Contra* Lindbeck
on the Status of Doctrinal Sentences," *RelS* 30(1994): 399–417; Hinze, *Narrating*, 95
n. 32; McGrath, *Genesis of Doctrine*, 22; Spiegler, *Eternal Covenant*, 136–56. The same
critique of Schleiermacher is found in Proudfoot, *Religious Experience*, 9–40.

[116] "First Letter to Lücke," *On the Glaubenslehre*, 53.

[117] *Brief Outline*, §203, where "orthodoxy" entails "holding fast to what is already
generally acknowledged, along with any inferences which may naturally follow." And
"heterodoxy" consists in "every element construed in the inclination to keep the
conception of doctrine mobile and to make room for still other modes of apprehension."
Cf. *CF*, §154, p. 690: "no definition of doctrine . . . can be regarded as irreformable
and valid for all time." On heresy, see *Brief Outline*, §§58, 61–62; *CF*, §21.

[118] This is the specific function of "polemics," a subdiscipline within the first of
his tripartite division of the theological task. See *Brief Outline*, §§54–62; Thiel,
Imagination, 38–44.

By "heterodoxy," Schleiermacher refers to that in the present which is not in the formulation of the past. Doctrine in his view is never something which is timeless and immutably fixed. It always contains within it the possibility of the unprecedented and the new. This is consistent with his hermeneutics. Just as every reading of a text is intrinsically provisional and potentially corrigible in the light of subsequent readings, similarly theological conclusions drawn on one's interpretations of Scriptures cannot *in principle* be closed to further refinement or development. Thiel explains what heterodoxy is in Schleiermacher's system:

> Heterodoxy is that element of doctrine without which there would "still be no conscious and free mobility" [*Brief Outline*, §204] in the development of doctrine. The heterodox dimension of doctrine captures the present determination of Christian faith in history and highlights the relationship of the most recent sensibilities of the tradition to the time-honored orthodox expressions of the past. Heterodoxy is the exploratory spirit in contemporary doctrine. It yearns to set sail from the familiar waters of its orthodox haven but only in order to plot a pioneering course through the uncharted seas of the tradition's present vitality and relevance. Heterodoxy is not a quality of doctrine to be avoided but an essential trait of all valid doctrine.[119]

The concept of heterodoxy thus has positive connotations. Be that as it may, we think that the use of the word "heterodoxy" is unfortunate since in popular understanding it is virtually synonymous with heresy. A less inflammatory approach might be to depict the relationship between orthodoxy and heterodoxy (or the not-yet-ortho-dox)[120] in terms of what we proposed in the last chapter: a dialectic of continuity and discontinuity in doctrinal development, or a dialectic involving fixity and openness. This allows one to maintain faithfulness to the essence of Christianity (as set forth in the doctrinal heritage of the past) while at the same time make room for the novel, creative and constructive in dogmatic definition.

---

[119] Thiel, *Imagination*, 49.

[120] Schleiermacher's own description gives ammunition for such a depiction. Speaking of his *Glaubenslehre*, he writes: "I am firmly convinced, however, that my position is an *inspired heterodoxy* that in due time will eventually become orthodox, although certainly not just because of my book and perhaps not until long after my death." *On the Glaubenslehre*, 53 (emphasis added). Nevertheless, he does not deny that heterodoxy can be potentially harmful and lead to heresy. He speaks of "false heterodoxy" whereby Christianity imbibes elements from its culture indiscriminately. *Brief Outline*, §206.

Experience in Schleiermacher must therefore be appraised in the light of an individual's situatedness in history and in the Church, both of which are strongly centred in Jesus Christ. Jacqueline Mariña maintains that

> Schleiermacher does not attempt to deduce the truth of revelation from human experience alone; rather is faith a response, in love, to revelation, one in which the contents of revelation are assimilated and lived by the innermost core of the person, and only as such is treated as experience. The experience of faith, then, can only occur within a pre-established context wherein that which is revealed in Jesus Christ sets up and governs both content and context of the experience.[121]

Religious affections are thus Christologically determined, the consequence of one's immersion in the life of the Christian community. Theology arises from the Church but has a responsibility towards it; it is both the child and servant of the church. Theology is the special responsibility of church leadership, and theological knowledge must always be a churchly discipline or it ceases to be theological.[122]

B. *Christology as Self-involving: Beyond the Mind-Heart Dichotomy*

In saying that "dogmatic treatment of doctrine is not possible without personal conviction",[123] Schleiermacher highlights the self-involving dimension of theological reflection. Christian dogmas are nurtured in the womb of "inner experience": "For there is an inner experience to which they may all be traced: they rest upon a *given*"; and "a true appropriation of Christian dogmas cannot be brought about by scientific means and thus lies outside the realm of reason: it can only be brought about through each man willing to have the experience for himself".[124] The distinction he makes between "scientific means" and "inner experience" in theological understanding is not only a romantic move to circumvent Kantian rationalism, but

---

[121] "Schleiermacher's Christology Revisited: A Reply to His Critics," *SJT* 49(1996): 182.

[122] See *Brief Outline*, §§3, 5–6; cf. Curran, *Schleiermacher's Glaubenslehre*, 140. On the importance of church leadership and theology in Schleiermacher, see Stephen W. Sykes, "Schleiermacher and Barth on the Essence of Christianity—an Instructive Disagreement," in James O. Duke & Robert F. Streetman, eds., *Barth and Schleiermacher: Beyond the Impasse?* (Philadelphia: Fortress, 1988), 100–104.

[123] *Brief Outline*, §196. Schleiermacher appeals to the primacy of individual conscience in matters of faith; see *CF*, §154.

[124] *CF*, §13.2, p. 67.

also an anticipation of the contemporary rejection of the dominance
of Enlightenment objectivism in lieu of a more personalistic but
tradition-shaped epistemic approach. Gadamer would have found in
Schleiermacher an ally here, for like Gadamer, the latter argues that
the detached and objective stance of science is not the only path to
understanding.[125] For theological understanding, like that in the human
sciences, cannot be distant and detached from its object but must
necessarily engage the interpreter.[126]

---

[125] The affinity between Schleiermacher and Gadamer gains further credence
when we consider how the former anticipates and the latter echoes Husserl's phenomenology. In this regard, it is interesting that Hinze, *Narrating*, 191f, describes
Schleiermacher's project in terms which are remarkably similar to Bernstein's depiction of Gadamer's hermeneutics. While Gadamer's proposal represents a move
"beyond objectivism and relativism," Schleiermacher's is situated somewhere "between
relativism and foundationalism," where the latter signifies Cartesian objectivism.
Schleiermacher has been accused of both relativism and foundationalism, the former
in the sense of sacrificing truth at the altar of modern thought, and the latter in
terms of an epistemological approach premised on the self-justifying, universal and
indubitable platform of direct experience or consciousness. On the charge of relativism,
see: Barth, *Protestant Theology*, 425–73; Chadwick, *Bossuet to Newman*, 104–11, 116;
Jan H. Walgrave, *Unfolding Revelation: The Nature of Doctrinal Development* (Philadelphia:
Westminster, 1972), 179–277, 282–9, 331, 401; on Schleiermacher's foundationalism of experience, see Lindbeck, *Doctrine*; and Thiemann, *Revelation and Theology*, 24.
   Both these criticisms fail to reckon with the nuanced way in which Schleiermacher
steers a middle course between them. The charge of relativism does not stick because
of Schleiermacher's (1) appeal to Scriptures and the creeds as norms for doctrinal
development, CF, §§27, 129–30; cf. *Brief Outline*, §83; and (2) his strong Christocentrism.
That relativism is excluded can be seen in the criteria which Schleiermacher employs
in doctrinal development. On these criteria, see Hinze, *Narrating*, 205–37. And the
charge of a foundationalism of experience does not apply either, because experience is rooted in the linguistic and ecclesial tradition emanating from the historicity of Jesus Christ. In his First Letter to Lücke, he specifically distances himself
from the kind of universalism which compromises the uniqueness of Christ, the
"view which leads to a common redemption of all through all, in which the Christ
is only one outstanding point." He laments: "But how anyone could attempt to
pass off some such view as my teaching, I can even less understand." *On the
Glaubenslehre*, 47. Moreover, his emphasis on the realization of the Kingdom of God
in history beginning with Christ and the apostolic church is contrary to the ahis-
toricality which lies at the heart of Enlightenment rationalism. One might say with
anachronistic verve that insofar as Schleiermacher rejects Cartesian objectivism and
epistemic relativism, he may be described as a proto-postmodern. Schleiermacher's
emphases on Word and Community have been seized upon in a recent essay by
Nicola Hoggard Creegan as potentially fruitful for a reclamation of Schleiermacher
as an apologist in a postmodern world. "Schleiermacher as Apologist: Reclaiming
the Father of Modern Theology", in Philips & Okholm, eds., *Christian Apologetics*, 59–74.
   [126] While this does not imply that theologians who do not personally believe and
practice the Christian religion are incapable of astute theological insights, it does
mean, as Brown, *Boundaries*, 146, asserts, that "in the long run effective theology
cannot be constructed in indifference or hostility to the communal feelings and

Schleiermacher's stubborn insistence on marrying theological assertions to experience or consciousness echoes the important connection between piety or *religio* and the knowledge of God among the
Reformers and the Protestant Orthodox. In a letter to his friend
Lücke, Schleiermacher looks to Luther for support by asking rhetorically: "Was not even our Luther such a person, and did he not
begin to reflect about his own piety . . . so that his theology is plainly
a daughter of his religion?"[127] The same support could just as well
be found in Calvin, "for whom the only knowledge of God with
which theology was to concern itself was given in 'piety'".[128] In making human experience and religiosity the entry point for his dogmatics, Schleiermacher might well be trying to appropriate Calvin
for his own purpose. While key concepts such as "consciousness,"
"feeling," and "piety" in Schleiermacher do not have a one-to-one
meaning-correspondence with what the Reformers considered as
"faith,"[129] his emphases are nevertheless largely in tune with the Protestant Orthodox who considered theology objectively as a divine
gift and subjectively as a *habitus mentis*, a mental disposition. Piety is
understood in terms of *recta Deum cognoscendi et colendi ratio*,[130] a right
way to know and honor God; and this, we suggest, is reflected in
what might be called Schleiermacher's Christology of the heart.[131]

---

practices that give such reflection its vitality". He notes further: "Much as literary
criticism must be connected to communities of writers (and often the critic will be
a writer), political science to politics (and often the scholar will be politically active),
anthropology to living communities (and often the investigator will be one of the
people being studied), and analyses of human relationships to concrete human interaction (and often . . .!), so, too, a theology somehow must have living interaction
with practicing religious groups—and often, of course, the theologian will be one
of their number." 147.

[127] First letter to Lücke in *On the Glaubenslehre*, 40–41.

[128] Gerrish, "Schleiermacher," 127, cf. Calvin, *Institutes*, I.2.1: "Piety is requisite
for the knowledge of God." See also B. A. Gerrish, "From Calvin to Schleiermacher:
The Theme and the Shape of Christian Dogmatics," *Continuing the Reformation*, 178–95.

[129] See Van A. Harvey, "A Word in Defense of Schleiermacher's Theological
Method," *JRel* 42(1962): 153–4. Gerrish observes: "Calvin . . . also used the terms
religio, sensus, and *pietas*; and while there are undoubted differences between his psychology of the religious consciousness and Schleiermacher's, it is exactly the parallels
of vocabulary that alert us to a possible similarity of method." "From Calvin," 188.

[130] Richard A. Muller, *Post-Reformation Reformed Dogmatics: Vol. 1: Prolegomena to
Theology* (Grand Rapids: Baker, 1987), 226. See also Muller on "religio" in *DLGTT*,
261–2.

[131] The expression, "Christology of the heart," is taken from Douglas F. Ottati's
characterization of the Christology he develops in his *Jesus Christ and Christian Vision*
(Minneapolis: Fortress, 1989), a work which has a strong Schleiermacherian flavour.

198 CHAPTER FOUR

In wanting to be a "modern" theologian, Schleiermacher has one foot in the Reformation heritage of Luther and Calvin, and the other in the romantic world of Schelling, Schlegel and Novalis.[132] And just as individual creativity is valorized in Romanticism alongside a stress on the necessary relation of the parts to the whole, *Schleiermacher's theological method may be regarded as an attempt to highlight (1) the affective dimension and (2) the contribution of the individual believer to theological and doctrinal definition, without severing his or her dialectical ties to ecclesial tradition and community.* His is a delicate balancing act between individuality and communality, between daring to be 'heterodox' (in the Schleiermacherian sense) in expanding the horizon of tradition, and remaining faithful to the givenness of "orthodoxy." We have already emphasized the ecclesial nature of Schleiermacher's view of subjectivity. Here we wish to accentuate the creative and contributory role of the individual in theological formulation. And the place in Schleiermacher where the two poles of individuality and traditionality intersect is in the redeemed imagination or "ecclesial piety"[133] of the theologian. It is thus instructive to reflect on the skein of elements comprising piety, creativity, individuality and fidelity to tradition entailed in theological formulation.

In his book *Imagination and Authority*, Thiel examines the concept of "theological authorship" and describes Schleiermacher's approach as an instantiation of "the romantic paradigm of theological responsibility," where the task of the individual theologian is conceived not so much "as the mimetic *representation* of an objective revelation but as the imaginative *construction* of the historical experience of salvation."[134] Instead of a simple reiteration of the received tradition, theological responsibility in the romantic paradigm involves "the creative presentation of divine truth through individual experience or original insight."[135] However, attending to the part played by the creative imagination in theological formulation should not be construed as (1) an alternate foundation to a doctrine of revelation, as Gordan

---

[132] For a discussion on Schleiermacher's relation to Romanticism, see Richard Crouter's "Introduction," to Schleiermacher's *On Religion*, 32–39.

[133] Hinze, *Narrating*, 209f.

[134] Thiel, *Imagination*, 21. Thiel's work (like Hinze's *Narrating*) considers the role of imagination in both Catholic and Protestant theology. Johann Sebastian Drey (1777–1853) is representative of the romantic paradigm in Catholic theology as Schleiermacher is in Protestant theology.

[135] Ibid., 19.

Kaufman seeks to do.[136] On the contrary, the fact of divine revelation in history necessitates a hermeneutical response which demands imaginative participation on the part of the recipient or interpreter of revelation. Neither should it be conceived as (2) a case of absolute self-referential iconoclasm, as though the individual's imagination is wholly unfettered or undisciplined. If imagination is a constituent part of consciousness as Schleiermacher understands it, then it is necessarily intersubjectively determined.[137]

This dialectical counterpoising of individuality over against received tradition recalls our earlier discussion about the tendency in Gadamer towards the sublation of individual critique within a strong linguistic ontology. Schleiermacher's stress on individual consciousness and its ability to criticise and contribute to the extension of the inherited theological horizon is necessary to provide that needed balance between individuality and traditionality. Having said that, one needs to keep in mind that while individual human experience can serve a reconstructivist agenda, as in the case of Schleiermacher's hermeneutical reconstruction of a text's meaning, it can also have a distortive, even deconstructive, effect. While Schleiermacher is right to point to the creational openness of all people to God, one wonders if he has not purchased this at the price of downplaying the malfunctional side of "un-creational" defiance against God. The fact that Schleiermacher lectured on NT doctrines, philosophy, hermeneutics, theology, and ethics, but never on the OT, coupled with his demythologization of the Genesis account of the Fall, may have inclined him towards the Irenaean view of sin as "arrested development" rather than sin as transgression and rebellion against God.[138] The noetic distortions of the "flesh" ($\sigma\acute{\alpha}\rho\xi$) which the apostle Paul warns about,[139] should put to rest any glib optimism about the innocence of the human perceptual faculty. The opposite of a feeling of absolute

---

[136] Gordan Kaufman, *An Essay on Theological Method*, 2d ed. (Missoula: Scholars Press, 1979); idem, *The Theological Imagination* (Philadelphia: Westminster, 1981); cf. Ronald Thiemann, "Revelation and Imaginative Construction," *JRel* 61(1981): 242–63; *Revelation and Theology*, 50f.

[137] For a study on imagination and theology, see Garrett Green, *Imagining God: Theology & the Religious Imagination* (San Francisco: Harper & Row, 1989).

[138] See George Nolan Boyd, *The Doctrine of Original Sin and the Fall in the Theology of Friedrich Schleiermacher* (Th.D. diss., Union Theological Seminary, 1970); and Walter E. Wyman, Jr., "Rethinking the Christian Doctrine of Sin: Friedrich Schleiermacher and Hick's 'Irenaean Type'," *JRel* 74(1994): 199–217.

[139] See Robert Jewett, *Paul's Anthropological Terms: A Study of Their Use in Conflict*

dependence is not a neutrality of indifference but a rebellious seeking after absolute *in*dependence from God. Sin has distortive noetic
effects which render suspect all interpretations based on an attempt
at penetrating the depths of human desire.

Schleiermacher's correlation of the theologian's pious consciousness and theological formulation may be understood as an example
of what Sykes calls the "tradition of inwardness" in Christian history.[140] The scriptural teaching on a requisite pure heart before one
can know and please God (e.g., Ps. 24:3–4; 51:6; Isa. 29:13; Mt.
5:8) figures in the literary output of the Judeo-Christian tradition.
The work of the Holy Spirit in penetrating into the depths of the
human heart or psyche, realigning it to the truth of the Gospel,
indwelling and infusing it with "holy affections" (Jonathan Edwards),
is an undeniable component of NT teaching (e.g., 1 Cor. 2:12; 3:16;
Gal. 3:2, 5; Rom. 5:5). What Schleiermacher says about the *Glau-
bensweise*, a particular mode of faith, as the principle of coherence
for Christian theology should be correlated with his view on the
activity of the Holy Spirit in the redemptive communication of Christ's
God-consciousness to believers.[141] Without the indwelling of the Holy
Spirit, he maintains, there can be no living fellowship with Christ
and no conformity to the image of Christ in the Church.

The need to reclaim the epistemic significance of the Spirit's inner
work in explicating the nature of theology is all the more urgent
when one considers how the practice of theology is often set apart
from spirituality. The dichotomization of theology as thought about
God and spirituality as the movement of the heart towards God is
evidence of a "dissociation of sensibility" in modern theology.[142] Louth
laments the one-sided way in which the search for truth and understanding has been construed within the scientific framework bequeathed
by the Enlightenment. Appealing to Vico's (1688–1744) notions of
fantasia (imagination) and the *sensus communis* against the Enlightenment
ideal of objective knowledge, Gadamer's protest against the domi-

---

Settings (Leiden: Brill, 1971), 49–166; and A. C. Thiselton, "The Meaning of σάρξ
in 1 Corinthians 5:5: A Fresh Approach in the Light of Logical and Semantic
Factors," *SJT* 26(1973): 204–28.

[140] Sykes, *Identity*, 35f.
[141] *CF*, §§116, 121–5, 148.
[142] Andrew Louth, *Discerning the Mystery: An Essay on the Nature of Theology* (Oxford:
Clarendon, 1983), 1–16. Louth's phrase, "dissociation of sensibility," is borrowed
from T. S. Eliot.

nance of method in the *Geisteswissenschaften*, and Polanyi's notions of personal knowledge and the "tacit dimension," Louth calls for a return to the holism of mind and heart in the knowledge of God exemplified by the patristic fathers.[143] The notion of the tacit, he suggests, has even deeper resonance in patristic thought than it has in Polanyi. In the Fathers,

> the tacit is interpreted as silence, the silence of presence, the presence of God who gives himself to the soul who waits on him in silence. The silence of the tacit makes immediate contact with the silence of prayer: and *prayer is seen in the Fathers to be, as it were, the amniotic fluid in which our knowledge of God takes form.*[144]

Tradition constitutes the tacit dimension for the Christian, and this tacitivity serves to orientate Christian experience. On this, one detects a substantive convergence between the notions of tacit knowledge in Polanyi, hermeneutical preunderstanding in Gadamer, and the "illative sense" in Newman. All three affirm the primacy of tradition in understanding, and each in his own way throws light on the nature of theological reflection.[145] Tradition is always experienced; and it is kept alive, according to Yves Congar, not only through the recollection of the mind, but also in the contemplation of the heart; it "involves not merely *a fidelity of memory*, but also *a fidelity of living, vital adherence.*"[146]

The indispensability of a believing heart in theological understanding which characterizes Schleiermacher's approach is a theme with pedigree in Augustine and Anselm. The location of theology within the heartland of devotion is exemplified in the *amor Dei* motif

---

[143] Ibid., 18–21, 29–44, 59–64.

[144] Ibid., 65; emphasis added.

[145] This does not mean that all three are alike in every way. Gadamer notes the affinity between his defense of the "personal" concept of experience and Polanyi. "Reflections," *PHG*, 36. See: Polanyi, *Personal Knowledge*; *The Tacit Dimension*; J. H. Newman, *An Essay in Aid of a Grammar of Assent* (Notre Dame: University of Notre Dame Press, 1979). Comparisons between the three have been made; e.g., Carr, *Newman & Gadamer*; Iain R. Torrance, "Gadamer, Polanyi and Ways of Being Closed," *SJT* 46(1993): 497–505. Note also Sykes's comparison of Newman and Schleiermacher in *Identity*, 118–22. On the theological appropriation of Polanyi's thought, see T. F. Torrance, *Theological Science* (London, New York & Toronto: Oxford University Press, 1969); idem, *Transformation and Convergence in the Frame of Mind* (Grand Rapids: Eerdmans, 1984); and Joan Crewdson, *Christian Doctrine in the Light of Michael Polanyi's Theory of Personal Knowledge: A Personalist Theology* (Lewiston: Edwin Mellen, 1994).

[146] Yves Congar, *Tradition and Traditions*, 15; cf. Louth, *Discerning*, 88–98.

in Augustine's ruminations on the longing of the human heart after
God, while Anselm's grounding of understanding in faith is captured
in his motto: *credo ut intelligam*, I believe that I may understand.
Theological understanding thus proceeds *from* belief and experience.
Accordingly, Lash suggests that "where the knowledge of God is concerned, it is discipleship which furnishes the necessary context of
experience."[147] Interestingly, Lash goes on to note, both Schleiermacher
and Barth took their bearings from Anselm, for they both knew that
it is only within the practice of discipleship or following Christ that
one is initiated into the mystery of the knowledge of God.

The importance of experience is evident in Rahner's essay, "The
Development of Dogma,"[148] which not only reprises the Augustinian
motif of love but is remarkably similar to Schleiermacher on the
nature of theological formulation. To Rahner, the process of doctrinal development is analogous to a lover coming gradually into a
sharper and fuller articulation of his experience of love. This sums
up nicely the relationship between the experience of the risen Christ
and the development of Christology. The person's love "may have
presuppositions . . . which are simply unknown to him. His love *itself* is
his 'experience'; he is conscious of it, lives through it with the entire
fullness and depth of a real love. He 'knows' much more about it
than he can 'state.'" In seeking to articulate what this love is, he
attempts to state "what he knows about his love, what he is already
aware of in the consciousness of simply possessing the reality (more
simply but more fully aware), so as finally to 'know'". The search
for a fuller articulation of a knowledge already possessed is "an
infinite search which only approaches its goal asymptotically."[149]

---

[147] Nicholas Lash, "Anselm Seeking," *The Beginning and the End of Religion* (Cambridge: Cambridge University Press, 1996), 155. Lash explains the rationale for the
choice of the word "discipleship": "I say 'discipleship', rather than 'believing', because
we will not hear what Anselm is saying if we indulge our pernicious modern habit
of *contracting* the sense of words like 'faith', 'hope' and 'love' until they refer to individual, private, psychic states or attitudes, rather than to shared and public patterns of conviction and behaviour." 155. This stricture is applicable as well to all
interpreters of Schleiermacher.

[148] Karl Rahner, "The Development of Dogma," *Theological Investigations, I: God,
Christ, Mary and Grace*, tr. Cornelius Ernst (London: Darton, Longman & Todd,
1961), 39–77; cf. idem, "Considerations on the Development of Dogma," *Theological
Investigations, IV: More Recent Writings*, tr. Kevin Smith (Baltimore: Helicon; London:
Darton, Longman & Todd, 1966), 3–35.

[149] Rahner, "Development of Dogma," 63–64. This is akin to Bernard Lonergan's
assertion that "Faith is the knowledge born of religious love." *Method in Theology*,

Rahner goes on to note that there is "a certain measure of reflexive articulateness" in love. The self-reflexion of the lover on his love adds to the love of the lover. Rahner contends that the progressive reflection on oneself

> in propositions . . . is thus a part of the progressive realization of love itself; . . . Original, non-propositional, unreflexive yet conscious possession of a reality on the one hand, and reflexive (propositional), articulated consciousness of this original consciousness on the other—these are not competing opposites but reciprocally interacting factors of a single experience necessarily unfolding in historical succession.[150]

What Rahner describes as self-reflexion is really the hermeneutical process of questioning experience with the aim of bringing about a more precise and fuller understanding. We submit that this setting forth in speech of the inner experience of love is comparable with Schleiermacher's analysis of the dynamics of doctrinal articulation, for like the latter's, Rahner's view of doctrinal development preserves the self-involving element which is integral to all theological articulations. And just as doctrinal development for Rahner is a reflective grasping after that "which only approaches its goal asymptotically", the goal of doctrinal validity for Schleiermacher is "neither a quality that can be absolutely fixed nor a normative constant with respect to which doctrinal expression must be aligned. Rather, doctrinal validity is an ideal that may be approximated dialectically but never reached."[151]

Just as the experience of the aliveness of Christ and the worship of Jesus by the early Christians formed the originating impulse for the development of primitive Christology, we maintain that *the*

---

115. The concept of love in the NT (ἀγάπη and ἀγαπάω) entails more than a subjective disposition; it points to the loving work of God in bringing about a new redemptive state of affairs. See Ethelbert Stauffer, "ἀγαπάω, ἀγάπη, ἀγαπητός," Gerhard Kittel, ed., *TDNT*, 10 vols., tr. & ed. Geoffrey Bromiley (Grand Rapids: Eerdmans, 1964), 1:21–55.

[150] Ibid., 64–65. Interestingly, Rahner's view of revelation as the gradual explication of the original experiential encounter with Christ in history can be read in terms of Gadamer's notion of *wirkungsgeschichtliches Bewusstsein*. Rahner, ibid., 66, writes: "Every explication which has been successfully established in propositional form illuminates the original experience, allows it to grow to its proper stature, and *becomes an intrinsic factor in the abiding life of this experience itself.*" (Emphasis mine.) See also his discussion on "Tradition" in "Considerations", 24–27. Expressions arise from the originating experience, and these in turn engender newer and fresher experiences as they become absorbed into that consciousness designated as the historical process.

[151] Thiel, *Imagination*, 48.

experiential appropriation of Christ through the Spirit's interior work today, and
the adoption of a worshipful stance towards Jesus now, are prerequisites for the
development of Christology today. It is in this sense of a contemplative
discipleship and an existential experience of the living Christ that
we speak of Christology as something done *from within.* If prayer is
indeed "the amniotic fluid in which our knowledge of God takes
form" (Louth), then the acuity of our interpretation of Christ is in
a sense related to, and even contingent on, our attitude towards
Christ. And true to the irony of faith, in the contemplative interpretation of Christ, one finds that the "object" of interpretation
becomes instead the "subject" who works to produce within the heart
of the interpreter a Spirit-effected subjectivity which is properly
responsive to Christ.

Such a description of the task of Christology may seem to some
the thin end of the wedge which leads to solipsism and subjectivism.
Yet as we have been at pains to show, *the experience of God and Christ*
is never abstracted from the web of tradition and ecclesial relationality. In his
discussion on the place of feeling in religion and religious assertions,
Macquarrie argues that feeling is never "mere feeling", a subjective
emotion void of cognitive content. That Schleiermacher's "feeling of
absolute dependence" is not a mere emotional state is compared to
Heidegger's claim that feeling-state is disclosive of man's condition
of existential thrownness, as well as R. Otto's "creaturely feeling."[152]
The symbiotic relationship between theology and the life and worship of the Christian community in Schleiermacher is an insight
which finds support in contemporary theologians like Louth, Hardy,
Ford, Wainwright, and Balthasar.[153] While the concern that truth

---

[152] John Macquarrie, "Feeling and Understanding," in *Studies in Christian Existentialism*
(London: SCM, 1965), 31–42. "The existential analysis of the disclosive character
of affective states seems to me an important contribution, and a corrective to a
one-sided reliance on the objective, detached thinking that is characteristic of the
sciences." 41.

[153] See: Louth, *Discerning*; Hardy & Ford, *Praising and Knowing God*; Wainwright,
Doxology; and Hans von Balthasar, *The Glory of the Lord: A Theological Aesthetics. Vol. 1:*
Seeing the Form, tr. Erasmo Leiva-Merikakis, ed. Joseph Fessio & John Riches
(Edinburgh: T&T Clark, 1982). That worship grants access to realms of knowledge
which are not otherwise open to us is a dominant theme in Balthasar, who argues
that a special perceptual ability is needed to apprehend the totality of the form of
theology. See Mark A. McIntosh, *Christology From Within: Spirituality and the Incarnation*
in Hans Urs Von Balthasar (Notre Dame: University of Notre Dame Press, 1996); and
David Brown, *Continental Philosophy and Modern Theology: An Engagement* (Oxford: Basil
Blackwell, 1987), 21.

should not collapse into solipsism and subjectivism is a legitimate one, one wonders if the apprehension about subjectivity in theology is not, among other things, symptomatic of a mind still labouring under the scientific objectivism of the Enlightenment. By contrast, we think experience is an integral part of the process of theological or doctrinal construction.[154]

Our proposal that Christology is necessarily self-involving and sub-jective clearly goes beyond the detached objectivism of empiricist sci-ence. To use Dilthey's distinction, what we suggest is more in line with the "indwelling" approach of the *Geisteswissenschaften* than that of the *Naturwissenschaften*. The contrast between these two can be seen in their different methodological goals. Louth observes that "concern for the mysterious is at the heart of the humanities, whereas at the heart of the sciences there is concern with the problematic."[155] The paradigm of the human sciences is that of an ongoing, self-involving and interactive engagement with the object of investigation, while that in the natural sciences is oriented toward a self-effacing and problem-solving approach. Without wanting to push this distinction too far, we think that the choice of paradigm here will have reper-cussions for one's interpretation of Christ.

If Christology is approached as a "problem" to be solved, we imme-diately run into the giant conundrum of the coinherence of the divine and human natures in a single person. The task of Christology then becomes strictly ratiocinatory, and the criterion of logic becomes the primary measure of Christological adequacy. The result is a reduc-tionistic constriction of understanding to just the workings of the intellect. Not only does this fail to reckon with the non-cognitive dimensions of human knowing, it has a low tolerance for mystery and is antipathetic to ambiguity. This propensity towards demystifica-tion and reductionism is typical of the methodology of science.

Now for the sake of argument, suppose that one day in the not too distant future we manage through some complex juggling of logic and reasoning to "solve" the problem of the incarnation. What then? In the problem-solving mode of scientism, once a problem has been

---

[154] On the place of experience in theology, see McGrath, *Genesis of Doctrine*, 66–72; idem, "Theology and Experience: Reflections on Cognitive and Experiential Approaches to Theology," *EJT* 2(1993): 65–74; Nicholas Lash, *Easter in Ordinary: Reflections on Human Experience and the Knowledge of God* (Notre Dame & London: University of Notre Dame Press, 1986).

[155] Louth, *Discerning*, 70.

resolved, there is no longer any need to dwell on it or return to it. It becomes another milestone in the history of scientific research; and scientists move on to other more intriguing pursuits. What then becomes of Christology in such a paradigm? Does it cease to be engaging? Clearly not.

By contrast, the approach of Christology from the heart is rooted in a deep respect for the mystery of the incarnation which manifests itself in a restless seeking after Christ. Instead of seeing Christ as a "problem" to be solved and then put *behind* us, Christ, in the paradigm of a Christology of the heart, is ever *before* us, beckoning us to contemplate the mystery of the Incarnation. In short, it is the restlessness of an Anselmian faith ever in search of understanding. In setting out the contrast between Christology done under the paradigm of science and that of the humanities, our intention is not to (further) dichotomize mind and heart. What we wish to do instead is to transcend the either-or situation (i.e., either a rationalism of the mind or a mysticism of the heart), and espouse an epistemological approach characterized by what William Wainwright calls "passional reason."[156] Such a position is not unlike the fine balance which Schleiermacher maintains between the objectivity of linguistic and ecclesial tradition on the one hand, and the subjectivity of God-consciousness on the other. Stell's description of the dialectical relationship between experience and tradition applies aptly to his position: "There is no tradition, but an *experienced* tradition. And there is no experience, but a *traditioned* experience."[157]

A Christology of the heart (Schleiermacher) goes hand in hand with a Christology mediated through tradition (Gadamer). The individual creative dimension involved in articulating one's belief concerning Christ must be seen alongside the corporate dimension of

---

[156] William J. Wainwright, *Reason and the Heart: A Prolegomenon to a Critique of Passional Reason* (Ithaca & London: Cornell University Press, 1995).

[157] Stell, "Hermeneutics in Theology," 687. Stephen Stell's essay is a critique of the way tradition and experience are dichotomized in Lindbeck's and D. Tracy's views on the significance of experience. Though both Lindbeck and Tracy affirm in theory a dialectical relationship between experience and tradition, in practice they consistently allow one of these poles to take precedence over the other. Lindbeck comes down in his bias on the side of cultural-linguistic tradition over experience, while Tracy does the opposite. See 680–7. Stell rightly points out that "there is an inherent relationality of experience and tradition which actually constitutes their individual identities." While Stell does not discuss Schleiermacher per se, his construal of the relationship between experience and tradition is not unlike our reading of Schleiermacher.

ecclesiality. Common to both, we suggest, is the work of the Holy Spirit, who not only superintends the disclosure of revelatory truth in Scripture, Church and history, but is the epistemological or hermeneutical bridge linking the contemplative (divinatory) heart of the Christian interpreter to the truth concerning Jesus Christ. The activity of the Spirit unites the creational sense of God inscribed on all human hearts, and that redemptive knowledge of God centred in the particularity of Christ, mediated through tradition, and enlivened within the heart of the individual.[158] Looked at in this light, we think that Schleiermacher's theological method is pertinent to our contention that Christology must be correlated with a vital experience of Jesus Christ made possible through the interior work of the Holy Spirit.

We have examined Schleiermacher's seminal reflections on hermeneutics and traced the contours of his theology of subjectivity. The balance which he maintains between the grammatical-linguistic and the psychological-divinatory in his hermeneutics is true of his theological method as well. There we find his assumption about the objective givenness of ecclesial tradition finely matched by a concern for the subjective and the experiential. Seen in this light, his position is not as radically different from Gadamer's as the latter thinks it is.[159] The stress on individuality and creativity in no way contravenes the situatedness of his understanding. On the contrary, we maintain that Schleiermacher's reflections have firm theological roots, particularly in theological anthropology and the redemptive realization of the Kingdom of God in history set in motion by Jesus Christ.

His understanding of doctrinal development as a dynamic process of interaction between orthodoxy and "heterodoxy," between continuity and discontinuity, traverses a middle path between the fixity of doctrine and an openness to change. He seeks to steer clear of the kind of objectivism in doctrine which stifles any creative contribution

---

[158] For a helpful discussion on the Spirit's work in hermeneutics and theological understanding, see Stephen Stell, "Hermeneutics in Theology," and idem, *Hermeneutics and the Holy Spirit: Trinitarian Insights into a Hermeneutical Impasse* (Ph.D. diss., Princeton Theological Seminary, 1988).

[159] Andrew Bowie's reading of Schleiermacher against the backdrop of romanticism and its linkage to modern literary theory leads him to conclude that Gadamer's view of Schleiermacher needs to be amended. See his *Aesthetics and Subjectivity: From Kant to Nietzsche* (Manchester & New York: Manchester University Press, 1990), 146–75; and *From Romanticism to Critical Theory: The Philosophy of German Literary Theory* (London & New York: Routledge, 1997).

on the part of the individual, without collapsing theology into relativism. Whether he succeeds in doing so will continue to be a debated
point. Yet in wanting to be faithful and creative simultaneously, in
seeking a *via media* between objectivism and relativism, Schleiermacher
anticipates the postmodern temper of our times.

He initiated a paradigm shift in theology by moving the focus
"from the external to the internal, from concentration on the external observance of Bible and Church to the internal persuasion of
the presence of God in the individual and community."[160] This shift
from being text-based to person-based is not without problems;[161] yet
it is precisely in the provocativeness of his proposals that we have
the measure of his significance. While we do not necessarily endorse
all his conclusions, his emphasis on individual experience supports
our case for doing Christology *from within* experience. Such an approach
we contend is consistent with the "tradition of inwardness" in Christian
theology.

---

[160] George Newlands, *Generosity and the Christian Future* (London: SPCK, 1997), 61.
So significant is Schleiermacher for theology today, that Newlands predicts that he
will be "a theologian of the future."
[161] Ibid., 60.

CHAPTER FIVE

A CHRISTOLOGY FROM AHEAD:
ESCHATOLOGICAL PROLEPSIS AND CHRISTOLOGY AS UNIVERSAL TRUTH

In response to the emphasis on the ineluctable historicality of knowledge in post-Cartesianism, we have begun in the preceding chapters to argue for an approach to Christology which is hermeneutically sensitive and attends to the formative roles of tradition and experience on the one hand, and eschatology on the other. We have designated these approaches, Christology *from within* and *from ahead* respectively. To recapitulate, Christology is *from within* in the dual sense of being situated within tradition and the inner (Spirit-engendered, tradition-mediated) experience of the theologian. As we have shown in chapters two to four, there is a dialectical relationship between the givenness of tradition and the expandability of tradition, the former accentuating continuity while the latter discontinuity.

Alongside this dialectic between corporate mediation and individual contribution, between the pastness of tradition and the contemporaneity of tradition-expansion, is another dialectic: that between the present and the future. Assertions about truth are made in the *now* in the light of the final realization of truth *then* in the Eschaton. This historical present-future tension brings the question of truth into the ambit of Eschatology. Christology oriented to the temporal nature of truth will inevitably take on an eschatological character, insofar as it focusses on the manifestation of truth *within history before the end of time*. In view of this, we propose that Christology as a truth-claim be done *from ahead*.

We shall attempt in this chapter to explicate what is meant by a Christology *from ahead* through a critical engagement with Wolfhart Pannenberg (1928–), whose approach to theology is orientated to the historicity of divine revelation and eschatological fulfilment. In the collection of essays, *Offenbarung als Geschichte*,[1] (1961) Pannenberg sets

---

[1] ET: W. Pannenberg *et al.*, *Revelation as History* (New York: Macmillan; London: Collier-Macmillan, 1968; hereafter *RaH*).

out his "dogmatic theses on the doctrine of revelation" which serve as a programmatic statement for the subsequent development of his theology. After laying the foundation with a series of works, some of which aimed at situating the discipline of theology in the context of the sciences,[2] he has since gone on to erect a three-volume *Systematische Theologie* (1988–1993)[3] edifice which sets forth his mature arguments. His linking of theological truth with an eschatological understanding of God and history has far-reaching ramifications for the task of theological construction, hence our dialogue with him here.

This chapter is divided into two halves. We will examine in the first Pannenberg's understanding of theological truth in terms of eschatological temporality. This will be in three parts: (1) an overview of the striking features of Pannenberg's theological method and hermeneutics; (2) a consideration of his Christology as the proleptic disclosure of the end of history; and (3) an examination of what might be described as Pannenberg's *eschatological trinitarian ontology* and its implications for Christological development. In the second half, we will critically appropriate Pannenberg's insights and apply them to Christological formulation. The chapter will end by spelling out what is entailed in a Christology *from ahead*.

I. *Eschatological Temporality and Theological Truth*

The theological landscape of the post-First World War period onto which Pannenberg[4] emerged as a young theologian was dominated

[2] W. Pannenberg, *Basic Questions in Theology*, 3 vols. (London: SCM, 1970–73; hereafter *BQT*), note that the American edition of *BQT* 3 is published as *The Idea of God and Human Freedom* (Philadelphia: Westminster, 1973); *What is Man? Contemporary Anthropology in Theological Perspective* (Philadelphia: Fortress, 1970); *Theology and the Kingdom of God* (Philadelphia: Westminster, 1969; hereafter *TKG*); *The Apostles' Creed in the Light of Today's Questions* (Philadelphia: Westminster, 1972); *Jesus—God and Man* (Philadelphia: Westminster, 1974; hereafter *JGM*); *Theology and the Philosophy of Science* (Philadelphia: Westminster, 1976; hereafter *TPS*); *Human Nature, Election and History* (Philadelphia: Westminster, 1977); *Faith and Reality* (Philadelphia: Westminster, 1977; hereafter *FR*); *Anthropology in Theological Perspective* (Philadelphia: Westminster, 1985; hereafter *ATP*); *Metaphysics and the Idea of God* (Edinburgh: T&T Clark, 1990; hereafter *MIG*).
[3] *Systematische Theologie*, 3 vols. (Göttingen: Vandenhoeck & Ruprecht, 1988–1993), ET: *Systematic Theology*, 3 vols. (Grand Rapids: Eerdmans, 1991, 1994, 1997; hereafter *ST*).
[4] For biographical reflections on Pannenberg, see Richard John Neuhaus, "Wolfhart Pannenberg: Profile of a Theologian," *TKG*, 9–50; cf. W. Pannenberg, "God's

by Karl Barth and Rudolf Bultmann, both of whom sought in their own ways to respond to the challenge of critical historical studies. Barth's emphasis on the world-transcending Word of God and disavowal of natural theology may have ransomed theology from abduction by liberalism, but it also led to the unwitting immunization of theology from history. The same may be said of the Heideggerian existentialist approach of Bultmann. Pannenberg laments these attempts to escape history and seek cover in the safe haven of a segmented "ghetto" known only to faith and impervious to the challenge of historical criticism. Such a Kierkegaardian turn toward a subjective validation of truth was rejected by Pannenberg alongside a disavowal of authoritarianism as a basis for theology. Theology cannot, to his mind, be based on a pietistic "decision of faith." Pannenberg's grounding of theology in the framework of God's history with humanity represents not only a *"return* to history," but also "a decisive *turn* toward an eschatological theology of history."[5] We go on now to survey the key features of his eschatological approach to theology.

A. *Revelation, History and Truth in Wolfhart Pannenberg*

We shall discuss the theological methodology of Pannenberg under four headings: the historicality of revelation; the universality of history and unity of truth; theology as the universal science of God; and history and hermeneutics.

Presence in History," James Wall, ed., *Theologians in Transition* (New York: Crossroad, 1981), 93–99; idem, "An Autobiographical Sketch," Carl E. Braaten & Philip Clayton, eds., *The Theology of Wolfhart Pannenberg: Twelve American Critiques, with an Autobiographical Essay and Response* (Minneapolis: Augsburg, 1988; hereafter *TWP*), 11–18; idem, "Theta Phi Talkback Session with Wolfhart Pannenberg," *ATJ* 46(1991): 37–41.
    [5] E. Frank Tupper, *The Theology of Wolfhart Pannenberg* (London: SCM, 1973), 20. Pannenberg's early espousal of eschatology as the framework for theological understanding coincided with the efforts of Jürgen Moltmann, Johannes Metz and Carl Braaten associated with the so-called "theology of hope" movement. While Pannenberg has never warmed to being so categorized, his rise to theological prominence, according to Stanley J. Grenz & Roger E. Olson, "occurred in the context of the advent of the theology of hope." *Twentieth-Century Theology: God & World in a Transitional Age* (Downers Grove: InterVarsity, 1992), 186. Pannenberg and Moltmann were colleagues for three years at Wuppertal, and they probably exerted influence on each other then. See David P. Polk, *On the Way to God: An Exploration into the Theology of Wolfhart Pannenberg* (Lanham: University Press of America, 1989), 10, 14 n. 41. Note that Gerhard von Rad's work on the biblical views of revelation and history exerted an important influence on both Pannenberg and Moltmann. See M. Douglas Meeks, *Origins of the Theology of Hope* (Philadelphia: Fortress, 1974), 68.

1. *The Historicality of Revelation*

Pannenberg affirms the fundamental historicality (*Geschichtlichkeit*) of
reality and speaks of "the historicness of truth."[6] Instead of escaping from critical history and seeking "sanctuary in the fortress of
specialized language and subjective experience surrounded by the
moat of revealed knowledge",[7] he wants to return theological truth
to history and work towards a positive correlation between theology
and historical inquiry.[8] Faith cannot "ascertain anything about events
of the past that would perhaps be inaccessible to the historian"[9]
because historical investigation and the inquiry of faith are not two
separate tracks, but one and the same. God is known within history,
and our normal epistemic equipment is not bypassed in grasping the
knowledge of God.

Pannenberg asserts that divine revelation should be understood
not just as something coming *in* history but *as* history.[10] While he
agrees with Barth that revelation has to do with the self-disclosure
of God, he nevertheless argues that in the biblical tradition, God
does not reveal himself directly but indirectly through his acts in
history.[11] All of history is as such the very medium of God's self-
revelation; and because revelation is the activity of God in human
history, it is universally available to "anyone who has eyes to see".[12]
To his mind, the "salvation-history" approach has turned redemp-

---

[6] Pannenberg, *BQT*, 2:58–59.

[7] Neuhaus, "Profile," *TKG*, 48.

[8] Besides Tupper, *Pannenberg*, see the following on Pannenberg's theology: Braaten
& Clayton, eds., *TWP*; Allan D. Galloway, *Wolfhart Pannenberg* (London: George
Allen & Unwin, 1973; Stanley J. Grentz, *Reason for Hope: The Systematic Theology of
Wolfhart Pannenberg* (New York & Oxford: Oxford University Press, 1990); William
Hamilton, "The Character of Pannenberg's Theology," in James M. Robinson &
John B. Cobb, eds., *New Frontiers in Theology, Vol. 3: Theology as History* (New York:
Harper & Row, 1967; hereafter *TaH*), 176–96; David McKenzie, *Wolfhart Pannenberg
and Religious Philosophy* (Washington: University Press of America, 1980); Reginald
Nnamdi, *Offenbarung und Geschichte: Zur hermeneutischen Bestimmung der Theologie Wolfhart
Pannenbergs* (Frankfurt/Main: Peter Lang, 1993); Don H. Olive, *Wolfhart Pannenberg*
(Waco: Word, 1973); Polk, *On the Way*; Christoph Schwöbel, "Wolfhart Pannenberg,"
in Ford, ed., *Modern Theologians*, 180–208.

[9] Pannenberg, *JGM*, 109.

[10] Besides Pannenberg's essay in *RaH*, see also: "Redemptive Event and History,"
BQT, 1:15–95, and his focal essay, "The Revelation of God in Jesus of Nazareth,"
in *TaH*, 101–33.

[11] *ST*, 1:227, 230–57; *RaH*, 13, 125–31; *FR*, 56; cf. Tupper, *Pannenberg*, 84–86.

[12] *RaH*, 135. Pannenberg clarifies in *ST*, 1:249f, his earlier thesis in *RaH* that
God's revelation "is open to anyone who has eyes to see". Only at the end, will
God's deity be universally patent.

tive history into a "ghetto" within the universal interconnectedness of human history.[13]

That God's revelation can be discerned in history not only shifts the focus of revelatory validity away from inner subjective experience to the public arena, it also frees it from reliance on the inspired testimony of human institutions.[14] History is "the most comprehensive horizon of Christian theology. All theological questions and answers are meaningful only within the framework of the history which God has with humanity and through humanity with his whole creation".[15] Thus insofar as theology rests on God's revelation as history, it must be a public discipline. Against Barth, Pannenberg contends that theology is not discontinuous with other forms of knowledge. It cannot opt for epistemological isolation or immunization by a "retreat to commitment."[16] Faith does not have access to knowledge shielded from the normal enquiry of reason. A retreat to "revealed truth" would, in his assessment, seriously jeopardize the universality of theology.

The focus on historical knowledge immediately raises the question as to how revelatory events may be perceived. Pannenberg rejects the epistemological dualism of public facts (*Historie*) and faith's apprehension or interpretation of these facts (*Geschichte*), and seeks to close the neo-Kantian gap between event and interpretation.[17] With an eye on the positivist's argument, he repudiates the idea that history

---

[13] *BQT*, 1:41. Pannenberg's concern to move away from a "decision of faith" approach to theology which sets it apart from general scientific enquiry is clearly seen in his early essays: "Insight and Faith," *BQT*, 2:43; "Faith and Reason," *BQT*, 2:52–53; "Eschatology and the Experience of Meaning," *BQT*, 3:208. This concern comes out of his desire to combat atheism as an alternative to Christian belief. See e.g., "Types of Atheism and their Theological Significance," and "The Question of God," *BQT*, 2:184–233; "Speaking about God in the face of Atheist Criticism," *BQT*, 3:99–115.

[14] In his "Response to the Discussion," *TaH*, 226, Pannenberg says: ". . . for men who live in the sphere in which the Enlightenment has become effective, authoritarian claims are no longer acceptable, in intellectual as little as in political life. All authoritarian claims are on principle subject to the suspicion that they clothe human thoughts and institutions with the splendor of divine majesty." See also, "Faith and Reason," *BQT*, 2:46–64.

[15] *BQT*, 1:15.

[16] Pannenberg seems haunted by William Bartley's charge that twentieth-century Protestant theology suffers from a retreat to an irrational commitment with a corresponding evasion of any form of critical debate. See Bartley, *Retreat to Commitment*; Pannenberg, *TPS*, 44f; "Revelation of God," *TaH*, 131–3.

[17] *TaH*, 126–28; Galloway, *Pannenberg*, 43.

is a collection of "brute facts," and affirms that facts are always experienced in context, and therefore already and always interpreted. Interpretation is part of any given event. The content or significance of events is given objectively with the events themselves. Revelation is embedded firmly in the medium of historical events. For Pannenberg, the medium of history is the message of revelation.[18] And since events are invariably presented in the context of particular traditions, history should be seen as "a history of the transmission of traditions".[19] This leads us to another key element in Pannenberg's theology.

2. *Universality of History and Unity of Truth*
A central and recurrent feature in Pannenberg's writings is the notion of universal history, an idea which comes out of his creative appropriation of Hegel,[20] Dilthey[21] and Collingwood,[22] as well as, if not more so, the OT—particularly Gerhard von Rad's interpretation of it—and Jesus's proclamation of the imminent Kingdom of God.[23] In

[18] The comparison between Pannenberg's approach and Marshall McLuhan's "the medium is the message" is made by Helmut G. Harder & W. Taylor Stevenson, "The Continuity of History and Faith in the Theology of Wolfhart Pannenberg: Toward an Erotics of History," *JRel* 51(1971): 34–56.

[19] "What is a Dogmatic Statement?" *BQT*, 1:199.

[20] See Pannenberg, "The Significance of Christianity in the Philosophy of Hegel," *BQT*, 3:144–77; *ST*, 1:228–9; also Polk, *On the Way*, 34–35; Grenz, *Reason for Hope*, 108; Galloway, *Pannenberg*, 112–4. Pannenberg parts company with Hegel on account that his view of universal history has no room for (1) the idea of Jesus as God's final revelation, and (2) contingent events. *RaH*, 16–18; cf. his essay, "What is Truth?" in *BQT*, 2:1–27. Pannenberg rebuts the charge that he is simply espousing Hegelianism: "I am not a Hegelian. I just happen to think that [Georg] Hegel was one of the outstanding minds in the history of modern thought, one whose work sets a high standard for us to follow.... But very few of my ideas did I actually get from Hegel—very few"; writing in Michael Bauman, *Roundtable: Conversations with European Theologians* (Grand Rapids: Baker, 1990), 48.

[21] *BQT*, 1:162–6; *TPS*, 103–16; *MIG*, 7–8, 74–5, 104–5, 162–7; *ST*, 1:54.

[22] See John P. Hogan, *Collingwood and Theological Hermeneutics* (Lanham: University Press of America, 1989), 185, 195; idem, "The Historical Imagination and the New Hermeneutic: Collingwood and Pannenberg," in Robert Masson, ed., *The Pedagogy of God's Image* (Chico: Scholars Press, 1981); and Iain G. Nicol, "Facts and Meanings: Wolfhart Pannenberg's Theology as History and the Role of the Historical-Critical Method," *RelS* 12(1976): 129–39.

[23] Pannenberg acknowledges his debt to von Rad for the insight that God's presence is revealed in history; see "God's Presence in History," 95. Pannenberg asserts: "Jesus' message of the imminent Kingdom of God precedes every Christology and every new qualification of human existence and thus becomes the foundation of both.... This resounding motif of Jesus' message—the imminent Kingdom of God—must be recovered as a key to the whole of Christian theology." *TKG*, 52–53. Acknowledging the huge influence these scriptural perspectives have on Pannenberg

contrast to other nations in the ancient near east, there was in Israel's faith, a historical consciousness which looked expectantly to Yahweh's continuing activities on their behalf in history. This confidence that God was working in *their* history eventually developed into a belief which saw *all* history as the arena of God's activity.[24] The eschatological vision of final salvation, discernible in Israel's exilic prophets, encompasses not only Israel as a nation, but also the earth. The world-wide scope of ultimate salvation in Jewish apocalypticism indicates a transformation of Israel's "salvation history" into "universal history."[25]

It is critical that we think of history as a totality because the meaning of any individual part can only be grasped in relation to the whole to which it belongs. To think historically necessitates positing an overarching universal history.[26] This projected (and provisional) view of the whole in turn influences the way reported historical events are interpreted. It is from this vantage point that we can speak meaningfully of the revelation of God in history. History as the medium of God's self-disclosure is however still in process, and will not yield its full meaning, i.e., the totality of God's revelation, until it is completed. Only from the eschatological end of history will the meaning of history be made known.[27] Here Pannenberg

---

need not preclude the presence of other influences. Besides Hegel and von Rad, others who helped shape Pannenberg's thinking include: Heidegger, Dilthey, Ernst Bloch, Karl Löwith, Hans von Campenhausen and Günther Bornkamm. See Herbert Neie, *The Doctrine of the Atonement in the Theology of Wolfhart Pannenberg* (Berlin & New York: Walter de Gruyter, 1979), 94–101, regarding influences on Pannenberg.

[24] *BQT*, 1:18.

[25] *RaH*, 133; *FR*, 15; see Tupper, *Pannenberg*, 89f.

[26] Pannenberg, "Response to the Discussion," *TaH*, 241f; *BQT*, 1:199. See also: Pannenberg, "The Significance of the Categories 'Part' and 'Whole' for the Epistemology of Theology," *JRel* 66(1986): 369–85.

[27] Thesis §2 of his "Dogmatic Theses on the Doctrine of Revelation" says: "Revelation is not comprehended completely in the beginning, but at the end of the revealing history." *RaH*, 131. Pannenberg appeals to Dilthey's observation that experience is a matter of the relationship between part and whole, and that the significance of any individual phenomenon can only be apprehended within a larger context. Thus for instance, Dilthey contends that the final significance of a life can only be measured after the person has died. While this supports Pannenberg's line of argument, he goes beyond Dilthey to posit that the "final future which constitutes the totality of life . . . cannot be identified with death." While death in a sense brings the totality of *a* life to completion, it is not until the entire history of humankind is wrapped up, that the meaning of history is evident. See Pannenberg, "Eschatology and the Experience of Meaning," *BQT*, 3:201–2; cf. 2:61–62; idem, *Apostles' Creed*, 35; and Philip Clayton, "Anticipation and Theological Method," *TWP*, 122–50.

makes a distinctive contribution with his notion of eschatological prolepsis. Drawing on the future-orientation of Jewish apocalypticism,
he sees in the history of Jesus Christ, in particular his resurrection,
a proleptic actualization of God's eschatological self-demonstration.[28]
The destiny of Jesus is the pre-actualization of the End. Revelation
is thus decidedly Christological.

For Pannenberg, the question of truth is wrapped up with the
notion of the totality of history since it is in history that God has
revealed himself. Talk about God, he asserts, "has the totality of the
world as its theme as well as God's own existence."[29] Like Hegel,
he sees truth as something which emerges in the temporal process
of history, not as a static given. Unlike Hegel, however, Pannenberg
would not allow the horizon of the future to be closed off as Hegel
did by identifying it with his own (German Idealistic) position. Such
a move would compromise the openness of history with regards to
its future.[30] In that God's revelation comes as history, and in that
history necessarily entails a contingent openness to the future, the
question of truth cannot be raised without first dealing with the complex relationship between unity and contingency in history or reality.

We do this, Pannenberg suggests, by viewing contingency retrospectively. As Tupper notes: "Unforeseen contingent events are retroactively joined to the past, transform it, and thereby restructure history's
continuity. Precisely through such *retroactive integration*, which continually reconstitutes the unity of history, the faithfulness of God expresses
itself."[31] History according to this eschatological scheme is understood as flowing from the future into the past. This calls for a standpoint which transcends history, one from which we may retroactively
integrate all contingencies. And since God as Creator is "the origin
of contingency in the world" as well as "the ground of the unity
which comprises the contingencies as history",[32] he is indispensable
to the question of truth in history. Insofar as revelation is speech
about God, "the power that determines everything that exists",[33] it
is speech about the totality of reality.

---

[28] *RaH*, 139; "The Revelation of God in Jesus of Nazareth," *TaH*, 101–123;
JGM, 53f, especially "The Significance of Jesus' Resurrection," 66–73.
[29] *ST*, 1:253.
[30] "What is Truth?", *BQT*, 2:22.
[31] Tupper, *Pannenberg*, 99.
[32] "Redemptive Event and History," *BQT*, 1:75.
[33] *BQT*, 1:1; "Speaking about God and speaking about the whole of reality are
not two entirely different matters, but mutually condition each other. Presumably

At this point, we see the different components of Pannenberg's thoughts overlapping and intersecting with each other. His notions of universal history, revelation as history, truth, and eschatological prolepsis converge in the idea of God, which is essential to both the theologian and the historian, or in Pannenbergian perspective, the theologian-historian. In this confluence of concepts, we can appreciate Pannenberg's operative view that God is the proper and all-embracing Object of Theology.

3. *Theology as the Universal Science of God*
The historical orientation in Pannenberg's theology is an integral part of his belief that theology is a discipline which seeks universal truth. This follows from the fact that God as *die alles bestimmende Wirklichkeit* (the all-determining reality) is the proper object of theology. Not only must Systematic Theology be true to its own scriptural tradition by expounding the revelation of God in Jesus Christ, it must attend to the question of universal truth as well. It is the task of theology "to understand all being [*alles Seienden*] in relation to God, so that without God they simply could not be understood. This is what constitutes theology's universality."[34] Theology, as a public discipline,[35] cannot be pursued in isolation from the broader field of human inquiry. Pannenberg exemplifies this holism in his own work, as evidenced not only by his familiarity with the human and natural sciences, but also his insistence that theology should actively engage these in conversation.[36]

God must first be seen as a problem for theology rather than as an accepted dogma—"God is the object of theology only as a problem, not as established fact."[37] And since God is the all-determining

---

it is not even possible to speak of the whole of reality without in some way thinking of God." 1:156.

[34] *BQT*, 1:1; see also *TPS*, 297f; *ST*, 1:4.

[35] See Richard John Neuhaus, "Reason Public and Private: The Pannenberg Project," *FT* 21(1992): 55–60.

[36] See Pannenberg, *TPS; ATP*; and essays on the interface between theology and the natural sciences in Carol Rausch Albright & Joel Haugen, eds., *Beginning with the End: God, Science, and Wolfhart Pannenberg* (Chicago 8 La Salle: Open Court, 1997), 37–89; also *ST*, 2:76–115; W. Pannenberg, "Gott und die Natur," *TuP* 58(1983): 481–500; idem, "The Doctrine of Creation and Modern Science," *Zygon* 23(1988): 3–21; also W. Pannenberg & A. M. Klaus Müller, *Erwägungen zu einer Theologie der Natur* (Gütersloh: Gütersloher Verlagshaus Gerd Mohn, 1970). Cf. Philip Hefner, "The Role of Science in Pannenberg's Theological Thinking," in *TWP*, 266–86.

[37] *TPS*, 300.

reality, we can, through careful reflection on objects and experiences in our world, come to an understanding of God. Pannenberg suggests that the principles used in scientific investigation should apply to theological investigation as well. Theology may be construed as a science in that it sets forth cognitive propositions (e.g., God as the determinant of all things and of reality) which are "hypotheses" or provisional assertions subject to confirmation or falsification by subsequent experience.[38]

Since the totality of reality is as yet unfinished, we can only glimpse experiences in life which anticipate this totality. Such intimations of ultimate reality can be found in the fundamental exocentricity of human life,[39] the essential openness of human beings to God which is manifested most clearly in the realm of religion. Hence the investigation of the 'problem' of God must take place among the historic religions of the world. "Theology as a science of God", Pannenberg contends, "is therefore possible only as a science of religion."[40] Out of the struggle of rival religious truth claims which takes place on the plane of religious history, true religion will emerge. For Pannenberg, the significance of any one religion in its particular stage of development can only be appraised within the framework of a history of world religions. The science of religion is a "fundamental theologi-

---

[38] *ST*, 1:56f. While theological assertions cannot be verified directly against God as object, it is possible to test assertions by their implications. See *TPS*, 332, 310. On Pannenberg's view on theology as science, see Wentzel van Huyssteen, *Theology and the Justification of Faith: Constructing Theories in Systematic Theology*, tr. H. F. Snijders (Grand Rapids: Eerdmans, 1989), 71–100; N. Murphy, *Theology in the Age of Scientific Reasoning*, 18–34; idem, "What Has Theology to Learn from Scientific Methodology?" in Murray Rae, Hilary Regan & John Stenhouse, eds., *Science and Theology: Questions at the Interface* (Edinburgh: T&T Clark, 1994), 101–126; Harvey W. White, "A Critique of Pannenberg's *Theology and the Philosophy of Science*," *SR* 11(1982): 419–36.
[39] See Pannenberg, *What is Man?*, 1–13; "Anthropology and the Question of God," *BQT*, 3:80–98; *ATP*, 43–79, 524; cf. *ST*, 1:430.
[40] *TPS*, 314. Pannenberg adds: "A theological investigation of historically given religion . . . would examine how far the conception of reality as a whole expressed in the religious tradition in fact takes account of all the currently accessible aspects of reality and is therefore able to identify the God described and worshipped in the religion as the all-determining reality." 315. In grounding theology in the religions, Pannenberg is developing his earlier reflections on anthropology as a starting point for theology. See *ST*, 1:119–88; cf. W. Pannenberg, "Religious Pluralism and Conflicting Truth Claims," G. D'Costa, ed., *Christian Uniqueness Reconsidered* (Maryknoll: Orbis, 1990), 96–106; Grentz, *Reason for Hope*, 33–36; Carl E. Braaten, "The Place of Christianity Among the World Religions: Wolfhart Pannenberg's Theology of Religion and the History of Religions," *TWP*, 287–312.

cal discipline" which investigates "the reality experienced in religious life and its history."[41]

Consistent with his aversion to immunizing religions from critical inquiry, Pannenberg wants to subject the claims of religions to scrutiny. He is not so much interested in how religious adherents feel or what notions of God they have, as in ascertaining what is revealed about God in the religions. Assertions within the religions (Christianity included) are "tested for their power to illuminate reality."[42] And given that final truth awaits eschatological unveiling, all theological assertions are necessarily provisional and hypothetical. This does not mean that they do not make any genuine truth claims, only that the ultimate veracity of these claims awaits eschatological verification.

As a universal science, the work of theology demands a critical use of reason.[43] True to his premise that truth is historical, Pannenberg contends that reason too is historical in that it involves a process of reflection which moves ever forward until the end of time. Theology cannot be justified by appeals to authority or faith; it must rest on a grasping of God's revelation in history which is accessible through the use of human rationality. He is not doing away with faith altogether in favour of a thoroughgoing rationalism. What he disavows is the turning of faith into "subjectivity's fortress into which Christianity could retreat from the attacks of scientific knowledge."[44] Faith must rest on the knowledge of God's revelation proleptically actualized in Christ. It involves risk and the entrusting of one's life upon the promissory character of the Christ-event.

To sum up, Pannenberg believes that a rational theology not only demonstrates its scientific nature, but is more importantly consonant with the nature of its subject matter, namely God. Furthermore, judging from his argumentative style of theologizing, it is clear that he believes in the universal intelligibility of reality, where people from differing traditions can debate and talk. In this, he is espousing a view not unlike the transcendental pragmatics of Apel.

---

[41] *TPS*, 363, cf. 386; see also: Edmund J. Dobbin, "Seminar on Foundations: Pannenberg on Theological Method," *CTSAP* 32(1977): 212.

[42] Ibid., 364.

[43] Pannenberg, "Faith and Reason," *BQT*, 2:46–64. For an exposition on Pannenberg and rationality, see D. Holwerda, "Faith, Reason, and the Resurrection in the Theology of Wolfhart Pannenberg," Plantinga & Wolterstorff, eds., *Faith and Rationality*, 265–316.

[44] Pannenberg, "Revelation of God," *TaH*, 131.

4. *History and Hermeneutics*

Pannenberg's understanding of universal history gives his hermeneutics its particular shape. The relationship between history and hermeneutics cannot be explored without recourse to theology. Hermeneutics is more than textual interpretation, it encompasses within it the larger question of the totality of history. As such, it is inescapably theological. Pannenberg engages Gadamer[45] and argues for a hermeneutics based on the universality of history. In seeking to bridge the gap between the present interpreter and the originating events which stand behind the texts, hermeneutics entails historical investigation, which in turn makes it necessary to posit the notion of universal history.[46] The meaning of an event is discovered by inquiring into its original setting in history. Yet this life-setting cannot be understood except in view of its place in the continuities of history.[47] Hence for Pannenberg, the question of hermeneutics leads to the question of the universality of history. Historical investigation and hermeneutical reflection are therefore really two aspects of a single theme.[48]

While Pannenberg agrees with Gadamer on: (1) the need to distinguish between the horizon of the interpreter and that of the text; (2) understanding as something which results from a fusion of the horizons of interpreter and text; and (3) the dynamic nature of the

---

[45] See: "Hermeneutic and Universal History," *BQT*, 1:96–136; *TPS*, 163f; cf. Ted Peters, "Truth in History: Gadamer's Hermeneutics and Pannenberg's Apologetic Method," *JRel* 55(1975): 36–56; Thiselton, *NHH*, 331–38.

[46] Following Gadamer, Pannenberg recognizes the historical distance between the horizon of the past and that of the present interpreter, and agrees that the two cannot be prematurely collapsed. It is in accepting the strangeness of the past or the historical particularity of the text that hermeneutical understanding can begin. As Pannenberg sees it, there are two gaps which must be crossed in hermeneutics: (1) the gap between the biblical writings and the historical events to which they refer; and (2) the gap between our period and the theology of primitive Christianity. *BQT*, 1:96.

[47] Pannenberg, *BQT*, 1:98, asserts: "Even significant individual occurrences and historical figures require for their evaluation a view of the broader continuities that extend beyond their narrower life-setting and epoch. The more significant an occurrence or a figure is, the more comprehensive must be the nexus of events to which one has to relate it in order to do justice to its true significance, at least in an appropriate way. . . . To that extent, we can justify in a general way our assertion that the event sought for in inquiring behind the texts reveals its true visage only within universal continuities of events and of meaning."

[48] See James Clark McHaan, Jr., *The Three Horizons: A Study in Biblical Hermeneutics with Special Reference to Wolfhart Pannenberg* (Ph.D. diss., University of Aberdeen, 1987), 294f.

interpreter's horizon in that it is always moving;[49] he disagrees with Gadamer's use of a conversation as a model for understanding the fusion of horizons. Unlike a conversation, in textual interpretation, the text is mute and cannot speak (back) to the interpreter. The interpreter has to put questions to it, and formulate the answers himself. Furthermore, in a conversation, the comprehensive new horizon arising from the "fusion of horizons" can remain unarticulated (conversationists are not obliged to articulate it explicitly) since there is fair agreement on the particulars of the moment. This is not so with textual interpretation.

Unlike Gadamer who shies away from making assertions for fear that it might contradict the finitude of all human understanding (the potential "infinity of the unsaid") and lead to propaganda,[50] Pannenberg thinks it is necessary to translate the new emerging horizon into assertions. We cannot restore a text to its original context of meaning (even granting that it is unspoken) without grasping what is stated there. Access to this understanding is only on the basis of assertions, not without them. Furthermore, the background for what is stated is again accessible only in assertions.[51]

Universal history is the most comprehensive horizon given our understanding of reality as historical. Since both interpreter and text are located in history, there is already a bridge connecting the two. We can build a hermeneutical bridge by "investigating the historical continuity between the present and the past situation from which the text stems."[52] For instance, the Christ-Event as a historical occurrence is mediated to us today through a tradition which links interpreters today to the past. This understanding of history as "the history of the transmission of traditions" or *Überlieferungsgeschichte* is not unlike Gadamer's notion of *Wirkungsgeschichte*.[53] The individuality of the historical Jesus and the "history of influences" arising from him belong together; fact and interpretation are inseparably bound.

---

[49] *BQT*, 1:117f.

[50] See Sullivan, *Political Hermeneutics*.

[51] Pannenberg notes: "[T]he interpreter can only become clearly conscious of the unity of that background of meaning made accessible by assertions, if this unity, for its part, also becomes the content of assertions." Ibid., 126.

[52] Ibid., 129.

[53] Theodore F. Peters, *Method and Truth: An Inquiry into the Philosophical Hermeneutics of Hans-Georg Gadamer and the Theology of History of Wolfhart Pannenberg* (Ph.D. diss., University of Chicago, 1973), 208–9, 218–20.

Unlike Gadamer who seems to focus exclusively on linguisticality or the language-event of understanding as the hermeneutical bridge which links the present to the past, Pannenberg wants to see universal history as that which provides the hermeneutical mediation of past and present. History is the ultimate horizon for hermeneutics. To apply a text from *then* to *now* necessitates bringing together different historical sources into a totality. Such a unified tradition requires a speculative projection of the whole of reality, i.e., universal history. This projection, which carries the risk of obscuring particulars, nevertheless has great potential to open up new possibilities of understanding. Pannenberg applies Gadamer's notion of preunderstanding to the question of the individual's anticipatory wholeness. Preunderstanding in Pannenberg is explicated in terms of a widening series of concentric circles of interaction, which moves from human individuality to societal context, the totality of humankind, and finally to universal history. Human individuality cannot be understood without reference to the society in which it is found, and this societal context in turn has meaning only in relation to the universal history of humankind. Following the logic of this "expanding context of meaning",[54] he shows that only when history has been consummated will the meaning of the present be fully seen.

B. *Pannenberg's Christology*

Christology is a key component in Pannenberg's theological edifice, and is integral to his view of reality, God, and the relationship between God and history.[55] Significantly, the first major work he produced after setting out his case for revelation as history was his Christology, *Grundzüge der Christologie*. He applies his earlier insights on revelatory history to the question of Christology in the book, and argues forcefully that Christology must be historically grounded. Christology, he suggests, is concerned "not only with *unfolding* the Christian community's confession of Christ, but above all with *grounding* it in the activity and fate of Jesus in the past."[56]

---

[54] Peters, "Truth in History," 46. This argument figures prominently in Pannenberg's writings, e.g., *BQT*, 1:68, 170; 2:61–62.

[55] See Elizabeth Johnson's assessment of the importance of Christology in Pannenberg, "The Ongoing Christology of Wolfhart Pannenberg," *Horizons* 9(1982): 237–50.

[56] *JGM*, 28.

The work precipitated much discussion and signaled a major shift in direction in Christology, away from the neo-orthodox Christocentrism of Barth and the existential-demythologizing Christology of Bultmann. Its main arguments are subsequently restated and expanded in volume two of his *Systematic Theology*, where he clarifies his view by way of a response to criticisms made about his earlier position. These modifications or refinements are noted by Schwöbel and Grenz.[57]

1. *Genesis of Christology and the Historical Jesus*

Unlike Kähler and Bultmann who sought to safeguard Christology from the unstable results of historical research by separating the Jesus of history from the Christ of faith, Pannenberg roots the kerygma boldly and without embarassment in the historical Jesus. He turns the Bultmannian thesis on its head by locating the genesis of Christology in the history of Jesus, particularly his resurrection, rather than in the Church's proclamation. It was not the Church that invented the resurrection, he argues, but the resurrection which made possible the

---

[57] Christoph Schwöbel, "Rational Theology in Trinitarian Perspective: Wolfhart Pannenberg's *Systematic Theology*," *JTS* 47(1996): 511f; and Grenz, *Reason for Hope.* Grenz enumerates several areas where Pannenberg moves beyond his earlier work (bracketed numbers are page references to Grenz's work): (a) While reaffirming his Christology "from below" approach, Pannenberg acknowledges that assertions about God cannot be derived solely from anthropology alone, and since Christology presupposes talk about God, it must proceed from the idea of God. (113, 135–6) There is thus in the *ST* a more nuanced exposition of his Christology "from below." Schwöbel notes that in the *ST*, the "from below" and "from above" approaches are seen as strictly complementary. "Rational Theology," 511. (b) Whereas *JGM* focusses on the background of the resurrection in apocalyptic literature (242, n. 30), the emphasis in *ST* is on the way in which the metaphoric term "resurrection" "is expressed nonmetaphorically in the New Testament by means of the religious concept of life." (118) (c) The role of the cross is given greater attention in the *ST* (120, 147). Pannenberg considers it "grotesque" to suggest that his focus on the resurrection in *JGM* entails a depreciation of the significance of the crucifixion of Christ. He states categorically: "The resurrection . . . presupposes his death; it is the raising again of the Crucified." *ST*, 2:338. (d) There is a gentle shift from the Christocentricity of *JGM* to a more conscious attempt at integrating Christology with the doctrine of God. "Pannenberg's goal in the dogmatics . . . is to unfold all doctrine, including the doctrine of Christ, in terms of the connection to the doctrine of God. Christology may lie at the heart of theology and form its middle point, but for Pannenberg the center of theology clearly is the doctrine of God, more specifically the doctrine of the Trinity." (134) (e) The logos-concept which was jettisoned in favour of the concept of revelation as the starting point for Christology in *JGM* is reintroduced in the dogmatics, albeit in a (revised) historicized form. (114–5, 137) (f) He revises the largely negative evaluation of the three offices of Christ in *JGM*. (127).

Church.[58] He wants to move the basis of Christology away from the authoritarianism of ecclesiastical confessions or reliance on personal experiences.

Instead of the "from above to below" schema of traditional Incarnational Christology, Pannenberg recommends that we build our Christology "from below" by beginning with the historical phenomenon of the Jesus-event. This procedural approach fits the main task of Christology, which is essentially an apologetic one: "to assure faith of its own foundations."[59] Pannenberg asserts, "Christology must begin with the man Jesus, its first question has to be that about his unity with God. Every statement about Jesus taken independently from his relationship to God could result only in a crass distortion of his historical reality."[60] Such an approach is a concommitant of Pannenberg's understanding of revelation as history. If God has indeed revealed himself in the history of Jesus, then an examination of that history should lead one to discern the revelation of God mediated therein.

An approach "from below" commends itself for three reasons:[61] (1) The task of Christology is to demonstrate the divinity of Christ, not to presuppose it. Consistent with Pannenberg's refusal to dichotomize faith and reason, he maintains that Christology can only be the *conclusion* of a consciously methodological approach "from below," it cannot be the starting point for the investigation.[62] (2) The distinctive historical and human features of Jesus tend to be eclipsed in a "from above" approach. (3) In order to construct a "from above" Christology, we would need to stand in the place of God himself.

---

[58] "Not infrequently the response of faith to the proclamation of Jesus is seen as the origin and basis of the confession of faith in the Easter event, though in fact the biblical testimony presents the Easter event as the basis of the faith of the disciples." *ST*, 2:286. Pannenberg states categorically: "[T]o maintain that apostolic proclamation has a *constitutive* function for the Christ event is not in keeping with the apostolic witness itself. The Easter message *follows* the Easter event; it does not constitute it." 288.

[59] Johnson, "Ongoing Christology," 242. See also G. G. O'Collins, "The Christology of Wolfhart Pannenberg," *RelS* 3(1967): 369–76.

[60] *JGM*, 36; cf. Tupper, *Pannenberg*, 129f.

[61] See summary in Richard Sturch, *The Word and the Christ: An Essay in Analytic Christology* (Oxford: Clarendon, 1991), 115f.

[62] See *BQT*, 2:46–64 on the correlation of "Faith and Reason." Pannenberg writes: "To be sure, all Christological considerations tend toward the idea of the incarnation; it can, however, only constitute the conclusion of Christology. If it is put instead at the beginning, all Christological concepts . . . are given a mythological tone." *JGM*, 279.

Christology "from below" seeks to bring to the surface a historical assumption implicit in the classical model. Mindful of the criticisms leveled at his "from below" approach, Pannenberg restates his
case in the later dogmatics, and essentially agrees that a "from below"
approach cannot be absolutized.[63] He distinguishes between methodological precedence and material primacy, the former signifying an
argument from below approach, while the latter points to the incarnation of the eternal Son in Jesus of Nazareth. The two lines of
argument "from above and from below are complementary" since
a "from below" approach necessarily entails making some assumptions about God and about humanity.[64] How else would we explicate the divinity and the humanity of Jesus unless we have some
idea as to what divinity and humanity involve? Yet the concept of
God (theology) and the concept of human nature and destiny (anthropology) cannot be arrived at independent from the revelation which
is the historical Jesus. This leads to a circular relation of reciprocal
conditioning between, on the one hand, our theological and anthropological underpinnings, and on the other, the historical Jesus.[65]

2. The Retroactive Power of the Resurrection

Pannenberg's Christology depends on his case for the resurrection.[66]
Unlike traditional Christology which tends to either locate the constitutive event in Jesus's life at the beginning of his life (the Incarnation),
or in the authoritative mien of his pre-Easter days, Pannenberg looks
to his resurrection instead as constitutive of Christology. Without the
historical resurrection of Jesus the rise of the primitive Church cannot

---

[63] *ST*, 2:277f. The refinement of a "from below" approach is first hinted at in
Pannenberg's "Afterword" to the 5th German edition of *JGM*, which is included
in the 2nd English edition (Philadelphia: Westminster, 1977), 399–410. See Philip
Clayton, "The God of History and the Presence of the Future," *JRel* 65(1985):
98–99.

[64] *ST*, 2:289; cf. Lash, "Up and Down in Christology," for a critique of the polarization of Christological approach into an either "from above" or "from below."

[65] *ST*, 2:290.

[66] John B. Cobb in his review of *JGM*, *JRel* 49(1969): 201, observes: "Nowhere
in the whole history of theology has the historical resurrection of Jesus been treated
as more determinative of every christological problem. Hence the reader's final judgment of the systematic value of the book must rest on his judgment on the adequacy of Pannenberg's case for the historicity of Jesus' rising from the dead." See
W. Pannenberg, "Did Jesus Really Rise from the Dead?" *Dialog* 4(1965): 128–35;
Herbert Burhenn, "Pannenberg's Argument for the Historicity of the Resurrection,"
JAAR 40(1972): 368–79; G. E. Michalson, Jr., "Pannenberg on the Resurrection
and Historical Method," *SJT* 33(1980): 345–59.

be plausibly accounted for.[67] He distinguishes between two strands of traditions which support the historicity of the resurrection: the tradition of the appearances of the resurrected Jesus and that of the empty grave. The purpose behind Paul's enumeration of the resurrection appearances in 1 Cor. 15:1–11 is to marshall proof for the historicity of Jesus's resurrection. These reports of appearances may be deemed historically reliable since Paul was not only chronologically close to the events themselves, but was also drawing on traditions already in circulation at the time of his writing.[68] The tradition of the empty tomb, which developed independently from the tradition concerning the resurrection appearances, provides complementary historical support.

Pannenberg dismisses the suggestion that the resurrection appearances were subjective visionary experiences on the part of the disciples, arguing that it was psychologically implausible that their faith could have survived Jesus's death. It was precisely because of the reality of Jesus's return from the dead that made possible the faith of the disciples. "The Easter appearances," Pannenberg asserts, "are not to be explained from the Easter faith of the disciples; rather, conversely, the Easter faith of the disciples is to be explained from the appearances."[69] The lack of a coherent and plausible (naturalistic) account for the transition from the activity of Jesus to the faith of the primitive Church other than the appearances of the resurrected Jesus and the phenomenon of the empty grave points, in Pannenberg's opinion, to the historicity of the resurrection.

Pannenberg takes historians to task for rejecting outright the possibility of the resurrection simply because it does not conform to their narrow concept of reality, a concept which says that "dead men do not rise."[70] Such an a priori dismissal of the resurrection of

---

[67] See Pannenberg, "Jesus' Resurrection as a Historical Problem," in *JGM*, 88–106; *ST*, 2:352–59. Pannenberg states: "Only the resurrection of Jesus, conceived in the framework of the cultural situation of primitive Christianity, renders intelligible the early history of Christian faith up to the confessions of Jesus' true divinity. If the resurrection of Jesus cannot be considered to be a historical event, then the historical aspect of the primitive Christian message and its different forms, both of which have crystallized into the New Testament, fall hopelessly apart." "The Crisis of the Scripture Principle," *BQT*, 1:8. See also W. Pannenberg, "*Dogmatische Erwägungen zur Auferstehung Jesu*," *KuD* 14(1968): 105–18.

[68] *JGM*, 90.

[69] Ibid., 96.

[70] Ibid., 109.

Jesus smacks of a positivistic historiography which does not do justice to the historical evidence. Here he develops his historiography
in dialogue with Troeltsch, rebutting specifically his use of the principle of analogy.[71] He rejects the notion that "what is said to have
taken place historically must be like other known events."[72] It is
entirely possible, on the grounds of historical argumentation, to regard
the resurrection of Jesus as an event without analogy in history.
Nevertheless, one should note that Pannenberg is not denying that
analogy can be a legitimate methodological principle of historical
inquiry.[73] His description of the resurrection as a metaphor, analogous to sleep,[74] indicates that he is not averse to the heuristic use
of analogy. What he objects to is the negative use of analogy in a
way which translates the principle as "a method of inquiry into a
view of reality as a whole".[75] Such an approach privileges an anti-
theistic and anti-supernatural ontological worldview.

Pannenberg is not saying that the fact of the resurrection alone

[71] *BQT*, 1:44–49, 53f; *TPS*, 103–16; cf. Daniel P. Fuller, "The Resurrection of
Jesus and the Historical Method," *JBR* 34(1966): 18–24. For discussions on Pannen-
berg's use of analogy, see: Langdon Gilkey, "'Pannenberg's *Basic Questions in Theology*:
A Review Article," *Perspectives* 14(1973): 37; V. A. Harvey, *The Historian and the Believer*
(London: SCM, 1967), 14–15; Elizabeth A. Johnson, *Analogy/Doxology and Their
Connection with Christology in the Thought of Wolfhart Pannenberg* (Ph.D. diss., Catholic
University of America, 1981); Michael Nevin, "Analogy: Aquinas and Pannenberg,"
Porter, ed., *Nature of Religious Language*, 201–11; Hiroshi Obayashi, "Pannenberg and
Troeltsch: History and Religion," *JAAR* 38(1970): 401–19; Ted Peters, "The Use of
Analogy in Historical Method," *CBQ* 35(1973): 475–482; "Jesus' Resurrection: An
Historical Event Without Analogy," *Dialog* 12(1973): 114f; Tupper, *Pannenberg*, 151.
[72] *ST*, 2:360.
[73] Pannenberg writes: "There is obviously an anthropocentric structure in the
way in which analogizing deliberations proceed from what lies closest to the investigator's current state of knowledge. This structure is fundamental for the methodological value of analogy as a means of knowing. Only because something about
the unknown can be concluded from what is already known can analogy prove its
power of disclosure." *BQT* 1:44. Also: "[I]n every historical judgment the evaluator's
whole experience of the world and himself plays a part. . . . What this or that historian believes to be in any way possible depends on his own picture of reality and
on the way in which he absorbs into this picture the points of view contributed by
the various sciences, from physics to anthropology and sociology." *Apostles' Creed*, 109.
[74] *JGM*, 74–75; Pannenberg, "Revelation of God," *TaH*, 115; *ST*, 2:346.
[75] Peters, "Use of Analogy," 477. "My criticism," Pannenberg writes, "is not
directed against the critical use of the principle of analogy, which is basic to the
critical historical method. This use is merely restricted. The instrument of analogy
gains precision, if judgments about the historicity or nonhistoricity of events asserted
in the tradition are based only on *positive* analogies between the tradition which is
being studied and situations known elsewhere, but not on the *lack* of such analogies." "Response to the Discussion," *TaH*, 264 n. 75.

is grounds enough for the Christian faith.[76] Only within the context
of Jewish eschatological expectation regarding the resurrection of the
dead and an apocalyptic scheme of cosmic salvation, will we understand the full and foundational significance of Jesus's resurrection.
Conceding that there is no parallel within Jewish apocalypticism to
the resurrection of an individual, he nevertheless sees in the resurrection of Jesus a proleptic realization of the final consummation
which is yet to come.[77] As a historical event, the resurrection-event
throws light on the rest of history and represents an eschatological
manifestation of God and a proleptic realization of the end. There
is in the resurrection of Jesus a manifestation of the *telos* of cosmic
history.[78] With Christ's resurrection,

> the end of history has already occurred, although it does not strike us
> in this way. It is through the resurrection that the God of Israel has
> substantiated his deity in an ultimate way and is now manifest as the
> God of all men. It is only the eschatological character of the Christ
> event that establishes that there will be no further self-manifestation
> of God beyond this event. Thus, the end of the world will be on a
> cosmic scale what has already happened in Jesus.[79]

Within this proleptic-eschatological framework, Pannenberg proposes
Christology as a development arising from the "retroactive force"
(*rückwirkende Kraft*) of the resurrection.[80] The exposition of the person
of Christ must be conducted from the standpoint of Jesus's resurrection. Insofar as the resurrection of Jesus is the pre-arrival of the
eschaton, the prehappening in the one man of that which is the destiny of all, we have in it a vantage point from which to evaluate all
things now, including the person of Jesus. The resurrection not only
vindicated the earthly Jesus, but showed us that the pre-Easter Jesus
was in fact the revelation of the Father, and in that revelation showed
himself as one with God.

The resurrection has both a retrospective significance for the sta-

---

[76] *JGM*, 111, n. 121.
[77] *ST*, 2:350; cf. *TKG*, 52. For the early Christians, the expression, "resurrection
from the dead" meant "a very particular reality expected by postexilic Judaism in
connection with the end of history." *JGM*, 74; cf. *BQT*, 3:197 n. 1.
[78] See R. David Rightmore, "Pannenberg's Quest for the Proleptic Jesus," *ATJ*
44(1989): 59.
[79] *RaH*, 142; cf. *Apostles' Creed*, 96–115.
[80] *JGM*, 133–158; *ST*, 2:303 n. 92; see Brian McDermott, "Pannenberg's Resurrection Christology: A Critique," *TS* 35(1974): 711–721.

tus of Jesus as divine, as well as "an ontologically constitutive force."[81]
Easter set in motion the process of Christian reflection which led
eventually to the Incarnation as "the conclusion of Christology".[82]
Only from the viewpoint of Easter do we appreciate the sinlessness
of Jesus, since it is impossible, in Pannenberg's opinion, to penetrate
into the inner life of the historical Jesus to establish his sinlessness.
Only by the light of the resurrection "shed backward upon his earthly
life" that we recognize God's verdict on his sinlessness.[83] This consideration of the retroactive power of the resurrection applies to the
understanding of the divinity of Christ as well.

3. *Christology and Anthropology*

Pannenberg's Anthropology and his Christology are closely connected.
This is clearly evident in the order in which his materials are organ-
ized in volume two of his *Systematic Theology*.[84] In proceeding from
Anthropology to Christology, he not only conforms to the traditional
sequence in dogmatic presentation, but is consciously working according to a "from below" paradigm. His desire is to show that Christological affirmations are not necessarily at odds with what the human
sciences are saying. This is so precisely because anthropology is determined by the doctrine of God.

Made in the image of God, there is built into the very constitution of human beings an "openness to God" which orientates all
people to a destiny (*Bestimmung*) of fellowship with God.[85] Consistent
with his view on the ontological priority of the future, Pannenberg

[81] Timothy Bradshaw, *Trinity and Ontology: A Comparative Study of the Theologies of Karl Barth and Wolfhart Pannenberg* (Edinburgh: Rutherford House Books, 1988), 158; cf. *JGM*, 136, 153.
[82] *JGM*, 279; Johnson, "Ongoing," 244.
[83] *JGM*, 363; *ST*, 2:306.
[84] Stanley Grenz's observations are instructive: "The delineation of the doctrine of Christ in the dogmatics is divided into three chapters. The first forms a bridge to the preceding anthropology section. In the second Pannenberg develops the central themes of Christology itself in the context of the doctrine of God. And the third provides a link between this section and the ecclesiology that follows. In this way the main delineation of Christology (chapter 10) is encompassed by two chap-
ters that place Jesus in connection with humanity (chapters 9 and 11). The basic content of this section may be summarized by three phrases relating to three aspects of the person and work of Jesus emphasized respectively in these chapters—the eschatological new human, the man united with God, and God's reconciliation of humanity." *Reason for Hope*, 112.
[85] *ST*, 2:203–210; *JGM*, 193. See also *ATP*, 43f.

regards the image of God in humanity as something which is realized only in the future destiny of humankind. And insofar as Christ
is the eschatological or last Adam, in him lies the true destiny of
the human race. "In Jesus himself the ultimate destiny of man for
God, man's destiny to be raised from the dead to a new life, had
been fulfilled."[86] This, as Pannenberg alludes to, is the thrust of Paul's
understanding of Christ as the true Image of God. Christology and
Anthropology are thus intertwined.

Just as the resurrection, understood within the apocalyptic framework, signals the proleptic dawning of the eschaton which has
significance for the whole world, there is a cosmic and universal
impact to Christ as the eschatological Man. Pannenberg notes: "By
depicting Jesus as the new eschatological Adam, and therefore as the
definitive form of humanity, the apostle Paul has given expression
to the universal significance of the person and history of Jesus in the
light of the Easter event—a significance that reaches far beyond the
people of Israel."[87]

4. *The Divinity of Christ and the Trinity*

The resurrection is the hermeneutical key to the identity of Jesus as
the eternal Son of God. On the basis of the resurrection, he is shown
to be in fact essentially one with God. Pannenberg does not mean
by this that Jesus received his divinity only at the resurrection. Nor
does he mean to depreciate his pre-Easter life and claims.[88] He seeks
instead to delineate the methodological route upon which we may
arrive at the knowledge of the divinity of Christ. Consistent with his
view of God's self-revelation as indirect rather than direct, Pannenberg's
approach to the question of the divine identity of Jesus is via what
he calls a "detour," for the question cannot be answered directly.

> The unity of the man Jesus with the eternal Son of God results rather
> only by the way of a *detour*. In the course of this detour, we must also
> find the justification for using the conception of a "Son of God" at
> all. It is a detour by way of Jesus' relation to the "Father," i.e., to the
> God of Israel whom he called Father. Only the personal community

---

[86] *JGM*, 192.
[87] *ST*, 2:315.
[88] Pannenberg, *JGM*, 137: "Jesus' unity with God, established in the Easter event,
does not begin only with this event—it comes into force retroactively from the perspective of this event for the claim to authority in the activity of the earthly Jesus."
Cf. McDermott, "Pannenberg's Resurrection Christology," 712.

of Jesus with the Father shows that he is himself identical with the Son of this Father.[89]

Pannenberg regards the "two-natures" Christology of Chalcedon as a futile attempt at holding together the mutually incompatible Alexandrian "unification Christology" and the Antiochean "disjunction Christology," the former divinizes the humanity of Jesus while the latter undermines the divinity of Christ.[90] To persist in positing the simultaneity of two natures in a single person would only lead to an "impasse" from which there is no escape. Furthermore, it does not take seriously enough the concrete human person of Jesus.

The way out of this impasse is to understand Jesus's unity with God in terms of his filial relationship with the Father, to interpret "divinity" in terms of the absolute obedience of Jesus as Son to God as Father. It is in the total dedication of his self to the will of the Father—the mark of true and authentic humanity—that we perceive the unity of Jesus with God. In the conscious self-distinction of Jesus from the Father we have the inner basis of his divine sonship.[91] Such an approach, Grenz observes, is in line with Pannenberg's overarching programme. "It fulfills the methodological requirement that the ontological constitution of the unity of the person of Jesus not bypass the history of Jesus . . . but be derived from the relationship of the historical Jesus to the Father found in the unfolding of Jesus' history."[92]

The divinity of Jesus is thus seen in his unity with the Father apprehended retroactively from his resurrection. This retroactive force indicates that Jesus did not die the deserved death of a sinner,[93] and it extends even further back through the pre-Easter Jesus to Christ's preexistence,[94] so that a Christology "from below" moves on logically to a Christology "from before". Probing the history of Jesus, one is led to posit the preexistence of the eternal Son of God who became incarnate in Jesus of Nazareth.

To be sure, Pannenberg, like Chalcedonian Christology, wants to preserve the full and true humanity and divinity of Jesus. He boldly

---

[89] *JGM*, 335.
[90] *JGM*, 283f; *ST*, 2:379f.
[91] *ST*, 2:372.
[92] Grenz, *Reason for Hope*, 120.
[93] *ST*, 2:374.
[94] *ST*, 2:367–71.

asserts: "Jesus is no synthesis of human and divine of which we can only see the human side in the historical Jesus. Rather, *as this man, Jesus is God*."[95] The thrust of his Christology is to show that precisely *in* the particularity of his humanity, a humanity distinguished by a self-differentiation from and submission to the Father, that Jesus is the Son of God.[96] And in the light of Easter, we recognize that Jesus has always been the Son of the Father. We cannot restrict the incarnation only to the conception of Jesus, but must take into account the entire life of Jesus. "Only in his life as a whole is he the Son."[97] The divinity of Jesus does not consist in his relation to a preexistent Logos or Son of God distinct from himself, but in his relation to the Father. Jesus's divinity may be seen as "his revelatory unity with God."[98] This brings the discussion on Christology back to Theology proper, since revelation is understood as God's self-revelation through the history and fate of Jesus. The integration of Christology and the doctrine of God is evident in Pannenberg's view of the incarnation of the Son as God's self-actualization in the world.[99] The self-differentiation of the Son from the Father eventually paved the way to a Trinitarian theology, for the latter arose out of primitive Christology.

It is significant that Pannenberg begins his exposition on the doctrine of the Trinity with the message of Jesus.[100] The doctrine of the

---

[95] *JGM*, 323 (emphasis added).

[96] *JGM*, 342. To speak of Jesus' personal and revelatory unity with God necessarily raises the question of the nature of the self-understanding of the pre-Easter Jesus. This issue cannot be avoided in Christology, even though establishing it is both exegetically and historically difficult. See *JGM*, 325–34. Agreeing with critical biblical scholarship after D. F. Strauss and F. C. Baur, Pannenberg regards the "I" sayings in John's Gospel as well as the alleged claim by Jesus, "My father and I are one" (Jn 10:30), as attributions by the post-Easter Christian community rather than authentic sayings of the historical Jesus. (326–7) He is sceptical that we can access Jesus' self-consciousness through the Christological titles. Instead, he proposes that we broaden "the circle of relevant traditional material" and take into account Israel's understanding of salvation, of God, and the expectation of the coming of the Kingdom of God. While the claim that Jesus applied the traditional Christological titles to himself is historically untenable, it is almost certain that Jesus' consciousness was "decisively stamped by his message of the nearness of God and his Kingdom." (332) The pre-Easter Jesus did not preach himself as Lord, but proclaimed the Lordship of the Father, the coming King. (365–6)

[97] *ST*, 2:384.

[98] *JGM*, 115.

[99] *ST*, 2:389f.

[100] Note the section headings in *ST*, 1: "The God of Jesus and the Beginnings of the Doctrine of the Trinity" (259); "The Revelation of God in Jesus Christ as the Starting Point, and the Traditional Terminology of the Doctrine of the Trinity"

Trinity must be based on the revelation of God in Christ, specifically in his relation to the Father and message of the divine rule.[101] The confirmatory effect of the resurrection renders Jesus's claims during his earthly ministry true and eternally valid. Hence construction of the doctrine of the Trinity must have as its source the examination of the revelation of God in Christ; it must be grounded in the economy of salvation. Operating with a social model of the Trinity, Pannenberg argues for an ontological equality of Father, Son and Spirit from the principle of relationality or mutual self-differentiation and submission,[102] a principle derived from the revelatory history of Jesus Christ.

Instead of inferring the Trinity from the presupposed unity of God (following Aquinas), Pannenberg, true to his historicizing methodology, looks to the revelation of the threeness of God in history and from there moves on to a unity of divine essence. In other words, for Pannenberg, as it is for Moltmann, the economic Trinity (God as he is revealed in salvation history) provides the basis for speech about the immanent Trinity (God as he is in himself). The link between Trinity and Christology is clear: Jesus Christ as the revelation of God in history occupies a central spot in the divine economy of salvation (*Heilsokönomie*), hence he is integral to the understanding of God as Triune in himself.

In summary, we underscore again the interconnectedness between Pannenberg's Christology, his view of revelation as history and his doctrine of God. In Christology, particularly in the Easter-event, all

---

(300). On Pannenberg's view of the Trinity see: Bradshaw, *Trinity and Ontology*, 137–233; Grenz, *Reason for Hope*, 44f; Roger Olson, "Trinity and Eschatology: The Historical Being of God in Jürgen Moltmann and Wolfhart Pannenberg," *SJT* 36(1983): 213–27; idem, "Wolfhart Pannenberg's Doctrine of the Trinity," *SJT* 43(1990): 175–206; Robert W. Jenson, "Jesus in the Trinity: Wolfhart Pannenberg's Christology and Doctrine of the Trinity," in *TWP*, 188–206; Chuck Gutenson, "Father, Son and Holy Spirit—The One God: An Exploration of the Trinitarian Doctrine of Wolfhart Pannenberg," *ATJ* 49(1994): 5–21.

[101] *ST*, 1:304.

[102] Just as Jesus differentiated himself as Son from the Father, Pannenberg suggests that there is a similar self-distinction on the part of the Father in relation to the Son as well. As Jesus is Son only in relation to the Father as Son, so the Father is Father in relation to Jesus as Son. This mutuality does not yield a binitarian doctrine of God because the principle of inner-relationship applies to the Spirit as well. Pannenberg rejects the Western church's addition of the *filioque* to the Nicene-Constantinopolitan Creed. See *ST*, 1:311–27; Jenson, "Jesus in the Trinity," 199; Guteson, "Father, Son and Holy Spirit," 11.

the major elements of his system intersect: the self-revelation of God in and as history, the nature of reality, the rise of primitive Christianity, the doctrine of the Trinity, eschatological fulfillment, human identity and destiny. All of these revolve around the historical figure of Jesus. We turn next to examine Pannenberg's eschatological and trinitarian ontology.

C. *Eschatological Trinitarian Ontology and Truth*

If one may speak of a principal leitmotif in Pannenberg's prodigious theological output, it might arguably be his idea of God rooted in an eschatological and trinitarian ontology. To appreciate the overall coherence of his arguments and apply his insights to our project, one would need to first understand his ontological assumptions or framework.[103] We begin with the strongly trinitarian nature of Pannenberg's theology.[104]

Like many in the recent renaissance of Trinitarian studies,[105] Pannenberg, in concert with Moltmann, Jüngel, Jenson and others,[106]

---

[103] B. J. Walsh, "Pannenberg's Eschatological Ontology," *CSR* 11(1982): 229–49.

[104] Herbert Burhenn's contention in his 1975 article, "Pannenberg's Doctrine of God," *SJT* 28(1975): 536–7, that the Trinity "cannot function for Pannenberg, as it does for Barth, as a structural principle of theology", is no longer viable in view of Pannenberg's published works since then, particularly in *ST*, 1:259–336. Pannenberg clearly states that the trinitarian conception of God "is not a doctrine of only secondary importance. . . . It has been in the center of my own project of developing a systematic presentation of the Christian doctrine." "The Christian Vision of God: The New Discussion on the Trinitarian Doctrine," *ATJ* 46(1991): 28. Cf. Olson, "Pannenberg's doctrine of the Trinity," 177: "Pannenberg *does* make the doctrine of the Trinity a structural principle of theology, if not exactly the same way as Barth." Schwöbel observes: "It is one of the major achievements of Pannenberg's *Systematic Theology* that it is a consistently trinitarian theology in which everything that can be said in dogmatics must be seen in the framework of an understanding of God as Trinity." "Pannenberg," 195.

[105] The current resurgence of trinitarian interest can be traced to the work of Barth and Rahner. Barth's trinitarian characterization of God's revelatory and redemptive work in history in his *CD*, is usually identified as the vanguard of the trend in the second half of this century to gather up temporality into discussions about God as Trinity. See Claude Welch, *In This Name: The Doctrine of the Trinity in Contemporary Theology* (New York: Charles Scribner's Sons, 1952), who follows Barth in rooting the trinitarian doctrine in revelation. Karl Rahner offers what Peters calls, the "Rahner-Rule"—the economic Trinity is the immanent Trinity and vice-versa—which acts as a kind of rallying point for modern discussions on the Trinity. See K. Rahner, *The Trinity* (New York: Herder & Herder, 1970); and Ted Peters, *God as Trinity: Relationality and Temporality in Divine Life* (Louisville: Westminster/John Knox, 1993), 96f.

[106] See Jürgen Moltmann, *The Trinity and the Kingdom of God* (San Francisco: Harper

argues for an ontological relationality between the persons of the Godhead and seeks to root the doctrine of the Trinity in the economy (*oikonomia*) of God's redemptive work in history. Contrary to classic trinitarianism, which tends to stress the oneness of *ousia* over the threeness of the *hypostases*, Pannenberg emphasizes the distinctness of the three persons of God. He is critical of any attempt to deduce the threeness of God from an a priori concept of divine essence. By beginning with a single subject or identifying the Father as the essence of deity, he argues, one invariably ends up with Modalism or even subordinationism. His suggestion, as noted earlier, is to ground the Trinity in the singular event of Jesus's sonship to the Father. Like his Christology, his Trinity is 'from below' in that he works from the revelation of God in the life and message of the historical Jesus.[107]

What is of interest here is that Pannenberg's ontological assumption about the nature of reality seems to simultaneously come out of, and shape, his distinctive interpretations of Christology and the Trinity. The linchpin of his ontological theology or theological ontology is that truth is eschatologically determined. Thus God's essence is neither *a se* nor prior to, or apart from, the historical work of the Son and the Spirit. The truth of God as eschatological means an historicization of the divine essence, the self-realization of God in history,[108] not in the sense of process metaphysics where the distinction between God and the world process is smudged,[109] but in the

---

& Row, 1981); Eberhard Jüngel, *The Doctrine of the Trinity: God's Being is in Becoming* (Grand Rapids: Eerdmans, 1976); idem, *God as the Mystery of the World* (Grand Rapids: Eerdmans, 1983); Robert W. Jenson, *The Triune Identity: God According to the Gospel* (Philadelphia: Fortress, 1982); Colin E. Gunton, *The Promise of Trinitarian Theology* (Edinburgh: T&T Clark, 1991); idem, *The One, the Three and the Many: God, Creation and the Culture of Modernity* (Cambridge: Cambridge University Press, 1993). For overviews on modern Trinitarian scholarship, see Peters, *God as Trinity*; John Thompson, *Modern Trinitarian Perspectives* (New York & Oxford: Oxford University Press, 1994); and Thomas R. Thompson, "Trinitarianism Today: Doctrinal Renaissance, Ethical Relevance, Social Redolence." *CTJ* 32(1997): 9–42.

[107] Olson, "Pannenberg on the Trinity," 185. In addition to Olson's treatment of Pannenberg's trinitarian doctrine, see Peters, *Trinity*, 135–42; John O'Donnell, "Pannenberg's Doctrine of God," *Greg* 72(1991): 73–98.

[108] Roger E. Olson, "The Human Self-Realization of God: Hegelian Elements in Pannenberg's Christology," *PRS* 13(1986): 207–23.

[109] See: John B. Cobb, Jr., "Pannenberg and Process Theology," *TWP*, 54–74; Lewis S. Ford, "The Nature of the Power of the Future," *TWP*, 75–94; David P. Polk, "The All-Determining God and the Peril of Determinism," *TWP*, 152–68; McKenzie, *Pannenberg*, 133, 137; Wolfhart Pannenberg and Lewis S. Ford, "A

sense of God's deliberate self-revelation through history so that the God encountered at the end is shown to be the same God all along.

Olson designates this as "Pannenberg's Principle": *God's deity is his rule.*[110] The divinity of God and the reign of God in the world are inseparable. The fundamental thesis in Pannenberg's eschatological ontology is that the essence of a being is constituted by its future. Thus God's essence, instead of being an eternal Platonic and Parmenidean timelessness, is interwoven with history until it is fully manifested in the Eschaton.[111] Pannenberg's is truly a futuristic ontology. God is not *vorhanden* ("at hand") in the sense that he is an item within history.[112] So emphatic is Pannenberg's stress on God as transcendentally futural, that at one point he boldly declares that "in a restricted but important sense, *God does not yet exist.*"[113] Yet paradoxically, God is not simply consigned to the future. Because in him *all* of history is wrapped up, God, as the power of the future, "dominates the remotest past" as well.[114] There is thus a sense in which God is *always, but not yet fully, present.* In Pannenberg's ontology, *appearance* and *essence* are conjoined.[115]

Dialogue about Process Philosophy," *Encounter* 38(1977): 318–24; Pannenberg, *MIG*, 113–29.

[110] Olson, "Pannenberg on the Trinity," 199.

[111] Pannenberg differentiates between Greek and Hebrew thought, the former he construes as depreciatory of temporality and contingency with an emphasis on the unchangeable nature of reality (to speak of Greek thought as uniformly such is no doubt a heuristic generalization on his part) in contrast to the latter which accentuates history. *BQT*, 2:137–38; *FR*, 10. The difference between the two is characterized by Walsh as a distinction between what he calls a "structuralist" ontology (not Structuralism as in modern philosophy and literary criticism, but a structural or static, immutable ontology), and a "geneticistic" ontology of Hebrew thought, which "places emphasis on the provisionality, temporality, and constant flux of life." "Pannenberg's Eschatological Ontology," 236.

[112] *BQT*, 2:171–2, 242; cf. Bradshaw, *Trinity and Ontology*, 144–5. Pannenberg says: "A God conceived as a thing at hand, even as a thingified person . . . is no longer credible." *BQT*, 2:241.

[113] *TKG*, 56 (emphasis added). God can no longer be thought of as "an existent being". *BQT*, 3:110.

[114] *TKG*, 62.

[115] Walsh, "Pannenberg's Eschatological Ontology," 239. The inseparability of *appearance* and *essence* in Pannenberg's ontology, means that the Christ-event as a proleptic appearance in history is inseparably tied to God as the all-determining reality which will be wholly manifested at the end of history. Such a view enables one to overcome the Kantian duality of the noumenal and phenomenal. Essence and temporality, the infinite and the finite, are not mutually exclusive. They are correlated in a revised Hegelian historical synthesis so that the temporal flow of the phenomenal carries within it the noumenal. The division between transcendence and immanence is thus overcome. See Bradshaw, *Trinity and Ontology*, 156, 177.

While history is determined by the God who is from ahead, there is at the same time built into the very constitution of the created order a self-transcending orientation. All of life, including human life, is characterized by an "ecstatic" dimension, a self-transcendence, a *Weltoffenheit* or openness to the world. Man is able to transcend his environment, able to have new experiences because of the openness of possibilities in relation to the world. His destiny (*Bestimmung*) lies ahead for him, and he constantly searches for it.[116] This tendentious-ness is part of the creation-wide propendent directionality in which all things are en route to the unitive Eschaton, and the ground of this ecstatic self-transcendence lies in the activity of the Spirit of God. There is thus a fundamental correlation between the spirit of humans—and by extension, the "spirit" of all of creation—and God's Spirit.

Pannenberg regards the Spirit not only as the giver of the new life of faith in salvation but also the origin of all life in creation.[117] The soteriological work of the Spirit is understood as the comple-tion of the Spirit's work in creation. The Spirit of salvation, Grenz notes, "is the eschatological Spirit who makes present the future real-ity of the kingdom of God."[118] We shall say more on this below when we look at the church as the prolepsis of a new humanity.

What is important for our thesis is the sophisticated way in which Pannenberg grounds Christology within an eschatological trinitarian ontological framework, so that truth can be construed as both his-torical, contingent and finite on the one hand, and transcendent and universal on the other. Pannenberg eschews a dualistic ontology

---

[116] Pannenberg, *FR*, 36–37; *BQT*, 2:104. H. Neie, *Atonement*, 108, describes it thus: "*Man's Weltoffenheit enforces such hope and quest since man's quest for his Bestimmung finds no conclusive answer within this life!* His *Weltoffenheit* forces him to think both God as the infinite vis-a-vis ('*das unendliche Gegenüber*') and such life beyond death." See Pan-nenberg, *What is Man?*, 44.

[117] See Pannenberg, "The Doctrine of the Spirit and the Task of a Theology of Nature," *Theology* 75(1972): 8–21; "The Spirit of Life," *FR*, 20–38; *ST*, 2:76–115. Pannenberg sees a correspondence between force-field theories in physics and the Christian doctrine of the dynamic work of God's Spirit in creation. *ST*, 1:382–3; 2:82f. On this correlation between the spirit of human beings and the divine Spirit, see Robert K. Johnston, "God in the Midst of Life: The spirit and the Spirit," *EA* 12(1996): 76–93. Pannenberg's discussion on pneumatology is not restricted to chap-ter 12 of *ST*, 3 where he deals with the Spirit in relation to ecclesiology and the Kingdom of God, but also in connection with the doctrines of Trinity and Christology in *ST*, 1 and creation in *ST*, 2.

[118] Grenz, *Reason for Hope*, 151.

which divides sacred revelation and secular history. The key lies in the notion of prolepsis, which provides the conceptual means by which one may affirm the simultaneous historical-contextuality *and* transcontextuality of truth in Christology, to hold together the ultimate coherence and finality of truth-claims and the contingency of understanding.[119]

In Pannenberg's system, the full realization of the trinitarian *Theos* is coterminous with the dawning of the world's *telos* in the Kingdom of God. God's deity is indeed his rule. Yet history does not subsist independently of God, but is rather "constituted by the active presence of the infinite God".[120] The historical movement towards the denouement at the Eschaton is animated by the unitive work of the Father, the Son and the Spirit in history, a work aimed at gathering up humanity into the perichoretic fellowship of the Trinity. The doctrine of the Trinity thus allows Pannenberg to formulate the concept of God as a historically experienced revelation. His trinitarian doctrine is foundational for his ontology as well as his epistemology, for it constitutes the condition for thought about God in relation to the world.

Pannenberg's economic trinitarianism serves as a potentially fruitful framework for speech about truth in a postmodern era. His refusal to privilege the oneness of God in favour of the differentiated activity of the persons of the Trinity in history, alongside his dialectical construal of proleptic finality and openness of truth, makes it possible for one to identify with the emphasis on historical particularity and contingency in postmodernity without giving up on truth as universal. The same line of argument based on the economic trinity is pursued by Colin Gunton. Like Pannenberg, he criticizes the elevation of the one over the many in respect of transcendental status in the Origen-Augustinian tradition, and seeks to develop instead "a trinitarian analogy of being (and becoming): a conception of the structures of the created world in the light of the dynamic of the being of the triune creator and redeemer."[121]

---

[119] As Tupper, *Pannenberg*, 121, notes, Pannenberg's modification of Hegel's philosophy of history in the direction of apocalyptic and eschatology enables him to "preserve the finitude of human experience, the openness of the future, and the intrinsic validity of the particular." These latter elements: finitude, openness, and validity of the particular, invite further reflection, particularly as they relate to theological development.

[120] Pannenberg, "Response to the Discussion," *TaH*, 253.

[121] Gunton, *The One, the Three and the Many*, 141.

Gunton seeks to bring the unity (one) and diversity (many) of reality together by means of a concept of relationality grounded in God's economic involvement in the world. His correlation of universality and particularity in a trinitarian framework is broadly consistent with Pannenberg. It will lead us too far afield to embark on a full comparison of Gunton and Pannenberg at this point. Suffice it to note that key elements in Gunton, particularly his views on creation, the trinitarian structure of God's activity and relation to the world, and the notion of "open transcendentals" which are trinitarianly developed, have conceptual resonance with Pannenberg's project, even though Gunton is not uncritical of him.[122]

We shall turn to the implications of Pannenberg's eschatological and trinitarian ontology for the nature of theological reflection in the final segment of this chapter. Before doing that, we will look at some criticisms raised against Pannenberg's proposals to see what adjustments are needed before we appropriate his insights for our own project.

II. *The Proleptic Truthfulness of Christology*

Building on the above analyses of Pannenberg's theological methodology, his Christology, and ontological commitments, we turn next to an enquiry into the viability of his proposals for our project of developing a model of Christology *from ahead*. This section is in two parts: (1) we will first look at some controverted areas in Pannenberg's work and offer our own critique, before (2) moving on to sketch a profile of a Christology *from ahead* based on what we think are needed conceptual adjustments to Pannenberg's proposals. It is hoped that this exercise will lead to a rapprochement between an eschatological emphasis on truth as futural and our observations in the previous chapters on the traditionary and experiential dimensions of doctrinal formulation.

A. *A Critical Appropriation of Pannenberg*

Pannenberg's attempt to correlate faith and reason has won him both admirers and critics.[123] It is a mark of the provocativeness of

---

[122] Ibid., 92–93; 159–60 n. 5.

[123] For a survey of theological attitudes towards Pannenberg, see Carl E. Braaten, "The Current Controversy on Revelation: Pannenberg and His Critics," *JRel* 45(1965):

his theses that they continue to precipitate questions and critiques. Such questioning of his theology serves a positive function, for in true Gadamerian fashion, it is only by means of dialogical engagement that understanding is enhanced. Thus before applying his insights to our own project, it is necessary to respond critically to three areas in Pannenberg: *history, fact and meaning*; and *faith and rationality*.

1. *History, Revelation and Theological Truth*
Pannenberg's exposition of revelation and truth raises two issues: the first concerns the proleptic finality of Christ, and the second the place of Scripture. We will examine these in turn. First, if the totality of history constitutes God's self-revelation, the question is raised as to how a particular event within history, i.e., Christ's resurrection, can be singled out as possessing absolute revelatory significance. The difficulty is not mitigated by an appeal to the notion of proleptic fulfillment. As a judgment made within history, the assertion about the prolepticality of Christ's resurrection is on Pannenberg's own reckoning a provisional, and hence corrigible, assertion. Does it mean then that it can be superseded later in time? If so, how can one speak of the Christ-event as *the* one point in history where the end has arrived ahead of time? How does one know if a particular event is eschatologically decisive and anticipatory of the totality of reality?[124] And if no other event apart from Christ's resurrection can have the same proleptic finality, would that not jeopardize the openness of history, a point Pannenberg is wont to maintain? Is revelation absolute in terms of a proleptic Christology but incomplete in terms of the openness of history?

While not everything in history is revelatory, Pannenberg wants to say that everything will in the end be shown to be revelatory.[125]

233–34; Stanley J. Grenz on "The Appraisal of Pannenberg: A Survey of the Literature," *TWP*, 19–52; and Kurt Koch, *Der Gott der Geschichte: Theologie der Geschichte bei Wolfhart Pannenberg als Paradigma einer philosophischen Theologie in ökumenischer Perspektive* (Mainz: Matthias Grünewald Verlag, 1988), 45–53.

[124] John V. Apczynski, "Truth in Religion: A Polanyian Appraisal of Wolfhart Pannenberg's Theological Program," *Zygon* 17(1982): 60.

[125] Pannenberg: "Modern history is not however divine revelation so to speak of itself. The connexion between revelation and history is not to be taken in the sense that revelation is necessarily to be encountered wherever one gains entry to history. Yet the revelation of the divinity of the biblical God has to do with history as a whole. It is disclosed only in history as a whole; not uniformly in every specific event, but only . . . in an end-perspective." *FR*, 89.

Meanwhile, perhaps all one can say is that everything is *potentially* revelatory. This ambivalence makes it difficult, on this side of the Eschaton, to discern what is truly revelatory, i.e., anticipatory of the end, and what is non-revelatory. The problem is compounded when faced with a plurality of truth-claims,[126] particularly on the issue of the uniqueness of Christ vis-à-vis the world religions. At times, Pannenberg seems to echo John Hick in musing that perhaps the same God is worshipped under other names![127] Even if one believes in eschatological verification, the question remains as to how we are to judge claims to truth *in the present*.

Second, the difficulty confronting Pannenberg is exacerbated by a degree of ambiguity in his stance on the authority of Scripture,[128] which deprives him of an "objective" criterion by which to differentiate the revelatory from the non-revelatory. As Hasel notes, his view of Scripture is shaped by his anthropology, concept of God, and view of revelation.[129] His refusal to justify theology on the basis of authority seems to imply that *sola scriptura* is no longer accepted as a normative principle.[130] Scripture for him is not so much direct communication from God in verbal and propositional form, as it is a historical sourcebook for the specific Judeo-Christian tradition. It is therefore descriptive of experiences rather than prescriptive.[131]

---

[126] Braaten asks "whether Pannenberg has found a clear enough way to speak of the distinction between God's revelation in the religions and God's unique revelation in Jesus Christ, which the New Testament calls 'the gospel.'" "The Place of Christianity Among the World Religions: Wolfhart Pannenberg's Theology of Religion and the History of Religions," *TWP*, 309.

[127] Pannenberg seems open to the idea that "in other religions God is worshipped under different names and in variously refracted forms and even in forms of perversion," yet "these religions are still related to the reality of the one God". "The Religions from the Perspective of Christian Theology and the Self-Interpretation of Christianity in Relation to the Non-Christian Religions." *MTh* 9(1993): 290. Nevertheless, sharp differences remain between Pannenberg and Hick, as the continuation of the exchange between them on eschatology in ch. 15 of *ST*, 3 indicates.

[128] Fred H. Klooster, "Aspects of Historical Method in Pannenberg's Theology," in J. T. Bakker *et al.*, eds., *Septuagesimo Anno: G. C. Berkouwer* (Kampen: Kok, 1973), 116, 122; cf. Grentz, *Reason for Hope*, 37–38; idem, "Appraisal of Pannenberg," *TWP*, 19–52. For a helpful analysis of Pannenberg's view of Scripture, see Frank Hasel, *Scripture in the Theologies of W. Pannenberg and D. G. Bloesch* (Frankfurt am Main: Peter Lang, 1996).

[129] Hasel, *Scripture*, 154–58; cf. Grenz, *Reason for Hope*, 37f.

[130] W. Pannenberg, *An Introduction to Systematic Theology* (Grand Rapids: Eerdmans, 1991), 14–17. Appeals to the Word of God involve for Pannenberg an "authoritarian style of theological argumentation" which inevitably stems from "faith subjectivism". *ST*, 1:242. Cf. Braaten, "Place of Christianity," *TWP*, 307.

[131] Hasel, *Scripture*, 157. See: Pannenberg, "Frage und Antwort—Das Normative

This does not however mean that the Bible is not central in Pannenberg, even though his *Systematic Theology* contains proportionately more history than exegesis.[132] He asserts that the authority of the Bible is parasitic on the authority of the gospel, which is centred in Jesus Christ. And even though our knowledge of Christ is mediated in the apostolic writings, the basis of authority is not coextensive with Scripture but goes beyond it.[133] Scripture functions as authoritative in the context of the life of the church, but not as guarantor of truth in terms of the problem of the relationship between authority and reason.[134] He is no doubt reacting in part to an ahistorical view of Scripture as a collection of propositions which has as it were been "dropped" from heaven, whose authority is a foregone conclusion. Perhaps like his Christology, he wants to see the authority of Scripture established "from below".

It is unclear how Scripture can exercise a criteriological role on matters of faith and doctrine given Pannenberg's ambivalent stand on its authority. He wants somehow to privilege the Scripture of the Judeo-Christian tradition, yet if one follows the train of his thought, it is uncertain why this ought to be so. Just as one queries the basis for the ascription of finality to Christ's resurrection, the same may be asked about the privileging of Scripture. The seeming unavoid-

---

in Christlicher Überlieferung und Theologie," Manfred Fuhrmann, Hans Robert Jauss & Wolfhart Pannenberg, eds., *Text und Applikation: Theologie, Jurisprudenz und Literaturwissenschaft im Hermeneutischen Gespräch* (Munich: Wilhelm Fink Verlag, 1981), 416. Pannenberg's view of the Bible as a human and historical document may account for his apparent nonchalance about the historicity of many of the records concerning Christ's words and activities in the Gospels, particularly the miraculous elements. In this respect, he tends to accept the findings of the more sceptical wing of New Testament scholarship, and accepts rather too readily the conclusions of form-criticism and redaction-criticism that the sayings of Jesus recorded in the Gospels are *vaticinia ex eventu*, confessions of the primitive church.

[132] Nevertheless, a cursory look at the indices of scriptural references in *ST*, 1–3 indicates extensive interaction with the Bible. For Pannenberg's view on Scripture, see: "The Crisis of the Scripture Principle," "Hermeneutics and Universal History," and "What is a Dogmatic Statement?" in *BQT*, 1:1–14, 96–136, 184–98. He essentially retains the view articulated in these essays in the later *Systematic Theology*.

[133] Pannenberg contends that we may accept Scripture and the apostolic proclamation as inspired by the Spirit of God, but this is "no guarantee of the truth of individual sayings. On the contrary, the statement that *scripture is inspired presupposes conviction as to the truth of the revelation of God* in the person and history of Jesus, the deity of Jesus, and the action of the triune God in the reconciling event of the death of Jesus Christ, his resurrection from the dead, and the apostolic ministry of reconciliation. *This conviction has its basis elsewhere.*" *ST*, 2:463–64 (emphasis added).

[134] Pannenberg's personal communication to F. Hasel, recounted in Hasel, *Scripture*, 230.

ability of fundamental assumptions should caution one against a premature dismissal of the Scripture principle. A way forward may be
to suggest, on Pannenberg's own terms, that Scripture is the proleptically authoritative Word of God, whose revelatory ultimacy will
only be fully manifested at the Eschaton. In other words, the same
privileging of the resurrection can just as well be extended to Scripture.

2. *Fact and Meaning in the Resurrection*

Critiques of Pannenberg's case for the resurrection range from those
that question the cogency and persuasiveness of his historical arguments, to those who think that his position on the relationship between
event (what really happened at the resurrection) and meaning (interpretation) is equivocal.[135] Whatever its merits, his view on the resurrection raises the question: What is the relation between fact and
meaning in assessing the significance of historical events? Is there
only one meaning attached to a particular historical occurrence? Or
can we speak of polyvalent signification? Is apocalypticism the only,
the best and the necessary interpretive grid for the Jesus-event, especially in view of the ambiguity surrounding it's definition?[136]

While Pannenberg attacks the a priori dismissal of the resurrection
on account of it being disanalogous to anything in present experience, he is not rejecting the use of critical tools in historical investigations. On the contrary, he thinks an open-minded historiography,
including the positive application of the principle of analogy, can
demonstrate not only the historicity of Jesus's resurrection but also
its nature as a proleptic realization of the eschaton. The latter he
does by positing the unity of fact and meaning in any historical
investigation. All events in history come with their own historically

---

[135] Peter Carnley, *The Structure of Resurrection Belief* (Oxford: Clarendon, 1987),
35–93; Burhenn, "Historicity of the Resurrection," 372; Braaten, "Current Controversy
on Revelation," 232–35; Laurence Wood, "History and Hermeneutics: A Pannenbergian Perspective," *WesTJ* 16(1981): 12–13; Peter C. Hodgson points out in his
review of *JGM* the ambiguity in Pannenberg's distinction between resurrection-
reality and resurrection-*event*. "Pannenberg on Jesus: A Review Article," *JAAR* 36(1968):
376; cf. W. Pannenberg, "Response to the Discussion" *TaH*, 266 n. 76. Frederick
Herzog wonders if the resurrection-event was as theologically perspicuous as Pannenberg would have us believe. The resurrection was no less puzzling to the disciples
as the cross was. The full significance of the resurrection had, for instance, to be
revealed to the disciples on the Emmaus Road. *Understanding God* (New York: Scribner's, 1966), 62–63.

[136] See William P. Murdock, "History and Revelation in Jewish Apocalypticism,"
Int 21(1967): 167–87.

conditioned or given meaning. In the case of the resurrection, it is the Jewish apocalyptic expectation of cosmic salvation.

Despite Pannenberg's intentions, it is not clear if he succeeds in his attempt to establish the resurrection, as he defines it, from strict historical argumentation alone. He brings to his historical investigation assumptions such as the nature of revelation, God as the all-determining reality, universal history, the universal validity of apocalyptic expectation, etc., which amounts to presupposing what he sets out to prove. For instance, from a historical-critical standpoint, the opposite of the positivistic maxim that "the dead do not rise" is the coming back to life again of one who is dead, vis-à-vis the resuscitation or revivification of the corpse of Jesus. This would meet the criteria of historiography which Pannenberg himself would consent to.[137] Yet as Michalson correctly notes, Pannenberg is not arguing for the resuscitation of a corpse, but the resurrection of Jesus.

In other words, historical investigation may tell us that something did in fact happen in the experience of the early disciples to convince them that Jesus was raised from the dead, but it is quite something else to move from this to the view that the resurrection signals the proleptic realization of the eschatological destiny of the universe. There seems to be in Pannenberg an undifferentiated commingling of historical argumentation and presuppositional imposition.[138] While he accepts that revelatory understanding cannot be read off directly from the historical evidence, one is not sure if he has not read the former into the evidence. As Iain Nicol observes: "To concede that the resurrection was a fact, that 'it really happened', is one thing.

[137] Michalson, "Pannenberg on the Resurrection," 355–56, notes: "Resuscitation is the only event that would satisfy the three requirements implicitly or explicitly established by Pannenberg's theological and historiographical standpoint: (1) it would constitute the objective, extra-mental occurrence which he insists is the necessary condition for the Easter witness; (2) it would constitute the *opposite* of the 'dead men do not rise' principle which, in his attack on the principle of analogy, Pannenberg specifically locates as an illicit limiting concept for historiography; and (3) even as a violation of natural law, resuscitation would be free from the 'prejudgment' of the natural scientist if the historian has good grounds for claiming its occurrence."

[138] This is the thrust of Burhenn's critique of Pannenberg. From a strict historiographic standpoint, it is one thing to say that no coherent naturalistic account can be given for the rise of resurrection faith in the early church, and quite another to appeal to Jewish apocalyptic as the necessary hermeneutical background for the resurrection. "Pannenberg's Argument for the Historicity of the Resurrection," 371–2. See also David Pailin, "Lessing's Ditch Revisited: The Problem of Faith and History," in Ronald H. Preston, ed., *Theology and Change: Essays in Memory of Alan Richardson* (London: SCM, 1975), 78–103.

To establish *what* really happened is another."[139] The transition from historical fact to faith is not as unequivocal as Pannenberg makes it out to be.

In seeking the meaning of past events, the historian invariably brings a set of assumptions to the task and projects an imaginative explanation upon the data in order to understand them.[140] The hermeneutics of historical meaning, like that of textual meaning, cannot escape the influence of the interpreter's pre-understanding. Historical investigation *alone* cannot reveal that Christ's resurrection is the key to the meaning of history. The way forward is to recognize that *what happened in Christ set in motion a history of effects which enables one who stands within this history to appreciate the pivotal significance of the resurrection and assent to it.*

What then of the unity of event and interpretation or meaning? Is the resurrection incomprehensible unless understood against the backdrop of Jewish apocalypticism? Leaving aside for now the question as to whether apocalyptic is the best interpretive background, we want to look first at the thesis that there is one meaning which is incontrovertably attached to any given event when it is appraised against its historical context.

To begin with, if Pannenberg is right that there is a necessary intertwining of the eventfulness of the resurrection and its meaning within its apocalyptic context in history, and if this marriage of fact and meaning is strong enough to remain inviolable and stable as it travels down through the undulating corridor of time, then surely it is possible to speak of this core meaning as a transhistorical and transcontextual criterion in Christology. The meaning of the Christ-event, understood against the Jewish apocalyptic milieu, becomes the touchstone against which all subsequent Christological developments must be assessed. This reading opens the door to the possibility of theological measurement across history, across time and space. By looking to the history of the transmission of the tradition concerning Christ—the *überlieferungsgeschichtliche* of Christology—we should then be able to discern a certain doctrinal continuity despite the many and often tumultuous Christological controversies in history. We have already argued along this line when we proposed in chapter

---

[139] Nicol, "Facts and Meanings," 136.
[140] Hogan, "Collingwood and Pannenberg," 10f; also Pailin, "Lessing's Ditch Revisited," 89.

three that there is a retrospectively discernible, complex and composite directionality to Christology when appraised diachronically.

Nevertheless, one needs to look again at the idea that a particular event always carries within it a particular interpretation. While we agree with Pannenberg on the basic unity of fact and meaning (subject to the qualifications which we shall make below), we do not share his apparent confidence in zeroing in on apocalyptic as *the* one and proper meaning of the resurrection-event. This does not mean that we object to apocalypticism per se.[141] What we are calling for is a little more reserve and a little less peremptory confidence in pronouncing on the meaning of historical events. It is in the very nature of historical inquiry to be as exhaustive as possible in the testing of one's hypotheses while at the same time maintain a measure of tentativeness about one's findings. Such a stance is compatible with the provisionality and contestability of all theological claims prior to the Eschaton.[142]

The connection between the facticity of the resurrection and its meaning in apocalyptic is one of historical probability, rather than logical necessity. The connection between a particular interpretation and a given event is not ironclad. The resurrection as a fact of history is always an interpreted fact, and that interpretation is always open to revision or replacement, however satisfying it is as a hypothesis. In this sense, Pannenberg's thesis that there is a basic unity between fact and meaning must be qualified.

---

[141] Pannenberg's thesis that the meaning of the Christ-event is ineluctably tied to the worldview of Jewish apocalypticism has been controverted. See: Murdock, "Jewish Apocalypticism"; Hans D. Betz, "The Concept of Apocalyptic in the Theology of the Pannenberg Group," *JTC* 6(1969): 192–207; idem, "On the Problem of the Religio-Historical Understanding of Apocalypticism," *JTC* 6(1969): 134–56. The subject of apocalyptic itself is controversial and scholarly opinion on it is often divided. The type of apocalypticism which Pannenberg has in mind is one which is an outgrowth of the prophetic and eschatological tradition of the Old Testament. While accepting that the Jesus-event is apocalyptic throughout, he nevertheless notes differences between Jesus and the activity of apocalyptic visionaries. *JGM*, 61.

Ever since Johannes Weiss, *Jesus' Proclamation of the Kingdom of God* (Philadelphia: Fortress, 1971, German original, 1892) and Albert Schweitzer, *The Quest of the Historical Jesus* (London: Adam & Charles Black, 1911, German original 1906), it has been virtually accepted universally that Jesus preached an apocalyptic eschatology, and that historical inquiry into the Jesus of history will yield a thoroughly eschatological Christ. This consensus though has been challenged in recent works on the historical Jesus. On this change, see Stephen J. Patterson, "The End of Apocalypse: Rethinking the Eschatological Jesus," *TT* 52(1995): 29–48; cf. Dale C. Allison, Jr., "A Plea for Thoroughgoing Eschatology," *JBL* 113(1994): 651–68.

[142] *ST*, 2:351.

3. *Faith and Rationality*

Pannenberg wants to establish the credibility of the Christian message in the modern world by means of rational argument rather than validation through authoritarianism or subjectivism. He is positively convinced that theology cannot seek sanctuary in fideism. To his mind, theology must be publicly debatable. It is therefore arguable that reason (or historical reasoning) in Pannenberg tends to take priority over faith-commitment in theology. Despite his strenuous attempt to distance himself from the revelational positivism of Barth, one wonders if he has not overstated his case and exaggerated the independence of rationality from faith; for there is implicit in his rational arguments an underlying faith stance.

If our reading of Pannenberg is correct, it may well be that knowledge for him is ultimately based on a value-judgment or a stance which is generated by a pre-judgment checked by coherence and plausibility. And the criteria for such a presuppositional stance are bound up with a view of history which is decidedly slanted in favour of Judaeo-Christian theism. On this, Michalson points out that Pannenberg "arrives at a position on historical knowledge *subsequent* to establishing an angle of vision on, first, the issue of historical revelation and, second, the question of the relationship between Christianity's truth claims and natural human modes of insight or wisdom."[143]

Many of the axioms of rational historical research which Pannenberg takes for granted are in fact assumptions or even faith statements in themselves,[144] e.g., concepts such as: God as the all-determining reality, resurrection and eschatological prolepsis, the ontological priority of the future, ec-static character of religions, etc. Commenting on his case for the resurrection of Christ, Holwerda wonders if Pannenberg's own faith intuition regarding the resurrection may not have in fact predisposed him to favour some arguments over others. "Has Pannenberg demonstrated by his historical arguments for the resurrection that faith depends upon reason, or has faith in fact subtly

---

[143] Michalson, *Lessing's "Ugly Ditch"*, 128. See also Gilkey, "Pannenberg's *Basic Questions in Theology*," and Nicol, "Facts and Meanings".

[144] Stanley Obitts, "Apostolic Eyewitnesses and Proleptically Historical Revelation," in Morris Inch & Ronald Youngblood, eds., *The Living and Active Word of God* (Winono Lake: Eisenbrauns, 1983), 137–148. Jentz, "Personal Freedom," 152, fears that Pannenberg "appeals to reason and metaphysics but plays philosophy with a loaded deck: a deck marked with cards bearing 'authoritative truth' stamped all over them, and derived from Scripture, creed, and ecclesiastical tradition."

or even basically affected the rational weighing of the historical evidence?"[145] Despite his disclaimer, it would appear that Pannenberg is working out of an implicit and *a priori* notion of the resurrection.

Holwerda sums up the tension between faith and reason in Pannenberg:

> [I]f faith requires certainty, Pannenberg must either assume an epistemology contrary to his dominant thesis that faith is not an avenue of knowledge but is dependent upon reason for its foundation, or acknowledge that he has not fully escaped the charge of subjectivism as he himself defines it. The only way out of this dilemma is to challenge the epistemology assumed by the autonomy of reason. Does reason, in fact, establish autonomously its own criteria for validating claims to truth, or is there a prior element of commitment, trust, or belief within which reason functions and on the basis of which it develops criteria for validating claims to truth?[146]

In our opinion, the viability of Pannenberg's theological method does not depend on an absolute independence of reason from a prior "faith" commitment. From a hermeneutical standpoint, a forced prioritization of reason over presuppositional commitment, or vice-versa, is unnecessary and ultimately fallacious. Pannenberg wants to move theology from the "inner" of faith commitment to the "outer" of public discourse and verification.[147] Such a polarization of inside-outside, of subjective faith and objective historical inquiry, must give way to a stance where faith and reason, subjective commitment and objective rationality, are held on to simultaneously.

Following Pannenberg's own emphasis on the historicality of hermeneutics, one might argue that the very notion of rationality itself is inescapably historical, and therefore partakes necessarily of some prior contextually mediated beliefs or commitments. Pannenberg would no doubt concur with such a Gadamerian observation. This raises the question as to whether Pannenberg can still be justified in his call for rational plausibility in theology while at the same time repudiating the kind of epistemological ghettoism represented by

---

[145] D. Holwerda, "Faith, Reason, and the Resurrection," 304; see also Michalson, "Pannenberg on the Resurrection," 345–59.

[146] Holwerda, "Faith, Reason, and the Resurrection," 309.

[147] As Michalson, describes it: "Pannenberg is attempting to reorient us toward the "outer" history that was displaced by the attention devoted to the "inner," personal history in the traditions of Lessing and Kierkegaard. To be interested in knowledge of historical events as the true basis of faith is simultaneously to suspect whatever is private, hidden, and individualistic." *Lessing's "Ugly Ditch"*, 123.

neo-orthodox and existential theology. What then is the status and nature of such rationality vis-à-vis the interpreter's inescapable prior commitments?

The answer we suggest is to seek a correlation, rather than a polarization, of faith and reason. We shall examine such a correlation in terms of: (1) the idea of provisionality; and (2) knowledge as self-involving. First, Pannenberg's notion of the necessary provisionality of all theological constructs before the Eschaton gives us the boldness to publicly acknowledge our faith stance and at the same time submit our theological beliefs to the public square for rational debate. Instead of bending backward to argue that reason is sufficient to demonstrate our theological beliefs, we can be explicit about our prior commitments and lay them out for intersubjective scrutiny. It is possible to argue consistently from Pannenberg, that eschatological provisionality extends not only to the contents of our theological exposition, but also to our faith-presuppositions as well as the canons of rationality we are operating with.[148] So, for instance, on the question of the resurrection, charges that Pannenberg has smuggled Christian beliefs into his rational justification for the resurrection will no longer threaten, since these convictional bases will not count as "smuggled" once the provisionality of our claims is openly acknowledged. This need not imply any diminishing of the force of our rational arguments for the resurrection, only that we put both our rationality and our faith on the table for examination.

A second approach is to draw on the notion of knowledge as inherently self-involving and personal, a notion which D. Evans, Lonergan, J. Newman, Polanyi have expressed in their different ways; e.g., Polanyi's idea that all knowing involves a tacit and subjective dimension.[149] Pannenberg's notion of universal history as the framework for the interpretation of the present has been compared with Polanyi's works on personal knowledge. Polanyi challenges the assumption of positivistic science that knowledge, if it is to be true and accepted, must be empirically verifiable, impersonal and thoroughly

[148] Rory A. A. Hinton, "Pannenberg on the Truth of Christian Discourse: A Logical Response," *CTJ* 27(1992): 317–8.

[149] See Donald Evans, *Logic of Self-Involvement*; John H. Newman, *Grammar of Assent*; Lonergan, *Method in Theology*; M. Polanyi, *Personal Knowledge*; and *The Tacit Dimension*. Cf. Apczynski, "Truth in Religion"; Durwood Foster, "Pannenberg's Polanyianism: A Response to John V. Apczynski," *Zygon* 17(1982): 75–81; Thomas A. Langford, "Michael Polanyi and the Task of Theology," *JRel* 46(1966): 45–55.

objective. To Polanyi, the personal is an unavoidable part of the
very process of knowing. In the very act of knowing something,
Polanyi suggests, a heuristic vision is at work. The knowing subject
apprehends the object of knowledge, namely the whole, through a
tacit comprehension of the particulars which together form the whole.
Like Pannenberg's, Polanyi's view of knowledge is eschatological
(though he may not describe it as such)[150] in that the process of
knowing invariably begins with a pre-conception, a heuristic vision,
of the whole. If Polanyi is correct, then there is no need to polarize between the subjective and experiential dimension of faith on the
one hand, and the allegedly more objective dimension of reason.

While one may get the impression that Pannenberg seems to accentuate reason over faith in his early writings, this is more perception
than content, especially in the light of his later arguments in his
Systematic Theology. In his earlier works, he was reacting to the tendency in dialectical and Bultmannian theology to ground faith in
mere "decisionism," and he wanted to call theology to history. It is
arguable that Pannenberg is not against the decision of faith per se,
and that he sees faith (*fiducia*) as based on knowledge (*notitia*) and
assent (*assensus*). Thus knowledge (historical knowledge) and reason
are included in the exercise of faith. It is not necessary to distinguish too sharply between the subjectivity of faith and the objectivity of reason. It is entirely possible that faith's way into truth is via
the stringent application of the mind and the vigorous use of critical tools. Faith's apprehension of truth is through, not apart from,
the exercise of reason.[151] The reverse is equally true. True rational-

---

[150] See Robert T. Osborn, "Christian Faith as Personal Knowledge," *SJT* 28(1975):
101–26. Osborn observes: "knowledge of the meaning of facts (the comprehensive
whole) comes not after the facts (given and past), but after a vision of yet unknown
and future unity. Knowledge is not after the fact but after the future, a future possessed only in the vision of the knower; knowledge is eschatological and personal."
107. Polanyi's emphasis on the "tacit dimension" in epistemology and on knowledge as personal provides a corrective to the illusion of objectivity in scientific
research. Pannenberg's concern on the other hand is somewhat different. He is
responding to what he considers an overreaction on the part of dialectical and existential theology to the objectification of knowledge. The result of that has been "a
retreat to commitment" and a virtual fideism. The difference between Pannenberg
and Polanyi is succinctly summed up by Durwood Foster: "whereas Polanyi has
wanted to qualify reason to make room for faith, Pannenberg's intention is to qualify faith to make room for reason." "Pannenberg's Polanyianism," 76.

[151] Such an understanding is in line with the NT view of the "heart" (καρδία)
as both the seat of all the passional forces of a person's inner life, and the seat of
understanding, thought, and reflection. See T. Sorg, "Heart" in *NIDNTT*, 2:180–84.

ity, a rationality which penetrates to the heart of the universe and grasps the truth, is possible only through embracing with critical rationality a dimension of understanding which entails a stance of faith and belief. Such an approach has much to commend itself on the question of theological construction.

To orientate our discussion thus far, we have been engaging critically with Pannenberg, and have focussed our attention on three main questions: the question of history, revelation and theological truth; the relationship between fact and meaning in the resurrection; and between faith and rationality. Bearing in mind the above critiques, we shall move on to propose an outline for a (Pannenbergian) Christology *from ahead*.

B. *Profile of a Christology From Ahead*

What does a Christology *from ahead* look like? In what follows we shall attempt to sketch out a response which would take into consideration the above dissection of Pannenberg's approach. We shall organize this in three interrelated assertions:

1. *The Presence of the Future—Christology from ahead is situated in the temporal bridge between the "already" of Christ's resurrection and the "not-yet" of the Eschaton, and bears witness to the proleptic incurrence of final truth through the contingent within history and tradition.*

The truth of Christology for Pannenberg is syncategorematic with the truth of eschatological fulfilment, understood in terms of proleptic arrival of that which still lies ahead along the timeline of history. Christology between the tensive span of proleptic arrival and consummation has the character of being both contingent and universal. Christology *from ahead* is proleptic in that it is marked by a simultaneous openness to the future and a referentiality to the pastness of the Christ-event.

In fact, following Pannenberg's own nomination of Jesus Christ as the pre-arrival of the Eschaton, one might argue that the way the future shapes the present is by means of the Spirit's mediation of

---

The Greek νοῦς (mind, reason, understanding) is used sparingly in the LXX; it occurs 6 times in connection with the Hebrew word for heart (*leb, lebab*), suggesting that *nous* is closely connected to the will. This is true of its use in the NT, where understanding is seen as a disposition, i.e., a standpoint of faith. See "Nous" in *NIDNTT*, 3:122–30.

the history of Jesus through participation in the life of Christian community and tradition. Such a reading is broadly in tune with Pannenberg's ecclesiology. The accent placed on the impingement of the future on the present should be counterbalanced by paying equal attention, first, to the influence of the past on the present, and second, to the experience which that influence engenders. In short, Christology *from ahead* must be correlated with Christology *from within* in the dual sense of tradition and experience.

One needs to attend to *the role of the past in the shaping of the present by the future.* Though the resurrection of Christ is the epicentre of the proleptic arrival of the end, in a real sense, the ongoing corporate life and ministry of the Church, and Christian tradition emanating from Jesus Christ, has transmuted prolepsis from being a *point* in time to a *process* in time leading up to the Eschaton. The church as the community constituted by Christ's resurrection shares in the proleptic character of the latter. We might describe this as a kind of *post-resurrection proleptic historical consciousness,* an *a posteriori* development arising from the resurrection of Christ and all that that entails.[152]

The pastness of the proleptic event in the form of Christian tradition now exerts a shaping impact on the present as it moves into the future. This is compatible with our argument in chapter three that theological development entails a dialectic of continuity and discontinuity, of fidelity to the ecclesial heritage on the one hand, and a creativity oriented to the future on the other. Christology, we suggest, takes place in that "space" between the effectivity coming out of the past and the eschatological pull of the future. Pannenberg says as much when he argues that knowledge about Jesus's resurrection and exaltation is mediated through the history of apostolic proclamation[153] and participation in the church, specifically in the

---

[152] Scott Cowdell thinks that Pannenberg, in locating the origin of Christian believing solely in the past event of the resurrection, has unhelpfully separated "the object of faith from the believing subject; and although his motive is to get away from the liberal subjectivism of Kant's legacy in theology, he creates his own subject-object divide nonetheless." *Is Jesus Unique? A Study of Recent Christology* (New York & Mahwah: Paulist Press, 1996), 132. Cowdell suggests a way forward for Pannenberg: "He could overcome the criticism that present ecclesial experience is overlooked in his approach *by allowing the resurrection to include its reception in the life of the faith community.*" 134 (emphasis added).

[153] Citing Paul in Rom. 5:11 and 2 Cor. 5:20, Pannenberg argues that the reconciliation through Jesus which Paul speaks about as coming through to him "now", is the "now of apostolic proclamation". "It is Jesus Christ himself, the exalted Kyrios,

eucharistic communion.[154] Nevertheless, the mediated character of the truth concerning Christ, though not absent in Pannenberg,[155] tends to be overshadowed by his emphasis on the futurity of truth. What we hope to do here is perhaps draw attention to the extent in which the logic of Pannenberg's argument can be made compatible with the Gadamerian (or for that matter, the Lindbeckian) stress on the tradition-mediatedness of understanding.

Once it is granted that (proleptic) truth comes out of the historical effects of Jesus's resurrection mediated through the history of the transmission of tradition, we are led back to the question of criteriological determination of the direction of this historical development. At this point, the biblical witness to God's activity in the world, centering specifically in Jesus Christ and interpreted in dialogue with tradition in the church,[156] has a part to play in disciplining the trajectorial passage of tradition between Christ's resurrection and the Eschaton. As indicated earlier, this is where we part company with Pannenberg, even though we agree with him that the mere citation of scriptural texts is not enough to guarantee the truth. Christology *from ahead* is Christology done coherently with the teachings of Scripture. The belief that God has revealed himself through an inscripturated Word is not *ipso facto* irrational. Neither does it remove the need for the rational articulation of Christian beliefs. It is possible to argue in Pannenbergian fashion that the truthfulness of this

who "now" gives us reconciliation through the ministry of the apostles and the preaching of the church—the reconciliation proleptically accomplished once and for all in his death." *ST*, 2:440; also 1:249f.

[154] See discussion on the relationship between the individual and the Church as the messianic community in *ST*, 3:97–434; see also W. Pannenberg, *Christian Spirituality and Sacramental Community* (London: Darton, Longman & Todd, 1983).

[155] Pannenberg does argue that the church plays an important role in the transmission and interpretation of the history of Jesus. See *ST*, 3:122f. This element of his exposition though tends not to be noted, probably because of his repeated insistence that theology be done in the public square rather than within the precinct of the church. See: Stanley J. Grenz, "The Irrelevancy of Theology: Pannenberg and the Quest for Truth," *CTJ* 27(1992): 310–1.

[156] The ability of Scripture to exercise an authoritative criteriological function is never abstracted from the hermeneutical community of the Church and Christian tradition. Scripture is always interpreted, and this makes the present apprehension of the truth about Christ in Scripture a hermeneutical exercise. As such, attention must be paid not only to the linguistic tradition but also the historical context as well. In this, we are in tune with Pannenberg's hermeneutics, about which Thiselton notes: he is "deeply concerned with *the extra-linguistic realities of history*, and with *the interaction and intertwining of language and patterns of events in the context of historical traditions*." *NHH*, 337 (emphasis author's).

belief, like that of the resurrection, awaits eschatological vindication.

Meanwhile, the ongoing reception of the Scripture-mediated tradition concerning Jesus Christ, under the superintendence of God's Spirit, forms a bridge in the present upon which the proleptic arrival of the future in the past is made alive again. This is how, we suggest, Pannenberg's belief that the truth of God must be proved anew[157] can be profitably understood. The dynamism of the movement of universal truth through contingent history makes it necessary for systematic theology to be done all over again in each new historical epoch.[158] And this is always carried out at the juncture where the future and the past meet. A Christology *from ahead* is thus a Christology done in the present, a present shaped by a past in which the future truth about God has arrived, albeit proleptically.

2. *The Church in the Spirit for the Kingdom—Christology from ahead comes out of the experience of the eschatological Spirit of God within the life of Christian community, and expresses itself in service to the future Kingdom of God.*

To recapitulate, the formulation of Christology is done *from within* (1) the historical trajectory of Christian tradition emanating from the Jesus-event, and (2) comes out of the Christian's experiential appropriation of Christ. In Pannenberg's opinion, these two elements converge in an understanding of the Spirit of God whose work it is to lift individuals above their particularity "into an ecstatic existence *extra se* in Christ"[159] (thus constituting the church). This work, already begun, will culminate at the Eschaton, when the Spirit's eschatological work in both redemption and creation will be consummated. This eschatological reality of the Spirit's work not only makes it possible for us to be in Christ and in the Church, it must also inform all our attempts to speak of the significance of Christ.

Christology *from ahead* is rooted in a living tradition made alive by the Spirit of God through the ongoing hermeneutical appropriation of tradition in the church. Whereas the emphasis in our first point is on the mediation of that which is from the future in the tradition of the past ("living *tradition*"), our concern in this second point is on the present aliveness of this tradition ("*living* tradition").

---

[157] *BQT*, 2:8.
[158] Pannenberg, *Introduction*, 7.
[159] Grenz, *Reason for Hope*, 159.

And this experiential animation of the mediated reality of Christ is testimony to the work of the eschatological Spirit in "presencing" the futural truth of God. The Spirit is the down payment, the deposit, of what is in store for all who are in Christ in the Eschaton. What the Christian believer experiences *within* attests to the reality of what is *ahead*. Pannenberg provides what Grenz describes as "a far more pneumatocentric theology in which the kingdom is understood as made present through the Spirit."[160] We have already examined the place of experience in Christological reflection in chapter four, and need not retrace our steps. Building on that discussion, we contend that a Christology *from ahead* is eschatologically oriented in that it is confession about Christ arising from, and validated by, the experience of the risen Christ made present by the inner work of the Spirit in the Christian believer.

There is thus a sense in which the human spirit, as it is enlivened by the Spirit of God, comes to recognize the truth that in Christ the end has arrived. Here one may speak of a recapitulation of the Spirit's work at creation, this time in the re-creative work of redemption. At the same time, there is brought forth in the human heart a receptiveness to the testimony concerning Christ in Scripture and tradition. It is important to underscore the fact that this experience of the eschatological Spirit is neither abstracted from life in the community of faith,[161] nor the work of God in the world. Both these emphases, namely the ecumenical church as the people of God and an active engagement with the world, are interrelated themes in Pannenberg's Kingdom-oriented ecclesiology.[162]

---

[160] Ibid., 154.

[161] The believers' communion with Christ is inextricably tied to their communion with each other. See *ST*, 3:99–110. The unity of believers and churches is of paramount importance for Pannenberg because of the anticipatory function of the Church for the unified destiny of humanity. This, according to Schwöbel, may be the reason for the disproportionate amount of space devoted to ecclesiology in *ST*, 3. "Rational Theology," 520–21.

[162] Pannenberg's ecclesiology may be seen in the early collection of essays, *Ethik und Ekklesiology* (Göttingen: Vandenhoeck & Ruprecht, 1977); ET by Keith Crim in two separate volumes: *Ethics* (Philadelphia: Westminster, 1981) and *The Church* (Philadelphia: Westminster, 1983). The broad themes of his ecclesiology in *ST*, 3 are anticipated in earlier works, e.g., "The Kingdom of God and the Church," *TKG*, 72–101; *Apostles' Creed*, 144–59; *Christian Spirituality*, 31–49; and *Human Nature, Election, and History* (Philadelphia: Westminster, 1977). See also: W. Pannenberg, "The Church Today," *ATJ* 46(1991): 7–16; idem, "Baptism as Remembered 'Ecstatic' Identity," David Brown & Ann Loades, eds., *Christ: The Sacramental Word. Incarnation, Sacrament and Poetry* (London: SPCK, 1996), 77–88.

Pannenberg has long argued for the importance of the church as the messianic fellowship and the proleptic sign of the Kingdom of God,[163] and his long involvement in the ecumenical movement is testimony to this concern for ecclesiology. He provides an elaborate treatment on ecclesiology in volume three of his *Systematic Theology* which brings together his earlier fragmentary writings on the subject. We cannot delve into this in detail here, except to draw attention to the interconnections between the Church, its involvement in the world, and the coming Kingdom of God in Pannenberg's exposition.

The Church must point beyond itself to the universal reign of God, and it does so, not by fleeing the world, but by engaging it.[164] This provides an important ballast against theology collapsing unwittingly into other-worldiness or a radical futurity. Not that the Church can, by the works of its hands, bring about the Kingdom; for only God can establish it. The Kingdom is, after all, as Pannenberg reminds us, *of God*.[165] Yet he insists that to believe in the imminent dawn of the Kingdom of God is not escapism but engagement with this world. His reflections on the Church and the world vis-à-vis the Kingdom of God[166] bear out our contention that the confession of Christ today cannot be abstracted from the Church's mandate "to participate now in the ultimate destiny of human life."[167]

Given this backdrop, Christology *from ahead* must therefore reflect the Church's active engagement with the world in the *here and now*. Insofar as it takes its bearing from the anticipated manifestation of the Kingdom of God in the future, Christology *from ahead* confesses the significance of Christ in conscious dialogue with the concerns of society, bearing in mind the final destiny of humanity. Pannenberg

---

[163] See Pannenberg, "Society and the Christian Faith," *Ethics*, 7–22; *TKG*, 72–101; *JGM*, 372–73; *ATP*, 444–48; *Apostles' Creed*, 152–55.

[164] Pannenberg, "Constructive and Critical Functions of Christian Eschatology." *HTR* 77(1984): 119–39; *BQT*, 3:195–6.

[165] *TKG*, 82. This is the primary reason for Pannenberg's critique of liberation theology, for in the latter's positive embrace of Marxist anthropology, it has blurred the distinction between human political order and the Kingdom of God. See Pannenberg, "Christianity, Marxism and Liberation Theology," *CSR* 18(1989): 215–26; idem, "Sanctification and Politics," *Christian Spirituality*, 50–70; cf. *TKG*, 81–82.

[166] Pannenberg connects Church and society by means of the concept of justice, and places both under the Kingdom of God. *ST*, 3:27–57. Both Church and society in history are thus judged against the coming Kingdom of God. God's self-revelation in history not only makes it the most comprehensive horizon for theological understanding, but also the framework for the Church's involvement in the world.

[167] *TKG*, 86.

asserts, "All the words and formulas of Christology have truth to the degree they express how the future of God's Kingdom became determinative for the present of Jesus's life and, through him, *for the history of mankind*."[168] This focus on the history of the world is precisely what is entailed in the Kingdom of God; and the Church, as the community of the Spirit of God, is *for* the Kingdom. Christology, as the Church's speech about Christ, must therefore reflect a commitment to the world in the light of the already-but-not-yet Kingdom.

3. *The Historicality, Referentiality and Universality of Truth—A Christology from ahead eschews any fideistic reduction of the universal and transcontextual truth of Christology and seeks to commend the truth of God in Christ within the public arena of rational discourse.*

Two elements in Pannenberg's eschatological approach to theology may be enlisted to help build our case for a Christology *from ahead*: (i) a positive embrace of history and contextuality, and (ii) a realist view of truth as unitary and universal. Both of these have implications for Christological inquiry.

First, revelation as history signals a positive attitude towards the historical process. As noted above, Pannenberg rejects a substantialist Hellenistic metaphysics in favour of a temporalized ontology, and situates the truth of God firmly within the temporality and concreteness of time and space. In the Incarnation God has acted and revealed himself under the conditions of existence and history. And a Pannenbergian Christology *from ahead* likewise is incarnational in that it is rooted in the specificity of a particular historical and social context. Just as Jesus's divine identity is fully compatible with his humanity in the prolepticality of the incarnation, Christology *from ahead* expresses the Truth even when it is clothed with garments fashioned from the fabric of contingent conceptuality. Christological confessions as human formulations about divine truth have a Chalcedonian character.[169]

---

[168] *TKG*, 81 (emphasis added).

[169] Carl E. Braaten, "Scripture, Church, and Dogma: An Essay on Theological Method," *Int* 50(1996): 153, speaks of a "chalcedonian hermeneutic" which affirms the revelation of God centred in Jesus Christ as well as the time-conditionedness of the Bible. He asserts this in connection with a comparative look at two different ways of doing theology. The first is represented by Pannenberg, who begins with a self-transcending anthropology established through reason, and moves from the world into the church. The second is that of E. Jüngel, who begins in Barthian fashion with the postulate of revelation, and moves from the church into the world.

Second, in an age of hesitancy about positing the reality of truth, Neuhaus observes that Pannenberg's work reflects a greater readiness to endorse "the audacity of truth."[170] His unabashed affirmation about the unitary nature of reality (a single meta-language game?) and the possibility of truth, goes against the grain of the parochialization of truth in postmodernity.[171] The truth of Christology is not just the private truth of the church, but the universal truth of the world. The Christ of the NT is a cosmic Christ (Col. 1:20; Eph. 1:9, 10, cf. 22–23). The idea that there are multiple truths ensconced on un-connected islands floating across a fideistic sea does not, in Pannenberg's view, do justice to the fact that people everywhere share in a common history, a common destiny. It is surely counter-intuitive to believe otherwise, especially when one considers the way the world is economically intermeshed and ecologically interdependent.

The unitary nature of reality and the impingement of the future in the present means embracing an active stance of discerning the reality of the future in the reality of the present. Pannenberg would undoubtedly warm to the idea that "all truth is God's truth," and such an attitude is amenable to a dialogical engagement between theology and other disciplines, not to mention the ways in which the different facets of experienced reality provide conceptual tools by which to formulate one's Christology. By the same token, theology can throw light on the concerns of everyday life as well as take its place at the roundtable of intellectual enquiry, with the bold conviction that it has something important to contribute. Pannenberg's theological overtures to anthropology, philosophy, the natural sciences, etc., exemplify the belief in the unitary and universal nature of truth.[172]

While Braaten is inclined towards Pannenberg's approach, he thinks that both of them are not materially different in their doctrine of God and the place of Jesus in the Trinity, which is Christology proper. 145. Arguing along the same lines as Pannenberg, he avers that "we have treasures of divine revelation in vessels of human language and history." 153. The same Chalcedonian characteristic applies, we suggest, to dogmatic Christology as well.

[170] Richard John Neuhaus, "Theology for Church and Polis," *TWP*, 238.
[171] It is therefore surprising that Scott Cowdell, *Is Jesus Unique?*, 114–5, should, on the basis of Pannenberg's anthropological musings in *What is Man?*, consider Pannenberg as "postmodern". The fact that Pannenberg is openly committed to a rational search for universal truth and has offered a sustained argument for the coherence of metanarratival Truth (albeit eschatologically-determined) over three volumes of *Systematic Theology* makes Cowdell's charge less than convincing.
[172] Pannenberg: "As soon as Christianity's appeal to God's revelation is taken

Christology *from ahead* presupposes the universality of truth and seeks to be a word about Christ uttered from within the interconnectedness of life. If indeed we have in Christ the proleptic arrival of ultimate truth, then that belief has extensive implications for all areas of life. It is therefore incumbent on the theological community to probe the significance of Christ in relation to the questions posed by, and confronting, the world; for as Pannenberg believes, reality is in the profoundest sense incomprehensible without God. And in the light of what we said earlier about the Christian community being the proleptic sign of the coming Kingdom, the Church must not only *proclaim a message about Christ* which comes out of its entanglement with the world, it must also *embody a Christocentric form of life* which actively engages in acts of justice and love, thus alerting the world to the possibility of life premised on the sovereign reign of God. Christology *from ahead* is thus both world-embracing and world-transforming.

Pannenberg adopts an argumentative rather than a dogmatically axiomatic approach to theology. He is surely correct to insist that assertions of faith are never simply expressions of ineffable subjective states which are absolutely beyond rational scrutiny and debate. All statements of faith "contain an *element of assertion*, reality depiction, or reference," and Pannenberg is justified in concluding that "all statements of faith in this sense have a *cognitive* core."[173] Assertions about God are hypotheses which are testable in terms of their implications for reality.

This does not mean that Pannenberg is an arrant rationalist who looks to reason as the final arbiter of truth. What he seeks instead is to demonstrate that the Christian faith is intellectually credible. As we have already suggested in our critique, Pannenberg does operate with a privileged belief in God even as he seeks to be rigorously rationalistic in his argumentative theology.[174] This allows one to adopt

---

seriously, then the subject of theology cannot be confined to a particular subject side by side with other subjects of other disciplines. Theology must then broach many other subjects as well as its particular concern with religious experience and Christianity." *TPS*, 264–65.

[173] J. Wentzel van Huyssteen, "Truth and Commitment in Theology and Science: An Appraisal of Wolfhart Pannenberg's Perspective," in *Essays in Postfoundationalist Theology* (Grand Rapids: Eerdmans, 1997), 62.

[174] To Pannenberg, the theologian's subjective religious commitment, and the social and historical framework it is grounded in, fall within the "context of discovery" but not the "context of justification." By this distinction, he seeks to affirm

an open stance with regards one's preunderstanding or pretheoretical commitment and still provide a cogent and rational explication of the meaning of Christ.

To summarise, we began with an overview of the salient features of Pannenberg's theological methodology before moving on to examine how this is worked out in terms of his Christology. This is followed by an analysis of what we call his eschatological trinitarian ontology, focussing in particular on how this enables him to speak of truth in temporal terms. This eschatologically informed temporalization of reality serves as a helpful framework for our project of developing a Christology *from ahead*. Before applying Pannenberg's insights to our task, a critique was mounted with reference to three areas in Pannenberg. This exercise set the stage for the attempt in the final section to offer a profile of what a broadly Pannenbergian Christology *from ahead* might look like. We have consciously correlated this discussion with our earlier arguments for a Christology "from within" both in terms of tradition and experience. How these two models—Christology *from within* and *from ahead*—may be further integrated will be the theme of our next chapter, where we shall argue that in Paul's theology, we find these two models coming together in a Christological convergence of tradition, experience and eschatology.

the contingency of argumentation without as it were taking the teeth out of the bite of rational justification. See *TPS*, 293–94, 321. According to Huyssteen, "Pannenberg concedes not only that the nature and origins of scientific and of theological statements are rooted in the socio-cultural context of the individual researcher (the context of discovery), but also that theological statements as such (the context of justification) are founded indirectly on general worldviews." "Truth and Commitment," 68.

CHAPTER SIX

CHRISTOLOGY FROM WITHIN AND AHEAD:
TRADITION, EXPERIENCE AND ESCHATOLOGY
IN PAUL'S HERMENEUTICAL CHRISTOLOGY

In our attempt to develop a hermeneutical approach to Christology
which takes seriously the temporality of understanding, we have proposed in the previous chapters that Christology be done *from within*
and *from ahead*, meaning that any formulation of belief concerning
Christ is necessarily rooted in tradition and experience, and takes
place within a framework of proleptic eschatological fulfilment brought
about by the resurrection of Christ. In this chapter, we shall put this
thesis to the test by applying it to the Christology of the apostle
Paul, drawing insights principally from his *methodological approach* as
well as relevant substantive elements from the *content* of his theology.
It is hoped that this will demonstrate the convergence of tradition,
experience and eschatological commitment in the development of
Christology.

No attempt is made here to survey the multi-faceted theology of
Paul; our agenda is more limited: to explore Paul's Christology as
a case study for our proposed models of Christological formulation.
This chapter is in two parts, which together demarcate the flow of
our argument: (1) we begin by examining the impact of the Damascus
Christophany on the shape of Paul's theology in general and his
Christology in particular. The importance of this experiential encounter
with the risen Christ will serve to support our thesis about the transformative significance of experience in hermeneutical understanding.
The consideration of which leads us to reaffirm our earlier observation that experience is always conditioned by one's background
and theoretical framework. This leads us then to explore (2) Paul's
methodological approach in terms of a hermeneutical interplay between
coherence and contingency in his theology. Attention will be given
to the way in which Paul develops his argument in critical dialogue
with tradition and his inherited Jewish assumptions. The eschatological character of Paul's Christology will then be examined in the
hope that both hermeneutical engagement with tradition and the

experience of Christ through the Spirit will expose an eschatological dimension which coheres with our argument up to this point. As
will become evident, these sections are interrelated, with the exposition of each dependent on and pointing to the other.

Before proceeding, a note must be made about the current state
of Pauline studies. We have been arguing that a hermeneutical approach to Christology entails a critical and dialogical engagement
with an interpretative preunderstanding or given tradition. This
Gadamerian stance is, we suggest, eminently compatible with developments in Pauline scholarship since the publication of E. P. Sanders's
Paul and Palestinian Judaism,[1] where we find a greater sensitivity to
the *difference within continuity* between the pre-Christian Saul and the
post-Damascus Paul. This Sanders-inspired "new perspective on Paul"[2]
calls for a fundamental revision in the way Paul's thought is understood vis-à-vis Judaism. The largely negative view of Judaism as a
legalistic religion (pervasive since Luther and the Reformation) and
the notion that Paul was troubled in his conscience prior to his conversion and struggling to lift himself up by his own moral rigour
have been called into question by Sanders, Stendahl, Davies and

---

[1] *Paul and Palestinian Judaism: A Comparison of Patterns of Religion* (London: SCM,
1977). See also his follow-up works: *Paul, the Law, and the Jewish People* (Philadelphia:
Fortress, 1983); and *Judaism: Practice and Belief 63 B.C.E–66 C.E* (London: SCM;
Philadelphia: Trinity Press International, 1992), 262–78, 377–78, 415–17.

[2] James D. G. Dunn, "The New Perspective on Paul," first published in *BJRL*
65 (1983): 95–122, and reprinted with "An Additional Note" (a response to his critics) in *Jesus, Paul and the Law: Studies in Mark and Galatians* (Louisville: Westminster/John
Knox, 1990), 183–214. Dunn rehearses the key features of Sanders's view in his
essay. N. T. Wright asserts that since Sanders's work, "the entire flavour of Pauline
studies has been changed quite probably permanently." Stephen Neill & N. T.
Wright, *The Interpretation of the New Testament: 1861–1986* (Oxford & New York:
Oxford University Press, 1988), 424. On this controversial proposal, see Stephen
Westerholm, *Israel's Law and the Church's Faith* (Grand Rapids: Eerdmans, 1988); N. T.
Wright, *The Climax of the Covenant: Christ and the Law in Pauline Theology* (Edinburgh:
T&T Clark, 1991), 1–17; Terence L. Donaldson, *Paul and the Gentiles: Remapping the
Apostle's Convictional World* (Minneapolis: Fortress, 1997), 8–21; and articles listed in
Watson E. Mills, *An Index to the Periodical Literature on the Apostle Paul* (Leiden: E. J.
Brill, 1993), 277–80. While Sanders is often credited with this 'paradigm shift' in
Pauline scholarship, key elements of his proposals are already anticipated in earlier
works, e.g., in Wrede's and Schweitzer's displacement of the doctrine of justification
by faith as the heart of Pauline thought; and Davies's and Schoeps's insistence on
the essentially Jewish and Rabbinic background of Paul's thought. W. Wrede, *Paul*,
tr. Edward Lumis (London: Philip Green, 1907); Albert Schweitzer, *Paul and His
Interpreters* (London: Adam & Charles Black, 1950); idem, *The Mysticism of Paul the
Apostle* (New York: Seabury, 1931); W. D. Davies, *Paul and Rabbinic Judaism: Some
Rabbinic Elements in Pauline Theology*, 4th ed. (London: SPCK, 1948, 1981); Hans

others.[3] Such a view of Judaism is, to them, historically inaccurate. Keeping the law in first-century Rabbinic Judaism is understood not so much as a means of gaining salvation as it is an outgrowth of Israel's covenantal response to the elective grace of God. Sanders describes this as "covenantal nomism," where Torah-observance is seen as the God-given means of "staying in," rather than a way of "getting into," the covenant.[4] Alongside this covenantal nomist interpretation, Sanders asserts, is the displacement of justification by faith as the centre of Paul's theology. Rather than construing the latter in terms of Luther's struggle to find faith, Sanders suggests, it should be characterized as a movement "from solution to plight",[5] in that it was from his discovery of Christ as the "solution" that Paul saw the "plight" nature of his misguided zeal.

This 'new perspective' on Paul is by no means a homogenous phenomenon, and Sanders's thesis is not without its dissenters,[6] with criticisms ranging from those targetted at its portrayal of Judaism to those of an exegetical nature. Even sympathetic voices (such as Dunn and Wright) are not uncritical; they point to lacunae in Sanders's

Joachim Schoeps, *Paul: The Theology of the Apostle in the Light of Jewish Religious History* (Philadelphia: Westminster, 1961). Other early anticipations of this "new perspective on Paul" are noted by Moises Silva, "The Law and Christianity: Dunn's New Synthesis," *WTJ* 53(1991): 339–53; Donald A. Hagner, "Paul and Judaism. The Jewish Matrix of Early Christianity: Issues in the Current Debate," *BBR* 3(1993): 111–30.

[3] Krister Stendahl, *Paul Among Jews and Gentiles* (Philadelphia: Fortress, 1976); Davies, *Rabbinic Judaism*; idem, "Paul and the People of Israel," *NTS* 24(1977–78): 4–39; Frank Thielman, *From Plight to Solution: A Jewish Framework for Understanding Paul's View of the Law in Galatians and Romans* (Leiden: E. J. Brill, 1989).

[4] Sanders, *Palestinian Judaism*, 75, 236. See Morna D. Hooker, "Paul and 'Covenantal Nomism'," in her *From Adam to Christ: Essays on Paul* (Cambridge: Cambridge University Press, 1990), 155–64.

[5] Sanders, *Palestinian Judaism*, 442–43.

[6] Richard H. Bell for instance states categorically that "As far as Paul is concerned, Sanders is certainly wrong", and questions Sanders's reading of Rabbinic texts. *Provoked to Jealousy: The Origin and Purpose of the Jealousy Motif in Romans 9–11* (Tübingen: J. C. B. Mohr (Paul Siebeck), 1994), 193. See: R. H. Gundry, "Grace, Works, and Staying Saved in Paul," *Bib* 66(1985): 1–38; Hans Hübner, "Pauli Theologiae Proprium," *NTS* 26(1979–80): 445–73; Heikki Räisänen, "Galatians 2:16 and Paul's Break with Judaism," *NTS* 31(1985): 543–53; idem, *Paul and the Law* (Philadelphia: Fortress, 1986); Thomas R. Schreiner, "The Abolition and Fulfilment of the Law in Paul," *JSNT* 35(1989): 47–74; idem, *The Law and Its Fulfillment: A Pauline Theology of Law* (Grand Rapids: Baker, 1993); Klyne Snodgrass, "Justification by Grace—to the Doers: An Analysis of the Place of Romans 2 in the Theology of Paul," *NTS* 32(1986): 72–93. See also: M. Hengel & R. Deines, "E. P. Sanders' 'Common Judaism', Jesus and the Pharisees. A Review Article," *JTS* 46(1995): 1–70.

overall argument, and seek to go beyond him in rethinking Paul's theology. Without entering fully into the discussion of post-Sanders Pauline theology, we think that these developments are remarkably amenable to a hermeneutical approach to Christological formulation. Our thesis does not stand or fall with the viability of a covenantal nomist reading of Paul. It is possible to argue for continuity and dis-continuity between the pre- and post-Damascus Paul without sign-ing up to the "Sanders revolution." Nevertheless, we think our case is strengthened when it can be shown that Paul's Christology developed in concert with the expansion of his (Jewish messianic) horizon of understanding as a result of his encounter with the risen Christ.

Whatever one's assessment of post-Sanders thought on Paul, the fact remains that the greater sensitivity to Paul as a first-century Jew, and to the way he articulated his non-Torah, Christ-centred theol-ogy *from within* the framework of Second Temple Judaism, is con-gruent with our thesis that theological development takes place along a trajectory of continuity and discontinuity, within the dialectic of fidelity to tradition and creative extension.[7] Just as understanding takes off from an already preconditioned stance, Paul's Christology developed within the conceptual framework of his pharisaical Judaism. To acknowledge that there are strands of continuity between the pre- and post-Damascus Paul is not to underplay the radically new departure in his theological thinking. On the contrary, we shall argue that it is the condition for such a departure.

I. *The Impact of the Damascus Christophany*

A. *Paul's Conversion and its Aftermath*

Paul's conversion experience is recounted both in his letters, princi-pally in 1 Cor. 9:1; 15:8–10; Gal. 1:13–17; Phil. 3:4–11, and (leav-ing aside for the moment issues of dating and authorship) in Acts 9:1–28; 22:1–21; and 26:4–23.[8] Whether understood as a radical

---

[7] The "new perspective" is, in Dunn's assessment, "a historical conclusion of some importance, since it begins to clarify with more precision what were the con-tinuities and discontinuities between Paul, his fellow Jewish Christians and his own Pharisaic past, so far as justification and grace, covenant and law are concerned." "New Perspective," 194.

[8] Though it is best methodologically to begin with Paul's own accounts of his experience, and then move on to the Acts accounts, seeing that the latter repre-

conversion or a prophetic commissioning,[9] the Damascus Christophany was a decisive transforming event for him, marking the starting point of Paul as missionary, pastor and theologian. How, and to what extent, his conversion experience affected the shape of his theology continues to be a matter of debate, with opinions ranging from a

sent later perceptions or interpretations (probably of an established tradition), one should not dismiss too quickly their value as a source of historical information on Paul's conversion. It is arguable that Luke's accounts have roots in Pauline traditions; see Carey C. Newman, *Paul's Glory-Christology: Tradition and Rhetoric* (Leiden: E. J. Brill, 1992), 223 n. 24; M. Hengel (in collaboration with Roland Deines), *The Pre-Christian Paul* (London: SCM; Philadelphia: Trinity Press International, 1991), 18f, points to the remarkable correspondence and compatibility between Luke's accounts and Paul's own letters. Also: Martin Hengel and Anna Maria Schwemer, *Paul Between Damascus and Antioch: The Unknown Years* (London: SCM, 1997), 6–11, 15–21, 38f; Alan F. Segal, "Paul and Luke" in his *Paul the Convert: The Apostolate and Apostasy of Saul the Pharisee* (New Haven & London: Yale University Press, 1990), 3–33.

[9] Stendahl famously contends that Paul was *called* and *not converted* in his essays, "Call Rather than Conversion," and "The Apostle Paul and the Introspective Conscience of the West," in *Paul Among Jews and Gentiles*, 7–23, 78–96. James D. G. Dunn argues along similar lines in "The Justice of God: A Renewed Perspective on Justification by Faith," *JTS* 43(1992): 1–22; cf. Segal, *Paul*, 6–7; R. F. Collins, "Paul's Damascus Experience: Reflections on the Lukan Account," *LS* 11(1986): 99–118. Stendahl's view is anticipated in Johannes Munck, *Paul and the Salvation of Mankind* (London: SCM, 1959), 11–35; and taken up in Karl Olav Sandness, *Paul—One of the Prophets?* (Tübingen: J. C. B. Mohr [Paul Siebeck], 1991). It is argued that Paul's account is couched in language reminiscent of the calling of the OT prophets: Gal. 1:15–16, cf. Jer. 1:4–5; Isa. 42:7; 49:1–6, especially significant is the verbal similarity between Gal. 1:15 and Isa. 49:1 in the LXX. Parallels between Paul's conversion-experience and Isa 6 have also been made. Bell, *Provoked*, 329f; Otto Betz, *Was wissen wir von Jesus* (Stuttgart: Kreuz-verlag, 1965), 69. In our opinion, there is no necessity to pit conversion against prophetic calling. It is best to hold both together since the two elements are intertwined. Paul's calling to the Gentiles makes perfect sense against the backdrop of the radical turnaround that the risen Lord effected in his life. Without that radical transformation, Paul would not have budged from his Israel-centred faith. His conversion was not just a conversion away *from* his past, but also a conversion *to* a universalisation of redemption.

On the nature of Paul's conversion, see: Donaldson, *Gentiles*, 17–18, 249–60; J. D. G. Dunn, "'A Light to the Gentiles': The Significance of the Damascus Road Christophany for Paul," in L. D. Hurst & N. T. Wright, eds., *The Glory of Christ in the New Testament: Studies in Christology in Memory of George Bradford Caird* (Oxford: Clarendon Press, 1987), 251–66, rpt. with "Additional Note" in *Jesus, Paul and the Law*, 89–107; J. Dupont, "The Conversion of Paul, and Its Influence on the Understanding of Salvation by Faith," in W. Ward Gasque & Ralph P. Martin, eds., *Apostolic History and the Gospel* (Grand Rapids: Eerdmans, 1970), 176–94; J. M. Everts, "Conversion and Call of Paul," in Gerald F. Hawthorne *et al.*, eds., *Dictionary of Paul and His Letters* (Downers Grove & Leicester: InterVarsity Press, 1993; henceforth *DPL*), 162–163; Larry W. Hurtado, "Convert, Apostate or Apostle to the Nations: The 'Conversion' of Paul in Recent Scholarship," *SR* 22(1993): 273–84; Seyoon Kim, *Origin of Paul's Gospel*; Richard N. Longenecker, ed., *The Road From Damascus: The Impact of Paul's Conversion on His Life, Thought, and Ministry* (Grand Rapids: Eerdmans, 1997).

focus on the fissure between Paul's thought and his Jewish background (conversion) to one which accentuates the continuity between
them (call). There is no need to dichotomize conversion and calling, for the verb καλέω (including the cognate adjective κλητόξ) is
used to describe both God's calling of people to salvation (Rom.
8:30; 1 Cor. 1:9; 7:15; Gal. 1:16; 5:13) as well as God's call to be
an apostle (Rom. 1:1).[10] As we shall argue below, Paul's conversion
and calling to a Gentile mission are intertwined within a theological
framework characterised by radical change and discernible continuity.

That Paul's conversion-experience en route to Damascus was sudden and unexpected is attested in both his own and Luke's recount-
ing (Gal. 1:15–16; Ac. 9:3) of the event. The emphasis in both is
on the overwhelming and unconditional electing grace of God. It
was this, rather than any psychological or sociological reasons per se,[11]
which led to Paul's conversion. He recognized that it was only because
it "pleased" (ὅτε δὲ εὐδόκησεν)[12] God, and through his grace (διὰ τῆς
χάριτος αὐτοῦ), that he was given the revelation of his Son (ἀποκαλύψαι
τὸν υἱὸν αὐτοῦ), Gal. 1:15, cf. 12).[13] On his own accounting (Phil.

---

[10] Paul describes himself and his converts as "called" (Rom. 9:24; 1 Thess. 4:7),
and believers as "called ones" (Rom. 1:6; 8:28; 1 Cor. 1:2, 24). P. T. O'Brien,
Gospel and Mission in the Writings of Paul: An Exegetical and Theological Analysis (Grand
Rapids: Baker; Carlisle: Paternoster, 1993, 1995), 7–8.

[11] Doubts about accepting uncritically Paul's autobiographical accounts of his pre-
Christian life and conversion have been expressed by Beverly R. Gaventa, *From
Darkness to Light: Aspects of Conversion in the New Testament* (Philadelphia: Fortress, 1986),
23; and Paula Fredriksen, "Paul and Augustine: Conversion Narratives, Orthodox
Traditions, and the Retrospective Self," *JTS* 37(1986): 3–34. J. G. Gager, "Some
Notes on Paul's Conversion," *NTS* 27(1981): 697–704, seeks to interpret Paul's conversion experience in terms of what L. Festiger calls, the phenomenon of "postde-
cision dissonance" in his *A Theory of Cognitive Dissonance* (Evanston: Row Peterson,
1957). According to this socio-psychological view, dissonance invariably sets in after
a person has chosen one option over another equally attractive option. In order to
reduce this dissonance, the person downplays the attractiveness of the rejected option
so as to confirm the wisdom of his or her choice. Allegedly something akin to this
led to Paul's rejection of the Law and fervent commitment to Christ. While this
may be a legitimate insight into the workings of the human psyche, I wonder if
that was Paul's concern at all. His focus was on the supremacy of God's saving
grace in Christ, not the downplaying of the attractiveness of the Law. The latter
flows from the former. It was the priority and attractiveness of grace that eclipsed
all else.

[12] Hengel suggests that behind this stands the Hebrew רצה, *raṣah*, "which denotes
God's free, underivable decision." *Damascus*, 41, 343 n. 186. That the verb εὐδοκέω
points to the freedom of God's gracious choice is also noted by C. Dietzfelbinger,
Die Berufung des Paulus als Ursprung seiner Theologie (Neukirchen-Vluyn: Neukirchener,
1985), 61.

[13] This conviction stayed with Paul throughout his life and influenced his theol-

3:4b–6; Gal. 1:14), he was proud of his heritage and achievements as a Hebrew of Hebrews; his conscience was "robust" rather than "uneasy"[14] (though this need not mean that he had no doubts or struggles with the demands of the law).[15] Yet by his own reckoning, his punctilious observance of the Law and impeccable pharisaic credentials had nothing to do with his being saved; it was due purely to God's grace. Such an experience of grace undoubtedly served as a catalyst to rethink the basis of human justification before God. We think such a reading comports with our thesis that the experiential dimension plays a critical role in the formation of theological beliefs.

The "revelation" consists in a blinding light and an audible word (Ac. 9:3–5; 22:7–8; 26:13–15). The description is akin to that of an OT epiphany, and is understood in the light of Paul's Christological statements in his letters as a theophanic revelation of God himself to Paul. Paul claims to have seen the Lord in 1 Cor. 9:1, and this may well allude to his experience on the road to Damascus, a story which was apparently known to the Corinthians, judging by the almost off-handed way in which Paul reminded them of it in 1 Cor. 15:8.[16] It is likely that Paul understood the vision of the risen Christ on the road to Damascus as a manifestation of the יהוה כבוד, *kabod* or glory of God.[17] The association and depiction of Christ with and in terms of the divine δόξα is reflected in Paul's description of Christ as τὸν κύριον τῆς δόξης (1 Cor. 2:8), raised through τῆς δόξης τοῦ πατρός (Rom. 6:4; cf. Phil. 2:11), and into whose σῶμα τῆς δόξης believers are to be joined (Phil. 3:21). Significantly, the word δόξα, used frequently in the LXX of the nature of God, is applied to Christ, indicating that there is a blurring of the line of distinction between God and Christ in Paul's language.[18] This Glory-Christology probably has its roots in Paul's experience on the road to Damascus,

---

ogy (1 Cor. 15:10). James D. G. Dunn notes, "it was his [Paul's] own *experience of grace* which made 'grace' a central and distinctive feature of his gospel". *Unity and Diversity in the New Testament* (Philadelphia: Westminster, 1977), 190.

[14] Stendahl, *Paul*, 14–15.

[15] See J. M. Espy's call to reconsider Stendahl's view on Paul prior to his conversion. "Paul's 'Robust Conscience' Re-Examined," *NTS* 31(1985): 161–88.

[16] According to Kim, an account of his conversion was probably included in Paul's teaching to the churches he founded. *Origin*, 28–29.

[17] Newman, *Glory-Christology*, 17. The notion of the divine "glory" is found in ancient Jewish sources to describe God's visible manifestations. See Newman's semantic observations of the word *kabod* both in the Hebrew Bible and in Jewish apocalyptic literature in *Glory-Christology*, 17–133; cf. Segal, *Paul*, 8–11, 34–71.

[18] See Neil Richardson, *Paul's Language about God*, 158–59.

with the main lines of his theology conceivably formulated, as Seyoon
Kim has tried to show, under the impact of that experience.[19]

The "revelation" which Paul received thus led to a reassessment
of the significance of Jesus, which resulted in a reinterpretation of
his notion of God and the Messiah. To the pre-Christian Saul, the
fact that Jesus was crucified was proof enough that he could not be
the Messiah, since exposure on a tree of a man condemned to die
is a sign of being cursed (Dt. 21:22–23).[20] However, in raising Jesus
from the dead, God vindicated him and essentially overturned the
verdict of the law. While this alone may not be sufficient to explain
the rise of the sharp Torah-Christ antithesis in Paul and early Christianity,[21] it is nevertheless congruent with the belief that God in

---

[19] According to Kim, key elements in Paul's Christology, soteriology, and understanding of mission, have their genesis in the Damascus Road encounter. See *Origin*,
and his "2 Cor. 5:11–21 and the Origin of Paul's Concept of 'Reconciliation',"
NovT 39(1997): 360–84. See Newman's analysis of δόξα as a Christological concept
in Paul, *Glory-Christology*, 3–7, 157–247. Newman contends that the revelation of
doxa in the Damascus Christophany constitutes the origin of Paul's Glory-Christology
and the "deepest level" of his theological enterprise. Cf. Dunn's critique of Kim,
"Light to the Gentiles," 93–98. See also: H. Schlier, "*Doxa* bei Paulus als heilsgeschichtlicher Begriff," in *Studiorum Paulinorum Congressus Internationalis Catholicus*,
2 vols. (Analecta Biblica 17–18; Rome: Pontifical Biblical Institute, 1963), 1:45–56.

[20] We know from the Qumran texts, 4QpNahum 3–4, I.7–8 and 11QTemple
64:6–13, that Dt. 21:23 was read in connection with crucifixion by the first century.

[21] Donaldson, *Gentiles*, 170–71, does not think the conventional explanation that
the scandal of a crucified Messiah and the belief that God is on the side of Christ
led to the rejection of the Law is convincing for the following reasons: (i) It is not
clear that a first-century Jew like Paul would have immediately concluded from the
sight of a crucified man that he is cursed. The Hebrew text of Dt. 21:23 which the
LXX renders as, "cursed by God" could also read, "an affront to God." If hanging
or crucifixion constitutes a curse, then Saul and Jonathan (2 Sam. 21:12), the eight
hundred crucified by Jannaeus (Josephus' *Antiquities of the Jews* 13.380), and the
many crucified by the Romans, would all have died under God's curse. Furthermore,
there are literary and archaeological evidence to suggest that first-century Jews did
not normally regard a crucified Jew as cursed by God. See N. Elliott, *Liberating
Paul: The Justice of God and the Politics of the Apostle* (Maryknoll: Orbis, 1994), 145,
268 n. 25; and Paula Fredriksen, *From Jesus to Christ: The Origins of the New Testament
Images of Jesus* (New Haven & London: Yale University Press, 1988), 147. (ii) There
are ways for a Jewish Christian to resolve the 'problem' of a crucified Messiah
other than repudiating the Torah. One could say that the court made a mistake;
Jesus was not guilty. Or that he died the death of a martyr since it was the Romans
who executed him. Alternatively, one could invoke Deutero-Isaiah's suffering servant or the righteous sufferer of the Psalms. Donaldson contends that Paul, being
a zealot for the law, would have found "a *resolution* of any perceived tension between
Christ and the law, before concluding . . . that 'if Torah had no room for Christ's
crucifixion, so much the worse for Torah'" (171, quoting Ben Meyer, *The Early
Christians: Their World Mission and Self-discovery* [Wilmington: Michael Glazier, 1986],
163). Further to Donaldson, we may add (iii) the observation that "the Torah had

Christ has the last word, not the law. The idea of a crucified Messiah became the core of Paul's preaching (1 Cor. 1:23)[22] as he identified with the suffering of the cross (Gal. 2:20). The encounter with the exalted Jesus was thus the generative event which shaped Paul's theology, leading him to join the early Christians in acclaiming Jesus as κύριος, a title regularly used in the LXX in the place of the divine tetragrammaton.[23]

Not only was Paul's concept of 'Messiah' changed as a result of his encounter with the exalted Jesus, his view of salvation history, particularly the outworking of God's messianic promises in history, was transformed as well. The significance of Jesus's resurrection could not at all have been lost on Paul the pharisee, steeped as he undoubtedly was in the eschatological expectation of Judaism; for resurrection meant the dawning of the eschaton.[24] In the raising of Jesus from the dead, *the age to come* has invaded *this age*. This eschatological two-age schema, where the end has encroached upon history proleptically in Jesus's resurrection serves as an important interpretive grid for Paul's theology. And as we shall see below, this eschatological and Christological orientation, arguably attributable to Paul's conversion/call experience, is evident in his hermeneutical reading of the Hebrew Scriptures.

To accept this eschatological interpretation of Jesus Christ is already to emphasize the continuity between Paul's new found faith and the

---

not condemned Jesus, nor does Paul ever suggest Jesus died because he had violated the Torah." Elliott, *Liberating Paul*, 144; H. Räisänen, *Paul and the Law*, 249–50. Cf. W. R. G. Loader, "Christ at the Right Hand: Ps. 110:1 in the NT," *NTS* 24(1977–8): 199–217.

[22] See W. Schrage, "Das 'Wort vom Kreuz' als Grund und Kriterium von Gemeinde und Apostel (1:18–2:5)," *Der erste Brief an die Korinther*, 2 vols. (EKKzNT VII, i, ii; Zürich: Benziger; Neukirchen: Neukirchener Verlag, 1991, 1993), 1:165–203.

[23] On the ascription of the title κύριος to Christ, see: J. A. Fitzmyer, "The Semitic Background of the New Testament *Kyrios*-Title," in *A Wandering Aramean* (Missoula: Scholars Press, 1979): 115–42; Larry Hurtado, *One God, One Lord: Early Christian Devotion and Ancient Jewish Monotheism* (Philadelphia: Fortress, 1988); Richard N. Longenecker, *The Christology of Early Jewish Christianity* (Grand Rapids: Baker, 1970), 120f; I. Howard Marshall, *The Origins of New Testament Christology* (Downers Grove: InterVarsity, 1976), 97–110; C. F. D. Moule, *The Origin of Christology* (Cambridge: Cambridge University Press, 1977), 35–46; Wright, *Climax*, 120–36.

[24] J. Christiaan Beker, *Paul the Apostle: The Triumph of God in Life and Thought* (Philadelphia: Fortress, 1980, 1984 pbk ed. with a new preface by the author), 135f; Leander E. Keck, "Paul as Thinker," *Int* 47(1993): 30f; L. J. Kreitzer, "Eschatology," *DPL*, 256–7. See also: Ben Witherington III, *Jesus, Paul, and the End of the World: A Comparative Study in New Testament Eschatology* (Downers Grove: InterVarsity, 1992).

faith of his Jewish forebears. The revelatory appearance of God's
Son to Paul, with all of its eschatological overtones, was given ἵνα
εὐαγγελίζωμαι αὐτὸν ἐν τοῖς ἔθνεσιν (Gal. 1:16). The purposive force
of the ἵνα should not be diluted.[25] Such was the clarity with which
Paul perceived the connection between the Christophany and his
call, that he became committed to a Gentile-mission from the very
beginning. The turn to the Gentiles was neither an insight which
developed over time,[26] nor a result of the unresponsiveness of the
Jews;[27] it was part and parcel of Paul's intentions from the very start.
Among the things he may have done when he went to Arabia (or
the territory of the Nabateans) soon after his Damascus experience
(Gal. 1:17) was preach Christ there.[28]

   Paul's mission to the Gentiles however cannot be adequately appraised in isolation. It must be seen within a network of interconnected issues which include: the role of the law vis-à-vis faith; the
nature of God's covenantal relationship with Israel; the place of
empirical Israel and the Gentile nations in eschatological fulfilment;
etc. These are huge questions which we obviously cannot take up
here. What engages our main concern in this context is the way in
which Paul's horizon of understanding, a horizon shaped by the religion of Judaism, is expanded and transformed while simultaneously
providing the terms and categories by which Christ is interpreted.
Paul's new found discovery of Jesus as Messiah at the Damascus
Christophany necessitated a remapping of his convictional world,[29]

---

[25] Dunn, "Light to the Gentiles," 89; cf. Donald Senior & Carroll Stuhlmueller, *The Biblical Foundations for Mission* (Maryknoll: Orbis, 1984), 165f.
[26] Dupont, "Conversion of Paul," 193.
[27] For instance: Segal, *Paul*, 8, 142–43; Francis B. Watson, *Paul, Judaism and the Gentiles* (SNTSMS 56; Cambridge: Cambridge University Press, 1986), 28–38.
[28] Jerome Murphy-O'Connor, *Paul: A Critical Life* (Oxford: Clarendon Press, 1996), 81–82, observes that Paul must have done something to antagonize the Nabateans, for even after three years, the Nabatean authorities were still intent on arresting him (2 Cor. 11:32–33). While Paul may have gone to Arabia to reflect, study and work out the full implications of what had just happened to him, e.g., R. N. Longenecker, *Galatians*, WBC (Dallas: Word, 1990), 34, this is unlikely according to Donaldson: "One does not rouse the anger of a ruler by engaging in a 'period of silence and seclusion,' as the Arabian sojourn has sometimes been romantically portrayed." *Gentiles*, 271. The most plausible explanation is that Paul tried to evangelize the Nabateans. See also: J. Murphy-O'Connor, "Paul in Arabia," *CBQ* 55(1993): 732–37; F. F. Bruce, *Paul: Apostle of the Free Spirit* (Exeter: Paternoster, 1977), 81–82.
[29] The subtitle of Donaldson's book, *Paul and the Gentiles* is "Remapping the Apostle's Convictional World." Donaldson applies Kuhn's notion of paradigm shift to describe the fundamental change in Paul's theological frame of reference. By

which comes into sharp relief when one investigates the origin and nature of his Gentile-mission. We will examine this briefly as a way of clarifying the dynamics involved in Paul's hermeneutical reconfiguration.

B. *The Convictional Reconfiguration of Paul's Theology*

As indicated earlier, Paul's Damascus road experience was both a conversion and a call. Given the extensive changes which came upon Paul, it is entirely appropriate to describe the experience as a conversion. At the same time, one can argue that *Paul did not so much change religion*[30] *after the Christophany as change his understanding of his religion.* There was of course a clear transfer of allegiance on Paul's part: he moved from being a persecutor to being persecuted. Yet he remained a Jewish man seeking to make sense of what happened in terms of his worldview, a worldview thrown into disarray by the unexpected encounter with the risen Lord. It is in considering Paul's fundamental reordering of his convictional world that we appreciate the shaping of his theology.

Paul describes his "earlier life in Judaism" as one marked by extreme zeal for the traditions of his fathers, a zeal which drove him to perpetrate violence upon the early Christians (Gal. 1:13–14; Phil. 3:6; Ac. 9:1). In all probability, Paul was, prior to his conversion, party to the more dominant and aggressive faction of pre-70 A.D. Pharisaism, the Shammaites. In contrast to the more lenient Hillelites, the Shammaites were prepared to use violence to defend the honour of God and Torah.[31] They drew inspiration from heroes of zeal

---

"convictional world" is meant a set of basic convictions which together constitute a tacit semantic universe. Donaldson however acknowledges that the notion of "conviction" or "convictional pattern" is already anticipated in Daniel Patte, *Paul's Faith and the Power of the Gospel: A Structural Introduction to the Pauline Letters* (Philadelphia: Fortress, 1983), 10–25. See also Alexandra R. Brown, *The Cross & Human Transformation: Paul's Apocalyptic Word in 1 Corinthians* (Minneapolis: Fortress, 1995).

[30] Hagner concurs with this: "I do *not* think that it is correct to say that he converted to a new religion, or that Paul himself would ever have thought so. Christianity, for Paul, is nothing other than the faith of his ancestors come to an eschatological phase of fulfillment before the final consummation." "Paul and Judaism," 123.

[31] On Shammaite and Hillelite Pharisaism, see N. T. Wright, *The New Testament and the People of God* (London: SPCK, 1992), 181–203; idem, *What Saint Paul Really Said* (Oxford: Lion, 1997), 25–35. See also: Kim, *Origin*, 41–44; Lloyd Gaston, "Paul and the Torah," Alan T. Davies, ed., *Antisemitism and the Foundations of Christianity*. (New York & Toronto: Paulist Press, 1979), 61; Klaus Haacker, "Die Berufung des Verfolgers und die Rechtfertigung des Gottlosen: Erwägungen zum Zusammenhang zwischen Biographie und Theologie des Apostels Paulus," *TB* 6(1975): 1–19.

like Phinehas (Nu. 25:7–13; cf. Sir. 45:23–24; 1 Macc. 2:26, 54; 4
Macc. 18:12), Elijah (1 Kgs. 18–19; Sir. 48:1–2; 1 Macc. 2:58),
Simeon and Levi (Gen. 34; Jub. 30:18; T. Levi 6:3; Jdt. 9:2–4).[32] If
this is the case, it follows that whatever it was that drove Saul to
persecute the early church, it was something which he perceived to
be a threat to the faith of his fathers. What was it then about the
Christian message that made it such a threat that it must be opposed?

Different reasons have been suggested as motivations for Paul's
persecution of the early Christians.[33] An important key to this question lies in Paul's characterization of his persecuting activity as a
demonstration of "zeal."[34] This is not simply a report of an emotional state; it presupposes a specific theological framework in which
the righteous status of the covenantal community is maintained by
its upholding of the Torah. Any aspersion cast on the Torah must
be confronted with asperity, and the zealous are willing to suffer and
die for the sake of the law, believing that God will reward their
efforts at defending it.[35] At stake is the identity of the community;
for God's judgment will come upon his people if the impediment is
not excised. By acting zealously, God's wrath might be turned away
from his people (Nu. 25:11).

Significantly, it was precisely because Paul understood the Christian
message to be about the God of Israel, the *same God* he worshipped
and served, that he embarked on his persecuting campaign. If the
Christians were simply talking about Jesus as a divine mediator, with
no reference to the Hebrew Scriptures, to the Messiah and God's
covenant with Israel, Saul would not have been galvanized into
action—the Greco-Roman world was after all awashed with gods
and mediators. But Paul recognized that the Christ of the kerygma

---

[32] See: Terence L. Donaldson, "Zealot and Convert: The Origin of Paul's Christ-
Torah Antithesis," *CBQ* 51(1989): 655–82; idem, *Gentiles*, 285–86; N. T. Wright,
"Paul, Arabia, and Elijah (Galatians 1:17)," *JBL* 115(1996): 683–92; cf. M. Hengel,
*The Zealots: Investigations into the Jewish Freedom Movement in the Period from Herod I until
70 A.D.* (Edinburgh: T&T Clark, 1961, rpt. 1989), 149–77.

[33] On possible reasons for Saul's persecution of the church, see Donaldson, *Gentiles*,
284–92; Elliott, *Liberating Paul*, 143–49; Murphy-O'Connor, *Paul*, 65–70.

[34] See Robert Jewett, "The Basic Human Dilemma: Weakness or Zealous Violence?
Romans 7:7–25 and 10:1–18," *Ex Auditu* 13(1997): 96–109.

[35] 1 Macc. 2:50–64; 2 Macc. 7:2; 8:21; 14:37–46; 4 Macc. 17:20–22; 18; cf.
Josephus, *Antiquities* 18.23–24; *Jubilees* 30.18–20; *Syriac Apocalypse of Baruch* 66.6. On
the significance of zeal, see Dupont, "Conversion of Paul," 183–85; Hengel, *Pre-
Christian Paul*, 70.

represented a rival to the Torah *from within* the one tradition of Judaism, and that the basis of entry into covenantal membership had shifted from the law to Christ. In other words, Paul saw that the entire edifice of the Jewish faith, founded as it was on God's mighty acts in their history and promises for the future, was put at risk by the message about Jesus as the Christ or Messiah. To the mind of this Shammaite pharisee, this was tantamount to theological treason and had to be set right.

What is interesting for our purposes is Donaldson's contention that the Christ-Torah antithesis, so evident in Paul's letters, was already present in his convictional make-up even before his conversion, albeit understood quite differently then. That Christ was perceived as a rival to the Torah as a boundary marker for the covenant was precisely what stirred the zealous blood of Paul. However, at the Damascus encounter, he realized that salvation was to be found in Christ alone, and not within the regime under the law. This new conviction led to a switch in his allegiance, and the Christ-Torah antithesis in Paul's subsequent set of Christian convictions can be seen as "an inversion of his preconversion perceptions of the Christian message."[36] Donaldson asserts:

> Paul's conversion experience ... resulted not so much in a new perception of the relationship between Christ and Torah, as in a new perspective on that relationship as he already perceived it. The incompatibility of Christ and Torah was the constant element in a syllogism that, on one side of the conversion experience, led to persecution of the church and, on the other, resulted in fierce resistance to the Judaizers. This argument is characterized by the assumption that a tight convictional or cognitive connection can be found to link together Paul's persecution of the church, his conversion, and his later pattern of thought.[37]

There is thus a sense in which there is continuity as well as change in Paul's thinking. While the encounter with Christ made all the difference to him, that difference makes sense only within some sort of continuity in his conceptual framework. The commonality which links the pre- and post-conversion Paul is the concept of the covenant: whereas Torah-observance marks one's membership in the covenant previously, now it is faith in Christ that determines one's acceptance

---

[36] Donaldson, *Gentiles*, 285.
[37] Ibid., 289–90.

into the ranks of God's covenantal people. And this same phenomenon of continuity and difference is possibly evident in Paul's view of the Gentiles as well.

Paul's call to a Gentile-mission, while clearly given as part of his conversion experience, may have roots extending back to his pre-Christian attitude towards the Gentiles.[38] While Second Temple Judaism was not a "missionary religion" in the Christian sense of conscientious outreach,[39] it nevertheless had strands of universalism within it.[40] Evidently, Gentile προσήλυτοι, "incomers" to Israel, were drawn to Judaism by the "power of attraction."[41] There were those in first-century Judaism who believed that salvation for the Gentiles in the age to come depends on their becoming proselytes to Judaism in this age.[42] And membership into Abraham's family was through embracing the Torah. Donaldson argues on the basis of Gal. 5:11, that Paul may well have been involved in proselytizing activities prior to his conversion, though not in the same way and with the same intensity as in his later missionary work. The expression, "still preaching circumcision" (περιτομὴν ἔτι κηρύσσω) implies that there was a time (the temporal force of the adverb, ἔτι) when he preached circumcision. Since it is unlikely that this took place *after* his conversion, it is reasonable to suppose that he is here referring to an activity

---

[38] Ibid., 275–84; idem, "Israelite, Convert, Apostle to the Gentiles: The Origin of Paul's Gentile Mission," *Road From Damascus*, 62–84.

[39] See Scot McKnight, *A Light Among the Gentiles: Jewish Missionary Activity in the Second Temple Period* (Minneapolis: Fortress, 1991); Martin Goodman, *Mission and Conversion: Proselytizing in the Religious History of the Roman Empire* (Oxford: Clarendon Press, 1994). L. H. Feldman however contends that "mission" was present in Judaism and argues his case against McKnight and Goldman in *Jew and Gentile in the Ancient World: Attitudes and Interactions from Alexander to Justinian* (Princeton: Princeton University Press, 1993).

[40] Jewish universalistic strands include: the belief that God is Creator and sovereign over all humanity (Gen. 12:1–3; Isa. 42; 49; 56; Ecclus. 13:15; 18:13); the tradition of the eschatological pilgrimage of the nations (Isa. 2:2–4; 25:6–10a; 56:6–8; Zech. 8:20–23; Tob. 14:5–7; *Sib. Or.* 3.716–20); righteous Gentiles (*Tosephta Sanhedrin* 13:2) or God-fearers (Josephus, *Jewish War* 4.262, 275); and Gentile proselytism (*2 Baruch* 30:4–5; 44:15; 51:6; 72.1–6; 82:3–9; *'Aboda Zara* 3b; *b. Yebamot* 24b). See Y. Cohen, "The Attitude to the Gentile in the Halakah and in Reality in the Tannaitic Period," *Immanuel* 9(1979): 32–41; Donaldson, *Gentiles*, 224–26, 275–84; McKnight, *Light*, 13–19; Segal, *Paul*, 205.

[41] Hengel, *Damascus*, 75.

[42] Gentiles would have to flee "under the wings" of Israel's God—this is the language of *2 Baruch* 41:1–6, where Gentiles are said to await eternal punishment unless they take upon themselves the yoke of the law.

before his conversion.[43] While this is admittedly conjectural, it is not inconceivable that the pre-Christian Paul may have been involved in instructing both Jews and God-fearers on matters pertaining to the Torah.[44]

Arguably there is a putative compatibility at the level of presuppositional framework between Paul's pre- and post-conversion stance towards Gentiles, without minimizing in any way the clear difference between his (alleged) pre-Christian proselytizing activity and his later work as an apostolic missionary. The divine endorsement of Jesus Christ which Paul became convinced of at and after the Damascus Christophany led not only to the conviction that Christ, and not the Torah, is the boundary marker for covenantal membership, but also to an inversion of the Jewish eschatological-pilgrimage tradition. Instead of Gentiles streaming *to* Zion, it is now a movement *from* Zion to the nations. Christology and Gentile-mission are integrally related.

Paul's Christology thus developed *from within* the particularity of Jewish tradition even though it was radically reconfigured under the impact of Christ's revelation.[45] This supports our contention that there is a dialectic of continuity and discontinuity in the development of his thought. There is a discernible expansion of Paul's horizon of understanding as it moves along a trajectory coming out of the Hebrew messianic tradition. This stems from a basic Christocentric and eschatological perspective, which serves as the hermeneutical grid for his theological interpretation of scriptures. To this we now turn.

II. *Paul's Hermeneutical Development of Christology*

A. *Paul's Christocentric-Retrospective Hermeneutics*

That eschatology figures prominently in Paul is noted in all the standard introductions to his theology.[46] Eschatological concerns are found

---

[43] Donaldson rejects F. Watson's thesis in *Paul, Judaism and the Gentiles*, that this refers to an early phase of Paul's activity. In the context of Galatians, "preaching circumcision" "*means* insisting that Gentiles be circumcised if they want to be members of Abraham's family." Donaldson, *Gentiles*, 270, also 278f.

[44] See Hengel, *Pre-Christian Paul*, 54–62.

[45] Donaldson, *Gentiles*, 297, "Paul did not so much as abandon his native convictional world as reconstruct it around a new center."

[46] E.g., Bruce, *Paul*; D. E. H. Whiteley, *The Theology of St. Paul* (Philadelphia: Fortress, 1966); H. Ridderbos, *Paul: An Outline of His Theology* (Grand Rapids: Eerdmans, 1975); G. Bornkamm, *Paul* (New York: Harper & Row, 1969).

in virtually all of Paul's letters, with the exception of Philemon and perhaps Galatians.[47] In recent times, Beker, building on Käsemann, has argued vigorously that apocalyptic lies at the very heart of Paul's gospel.[48] The eschatological dualism of two aeons is evident in Paul's juxtaposing of "this age" (Rom. 12:2; 1 Cor. 1:20; 2:6–8; 3:18; 2 Cor. 4:4) and "the new creation" (2 Cor. 5:17; Gal. 6:15) in Christ. We shall argue below that apocalyptic eschatology forms the background against which Paul's Christology, his views on salvation, the church, human destiny, mission praxis, and hermeneutics may be understood.

As with other NT writers, the category of fulfilment is essential to Paul's theology, for whom Christ's resurrection is the pivotal sign of eschatological fulfilment. The identity of the Son of God is inseparably tied to the facticity of his resurrection (Rom. 1:3–4). The eschatological overlapping of the ages serves as hermeneutical grid for Paul's development of his Christology. A good example of this is the almost seamless way in which eschatological exposition on the resurrection and Christology are conjoined in 1 Cor. 15. Against the over-realized eschatology of the Corinthian enthusiasts,[49] Paul asserts that the full and final realization of God's purposes for history remains in the future, when all who are "in Christ" (v 22b) will be resurrected. Christ raised as "first fruits" (vv 20, 23) meant that the believers' future is secured. In explaining Christ's relationship with believers, Paul develops his Adam-Christ typology (vv 20–21, 44b–45; cf. Rom. 5) by going back to the beginning of history and presenting a Christ who transcends all human divides, including that between Jew and Gentile. With Christ's coming, humanity is bifurcated into those who

---

[47] Even the disputed 2 Thessalonians, Colossians, Ephesians and the Pastorals show distinctively Pauline eschatological commitments. And even though the Day of the Lord is not explicitly mentioned in Galatians, it may be argued that the references to Abraham, the relativising of the ethnic division between Jews and Gentiles, and the sending of the Son in the fullness of time have a decidedly Pauline eschatological flavour.

[48] Beker, *Paul*; idem, *Paul's Apocalyptic Gospel: The Coming Triumph of God* (Philadelphia: Fortress, 1982); *The Triumph of God: The Essence of Paul's Thought* (Minneapolis: Fortress, 1990); "Recasting Pauline Theology: The Coherence-Contingency Scheme as Interpretive Model," in Jouette M. Bassler, ed., *Pauline Theology, Volume I: Thessalonians, Philippians, Galatians, Philemon* (Minneapolis: Fortress, 1991), 15–24; E. Käsemann, *New Testament Questions of Today* (Philadelphia: Fortress, 1969), 82–107. Beker's use of apocalypticism as an interpretive grid for Paul's theology follows a path demarcated by Wrede and Schweitzer.

[49] A. C. Thiselton, "Realized Eschatology at Corinth," *NTS* 24(1978): 510–24.

are "in Adam" and those "in Christ"; all other divisions have been
relativised by Christ. To be in Christ is to be a part of "an eschatological humanity".[50]

Passages from the OT are regularly invoked in Paul's letters, where
one discerns a hermeneutical or exegetical perspective which is strongly
Christological in orientation.[51] For instance, two passages from the
Psalms are alluded to in 1 Cor. 15:23–28; Ps. 110:1 is reflected in
the language of v 25—"For he must reign until he has put all his
enemies under his feet", while Ps. 8:7 lies behind v 27—"For God
has put all things in subjection under his feet." These passages have
been reworked and applied to Christ with a referent which is neither present nor intended in the original contexts.[52] Furthermore,
Paul's use of Gen. 2:7 in 1 Cor. 15:44–45 seems to go against modern exegetical practice. To the expression, "the man became a living being" in Gen. 2:7, Paul adds the words "first" and "Adam",
rendering it: "the *first* man, *Adam*, became a living being" (v 45a).
In so doing, he achieves a typological balance with what follows,
"the last Adam became a life-giving spirit" (v 45b). Paul evidently
felt it legitimate to add to a text which was no doubt readily identifiable
as a quote from Genesis.

Other examples where Paul apparently 'misreads' Scriptures to
make his point can be cited. The alteration of the citation of Isa.
59:20 in Rom. 11:26 is a case in point. In the Hebrew and Aramaic
of the Isaiah passage, the Redeemer or Deliverer will come "to
Zion"; while the LXX has, "for the sake of Zion" (ἕνεκεν Σίων). Paul

---

[50] Roger Scroggs, *The Last Adam* (Oxford: Basil Blackwell, 1966). Wright, *Climax*,
18–40, points out that the idea of last Adam was already present in Jewish speculation in the first century. The last Adam is identified as the nation of Israel, God's
true humanity, the eschatological people of God. This is the best background for
understanding Paul's Adam-Christology in 1 Cor. 15. Also: Dunn, *Christology in the
Making*, 98–128; C. K. Barrett, *From First Adam to Last* (London: A & C Black, 1962).
[51] See D. Moody Smith, "The Pauline Literature," in D. A. Carson & H. G.
M. Williamson, eds., *It is Written: Scripture Citing Scripture: Essays in Honour of Barnabas
Lindars* (Cambridge: Cambridge University Press, 1988), 265–91; A. T. Hanson,
Studies on Paul's Technique and Theology (Grand Rapids: Eerdmans, 1974), 202.
[52] J. Lambrecht, "Paul's Christological Use of Scripture in 1 Cor. 15:20–28,"
NTS 28(1982): 505; Matthew Black, "The Christological Use of the Old Testament
in the New Testament," *NTS* 18(1971): 6f; cf. Earle E. Ellis, "A Note on Pauline
Hermeneutics," *NTS* 2(1955–56): 127–33; idem, *Paul's Use of the Old Testament* (Grand
Rapids: Baker, 1981). The question as to whether the NT writers engage in contextual or noncontextual exegesis in their approach to the OT continues to be a
debated point. See G. K. Beale, ed., *The Right Doctrine from the Wrong Text? Essays
on the Use of the Old Testament in the New* (Grand Rapids: Baker, 1994).

steers away from both these renditions, and changes the preposition
to "*from* Zion" or "*out of* Zion" (ἐκ Σίων), thereby retaining some ties
between the Deliverer and Israel without limiting redemption to Zion.
Such an argument fits the the overall thrust of Rom. 9–11, where
Paul works out the repercussions of the restoration of Israel (which
had already begun with the resurrection of Christ), and demonstrates
that the redemptive inclusion of the Gentiles is one of a piece with
God's dealings with Israel, her unbelief notwithstanding.[53] If this reading is correct, then it is clear that Paul does not simply cite scriptures, he interprets them for his situation and in such a way as to
reinforce his points.

Paul's hermeneutics may be characterized as retrospective and teleological. It involves looking at the past from the vantage point of a
future consummation, the realization of which has already begun in
the present. In short, Paul legitimatizes his use of scriptures on
account of the proleptic arrival of the End in Christ. Paul's hermeneutics is teleological in that it is oriented to the τέλος or purpose of
the Law (Rom. 10:4);[54] and it is retrospective in that it seeks the
meaning of the past in terms of the new which has impinged upon
the present. It is axiomatic for Paul that the true meaning of scriptures
lies hidden until made known in Christ.[55] Christ is the "hermeneutical

---

[53] See Bell, *Provoked*, 142 n. 195; N. T. Wright, *Climax*, 231–57; idem, "Romans
and the Theology of Paul," David M. Hay & E. Elizabeth Johnson, eds., *Pauline
Theology, Volume 3: Romans* (Minneapolis: Fortress, 1995), 61; James W. Aageson,
"Scripture and Structure in the Development of the Argument in Romans 9–11,"
CBQ 48(1986): 268–89; idem, "Typology, Correspondence, and the Application of
Scripture in Romans 9–11," JSNT 31(1987): 51–72; and *Written Also for Our Sake:
Paul and the Art of Biblical Interpretation* (Louisville: Westminster/John Knox, 1994), 89f.

[54] We cannot deal with the question in any detail here as to whether the phrase,
"end of the law" (Rom. 10:4) should be understood in terms of Christ being the
termination or the *goal* of the Torah. While the first interpretation is semantically possible, we think the second fits the context and flow of Paul's argument in Rom.
9–11 better, and is the interpretation adopted here. Paul's concern in Rom. 9–11
is to demonstrate that God's promises to Israel are irrevocable (Rom. 11:29, cf.
9:4), and that these, rather than being a failure, have in fact been fulfilled in Christ.
With Wright, *Climax*, 241, and Frank Thielman, *Paul & the Law: A Contextual Approach*
(Downers Grove: InterVarsity, 1994), 207, we regard Christ as the climax of the OT
covenant and the goal of the Torah. On this issue, see R. Badenas, *Christ the End
of the Law: Romans 10:4 in Pauline Perspective* (Sheffield: Sheffield Academic Press, 1985).

[55] Paul is not alone in this; other NT writers appropriate the OT in similar fashion, sometimes even using the same passages cited in Paul; e.g., Peter's use of Isa.
8:14; 28:16 in 1 Pet. 2:6–8, passages which are also alluded to in Rom. 9:33. See
Barnabas Lindars, *New Testament Apologetic: The Doctrinal Significance of the Old Testament
Quotations* (London: SCM, 1961), 169–86.

key" to the OT; and the latter is understood as pointing to the new dispensation inaugurated by the Messiah (Rom. 4:23f; 15:4; 1 Cor. 9:10; 10:11).

The modern notion of eisegesis is not Paul's concern, since he does not see himself as importing into the text something which is not there in the first place. His experience of Christ led him to find Christ in the scriptures.[56] He sees Christ as the fulfilment of what scripture has prophesied, not on a strict one-to-one, prediction-specific fulfilment model, but more along the line of a typological correspondence. Thus he sees Christ as the true seed of Abraham (Gal. 3:16), using the Abraham argument to demonstrate that justification is not by the works of the law, and that there is scriptural warrant for the inclusion of the Gentiles and for his Gentile-mission.[57] Paul's experiences with Gentiles in his congregations certainly shaped his reading of Gen. 12:3 & 22:18 in Gal. 3:7. Abraham is interpreted within the eschatological framework inaugurated in Christ. For Paul, the experience of oneness in Christ, regardless of racial background, is a hermeneutical paradigm by which scripture is interpreted.[58] This new understanding is grounded in his Christology. Paul's use of the OT, while formally soteriological, is presuppositionally Christological. There is really no need to pit one against the other.

Equally significant is the way in which OT passages which in their original contexts refer to God are applied to Christ, particularly those having to do with final judgment.[59] The OT concept of the Day of Yahweh is "Christified",[60] leading to a referential shift of "Lord"

---

[56] Morna D. Hooker notes that "Paul starts from Christian experience and expounds Scripture in the light of that experience, quarrying the Old Testament where he will." "Beyond the Things That Are Written? Saint Paul's Use of Scripture," in *Right Doctrine from the Wrong Text?*, 291.

[57] Different proposals have been made on the purpose of the Abraham pericope in Galatians. See discussion and references in G. Walter Hansen, *Abraham in Galatians: Epistolary and Rhetorical Contexts* (Sheffield: Sheffield Academic Press, 1989). Also: Segal, *Paul*, 121; and J. Louis Martyn, "A Law-observant Mission to Gentiles: The Background of Galatians," *SJT* 38(1985): 307–24. They argue that Paul is not saying that the Torah is wrong, only that the belief which he and other Jewish zealots (including his opponents?) hold to is not all together correct. Hence the reclamation of Abraham in support of his Christologically corrected interpretation.

[58] Richard B. Hays, *Echoes of Scripture in the Letters of Paul* (New Haven & London: Yale University Press, 1989), 104.

[59] See the helpful study by Neil Richardson, *Paul's Language about God*, on the fluid interchange between God and Christ references in Paul.

[60] D. R. de Lacey, "'One Lord' in Pauline Christology" in Rowdon, ed., *Christ the Lord*, 198.

from God to Jesus Christ (Joel 2:32/Rom. 10:13; Isa. 45:23/Phil.
2:10–11; Zech. 14:5/1 Thess. 3:13, etc).[61] Once again, we find in
Paul the interpenetrative way in which eschatology and Christology
are related in his hermeneutics. Paul declares emphatically that in
Christ, a καινὴ κτίσις (2 Cor. 5:17) has been effected; and part of
being "a new creation" involves the reception of new "eyes" with
which to see scriptures and to grasp the truth. An inextricable connection exists between eschatology (Christological fulfilment), hermeneutics and epistemology in Paul. Christ is appraised from the perspective
of the turning of the ages; specifically, in terms of the dawning of
the new age, and not that of the old-age, which has been eclipsed.
This is the force of what he means by not knowing κατὰ σάρκα
Χριστόν (2 Cor. 5:16).[62]

Paul's hermeneutics may be understood as a conversation which
he carries out with the text of the OT. While the latter provides
the conceptual and linguistic categories for the construction of his
Christology,—and thus influences his understanding of the significance
of the Christ-event—the recognition that in Christ the End has
arrived in turn affects and shapes his reading of the OT. As a pharisee, Paul was undoubtedly acquainted with the Jewish exegetical
practices of his day, e.g., peshat, midrash, pesher, allegorical, etc.
These skills remained in tact even after his conversion/call, even
though they were radically turned on their heads on account of
Christ.[63] And like the Jews of his day, Paul sees the OT as the "ora-
cles of God" (Rom. 3:1f) which have something to say to the present (Rom. 4:23; 15:4). He introduces his citations of scriptures in
2 Cor. 6:16 with the expression, "as God said . . .". That the scriptures were deemed authoritative for Paul is seen in his reliance on
them as the basis for theological justification.[64] So saturated was his

---

[61] L. Joseph Kreitzer, *Jesus and God in Paul's Eschatology* (Sheffield: Academic Press,
1987), 112–28; also Moule, *Origin*, 41–44.

[62] J. Louis Martyn, "Epistemology at the Turn of the Ages," *Theological Issues in
the Letters of Paul* (Edinburgh: T&T Clark, 1997), 89–110.

[63] Segal, *Paul the Convert*, 118. According to Moody Smith, "Pauline Literature,"
277, though Paul's exegetical methodology has precedence in rabbinic and inter-
testamental literature, it differs in two ways: (1) Paul is not primarily interested in
the interpretation of the OT as law, i.e., casuistry and legal sanctions; (2) he emphasizes the present prophetic function of Scripture, not just as law per se.

[64] See C. D. Stanley, *Paul and the Language of Scripture: Citation Technique in the Pauline
Epistles and Contemporary Literature* (SNTSMS 69; Cambridge: Cambridge University
Press, 1992).

mind with the Hebrew Scriptures that they emerged in all sorts of ways in his letters, often as allusions which are either clearly evident in the text or simmering just below the surface. Such "echoes" of the OT in Paul's letters are noted in Richard Hays' *Echoes of Scripture*, where he understands Paul's hermeneutics in terms of an intertextual conversation with the OT.[65]

Alongside the apocalyptic strand of a cosmic turning point in history, there is also discernible in Paul's Christology indications of the Jewish belief in divine agency. Jewish thought in the Hellenistic environment of the first-century had a very high view of God's transcendence. He is above and beyond the world. How then does one speak of God acting in the world, without running the risk of idolatrous representation? To an educated and sophisticated Jewish thinker, e.g., Philo, the way God manifests himself in the world is by means of intermediaries, agents or personified hypostases, such as his Word, Spirit, and Wisdom. It is the measure of Paul's genius that he blends this mediation divine agency language with that of the apocalyptic new-creation language to speak of the cosmic significance and supremacy of Christ as God's agent (*shaliach*).[66] The idea of divine agency, so closely aligned with that of Wisdom, was appropriated by Paul (and the other NT writers, e.g., John) to articulate an eschatological Christology.[67]

The personification of Wisdom in Jewish literature has conceptual parallels with a divine agency Christology. The sending language of Gal. 4:4 is akin to the sending of the preexistent Wisdom of God[68] described in Wisdom 9:10. Wisdom is represented in Jewish understanding as existing prior to creation, as one in close relationship

---

[65] For a response to Hays' proposal, see Jouette Bassler, "Paul's Theology: Whence and Whither?" in David M. Hay, ed., *Pauline Theology, Volume II: 1 & 2 Corinthians* (Minneapolis: Fortress, 1993), 9.

[66] See: P. G. Davis, "Divine Agents, Mediators, and New Testament Christology," *JTS* 45(1994): 479–503; A. T. Harvey, "Christ as Agent" in L. D. Hurst & N. T. Wright, eds., *The Glory of Christ in the New Testament: Studies in Christology* (Oxford: Clarendon, 1987), 239–50; Hurtado, *One God, One Lord*; C. A. Wanamaker, "Christ as Divine Agent in Paul," *SJT* 39(1986): 517–28; cf. J. H. Charlesworth, "From Jewish Messianology to Christian Christology: Some Caveats and Perspectives," J. Neusner *et al.*, eds., *Judaisms and Their Messiahs at the Turn of the Christian Era* (Cambridge: Cambridge University Press, 1987), 225–64.

[67] See A. van Roon, "The Relationship Between Christ and the Wisdom of God According to Paul," *NovT* 16(1974): 207–39; Witherington, *Jesus the Sage*, 296f; 330–33.

[68] See discussion in Dunn, *Christology*, 38f; Hamerton-Kelly, *Pre-existence*.

with God and having a role in creation (Pr. 8:22–30; Sir. 24:9; Wis.
7:21, 25; 8:3–6; 9:1–2, 9–10). Of special significance are the references to God sending pre-existent Wisdom (Wis. 9:10–17) and
Wisdom's descent from heaven to earth in search of a "resting place"
but finding none (Sir. 24:3–8; 1 En. 42; also 48:1–7). It is note-
worthy that Paul's teaching on the *pre-existence* of the Son may well
have been prompted by his experience of Christ as the resurrected
Lord. As Moule suggests, it is neither difficult nor illogical to move
from reflection on Christ's "post-existence" to his pre-existence. "If
he is Lord of the End, is he not Lord of the Beginning also?"[69] In
this sense, eschatological considerations led to protological assertions.
Hengel writes:

> by virtue of the dignity of the revelation which took place through
> him [i.e. Christ], the unrestricted eschatological plenipotentiary of God
> must at the same time also have been the protological 'plenipoten-
> tiary', since God's words and actions in the end-time and the begin-
> ning of time form a unity by virtue of God's truth. This step was not
> a gnostic, syncretistic falsification but a necessary last consequence of
> primitive Christian thinking.[70]

This brings us full circle to the starting point of Paul's theological
enterprise: his encounter with the risen Lord on the road to Damascus.
The realization that the eschatological end has invaded the present
in Christ, a point analogous to the teaching of the Kingdom of God
in the Synoptics, provided a hermeneutical paradigm for Paul. One
detects in his letters a dynamic interplay between eschatology, exegesis, experience, and pastoral controversy, the last of these providing the context in which Paul worked out his Christology.

It was often in controversy with those who preached different
"gospels" that Paul looked to Israel's scriptures to authenticate his
message, and in the process developed his theology. His Adam and
First Fruits Christology in 1 Cor. 15 was formulated in the context
of correcting the over-realized eschatological enthusiasm of some
within the Corinthian church. Pastoral correction and Christological
development often go hand in hand. Paul's hermeneutics operates
within the reciprocity which exists between Christ, scriptures, and
contingent situations.

---

[69] *Origin*, 139, 154.
[70] Martin Hengel, *Between Jesus and Paul* (Philadelphia: Fortress, 1983), 95; cf.
idem, *Studies in Early Christology* (Edinburgh: T&T Clark, 1995), 73–117.

One way to explicate the interdependence between exposition and experience is to inquire into the relationship between Paul's view of the law and his Gentile-mission. Did Paul first recognize the displacement of the law by Christ and then move on from that to his mission to the Gentiles, or did his experiences with the Gentiles lead him to rethink the role of the Law?[71] If one concedes that Paul's own experience with Christ led to a change in his theological mindset, does it not stand to reason that his encounters with Gentile believers may have affected his thinking on the Law? Many years separate the beginning of Paul's ministry and the writing of his epistles. Is it not conceivable that in those intervening years, Paul witnessed for himself the clear manifestations of the Spirit's presence among Gentile believers, which reinforced for him the reality of eschatological fulfilment? And if we believe that the rudiments of his (mature) theology of the Holy Spirit and Christ were already there at the beginning of his ministry, it is entirely possible that he would have understood the reality of the Spirit's work among the Gentiles as a sign of the dawning of the messianic age.[72] One should not underestimate the impact of Paul's mission experiences on the development of his theology.

Yet despite the contingency of the various pastoral situations, there is a coherent centre (Beker) out of which Paul works, a foundational kergymatic narrative or story (Hays) about Jesus Christ. It is the touchstone upon which message and praxis are judged and pastoral disputes resolved. Though the fundamentals of this coherent Gospel were already in place in the kerygma of the church (oral traditions), the Gospel itself had not yet acquired canonical status when Paul preached. His Gospel was in one sense still in process of formation, a process to which he contributed much. That is why Paul's appeal was to the Gospel he preached, rather than some fixed doctrinal canon, since this was as yet unformalized. Nevertheless, though developmentally provisional, Paul's Gospel had sufficient coherence to it that it was capable of adjudicating between the true Gospel and aberrant versions of it. We turn next to consider the question of the relationship between coherence and contingency in Paul's theology.

---

[71] Stephen G. Wilson, *The Gentiles and the Gentile Mission in Luke-Acts* (SNTSMS 23; Cambridge: Cambridge University Press, 1973), 156.

[72] Senior & Stuhlmueller, *Foundations for Mission*, 178. See also J. Jeremias, "Paul and James," *ExpT* 66(1955): 368–71; idem, *The Central Message of the New Testament* (London: SCM, 1965).

B. *Paul's Coherent Gospel as Interpretive Framework*

It can hardly be disputed that Paul's letters are occasional in nature, prompted as they were by specific situations in churches or relationships with individuals. Even Romans, which at first sight appears to be a thoroughgoing theological treatise, can arguably be situated in the contingencies of Paul's missionary concerns.[73] Consensus, however, does not seem to be the case on the question of what constitutes the heart of Paul's theology, or whether it is even possible to derive a coherent theology from his letters.[74]

Justification by faith has been widely regarded as the heart of Paul's gospel ever since Luther. Paul's thought was perceived as essentially doctrinal in nature and construed as a polemic against his former religion. With F. C. Baur and the history-of-religions school, a noticeable shift can be discerned. Paul began to be interpreted more as a mystic or religious genius, than as a doctrinal thinker or writer.[75] And as we have noted, the centrality of justification by faith has been called into question by the 'new perspective on Paul.' To be sure, justification by faith continues to garner votes from Pauline scholars, particularly the Lutherans among them,[76] but definite challenges have been mounted from other quarters.

Since Wrede and Schweitzer, the notion of eschatological mysticism or apocalyptic fulfilment as the key theme in Paul's thought

---

[73] On the occasion of Romans, see K. P. Donfried, ed., *The Roman Debate*, rev. exp. ed. (Peabody: Hendricksen, 1977, 1991), especially F. F. Bruce, "The Roman Debate Continued," 175–94, originally in *BJRL* 64(1981–82): 334–59. See also: N. Elliott, *The Rhetoric of Romans* (Sheffield: Sheffield Academic Press, 1990); L. A. Jervis, *The Purpose of Romans* (Sheffield: Sheffield Academic Press, 1991); G. Smiga, "Rm 12:1–2; 15:30–32: Occasion of Romans," *CBQ* 53(1991): 257–73.

[74] G. A. Deissmann, for instance, considers it misguided to regard Paul as a systematic thinker-theologian or to seek a coherent theology within the Pauline corpus. *Paul: A Study in Social and Religious History*, 2d ed. (London: Hodder and Stoughton, 1926).

[75] F. C. Baur, *Paul, the Apostle of Jesus Christ; His Life and Work, His Epistles and His Doctrine: A Contribution to a Critical History of Primitive Christianity*, 2 vols., 2d ed. (London & Edinburgh: Williams and Norgate, 1876). Richard Reitzenstein sees Paul as a Gnostic, *Hellenistic Mystery Religions: Their Basic Ideas and Significance* (Pittsburgh: Pickwick, 1978); Wilhelm Bousset, *Kyrios Christos: A History of the Belief in Christ from the Beginnings of Christianity to Irenaeus* (Nashville: Abingdon, 1970), 104–54; also Deissmann, *Paul*, 4–26.

[76] E.g. J. Reumann in J. Reumann, J. Fitzmyer & J. Quinn, *Righteousness in the New Testament: "Justification" in the United States Lutheran-Catholic Dialogue* (Philadelphia: Fortress, 1982), 105–23, 185.

has attracted many.[77] Other candidates for the heart of Paul's theology include: righteousness of God,[78] reconciliation,[79] a pattern of religion or participation in Christ,[80] being in Christ,[81] Christ the Son of God, or Christocentric soteriology,[82] etc. Despite the obvious disagreement on what constitutes the centre of Paul's theology, there is nevertheless agreement that a centre does exist. The search for a coherent centre is a complex one involving many issues which we cannot engage with here.[83] In what follows, we will (1) seek to discern the nature of Paul's coherent theology or narrative thought-world in dialogue with Beker and Witherington.[84] We will limit ourselves to just these two sample studies. This leads us then (2) to argue on the basis of H. H. Price's notion of belief as disposition,[85] that Paul's coherent theology is a multi-dimensional web of inter-connecting beliefs.

1. Construals of Coherence

We begin with the J. Christiaan Beker's attempt in his *Paul the Apostle* to understand Paul's overarching theology. He suggests that Paul's thought is best understood as a hermeneutical interaction that goes

---

[77] Wrede, *Paul*; Schweitzer, *Mysticism*; Beker, *Paul*; C. J. A. Hickling, "Center and Periphery in Paul's Thought," in E. A. Livingstone, ed., *Studia Biblica III: Papers on Paul and Other NT Authors* (Sheffield: Sheffield Academic Press, 1978), 199–214.

[78] This is often closely associated with justification by faith, and may be regarded as a more nuanced version of it. Examples: Ernst Käsemann, "'The Righteousness of God' in Paul," in *New Testament Questions of Today* (Philadelphia: Fortress, 1969), 168–82; Peter Stuhlmacher, *Gerechtigkeit Gottes bei Paulus* (Göttingen: Vandenhoeck & Ruprecht, 1966); N. T. Wright, "On Becoming the Righteousness of God," *Pauline Theology, Volume II*, 200–208; idem, *People of God*, 271f; *Climax*, 234–46; "Romans and the Theology of Paul."

[79] Ralph P. Martin, *Reconciliation: A Study of Paul's Theology*, rev. ed. (Grand Rapids: Zondervan, 1990).

[80] Sanders, *Palestinian Judaism*, 432–47, 520.

[81] Davies, *Rabbinic Judaism*, 221f.

[82] J. Fitzmyer, *Pauline Theology: A Brief Sketch* (Englewood Cliffs: Prentice-Hall, 1967), 16. The tendency in Catholic scholarship is to posit Christ as the key or heart of Paul's gospel. See L. Cerfaux, *Christ in the Theology of St Paul* (New York: Herder and Herder, 1959).

[83] Questions which readily come to mind include: What criteria do we use to determine what qualifies as a centre? What makes a centre a centre? How large a base do we work with, the letters which are commonly accepted as genuinely Paul's, or do we include the so-called deutero-Pauline epistles as well?

[84] Beker, *Paul the Apostle*; Ben Witherington III, *Paul's Narrative Thought-World: The Tapestry of Tragedy and Triumph* (Louisville: Westminster/John Knox, 1994).

[85] H. H. Price, *Belief* (London: George Allen & Unwin; New York: Humanities Press, 1969).

on between the contingency of his letters and the coherence of this
theology. There is in his letters, a "constant interaction between the
coherent center of the gospel and its contingent interpretations."[86]
Drawing on structuralism, Beker distinguishes between "deep structure" (paradigmatic) and "surface structure" (syntagmatic) in the
Pauline corpus, the former refers to the coherent "symbolic structure" of Paul's overall theology, while the latter refers to the contingent expressions which are Paul's epistolary responses to particular
pastoral situations.[87] The deep symbolic structure, Beker suggests, is
Christian apocalyptic, or the triumph of God inaugurated in the
death and resurrection of Jesus Christ, a triumph which will be fully
realized at the Parousia.[88] According to Beker, "the *character* of Paul's
contingent hermeneutic is shaped by his apocalyptic core in that in
nearly all cases the contingent interpretation of the gospel points—
whether implicitly or explicitly—to the imminent cosmic triumph of
God."[89] Beker wants to give to Paul's coherence a theocentric focus,
for Christology, in his view, must be appraised theocentrically.

In Beker's opinion, Paul's genius lies not in his doctrinal architecture but in his hermeneutics. While he stood within the accepted
traditions of the early church, his ministry was marked by a revelatory immediacy which authorized his Christological (re)interpreta-

---

[86] Beker, *Paul*, 11.

[87] To demonstrate that contingency marks all of Paul's letters, Beker selects for
scrutiny Galatians and Romans, two letters often regarded as the most systematic
and least occasional of Paul's epistles. Paul's exposition in Galatians, particularly
the Abraham story, was given in conscious debate with Judaizers in the church;
while Romans, Beker argues, should be understood not primarily as a theological
handbook, but a situational missive targeted at the Jewish-Gentile congregation of
Rome, to whom Paul was appealing for assistance. Beker, *Paul*, 71–74.

[88] Ibid., 128: "Paul identifies a specific apocalyptic 'core' of the gospel amid a
variety of theological traditions in the early church and interprets that specific core—
'Jesus Christ and him crucified' (1 Cor. 2:3)—as the prelude to God's triumph
within a variety of contingent situations."

[89] Ibid., 19. In the new preface to the 1984 edition of the book, xviii, Beker
explains what he means by this: "Paul's Christian apocalyptic is a symbolic expression of two basic interdependent constituents: the experiential reality of his call on
the Damascus road—which Paul himself calls an *apokalypsis* (Gal. 1:12; cf. 1:15)—
and the traditional "in-house" apocalyptic language of the world in which he lived
and thought as a Pharisaic Jew. Paul's coherent center then is created by the "transforming moment" of his call. At that moment his "routinized" apocalyptic world
was both disconfirmed and confirmed by the revelation of Christ. Concretely, the
event of Christ could achieve meaningful expression only within Paul's own lan-
guage-world, and yet the specificity of his Christ-experience necessitated a reordering of this language world."

tion of the Hebrew scriptures. Paul's hermeneutics is distinctive in two ways: (1) he is able to focus on a coherent core within the multiple traditions in the early church, and interpret this "essence" in terms of its apocalyptic setting; (2) he sees in the traditions a deeper or "different" meaning not evident on the surface. The apocalyptic interpretation of the Christ-event, the genesis of which goes back to Paul's conversion, is the deep symbolic structure in Paul's thought. Coherence for Paul is not a "frozen text or a creedal sacred formula but a symbolic structure"[90] which is always in an active relationship with contingent events. In fact, it is conceptually available to us only through interaction and application to historical contingent situations. Coherence denotes a field of meaning, a network of symbolic relations.[91]

The contingency and coherence dialogue is really in Paul an interaction between context (contingency) and text (coherence). It is Paul's hermeneutical genius that he is able to combine both particularity and universality, diversity and unity. Coherence is "the stable, constant element which expresses the convictional basis of Paul's proclamation of the gospel", while contingency is the variable element and has to do with "the variety and particularity of sociological, economic, and psychological situations which Paul faces in his churches and on the mission field."[92]

Like Beker, Ben Witherington argues that there is a coherent "narrative thought world" connecting Paul's different letters, and that one needs to step back from detailed analyses of individual letters to take in the whole tapestry of his thought. His writings presuppose a grand multi-layered narrative or story,[93] and cannot be reduced to just ideas and propositions. This narrative comprises elements from the Hebrew scriptures, Jewish and Greco-Roman traditions, elements of logic, and Paul's personal experience of God in Christ, as well as the experiences of others in the nascent church. All of

---

[90] Ibid., 351.

[91] In a later article, J. Christiaan Beker, "Recasting Pauline Theology: The Coherence-Contingency Scheme as Interpretive Model," in Jouette M. Bassler, ed., *Pauline Theology, Volume I: Thessalonians, Philippians, Galatians, Philemon* (Minneapolis: Fortress, 1991), 17, indicates a preference for the word "coherence" over "core" because he feels that the latter suggests a fixed and non-pliable substance whereas the former allows for fluidity and flexibility.

[92] Ibid., 15.

[93] Here Witherington's proposal coheres with Hays, *Echoes of Scripture.*

Paul's ideas, arguments, practical advice, social arrangements are ultimately grounded in this grand narrative.[94] Witherington identifies
four interrelated stories which together comprise the one large drama
that is Paul's narrative thought world:

> (1) the story of a world gone wrong; (2) the story of Israel in that
> world; (3) the story of Christ, which arises out of the story of Israel
> and humankind on the human side of things, but in a larger sense
> arises out of the very story of God as creator and redeemer; and (4)
> the story of Christians, including Paul himself, which arises out of all
> three of these previous stories and is the first full installment of the
> story of a world set right again. Christ's story is the hinge, crucial
> turning point, and climax of the entire larger drama, which more than
> anything else affects how *the* Story will ultimately turn out.[95]

Paul's theology, in Witherington's opinion, did not simply arise from
contingent situations; it was already there prior to his engagement
with these contingencies. Historical situations may have caused him to
articulate his thoughts in a certain way, but the content or substance
of his theology had already arisen from his narrative thought world.

Witherington seeks to gather Paul's diverse thoughts scattered across
his various epistles into a narrative plot suggested by the above-
mentioned fourfold "grand narrative." Beginning with the story of
creation gone wrong, he suggests that Rom. 7:7–25 may well be
Paul's reflection on the temptation of Adam, his subsequent fall, and
humanity's fall with him in Gen. 3. The calling of Abraham signals
God's remedy for the despoliation of his good creation. Paul's Christological re-reading of the Torah comes next as Witherington examines its place in Paul's gospel. As with ethnic Israel, the Law is
understood to have a specific role for a specific time period within
the broader story of God's salvation plan for humanity.[96] One dis-

---

[94] It should be noted that the concept of "grand narrative" is utilized by Northrop
Frye in his *The Great Code: The Bible and Literature* (New York & London: Harcourt
Brace Jovanovich, 1982) as an interpretive backdrop against which the Bible may
be understood. Frye's use however, is less sensitive to particularities and to the temporal nature of history, focussing instead on structuralized and archetypal patterns.
By contrast, P. Ricoeur pays greater attention to the contingency and temporality
of narrative. See his *Time and Narrative*, 1:5–90; 3:60–126.

[95] Witherington, *Narrative*, 5. This emphasis on an overarching narrative is congruent with Wright's view in *New Testament and the People of God*; and *Climax of the
Covenant*, as well as Gerard Loughlin's thesis in *Telling God's Story*, (cf. chapter 3
above).

[96] Witherington, *Narrative*, 65.

cerns a narrative shape to Paul's Christology in Phil. 2:6–11. There is movement in the condescension of Christ to take the form and status of a slave, his death as a slave, and his eventual exaltation by God. Christology's story is also the story of God as Creator and Redeemer. It is at the same time the story of Israel in that Christ was born under the law (Gal. 4:4), and insofar as Christ's work is for humanity's salvation, it is the story of the world as well.

Paul's Damascus road experience is another factor contributing to the shape of his narrative world. In addition, Christian worship and Christian-Jewish traditions, including that of Wisdom, provided him with the basic materials with which to construct his theology. Witherington points to the remarkable parallels between the Christological hymns (Phil. 2:6–11 & Col. 1:15–20) and the wisdom writings.[97] The concepts of Messiahship, Eschatological Adam ("the Omega Man"), the resurrection of Jesus, and the "royal return" of Christ are then examined. On the resurrection of Christ, Witherington notes that Paul's teaching is always expounded in connection with eschatological events and never as an isolated event. This is clearly seen in 1 Cor. 15, where Christ's resurrection is a pledge of the Christians' (vv 12, 20, 23). On this linkage between Christ's resurrection and the eschatological destiny of Christian believers, Witherington is in agreement with Beker.[98]

Paul's own story and self-understanding as an apostle are correlated with the story of God's salvific work in Christ, by means of the Jewish tradition of *shaliach* (which lies behind the concept of apostleship). The act of the *shaliach* or agent, and the act of the one who sends the agent, are one and the same. Paul's sense of his special mission to the Gentiles is one of a piece with a story of redemption which reaches out to the nations beyond the boundaries of Israel.

The basic contours of the larger story world of Paul are evident even though it is a complex story involving many individuals, events, and subplots. This story "is progressive rather than cyclical; it is also teleological" in that it is moving "forward toward the goal of the return of Christ, the resurrection of believers, the coming of the

---

[97] "The juxtaposition of (1) preexistence language; (2) servant language; (3) humility and exaltation language; and (4) the bestowal of kingship and kingdom is found in both the Christ hymn in Philippians 2 and also in the sapiential material in Sirach and the Wisdom of Solomon." Ibid., 100. In the case of Col. 1:15–20, the parallels are even more striking. See comparison chart on p. 105.

[98] Ibid., 170–71; cf. Beker, *Paul*, 152, 155–56.

kingdom on earth, and thus the new creation. The story is basically about the points of intersection between the story of God and the story of humankind."[99] In Paul's "storied world," the key figures are Adam, Abraham, Moses and Christ. "When Paul thinks of Adam he thinks of sin; when he thinks of Abraham he thinks of faith; when he thinks of Moses he thinks of Law; and when he thinks of Christ he thinks of grace and redemption."[100] In that the parousia awaits us in the future, the story of Christ and of Christians is as yet incomplete.

We have glanced briefly at two construals of coherence in Paul's theology. If the key words in Beker's work are: *contingency, coherence* and *apocalyptic*; the key word in Witherington's is *story*. To the latter, Paul's theology has coherence, not in the sense of there being a single idea or element at the heart of his thought, but in the sense that there is embedded within the various components of his thought an overall narrative structure. This is not unlike Beker's thesis. His depiction of Paul's theology as a "symbolic structure" or network of symbolic relations is compatible with Witherington's narrative structure in that both seek a unity or a unifying possibility in the midst of the diversity inherent in the contingency of Paul's letters.

2. Coherence as Disposition

Paul uses the word "gospel" as a shorthand for his multi-dimensional message. Beker's nomination of a Christianized Jewish apocalyptic as the organizing principle which gives coherence to Paul's thought is not without its detractors.[101] Whether apocalyptic is helpful as an

---

[99] Witherington, *Narrative*, 352.

[100] Ibid., 353.

[101] To begin with, features integral to apocalyptic thinking do not seem to figure much in Galatians and 2 Corinthians, a point which Beker himself admits, *Paul*, 58. If apocalyptic is the coherent centre of Paul's thought, it is reasonable that one should expect, as Margaret E. Thrall points out in her review of Beker's book, that the structure of the coherent centre of Paul's thought should "appear with reasonable clarity in at least the four major epistles and also to have some direct bearing on the main thrust of his arguments?" *JTS* 33(1982): 269. But this does not seem to be the case. If Thrall's observation is true that apocalyptic does not figure consistently in Paul's writings, then it is not unfair to question its credential as the *centrum Paulinum*. Cf. R. P. Martin's review in *JBL* 101(1982): 463–6. Furthermore, how does one distinguish a primary (deep) structure from a surface structure? And what if apocalyptic is but another surface structure concept? In any case, on what basis does one decide that apocalyptic is the primary symbolic structure?

One detects an unwitting subordination of Christology to an apocalyptic framework, even though Beker affirms without reservation the importance of the death and resurrection of Christ in Paul's theology. While Beker wants to say that

overarching category to describe Paul's theology largely depends on how it is defined, which in itself is not a straightforward matter given its polymorphous character.[102] Given the ambiguity and the risks of misunderstanding entailed by the use of the word *apocalyptic*, it may be more advantageous to speak of Paul's theology as *eschatological* instead.[103] Beker's emphasis on (apocalyptic) eschatological fulfilment or triumph of God and Witherington's proposal of a narrative-world may be correlated within a salvation history framework, where God is seen as the central actor in history whose plan of salvation for the world, begun in Abraham and Israel, has come to fulfilment in the proleptic arrival of the End in Christ's resurrection. This salvation-history framework, we submit, forms the coherent backdrop of Paul's theology.

Rather than isolate a single element as the *Mitte* of Paul's theology,

---

Christology affirms and modifies Jewish apocalyptic thought (which would make Christology the primary language and apocalyptic the derivative), in practice, he tends to make Jewish apocalyptic primary. See H. D. Betz's review in *JRel* 61(1981): 459. "When futurist, cosmic eschatology is minimized or neutralized," Beker warns, "the final triumph of God at the end of history becomes so identified with the triumph of God in the Christ-event that the theocentric apocalyptic focus of Paul is absorbed into the Christocentric triumph of Christ." *Paul*, 356. But such a polarization of eschatological theocentricity and Christocentricity is really unwarranted when one considers that for Paul, the entire eschatological landscape has been overturned by the climactic event of Christ. Witherington correctly points out that Beker has high-lighted Paul's eschatological framework at the expense of Christology. *Narrative*, 171.

Despite Beker's qualifications, it seems that his apocalyptic canopy is not quite big enough. As J. Plevnik, "The Center of Paul's Theology," *CBQ* 51(1989): 473–74, observes, some essential features in Paul's Christology cannot be accounted for by an apocalyptic interpretation. These include: "(1) Christ's filial relationship with God, his being "in the form of God" (Phil. 2:6), his role as the preexisting means of creation and salvation (1 Cor. 8:6); (2) Christ's inclusive and representative role, affirmed in connection with the universal significance of his death and resurrection; (3) the believer's conformation with Christ, affirmed in connection with Christ's parousia; (4) the present participation in Christ, above all the sacramental sharing through Baptism and the Eucharist."

[102] "Apocalyptic," in Leander E. Keck's view, "may be the most misused word in the scholar's vocabulary because it resists definition". "Paul and Apocalyptic Theology," *Int* 38(1984): 230. On apocalyptic interpretations in/of Paul, see R. Barry Matlock, *Unveiling the Apocalyptic Paul: Paul's Interpreters and the Rhetoric of Criticism* (Sheffield: Sheffield Academic Press, 1996). On the relevance of apocalypticism in general, see H. H. Rowley, *The Relevance of Apocalyptic: A Study of Jewish and Christian Apocalypses from Daniel to Revelation*, 3rd rev. ed. (Greenwood: Attic Press, 1944, 1963); Christopher C. Rowland, *The Open Heaven: A Study of Apocalyptic in Judaism and Early Christianity* (New York: Crossroad, 1982); Wright, *People of God*, 280–338.

[103] Witherington discusses some of the difficulties involved in the use of apocalypticism and why the category of the eschatological is preferable. *End of the World*, 16–20.

we have in Paul a cluster of interpenetrating core ideas.[104] J. Paul
Sampley observes that Paul is constantly seeking to hold truths in
delicate balance and to keep them in equilibrium, e.g., the faithfulness of God with the freedom of God, the "already" with the "not
yet", the special place of Israel in salvation history with the universality of the gospel.[105] To make any single pole the primary one
would not adequately represent Paul's thought. He suggests instead
the use of the analogy of an electromagnetic field as a model for
Paul's thought. No single charge is sufficient to set up an electromagnetic field; we need two or more charges held in tension with
each other. In Paul, we have a series of electromagnetic fields, each
in tension within itself and in tension with each other. In this model,
no one notion (e.g., righteousness of God or justification by faith) is
at the centre. In this, Sampley's model is not unlike the multi-tiered
narrative world which Witherington proposes, or for that matter, the
apocalyptic and eschatological framework in Beker.[106]

Such a depiction of Paul's coherent theology—the interconnectivity of convictions within an overall belief system of a person—is
essentially what H. H. Price describes as a *disposition*. According to
Price, belief is really a disposition, a certain constant in the midst
of varying circumstances.[107] It is neither an occurrence nor a mental act. If this were the case, one would be bereft of beliefs when
unconscious or asleep. Belief as disposition is more akin to being a
definition of who we are and what we stand for. It is an attitude,
an inner coherence out of which, and in accordance with which,
one engages the world; and this disposition is manifested in one's
action or inaction, emotional states, ability to draw inferences, etc.

Applying this to Paul, Price would say that Paul did not have a
theology only when he was consciously rebutting challenges to his
apostleship, or dispensing apostolic advice to a congregation in need.
Rather, he operated out of a basic dispositional belief system which

---

[104] Plevnik, "Center of Paul's Theology," 460–78.

[105] J. Paul Sampley, "From Text to Thought World: The Route to Paul's Ways,"
in *Pauline Theology, Volume I*, 3–14.

[106] The recognition that there is an interconnectivity or a narrative-world or struc-
ture within Paul's letters is also found in Richard B. Hays, *The Faith of Jesus Christ*
(Chico: Scholars Press, 1983); Wright, *People of God*, 47–80; S. Fowl, *The Story of
Christ in the Ethics of Paul* (Sheffield: JSOT Press, 1990); & Norman R. Petersen,
Rediscovering Paul: Philemon and the Sociology of Paul's Narrative World (Philadelphia:
Fortress, 1985).

[107] Price, *Belief*, 243f.

defined him, and enabled him to define whatever situations he was confronting. There is arguably a certain conceptual compatibility between his various letters so that one may speak of a unified disposition underlying Paul's thought. His disposition is his narrative thought world. If Price's observation is true, then we have added support for saying that there is coherence in Paul's theology. While a disposition is stable, it is also dynamic in the sense that it leaves room for growth and variation. To apply Beker's coherence-contingent schema, influence is from coherence to contingency and vice-versa.

The dynamic nature of a convictional disposition can be seen in Paul's pastoral relationship with his churches. As John D. Moores pointedly argues, the kind of rationality at work in Paul's epistolary appeal to his churches is never simply a matter of deductive or inductive logic, as though he is inviting his readers "to weigh the gospel evidence on the probability scales."[108] What we have instead is an appeal based on a shared convictional framework. "Paul's discourse," Moores notes, "presumes its addressees to have at their disposal *a code* which nothing other than the experience of Christ *which he and they share together* . . . will suffice to supply."[109] "Premises are constantly being taken for granted"[110] in Paul's discursive appeal, indicating that both he and his readers are inhabiting the same narrative world. Paul's constant use, for instance, of the refrain, οὐκ οἴδατε ὅτι in 1 Corinthians (3:16; 5:6; 6:2, 3, 9, 15, 16, 19; 9:13, 24) suggests that the Corinthians were in all likelihood apprised of a body of Christian teachings, teachings which Paul and/or his co-workers had probably imparted to them earlier.[111] The same may be said of Galatians. Dunn correctly points out that there are a number of "shared convictions"[112] between Paul and the Galatians. Paul appeals to this "submerged and hidden theology". "[T]he theology

---

[108] *Wrestling with Rationality in Paul: Romans 1–8 in a New Perspective* (SNTSMS 82; Cambrdige: Cambridge University Press, 1995), 21.

[109] Ibid., 25; emphasis added.

[110] Ibid., 28.

[111] E. Earle Ellis, "Traditions in 1 Corinthians," *NTS* 32(1986): 487. The oblique way in which Paul weaves and enlists traditions in his arguments suggests that he and his readers shared similar presuppositions. Allusions are easily caught when both parties in the communication process share a common conceptual base.

[112] James D. G. Dunn, *New Testament Theology: The Theology of Paul's Letters to the Galatians* (Cambridge: Cambridge University Press, 1993), 35. This coheres with the qualified use of structuralism to describe the underlying "conviction" or "faith" of Paul in D. Patte's *Paul's Faith and the Power of the Gospel*.

of Galatians is like a basin of water drawn from a larger cistern."[113]
This "larger cistern" is the coherence which holds together all of
Paul's convictions.

A shared convictional frame of reference however is not immune
to change, as the case of the Corinthians shows. There was a time
when Paul shared a common convictional disposition with them.
They once walked as it were on the same road; perhaps when the
message of Christ was first preached to, and welcomed by, them.
But when they began to be enamored by the flamboyant sophistry
of Greek wisdom rather than the foolishness of the cross as the true
wisdom of God, that commonality which they shared with Paul was
threatened. To Paul's mind, they were beginning to tread a different
path. It was precisely because they were in danger of deviating from
their shared convictional world that Paul felt the need to re-preach
the message of the cross in his letter to them. Yet interestingly, the
basis of Paul's appeal continues to be based on that which they held
in common: the gospel of the cross of Jesus Christ. The discursive
force of Paul's arguments rests on an agreed upon belief-disposition.
Not only does this indicate that a disposition (whether belonging to
an individual or shared) necessarily serves as interpretive grid, it also
highlights the fact that it is dynamic and open to change. This is
in the nature of the temporality of all beliefs or the overall pattern
of convictions.

Such an understanding of Paul's coherent theology in terms of a
disposition which manifests itself in various contingencies, explains
the presence of apparent contradictions or changes in Paul's thoughts.
The oft-repeated observation that there is a mutation in Paul's eschatology from a futuristic focus in his earlier letters, to a more realized eschatology in his later writings[114] need not be construed as Paul
jettisoning an earlier (immature?) view for something else. In view
of the constant dialogical interaction between coherence and contingency in Paul's thought, the perceived difference may be seen as
a difference in emphasis rather than in kind. With a multi-dimensional and dispositional understanding of Paul's coherent theology,

---

[113] Dunn, *Galatians*, 34.
[114] C. H. Dodd, "The Mind of Paul," in *New Testament Studies* (Manchester:
Manchester University Press, 1953), 67–128. See response by John Lowe, "An
Attempt to Detect Development in St Paul's Theology," *JTS* 42(1941): 129–42.
Cf. William Baird, "Pauline Eschatology in Hermeneutical Perspective," *NTS*
17(1970–71): 314–27.

one does not need to be locked into a single linear evolutionary schema to account for variation in Paul's thought.

The above dispositional account of Paul's coherent theology is congruent with our earlier observation about the situatedness of Paul's thought within the messianic tradition of Judaism and the Christological reconfiguration of his theological frame of reference. Whether we describe his coherent theology as "faith" or "conviction" (Patte), "narrative thought-world" (Witherington), or "convictional world" (Donaldson), Paul's Christologically transvaluated semantic or symbolic universe constitutes his hermeneutical pre-understanding (in the Heideggerian and Gadamerian sense).

This fundamental belief or disposition in Paul has five characteristics which together support our thesis of Christology *from within* and *from ahead*. It is a living, dynamic stance which is (1) precipitated by his *experience* of the risen Christ on the Damascus road, a point we have already covered earlier. (2) It is *traditional* in the sense that it is (a) rooted in the covenantal framework of the Jewish religion, and (b) dependent on early Christian traditions. We have already noted the continuity (in discontinuity) between the pre- and the post-conversion Paul. The second aspect of traditionality however, i.e., the use of *Christian* traditions, calls for comment.

Apart from his use of Hebrew scriptures and Jewish expositions of these, one finds also in Paul's letters evidence of early *Christian* traditions.[115] These include: traditions about the sayings of Jesus, including signs of knowledge of the traditions concerning the ministry and teachings of Jesus;[116] embryonic creeds (1 Cor. 15:3–5;

---

[115] F. F. Bruce, *Tradition: Old and New* (Exeter: Paternoster, 1970); K. Chamblin, "Revelation and Tradition in the Pauline *Euangelion*," *WTJ* 48(1986): 1–16; Oscar Cullmann, "The Tradition," A. J. B. Higgins, ed., *The Early Church* (London: SCM, 1956), 59–99; David L. Dungan, *The Sayings of Jesus in the Churches of Paul: The Use of the Synoptic Tradition in the Regulation of Early Church Life* (Oxford: Blackwell, 1971); R. P. C. Hanson, *Tradition*.

[116] It is true that we do not have extensive and explicit quotations from Jesus as such in the Pauline corpus. Nevertheless Paul evidently knew the traditions concerning the ministry and teachings of Jesus, and alluded to these in his letters, e.g., 1 Cor. 7:10; 9:14; 11:23–24; 1 Thess. 4:15–17; cf. Gal. 2:7; Rom. 13:8f; 1 Thess. 4:13–5:6). He was conscious of the distinction between his own view and that of his Lord (1 Cor. 7:12, 25). See D. Wenham's detailed analyses on possible links between Paul and the historical Jesus. *Paul: Follower of Jesus or Founder of Christianity?* (Grand Rapids: Eerdmans, 1995); also: Ellis, "Traditions," 486; A. J. M. Wedderburn, "Paul and Jesus: The Problem of Continuity," *SJT* 38(1985): 189–203; "Paul and Jesus: Similarity and Continuity," *NTS* 34(1988): 161–82; A. J. M. Wedderburn, ed., *Paul and Jesus* (Sheffield: JSOT Press, 1989).

Rom. 1:3–4; 3:24–26; 1 Thess. 1:9–10);[117] hymns and liturgical materials (Phil. 2:6–11; Col. 1:15–20; cf. Eph. 5:14); baptismal formulae, moral teaching or paraenesis (Rom. 12:1–15:13; Gal. 5:1–6:10; 1 Thess. 4:1–5:22; Col. 3:1–4:6); as well as lists of virtues and vices in circulation among the early churches. Paul adopts the rabbinic terminology of "deliver" (παραδιδόναι) and "receive" (παραλαμβανειν) to signal the citing of traditional materials,[118] e.g., παρέδωκα γὰρ ὑμῖν ἐν πρώτοισ, ὃ καὶ παρέλαβον (1 Cor. 15:3). Even though Paul argues strenuously in Galatians that his gospel is not derived from human sources but received "by revelation from Jesus Christ" (1:11–12, 16–17; 2:2),[119] he does not seem to regard appeals to accepted traditions as incompatible with the latter.

Paul not only received and made use of traditions, it is likely too that these traditions were passed on through his kerygmatic ministry. He was both recipient and bearer of tradition. For Paul, to preach Christ certainly involved conveying something *about* Christ.[120] Yet even in his use of tradition, we find Paul maintaining creative control. He did not simply transfer his rabbinic approach to the use of tradition into his epistolary appeals. In this sense, Paul theologizes from within tradition yet transcends it, and in so doing makes his contribution.

Paul's coherent disposition is (3) *cultural-contextual* in that his theology is constructed from materials mined from his Palestinian/Hellenistic

---

[117] See Neufeld, *Earliest Christian Confessions.*

[118] Ellis, "Traditions," 481.

[119] Paul's insistence that he "did not consult any man" (Gal. 1:16) should not be construed as his absolute independence from the other apostles. Undoubtedly Paul would have received information concerning Jesus when he visited Jerusalem (Gal. 1:18f). See J. D. G. Dunn, "The Relationship Between Paul and Jerusalem According to Galatians 1 and 2," *NTS* 28(1982): 461–78.

[120] Assuming that Colossians is accepted as genuinely Paul's, one detects a hint of a close connection between believing in Christ and believing in the traditions about Christ. Paul warned the Colossians against following those who operated κατὰ τὴν παράδοσιν τῶν ἀνθρώπων (Col. 2:8). Instead, they were to keep true to the "faith" they had been taught, and to live κατὰ χριστόν (Col. 2:8b). Given this context where the technical language for transmission of tradition is used, it is significant that Paul should describe the Colossians as those who have "*received* Christ". Ellis, "Traditions," 486, suggests that the expression "to receive Christ" in this context may well be a "shorthand for the 'Christ-tradition'". The reception of Christ is bound up with the reception of the tradition concerning Christ. This makes sense when we see the juxtaposition of those who are walking according to the faith in which they were "taught" (Col. 2:6), i.e., those who are κατὰ χριστόν, with those who are operating κατὰ τὴν παράδοσιν τῶν ἀνθρώπων (Col. 2:8). It is certainly probable that while Paul preached Christ, he also preached about Jesus.

environment,[121] and invariably rooted in the contextual contingencies of his missionary and pastoral ministry to the Gentiles. As indicated earlier, the appropriation of Jewish and Hellenistic wisdom speculation for Christological formulation is a case in point. Paul's missionary strategy to be "all things to all men" certainly prompted his use of Hellenistic categories to express his gospel. One might even appeal to the unmistakable correspondence between Paul's logic and persuasive strategy, and Greek rhetorical practice.[122] In short, we cannot discount the formative part Paul's background and his context played in determining the shape of his theology.

The fourth and fifth characteristics of Paul's coherent theological disposition are related: it is (4) *Christocentric* in that "the generative center"[123] of Paul's theology rests on the conviction that God has raised Jesus from the dead, which gives his theology a thoroughly (5) *eschatological* character. The confidence that in Christ we have the turning of the ages and the pre-arrival of the Eschaton is impressed upon the consciousness of Paul by the experience of the eschatological Spirit of God at the Damascus Christophany.[124] The Spirit as experienced reality, besides confirming Paul's apostolic status (Rom. 15:18–19), also serves as a sign that life in Christ is based on faith and not the Torah (Gal. 3:1–5; 4:6–7). The Holy Spirit is the eschatological Spirit in that he is experienced as the ἀρραβών, the "firstfruits" or "down payment" (Rom. 8:23) and σφραγή, "seal" (2 Cor. 1:21–22) of the believers' life in Christ. This presupposes the eschatological schema of *already* but *not yet*.[125]

---

[121] It is no longer possible to distinguish sharply between a Palestinian form of Judaism and a Hellenistic one. The Judaism of Palestine was already Hellenized by the time of the apostle Paul. See M. Hengel (in collaboration with Christoph Markschies), *The "Hellenization" of Judaea in the First Century after Christ* (London: SCM; Philadelphia: Trinity Press International, 1989).

[122] Ben Witherington III's analysis of the Corinthian correspondence in terms of Greco-Roman rhetoric and social customs. *Conflict & Community in Corinth: A Socio-Rhetorical Commentary on 1 and 2 Corinthians* (Grand Rapids: Eerdmans, 1995); also G. W. Hansen, "Rhetorical Criticism," *DPL*, 822–26.

[123] Paul J. Achtemeier, "The Continuing Quest for Coherence in St. Paul: An Experiment in Thought," Eugene H. Lovering, Jr. & Jerry L. Sumney, eds., *Theology & Ethics in Paul and His Interpreters: Essays in Honor of Victor Paul Furnish* (Nashville: Abingdon, 1996), 138.

[124] See Gordon Fee, "Paul's Conversion as Key to His Understanding of the Spirit," *Road From Damascus*, 166–83; and his thorough investigation of the Spirit in Paul's letters: *God's Empowering Presence: The Holy Spirit in the Letters of Paul* (Peabody: Hendrickson, 1994).

[125] See N. Q. Hamilton, *The Holy Spirit and Eschatology in Paul* (Edinburgh: Oliver Boyd, 1957).

Paul's coherent theology is thus a living and dynamic disposition which has five interrelated characteristics: *experiential, traditional, cultural-contextual, Christological* and *eschatological*. Together they underscore the confluence of historical contingency, tradition, experience and the framework of eschatological proleptic fulfilment in the formulation of Paul's Christology.

To summarise, we have held up Paul's hermeneutical Christology as a case study to illustrate our proposal that Christology be done *from within* and *from ahead*. It is clear that Paul's conversion/call experience made a deep impact on his thought and played a pivotal role in determining the shape of his Christology as well as his sense of calling, i.e., the Gentile-mission. Yet the experience of the risen Lord was not an uninterpreted experience; it depended on the covenantal and messianic categories of Paul's Jewish background. While there is structural continuity between the mindset of Saul the persecuting zealot and the theological framework of Paul the converted Christian, there is nevertheless material discontinuity between the Torah-centred Jewish religion and the Christ-centred early Church.

So powerful was the gracious revelation of God's Son on the Damascus road that it led to a radical reconfiguration of Paul's convictional world. The experience of Christ was thus for Paul both conditioned and transformative. It caused him to reappraise the faith of his fathers, the significance of the Torah, the trustworthiness of God in relation to Israel, the meaning of history, and humanity as a whole. All these were re-evaluated in the light of Christ. This led him to adopt a hermeneutical approach which is Christocentrically retrospective and eschatologically orientated. We suggested that Paul's hermeneutical development of Christology took place along a historical trajectory coming out of God's covenantal relationship with Israel and the messianic expectations of the Hebrew scriptures. As a result of Paul's encounter with Christ and the eschatological Spirit, his horizon of understanding was expanded and his zeal for the honour of God extended Christ-ward.

Paul's revamped convictional world provided him with a coherent theological framework which is a network of interconnecting beliefs. Using Price's view of belief as disposition, we argued that the web of convictions which is Paul's coherent theology can be meaningfully understood in terms of the grand narrative of God's salvific work in history which has come to climactic fulfilment in the history of Jesus Christ. It is hoped that the above considerations have shown that the distinction made between Christology *from within* in terms of tradition and experience, and Christology *from ahead* in terms of eschatological prolepsis, cannot be pressed too sharply. The features of one overlap with those of the other.

CONCLUSION

We have tried in the preceding pages to set out an approach to Christological formulation which takes into account the necessary temporality of all claims to knowledge. The repercussions for Christology of a strong commitment to historicism were explored in chapter one by way of a case study of Troeltsch's struggle against the rising tide of historicism in the nineteenth-century. That challenging tide of historical contingency continues to wash upon the shores of philosophy and theology today, albeit in a transmogrified form. With it comes a reinvigorated challenge of (a new) historicism for Christology.

Christology, we argued, must navigate the waters between the objectivism of truth as supposedly timeless postulates, and the relativism which gives absolute privilege to contextuality and thereby tribalizes truth. To come to terms with historical consciousness, Troeltsch acknowledged that theology must move out of the safe zone of an atemporal "house of authority." He succeeded in launching from the shore of objectivism, but despite his efforts, could not resist the currents of historicism which eventually brought him to grief upon the craggy rocks of an epistemic relativism. His undoing, from our point of view, lies in his presuppositional rejection of the possibility of the coinherence of the transcendental and the historical. When one has ruled out of court from the start the possibility of universal and transcontextual truth, it is hardly surprising that one should end up with only contextual and historicized particularities.

We submit that it is precisely in refusing to absolutize the separation between the transcendental and the historical, between transcontextuality and contingency, that we can forge a way forward in Christology. Such an approach is congruent with the belief that God has revealed himself and acted in universal history, particularly in Jesus Christ and the tradition emanating from him. One can hold on to such a conviction and still accept the necessary contingency of human knowledge. It is our contention that having a presuppositional framework, which in our case concerns the possibility and reality of transcontextual truth in history, remains not only compatible with the temporality of understanding but also necessary from

a hermeneutical standpoint. In any case, in dealing with phenomenological particularity, it is difficult, if not impossible, to escape the
need to postulate some sort of totality or universality. In acknowledging at the outset the possibility of transcendent or transcontextual
truth, we are doing no more than making explicit a preunderstanding
for which we have argued, as we approach the task of apprehending
the truth about Christ, and through him the truth about reality.

In view of this, we proposed an approach to Christology which
is hermeneutically sensitive, one which takes seriously the temporality of understanding. Instead of the conventionalized models of
Christology "from above" and "from below," we have tried in the
preceding chapters to develop a Christology *from within* and *from ahead*
which takes account of the impact of *tradition* and *experience*, and is
eschatologically oriented. The emphases on traditionality, history, interpretive horizons and experiential self-involvement in the hermeneutics tradition represented by Gadamer and Schleiermacher, together
with Pannenberg's notion of proleptic-eschatological fulfilment, help
to orientate the task of interpreting the significance of Christ today.
Our proposal seeks to reflect "the interpretive turn" in philosophy,
and operates from an eschatological temporal framework grounded
in a concept of divine transcendental immanence in history.

Drawing on the philosophical hermeneutics of Gadamer (chapter
two), we examined the dynamics of a traditionary Christology (chapter three) and argued that Christology must be done *from within* the
framework of a living tradition. Gadamer's view on the historicality
and linguisticality of understanding, and his Heideggerian stress on
the conditioning impact of preunderstanding or prejudice in interpretation, serve as resources to help us overcome the subject-object
dualism which has plagued Christological formulation since the
Enlightenment. Building on Gadamer's notion of *wirkungsgeschichtliches
Bewusstsein*, we looked at the dialectic of continuity and discontinuity in the development of Christology within tradition, and assessed
the impact of ecclesial life and praxis on Christological formulation.
Tradition, we argued, is both a *given* and a *task*, the *habitus* and *goal*
of theological reflection; we are at once tradition-bound and tradi-
tion-transcending. Any fresh articulation of Christology must therefore emerge from, and be in critical dialogue with, the tradition in
which the theologian stands.

In response to the plurality of Christologies in history, we maintained that there is arguably a *retrospectively discernible trajectory* within

the dialectic of continuity and discontinuity in Christological development. We raised in chapter three the possibility of a confluencing of the divergent trajectories of church history, such that one may discern *a complex and composite directionality* which unites different Christological interpretations. The idea of movement along the directional trajectory of time is in line with our thesis that Christological understanding takes place along a temporal axis. We submit that such a traditionary construal of Christology allows for new interpretive formulations of Christ to blossom, while at the same time disciplines all such developments in terms of their fidelity to the trajectorial directionality which comes out of the dogmatic achievements of the past. This is necessary not only to ensure that tradition is seen as a launching pad for new initiatives and not a prison to constrain theological creativity, but also to enable us to speak of Christianity as a faith with a coherent identity through the permutations of time. In the same way, the dialectic of continuity and discontinuity allows Christology, articulated in each new generation, to be similar to, yet different from, what had gone before.

Christology undertaken from within tradition cannot ignore or bypass engagement with the actualities of life in ecclesial community, for the latter play a pivotal part in the transmission of the "corporate memory" of the Church. Christological construction is to be carried out within the tradition-mediating ecclesial community and cannot be divorced from pious and practical performance of Christian identity. This performance however is not without a script or score. It is circumscribed by Scripture as canon for theological development, whose criteriological authority is to be found within the interpretive interaction between Scripture and the ongoing life of the Christian community. Just as tradition is capable of exerting a disciplining influence on theological development even as it is being critically extended, we argued that Scripture as a transcendental norm is dialectically related to Scripture understood as a contingent implicate of tradition. An inseparable interconnectedness thus emerges between Christ, Church and Scriptures. Christology from within tradition is situated within this network of interpenetrating convictions.

Gadamer's reflections on the dialogical fusion of horizons alert us to the need for Christology to engage fully with the context in which the hermeneutical community of faith is situated. Contextualization ensures that Christological formulae are always anchored to the specificity of time and place, as the horizon of the past is fused with that of the present. But before this can happen, we proposed that a prior move be made: what we call a process of *dialogical transcontextualization*. This is essentially an exercise in self-transcendence whereby one attains, through dialogical engagement with the other, to a perspective external to one's own situatedness. Through this process of transcontextualization, one discerns how and in what ways one's belief concerning Christ can undergo transformative development.

We turned in chapter four to the second of our dual understandings of Christology *from within*, vis-à-vis the experiential dimension, and sought to develop a Christology of the human heart in dialogue with Schleiermacher. The focus in chapters two and three on the communal and traditional in Christological reflection is balanced by the exploration of the existential and experiential in chapter four. We tried to show that Christological confession is a self-involving undertaking which entails an interpenetration of the inward dimension of faith and the outward dimension of cultural-linguistic ecclesiality. As such, it is important to reiterate that by "experience," we do not mean a mere interiority or subjective emotional state. Experience, as we said earlier, is necessarily traditioned, and tradition must be experienced.

True to the "tradition of inwardness" discernible in the history of Christian thought, Schleiermacher raises into prominence the role of a believing subjectivity in the apprehension of God. Theology as reflection animated by the Christian's experience of redemption in Christ suggests that the former can never be undertaken in a detached manner. In this, Schleiermacher's theological method, we argued, is not unlike the Anselmian view of faith seeking understanding. The theologian confesses Christ from within the circle of faith or personal appropriation of Christ; he or she is hardly an uninvolved observer. Yet this experience of God is not something given apart from the common life of faith. That experience is necessarily ecclesial and historical in nature is a Schleiermacherian emphasis, which may need to be rescued from undue neglect, especially in terms of the specific agenda which Schleiermacher proposes. We have attempted to show that he operated with an empiricism oriented to the phenomenology of religious experience situated within the communion of Christian believers. Experience for Schleiermacher, far from being an ineffable interiority, is caught up in the web of intersubjectivity.

We suggested too that Schleiermacher's stubborn refusal to divorce theological assertions from experience or consciousness, echoes the

Reformers' insistence on the importance of *religio* in the knowledge of God. The conjoining of thought about God (theology) and a heart for God (spirituality) in Schleiermacher recalls the patristic holism of heart and mind in the knowledge of God. Not only does his theological method highlight the affective dimension of theological reflection, it draws attention to the contribution of the individual to theological and doctrinal definition, without denying his or her situatedness in ecclesial tradition. He instantiates the romantic paradigm of theological authorship whereby the individual imaginatively and creatively reappropriates the received tradition and extends that inherited theological horizon. Despite our reservations about certain aspects of his program, we find in Schleiermacher's approach to theological formulation a laudable convergence of piety, creativity, individuality and fidelity to tradition.

Alongside the tension between the corporate (tradition) and the individual (experience) in our construal of Christology *from within*, there is a further dialectic between the present and the future. With Pannenberg as our conversation partner, we took up this tension and developed in chapter five a Christology *from ahead* which utilizes the eschatological notion of proleptic fulfilment. A Christology oriented to the temporality of truth and understanding, inevitably takes on an eschatological character, insofar as it affirms that God and truth are manifested within history. The truth of Christology is correlated with the truth of eschatological fulfilment. Christology is *from ahead* in that it is carried out along the temporal bridge between the "already" of Christ's resurrection and the "not yet" of the Eschaton. Situated in this tensive period between proleptic arrival and consummation, Christology is characterized as both contingent and universal.

We have tried to show that Christology *from ahead* is proleptic in that it is marked by a simultaneous openness to the future and a referentiality to the pastness of the Christ-Event. This eschatological vantage point is situated in a present shaped by the tradition of effective history which stems from the proleptic eventfulness of Christ's resurrection in the past. Such a tradition-centered orientation in turn orientates us to the future. This proleptic reality is made real by the eschatological Spirit of God within the life of Christian community. Christology *from ahead* is thus bound up with a Christology *from within* in the dual sense of ecclesial tradition and experience. Furthermore, Christology *from ahead* eschews fideism and seeks to commend the truth about Christ within the public arena. Pannenberg's positive embrace of history and contextuality, and his realist view of truth as unitary and universal, are elements which cohere with our case for Christology. Unlike those who shy away from making universal truth claims, Pannenberg unabashedly affirms that there is truth, and that truth is unitary. In his readiness to speak of the cosmic significance of Christ, he stands firmly within the tradition of the apostles reflected in the New Testament.

It is hopefully patent from the above summaries that the twin models of Christology *from within* and *from ahead* are more than inter-related. This is especially evident in chapter six where we discerned the intricate interconnections between tradition, experience and eschatology in Paul's hermeneutical Christology. The impact of Paul's conversion/call experience at the Damascus Christophany on the shape of his Christology plays a significant role in our argument. Paul perceived the significance of this experiential encounter with the risen Christ in terms of the apocalyptic tradition of eschatological fulfilment; it was not just a bare uninterpreted experience. His Jewish preunderstanding provided him the conceptual categories with which to make sense of his experience. This led to a radical reconfiguration of his convictional world. Such a reading supports our thesis on the dialectic of continuity and discontinuity in theological formulation. Paul developed his Christology *from within* tradition, and in the process found the constitution of that tradition Christologically transformed or transvalued.

The importance of eschatological fulfilment can be seen not only in the substance of Paul's epistles, but also in his hermeneutics. The recognition that in Christ the age to come has invaded this age served as hermeneutical grid for his Christological reinterpretation of the Hebrew Scriptures. His hermeneutics, we maintained, may be understood as both retrospective and teleological: his approach looks back to the past from the vantage point of the future. In that Paul's Christology is inseparable from the horizon of eschatological fulfilment, it may be described as *from ahead*. We then considered the nature of Paul's coherent theology or narrative thought-world, and its relation to contingent situations. In the light of Price's notion of belief as disposition, we proposed that Paul's coherent gospel entails a cluster of ideas which together constitute an overall disposition or pattern of belief. This Christocentric disposition, the result of the reconfiguration

of his interpretive horizon after his conversion, in turn became the
framework from which he grappled with the contingencies of his
ministry.

We have characterized our attempt in this study as a "quest" for
transcontextual criteria in Christology because we are mindful of the
difficulties involved in the assertion of universality given the indisputable contingency of all theological claims. Yet we must press on
in this quest if Christology is not to lose its universal character.
Unless one is prepared to accept that the claims which Christian
tradition makes about Christ are simply parochial expressions of
what is *true only for* the Christian believer, and have no extra-systemic
validity or reference, it is incumbent upon us to seek that which is
transcontextual within the contextual. Returning to the static and
atemporal objectivism of understanding is no longer tenable. Neither
is the option of an epistemic relativism which denies the universal
claim of the gospel of Christ a live option; not if we want to remain
faithful to the tradition of the Christian faith. We submit that if it
is to be viable in an age of historical consciousness, a constructive
Christology is best served by proceeding along a hermeneutical path
between objectivism and relativism. The quest continues.

BIBLIOGRAPHY

Aageson, James W. "Scripture and Structure in the Development of the Argument in Romans 9–11." *CBQ* 48(1986): 268–89.
———. "Typology, Correspondence, and the Application of Scripture in Romans 9–11." *JSNT* 31(1987): 51–72.
———. *Written Also for Our Sake: Paul and the Art of Biblical Interpretation*. Louisville: Westminster/John Knox, 1994.
Abraham, William J. *Divine Revelation and the Limits of Historical Criticism*. Oxford: Oxford University Press, 1982.
Achtemeir, Paul J. "The Continuing Quest for Coherence in St. Paul: An Experiment in Thought." Eugene H. Lovering, Jr. & Jerry L. Sumney, eds. *Theology and Ethics in Paul and His Interpreters*. Nashville: Abingdon, 1996. 132–45.
———. *The Inspiration of Scripture: Problems and Proposals*. Philadelphia: Westminster, 1980.
Adams, James Luther. "Ernst Troeltsch as Analyst of Religion." *JSSR* 1(1961): 98–109.
Albright, Carol Rausch & Joel Haugen, eds. *Beginning with the End: God, Science, and Wolfhart Pannenberg*. Chicago & La Salle: Open Court, 1997.
Allen, Diogenes. *Christian Belief in a Postmodern World: The Full Wealth of Conviction*. Louisville: Westminster/John Knox, 1989.
Allen, L. "From Dogmatik to Glaubenslehre: Ernst Troeltsch and the Task of Theology." *FH* 12(1980): 37–60.
Allison Jr., Dale C. "A Plea for Thoroughgoing Eschatology." *JBL* 113(1994): 651–68.
Alston, William P. *A Realist Conception of Truth*. Ithaca & London: Cornell University Press, 1996.
———. "Two Types of Foundationalism." *JP* 73(1976): 165–85.
Altizer, Thomas J. J., Max A. Myers, Carl A. Raschke, Robert P. Scharlemann, Mark C. Taylor & Charles Winquist. *Deconstruction and Theology*. New York: Crossroad, 1982.
Ambrosio, Francis J. "Dawn and Dusk: Gadamer and Heidegger on Truth." *MW* 19(1986): 21–53.
Anderson, Walter Truett. *Reality Isn't What It Used to Be: Theatrical Politics, Ready-to-Wear Religion, Global Myths, Primitive Chic, and Other Wonders of the Postmodern World*. San Francisco: Harper & Row, 1990.
Apczynski, John V. "Truth in Religion: A Polanyian Appraisal of Wolfhart Pannenberg's Theological Program." *Zygon* 17(1982): 49–73.
Apel, Karl-Otto. "The Problem of Philosophical Foundations in Light of a Transcendental Pragmatics of Language." Kenneth Baynes, James Bohman & Thomas McCarthy, eds. *After Philosophy: End or Transformation?* Cambridge & London: MIT Press, 1987. 250–90.
———. "Regulative Ideas or Truth-Happening?: An Attempt to Answer the Question of the Conditions of the Possibility of Valid Understanding." Lewis Edwin Hahn, ed. *The Philosophy of Hans-Georg Gadamer*. Chicago & La Salle: Open Court, 1997. 67–94.
———. *Towards a Transformation of Philosophy*, tr. Glyn Adey & David Frisby. London, Boston & Henley: Routledge & Kegan Paul, 1980.
Apel, Karl-Otto *et al.*, eds. *Hermeneutik und Ideologiekritik: Theorie-Diskussion*. Frankfurt: Suhrkamp, 1971.

Apfelbacher, K. A. *Frömmigkeit und Wissenschaft: Ernst Troeltsch und sein theologisches Program*. Munich: Paderborn, 1978.

Arens, Edmund. *Christopraxis: A Theology of Action*. Tr. John F. Hoffmeyer. Minneapolis: Fortress, 1995.

Austin, J. L. *How To Do Things With Words*. 2d. ed. Edited by J. O. Urmson & Marina Sbisà. Cambridge: Harvard University Press, 1962, 1975.

Avis, Paul. "Divine Revelation in Modern Protestant Theology." Paul Avis, ed. *Divine Revelation*. London: Darton, Longman & Todd, 1997. 45–66.

Badenas, Robert. *Christ the End of the Law: Romans 10:4 in Pauline Perspective*. Sheffield: Sheffield Academic Press, 1985.

Baird, William. *History of New Testament Research. Volume 1: From Deism to Tübingen*. Minneapolis: Fortress, 1992.

———. "Pauline Eschatology in Hermeneutical Perspective." *NTS* 17(1970–71): 314–27.

Balchin, John. "Paul, Wisdom and Christ." H. H. Rowden, ed. *Christ the Lord: Studies in Christology presented to Donald Guthrie*. Leicester: InterVarsity, 1982. 204–19.

Balthasar, Hans Urs Von. *The Glory of the Lord: A Theological Aesthetics. Vol. 1: Seeing the Form*. Tr. Erasmo Leiva-Merikakis. Ed. Joseph Fessio & John Riches. Edinburgh: T&T Clark, 1982.

Barbour, Ian G. *Myths, Models and Paradigms: The Nature of Scientific and Religious Language*. London: SCM Press, 1974.

———. *Religion in An Age of Science*. The Gifford Lectures, 1989–1991, Vol. 1. New York: HarperCollins, 1990.

Barclay, John & John Sweet, eds. *Early Christian Thought in its Jewish Context*. Cambridge: Cambridge University Press, 1996.

Barr, James. *The Bible in the Modern World*. London: SCM, 1973.

Barrett, C. K. *From First Adam to Last*. London: A & C Black, 1962.

Barrett, Lee C. "Theology as Grammar: Regulative Principles or Paradigms and Practices." *MTh* 4(1988): 155–72.

Barth, Karl. *Church Dogmatics*. 12 vols. G. W. Bromiley & T. F. Torrance, eds. Edinburgh: T&T Clark, 1936–1962.

———. *The Humanity of God*. Atlanta: John Knox, 1960.

———. *Protestant Theology in the Nineteenth Century: Its Background and History*. Valley Forge: Judson Press, 1973.

———. *The Theology of Schleiermacher: Lectures at Göttingen, 1923–24*. Ed. Dietrich Ritschl. Grand Rapids: Eerdmans, 1982.

Bartley, William Warren, III. *The Retreat to Commitment*. 2d. rev. ed. La Salle & London: Open Court Publishing Company, 1984.

Bassler, Jouette M., ed. *Pauline Theology, Volume I: Thessalonians, Philippians, Galatians, Philemon*. Minneapolis: Fortress, 1991.

———. "Paul's Theology: Whence and Whither?" David M. Hay, ed. *Pauline Theology, Volume II: 1 & 2 Corinthians*. Minneapolis: Fortress, 1993. 3–17.

Bauckham, Richard. "Tradition in Relation to Scripture and Reason." Richard Bauckham & Benjamin Drewery, eds. *Scripture, Tradition and Reason*. Edinburgh: T&T Clark, 1988. 117–45.

Bauckham, Richard and Benjamin Drewery, eds. *Scripture, Tradition, and Reason: A Study in the Criteria of Christian Doctrine*. Edinburgh: T&T Clark, 1988.

Bauer, Walter. *Orthodoxy and Heresy in Earliest Christianity*. Edited by Robert A. Kraft & Gerhard Krodel. Philadelphia: Fortress, 1971. From 2d. German ed. of *Rechtgläubigkeit und Ketzerei im ältesten Christentum*. Tübingen: J. C. B. Mohr, 1934.

Michael Bauman. *Roundtable: Conversations with European Theologians*. Grand Rapids: Baker, 1990.

Bauman, Zygmunt. *Hermeneutics and Social Science: Approaches to Understanding*. London: Hutchinson, 1978.

————. *Intimations of Postmodernity*. London & New York: Routledge, 1992.

Baur, Ferdinand C. *Paul, the Apostle of Jesus Christ; His Life and Work, His Epistles and His Doctrine: A Contribution to a Critical History of Primitive Christianity*. 2 vols. 2d. ed. London & Edinburgh: Williams and Norgate, 1876.

Baynes, Kenneth, James Bohman & Thomas McCarthy, eds. *After Philosophy: End or Transformation?* Cambridge & London: MIT Press, 1987.

Beale, G. K., ed. *The Right Doctrine from the Wrong Texts? Essays on the Use of the Old Testament in the New*. Grand Rapids: Baker, 1994.

Behrens, Georg. "Schleiermacher *Contra* Lindbeck on the Status of Doctrinal Sentences." *RelS* 30(1994): 399–417.

Beisser, Friedrich. *Schleiermachers Lehre von Gott dargestellt nach seinen Reden und seiner Glaubenslehre*. Göttingen: Vanderhoeck & Ruprecht, 1970.

Beker, J. Christiaan. *Paul's Apocalyptic Gospel: The Coming Triumph of God*. Philadelphia: Fortress, 1982.

————. *Paul the Apostle: The Triumph of God in Life and Thought*. Edinburgh: T&T Clark, 1980.

————. "Recasting Pauline Theology: The Coherence-Contingency Scheme as Interpretive Model." Jouette M. Bassler, ed. *Pauline Theology, Volume I: Thessalonians, Philippians, Galatians, Philemon*. Minneapolis: Fortress, 1991. 15–24.

————. *The Triumph of God: The Essence of Paul's Thought*. Minneapolis: Fortress, 1990.

Bell, Richard H. *Provoked to Jealousy: The Origin and Purpose of the Jealousy Motif in Romans 9–11*. Tübingen: J. C. B. Mohr (Paul Siebeck), 1994.

Bellah, Robert N. With Richard Madsen, William M. Sullivan, Ann Swidler & Steven M. Tipton. *Habits of the Heart*. Berkeley: University of California Press, 1985.

Bender, Wilhelm. "Schleiermachers Lehre vom schlechthinigen Abhängigkeitsgefühl im Zusammenhang seiner Wissenschaft." *Jahrbücher für deutsche Theologie*. 16 (Gotha: Rudolf Besser, 1871), 79–146.

Berger, Peter & Thomas Luckmann. *The Social Construction of Reality: A Treatise in the Sociology of Knowledge*. London: Penguin, 1966.

Berkouwer, G. C. *Studies in Dogmatics: Holy Scripture*. Grand Rapids: Eerdmans, 1975.

Berkowitz, Peter. *Nietzsche: The Ethics of an Immoralist*. Cambridge & London: Harvard University Press, 1995.

Bernstein, Richard J. *Beyond Objectivism and Relativism: Science, Hermeneutics, and Praxis*. Philadelphia: University of Pennsylvania Press, 1991.

————. "From Hermeneutics to Praxis." Brice R. Wachterhauser, ed. *Hermeneutics and Modern Philosophy*. Albany: State University of New York Press, 1986. 87–110.

————. ed. *Habermas and Modernity*. Cambridge: Polity Press, 1985.

————. "Hermeneutics and its Anxieties." Daniel Bahltron, ed. *Hermeneutics and the Tradition*. Proceedings of the American Catholic Philosophical Association, 1988, 58–70.

————. *The New Constellation: The Ethical-Political Horizons of Modernity/Postmodernity*. Cambridge: Polity Press, 1991.

————. *Praxis and Action: Contemporary Philosophies of Human Activity*. Philadelphia: University of Pennsylvania Press, 1971.

Best, Steven & Douglas Kellner. *Postmodern Theory: Critical Interrogations*. Basingstoke & London: Macmillan, 1991.

Betti, Emilio. *Allgemeine Auslegungslehre als Methodik der Geisteswissenschaften*. Tübingen: Mohr, 1967.

————. *Die Hermeneutik als allgemeine Methodik der Geisteswissenschaften*. 2d. ed. Tübingen: Mohr, 1972. ET: "Hermeneutics as the General Methodology of the Geisteswissenschaften." J. Bleicher. *Contemporary Hermeneutics: Hermeneutics as Method, Philosophy and Critique*. London, Boston & Henley: Routledge & Kegan Paul, 1980. 51–94.

Betz, Hans D. "The Concept of Apocalyptic in the Theology of the Pannenberg Group." *JTC* 6(1969): 192–207.

————. "On the Problem of the Religio-Historical Understanding of Apocalypticism." *JTC* 6(1969): 134–56.

Betz, Otto. *Was wissen wir von Jesus.* Stuttgart: Kreuz-verlag, 1965.

Bevans, Stephen B. *Models of Contextual Theology.* New York: Orbis, 1992.

Bhaskar, Roy. *Philosophy and the Idea of Freedom.* Oxford & Cambridge: Blackwell, 1991.

Birkner, Hans-Joachim. *Historisches Wörterbuch der Philosophie.* Vol. 3. Ed. J. Ritter & K. Gründer. Darmstadt: Wissenschaftliche Buchgesellschaft, 1974.

Black, Matthew. "The Christological Use of the Old Testament in the New Testament." *NTS* 18(1971): 1–14.

Bleicher, Josef. *Contemporary Hermeneutics: Hermeneutics as Method, Philosophy and Critique.* London, Boston & Henley: Routledge & Kegan Paul, 1980.

Bockmuehl, Markus N. A. *Revelation as Mystery in Ancient Judaism and Pauline Christianity.* Tübingen: J. C. B. Mohr (Paul Siebeck), 1990.

Boderstein, Walter. *Neige des Historismus: Ernst Troeltschs Entwicklungsgang.* Gütersloh: Gütersloher Verlaghaus Gerd Mohn, 1959.

Boff, Clodovis. *Theology and Praxis: Epistemological Foundations.* Maryknoll: Orbis, 1987.

Bohman, James F. "Holism Without Skepticism: Contextualism and the Limits of Interpretation." David R. Hiley, James F. Bohman & Richard Shusterman, eds. *The Interpretive Turn: Philosophy, Science, Culture.* Ithaca & London: Cornell University Press, 1991. 129–154.

Borgmann, Albert. *Crossing the Postmodern Divide.* Chicago: University of Chicago Press, 1992.

Bornkamm, G. *Paul.* New York: Harper & Row, 1969.

Bousset, Wilhelm. *Kyrios Christos: A History of the Belief in Christ from the Beginnings of Christianity to Irenaeus.* Nashville: Abingdon, 1970.

Bowie, Andrew. *Aesthetics and Subjectivity: From Kant to Nietzsche.* Manchester & New York: Manchester University Press, 1990.

————. *From Romanticism to Critical Theory: The Philosophy of German Literary Theory.* London & New York: Routledge, 1997.

————. *Schelling and Modern European Philosophy: An Introduction.* London & New York: Routledge, 1993.

Boyd, George Nolan. *The Doctrine of Original Sin and the Fall in the Theology of Friedrich Schleiermacher.* Th.D. diss., Union Theological Seminary, 1970.

Braaten, Carl E. "The Current Controversy on Revelation: Pannenberg and His Critics." *JRel* 45(1965): 225–37.

————. *History and Hermeneutics. New Directions in Theology Today,* Vol. 2. London: Lutterworth, 1968.

————. "The Place of Christianity Among the World Religions: Wolfhart Pannenberg's Theology of Religion and the History of Religions." *The Theology of Wolfhart Pannenberg.* Minneapolis: Augsburg, 1988. 287–312.

————. "Scripture, Church, and Dogma: An Essay on Theological Method." *Int* 50(1996): 142–55.

Braaten, Carl E. & Philip Clayton, eds. *The Theology of Wolfhart Pannenberg: Twelve American Critiques, with an Autobiographical Essay and Response.* Minneapolis: Augsburg, 1988.

Bradshaw, Timothy. *Trinity and Ontology: A Comparative Study of the Theologies of Karl Barth and Wolfhart Pannenberg.* Edinburgh: Rutherford House Books, 1988.

Brandt, Richard B. *The Philosophy of Schleiermacher: The Development of His Theory of Scientific and Religious Knowledge.* New York: Greenwood Press, 1968.

Brown, Alexandra R. *The Cross & Human Transformation: Paul's Apocalyptic Word in 1 Corinthians.* Minneapolis: Fortress, 1995.

Brown, Colin. "Christology and the Quest of the Historical Jesus." Donald Lewis & Alister McGrath, eds., *Doing Theology for the People of God: Studies in Honour of J. I. Packer.* Leicester: Apollos, 1996. 67–83.

————. *History and Faith: A Personal Exploration.* Leicester: InterVarsity, 1988.

————. *Jesus in European Protestant Thought: 1778–1860.* Durham: Labyrinth Press, 1985.

————. *Miracles and the Critical Mind.* Grand Rapids: Eerdmans, 1984.

————, ed. *The New International Dictionary of New Testament Theology.* 3 vols. Exeter: Paternoster, 1976.

————. "Synoptic Miracle Stories: A Jewish Religious and Social Setting." *Foundations & Facets Forum* 2(1986): 55–76.

————. "Trinity and Incarnation: In Search of Contemporary Orthodoxy." *EA* 7(1991): 83–100.

Brown, David. *Continental Philosophy and Modern Theology: An Engagement.* Oxford: Basil Blackwell, 1987.

Brown, Delwin. *Boundaries of Our Habitation: Tradition and Theological Construction.* Albany: State University of New York Press, 1994.

————. "Struggle Till Daybreak: On the Nature of Authority in Theology." *JRel* 65(1985): 15–32.

Brown, Delwin & Sheila Greeve Davaney, "Postliberalism." Alister E. McGrath, ed. *Encyclopedia of Modern Christian Thought.* Oxford: Basil Blackwell, 1993. 325–30.

Bruce, F. F. *Paul: Apostle of the Free Spirit.* Exeter: Paternoster, 1977.

————. "The Roman Debate Continued." Karl P. Donfried, ed. *The Roman Debate.* Rev. exp. ed. Peabody: Hendricksen, 1977, 1991. 175–94.

————. *Tradition: Old and New.* Exeter: Paternoster, 1970.

Brunner, Emil. *Die Mystik und das Wort: Der Gegensatz zwischen moderner Religionsauffassung und christlichen Glauben dargestellt an der Theologie Schleiermachers.* Tübingen: J. C. B. Mohr [Paul Siebeck], 1924.

Bruns, Gerald L. "What is Tradition?" *NLH* 22(1991): 1–21.

Bryant, David J. "Christian Identity and Historical Change: Postliberals and Historicity." *JRel* 73(1993): 31–41.

Buck, Günther. "The Structure of Hermeneutic Experience and the Problem of Tradition." *NLH* 10(1978–79): 31–47

Burhenn, Herbert. "Pannenberg's Argument for the Historicity of the Resurrection." *JAAR* 50(1972): 368–79.

————. "Pannenberg's Doctrine of God." *SJT* 28(1975): 535–49.

Burnham, Frederic B., ed. *Postmodern Theology: Christian Faith in a Pluralist World.* San Francisco: Harper & Row, 1989.

Calvin, John. *Institutes of the Christian Religion.* 2 vols. Ed. John T. McNeill. Tr. Ford Lewis Battles. London: SCM, 1961.

Caputo, John D. "Beyond Aestheticism: Derrida's Responsible Anarchy." *RP* 18(1988): 59–73.

————. "Gadamer's Closet Essentialism: A Derridean Critique." Diane P. Michelfelder & Richard E. Palmer, eds. *Dialogue and Deconstruction: The Gadamer-Derrida Encounter.* Albany: State University of New York Press, 1989. 258–64.

————. *Radical Hermeneutics.* Bloomington: Indiana University Press, 1987.

Carnley, Peter. *The Structure of Resurrection Belief.* Oxford: Clarendon, 1987.

Carpenter, David. "Emanation, Incarnation, and the Truth-Event in Gadamer's *Truth and Method.*" Brice R. Wachterhauser, ed. *Hermeneutics and Truth.* Evanston: Northwestern University Press, 1994. 98–122.

Carr, Thomas K. *Newman & Gadamer: Toward a Hermeneutics of Religious Knowledge.* Atlanta: Scholars Press, 1996.

Carson, D. A. *The Gagging of God: Christianity Confronts Pluralism.* Grand Rapids: Zondervan, 1996.

Carson, D. A. and H. G. M. Williamson, eds. *It is Written: Scripture Citing Scripture: Essays in Honour of Barnabas Lindars.* Cambridge: Cambridge University Press, 1988.

Carson, D. A. and John D. Woodbridge, eds. *Hermeneutics, Authority, and Canon.* Grand Rapids: Zondervan, 1986.

Cerfaux, L. *Christ in the Theology of St Paul*. New York: Herder and Herder, 1959.
Chadwick, Owen. *From Bossuet to Newman: The Idea of Doctrinal Development*. Cambridge: Cambridge University Press, 1957.
Chamblin, K. "Revelation and Tradition in the Pauline *Euangelion*." *WTJ* 48(1986): 1–16.
Charlesworth, J. H. "From Jewish Messianology to Christian Christology: Some Caveats and Perspectives." J. Neusner, W. S. Green & E. S. Frerichs, eds. *Judaisms and Their Messiahs at the Turn of the Christian Era*. Cambridge: Cambridge University Press, 1987. 225–64.
Childs, Brevard S. *The New Testament as Canon: An Introduction*. Philadelphia: Fortress, 1984.
Christian, C. W. *Friedrich Schleiermacher*. Waco: Word, 1979.
Clayton, John Powell, ed. *Ernst Troeltsch and the Future of Theology*. Cambridge: Cambridge University Press, 1976.
Clayton, Philip. "The God of History and the Presence of the Future." *JRel* 65(1985): 98–99.
Clements, Keith W., ed. *Friedrich Schleiermacher: Pioneer of Modern Theology*. The Making of Modern Theology: Nineteenth- and Twentieth-Century Texts. Minneapolis: Fortress, 1991.
Clifford, James. *The Predicament of Culture: Twentieth-Century Ethnography, Literature, and Art*. Cambridge: Harvard University Press, 1988.
Coakley, Sarah. *Christ Without Absolutes: A Study of the Christology of Ernst Troeltsch*. Oxford: Clarendon Press, 1988.
Coakley, Sarah & David A. Pailin, eds. *The Making and Remaking of Christian Doctrine: Essays in Honour of Maurice Wiles*. Oxford: Clarendon Press, 1993.
Cohen, Y. "The Attitude to the Gentile in the Halakah and in Reality in the Tannaitic Period." *Immanuel* 9(1979): 32–41.
Cohn-Sherbok, Daniel. "Paul and Rabbinic Exegesis." *SJT* 35(1982): 117–32.
Collier, Peter & Helga Geyer-Ryan, eds. *Literary Theory Today*. Oxford: Polity Press, 1990.
Collingwood, R. G. *The Idea of History*. Oxford: Oxford University Press, 1946, 1992.
Collins, R. F. "Paul's Damascus Experience: Reflections on the Lukan Account." *LS* 11(1986): 99–118.
Congar, Yves. *Tradition and Traditions: An Historical and a Theological Essay*. New York: Burns and Oates, 1966.
Cordes, Martin. "Der Brief Schleiermachers an Jacobi: Ein Beitrag zu seiner Entstehung und Überlieferung." *ZTK* 68(1971): 195–212.
Corliss, Richard L. "Schleiermacher's Hermeneutics and Its Critics." *RelS* 29(1993): 363–79.
Corrington, Robert S. *The Community of Interpreters: On the Hermeneutics of Nature and the Bible in the American Philosophical Tradition*. Marcon: Mercer University Press, 1987, 1995.
Cousins, Ewert H., ed. *Hope and the Future of Man*. Philadelphia: Fortress, 1972.
Cowdell, Scott. *Is Jesus Unique? A Study of Recent Christology*. New York & Mahwah: Paulist, 1996.
Creegan, Nicola Hoggard. "Schleiermacher as Apologist: Reclaiming the Father of Modern Theology." Timothy R. Phillips & Dennis L. Okholm, eds. *Christian Apologetics in the Postmodern World*. Downers Grove: InterVarsity Press, 1995. 59–74.
Crewdson, Joan. *Christian Doctrine in the Light of Michael Polanyi's Theory of Personal Knowledge: A Personalist Theology*. Toronto Studies in Theology, Vol. 66. Lewiston: Edwin Mellen Press, 1994.
Crouter, Richard. "Friedrich Schleiermacher: A Critical Edition, New York, and Perspectives." *RSR* 18(1992): 20–27.

———. "Hegel and Schleiermacher at Berlin: A Many-Sided Debate." *JAAR* 48(1980): 19–43.

Cullmann, Oscar. *Christ and Time.* London: SCM, 1951.

———. *Early Christian Worship.* Tr. A. Stewart Todd & James B. Torrance. London: SCM, 1953.

———. *The Earliest Christian Confessions.* London: Lutterworth, 1949.

———. *The Early Church.* Ed. A. J. B. Higgins. London: SCM, 1956.

Cunningham, David S. *Faithful Persuasion: In Aid of a Rhetoric of Christian Theology.* Notre Dame & London: University of Notre Dame Press, 1990, 1991.

Curran, Thomas H. *Doctrine and Speculation in Schleiermacher's Glaubenslehre.* Berlin & New York: Walter de Gruyter, 1994.

Dahl, Nils Alstrup. *Jesus the Christ: The Historical Origins of Christological Doctrine.* Ed. Donald H. Juel. Minneapolis: Fortress, 1991.

Dallmayr, Fred & Thomas A. McCarthy, eds. *Understanding and Social Inquiry.* Notre Dame: University of Notre Dame Press, 1977.

Dancy, Jonathan. *An Introduction to Contemporary Epistemology.* Oxford: Blackwell, 1985.

Davidson, Donald. "On the Very Idea of a Conceptual Scheme." *PAAPA* 47(1974): 5–20.

Davies, W. D. *Paul and Rabbinic Judaism: Some Rabbinic Elements in Pauline Theology.* 4th ed. London: SPCK, 1948, 1981.

———. "Paul and the People of Israel." *NTS* 24(1977–78): 4–39.

Davis, P. G. "Divine Agents, Mediators, and New Testament Christology." *JTS* 45(1994): 479–503.

Dean, William. "The Challenge of the New Historicism." *JRel* 66(1986): 261–81.

Deissmann, Gustav Adolf. *Paul: A Study in Social and Religious History.* 2d. ed. London: Hodder & Stoughton, 1926.

De Lacey, Douglas R. "'One Lord' in Pauline Christology." H. H. Rowdon, ed. *Christ the Lord: Studies in Christology presented to Donald Guthrie* (Leicester: InterVarsity, 1982. 191–203.

Demson, David E. *Hans Frei & Karl Barth: Different Ways of Reading Scripture.* Grand Rapids & Cambridge: Eerdmans, 1997.

Descartes, René. *Discourse on the Method of Rightly Conducting the Reason and Seeking for Truth in the Sciences.* In *The Philosophical Works of Descartes. Vol. 1.* Tr. E. S. Haldane & G. R. T. Ross. New York: Dover Publications, 1955.

Desjardins, Michael. "Bauer and Beyond: On Recent Scholarly Discussions of *Hairesis* in the Early Christian Era." *SC* 8(1991): 65–82.

DiCenso, James. *Hermeneutics and the Disclosure of Truth: A Study in the Work of Heidegger, Gadamer, and Ricoeur.* Charlottesville: University Press of Virginia, 1990.

Dietzfelbinger, Christian. *Die Berufung des Paulus als Ursprung seiner Theologie.* Neukirchen-Vluyn: Neukirchener, 1985.

Diggins, John Patrick. *The Promise of Pragmatism: Modernism and the Crisis of Knowledge and Authority.* Chicago & London: University of Chicago Press, 1994.

Dobbin, Edmund J. "Seminar on Foundations: Pannenberg on Theological Method." *CTSAP* 32(1977): 202–20.

Doctrine Commission of the Church of England. *Believing in the Church: The Corporate Nature of Faith.* London: SPCK, 1981.

Dodd, C. H. "The Mind of Paul." *New Testament Studies.* Manchester: Manchester University Press, 1953. 67–128.

Donaldson, Terence L. "Israelite, Convert, Apostle to the Gentiles: The Origin of Paul's Gentile Mission." Richard Longenecker, ed. *The Road From Damascus: The Impact of Paul's Conversion on His Life, Thought, and Ministry.* Grand Rapids: Eerdmans, 1997. 62–84.

———. *Paul and the Gentiles: Remapping the Apostle's Convictional World.* Minneapolis: Fortress, 1997.

————. "Zealot and Convert: The Origin of Paul's Christ-Torah Antithesis." *CBQ* 51(1989): 655–82.

Donfried, Karl P. ed. *The Roman Debate*. Rev. exp. ed. Peabody: Hendricksen, 1977, 1991.

Doppelt, Gerald. "Kuhn's Epistemological Relativism: An Interpretation and Defense." *Inquiry* 21(1978): 33–86.

Dostal, Robert J. "The Experience of Truth for Gadamer and Heidegger: Taking Time and Sudden Lightning." Brice R. Wachterhauser, ed. *Hermeneutics and Truth*. Evanston: Northwestern University Press, 1994. 47–67.

Drescher, Hans-Georg. "Das Problem der Geschichte bei Ernst Troeltsch." *ZTK* 57(1960): 186–230.

————. *Ernst Troeltsch: His Life and Work*, tr. John Bowden. London: SCM, 1992.

Drews, Arthur. *Die Christusmythe*. Jena: E. Diedrichs, 1909. ET: *The Christ Myth*. Tr. C. Delisle Burns. London: Fisher Unwin, 1910.

Duke, James O. & Robert F. Streetman, eds. *Barth and Schleiermacher: Beyond the Impasse?* Philadelphia: Fortress, 1988.

Dulles, Avery. *The Craft of Theology: From Symbol to System*. New York: Crossroad, 1992.

————. *The Survival of Dogma: Faith, Authority, and Dogma in a Changing World*. New York: Crossroad, 1971, 1985.

Dungan, David L. *The Sayings of Jesus in the Churches of Paul: The Use of the Synoptic Tradition in the Regulation of Early Church Life*. Oxford: Blackwell, 1971.

Dunn, James D. G. *Christology in the Making: A New Testament Inquiry into the Origins of the Doctrine of the Incarnation*. Philadelphia: Westminster, 1980.

————. *Jesus, Paul and the Law: Studies in Mark and Galatians*. Louisville: Westminster/John Knox, 1990.

————. "The Justice of God: A Renewed Perspective on Justification by Faith." *JTS* 43(1992): 1–22.

————, ed. *Paul and the Mosaic Law*. Tübingen: J. C. B. Mohr (Paul Siebeck), 1996.

————. "The Relationship Between Paul and Jerusalem According to Galatians 1 and 2." *NTS* 28(1982): 461–78.

————. *Unity and Diversity in the New Testament*. Philadelphia: Westminster, 1977.

————. *New Testament Theology: The Theology of Paul's Letters to the Galatians*. Cambridge: Cambridge University Press, 1993.

Dupont, Jacques. "The Conversion of Paul and Its Influence on the Understanding of Salvation by Faith." W. Ward Gasque & Ralph P. Martin, eds. *Apostolic History and the Gospel*. Grand Rapids: Eerdmans, 1970. 176–94.

Dyson, A. O. *The Immortality of the Past*. London: SCM, 1974.

————. "Ernst Troeltsch and the Possibility of a Systematic Theology." John Powell Clayton, ed. *Ernst Troeltsch and the Future of Theology*. Cambridge: Cambridge University Press, 1976. 81–99.

Eagleton, Terry. *Literary Theory: An Introduction*. Minneapolis: University of Minnesota Press; Oxford: Blackwell, 1983.

————. *The Illusions of Postmodernism*. Oxford: Blackwell, 1996.

Elliott, Neil. *Liberating Paul: The Justice of God and the Politics of the Apostle*. Maryknoll: Orbis, 1994.

————. *The Rhetoric of Romans*. Sheffield: Sheffield Academic Press, 1990.

Ellis, Earle E. "A Note on Pauline Hermeneutics." *NTS* 2(1955–56): 127–33.

————. *Paul's Use of the Old Testament*. Grand Rapids: Baker, 1981.

————. "Traditions in 1 Corinthians." *NTS* 32(1986): 481–502.

Engel, Mary Potter and Walter E. Wyman, Jr., eds. *Revisioning the Past: Prospects in Historical Theology*. Minneapolis: Fortress, 1992.

Ermath, Michael. "The Transformation of Hermeneutics: 19th Century Ancients and 20th Century Moderns." *Monist* 64(1981): 175–94.

Espy, J. M. "Paul's 'Robust Conscience' Re-Examined." *NTS* 31(1985): 161–88.

Evans, Craig A. "The Historical Jesus and the Deified Christ: How Did the One Lead to the Other?" Stanley E. Porter, ed. *The Nature of Religious Language: A Colloquium.* Sheffield: Sheffield Academic Press, 1996. 47–67.

Evans, Donald. *The Logic of Self-Involvement. A Philosophical Study of Everyday Language with Special Reference to the Christian Use of Language about God as Creator.* London: SCM, 1963.

Evans, C. Stephen. *The Historical Christ and the Jesus of Faith: The Incarnational Narrative as History.* Oxford: Clarendon Press, 1996.

Everts, J. M. "Conversion and Call of Paul." *DPL.* 156–63.

Fackre, Gabriel. *The Doctrine of Revelation: A Narrative Interpretation.* Edinburgh: Edinburgh University Press, 1997.

Farley, Edward. *Ecclesial Man: A Social Phenomenology of Faith and Reality.* Philadelphia: Fortress, 1975.

———. *Ecclesial Reflection: An Anatomy of Theological Method.* Philadelphia: Fortress, 1982.

Farley, Edward & Peter C. Hodgson. "Scripture and Tradition." Peter C. Hodgson & Robert King, eds. *Christian Theology: An Introduction to Its Traditions and Tasks.* Second, revised and enlarged edition. Philadelphia: Fortress, 1982, 1985. 61–87.

Farrell, Frank B. *Subjectivity, Realism, and Postmodernism—The Recovery of the World.* Cambridge: Cambridge University Press, 1994.

Fee, Gordon D. *God's Empowering Presence: The Holy Spirit in the Letters of Paul.* Peabody: Hendrickson, 1994.

———. "Paul's Conversion as Key to His Understanding of the Spirit." Richard Longenecker, ed. *The Road From Damascus: The Impact of Paul's Conversion on His Life, Thought, and Ministry.* Grand Rapids & Cambridge: Eerdmans, 1997. 166–83.

Feldman, L. H. *Jew and Gentile in the Ancient World: Attitudes and Interactions from Alexander to Justinian.* Princeton: Princeton University Press, 1993.

Festiger, L. *A Theory of Cognitive Dissonance.* Evanston: Row Peterson, 1957.

Feyerabend, Paul. *Against Method.* London: New Left Books, 1975.

Fichte, J. G. *Darstellung der Wissenschaftslehre (1801/1802).* Ed. Reinhard Lauth & P. K. Schneider. Hamburg: Felix Meiner, 1977.

———. *Grundlage der gesamten Wissenschaftslehre: Als Handschrift für seine Zuhörer (1794).* Hamburg: Felix Meiner, 1988.

Figal, Günter. "*Phronesis* as Understanding: Situating Philosophical Hermeneutics." Lawrence K. Schmidt, ed. *The Spectre of Relativism: Truth, Dialogue, and Phronesis in Philosophical Hermeneutics.* Evanston: Northwestern University Press, 1995. 236–47.

Fiorenza, Francis Schüssler. *Foundational Theology: Jesus and the Church.* New York: Crossroad, 1984.

———. "The Crisis of Scriptural Authority." *Int* 44(1990): 353–68.

Fitzmyer, Joseph A. *Pauline Theology: A Brief Sketch.* Englewood Cliffs: Prentice-Hall, 1967.

———. "The Semitic Background of the New Testament *Kyrios*-Title," in *A Wandering Aramean.* Missoula: Scholars Press, 1979. 115–42.

———. "The Use of Explicit Old Testament Quotations in Qumran Literature and in the New Testament," in *Essays on the Semitic Background of the New Testament.* London: Geoffrey Chapman, 1971. 3–58.

Flückiger, Felix. *Philosophie und Theologie bei Schleiermacher.* Zollikon-Zurich: Evangelischer Verlag, 1947.

Ford, David F. Review of George Lindbeck's *The Nature of Doctrine. JTS* 37(1986): 277–82.

———, ed. *The Modern Theologians: An Introduction to Christian Theology in the Twentieth Century.* 2d. ed. Oxford: Blackwell, 1997.

Forstman, Jack. *A Romantic Triangle: Schleiermacher and Early German Romanticism.* AAR Studies in Religion 13. Missoula: Scholars Press, 1977.

Foster, Durwood. "Pannenberg's Polanyianism: A Response to John V. Apczynski." *Zygon* 17(1982): 75–81.

Foster, Matthew. *Gadamer and Practical Philosophy: The Hermeneutics of Moral Confidence.* Atlanta: Scholars Press, 1991.

Foucault, Michel. *The Archaeology of Knowledge.* New York: Random House, 1972.

———. *The Order of Things: An Archaeology of the Human Sciences.* London: Tavistock, 1970.

———. *Power/Knowledge.* New York: Pantheon Books, 1980.

Fowl, Stephen. *The Story of Christ in the Ethics of Paul.* Sheffield: Sheffield Academic Press, 1990.

France, R. T. "The Worship of Jesus." H. H. Rowden, ed. *Christ the Lord.* Leicester: InterVarsity, 1982. 19–23.

Frank, Manfred. *Das Individuelle Allgemeine: Textstrukturierung und interpretation nach Schleiermacher.* Frankfurt am Main: Suhrkamp, 1977.

———, ed. *Hermeneutik und Kritik.* Frankfurt am Main: Suhrkamp, 1977, 1990.

Fredriksen, Paula. *From Jesus to Christ: The Origins of the New Testament Images of Jesus.* New Haven & London: Yale University Press, 1988.

———. "Paul and Augustine: Conversion Narratives, Orthodox Traditions, and the Retrospective Self." *JTS* 37(1986): 3–34.

Frei, Hans W. *The Eclipse of Biblical Narrative. A Study in Eighteenth and Nineteenth Century Hermeneutics.* New Haven & London: Yale University Press, 1974.

———. "Epilogue: George Lindbeck and *The Nature of Doctrine*." Bruce D. Marshall, ed. *Theology and Dialogue: Essays in Conversation with George Lindbeck.* Notre Dame: University of Notre Dame Press, 1990. 275–82.

———. *The Identity of Jesus Christ: The Hermeneutical Bases of Dogmatic Theology.* Philadelphia: Fortress, 1975.

———. "The Relation of Faith and History in the Thought of Ernst Troeltsch," in Paul Ramsey, ed., *Faith and Ethics: The Theology of H. Richard Niebuhr.* New York: Harper & Brothers, 1957. 53–64.

———. *Theology and Narrative: Selected Essays.* Edited by George Hunsinger & William C. Placher. New York & Oxford: Oxford University Press, 1993.

———. *Types of Christian Theology.* Edited by George Hunsinger & William C. Placher. New Haven & London: Yale University Press, 1992.

Frye, Northrop. *The Great Code: The Bible and Literature.* New York & London: Harcourt Brace Jovanovich, 1982.

Fuller, Daniel P. "The Resurrection of Jesus and the Historical Method." *JBR* 34(1966): 18–24.

Funk, Robert W. *Language, Hermeneutics, and the Word of God: The Problem of Language in the New Testament and Contemporary Theology.* New York, Evanston & London: Harper & Row, 1966.

———, ed. *Schleiermacher As Contemporary: Journal for Theology and the Church, 7.* New York: Herder & Herder, 1970.

Gadamer, Hans-Georg. "The Continuity of History and the Existential Moment." *PhT* 16(1972): 230–40.

———. "*Destruktion* and Deconstruction." Diane P. Michelfelder & Richard E. Palmer, eds. *Dialogue and Deconstruction: The Gadamer-Derrida Encounter.* Albany: State University of New York Press, 1989. 102–13.

———. "The Eminent Text and Its Truth." *BMMLA* 13(1980): 3–10.

———. *The Enigma of Health: The Art of Healing in a Scientific Age.* Tr. Jason Gaiger & Nicholas Walker. Cambridge: Polity Press, 1996.

———. "Grenzen der Sprache." *Evolution und Sprache: Über Entstehung und Wesen der Sprache, Herrenalber Texte* 66(1985): 89–99.

————. *Hegel's Dialectic: Five Hermeneutical Studies.* New Haven & London: Yale University Press, 1976.

————. "Hermeneutics and Social Science." *CH* 2(1975): 307–16.

————. "The Hermeneutics of Suspicion." Gary Shapiro & Alan Sica, eds. *Hermeneutics: Questions and Prospects.* Amherst: University of Massachusetts Press, 1984. 54–65.

————. "Historical Transformations of Reason." Theodore Geraets, ed. *Rationality Today.* Ottawa: University of Ottawa Press, 1979. 3–14.

————. "Notes on Planning for the Future." *Daedalus* 95(1966): 572–89.

————. *Philosophical Apprenticeships.* Tr. R. R. Sullivan. Cambridge & London: MIT Press, 1977.

————. *Philosophical Hermeneutics.* Tr. & ed. David E. Linge. Berkeley, Los Angeles & London: University of California Press, 1976.

————. "Practical Philosophy as a Model of the Human Sciences." *RP* 9(1980): 74–85.

————. "The Problem of Historical Consciousness." Paul Rabinow & William M. Sullivan, eds. *Interpretive Social Science: A Reader.* Berkeley, Los Angeles & London: University of California Press, 1979. 103–60.

————. "The Problem of Language in Schleiermacher's Hermeneutics." Robert Funk, ed. *Schleiermacher As Contemporary: Journal for Theology and the Church, 7.* New York: Herder & Herder, 1970. 68–84.

————. *Reason in the Age of Science.* Tr. Frederick G. Lawrence. Cambridge & London: MIT Press, 1981.

————. "Reflections on my Philosophical Journey." Lewis Edwin Hahn, ed. *The Philosophy of Hans-Georg Gadamer.* Library of Living Philosopher. Vol. 24. Chicago & La Salle: Open Court, 1997. 3–63.

————. *The Relevance of the Beautiful.* Tr. N. Walker & ed. Robert Bernasconi. Cambridge: Cambridge University Press, 1986.

————. "Rhetorik, Hermeneutik und Ideologiekritik." *GW*, 2:232–50.

————. "Text and Interpretation." Brice R. Wachterhauser, ed. *Hermeneutics and Modern Philosophy.* Albany: State University of New York Press, 1986. 377–96.

————. *Truth and Method.* 2d. rev. ed. & translation revision by Joel Weinsheimer & Donald G. Marshall. London: Sheed & Ward, 1975. 1989. From *Wahrheit und Method: Grundzüge einer philosophischen Hermeneutik.* 4th edition. Tübingen: J. C. B. Mohr, 1960, 1975.

————. "Truth in the Human Sciences." Brice R. Wachterhauser, ed. *Hermeneutics and Truth.* Evanston: Northwestern University Press, 1994. 25–32.

————. "What is Truth?" Brice R. Wachterhauser, ed. *Hermeneutics and Truth.* Evanston: Northwestern University Press, 1994. 33–46.

————. "Zur Phänomenologie von Ritual und Sprache." *GW*, 8:400–440.

Gager, J. G. "Some Notes on Paul's Conversion." *NTS* 27(1981): 697–704.

Gallagher, Shaun. *Hermeneutics and Education.* Albany: State University of New York Press, 1992.

Galloway, Allan D. *Wolfhart Pannenberg.* London: George Allen & Unwin, 1973.

Gamwell, Franklin I. *The Divine Good: Modern Moral Theory and the Necessity of God.* Dallas: Southern Methodist University Press, 1990.

Gardiner, Patrick. "German Philosophy and the Rise of Relativism." *Monist* 64(1981): 138–53.

Gasque, W. W. & R. P. Martin, eds. *Apostolic History and the Gospel.* Grand Rapids: Eerdmans, 1970.

Gaston, Lloyd. "Paul and the Torah." Alan T. Davies, ed. *Antisemitism and the Foundations of Christianity.* New York & Toronto: Paulist Press, 1979. 48–71.

Gaventa, Beverly R. *From Darkness to Light: Aspects of Conversion in the New Testament.* Philadelphia: Fortress, 1986.

Geertz, Clifford. *Local Knowledge: Further Essays in Interpretive Anthropology.* New York: Basic Books, 1983.

———. *The Interpretation of Cultures.* New York: Basic Books, 1973.

Gelpi, Donald L. *The Turn to Experience in Contemporary Theology.* New York & Mahwah: Paulist, 1994.

Gergen, Kenneth J. *The Saturated Self: Dilemmas of Identity in Contemporary Life.* New York: Basic Books, 1991.

Gerhart, Mary & Allan Russell. *The Metaphoric Process: The Creation of Scientific and Religious Understanding.* Fort Worth: Texas Christian University Press, 1984.

Gerkin, Charles V. *The Living Human Document: Re-visioning Pastoral Counseling in a Hermeneutical Mode.* Nashville: Abingdon, 1984.

Gerrish, B. A. *A Prince of the Church: Schleiermacher and the Beginnings of Modern Theology.* Philadelphia: Fortress, 1984.

———. "The Nature and Theater of Redemption: Schleiermacher on Christian Dogmatics and the Christian Story." *Continuing the Reformation: Essays on Modern Religious Thought.* Chicago & London: University of Chicago Press, 1993. 196–216.

———. "Ernst Troeltsch and the Possibility of a Historical Theology." John Powell Clayton, ed. *Ernst Troeltsch and the Future of Theology.* Cambridge: Cambridge University Press, 1976. 100–35.

———. "Friedrich Schleiermacher." Ninian Smart et al. *Nineteenth Century Religious Thought in the West.* 3 vols. Cambridge: Cambridge University Press, 1985. 1:123–56.

———. "From Calvin to Schleiermacher: The Theme and the Shape of Christian Dogmatics." *Continuing the Reformation: Essays on Modern Religious Thought.* Chicago & London: University of Chicago Press, 1993. 178–95.

———. "From 'Dogmatik' to 'Glaubenslehre': A Paradigm Change in Modern Theology?" Hans Küng & David Tracy, eds., *Paradigm Change in Theology: A Symposium for the Future.* New York: Crossroads, 1991, 161–73.

———. "Jesus, Myth, and History: Troeltsch's Stand in the 'Christ-Myth' Debate," *JRel* 55(1975): 13–35.

———. "Schleiermacher and the Reformation: A Question of Doctrinal Development." *The Old Protestantism and the New: Essays on the Reformation Heritage.* Edinburgh: T&T Clark, 1982. 179–95.

———. "Theology and the Historical Consciousness," and "Postscript to 'Theology and the Historical Consciousness'," in Mary Potter Engel & Walter E. Wyman, Jr., eds., *Revisioning the Past: Prospects in Historical Theology.* Minneapolis: Fortress, 1992, 281–306.

———. *Tradition and the Modern World: Reformed Theology in the Nineteenth Century.* Chicago: University of Chicago Press, 1978.

Gierke, Otto. *Natural Law and the Theory of Society, 1500–1800.* Cambridge: Cambridge University Press, 1934.

Gilkey, Langdon. "Pannenberg's *Basic Questions in Theology*: A Review Article." *Perspective* 14(1973): 34–55.

Glock, Hans-Johann. *A Wittgenstein Dictionary.* The Blackwell Philosopher Dictionary. Oxford: Blackwell, 1996.

Gogarten, Friedrich. "Wider die romantische Theologie." Jürgen Moltmann, ed. *Anfänge der dialektischen Theologie.* 2 vols. Munich: Chr. Kaiser Verlag, 1967. 2:140–53.

Goldingay, John. *Models For Scripture.* Grand Rapids: Eerdmans; Carlisle: Paternoster, 1994.

Goodman, Martin. *Mission and Conversion: Proselytizing in the Religious History of the Roman Empire.* Oxford: Clarendon Press, 1994.

Grant, Robert M. & David Tracy. *A Short History of the Interpretation of the Bible.* 2d. rev. & enl. ed. Philadelphia: Fortress, 1963, 1984.

Green, Garrett, ed. *Scriptural Authority and Narrative Interpretation*. Philadelphia: Fortress, 1987.

Green, Joel B. and Max Turner, eds. *Jesus of Nazareth: Lord and Christ: Essays on the Historical Jesus and New Testament Christology*. Grand Rapids: Eerdmans; Carlisle: Paternoster, 1994.

Grenz, Stanley J. *A Primer on Postmodernism*. Grand Rapids: Eerdmans, 1996.

————. "The Irrelevancy of Theology: Pannenberg and the Quest for Truth." *CTJ* 27(1992): 307–11.

————. *Reason for Hope: The Systematic Theology of Wolfhart Pannenberg*. New York: Oxford University Press, 1990.

————. *Revisioning Evangelical Theology: A Fresh Agenda for the 21st Century*. Downers Grove: InterVarsity Press, 1993.

————. *Theology for the Community of God*. Nashville: Broadman & Holman, 1994.

Grenz, Stanley J. & Roger E. Olson. *Twentieth-Century Theology: God & World in a Transitional Age*. Downers Grove: InterVarsity Press, 1992.

Griffin, David Ray, ed. *Varieties of Postmodern Theology*. Albany: State University of New York Press, 1989.

Grillmeier, Aloys. *Christ in Christian Tradition. Vol. I: From the Apostolic Age to Chalcedon (451)*. Tr. John Bowden. 2d. rev. ed. Atlanta: John Knox, 1975.

Grondin, Jean. "Hermeneutics and Relativism." Kathleen Wright, ed. *Festivals of Interpretation: Essays on Hans-Georg Gadamer's Work*. Albany: State University of New York Press, 1990. 42–62.

————. *Hermeneutische Wahrheit? Zum Wahrheitsbegriff Hans-Georg Gadamers*. Königstein: Forum Academicum, 1982.

————. *Introduction to Philosophical Hermeneutics*. Tr. Joel Weinsheimer. New Haven & London: Yale University Press, 1994.

————. "On the Composition of *Truth and Method*." Lawrence K. Schmidt, ed. *The Specter of Relativism: Truth, Dialogue, and* Phronesis *in Philosophical Hermeneutics*. Evanston: Northwestern University Press, 1995. 23–38.

————. *Sources of Hermeneutics*. Albany: State University of New York, 1995.

Guarino, Thomas. "Contemporary Theology and Scientific Rationality." *SR* 22(1993): 311–22.

Gundry, Robert H. "Grace, Works, and Staying Saved in Paul." *Bib* 66(1985): 1–38.

Gunton, Colin E. *A Brief Theology of Revelation*. Edinburgh: T&T Clark, 1995.

————, ed. *The Cambridge Companion to Christian Doctrine*. Cambridge: Cambridge University Press, 1997.

————. *The One, the Three and the Many: God, Creation and the Culture of Modernity*. Cambridge: Cambridge University Press, 1993.

————. *The Promise of Trinitarian Theology*. Edinburgh: T&T Clark, 1991.

————. *Yesterday & Today: A Study of Continuities in Christology*. Grand Rapids: Eerdmans, 1983.

Gustafson, James F. "The Sectarian Temptation: Reflections on Theology, the Church, and the University." *PCTS* 40(1985): 83–94.

Gutenson, Chuck. "Father, Son and Holy Spirit—The One God: An Exploration of the Trinitarian Doctrine of Wolfhart Pannenberg." *ATJ* 49(1994): 5–21.

Gutting, Gary, ed. *Paradigms and Revolutions: Appraisals and Applications of Thomas Kuhn's Philosophy of Science*. Notre Dame & London: University of Notre Dame Press, 1980.

Haacker, Klaus. "Die Berufung des Verfolgers und die Rechtfertigung des Gottlosen: Erwägungen zum Zusammenhang zwischen Biographie und Theologie des Apostels Paulus." *TB* 6(1975): 1–19.

Habermas, Jürgen. "A Review of Gadamer's *Truth and Method*." Fred Dallmayr & Thomas A. McCarthy, eds. *Understanding and Social Inquiry*. Notre Dame: University of Notre Dame Press, 1977. 335–63.

————. *On the Logic of the Social Sciences*. Tr. Shierry Weber Nicholsen & Jerry A. Stark. Cambridge: Polity Press, 1988.

————. "The Hermeneutic Claim to Universality." Joseph Bleicher, *Contemporary Hermeneutics: Hermeneutics as Method, Philosophy and Critique*. London, Boston & Henley: Routledge & Kegan Paul, 1980. 181–211.

————. "Modernity versus Post-Modernity." *NGC* 22(1981): 3–22.

————. *The Philosophical Discourse of Modernity: Twelve Lectures*. Tr. Frederick G. Lawrence. Cambridge: MIT Press, 1987, rpt. 1995.

————. *The Theory of Communicative Action*. 2 vols. Tr. Thomas A. McCarthy. Boston: Beacon Press, 1984.

Hagner, Donald A. "Paul and Judaism. The Jewish Matrix of Early Christianity: Issues in the Current Debate." *BBR* 3(1993): 111–30.

————. "Paul's Christology and Jewish Monotheism." Marguerite Shuster & Richard Muller, eds. *Perspectives on Christology: Essays in Honor of Paul K. Jewett*. Grand Rapids: Zondervan, 1991. 19–38.

Hahn, Lewis Edwin, ed. *The Philosophy of Hans-Georg Gadamer*. Library of Living Philosopher. Vol. 24. Chicago & La Salle: Open Court, 1997.

Haight, Roger. *Dynamics of Theology*. New York: Paulist, 1990.

Hall, Douglas John. *Thinking the Faith: Christian Theology in a North American Context*. Minneapolis: Augsburg, 1989.

Hamerton-Kelly, R. G. *Pre-existence, Wisdom, and the Son of Man*. SNTSMS 21. Cambridge: Cambridge University Press, 1973.

Hamilton, N. Q. *The Holy Spirit and Eschatology in Paul*. Edinburgh: Oliver Boyd, 1957.

Hamilton, Paul. *Historicism*. London & New York: Routledge, 1996.

Hamilton, William. "The Character of Pannenberg's Theology." James M. Robinson & John B. Cobb, eds. *New Frontiers in Theology. Vol. 3: Theology as History*. New York: Harper & Row, 1967. 176–96.

Hansen, G. Walter. *Abraham in Galatians: Epistolary and Rhetorical Contexts*. Sheffield: Sheffield Academic Press, 1989.

————. "Rhetorical Criticism." *DPL*, 822–26.

Hanson, Anthony T. *The Living Utterances of God: The New Testament Exegesis of the Old*. London: Darton, Longman & Todd, 1983.

————. *Studies on Paul's Technique and Theology*. Grand Rapids: Eerdmans, 1974.

Hanson, Norwood. *Patterns of Discovery*. Cambridge: Cambridge University Press, 1958.

Hanson, Richard P. C. *The Continuity of Christian Doctrine*. New York: Seabury, 1981.

————. *The New Testament Interpretation of Scripture*. London: SPCK, 1980.

————. *Tradition in the Early Church*. London: SCM, 1962.

Harder, Helmut G. & W. Taylor Stevenson. "The Continuity of History and Faith in the Theology of Wolfhart Pannenberg: Toward an Erotics of History." *JRel* 51(1971): 34–56.

Hardy, Daniel W. & David F. Ford. *Praising and Knowing God*. Philadelphia: Westminster, 1985.

Harnack, Adolf von. *History of Dogma*. 7 vols. Tr. From 3rd German ed. By Neil Buchanan. London: Williams & Norgate, 1905.

————. *What is Christianity?* Tr. Thomas Bailey Saunders. New York: Harper & Brothers, 1957.

Harré, Rom & Michael Krausz. *Varieties of Relativism*. Oxford & Cambridge: Blackwell, 1996.

Harrington, Daniel J. "The Reception of Walter Bauer's *Orthodoxy and Heresy in Earliest Christianity* During the Last Decade." *Harvard Theological Review* 73(1980): 289–98.

Harris, James F. *Against Relativism: A Philosophical Defense of Method*. LaSalle: Open Court, 1992.

Harris, Murray J. *Jesus as God: The New Testament Use of Theos in Reference to Jesus.* Grand Rapids: Baker, 1992.
Harrisville, Roy A. & Walter Sundberg. *The Bible in Modern Culture: Theology and Historical-Critical Method from Spinoza to Käsemann.* Grand Rapids: Eerdmans, 1995.
Hartman, Lars. "Early Baptism—Early Christology." Abraham J. Malherbe & Wayne Meeks, eds. *The Future of Christology: Essays in Honor of Leander E. Keck.* Minneapolis: Fortress, 1993. 191–201.
———. "'Into the Name of Jesus': A Suggestion concerning the Earliest Meaning of the Phrase." *NTS* 20(1973/4): 432–40.
Harvey, A. T. "Christ as Agent." L. D. Hurst & N. T. Wright, eds. *The Glory of Christ in the New Testament: Studies in Christology.* Oxford: Clarendon, 1987. 239–50.
Harvey, David. *The Condition of Postmodernity: An Enquiry into the Origins of Cultural Change.* 2d. ed. Oxford: Blackwell, 1989.
Harvey, Van A. "A Word in Defense of Schleiermacher's Theological Method." *JRel* 42(1962): 151–70.
———. *The Historian and the Believer.* London: SCM, 1967.
Hasel, Frank M. *Scripture in the Theologies of W. Pannenberg and D. G. Bloesch: An Investigation and Assessment of its Origin, Nature and Use.* Frankfurt am Main: Peter Lang, 1996.
Hassan, Ihab. *The Postmodern Turn: Essays in Postmodern Theory and Culture.* Columbus: Ohio State University Press, 1987.
Hauerwas, Stanley. *A Community of Character.* Notre Dame: University of Notre Dame Press, 1981.
———. "The Church as God's New Language." Garrett Green, ed. *Scriptural Authority and Narrative Interpretation.* Philadelphia: Fortress, 1987. 179–98.
———. "The Church's One Foundation is Jesus Christ Her Lord; Or, In a World Without Foundations: All We Have is the Church." in Stanley Hauerwas, Nancey Murphy & Mark Nation, eds. *Theology Without Foundations. Religious Practice & the Future of Theological Truth.* Nashville: Abingdon, 1994. 143–62.
Hauerwas, Stanley, Nancey Murphy and Mark Nation, eds. *Theology Without Foundations: Religious Practice & The Future of Theological Truth.* Nashville: Abingdon, 1994.
Hawthorne, Gerald F., Ralph P. Martin & Daniel G. Reid, eds. *Dictionary of Paul and His Letters.* Downers Grove & Leicester: InterVarsity Press, 1993.
Hay, David M., ed. *Pauline Theology, Volume II: 1 & 2 Corinthians.* Minneapolis: Fortress, 1993.
Hay, David M. & E. Elizabeth Johnson. *Pauline Theology, Volume III: Romans.* Minneapolis: Fortress, 1995.
Hays, Richard B. *Echoes of Scripture in the Letters of Paul.* New Haven & London: Yale University Press, 1989.
———. *The Faith of Jesus Christ.* Chico: Scholars Press, 1983.
Hebblethwaite, Brian. *The Incarnation: Collected Essays in Christology.* Cambridge: Cambridge University Press, 1987.
Hefner, Philip. "Theological Reflections: Questions for Moltmann and Pannenberg." *UnaS* 25(1968): 32–51.
Heidegger, Martin. *Basic Writings: From Being and Time (1927) to The Task of Thinking (1964).* Ed. F. Krell. London: Routledge & Kegan Paul, 1978.
———. *Being and Time.* Tr. John Macquarrie & Edward Robinson. Oxford & Cambridge: Blackwell, 1962, rpt. 1992.
———. *Discourse in Thinking.* New York: Harper & Row, 1966.
———. *Gesamtausgabe: Phänomenologische Interpretationen zu Aristoteles: Einführung in die phänomenologische Forschung.* Frankfurt: Klostermann, 1985.
———. *History of the Concept of Time: Prolegomena.* Tr. Theodore Kisiel. Bloomington: Indiana University Press, 1985.
———. *Ontologie: Hermeneutik der Faktizität.* Frankfurt: Klostermann, 1988.

——. "The Origin of the Work of Art." *Poetry, Language, Thought.* Tr. & intro. Albert Hofstadter. New York: Harper & Row, 1971. 15–87.

Hellwig, Monika. "Re-Emergence of the Human, Critical, Public Jesus." *TS* 50(1989): 466–80.

Helminiak, Daniel A. *The Same Jesus: A Contemporary Christology.* Chicago: Loyola University Press, 1986.

Hengel, Martin. *Between Jesus and Paul.* Philadelphia: Fortress, 1983.

——. (in collaboration with Christoph Markschies). *The "Hellenization" of Judaea in the First Century after Christ.* Tr. John Bowden. London: SCM; Philadelphia: Trinity Press International, 1989.

——. *Jews, Greeks and Barbarians.* London: SCM, 1980.

——. (in collaboration with Roland Deines). *The Pre-Christian Paul.* Tr. John Bowden. London: SCM; Philadelphia: Trinity Press International, 1991.

——. *The Zealots: Investigations into the Jewish Freedom Movement in the Period from Herod I until 70 A.D.* Edinburgh: T&T Clark, 1961, rpt. 1989.

Hengel, Martin & Anna Maria Schwemer. *Paul Between Damascus and Antioch: The Unknown Years.* Tr. John Bowden. London: SCM, 1997.

Hengel, Martin & R. Deines. "E. P. Sanders' 'Common Judaism', Jesus and the Pharisees. A Review Article." *JTS* 46(1995): 1–70.

Hensley, Jeffrey. "Are Postliberals Necessarily Antirealists? Reexamining the Metaphysics of Lindbeck's Postliberal Theology." Timothy R. Phillips & Dennis L. Okholm, eds. *The Nature of Confession: Evangelicals & Postliberals in Conversation.* Downers Grove: InterVarsity, 1996. 69–80.

Herzog, Frederick. *Understanding God.* New York: Scribner's, 1966.

Hesse, Mary. *Revolutions and Reconstructions in the Philosophy of Science.* Bloomington: Indiana University Press, 1980.

Hick, John. *God Has Many Names.* London: Macmillan, 1980.

——. *The Metaphor of God Incarnate.* London: SCM, 1993.

——, ed. *The Myth of God Incarnate.* Philadelphia: Westminster, 1977.

——. "Towards a Philosophy of Religious Pluralism." *NZTR* 22(1980): 131–49.

——. "Whatever Path Men Choose is Mine." John Hick & Brian Hebblethwaite, eds. *Christianity and Other Religions.* Philadelphia: Fortress, 1981. 171–90.

Hickling, C. J. A. "Center and Periphery in Paul's Thought." E. A. Livingstone, ed. *Studia Biblica III: Papers on Paul and Other NT Authors.* Sheffield: Academic Press, 1978. 199–214.

High, Dallas M. *Language, Persons, and Belief: Studies in Wittgenstein's* Philosophical Investigations *and Religious Uses of Language.* New York: Oxford University Press, 1967.

Higton, Mike. "Frei's Christology and Lindbeck's Cultural-Linguistic Theory." *SJT* 50(1997): 83–95.

Hiley, David R., James F. Bohman & Richard Shusterman, eds. *The Interpretive Turn: Philosophy, Science, Culture.* Ithaca & London: Cornell University Press, 1991.

Himes, Michael J. "The Ecclesiological Significance of the Reception of Doctrine." *HeyJ* 33(1992): 146–60.

Hinman, Lawrence. "Quid Facti or Quid Juris? The Fundamental Ambiguity of Gadamer's Understanding of Hermeneutics." *PPR* 40(1980): 512–35.

Hinton, Rory A. A. "Pannenberg on the Truth of Christian Discourse: A Logical Response." *CTJ* 27(1992): 312–18.

Hinze, Bradford E. *Narrating History, Developing Doctrine: Friedrich Schleiermacher and Johann Sebastian Drey.* Atlanta: Scholars Press, 1993.

——. "Narrative Contexts, Doctrinal Reform." *TS* 51(1990): 417–33.

Hirsch, E. D. *Validity in Interpretation.* New Haven: Yale University Press, 1967.

Hodgson, Peter C. *Jesus—Word and Presence: An Essay in Christology.* Philadelphia: Fortress, 1971.

——. *God in History: Shapes of Freedom.* Nashville: Abingdon, 1989.

Hodgson, Peter C. and Robert H. King, eds. *Christian Theology: An Introduction to Its Traditions and Tasks*, 2d. & enlarged ed. Philadelphia: Fortress, 1982, 1985.

Hogan, John P. *Collingwood and Theological Hermeneutics*. Lanham: University Press of America, 1989.

———. "Hermeneutics and the Logic of Question and Answer: Collingwood and Gadamer." *HeyJ* 28(1987): 263–84.

———. "The Historical Imagination and the New Hermeneutic: Collingwood and Pannenberg." Robert Masson, ed. *The Pedagogy of God's Image*. Chico: Scholars Press, 1981. 9–30.

Holleman, Warren Lee. "Schleiermacher's Liberalism." *JTSA* 62(1988): 29–42.

Hollinger, Robert, ed. *Hermeneutics and Praxis*. Notre Dame: University of Notre Dame Press, 1985.

Holmer, Paul. *The Grammar of Faith*. New York: Harper & Row, 1978.

Holub, Robert C. "Constance School of Reception Aesthetics." Irena R. Makaryk, ed., *Encyclopedia of Contemporary Literary Theory: Approaches, Scholars, Terms*. Toronto: University of Toronto Press, 1993. 14–18.

———. *Reception Theory: A Critical Introduction*. London: Methuen, 1984.

Holwerda, David E. "Faith, Reason, and the Resurrection in the Theology of Wolfhart Pannenberg." Alvin Plantinga & Nicholas Wolterstorff, eds. *Faith and Rationality: Reason and Belief in God*. Notre Dame & London: University of Notre Dame Press, 1983. 265–316.

———. *Jesus & Israel: One Covenant or Two?* Grand Rapids: Eerdmans, 1995.

Hooker, Morna D. "Beyond the Things that are Written? Saint Paul's Use of Scripture." G. K. Beale, ed. *The Right Doctrine from the Wrong Texts? Essays on the Use of the Old Testament in the New*. Grand Rapids: Baker, 1994. 279–94.

———. *Continuity and Discontinuity: Early Christianity in its Jewish Setting*. London: Epworth, 1986.

———. *From Adam to Christ: Essays on Paul*. Cambridge: Cambridge University Press, 1990.

Howell, Jr., Don N. "God-Christ Interchange in Paul: Impressive Testimony to the Deity of Jesus." *JETS* 36(1993): 467–79.

Hoy, David Couzens. *The Critical Circle: Literature, History, and Philosophical Hermeneutics*. Berkeley, Los Angeles & London: University of California Press, 1978.

———. "Taking History Seriously: Foucault, Gadamer, Habermas." *USQR* 34(1979): 85–95.

Hoyningen-Huene, Paul. *Reconstructing Scientific Revolutions: Thomas S. Kuhn's Philosophy of Science*. Chicago: University of Chicago Press, 1993.

Hübner, Hans. "Pauli Theologiae Proprium." *NTS* 26(1979–80): 445–73.

Hultgren, Arland J. *Paul's Gospel and Mission*. Philadelphia: Fortress, 1985.

———. *The Rise of Normative Christianity*. Minneapolis: Fortress, 1994.

Hurtado, Larry W. "Convert, Apostate or Apostle to the Nations: The 'Conversion' of Paul in Recent Scholarship." *SR* 22(1993): 273–84.

———. *One God, One Lord: Early Christian Devotion and Ancient Jewish Monotheism*. Philadelphia: Fortress, 1988.

Husserl, Edmund. *Crisis of European Science and Transcendental Phenomenology*. Tr. David Carr. Evanston: Northwestern University Press, 1970.

Iggers, Georg G. "Historicism: The History and Meaning of the Term." *JHI* 56(1995): 129–52.

Jackson, Timothy P. "Against Grammar" in "The Nature of Doctrine: Religion and Theology in a Postliberal Age." *RSR* 11(1985): 240–45.

Jameson, Frederic. *Postmodernism: Or, The Cultural Logic of Late Capitalism*. Durham: Duke University Press, 1991.

Jasper, David, ed. *The Interpretation of Belief: Coleridge, Schleiermacher and Romanticism*. New York: St Martin's Press, 1986.

Jauss, Hans Robert. *Aesthetic Experience and Literary Hermeneutics.* Minneapolis: University of Minnesota Press, 1982.
———. *Question and Answer: Forms of Dialogic Understanding.* Minneapolis: University of Minnesota Press, 1989.
———. "The Theory of Reception: A Retrospective of its Unrecognized Prehistory." Peter Collier & Helga Geyer-Ryan, eds. *Literary Theory Today.* Oxford: Polity Press, 1990. 53–73.
———. *Toward an Aesthetic of Reception.* Tr. Timothy Bahti. Minneapolis: University of Minnesota Press, 1982.
Jay, Martin. "Should Intellectual History Take a Linguistic Turn? Reflections on the Habermas-Gadamer Debate." Dominick LaCapra & Steven L. Kaplan, eds. *Modern European Intellectual History: Reappraisals and New Perspectives.* Ithaca: Cornell University Press, 1982. 86–110.
Jeanrond, Werner G. *Text and Interpretation as Categories of Theological Thinking.* Tr. Thomas J. Wilson. New York: Crossroad, 1988.
———. "The Impact of Schleiermacher's Hermeneutics on Contemporary Interpretation Theory." David Jasper, ed. *The Interpretation of Belief: Coleridge, Schleiermacher and Romanticism.* New York: St Martin's Press, 1986. 81–96.
———. *Theological Hermeneutics: Development and Significance.* London: SCM, 1991, 1994.
Jenson, Robert W. "Jesus in the Trinity: Wolfhart Pannenberg's Christology and Doctrine of the Trinity." Carl E. Braaten & Philip Clayton, eds. *The Theology of Wolfhart Pannenberg: Twelve American Critiques, with an Autobiographical Essay and Response.* Minneapolis: Augsburg, 1988. 188–206.
———. *The Triune Identity: God According to the Gospel.* Philadelphia: Fortress, 1982.
Jentz, Jr., Arthur H. "Personal Freedom and the Futurity of God: Some Reflections on Pannenberg's 'God of Hope'." *RR* 31(1978): 148–54.
Jeremias, Joachim. *The Central Message of the New Testament.* London: SCM, 1965.
———. "Paul and James." *ExpT* 66(1955): 368–71.
Jervis, L. A. *The Purpose of Romans.* Sheffield: Sheffield Academic Press, 1991.
Jewett, Robert. "The Basic Human Dilemma: Weakness or Zealous Violence? Romans 7:7–25 and 10:1–18." *EA* 13(1997): 96–109.
Jodock, Darrell. "The Reciprocity Between Scripture and Theology: The Role of Scripture in Contemporary Theological Reflection." *Int* 44(1990): 369–82.
Johnson, Elizabeth A. *Analogy/Doxology and Their Connection with Christology in the Thought of Wolfhart Pannenberg.* Ph.D. diss., Catholic University of America, 1981.
———. "The Ongoing Christology of Wolfhart Pannenberg." *Horizons* 9(1982): 237–50.
Johnston, Robert K. "God in the Midst of Life: The spirit and the Spirit." *EA* 12(1996): 76–93.
———. *The Use of the Bible in Theology: Evangelical Options.* Atlanta: John Knox, 1985.
Jüngel, Eberhard. *The Doctrine of the Trinity: God's Being is in Becoming.* Grand Rapids: Eerdmans, 1976.
———. "The Dogmatic Significance of the Question of the Historical Jesus." *Theological Essays II.* Edited by J. B. Webster. Tr. Arnold Neufeldt-Fast and J. B. Webster. Edinburgh: T&T Clark, 1995. 82–119.
———. *God as the Mystery of the World.* Grand Rapids: Eerdmans, 1983.
Kähler, Martin. *The So-Called Historical Jesus and the Historic Biblical Christ.* Ed. Ernst Wolf. Tr. Carl Braaten. Philadelphia: Fortress, 1964.
Kallenberg, Brad J. "Unstuck From Yale: Theological Method After Lindbeck." *SJT* 50(1997): 191–218.
Käsemann, Ernst. *New Testament Questions of Today.* Philadelphia: Fortress, 1969.
Kaufman, Gordan. *An Essay on Theological Method.* 2d. ed. Missoula: Scholars Press, 1979.
———. *The Theological Imagination.* Philadelphia: Westminster, 1981.

Kaufmann, Walter, ed. & tr. *The Basic Writings of Nietzsche*. New York: Modern Library, 1969.

———, ed. *The Portable Nietzsche*. New York: Penguin, 1976.

Keck, Leander E. "Paul and Apocalyptic Theology." *Int* 38(1984): 229–41.

———. "Paul as Thinker." *Int* 47(1993): 27–38.

Kellenberger, J. *The Cognitivity of Religion: Three Perspectives*. Berkeley & Los Angeles: University of California Press, 1985.

Kelly, J. N. D. *Early Christian Doctrines*. New York: Harper & Row, 1960.

Kelsey, David H. *The Uses of Scripture in Recent Theology*. Philadelphia: Fortress, 1975.

Kenneson, Philip D. "The Alleged Incorrigibility of Postliberal Theology, Or What Babe Ruth & George Lindbeck Have in Common." Timothy R. Phillips & Dennis L. Okholm, eds. *The Nature of Confession: Evangelicals & Postliberals in Conversation*. Downers Grove: InterVarsity, 1996. 93–106.

Ker, Ian T. *The Achievement of John Henry Newman*. London: Collins, 1990.

Kerr, Fergus. *Theology after Wittgenstein*. Oxford: Basil Blackwell, 1986.

Kim, Seyoon. *The Origin of Paul's Gospel*. Grand Rapids: Eerdmans, 1981.

———. "2 Cor. 5:11–21 and the Origin of Paul's Concept of 'Reconciliation'." *NovT* 39(1997): 360–84.

Kimmerle, Heinz. "Hermeneutical Theory or Ontological Hermeneutics." *Journal for Theology and the Church, 4: History and Hermeneutic*. Tübingen: Mohr; New York: Harper & Row, 1967. 107–21.

Kirkham, Richard L. *Theories of Truth: A Critical Introduction*. Cambridge & London: MIT Press, 1995.

Kisiel, Theodore. "The Happening of Tradition: The Hermeneutics of Gadamer and Heidegger." Robert Hollinger, ed. *Hermeneutics and Praxis*. Notre Dame: University of Notre Dame Press, 1985.

Klemm, David E. *The Hermeneutical Theory of Paul Ricoeur: A Constructive Analysis*. Lewisburg: Bucknell University Press; London & Toronto: Associated University Presses, 1983.

Klooster, Fred H. "Aspects of Historical Method in Pannenberg's Theology." J. T. Bakker *et al.*, eds. *Septuagesimo Anno: Festschrift for G. C. Berkouwer*. Kampen: Kok, 1973. 112–28.

Knitter, Paul F. *No Other Name? A Critical Survey of Christian Attitudes Toward the World Religions*. Maryknoll: Orbis, 1985.

Knox, John. *The Church and the Reality of Christ*. New York: Harper & Row, 1962.

Koch, Kurt. *Der Gott der Geschichte: Theologie der Geschichte bei Wolfhart Pannenberg als Paradigma einer philosophischen Theologie in ökumenischer Perspektive*. Mainz: Matthias Grünewald Verlag, 1988.

Kögler, Hans Herbert. *The Power of Dialogue: Critical Hermeneutics after Gadamer and Foucault*. Tr. Paul Hendrickson. Cambridge & London: MIT Press, 1996.

Köhler, Walter. *Ernst Troeltsch*. Tübingen: J. C. B. Mohr (Paul Siebeck), 1941.

Kordig, Carl R. *The Justification of Scientific Change*. Dordrecht: D. Reidel, 1971.

Krasevac, Edward L. "'Christology from Above' and 'Christology from Below'." *Thomist* 51(1987): 299–306.

Kreitzer, L. Joseph. *Jesus and God in Paul's Eschatology*. Sheffield: Academic Press, 1987.

Kuhn, Thomas S. *The Essential Tension: Selected Studies in Scientific Tradition and Change*. Chicago & London: University of Chicago Press, 1977.

———. *The Structure of Scientific Revolutions*. 2d. ed. Chicago: University of Chicago Press, 1962, 1970.

Küng, Hans. *Great Christian Thinkers*. Tr. John Bowden. London: SCM, 1994.

———. *On Being a Christian*. Tr. Edward Quinn. London: Collins, 1977.

Küng, Hans & David Tracy, eds. *Paradigm Change in Theology: A Symposium for the Future*. Tr. Margaret Köhl. New York: Crossroad, 1991.

Kuschel, Karl-Josef. *Born Before All Time? The Dispute over Christ's Origin*. Tr. John Bowden. New York: Crossroad, 1992.

Lakatos, Imre & Alan Musgrave, eds. *Criticism and the Growth of Knowledge*. Cambridge: Cambridge University Press, 1970.

Lambrecht, J. "Paul's Christological Use of Scripture in 1 Cor. 15:20–28," *NTS* 28(1982): 502–27.

Lamm, Julia A. "The Early Philosophical Roots of Schleiermacher's Notion of *Gefühl*, 1788–1794." *HTR* 87(1994): 67–105.

Lammi, Walter. "Hans-Georg Gadamer's 'Correction' of Heidegger." *JHI* 52(1991): 487–507.

Lane, Anthony N. S. "Scripture, Tradition and Church: An Historical Survey." *VE* 9(1975): 37–55.

————. "*Sola Scriptura?* Making Sense of a Post-Reformation Slogan." Philip E. Satterthwaite & David F. Wright, eds., *A Pathway into the Holy Scripture*. Grand Rapids: Eerdmans, 1994. 297–327.

Langford, Thomas A. "Michael Polanyi and the Task of Theology." *JRel* 46(1966): 45–55.

Lash, Nicholas. *The Beginning and the End of "Religion"*. Cambridge: Cambridge University Press, 1996.

————. *Change in Focus: A Study of Doctrinal Change and Continuity*. London: Sheed & Ward, 1973.

————. *Easter in Ordinary: Reflections on Human Experience and the Knowledge of God*. Notre Dame & London: University of Notre Dame Press, 1986.

————. *Newman on Development: The Search for an Explanation in History*. Shepherdstown: Patmos Press, 1975.

————. *Theology on the Way to Emmaus*. London: SCM, 1986.

————. "Up and Down in Christology." Stephen Sykes & Derek Holmes, eds. *New Studies in Theology*. London: Duckworth, 1980. 31–46.

Laudan, Larry. *Progress and Its Problems*. Berkeley: University of California Press, 1977.

Lawrence, Frederick. "Responses to 'Hermeneutics and Social Science'." *CH* 2(1975): 321–25.

Lawson, Hilary & Lisa Appignansesi, eds. *Dismantling Truth: Reality in the Post-Modern World*. New York: St Martin's Press, 1989.

Lentricchia, Frank. *After the New Criticism*. Chicago: University of Chicago Press, 1980.

Lessing, G. E. *Lessing's Theological Writings: Selections in Translation with an Introductory Essay*. Tr. Henry Chadwick. London: A & C Black; Stanford: Stanford University Press, 1956.

Liechty, Daniel. *Theology in a Postliberal Perspective*. London: SCM; Philadelphia: Trinity Press International, 1990.

Lindars, Barnabas. *New Testament Apologetic: The Doctrinal Significance of the Old Testament Quotations*. London: SCM, 1961.

Lindbeck, George A. "Atonement & The Hermeneutics of Intratextual Social Embodiment." Timothy R. Phillips & Dennis L. Okholm, eds. *The Nature of Confession: Evangelicals & Postliberals in Conversation*. Downers Grove: InterVarsity, 1996. 221–40.

————. "The Church's Mission to a Postmodern Culture." Frederic B. Burnham, ed. *Postmodern Theology: Christian Faith in a Pluralist World*. New York: Harper & Row, 1989. 37–55.

————. *The Nature of Doctrine: Religion and Theology in a Postliberal Age*. Philadelphia: Westminster Press, 1984.

————. "The Story-shaped Church: Exegesis and Theological Interpretation." Garrett Green, ed. *Scriptural Authority and Narrative Interpretation*. Philadelphia: Fortress, 1987. 161–78.

Loader, W. R. G. "Christ at the Right Hand: Ps. 110:1 in the NT." *NTS* 24(1977–8): 199–217.

Lobkowicz, Nicholas. *Theory and Practice: History of a Concept from Aristotle to Marx.* Notre Dame: University of Notre Dame Press, 1967.

Longenecker, Richard N. *Biblical Exegesis in the Apostolic Period.* Grand Rapids: Eerdmans, 1975.

———. *The Christology of Early Jewish Christianity.* Grand Rapids: Baker, 1970.

———, ed. *The Road from Damascus: The Impact of Paul's Conversion on His Life, Thought, and Ministry.* Grand Rapids & Cambridge: Eerdmans, 1997.

Lornegan, Bernard. *Method in Theology.* New York: Herder & Herder, 1972.

Loughlin, Gerard. *Telling God's Story: Bible, Church and Narrative Theology.* Cambridge: Cambridge University Press, 1996.

Louth, Andrew. *Discerning the Mystery.* Oxford: Oxford University Press, 1983.

Lovering, Eugene H., Jr. & Jerry L. Sumney. *Theology and Ethics in Paul and His Interpreters: Essays in Honor of Victor Paul Furnish.* Nashville: Abingdon, 1996.

Lowe, John. "An Attempt to Detect Development in St Paul's Theology." *JTS* 42(1941): 129–42.

Lundin, Roger. *The Culture of Interpretation: Christian Faith and the Postmodern World.* Grand Rapids: Eerdmans, 1993.

———, ed. *Disciplining Hermeneutics: Interpretation in Christian Perspective.* Grand Rapids: Eerdmans, 1997.

———. "The Pragmatics of Postmodernity." Timothy R. Phillips & Dennis L. Okholm, eds. *Christian Apologetics in the Postmodern World.* Downers Grove: Inter-Varsity Press, 1995. 24–38.

Luntley, Michael. *Reason, Truth and Self: The Postmodern Reconditioned.* London & New York: Routledge, 1995.

Lüthi, Kurth. *Feminismus und Romantik: Sprache, Gellschaft. Symbole, Religion.* Wien u.a.: Böhlau, 1985.

Lyon, David. *Postmodernity.* Buckingham: Open University Press, 1994.

Lyotard, Jean-François. *The Postmodern Condition: A Report on Knowledge.* Tr. Geoff Bennington & Brian Massumi. Minneapolis: University of Minnesota Press, 1984.

MacIntyre, Alasdair. "Epistemological Crises, Dramatic Narrative, and the Philosophy of Science." Gary Gutting, ed. *Paradigms and Revolutions: Appraisals and Applications of Thomas Kuhn's Philosophy of Science.* Notre Dame & London: University of Notre Dame Press, 1980. 54–74.

———. *After Virtue: A Study in Moral Theory.* 2d. ed. Notre Dame: University of Notre Dame Press, 1981, 1984.

MacKinnon, D. M. "'Substance' in Christology—A Cross-bench View." S. W. Sykes & J. P. Clayton, eds. *Christ, Faith and History: Cambridge Studies in Christology.* Cambridge: Cambridge University Press, 1972. 279–300.

Macquarrie, John. *Contemporary Religious Thinkers: From Idealist Metaphysicians to Existential Theologians.* London: SCM, 1968.

———. "Doctrinal Development: Searching for Criteria." Sarah Coakley & David A. Pailin, eds. *The Making and Remaking of Christian Doctrine: Essays in Honour of Maurice Wiles.* Oxford: Clarendon Press, 1993. 161–76.

———. *Jesus Christ in Modern Thought.* London: SCM; Philadelphia: Trinity Press International, 1990.

———. *Studies in Christian Existentialism.* London: SCM, 1965.

———. "Tradition, Truth and Christology." *HeyJ* 21(1980): 365–75.

———. "Truth in Theology." *Thinking about God.* London: SCM, 1975. 15–27.

Madison, G. B. *The Hermeneutics of Postmodernity: Figures and Themes.* Bloomington & Indianapolis: Indiana University Press, 1988.

Maddox, Randy L. "Contemporary Hermeneutic Philosophy and Theological Studies." *RelS* 21(1985): 517–29.

Makaryk, Irena R., ed. *Encyclopedia of Contemporary Literary Theory: Approaches, Scholars, Terms.* Toronto: University of Toronto Press, 1993.

Mariña, Jacqueline. "Schleiermacher's Christology Revisited: A Reply to His Critics." *SJT* 49(1996): 177–200.

Marshall, Bruce D. "Absorbing the World: Christianity and the Universe of Truths." Bruce D. Marshall, ed. *Theology as Dialogue: Essays in Conversation with George Lindbeck.* Notre Dame: University of Notre Dame Press, 1990. 69–102.

———. "Aquinas as Postliberal Theologian." *Thomist* 53(1989): 353–402.

———. "Hermeneutics and Dogmatics in Schleiermacher's Theology." *JRel* 67(1987): 14–32.

———, ed. *Theology as Dialogue: Essays in Conversation with George Lindbeck.* Notre Dame: University of Notre Dame Press, 1990.

———. "'We Shall Bear the Image of the Man of Heaven': Theology and the Concept of Truth." *MTh* 11(1995): 93–117.

Marshall, I. Howard. *The Origins of New Testament Christology.* Downers Grove: Inter-Varsity, 1976.

———. "Orthodoxy and Heresy in Earlier Christianity." *Them* 2(1976): 5–14.

Martin, Ralph P. *Reconciliation: A Study of Paul's Theology.* Rev. ed. Grand Rapids: Zondervan, 1990.

Martyn, J. Louis. "A Law-observant Mission to Gentiles: The Background of Galatians." *SJT* 38(1985): 307–24.

———. "Epistemology at the Turn of the Ages." *Theological Issues in the Letters of Paul.* Edinburgh: T&T Clark, 1997. 89–110.

Masterman, Margaret. "The Nature of a Paradigm." Imre Lakatos & Alan Musgrave, eds. *Criticism and the Growth of Knowledge.* Cambridge: Cambridge University Press, 1970. 59–89.

Matlock, R. Barry. *Unveiling the Apocalyptic Paul: Paul's Interpreters and the Rhetoric of Criticism.* Sheffield: Sheffield Academic Press, 1996.

McDermott, Brian. "Pannenberg's Resurrection Christology: A Critique." *TS* 35(1974): 711–721.

McFague, Sallie T. *Metaphorical Theology: Models of God in Religious Language.* Philadelphia: Fortress, 1982.

———. "The Theologian as Advocate." Sarah Coakley & David A. Pailin, eds. *The Making and Remaking of Christian Doctrine: Essays in Honour of Maurice Wiles.* Oxford: Clarendon, 1993. 143–59.

McGinley, John. "Heidegger's Concern for the Lived-World in his Dasein-Analysis." *PT* 16(1972): 92–116.

McGrath, Alister E. *A Passion for Truth: The Intellectual Coherence of Evangelicalism.* Leicester: Apollos, 1996.

———, ed. *Encyclopedia of Modern Christian Throught.* Oxford: Basil Blackwell, 1993.

———. *The Genesis of Doctrine: A Study in the Foundations of Doctrinal Criticism.* Oxford: Basil Blackwell, 1990.

———. *Iustitia Dei: A History of the Christian Doctrine of Justification. Vol. 2: From 1500 to the Present Day.* Cambridge: Cambridge University Press, 1986.

———. *The Making of Modern German Christology 1750–1990.* 2d. ed. Leicester: Apollos; Grand Rapids: Zondervan, 1987, 1994.

———. "Theology and Experience: Reflections on Cognitive and Experiential Approaches to Theology." *EJT* 2(1993): 65–74.

McHaan, Jr., James Clark. *The Three Horizons: A Study in Biblical Hermeneutics with Special Reference to Wolfhart Pannenberg.* Ph.D. diss., University of Aberdeen, 1987.

McIntosh, Mark A. *Christology From Within: Spirituality and the Incarnation in Hans Urs Von Balthasar.* Notre Dame: University of Notre Dame Press, 1996.

McKenzie, David M. *Wolfhart Pannenberg and Religious Philosophy.* Washington, D.C.: University Press of America, 1980.

McKnight, Scot. *A Light Among the Gentiles: Jewish Missionary Activity in the Second Temple Period.* Minneapolis: Fortress, 1991.

Meeks, M. Douglas. *Origins of the Theology of Hope.* Philadelphia: Fortress, 1974.

Megill, Allan. *Prophets of Extremity: Nietzsche, Heidegger, Foucault, Derrida.* Berkeley, Los Angeles, London: University of California Press, 1985.

Mendelson, Jack. "The Habermas-Gadamer Debate." *NGC* 18(1979): 44–73.

Mendieta, Eduardo. "Metaphysics of Subjectivity and the Theology of Subjectivity: Schleiermacher's Anthropological Theology." *Ph&T* 6(1992): 276–90.

———, ed. *Karl-Otto Apel: Selected Essays, Volume One: Towards a Transcendental Semiotics.* New Jersey: Humanities Press, 1994.

———. "Metaphysics of Subjectivity and the Theology of Subjectivity: Schleiermacher's Anthropological Theology." *Ph&T* 6(1992): 276–90.

Messer, Stanley B., Louis A. Sass & Robert L. Woolfolk, eds. *Hermeneutics and Psychological Theory: Interpretive Perspectives on Personality, Psychotherapy, and Psychopathology.* New Brunswick & London: Rutgers University Press, 1988.

Meyer, Ben. *The Early Christians: Their World Mission and Self-discovery.* Wilmington: Michael Glazier, 1986.

Michalson, Gordon E., Jr. "Faith and History." Alister E. McGrath, ed., *The Blackwell Encyclopedia of Modern Christian Thought.* Oxford: Blackwell, 1993. 210–14.

———. *Lessing's "Ugly Ditch": A Study of Theology and History.* University Park & London: Pennsylvania State University Press, 1985.

———. "Pannenberg on the Resurrection and Historical Method." *SJT* 33(1980): 345–59.

Michelfelder, Diane P. & Richard E. Palmer, eds. & trs. *Dialogue and Deconstruction: The Gadamer-Derrida Encounter.* Albany: State University of New York Press, 1989.

Middleton, J. Richard & Brian J. Walsh. *Truth is Stranger Than It Used to Be: Biblical Faith in a Postmodern Age.* Downers Grove: InterVarsity Press, 1995.

Milbank, John. *Theology & Social Theory: Beyond Secular Reason.* Oxford & Cambridge: Blackwell, 1990.

Mills, Watson E. *An Index to the Periodical Literature on the Apostle Paul.* Leiden: E. J. Brill, 1993.

Moltmann, Jürgen. *The Crucified God: The Cross of Christ as the Foundation and Criticism of Christian Theology.* London: SCM, 1974.

———. *The Trinity and the Kingdom of God.* Tr. Margaret Kohl. San Francisco: Harper & Row, 1981.

———. *The Way of Jesus Christ: Christology in Messianic Dimensions.* Tr. Margaret Kohl. San Francisco: Harper, 1990.

Moores, John D. *Wrestling with Rationality in Paul: Romans 1–8 in a New Perspective.* SNTSMS 82. Cambridge: Cambridge University Press, 1995.

Morgan, Robert & Michael Pye, eds. & trs. *Ernst Troeltsch: Writings on Theology and Religion.* London: Duckworth, 1977.

Moule, C. F. D. *The Origin of Christology.* Cambridge: Cambridge University Press, 1977.

Muller, Richard A. "The Christological Problem as Addressed by Friedrich Schleiermacher: A Dogmatic Query." Marguerite Shuster & Richard Muller, eds. *Perspectives on Christology: Essays in Honor of Paul K. Jewett.* Grand Rapids: Zondervan, 1991. 141–62.

———. *Dictionary of Latin and Greek Theological Terms: Drawn Principally from Protestant Scholastic Theology.* Grand Rapids: Baker, 1985.

———. *Post-Reformation Reformed Dogmatics. Vol. 1: Prolegomena to Theology.* Grand Rapids: Baker, 1987.

Munck, Johannes. *Paul and the Salvation of Mankind.* London: SCM, 1959.

Murdock, William P. "History and Revelation in Jewish Apocalypticism." *Int* 21(1967): 167–87.

Murphy, Nancey. *Beyond Liberalism & Fundamentalism: How Modern and Postmodern Philosophy set the Theological Agenda*. Valley Forge: Trinity Press International, 1996.

———. *Theology in the Age of Scientific Reasoning*. Ithaca & London: Cornell University Press, 1990.

———. "What Has Theology to Learn from Scientific Methodology?" Murray Rae, Hilary Regan & John Stenhouse, eds. *Science and Theology: Questions at the Interface*. Edinburgh: T&T Clark, 1994. 101–126.

Murphy, Nancey & James W. McClendon, Jr. "Distinguishing Modern and Postmodern Theologies." *MTh* 5(1989): 191–214.

Murphy-O'Connor, Jerome. *Paul: A Critical Life*. Oxford: Clarendon Press, 1996.

———. "Paul in Arabia." *CBQ* 55(1993): 732–37.

Musgrave, Alan. *Common Sense, Science and Scepticism: A Historical Introduction to the Theory of Knowledge*. Cambridge: Cambridge University Press, 1993.

Neie, Herbert. *The Doctrine of the Atonement in the Theology of Wolfhart Pannenberg*. Berlin & New York: Walter de Gruyter, 1979.

Neill, Stephen & Tom Wright. *The Interpretation of the New Testament: 1861–1986*. Oxford & New York: Oxford University Press, 1988.

Neufeld, Vernon H. *The Earliest Christian Confessions*. Grand Rapids: Eerdmans, 1963.

Neuhaus, Richard John. "Reason Public and Private: The Pannenberg Project," *FT* 21(1992): 55–60.

———. "Theology for Church and Polis." Carl E. Braaten & Philip Clayton, eds. *The Theology of Wolfhart Pannenberg: Twelve American Critiques, with an Autobiographical Essay and Response*. Minneapolis: Augsburg, 1988. 226–38.

———. "Wolfhart Pannenberg: Profile of a Theologian." Wolfhart Pannenberg. *Theology and the Kingdom of God*. Philadelphia: Westminster, 1969. 9–50.

Nevin, Michael. "Analogy: Aquinas and Pannenberg." Stanley J. Porter, ed. *The Nature of Religious Language: A Colloquium*. Sheffield: Sheffield Academic Press, 1996. 201–11.

Newlands, George. *Generosity and the Christian Future*. London: SPCK, 1997.

Newman, Carey C. *Paul's Glory-Christology: Tradition and Rhetoric*. Leiden: E. J. Brill, 1992.

Newman, John Henry. *An Essay in Aid of a Grammar of Assent*. Notre Dame: University of Notre Dame Press, 1979.

———. "An Essay on the Development of Christian Doctrine." *Conscience, Consensus, and the Development of Doctrine*. New York: Image Books, Doubleday, 1992. 38–385.

Nichols, Aidan. *A Grammar of Consent: The Existence of God in Christian Tradition*. Edinburgh: T&T Clark, 1991.

———. *From Newman to Congar: The Idea of Doctrinal Development from the Victorians to the Second Vatican Council*. Edinburgh: T&T Clark, 1990.

Nicol, Iain G. "Facts and Meanings: Wolfhart Pannenberg's Theology as History and the Role of the Historical-Critical Method." *RelS* 12(1976): 129–39.

Niebuhr, Richard R. *Schleiermacher on Christ and Religion*. New York: Scribners, 1964; London: SCM, 1965.

Nnamdi, Reginald. *Offenbarung und Geschichte: Zur hermeneutischen Bestimmung der Theologie Wolfhart Pannenbergs*. Frankfurt/Main: Peter Lang, 1993.

Norris, Christopher. *The Truth about Postmodernism*. Oxford: Blackwell, 1993.

———. *Reclaiming Truth: Contribution to a Critique of Cultural Relativism*. London: Lawrence & Wishart, 1996.

Norris, Frederick W. "Ignatius, Polycarp, and I Clement: Walter Bauer Reconsidered." *VC* 30(1976): 23–44.

Obayashi, Hiroshi. "Pannenberg and Troeltsch: History and Religion." *JAAR* 38(1970): 401–19.

Obitts, Stanley. "Apostolic Eyewitnesses and Proleptically Historical Revelation."

Morris Inch & Ronald Youngblood, eds. *The Living and Active Word of God.* Winono Lake: Eisenbrauns, 1983. 137–148.

O'Brien, Peter T. *Colossians, Philemon.* Word Biblical Commentary. Waco: Word, 1982.

————. *Gospel and Mission in the Writings of Paul: An Exegetical and Theological Analysis.* Grand Rapids: Baker; Carlisle: Paternoster, 1993, 1995.

O'Collins, Gerald. *Christology: A Biblical, Historical, and Systematic Study of Jesus.* Oxford: Oxford University Press, 1995.

————. "The Christology of Wolfhart Pannenberg." *RelS* 3(1967): 369–76.

————. *What Are They Saying About Jesus?* New York: Paulist, 1977.

Oden, Thomas C. *After Modernity . . . What? Agenda for Theology.* Grand Rapids: Zondervan, 1990.

O'Donnell, John. "Pannenberg's Doctrine of God." *Greg* 72(1991): 73–98.

Olive, Don H. *Wolfhart Pannenberg.* Waco: Word, 1973.

Olson, Roger E. "The Human Self-Realization of God: Hegelian Elements in Pannenberg's Christology." *PRS* 13(1986): 207–23.

————. "Trinity and Eschatology: The Historical Being of God in Jürgen Moltmann and Wolfhart Pannenberg." *SJT* 36(1983): 213–27.

————. "Wolfhart Pannenberg's Doctrine of the Trinity." *SJT* 43(1990): 175–206.

Ommen, Thomas B. *The Hermeneutic of Dogma.* Missoula: Scholars Press, 1975.

————. "Theology & The Fusion of Horizons." *Ph&T* 3(1988): 57–72.

O'Neill, Colman E. "The Rule Theory of Doctrine and Propositional Truth." *Thomist* 49(1985): 417–42.

Ormiston, Gayle L. & Alan D. Schrift, eds. *The Hermeneutic Tradition: From Ast to Ricoeur.* Albany: State University of New York Press, 1990.

Osborn, Robert T. "Christian Faith as Personal Knowledge." *SJT* 28(1975): 101–26.

Ottati, Douglas F. *Jesus Christ and Christian Vision.* Minneapolis: Fortress, 1989.

Pailin, David A. "Lessing's Ditch Revisited: The Problem of Faith and History." Ronald H. Preston, ed. *Theology and Change: Essays in Memory of Alan Richardson.* London: SCM, 1975. 78–103.

————. *The Anthropological Character of Theology: Conditioning Theological Understanding.* Cambridge: Cambridge University Press, 1990.

Palmer, Richard E. *Hermeneutics: Interpretation Theory in Schleiermacher, Dilthey, Heidegger, and Gadamer.* Evanston: Northwestern University Press, 1969.

Pannenberg, Wolfhart. "An Autobiographical Sketch." Carl. E. Braaten & Philip Clayton, eds., *The Theology of Wolfhart Pannenberg: Twelve American Critiques.* Minneapolis: Augsburg, 1988. 11–18.

————. *An Introduction to Systematic Theology.* Grand Rapids: Eerdmans, 1991.

————. *Anthropology in Theological Perspective.* Tr. Matthew J. O'Connell. Philadelphia: Westminster, 1985.

————. *The Apostles' Creed in the Light of Today's Questions.* Tr. Margaret Kohl. London: SCM, 1972.

————. "Baptism as Remembered 'Ecstatic' Identity." David Brown & Ann Loades, eds. *Christ: The Sacramental Word. Incarnation, Sacrament and Poetry.* London: SPCK, 1996. 77–88.

————. *Basic Questions in Theology.* 3 vols. Trs. George H. Kehm (vols. 1 & 2), R. A. Wilson (vol. 3). Philadelphia: Westminster, 1970, 1971, 1973.

————. "The Christian Vision of God: The New Discussion on the Trinitarian Doctrine." *ATJ* 46(1991): 27–36.

————. "Christianity, Marxism and Liberation Theology." *CSR* 18(1989): 215–26.

————. *The Church.* Tr. Keith Crim. Philadelphia: Westminster, 1983.

————. "The Church Today." *ATJ* 46(1991): 7–16.

————. "Constructive and Critical Functions of Christian Eschatology." *HTR* 77(1984): 119–39.

————. "Did Jesus Really Rise from the Dead?" *Dialog* 4(1965): 128–35.

————. "The Doctrine of Creation and Modern Science." *Zygon* 23(1988): 3–21.

————. "The Doctrine of the Spirit and the Task of a Theology of Nature." *Theology* 75(1972): 8–21.

————. "Dogmatische Erwägungen zur Auferstehung Jesu." *KuD* 14(1968): 105–18.

————. *Ethics*. Tr. Keith Crim. Philadelphia: Westminster, 1981.

————. *Faith and Reality*. Tr. John Maxwell. Philadelphia: Westminster, 1977.

————. "Frage und Antwort—Das Normative in Christlicher Überlieferung und Theologie." Manfred Fuhrmann, Hans Robert Jauss & Wolfhart Pannenberg, eds. *Text und Applikation: Theologie, Jurisprudenz und Literaturwissenschaft im Hermeneutischen Gespräch*. Munich: Wilhelm Fink Verlag, 1981. 413–21.

————. "Future and Unity." Ewert H. Cousins, ed. *Hope and the Future of Man*. Philadelphia: Fortress, 1972. 60–78.

————. "God's Presence in History." James Wall, ed. *Theologians in Transition*. New York: Crossroad, 1981. 93–99.

————. "Gott und die Natur," *TuP* 58(1983): 481–500.

————. *Human Nature, Election and History*. Philadelphia: Westminster, 1977.

————. *Jesus—God and Man*. 2d. ed. Tr. Lewis L. Wilkins & Duane A. Priebe. Philadelphia: Westminster, 1968, 1977.

————. *Metaphysics and the Idea of God*. Tr. Philip Clayton. Edinburgh: T&T Clark, 1990.

————. "The Religions from the Perspective of Christian Theology and the Self-Interpretation of Christianity in Relation to the Non-Christian Religions." *MTh* 9(1993): 285–97.

————. "Religious Pluralism and Conflicting Truth Claims." G. D'Costa, ed. *Christian Uniqueness Reconsidered*. Maryknoll: Orbis, 1990. 96–106.

————. "Response to the Discussion." James M. Robinson & John B. Cobb, Jr., eds. *Theology as History*. New York: Harper & Row, 1967. 221–76.

————, ed., in association with Rolf Rendtorff, Trutz Rendtorff, & Ulrich Wilkens. *Revelation as History*. Tr. David Granskou. New York: Macmillan; London: Collier-Macmillan, 1968.

————. "The Revelation of God in Jesus of Nazareth." James M. Robinson & John B. Cobb, Jr., eds. *Theology as History*. New York: Harper & Row, 1967. 101–33.

————. *Systematic Theology*. 3 vols. Tr. Geoffrey Bromiley. Grand Rapids: Eerdmans, 1991, 1994, 1997.

————. *Theology and the Kingdom of God*. Philadelphia: Westminster, 1969.

————. *Theology and the Philosophy of Science*. Tr. Francis McDonagh. Philadelphia: Westminster, 1976.

————. "Theta Phi Talkback Session with Wolfhart Pannenberg," *ATJ* 46(1991): 37–41.

————. *What is Man? Contemporary Anthropology in Theological Perspective*. Philadelphia: Fortress, 1970.

Pannenberg, W. & Lewis S. Ford. "A Dialogue about Process Philosophy." *Encounter* 38(1977): 318–24.

Pannenberg, W. & A. M. Klaus Müller. *Erwägungen zu einer Theologie der Natur*. Gütersloh: Gütersloher Verlagshaus Gerd Mohn, 1970.

Patte, Daniel. *Paul's Faith and the Power of the Gospel: A Structural Introduction to the Pauline Letters*. Philadelphia: Fortress, 1983.

Patterson, Stephen J. "The End of Apocalypse: Rethinking the Eschatological Jesus." *TT* 52(1995): 29–48.

Pelikan, Jaroslav. *The Christian Tradition: A History of the Development of Doctrine. Vol. 1: The Emergence of the Catholic Tradition (100–600)*. Chicago & London: University of Chicago Press, 1971.

———. *Development of Christian Doctrine: Some Historical Prolegomena*. New Haven & London: Yale University Press, 1969.

———. *Historical Theology: Continuity and Change in Christian Doctrine*. Philadelphia: Westminster, 1971.

———. *The Vindication of Tradition*. New Haven & London: Yale University Press, 1984.

Perkins, Darrell Davis, Jr. *Explicating Christian Faith in a Historically Conscious Age: The Method of Ernst Troeltsch's* Glaubenslehre. Ph.D. dissertation, Vanderbilt University, 1981.

Peters, Theodore F. *God as Trinity: Relationality and Temporality in Divine Life*. Louisville: Westminster/John Knox, 1993.

———. *Method and Truth: An Inquiry into the Philosophical Hermeneutics of Hans-Georg Gadamer and the Theology of History of Wolfhart Pannenberg*. Ph.D. dissertation, University of Chicago, 1973.

———. "Truth in History: Gadamer's Hermeneutics and Pannenberg's Apologetic Method." *JRel* 55(1975): 36–56.

———. "The Use of Analogy in Historical Method," *CBQ* 35(1973): 475–482.

Petersen, Norman R. *Rediscovering Paul: Philemon and the Sociology of Paul's Narrative World*. Philadelphia: Fortress, 1985.

Phillips, D. Z. *Faith After Foundationalism: Plantiga-Rorty-Lindbeck-Berger—Critiques and Alternatives*. Bounder, San Francisco & Oxford: Westview Press, 1988, 1995.

———. *Faith and Philosophical Enquiry*. London: Routledge & Kegan Paul, 1970.

Phillips, Timothy R. and Dennis L. Okholm, eds. *Christian Apologetics in the Postmodern World*. Downers Grove: InterVarsity Press, 1995.

———, eds. *The Nature of Confession: Evangelicals & Postliberals in Conversation*. Downers Grove: InterVarsity Press, 1996.

Placher, William C. "Postliberal Theology." David F. Ford, ed. *The Modern Theologians: An Introduction to Christian Theology in the Twentieth Century*. 2d. ed. Oxford: Blackwell, 1997. 343–56.

———. *Unapologetic Theology: A Christian Voice in a Pluralistic Conversation*. Louisville: Westminster/John Knox Press, 1989.

Plantinga, Alvin & Nicholas Wolterstorff, eds. *Faith and Rationality: Reason and Belief in God*. Notre Dame & London: University of Notre Dame, 1983.

Plevnik, J. "The Center of Paul's Theology." *CBQ* 51(1989): 460–78.

Polanyi, Michael. *Personal Knowledge*. London: Routledge and Kegan Paul, 1958.

———. *The Tacit Dimension*. London: Routledge and Kegan Paul, 1966.

Polk, David P. *On the Way to God: An Exploration into the Theology of Wolfhart Pannenberg*. Lanham: University Press of America, 1989.

Pope-Levison, Priscilla & John R. Levison. *Jesus in Global Contexts*. Louisville: Westminster/John Knox, 1992.

Porter, Stanley J., ed. *The Nature of Religious Language: A Colloquium*. Sheffield: Sheffield Academic Press, 1996.

Price, H. H. *Belief*. London: George Allen & Unwin; New York: Humanities Press, 1969.

Proudfoot, Wayne. *Religious Experience*. Berkeley, Los Angeles & London: University of California Press, 1985.

Prozesky, Martin H. "The Young Schleiermacher: Advocating Religion in An Age of Critical Reason (1768–1807)." *JTSA* 37(1981): 51–55.

Quigley, Michael A. "Ernst Troeltsch and the Problem of the Historical Absolute." *HeyJ* 24(1983): 19–37.

Quine, Willard V. O. *From a Logical Point of View*. 2d. rev. ed. New York: Harper & Row, 1963.

Rabinow, Paul & William M. Sullivan, eds. *Interpretive Social Science: A Reader*. Berkeley, Los Angeles & London: University of California Press, 1979.

Rae, Murray, Hilary Regan & John Stenhouse, eds. *Science ad Theology: Questions at the Interface*. Edinburgh: T&T Clark, 1994.

Rahner, Karl. "Considerations on the Development of Dogma." *Theological Investigations. Vol. IV: More Recent Writings*. Tr. Kevin Smyth. Baltimore: Helicon; London: Darton, Longman & Todd, 1966. 3–35.

———. "The Development of Dogma." *Theological Investigations. Vol. I: God, Christ, Mary and Grace*. Tr. Cornelius Ernst. London: Darton, Longman & Todd, 1961. 39–77.

———. "The Theology of the Symbol." *Theological Investigations. Vol. IV: More Recent Writings*. Tr. Kevin Smyth. Baltimore: Helicon; London: Darton, Longman & Todd, 1966. 221–52.

———. *The Trinity*. New York: Herder & Herder, 1970.

———. "The Two Basic Types of Christology," *Theological Investigations. Vol. XIII: Theology, Anthropology, Christology*. Tr. David Bourke. London: Darton, Longman & Todd, 1975. 213–23.

Räisänen, Heikki. "Galatians 2:16 and Paul's Break with Judaism." *NTS* 31(1985): 543–53.

———. *Paul and the Law*. Philadelphia: Fortress, 1986.

Raschke, Carl A. *The Alchemy of the Word: Language and the End of Theology*. Missoula: Scholars Press, 1979.

Redeker, Martin. *Schleiermacher: Life and Thought*. Tr. John Wallhausser. Philadelphia: Fortress, 1973.

Regan, Hilary & Alan J. Torrance, eds. *Christ in Context: The Confrontation between Gospel and Culture*. Edinburgh: T&T Clark, 1993.

Reist, Benjamin A. *Toward a Theology of Involvement: The Thought of Ernst Troeltsch*. London: SCM, 1966.

Reitzenstein, Richard. *Hellenistic Mystery Religions: Their Basic Ideas and Significance*. Pittsburgh: Pickwick, 1978.

Rendtorff, Trutz & Friedrich Wilhelm Graf. "Ernst Troeltsch." Ninian Smart, John Clayton, Patrick Sherry, & Steven T. Katz, eds. *Nineteenth Century Religious Thought in the West*. 3 vols. Cambridge: Cambridge University Press, 1985. 3:305–32.

Reumann, J., J. Fitzmyer & J. Quinn. *Righteousness in the New Testament: "Justification" in the United States Lutheran-Catholic Dialogue*. Philadelphia: Fortress, 1982.

Reynolds, Terrence. "Walking Apart, Together: Lindbeck and McFague on Theological Method." *JRel* 77(1997): 44–67.

Richards, Jay Wesley. "Truth and Meaning in George Lindbeck's *The Nature of Doctrine*." *RelS* 33(1997): 33–53.

Richardson, Neil. *Paul's Language about God*. Sheffield: Sheffield Academic Press, 1994.

Richardson, Ruth Drucilla. *The Role of Women in the Life and Thought of the Early Schleiermacher, 1768–1806: An Historical Overview*. Lewiston: Edwin Mellen Press, 1992.

Ricoeur, Paul. "Ethics and Culture: Habermas and Gadamer in Dialogue," *PhT* 17(1973): 153–65.

———. *Freedom and Nature: The Voluntary and the Involuntary*. Evanston: Northwestern University Press, 1966.

———. *Hermeneutics and the Human Sciences*. Tr., ed. & int. by John B. Thompson. Cambridge: Cambridge University Press; Paris: Editions de la Maison des Sciences de l'Homme, 1981.

———. "Hermeneutics and the Critique of Ideology." Brice R. Wachterhauser, ed. *Hermeneutics and Modern Philosophy*. Albany: State University of New York Press, 1986. 300–39.

———. "Life in Quest of Narrative." David Wood, ed. *On Paul Ricoeur: Narrative and Interpretation*. London & New York: Routledge, 1991. 20–33.

———. "On Interpretation." Alan Montefiore, ed. *Philosophy in France Today*. Cambridge: Cambridge University Press, 1983. 175–97.

————. "Schleiermacher's Hermeneutics." *Monist* 60(1977): 181–97.
————. *Time and Narrative.* ET 3 vols. Chicago & London: University of Chicago Press, 1984, 1988, 1990.
Ridderbos, H. *Paul: An Outline of His Theology.* Grand Rapids: Eerdmans, 1975.
Rightmore, R. David. "Pannenberg's Quest for the Proleptic Jesus." *ATJ* 44(1989): 51–75.
Risser, James. *Hermeneutics and the Voice of the Other: Re-Reading Gadamer's Philosophical Hermeneutics.* Albany: State University of New York Press, 1997.
Ritschl, Dietrich. *Memory and Hope: An Inquiry Concerning the Presence of Christ.* New York: Macmillan; London: Collier-Macmillan, 1967.
Roberts, David D. *Nothing But History: Reconstruction and Extremity after Metaphysics.* Berkeley, Los Angeles & London: University of California Press, 1995.
Robinson, James M. "Hermeneutic Since Barth." James M. Robinson & John B. Cobb, Jr., eds. *New Frontiers in Theology. Vol. 2: The New Hermeneutic.* New York: Harper & Row, 1964. 1–77.
Robinson, James M. & Helmut Koester. *Trajectories through Early Christianity.* Philadelphia: Fortress, 1971.
Robinson, James M. & John B. Cobb, Jr., eds. *Theology as History.* New York, Evanston & London: Harper & Row, 1967.
Robinson, John A. T. *The Human Face of God.* London: SCM, 1973.
Robinson, Thomas A. *The Bauer Thesis Examined: The Geography of Heresy in the Early Christian Community.* Lewiston: Edwin Mellen, 1988.
Root, Michael. "Schleiermacher as Innovator and Inheritor: God, Dependence, and Election." *SJT* 43(1990): 87–110.
————. "Truth, Relativism and Postliberal Theology." *Dialog* 25(1986): 175–80.
Rorty, Richard. *Consequences of Pragmatism.* Minneapolis: University of Minnesota Press, 1982.
————. *Contingency, Irony and Solidarity.* Cambridge: Cambridge University Press, 1989.
————. *Essays on Heidegger and Others. Philosophical Papers: Volume 2.* Cambridge: Cambridge University Press, 1991.
————. *Objectivity, Relativism, and Truth. Philosophical Papers: Volume 1.* Cambridge: Cambridge University Press, 1991.
————. *Philosophy and the Mirror of Nature.* Oxford & Cambridge: Blackwell, 1980.
Rowden, H. H., ed. *Christ the Lord: Studies in Christology presented to Donald Guthrie.* Leicester: InterVarsity, 1982.
Rowland, Christopher C. *Christian Origins: From Messianic Movement to Christian Religion.* Minneapolis: Augsburg, 1985.
————. *The Open Heaven: A Study of Apocalyptic in Judaism and Early Christianity.* New York: Crossroad, 1982.
Rowley, H. H. *The Relevance of Apocalyptic: A Study of Jewish and Christian Apocalypses from Daniel to Revelation.* 3rd rev. ed. Greenwood: Attic Press, 1944, 1963.
Roy, Louis. "Consciousness According to Schleiermacher." *JRel* 77(1997): 217–32.
Rupp, George. *Christologies and Cultures: Toward a Typology of Religious Worldviews.* The Hague: Mouton, 1974.
Rush, Ormond. "Living Reception of the Living Tradition: Hermeneutical Principles for Theology." Neil J. Byrne, ed., *Banyo Studies.* Banyo, Queensland: Pius XII Seminary, 1991. 242–90.
————. "Reception Hermeneutics and the 'Development' of Doctrine: An Alternative Model." *Pacifica* 6(1993): 125–40.
Sampley, J. Paul. "From Text to Thought World: The Route to Paul's Ways." Jouette M. Bassler, ed. *Pauline Theology, Volume I: Thessalonians, Philippians, Galatians, Philemon.* Minneapolis: Fortress, 1991. 3–14.
Sampson, Philip, Vinay Samuel & Chris Sugden, eds. *Faith and Modernity.* Oxford: Regnum Books International, 1994.

Sanders, E. P. *Judaism: Practice and Belief 63 B.C.E–66 C.E.* London: SCM; Philadelphia: Trinity Press International, 1992.

―――. *Paul and Palestinian Judaism: A Comparison of Patterns of Religion.* London: SCM, 1977.

―――. *Paul, the Law, and the Jewish People.* Philadelphia: Fortress, 1983.

Sanders, James A. *From Sacred Story to Sacred Text.* Philadelphia: Fortress, 1987.

Sandness, Karl Olav. *Paul—One of the Prophets?* Tübingen: J. C. B. Mohr (Paul Siebeck), 1991.

Satterthwaite, Philip E. and David F. Wright, eds. *A Pathway into the Holy Scripture.* Grand Rapids: Eerdmans, 1994.

Scalise, Charles J. *Hermeneutics as Theological Prolegomena: A Canonical Approach.* Macon: Mercer University Press, 1994.

Scheffler, Israel. *Science and Subjectivity.* 2d. ed. Indianapolis: Hackett, 1967, 1982.

Schillebeeckx, Eduard. *Jesus: An Experiment in Christology.* Tr. Hubert Hoskins. New York: Seabury, 1979.

―――. "Towards a Catholic Use of Hermeneutics." *God the Future of Man.* New York: Sheed and Ward, 1968. 1–51.

Schleiermacher, Friedrich. *Brief Outline on the Study of Theology.* Tr. with introductions and notes by Terrence N. Tice. Atlanta: John Knox, 1966, rpt. 1977.

―――. *The Christian Faith.* Tr. from 2d. German ed. H. R. Mackintosh & J. S. Stewart. Philadelphia: Fortress, 1928.

―――. *Christmas Eve: Dialogue on the Incarnation.* Tr. Terrence N. Tice. Richmond: John Knox, 1967.

―――. *A Critical Essay on the Gospel of Luke.* Tr. Connop Thirlwall. London: John Taylor, 1825.

―――. *Das Leben Jesu. Vorlesungen an der Universität Berlin im Jahr 1832.* Ed. K. A. Rutenik. Berlin: G. Reimer, 1864. ET: *The Life of Jesus.* Ed. J. C. Verheyden. Tr. S. M. Gilmour. Philadelphia: Fortress, 1975.

―――. *Dialektik 1814/15.* Ed. Andreas Arndt. Hamburg: Felix Meiner Verlag, 1988.

―――. *Die christliche Sitte.* Ed. L. Jonas. *Sämmtliche Werke.* I/12. 2d. ed. Berlin: G. Reimer, 1884.

―――. *Hermeneutics: The Handwritten Manuscripts.* Ed. Heinz Kimmerle, tr. James Duke & Jack Forstman. Atlanta: Scholars Press, 1977, rpt. 1986.

―――. *The Life of Schleiermacher, as Unfolded in His Autobiography and Letters.* Tr. Frederica Rowan. 2 vols. London: Smith, Elder & Co., 1860.

―――. *On Religion: Speeches to its Cultured Despisers.* Introduction, translation and notes by Richard Crouter. Cambridge: Cambridge University Press, 1988.

―――. *On the Glaubenslehre: Two Letters to Dr Lücke.* Tr. James Duke & Francis Fiorenza. Chico: Scholars Press, 1981.

―――. *Psychologie.* aus Schleiermachers handschriften Nachlasse und nachgeschreibenen Vorlesungen. *sämmtliche Werke.* III/6. Berlin: G. Reimer, 1862.

―――. *Soliloquies: An English Translation of the Monologen.* Tr. Horace Leleand Freiss. Westport: Hyperion Press, 1926.

―――. "Ueber den sogenannten ersten Brief des Paulos an den Timotheos. Ein kritisches Sendschreiben an J. C. Gass." *sämmtliche Werke.* 2:221–320.

Schlier, H. "*Doxa* bei Paulus als heilsgeschichtlicher Begriff." *Studiorum Paulinorum Congressus Internationalis Catholicus,* 2 vols. Analecta Biblica 17–18. Rome: Pontifical Biblical Institute, 1963. 1:45–56.

Schlink, Edmund. "Die Struktur der dogmatischen Aussage als Oekumenisches Problem." *KuD* 3(1957): 251–306.

Schmidt, Lawrence K., ed. *The Specter of Relativism: Truth, Dialogue, and Phronesis in Philosophical Hermeneutics.* Evanston: Northwestern University Press, 1995.

Schoeps, Hans Joachim. *Paul: The Theology of the Apostle in the Light of Jewish Religious History.* Philadelphia: Westminster, 1961.

Schrage, W. *Der erste Brief an die Korinther*. 2 vols. EKKzNT VII, i, ii. Zürich: Benziger; Neukirchen: Neukirchener Verlag, 1991, 1993.
Schreiner, Thomas R. "The Abolition and Fulfilment of the Law in Paul." *JSNT* 35(1989): 47–74.
———. *The Law and Its Fulfillment: A Pauline Theology of Law*. Grand Rapids: Baker, 1993.
Schreiter, Robert J. *Constructing Local Theologies*. Maryknoll: Orbis, 1985.
Schweitzer, Albert. *The Mysticism of Paul the Apostle*. New York: Seabury, 1931.
———. *The Quest of the Historical Jesus*. London: Adam & Charles Black, 1911.
Schwöbel, Christoph. "Christology and Trinitarian Thought." Christoph Schwöbel, ed. *Trinitarian Theology Today: Essays on Divine Being and Act*. Edinburgh: T&T Clark, 1995. 113–46.
———. "Wolfhart Pannenberg." David F. Ford, ed. *The Modern Theologians: An Introduction to Christian Theology in the Twentieth Century*. 2d. ed. Oxford: Blackwell, 1997. 180–208.
———. "Rational Theology in Trinitarian Perspective: Wolfhart Pannenberg's *Systematic Theology*." *JTS* 47(1996): 498–527.
———, ed. *Trinitarian Theology Today: Essays on Divine Being and Act*. Edinburgh: T&T Clark, 1995.
Scott, Charles E. "Schleiermacher and the Problem of Divine Immediacy." *RelS* 3(1967): 499–512.
Scroggs, Roger. *The Last Adam*. Oxford: Basil Blackwell, 1966.
Searle, John R. *The Construction of Social Reality*. New York: Free Press, 1995.
———. *Expression and Meaning: Studies in the Theory of Speech-Acts*. Cambridge: Cambridge University Press, 1979.
———. *Intentionality: An Essay in the Philosophy of Mind*. Cambridge: Cambridge University Press, 1983.
———. *Speech Acts: An Essay in the Philosophy of Language*. Cambridge: Cambridge University Press, 1969.
Segal, Alan. *Paul the Convert: The Apostolate and Apostasy of Saul the Pharisee*. New Haven & London: Yale University Press, 1990.
Sellars, Wilfred. *Science, Perception and Reality*. New York: Humanities Press, 1963.
Senior, Donald & Carroll Stuhlmueller. *The Biblical Foundations for Mission*. Maryknoll: Orbis, 1984.
Shalins, Marshall. *Islands of History*. Chicago: University of Chicago Press, 1985.
Shapere, Dudley. "The Structure of Scientific Revolutions." Gary Gutting, ed. *Paradigms and Revolutions: Appraisals and Applications of Thomas Kuhn's Philosophy of Science*. Notre Dame & London: University of Notre Dame Press, 1980. 27–38.
Shapiro, Gary & Alan Sica, eds. *Hermeneutics: Questions and Prospects*. Amherst: University of Massachusetts Press, 1984.
Sherry, Patrick. *Religion, Truth and Language-Games*. London & Basingstoke: Macmillan, 1977.
Shuster, Marguerite, and Richard A. Muller, eds. *Perspectives on Christology: Essays in Honor of Paul K. Jewett*. Grand Rapids: Zondervan, 1991.
Siegel, Harvey. *Relativism Refuted: A Critique of Contemporary Epistemological Relativism*. Dordrecht: D. Reidel Publishing Company, 1987.
Silva, Moises. "The Law and Christianity: Dunn's New Synthesis." *WTJ* 53(1991): 339–53.
Silverman, Hugh J., ed. *Gadamer and Hermeneutics. Continental Philosophy IV*. New York & London: Routledge, 1991.
Simon, Marianne. *La philosophie de la religion dans l'oeuvre de Schleiermacher*. Paris: Vrin, 1974.
Skarsaune, Oskar. *Incarnation: Myth or Fact?* Tr. Trygve R. Skarsten. St Louis: Concordia, 1991.

Skinner, Quentin. "Hermeneutics and the Role of History." *NLH* 7(1975): 209–32.
———, ed. *The Return of Grand Theory in the Human Sciences*. Cambridge: Cambridge University Press, 1985.
Small, Robin. "Nietzsche" in C. L. Ten, ed. *The Nineteenth Century. Routledge History of Philosophy. Vol. VII*. London & New York: Routledge, 1994. 177–205.
Smart, Ninian, John Clayton, Patrick Sherry & Steven T. katz, eds. *Nineteenth Century Religious Thought in the West*. 3 vols. Cambridge: Cambridge University Press, 1985.
Smiga, G. "Rm 12:1–2; 15:30–32: Occasion of Romans." *CBQ* 53(1991): 257–73.
Smith, D. Moody. "The Pauline Literature." D. A. Carson & H. G. M. Williamson, eds. *It is Written: Scripture Citing Scripture: Essays in Honour of Barnabas Lindars*. Cambridge: Cambridge University Press, 1988. 265–91.
Smith, P. Christopher. "Gadamer's Hermeneutics and Ordinary Language Philosophy." *Thomist* 43(1979): 296–321.
Snodgrass, Klyne. "Justification by Grace—to the Doers: An Analysis of the Place of Romans 2 in the Theology of Paul." *NTS* 32(1986): 72–93.
Sobrino, Jon. *Christology at the Crossroads: A Latin American Approach*. London: SCM, 1978.
Sommer, Wolfgang. "Cusanus und Schleiermacher." *NZSTR* 12(1970): 85–102.
Sosa, Ernest. "The Foundations of Foundationalism." *Nous* 14(1980): 547–64.
———. "The Raft and the Pyramid." *MSP* 5(1980): 3–25.
Soskice, Janet Martin. *Metaphor and Religious Language*. Oxford: Clarendon, 1985.
Spiegler, Gerhard. *The Eternal Covenant: Schleiermacher's Experiment in Cultural Theology*. New York: Harper & Row, 1967.
Sponheim, Paul R. *God—The Question and the Quest: Toward a Conversation Concerning Christian Faith*. Philadelphia: Fortress, 1985.
Stanley, Christopher D. *Paul and the Language of Scripture: Citation Technique in the Pauline Epistles and Contemporary Literature*. SNTSMS 69. Cambridge: Cambridge University Press, 1992.
Stanton, Graham N. "The Gospel Traditions and Early Christological Reflection." S. W. Sykes & J. P. Clayton, eds. *Christ, Faith and History*. Cambridge: Cambridge University Press, 1972. 191–204.
Stell, Stephen L. *Hermeneutics and the Holy Spirit: Trinitarian Insights into a Hermeneuetical Impasse*. Ph.D. diss. Princeton Theological Seminary, 1988.
———. "Hermeneutics in Theology and the Theology of Hermeneutics: Beyond Lindbeck and Tracy." *JAAR* 61(1993): 679–703.
Stendahl, Krister. *Paul Among Jews and Gentiles*. Philadelphia: Fortress, 1976.
Stiver, Dan R. *The Philosophy of Religious Language: Sign, Symbol and Story*. Cambridge & Oxford: Blackwell, 1996.
Stout, Jeffrey. *Flight from Authority: Religion, Morality, and the Quest for Autonomy*. Notre Dame: University of Notre Dame Press, 1983.
Strauss, Leo & Hans-Georg Gadamer. "Correspondence Concerning *Wahrheit und Methode*." *IJP* 2(1978): 5–12.
Streetman, Robert F. "Romanticism and the *Sensus Numinis* in Schleiermacher." David Jasper, ed. *The Interpretation of Belief: Coleridge, Schleiermacher and Romanticism*. New York: St Martin's Press, 1986.
Stroup, George W. *The Promise of Narrative Theology*. London: SCM, 1981, 1984.
Studer, Basil. *Trinity and Incarnation: The Faith of the Early Church*. Edinburgh: T&T Clark, 1993.
Stuhlmacher, Peter. *Gerechtigkeit Gottes bei Paulus*. Göttingen: Vandenhoeck & Ruprecht, 1966.
Sturch, Richard. *The Word and the Christ: An Essay in Analytic Christology*. Oxford: Clarendon, 1991.
Sullivan, Robert R. *Political Hermeneutics: The Early Thinking of Hans-Georg Gadamer*. University Park & London: Pennsylvania State University Press, 1989.

Surin, Kenneth. "'Many Religions and the One True Faith': An Examination of Lindbeck's Chapter Three." *MTh* 2(1988): 187–209.

Sykes, Stephen W. "Ernst Troeltsch and Christianity's Essence." John Powell Clayton, ed. *Ernst Troeltsch and the Future of Theology*. Cambridge: Cambridge University Press, 1976. 139–71.

———. "Schleiermacher and Barth on the Essence of Christianity—An Instructive Disagreement." James O. Duke & Robert F. Streetman, eds. *Barth and Schleiermacher: Beyond the Impasse?* Philadelphia: Fortress, 1988. 88–107.

———. *The Identity of Christianity: Theologians and the Essence of Christianity from Schleiermacher to Barth*. Philadelphia: Fortress, 1984.

Sykes, S. W. & J. P. Clayton, eds. *Christ, Faith and History: Cambridge Studies in Christology*. Cambridge: Cambridge University Press, 1972.

Sykes, S. W. & Derek Holmes, eds. *New Studies in Theology*. London: Duckworth, 1980.

Szondi, Peter. *Introduction to Literary Hermeneutics*. Tr. Martha Woodmansee. Cambridge: Cambridge University Press, 1995.

Taylor, Mark C. *Deconstruction in Context*. Chicago: University of Chicago Press, 1986.

———. *Erring: A Postmodern A/theology*. Chicago: University of Chicago Press, 1984.

Teigas, Demetrius. *Knowledge and Hermeneutic Understanding: A Study of the Habermas-Gadamer Debate*. Lewisburg: Bucknell University Press; London & Toronto: Associated University Presses, 1995.

Ten, C. L., ed. *The Nineteenth Century*. Routledge History of Philosophy, Vol. VII. London & New York: Routledge, 1994.

Thiel, John E. *God and World in Schleiermacher's "Dialektik" and "Glaubenslehre"*. Berne: Peter Lang, 1981.

———. *Imagination & Authority: Theological Authorship in the Modern Tradition*. Minneapolis: Fortress, 1991.

———. *Nonfoundationalism*. Minneapolis: Fortress, 1994.

———. "Orthodoxy and Heterodoxy in Schleiermacher's Theological Encyclopedia: Doctrinal Development and Theological Creativity." *HeyJ* 25(1984): 142–57.

Thielicke, Helmut. *Modern Faith and Thought*. Tr. Geoffrey Bromiley. Grand Rapids: Eerdmans, 1990.

Thielman, Frank. *From Plight to Solution: A Jewish Framework for Understanding Paul's View of the Law in Galatians and Romans*. Leiden: E. J. Brill, 1989.

———. *Paul and the Law: A Contextual Approach*. Downers Grove: InterVarsity Press, 1994.

Thiemann, Ronald F. "Piety, Narrative, and Christian Identity." *WW* 3(1983): 148–59.

———. "Revelation and Imaginative Construction." *JRel* 61(1981): 242–63.

———. *Revelation and Theology: The Gospel as Narrated Promise*. Notre Dame: University of Notre Dame, 1985.

Thiselton, Anthony C. "Authority and Hermeneutics: Some Proposals for a More Creative Agenda." Philip E. Satterthwaite & David F. Wright, eds. *A Pathway into the Holy Scripture*. Grand Rapids: Eerdmans, 1994. 107–41.

———. "Christology in Luke, Speech-Act Theory, and the Problem of Dualism in Christology after Kant." Joel B. Green & Max Turner, eds. *Jesus of Nazareth: Lord and Christ: Essays on the Historical Jesus and New Testament Christology*. Grand Rapids: Eerdmans; Carlisle: Paternoster, 1994. 453–72.

———. *Interpreting God and the Postmodern Self: On Meaning, Manipulation and Promise*. Grand Rapids: Eerdmans, 1995.

———. "Knowledge, Myth and Corporate Memory." *Believing in the Church*. A Report by the Doctrine Commission of the Church of England. London: SPCK, 1981. 45–78.

———. "The Meaning of *Sarx* in 1 Cor. 5:5. A Fresh Approach in the Light of Logical and Semantic Factors." *SJT* 26(1973): 204–28.

————. *New Horizons in Hermeneutics: The Theory and Practice of Transforming Biblical Reading.* Grand Rapids: Zondervan, 1992.
————. "Realized Eschatology at Corinth." *NTS* 24(1978): 510–24.
————. "Truth." Colin Brown, ed., *New International Dictionary of New Testament Theology*, 3 vols. Exeter: Paternoster, 1978. 3:874–902.
————. *The Two Horizons: New Testament Hermeneutics and Philosophical Description with Special Reference to Heidegger, Bultmann, Gadamer, and Wittgenstein.* Grand Rapids: Eerdmans, 1980.
Thomas, Brook. *The New Historicism and Other Old-Fashioned Topics.* Princeton: Princeton University Press, 1991.
Thompson, John. *Modern Trinitarian Perspectives.* New York & Oxford: Oxford University Press, 1994.
Thompson, Thomas R. "Trinitarianism Today: Doctrinal Renaissance, Ethical Relevance, Social Redolence." *CTJ* 32(1997): 9–42.
Thompson, William M. *The Struggle for Theology's Soul: Contesting Scripture in Christology.* New York: Crossroad, 1996.
Tice, Terrence N. *Schleiermacher Bibliography 1784–1984.* Princeton Pamphlets no. 101. Princeton: Princeton Theological Seminary, 1985.
Tilley, Terrence W. "Incommensurability, Intratextuality, and Fideism." *MTh* 5(1989): 87–111.
Tilley, Terrence W., with John Edwards, Tami England, H. Frederick Felice, Stuart Kendall, C. Brad Morris, Bruce Richey, Craig Westman. *Postmodern Theologies: The Challenge of Religious Diversity.* Maryknoll: Orbis, 1995.
Tillich, Paul. *Perspectives on Nineteenth and Twentieth Century Protestant Theology.* Ed. Carl E. Braaten. London: SCM, 1967.
Torrance, Iain R. "Gadamer, Polanyi and Ways of Being Closed." *SJT* 46(1993): 497–505.
Torrance, James B. "Interpretation and Understanding in Schleiermacher's Theology: Some Critical Questions." *SJT* 21(1968): 268–82.
Torrance, Thomas F. "Hermeneutics According to F. D. E. Schleiermacher." *SJT* 21(1968): 257–67.
————. *Theological Science.* London, New York & Toronto: Oxford University Press, 1969.
————. *Transformation and Convergence in the Frame of Mind.* Grand Rapids: Eerdmans, 1984.
Toulmin, Stephen. *Cosmopolis: The Hidden Agenda of Modernity.* New York: Free Press, 1990.
Tracy, David. *The Analogical Imagination: Christian Theology and the Culture of Pluralism.* New York: Crossroad, 1981.
————. "Hermeneutical Reflections in the New Paradigm." Hans Küng & David Tracy, eds. *Paradigm Change in Theology: A Symposium for the Future.* New York: Crossroad, 1991. 34–62.
————. "On Reading the Scriptures Theologically." Bruce D. Marshall, ed. *Theology as Dialogue: Essays in Conversation with George Lindbeck.* Notre Dame: University of Notre Dame Press, 1990. 35–68.
————. *Plurality and Ambiguity: Hermeneutics, Religion, Hope.* San Francisco: Harper & Row, 1987.
————. "Theological Method." Peter C. Hodgson & Robert H. King, eds. *Christian Theology: An Introduction to Its Traditions and Tasks.* 2d. rev. & enlarged ed. Philadelphia: Fortress, 1982, 1985. 35–59.
————. "Theology and the Many Faces of Postmodernity." *TT* 51(1994): 104–14.
Trigg, Roger. *Reality at Risk: A Defence of Realism in Philosophy and the Sciences.* Second edition. New York: Harvester Wheatsheaf, 1980, 1989.

Troeltsch, Ernst. *The Absoluteness of Christianity and the History of Religions.* Second edition. Tr. David Reid. London: SCM, 1972.

————. *Christian Thought: Its History and Application.* Ed. by Baron Friedrich von Hügel. London: University of London Press, 1923.

————. "Die christliche Weltanschauung und die wissenschaftlichen Gegenströmungen." *ZTK* 3(1893): 493–528.

————. "The Dogmatics of the 'Religionsgeschichte Schule'." *AJT* 17(1913): 1–21.

————. "Empiricism and Platonism in the Philosophy of Religion." *HTR* 5(1912): 401–22.

————. "Geschichte und Metaphysik." *ZTK* 8(1898): 1–69.

————. "Glaube: Glaube und Geschichte." *RGG.* F. M. Schiele and L. Zscharnack, eds. 5 vols. Tübingen: J. C. B. Mohr (Paul Siebeck), 1909–1914. 2:1437–56.

————. *Glaubenslehre nach Heidelberger Vorlesungen aus den Jahren 1911 und 1912.* Munich & Leipzig: Duncker & Humblot, 1925.

————. "Historiography" in John Macquarrie, ed. *Contemporary Religious Thinkers: From Idealist Metaphysicians to Existential Theologians.* London: SCM, 1968. 76–97.

————. "The Ideas of Natural and Humanity in World Politics." Tr. by Ernest Barker from "Naturrecht und Humanität in der Weltpolitik," *Weltwirtschaftliches Archiv* 18(1922): 485–501, and included as an appendix in Otto Gierke, *Natural Law and the Theory of Society, 1500–1800.* Cambridge: Cambridge University Press, 1934. 201–22.

————. "On the Historical and Dogmatic Methods in Theology." Tr. H. Jackson Forstman. *GS.* 4 vols. Tübingen: J. C. B. Mohr (Paul Siebeck), 1913. Vol. 2: *Zur religiösen Lage, Religionsphilosophie und Ethik,* 728–53.

————. "On the Possibility of a Liberal Christianity." *Unitarian Universalist Christian* 29(1974): 27–38.

————. "Religionswissenschaft und Theologie des 18. Jahrhundrets." *PJ* 114(1903): 30–56.

————. "Die Selbständigkeit der Religion." *ZTK* 5(1895): 361–436; 6(1896): 71–110, 167–218.

————. "The Significance of the Historical Existence of Jesus for Faith." R. Morgan & M. Pye, trs. & eds. *Ernst Troeltsch: Writings on Theology and Religion.* London: Duckworth, 1977. 182–207.

————. *The Social Teaching of the Christian Churches.* Tr. Olive Wyon. 2 vols. London: George Allen & Unwin; New York: Macmillan, 1931.

————. "What Does 'Essence of Christianity' Mean?" R. Morgan & M. Pye, trs. & eds. *Ernst Troeltsch: Writings on Theology and Religion.* London: Duckworth, 1977. 124–79.

————. "Zur Frage des religiösen Apriori." *GS.* 4 vols. Tübingen: J. C. B. Mohr (Paul Siebeck), 1913. Vol. 2: *Zur religiösen Lage, Religionsphilosophie und Ethik,* 754–68.

Tupper, E. Frank. *The Theology of Wolfhart Pannenberg.* London: SCM, 1974.

Turner, H. E. W. *The Pattern of Christian Truth: A Study in the Relations between Orthodoxy and Heresy in the Early Church.* London: Mowbray, 1954.

van Huyssteen, J. Wentzel. *Essays in Postfoundationalist Theology.* Grand Rapids & Cambridge: Eerdmans, 1997.

————. *Theology and the Justification of Faith: Constructing Theories in Systematic Theology.* Tr. H. F. Snijders. Grand Rapids: Eerdmans, 1989.

van Roon, A. "The Relationship Between Christ and the Wisdom of God According to Paul." *NovT* 16(1974): 207–39.

Vanhoozer, Kevin J. "A Lamp in the Labyrinth: The Hermeneutics of 'Aesthetic' Theology." *TJ* 8 NS(1987): 25–56.

————. *Biblical Narrative in the Philosophy of Paul Ricoeur: A Study in Hermeneutics and Theology.* Cambridge: Cambridge University Press, 1990.

————. "Exploring the World; Following the Word: The Credibility of Evangelical Theology in an Incredulous Age." *TJ* 16 NS (1995): 3–27.

————. "God's Mighty Speech-Acts: The Doctrine of Scripture Today." Philip E. Satterthwaite & David F. Wright, eds. *A Pathway into the Holy Scripture*. Grand Rapids: Eerdmans, 1994. 143–181.

————. "Philosophical Antecedents to Ricoeur's *Time and Narrative*." David Wood, ed. *On Paul Ricoeur: Narrative and Interpretation*. London & New York: Routledge, 1991. 34–54.

————. "The Spirit of Understanding: Special Revelation and General Hermeneutics." Roger Lundin, ed. *Disciplining Hermeneutics: Interpretation in Christian Perspective*. Grand Rapids: Eerdmans, 1997. 131–65.

Vattimo, Gianni. *The End of Modernity: Nihilism and Hermeneutics in Postmodern Culture*. Tr. John R. Snyder. Baltimore: John Hopkins University Press, 1988.

Veeser, H. Aram, ed. *The New Historicism*. New York & London: Routledge, 1989.

Veith, Gene Edward. *Guide to Contemporary Culture*. Leicester: Crossway Books, 1994.

Volf, Miraslav. "Theology, Meaning & Power: A Conversation with George Lindbeck on Theology & the Nature of Christian Difference." Timothy R. Phillips & Dennis L. Okholm, eds. *The Nature of Confession: Evangelicals & Postliberals in Conversation*. Downers Grove: InterVarsity, 1996. 45–66.

Wachterhauser, Brice R., ed. *Hermeneutics and Modern Philosophy*. Albany: State University of New York Press, 1986.

————, ed. *Hermeneutics and Truth*. Evanston: Northwestern University Press, 1994.

Wagner, Roy. *The Invention of Culture*. Rev. & exp. Ed. Chicago: University of Chicago Press, 1981.

Wainwright, Geoffrey. *Doxology: The Praise of God in Worship, Doctrine and Life*. New York: Oxford University Press, 1980.

Wainwright, William J. *Reason and the Heart: A Prolegomenon to a Critique of Passional Reason*. Ithaca & London: Cornell University Press, 1995.

Walgrave, Jan Hendrik. *Unfolding Revelation: The Nature of Doctrinal Development*. London: Hutchinson; Philadelphia: Westminster, 1972.

Wallace, Mark I. "The New Yale Theology." *CSR* 17(1987): 154–70.

————. *The Second Naiveté: Barth, Ricoeur, and the New Yale Theology*. Studies in American Biblical Hermeneutics, Vol. 6. Macon: Mercer University Press, 1990.

Walsh, Brian J. "Pannenberg's Eschatological Ontology." *CSR* 11(1982): 229–49.

Wanamaker, C. A. "Christ as Divine Agent in Paul." *SJT* 39(1986): 517–28.

Warnke, Georgia. *Gadamer: Hermeneutics, Tradition, and Reason*. Cambridge: Polity Press, 1987.

Watson, Francis B. "Is Revelation an 'Event'?" *MTh* 10(1994): 383–99.

————. *Paul, Judaism and the Gentiles*. SNTSMS 56. Cambridge: Cambridge University Press, 1986.

————. *Text, Church and World: Biblical Interpretation in Theological Perspective*. Grand Rapids: Eerdmans, 1994.

Weber, Otto. *Foundations of Dogmatics*. Tr. Darrell L. Guder. 2 vols. Grand Rapids: Eerdmans, 1981.

Wedderburn, A. J. M. "Paul and Jesus: The Problem of Continuity." *SJT* 38(1985): 189–203.

————. "Paul and Jesus: Similarity and Continuity." *NTS* 34(1988): 161–82.

————, ed. *Paul and Jesus*. Sheffield: JSOT Press, 1989.

————. *The Reasons for Romans*. Edinburgh: T&T Clark, 1988.

Weinsheimer, Joel C. *Gadamer's Hermeneutics: A Reading of* Truth and Method. New Haven & London: Yale University Press, 1985.

Weiss, Johannes. *Jesus' Proclamation of the Kingdom of God*. Philadelphia: Fortress, 1971.

Welch, Claude. *In This Name: The Doctrine of the Trinity in Contemporary Theology*. New York: Charles Scribner's Sons, 1952.

————. *Protestant Thought in the Nineteenth Century*. Vol. 1: *1799–1870*. New Haven & London: Yale University Press, 1972.

————. *Protestant Thought in the Nineteenth Century*. Vol. 2: *1870–1914*. New Haven & London: Yale University Press, 1985.

Welton, Donn & Hugh Silverman, eds. *Critical and Dialectical Phenomenology*. Albany: State University of New York Press, 1987.

Wenham, David. *Paul: Follower of Jesus or Founder of Christianity?* Grand Rapids & Cambridge: Eerdmans, 1995.

Werner, Martin. *The Formation of Christian Dogma: An Historical Study of Its Problems*. Tr. & intro. by G. F. Brandon. London: Adam & Charles Black, 1957.

Wessels, Anton. *Images of Jesus: How Jesus is Perceived and Portrayed in Non-European Cultures*. Grand Rapids: Eerdmans, 1990.

West, Cornel. "Schleiermacher's Hermeneutics and the Myth of the Given." *USQR* 34(1979): 71–84.

Westerholm, Stephen. *Israel's Law and the Church's Faith: Paul and His Recent Interpreters*. Grand Rapids: Eerdmans, 1988.

Westphal, Merold. "Hegel and Gadamer." Brice R. Wachterhauser, ed. *Hermeneutics and Modern Philosophy*. Albany: State University of New York Press, 1986. 65–86.

————. "Hegel, Pannenberg, and Hermeneutics." *MW* 4(1971): 276–93.

————. *Suspicion and Faith: The Religious Uses of Modern Atheism*. Grand Rapids: Eerdmans, 1993.

White, Harvey W. "A Critique of Pannenberg's *Theology and the Philosophy of Science*." *SR* 11(1982): 419–36.

Whiteley, D. E. H. *The Theology of St Paul*. Philadelphia: Fortress, 1966.

Wiles, Maurice. "The Patristic Appeal to Tradition." *Explorations in Theology 4*. London: SCM, 1979. 41–52.

Wilke, Sabine. "Authorial Intent versus Universal Symbolic Language: Schleiermacher and Schlegel on Mythology, Interpretation, and Communal Values." *Soundings* 74(1991): 411–25.

Wilken, Robert L. "Diversity and Unity in Early Christianity." *SC* 1(1981): 106–10.

Williams, Robert Roy. *Consciousness and Redemption in the Theology of Friedrich Schleiermacher*. Th.D. diss. Union Theological Seminary, 1971.

————. *Schleiermacher the Theologian: The Construction of the Doctrine of God*. Philadelphia: Fortress, 1978.

Williams, Rowan. *The Making of Orthodoxy: Essays in Honour of Henry Chadwick*. Cambridge: Cambridge University Press, 1989.

Williams, Stephen N. "Lindbeck's Regulative Christology." *MTh* 4(1988): 173–86.

————. *Revelation and Reconciliation: A Window on Modernity*. Cambridge: Cambridge University Press, 1995.

Wilson, Stephen G. *The Gentiles and the Gentile Mission in Luke-Acts*. SNTSMS 23. Cambridge: Cambridge University Press, 1973.

Winquist, Charles. *Epiphanies of Darkness: Deconstruction in Theology*. Philadelphia: Fortress, 1986.

Winslow, Donald F. "Tradition." Everett Ferguson, ed. *Encyclopedia of Early Christianity*. Chicago & London: St James Press, 1990. 906–10.

Witherington III, Ben. *Conflict & Community in Corinth: A Socio-Rhetorical Commentary on 1 and 2 Corinthians*. Grand Rapids: Eerdmans, 1995.

————. *Jesus, Paul, and the End of the World: A Comparative Study in New Testament Eschatology*. Downers Grove: InterVarsity, 1992.

————. *Jesus the Sage: The Pilgrimage of Wisdom*. Minneapolis: Fortress, 1994.

————. *Paul's Narrative Thought-World: The Tapestry of Tragedy and Triumph*. Louisville: Westminster/John Knox, 1994.

Wittgenstein, Ludwig. *The Blue and Brown Books*. New York: Harper, 1958.

————. *On Certainty*. New York: Harper Torchbooks, Harper & Row, 1969.

————. *Philosophical Investigations.* 2d. ed. Tr. G. E. M. Anscombe. Oxford: Basil Blackwell, 1953, 1958, rpt. 1963.

Wolterstorff, Nicholas. *Reason Within the Bounds of Religion.* 2d. ed. Grand Rapids: Eerdmans, 1976, 1984.

————. "Tradition, Insight and Constraint." *PAAPA* 66(1992): 43–57.

————. *What New Haven and Grand Rapids Have to Say to Each Other.* Stob Lectures of Calvin College and Calvin Theological Seminary. Grand Rapids: Calvin College, 1993.

Wood, Charles M. *The Formation of Christian Understanding.* Philadelphia: Westminster, 1981.

————. "The Nature of Doctrine: Religion and Theology in a Postliberal Age." *RSR* 11(1985): 235–40.

Wood, David, ed. *On Paul Ricoeur: Narrative and Interpretation.* London & New York: Routledge, 1991.

Wood, Laurence W. "Above, Within or Ahead Of? Pannenberg's Eschatologicalism as a Replacement for Supernaturalism." *ATJ* 46(1991): 43–72.

————. "History and Hermeneutics: A Pannenbergian Perspective." *WesTJ* 16(1981): 7–22.

Woodbridge, John D. and Thomas Edward McComiskey, eds. *Doing Theology in Today's World: Essays in Honor of Kenneth S. Kantzer.* Grand Rapids: Zondervan, 1991.

Wright, Kathleen, ed. *Festivals of Interpretations: Essays on Hans-Georg Gadamer's Work.* Albany: State University of New York Press, 1990.

Wrede, W. *Paul.* Tr. Edward Lumis. London: Philip Greem, 1907.

Wright, N. T. *The Climax of the Covenant: Christ and the Law in Pauline Theology.* Edinburgh: T&T Clark, 1991.

————. *The New Testament and the People of God.* London: SPCK, 1992.

————. "Paul, Arabia, and Elijah (Galatians 1:17)." *JBL* 115(1996): 683–92.

————. *What Saint Paul Really Said: Was Paul of Tarsus the Real Founder of Christianity.* Oxford: Lion, 1997.

Wyman, Jr., Walter E. *The Concept of* Glaubenslehre: *Ernst Troeltsch and the Theological Heritage of Schleiermacher.* Chico: Scholars Press, 1983.

————. "Rethinking the Christian Doctrine of Sin: Friedrich Schleiermacher and Hick's 'Irenaean Type'." *JRel* 74(1994): 199–217.

Yasukata, Toshimasa. *Ernst Troeltsch: Systematic Theologian of Radical Historicality.* Atlanta: Scholars Press, 1986.

Young, Frances. *The Art of Performance: Towards a Theology of Holy Scripture.* London: Darton, Longman & Todd, 1990.

————. *From Nicea to Chalcedon.* Philadelphia: Fortress, 1983.

INDEX OF NAMES

BIBLICAL INTERPRETATION SERIES

ISSN 0928-0731

The *Biblical Interpretation Series* accommodates monographs, collections of essays and works of reference that are concerned with the discussion or application of new methods of interpreting the Bible. Works published in the series ordinarily either give a practical demonstration of how a particular approach may be instructively applied to a Biblical text or texts, or make a productive contribution to the discussion of method. The series thus provides a vehicle for the exercise and development of a whole range of newer techniques of interpretation, including feminist readings, semiotic, post-structuralist, reader-response and other types of literary readings, liberation-theological readings, ecological readings, and psychological readings, among many others.

21. Rutledge, D. *Reading Marginally*. Feminism, Deconstruction and the Bible. 1996. ISBN 90 04 10564 6
22. Culpepper, R.A. (ed.). *Critical Readings of John 6*. 1997. ISBN 90 04 10579 4
23. Pyper, H.S. *David as Reader*. 2 Samuel 12:1-15 and the Poetics of Fatherhood. 1996. ISBN 90 04 10581 6
25. Amit, Y. *Hidden Polemics in Biblical Narrative*. Translated from the Hebrew by Jonathan Chipman. 2000. ISBN 90 04 10153 5
26. Brenner, A. *The Intercourse of Knowledge*. On Gendering Desire and 'Sexuality' in the Hebrew Bible. 1997. ISBN 90 04 10155 1
27. Beck, D.R. *The Discipleship Paradigm*. Readers and Anonymous Characters in the Fourth Gospel. 1997. ISBN 90 04 10700 2
28. Evans, C.A. & S. Talmon (eds.) *The Quest for Context and Meaning*. Studies in Biblical Intertextuality in Honor of James A. Sanders. 1997. ISBN 90 04 10835 1
29. van Wolde, E. (ed.) *Narrative Syntax and the Hebrew Bible*. Papers of the Tilburg Conference 1996. 1997. ISBN 90 04 10787 8
30. Dawes, G.W. *The Body in Question*. Metaphor and Meaning in the Interpretation of Ephesians 5:21-33. 1998. ISBN 90 04 10959 5
31. Neuenschwander, B. *Mystik im Johannesevangelium*. Eine hermeneutische Untersuchung aufgrund der Auseinandersetzung mit Zen-Meister Hisamatsu Shin'ichi. 1998. ISBN 90 04 11035 6
32. Resseguie, J.L. *Revelation Unsealed*. A Narrative Critical Approach to John's Apocalypse. 1998. ISBN 90 04 11129 8
33. Dyck, J.E. *The Theocratic Ideology of the Chronicler*. 1998. ISBN 90 04 11146 8
34. van Wieringen, A.L.H.M. *The Implied Reader in Isaiah 6–12*. 1998. ISBN 90 04 11222 7
35. Warning, W. *Literary Artistry in Leviticus*. 1999. ISBN 90 04 11235 9

36. Marais, J. *Representation in Old Testament Narrative Texts*. 1998.
    ISBN 90 04 11234 0
37. Siebert-Hommes, J. *Let the Daughters* Live! The Literary Architecture of
    Exodus 1-2 as a Key for Interpretation. 1998. ISBN 90 04 10778 9
38. Amit, Y. *The Book of Judges: The Art of Editing*. 1999. ISBN 90 04 10827 0
39. Ellis, E.E. *The Making of the New Testament Documents*. 1999.
    ISBN 90 04 11332 0
40. Hill, J. *Friend or Foe? The Figure of Babylon in the Book of Jeremiah MT*. 1999.
    ISBN 90 04 11434 3
41. Young, G.W. *Subversive Symmetry*. Exploring the Fantastic in Mark 6:45-56.
    1999. ISBN 90 04 11428 9
42. Liew, T-S. B. *Politics of Parousia*. Reading Mark Inter(con)textually. 1999.
    ISBN 90 04 11360 6
43. Kitzberger, I.R. *Transformative Encounters*. Jesus and Women Re-viewed.
    2000. ISBN 90 04 11311 8
44. Chatelion Counet, P.J.E., *A Postmodern Gospel*. Introduction to Deconstruc-
    tive Exegesis Applied to the Fourth Gospel. 2000.
    ISBN 90 04 11661 3
45. van Tilborg, S. and P.J.E. Chatelion Counet. *Jesus' appearances and
    disappearances in Luke 24*. 2000. ISBN 90 04 11757 1
46. Davies, A. Double *Standards in Isaiah*. Re-evaluating Prophetic Ethics and
    Divine Justice. 2000. ISBN 90 04 11581 1
47. Watt, Jan G. van der. *Family of the King*. Dynamics of Metaphor in the
    Gospel According to John. 2000. ISBN 90 04 11660 5.
48. Peterson, Dwight N. *The Origins of Mark*. The Markan Community in
    Current Debate. 2000. ISBN 90 04 11755 5
49. Chan, Mark L.Y. *Christology from within and ahead*. Hermeneutics, Contin-
    gency and the Quest for Transcontextual Criteria in Christology. 2001.
    ISBN 90 04 11844 6
50. Polaski, Donald C. *Authorizing an End*. The Isaiah Apocalypse and Inter-
    textuality. 2000. ISBN 90 04 11607 9
51. Reese, Ruth Anne. *Writing Jude*. The Reader, the Text, and the Author
    in Constructs of Power and Desire. 2000. ISBN 90 04 11659 1